The Autobiography of Bertrand Russell

London
UNWIN PAPERBACKS
Boston   Sydney

Volume One first published by George Allen & Unwin 1967
Volume Two first published by George Allen & Unwin 1968
Volume Three first published by George Allen & Unwin
1969

Paperback (separate volumes) edition 1971
One volume paperback edition 1975
First published in Unwin Paperbacks 1978

UNWIN ® PAPERBACKS
40 Museum Street, London WC1A 1LU

ISBN 0 04 921022 X

© George Allen & Unwin (Publishers) Ltd, 1967, 1968,
1971 1975

Printed in Great Britain
in 9pt Plantin type by
Cox & Wyman Ltd
London, Reading and Fakenham

'Three passions, simple but overwhelmingly strong, have governed my life: the longing for love, the search for knowledge, and unbearable pity for the suffering of mankind. These passions, like great winds, have blown me hither and thither ... over a deep ocean of anguish, reaching to the very verge of despair.'

Thinker, philosopher, mathematician, educational innovator and experimenter, champion of intellectual, social and sexual freedom, campaigner for peace and for civil and human rights, Bertrand Russell's life was one of incredible variety and richness. In keeping with his character and beliefs, his life-story is told with vigour, disarming charm and total frankness. His childhood was bitterly lonely but unusually rich in experience. His adult-life was spent grappling both with his own beliefs and the problems of the universe and mankind, and the pursuit of love and permanent happiness which resulted in no less than five marriages. The many storms and episodes of his life are recalled with the vivid freshness and clarity which characterised all Russell's writing and which make this perhaps the most moving literary self-portrait of the twentieth century.

To Edith

Through the long years
   I sought peace,
I found ecstasy, I found anguish,
   I found madness,
I found loneliness,
I found the solitary pain
   that gnaws the heart,
But peace I did not find.

Now, old & near my end,
   I have known you,
And, knowing you,
I have found both ecstasy & peace,
   I know rest,
After so many lonely years.
I know what life & love may be.
Now, if I sleep,
I shall sleep fulfilled.

Contents

Contents

Acknowledgements

Acknowledgements are due to the following for permission to include certain letters. In Part I: the letters from Joseph Conrad are included by permission of J. M. Dent Ltd and the Trustees of the Joseph Conrad Estate. In Part II: Les Amis d'Henri Barbusse; Margaret Cole, for the letters of Beatrice Webb; Joseph Conrad through J. M. Dent Ltd, for the letters of Joseph Conrad; Valerie Eliot, for the letters of T. S. Eliot; the Estate of Albert Einstein; the Executors of the H. G. Wells Estate (© 1968 George Philip Wells and Frank Wells); Pearn, Pollinger & Higham, with the concurrence of William Heinemann Ltd, for passages from the letters of D. H. Lawrence; the Public Trustee and the Society of Authors, for the letters of Bernard Shaw; the Trustees of the Will of Mrs Bernard Shaw; and the Council of Trinity College, Cambridge. Facsimiles of Crown-copyright records in the Public Record Office appear by permission of the Controller of H.M. Stationery Office. The above list includes only those who requested formal acknowledgement; many others have kindly granted permission to publish letters.

Acknowledgements are also due to the following for permission to include certain letters and articles in Part III: Baron Cecil Anrep, for the letters of Bernard Berenson; the Estate of Albert Einstein; Valerie Eliot, for the letters of T. S. Eliot; Dorelia John, for the letter of Augustus John; *The New York Times* Company, for 'The Best Answer to Fanaticism-Liberalism' (© 1951); *The Observer*, for 'Pros and Cons of Reaching Ninety'. The above list includes only those who requested formal acknowledgement; many others have kindly granted permission to publish letters.

1872–1914

What I have Lived for

Three passions, simple but overwhelmingly strong, have governed my life: the longing for love, the search for knowledge, and unbearable pity for the suffering of mankind. These passions, like great winds, have blown me hither and thither, in a wayward course, over a deep ocean of anguish, reaching to the very verge of despair.

I have sought love, first, because it brings ecstasy – ecstasy so great that I would often have sacrificed all the rest of life for a few hours of this joy. I have sought it, next, because it relieves loneliness – that terrible loneliness in which one shivering consciousness looks over the rim of the world into the cold unfathomable lifeless abyss. I have sought it, finally, because in the union of love I have seen, in a mystic miniature, the prefiguring vision of the heaven that saints and poets have imagined. This is what I sought, and though it might seem too good for human life, this is what – at last – I have found.

With equal passion I have sought knowledge. I have wished to understand the hearts of men. I have wished to know why the stars shine. And I have tried to apprehend the Pythagorean power by which number holds sway above the flux. A little of this, but not much, I have achieved.

Love and knowledge, so far as they were possible, led upward toward the heavens. But always pity brought me back to earth. Echoes of cries of pain reverberate in my heart. Children in famine, victims tortured by oppressors, helpless old people a hated burden to their sons, and the whole world of loneliness, poverty, and pain make a mockery of what human life should be. I long to alleviate the evil, but I cannot, and I too suffer.

This has been my life. I have found it worth living, and would gladly live it again if the chance were offered me.

Chapter 1

Childhood

My first vivid recollection is my arrival at Pembroke Lodge in February 1876. To be accurate, I do not remember the actual arrival at the house, though I remember the big glass roof of the London terminus, presumably Paddington, at which I arrived on my way and which I thought inconceivably beautiful. What I remember of my first day at Pembroke Lodge is tea in the servants' hall. It was a large, bare room with a long massive table with chairs and a high stool. All the servants had their tea in this room except the house-keeper, the cook, the lady's maid, and the butler, who formed an aristocracy in the house-keeper's room. I was placed upon the high stool for tea, and what I remember most vividly is wondering why the servants took so much interest in me. I did not, at that time, know that I had already been the subject of serious deliberation by the Lord Chancellor, various eminent Queen's Counsel, and other notable persons, nor was it until I was grown-up that I learned to know of the strange events which had preceded my coming to Pembroke Lodge.

My father, Lord Amberley, had recently died after a long period of gradually increasing debility. My mother and my sister had died of diphtheria about a year and a half sooner. My mother, as I came to know her later from her diary and her letters, was vigorous, lively, witty, serious, original, and fearless. Judging by her pictures she must also have been beautiful. My father was philosophical, studious, unworldly, morose, and priggish. Both were ardent theorists of reform and prepared to put into practice whatever theory they believed in. My father was a disciple and friend of John Stuart Mill, from whom both learned to believe in birth-control and votes for women. My father lost his seat in Parliament through advocacy of birth-control. My mother sometimes got into hot water for her radical opinions. At a garden-party given by the parents of Queen Mary, the Duchess of Cambridge remarked in a loud voice: 'Yes, I know who you are, you are the daughter-in-law. But now I hear you only like dirty Radicals and dirty Americans. All London is full of it; all the clubs are talking of it. I must look at your petticoats to see if they are dirty.'

The following letter from the British Consul in Florence speaks for itself:

Sept. 22, 1870

Dear Lady Amberley

I am *not* an admirer of M. Mazzini, but have an utter detestation and abhorrence of his character and principles. The public position which I hold, moreover, precludes me from being the channel for his correspondence. Not however wishing to disoblige you in this instance, I have taken the only course which was open to me with the view to his receiving your letter, viz. to put it in the Post to the care of the Procuratore del Re, Gaeta.

I remain,
Yours very faithfully,
A. Paget

Mazzini gave my mother his watch-case, which is now in my possession.

My mother used to address meetings in favour of votes for women, and I found one passage in her diary where she speaks of the Potter Sisterhood, which included Mrs Sidney Webb and Lady Courtenay, as social butterflies. Having in later years come to know Mrs Sidney Webb well, I conceived a considerable respect for my mother's seriousness when I remembered that to her Mrs Webb seemed frivolous. From my mother's letters, however, for example to Henry Crompton, the Positivist, I find that she was on occasion sprightly and coquettish, so that perhaps the face she turned to the world was less alarming than that which she presented to her diary.

My father was a free-thinker, and wrote a large book, posthumously published, called *An Analysis of Religious Belief*. He had a large library containing the Fathers, works on Buddhism, accounts of Confucianism, and so on. He spent a great deal of time in the country in the preparation of his book. He and my mother, however, in the earlier years of their marriage, spent some months of each year in London, where they had a house in Dean's Yard. My mother and her sister, Mrs George Howard (afterwards Lady Carlisle), had rival *salons*. At Mrs Howard's *salon* were to be seen all the Pre-Raphaelite painters, and at my mother's all the British philosophers from Mill downwards.

In 1867 my parents went to America, where they made friends with all the Radicals of Boston. They could not foresee that the men and women whose democratic ardour they applauded and whose triumphant opposition to slavery they admired were the grandfathers and grandmothers of those who murdered Sacco and Vanzetti. My parents married in 1864, when they were both only twenty-two. My brother, as he boasts in his autobiography, was born nine months and four days after the wedding. Shortly before I was born, they went to live in a very lonely house called Ravenscroft (now called Cleiddon Hall) in a wood just above the steep banks of the Wye. From the house, three days after I was born, my mother wrote a description of me to her mother: 'The baby weighed 8¾ lb. is 21 inches long and very fat and very ugly very like Frank everyone thinks, blue eyes far apart and not much chin. He is just like Frank was about nursing. I have lots of milk now, but if he does not get it at once or has wind or anything he gets into such a rage and screams and kicks and trembles till he is soothed off. . . . He lifts his head up and looks about in a very energetic way.'

They obtained for my brother a tutor, D. A. Spalding, of considerable scientific ability – so at least I judge from a reference to his work in William James's *Psychology*.[1] He was a Darwinian, and was engaged in studying the instincts of chickens, which, to facilitate his studies, were allowed to work havoc in every room in the house, including the drawing-room. He himself was in an advanced stage of consumption and died not very long after my father. Apparently upon grounds of pure theory, my father and mother decided that although he ought to remain childless on account of his tuberculosis, it was unfair to expect him to be celibate. My mother therefore, allowed him to live with her, though I know of no evidence that she derived any pleasure from doing so. This arrangement subsisted for a very short time, as it began after my birth and I was only two years old when my mother died. My father, however, kept on the tutor after my mother's death, and when my father died it was found that he had left the tutor and Cobden-Sanderson, both atheists, to be guardians of his two sons, whom he wished to protect from the evils of a religious upbringing. My grandparents, however, discovered from his papers what had taken place in relation to my mother. This discovery caused them the utmost Victorian horror. They decided that if necessary they would put the law in motion to rescue innocent children from the clutches of intriguing infidels. The intriguing infidels consulted Sir Horace Davey (afterwards Lord Davey) who assured them that they would have no case, relying, apparently, upon the Shelley precedent. My brother and I were therefore made wards in Chancery, and Cobden-Sanderson delivered me up to my grandparents on the day of which I have already spoken. No doubt this history contributed to the interest which the servants took in me.

Of my mother I remember nothing whatever, though I remember falling out of a pony carriage on an occasion when she must have been present. I know that this recollection is genuine, because I verified it at a much later time, after having kept it to myself for a number of years. Of my father I remember only two things: I remember his giving me a

[1] See also J. B. S. Haldane, *British Journal of Animal Behaviour*, Vol. II, No. I, 1954.

page of red print, the colour of which delighted me, and I remember once seeing him in his bath. My parents had themselves buried in the garden at Ravenscroft, but were dug up and transferred to the family vault at Chenies. A few days before his death my father wrote the following letter to his mother.

Ravenscroft,
Wednesday at night

My dear Mama

You will be glad to hear that I mean to see Radcliffe as soon as I am able – sorry to hear the cause. This is that I have a nasty attack of bronchitis which is likely to keep me in bed some time. Your pencil letter came to-day, and I was sorry to see that you too were knocked up. Exhausted as I am I may as well write, since I cannot sleep. It would be needless to say that this attack is not dangerous and I do not anticipate danger. But I have had too bitter experience of the rapidity with which illnesses may go to believe in absolute safety, or cry Peace when there is no peace. Both my lungs are inflamed and may grow worse. I beseech you not to telegraph or take any hasty action. We have a nice young Doctor in place of Audland, and for his own sake as just beginning to practise here, he will do all he can for me. I repeat that I expect to recover, but in case of a bad turn I wish to say that I look forward to dying as calmly and unmovedly as 'One who wraps the drapery of his couch About him and lies down to pleasant dreams'.

For myself, no anxiety nor even shrinking; but I do feel much pain for a few others whom I should leave, especially you. Writing in pain and weakness I can offer you only this most inadequate expression of my deep sense of your constant and immoveable love and goodness to me, even when I may appear not to have deserved it. It is a great matter of regret to me that I was sometimes compelled to appear harsh; I did not wish to show anything but affection. I have done very little of all I should like to have done, but I hope that little has not been of a bad kind. I should die with the sense that one great work of my life was accomplished. For my two darling boys I hope you would see them much, if possible, and that they might look on you as a mother. The burial you know would be here in my beloved wood and at the beautiful spot already prepared for me. I can hardly hope you would be there, but I wish it were possible to think of it.

Perhaps it is very selfish of me to give the pain of this letter; only I fear another day I might be too weak to write. If I can I shall let you know daily. I also have met with nothing but kindness and gentleness from my dear Papa all my life, for which I am deeply grateful. I do earnestly hope that at the end of his long and noble life he may be spared the pain of losing a son. I can only send my best love to Agatha and Rollo and poor Willy if possible.

> *Your loving son,*
> *A.*

Pembroke Lodge, where my grandfather and grandmother lived, is a rambling house of only two storeys in Richmond Park. It was in the gift of the Sovereign, and derives its name from the Lady Pembroke to whom George III was devoted in the days of his lunacy. The Queen had given it to my grandparents for their life-time in the forties, and they had lived there ever since. The famous Cabinet meeting described in Kinglake's *Invasion of the Crimea*, at which several Cabinet Ministers slept while the Crimean War was decided upon, took place at Pembroke Lodge. Kinglake, in later years, lived at Richmond, and I remember him well. I once asked Sir Spencer Walpole why Kinglake was so bitter against Napoleon III. Sir Spencer replied that they quarrelled about a woman. 'Will you tell me the story?' I naturally asked. 'No, sir,' he replied, 'I shall not tell you the story.' And shortly afterwards he died.

Pembroke Lodge had eleven acres of garden, mostly allowed to run wild. This garden played a very large part in my life up to the age of eighteen. To the west there was an enormous view extending from the Epsom Downs (which I believed to be the 'Ups and Downs') to Windsor Castle, with Hindhead and Leith Hill between. I grew accustomed to wide horizons and to an unimpeded view of the sunset. And I have never since been able to live happily without both. There were many fine trees, oaks, beeches, horse- and Spanish chestnuts, and lime trees, a very beautiful cedar tree, cryptomerias and deodaras presented by Indian princes. There were summer-houses, sweet briar hedges, thickets of laurel, and all kinds of secret places in which it was possible to hide from grown-up people so successfully that there was not the slightest fear of discovery. There were several flower-gardens with box-hedges. Throughout the years during which I lived at Pembroke Lodge, the garden was growing gradually more and more neglected. Big trees fell, shrubs grew over the paths, the grass on the lawns became long and rank, and the box-hedges grew almost into trees. The garden seemed to remember the days of its former splendour, when foreign ambassadors paced its lawns, and princes admired its trim beds of flowers. It lived in the past, and I lived in the past with it. I wove fantasies about my parents and my sister. I imagined the days of my grandfather's vigour. The grown-up conversation to which I listened was mostly of things that had happened long ago; how my grandfather had visited Napoleon in Elba, how my grandmother's great-uncle had defended Gibraltar during the American War of Independence, and how her grandfather had been cut by the County for saying that the world must have been created before 4004 BC because there is so much lava on the slopes of Etna. Sometimes the conversation descended to more recent times, and I should be told how Carlyle had called Herbert Spencer a 'perfect vacuum', or how Darwin had felt it a great honour to be visited by Mr Gladstone. My father and mother were dead, and I used to wonder what sort of people they had been. In solitude I used to wander about the garden, alternately collecting birds' eggs and meditating on the flight of time. If I may judge by my own recollections, the important and formative impressions of childhood rise to consciousness only in fugitive moments in the midst of childish occupations, and are never mentioned to adults. I think periods of browsing during which no occupation is imposed from without are important in youth because they give time for the formation of these apparently fugitive but really vital impressions.

My grandfather as I remember him was a man well past eighty, being wheeled round the garden in a bath chair, or sitting in his room reading Hansard. I was just six years old when he died. I remember that when on the day of his death I saw my brother (who was at school) drive up in a cab although it was in the middle of term, I shouted 'Hurrah!', and my nurse said: 'Hush! You must not say "Hurrah" today!' It may be inferred from this incident that my grandfather had no great importance to me.

My grandmother, on the contrary, who was twenty-three years younger than he was, was the most important person to me throughout my childhood. She was a Scotch Presbyterian, Liberal in politics and religion (she became a Unitarian at the age of seventy), but extremely strict in all matters of morality. When she married my grandfather she was young and very shy. My grandfather was a widower with two children and four step-children, and a few years after their marriage he became Prime Minister. For her this must have been a severe ordeal. She related how she went once as a girl to one of the famous breakfasts given by the poet Rogers, and how, after observing her shyness, he said: 'Have a little tongue. You need it, my dear!' It was obvious from her conversation that she never came anywhere near to knowing what it feels like to be in love. She told me once how relieved she was on her honeymoon when her mother joined her. On another occasion she lamented that so much poetry should be concerned with so trivial a subject as love. But she made my grandfather a devoted wife, and never, so far as I have been able to discover, failed to perform what her very exacting standards represented as her duty.

As a mother and a grandmother she was deeply, but not always wisely, solicitous. I do not think that she ever understood the claims of animal spirits and exuberant vitality. She demanded that everything should be viewed through a mist of Victorian sentiment. I remember trying to make her see that it was inconsistent to demand at one and the same time that everybody should be well housed, and yet that no new houses should be built because they were an eye-sore. To her each sentiment had its separate rights, and must not be asked to give place to another sentiment on account of anything so cold as mere logic. She was cultivated according to the standards of her time; she could speak French, German and Italian faultlessly, without the slightest trace of accent. She knew Shakespeare, Milton, and the eighteenth-century poets intimately. She could repeat the signs of the Zodiac and the names of the Nine Muses. She had a minute knowledge of English history according to the Whig tradition. French, German, and Italian classics were familiar to her. Of politics since 1830 she had a close personal knowledge. But everything that involved reasoning had been totally omitted from her education, and was absent from her mental life. She never could understand how locks on rivers worked, although I heard any number of people try to explain it to her. Her morality was that of a Victorian Puritan, and nothing would have persuaded her that a man who swore on occasion might nevertheless have some good qualities. To this, however, there were exceptions. She knew the Miss Berrys who were Horace Walpole's friends, and she told me once without any censure that 'they were old-fashioned, they used to swear a little'. Like many of her type she made an inconsistent exception of Byron, whom she regarded as an unfortunate victim of an unrequited youthful love. She extended no such tolerance to Shelley, whose life she considered wicked and whose poetry she considered mawkish. Of Keats I do not think she had ever heard. While she was well read in Continental classics down to Goethe and Schiller, she knew nothing of the Continental writers of her own time. Turgeniev once gave her one of his novels, but she never read it, or regarded him as anything but the cousin of some friends of hers. She was aware that he wrote books, but so did almost everybody else.

Of psychology in the modern sense, she had, of course, no vestige. Certain motives were known to exist: love of country, public spirit, love of one's children, were laudable motives; love of money, love of power, vanity, were bad motives. Good men acted from good motives always; bad men, however, even the worst, had moments when they were not wholly bad. Marriage was a puzzling institution. It was clearly the duty of husbands and wives to love one another, but it was a duty they ought not to perform too easily, for if sex attraction drew them together there must be something not quite nice about them. Not, of course, that she would have phrased the matter in these terms. What she would have said, and in fact did say, was: 'You know, I never think that the affection of husbands and wives is quite such a good thing as the affection of parents for their children, because there is sometimes something a little selfish about it.' That was as near as her thoughts could come to such a topic as sex. Perhaps once I heard her approach a little nearer to the forbidden topic: that was when she said that Lord Palmerston had been peculiar among men through the fact that he was not quite a good man. She disliked wine, abhorred tobacco, and was always on the verge of becoming a vegetarian. Her life was austere. She ate only the plainest food, breakfasted at eight, and until she reached the age of eighty never sat in a comfortable chair until after tea. She was completely unworldly, and despised those who thought anything of worldly honours. I regret to say that her attitude to Queen Victoria was far from respectful. She used to relate with much amusement how one time when she was at Windsor and feeling rather ill, the Queen had been graciously pleased to say: 'Lady Russell may sit down. Lady So-and-So shall stand in front of her.'

After I reached the age of fourteen, my grandmother's intellectual limitations became trying to me, and her Puritan morality began to seem to me to be excessive; but while I was a child her great affection for me, and her intense care for my welfare, made me love her and gave me that feeling of safety that children need. I remember when I was about four or five years old lying awake thinking how dreadful it would be when my grandmother was dead. When she did in fact die, which was after I was married, I did not mind at all. But in retrospect, as I have grown older, I have realised more and more the importance she had in moulding my outlook on life. Her fearlessness, her public spirit, her contempt for convention, and her indifference to the opinion of the majority have always seemed good to me and have impressed themselves upon me as worthy of imitation. She gave me a Bible with her favourite texts written on the fly-leaf. Among these was 'Thou shalt not follow a multitude to do evil'. Her emphasis upon this text led me in later life to be not afraid of belonging to small minorities.

My grandmother, when I was a boy, had four surviving brothers and two surviving sisters, all of whom used to come to Pembroke Lodge from time to time. The oldest of the brothers was Lord Minto, whom I knew as Uncle William. The second was Sir Henry Elliot, who had had a respectable diplomatic career, but of whom I remember little. The third, my Uncle Charlie, I remember chiefly because of the length of his name on an envelope: he was Admiral the Hon. Sir Charles Elliot, KCB, and he lived at Devonport. I was told that he was Rear Admiral and that there is a grander sort of admiral called Admiral of the Fleet. This rather pained me and I felt he should have done something about it. The youngest, who was a bachelor, was George Elliot, but was known to me as Uncle Doddy. The chief thing that I was asked to notice about him was his close resemblance to his and my grandmother's grandfather, Mr Brydon, who had been led into regrettable heresy by the lava on Etna. Otherwise, Uncle Doddy was undistinguished. Of Uncle William I have a very painful recollection: he came to Pembroke Lodge one June evening at the end of a day of continual sunshine, every moment of which I had enjoyed. When it became time for me to say good-night, he gravely informed me that the human capacity for enjoyment decreases with the years and that I should never again enjoy a summer's day as much as the one that was now ending. I burst into floods of tears and continued to weep long after I was in bed. Subsequent experience has shown me that his remark was as untrue as it was cruel.

The grown-ups with whom I came in contact had a remarkable incapacity for understanding the intensity of childish emotions. When, at the age of four, I was taken to be photographed in Richmond, the photographer had difficulty in getting me to sit still, and at last promised me a sponge cake if I would remain motionless. I had, until that moment, only had one sponge cake in all my life and it had remained as a high point of ecstasy. I therefore stayed as quiet as a mouse and the photograph was wholly successful. But I never got the sponge cake.

On another occasion I heard one of the grown-ups saying to another 'When is that young Lyon coming?' I pricked up my ears and said 'Is there a lion coming?' 'Yes,' they said, 'he's coming on Sunday. He'll be quite tame and you shall see him in the drawing-room.' I counted the days till Sunday and the hours through Sunday morning. At last I was told the young lion was in the drawing-room and I could come and see him. I came. And he was an ordinary young man named Lyon. I was utterly overwhelmed by the disenchantment and still remember with anguish the depths of my despair.

To return to my grandmother's family, I remember little of her sister Lady Elizabeth Romilly except that she was the first person from whom I heard of Rudyard Kipling, whose *Plain Tales from the Hills* she greatly admired. The other sister, Lady Charlotte Portal, whom I knew as Aunt Lottie, was more colourful. It was said of her that as a child she had tumbled out of bed and without waking up had murmured, 'My head is laid low, my pride has had a fall.' It was also said that having heard the grown-ups talking about somnambulism she had got up during the following night and walked about in what she hoped was a sleep-walking manner. The grown-ups, who saw that she was wide awake, decided to say nothing about it. Their silence next morning so disappointed her that at last she said, 'Did no one see me walking in my sleep last night?' In later life she was apt to express herself unfortunately. On one occasion when she had to order a cab for three people, she thought a hansom would be too small and a four-wheeler too large, so she told the footman to fetch a three-wheeled cab. On another occasion, the footman, whose name was George, was seeing her off at the station when she was on her way to the Continent. Thinking that she might have to write to him about some household matter she suddenly remembered that she did not know his surname. Just after the train had started she put her head out of the window and called out, 'George, George, what's your name?' 'George, My Lady', came the answer. By that time he was out of earshot.

Besides my grandmother there were in the house my Uncle Rollo and my Aunt Agatha, both unmarried. My Uncle Rollo had some importance in my early development, as he frequently talked to me about scientific matters, of which he had considerable knowledge. He suffered all his life from a morbid shyness so intense as to prevent him from achieving anything that involved contact with other human beings. But with me, so long as I was a child, he was not shy, and he used to display a vein of droll humour of which adults would not have suspected him. I remember asking him once why they had coloured glass in church windows. He informed me very gravely that in former times this had not been so, but that once, just after the clergyman had gone up into the pulpit, he saw a man walking along with a pail of whitewash on his head and the bottom of the pail fell out and the man was covered with whitewash. This caused in the poor clergyman such an uncontrollable fit of laughter that he was unable to proceed with the sermon, and ever since this they had had coloured glass in church windows. He had been in the Foreign Office, but he had trouble with his eyes, and when I first knew him he was unable to read or write. His eyes improved later, but he never again attempted any kind of routine work. He was a meteorologist, and did valuable investigations of the effects of the Krakatoa eruption of 1883, which produced in England strange sunsets and even a blue moon. He used to talk to me about the evidence that Krakatoa had caused the sunsets, and I listened to him with profound attention. His conversation did a great deal to stimulate my scientific interests.

My Aunt Agatha was the youngest of the grown-up people at Pembroke Lodge. She was, in fact, only nineteen years older than I was, so when I came there she was twenty-two. During my first years at Pembroke Lodge, she made various attempts to educate me, but without much success. She had three brightly coloured balls, one red, one yellow, and one blue. She would hold up the red ball and say: 'What colour is that?' and I would say, 'Yellow'. She would then hold it against her canary and say: 'Do you think that it is the same colour as the canary?' I would say, 'No', but as I did not know the canary was yellow it did not help much. I suppose I must have learned the colours in time, but I can only remember not knowing them. Then she tried to teach me to read, but that was quite beyond me. There was only one word that I ever succeeded in reading so long as she taught me, and that was the word 'or'. The other words, though equally short, I could never remember. She must have become discouraged, since shortly before I was five years old I was handed over to a kindergarten, which finally succeeded in teaching me the difficult art of reading. When I was six or seven she took me in hand again and taught me English Constitutional history. This interested me very much indeed, and I remember to this day much of what she taught me.

I still possess the little book in which I wrote down her questions and answers, both dictated. A few samples will illustrate the point of view.

Q. What did Henry II and Thomas Becket quarrel about ?
A. Henry wished to put a stop to the evils which had arisen in consequence of the Bishops having courts of their own, so that the church law was separated from the common law of the land. Becket refused to lessen the power of the Bishops' Courts, but at last he was persuaded to agree to the Constitutions of Clarendon (the provisions of which are then given).
Q. Did Henry II try to improve the government of the country or not ?
A. Yes, throughout his busy reign he never forgot his work of reforming the law. The itinerant justices grew in importance, and not only settled money matters in the counties as at first, but heard pleas and judged cases. It is to Henry II's reforms that we owe the first clear beginnings of trial by jury.

The murder of Becket is not mentioned. The execution of Charles I is mentioned, but not blamed.

She remained unmarried, having once become engaged to a curate and suffered from insane delusions during her engagement, which led to its being broken off. She became a miser, living in a large house, but using few of the rooms in order to save coal, and only having a bath once a week for the same reason. She wore thick woollen stockings which were always coming down in rumples over her ankles, and at most times talked sentimentally about the extreme goodness of certain people and the extreme wickedness of certain others, both equally imaginary. Both in my brother's case and in mine, she hated our wives so long as we lived with them, but loved them afterwards. When I first took my second wife to see her, she put a photograph of my first wife on the mantelpiece, and said to my second wife: 'When I see you I cannot help thinking of dear Alys, and wondering what would happen should Bertie desert you, which God forbid.' My brother said to her once: 'Auntie, you are always a wife behind.' This remark, instead of angering her, sent her into fits of laughter, and she repeated it to everybody. Those who thought her sentimental and doddering were liable to be surprised by a sudden outburst of shrewdness and wit. She was a victim of my grandmother's virtue. If she had not been taught that sex is wicked, she might have been happy, successful, and able.

My brother was seven years older than I was, and therefore not much of a companion to me. Except in holiday time he was away at school. I admired him in the way natural to a younger brother, and was always delighted when he returned at the beginning of the holidays, but after a few days I began to wish the holidays were over. He teased me, and bullied me mildly. I remember once when I was six years old he called in a loud voice: 'Baby!' With great dignity I refused to take any notice, considering that this was not my name. He afterwards informed me that he had had a bunch of grapes which he would have given me if I had come. As I was never in any circumstances allowed to eat any fruit at all, this deprivation was rather serious. There was also a certain small bell which I believed to be mine, but which he at each return asserted to be his and took from me, although he was himself too old to derive any pleasure from it. He still had it when he was grown-up, and I never saw it without angry feelings. My father and mother, as appears from their letters to each other, had considerable trouble with him, but at any rate my mother understood him, as he was in character and appearance a Stanley. The Russells never understood him at all, and regarded him from the first as a limb of Satan.[1] Not unnaturally, finding himself so viewed, he set out to live up to his reputation. Attempts were made to keep him away from me, which I resented as soon as I became aware of them. His personality was, however, very overpowering, and after I had been with him some time I began to feel as if I could not breathe. I retained throughout his life an attitude towards him consisting of affection mixed with fear. He passionately longed to be loved, but was such a bully that he never could keep the love of anyone. When he lost anyone's love, his heart was wounded and he became cruel and unscrupulous, but all his worst actions sprang from sentimental causes.

During my early years at Pembroke Lodge the servants played a larger part in my life than the family did. There was an old housekeeper named Mrs Cox who had been my grandmother's nursery-maid when my grandmother was a child. She was straight and vigorous and strict and devoted to the family and always nice to me. There was a butler named MacAlpine who was very Scotch. He used to take me on his knee and read me accounts of railway accidents in the newspaper. As soon as I saw him I always climbed up on him and said: 'Tell me about an accident-happen.' Then there was a French cook named

[1] My grandfather on one occasion wrote to my father telling him not to take my brother's naughtiness too seriously, in view of the fact that Charles James Fox had been a very naughty boy, but had nevertheless turned out well.

Michaud, who was rather terrifying, but in spite of her awe-inspiring qualities I could not resist going to the kitchen to see the roast meat turning on the old-fashioned spit, and to steal lumps of salt, which I liked better than sugar, out of the salt box. She would pursue me with a carving knife, but I always escaped easily. Out-of-doors there was a gardener named MacRobie of whom I remember little as he left when I was five years old, and the lodge-keeper and his wife, Mr and Mrs Singleton, of whom I was very fond, as they gave me baked apples and beer, both of which were strictly forbidden. MacRobie was succeeded by a gardener named Vidler, who informed me that the English are the lost Ten Tribes, though I do not think I quite believed him. When I first came to Pembroke Lodge, I had a German nursery governess named Miss Hetschel, and I already spoke German as fluently as English. She left a few days after my arrival at Pembroke Lodge, and was succeeded by a German nurse named Wilhelmina, or Mina for short. I remember vividly the first evening when she bathed me, when I considered it prudent to make myself stiff, as I did not know what she might be up to. She finally had to call in outside assistance, as I frustrated all her efforts. Very soon, however, I became devoted to her. She taught me to write German letters. I remember, after learning all the German capitals and all the German small letters, saying to her: 'Now it only remains to learn the numbers', and being relieved and surprised to find that they were the same in German. She used to slap me occasionally, and I can remember crying when she did so, but it never occurred to me to regard her as less of a friend on that account. She was with me until I was six years old. During her time I also had a nursery maid called Ada who used to light the fire in the morning while I lay in bed. She would wait till the sticks were blazing and then put on coal. I always wished she would not put on coal, as I loved the crackle and brightness of the burning wood. The nurse slept in the same room with me, but never, so far as my recollection serves me, either dressed or undressed. Freudians may make what they like of this.

In the matter of food, all through my youth I was treated in a very Spartan manner, much more so, in fact, than is now considered compatible with good health. There was an old French lady living in Richmond, named Madame D'Etchegoyen, a niece of Talleyrand, who used to give me large boxes of the most delicious chocolates. Of these I was allowed only one on Sundays, but Sundays and week-days alike I had to hand them round to the grown-ups. I was very fond of crumbling my bread into my gravy, which I was allowed to do in the nursery, but not in the dining-room. I used often to have a sleep before my dinner, and if I slept late I had dinner in the nursery, but if I woke up in time I had it in the dining-room. I used to pretend to sleep late in order to have dinner in the nursery. At last they suspected that I was pretending, and one day, as I was lying in my bed, they poked me about. I made myself quite stiff, imagining that was how people would be if they were asleep, but to my dismay I heard them saying: 'He is not asleep, because he is making himself stiff.' No one ever discovered why I had pretended to be asleep. I remember an occasion at lunch when all the plates were changed and everybody except me was given an orange. I was not allowed an orange as there was an unalterable conviction that fruit is bad for children. I knew I must not ask for one as that would be impertinent, but as I had been given a plate I did venture to say, 'a plate and nothing on it'. Everybody laughed, but I did not get an orange. I had no fruit, practically no sugar, and an excess of carbohydrates. Nevertheless, I never had a day's illness except a mild attack of measles at the age of eleven. Since I became interested in children, after the birth of my own children, I have never known one nearly as healthy as I was, and yet I am sure that any modern expert on children's diet would think that I ought to have had various deficiency diseases. Perhaps I was saved by the practice of stealing crab-apples, which, if it had been known, would have caused the utmost horror and alarm. A similar instinct for self-preservation was the cause of my first lie. My governess left me alone for half an hour with strict instructions to eat no blackberries during her absence. When she returned I was suspiciously near the brambles. 'You have been eating blackberries', she said. 'I have not', I replied. 'Put out your tongue!' she said. Shame overwhelmed me, and I felt utterly wicked.

I was, in fact, unusually prone to a sense of sin. When asked what was my favourite hymn, I answered 'Weary of earth and laden with my sin'. On one occasion when my grandmother read the parable of the Prodigal Son at family prayers, I said to her afterwards: 'I know why you read that – because I broke my jug.' She used to relate the anecdote in after years with amusement, not realising that she was responsible for a morbidness which had produced tragic results in her own children.

Many of my most vivid early memories are of humiliations. In the summer of 1877 my grandparents rented from the Archbishop of Canterbury a house near Broadstairs, called Stone House. The journey by train seemed to me enormously long, and after a time I began to think that we must have reached Scotland, so I said: 'What country are we in now?' They all laughed at me and said: 'Don't you know you cannot get out of England without crossing the sea?' I did not venture to explain, and was left overwhelmed with shame. While we were there I went down to the sea one afternoon with my grandmother and my Aunt Agatha. I had on a new pair of boots, and the last thing my nurse said to me as I went out was: 'Take care not to get your boots wet!' But the in-coming tide caught me on a rock, and my grandmother and Aunt Agatha told me to wade through the water to the shore. I would not do so, and my aunt had to wade through and carry me. They supposed that this was through fear, and I never told them of my nurse's prohibition, but accepted meekly the lecture on cowardice which resulted.

In the main, however, the time that I spent at Stone House was very delightful. I remember the North Foreland, which I believed to be one of the four corners of England, since I imagined at that time that England was a rectangle. I remember the ruins at Richborough which greatly interested me, and the *camera obscura* at Ramsgate, which interested me still more. I remember waving corn-fields which, to my regret, had disappeared when I returned to the neighbourhood thirty years later. I remember, of course, all the usual delights of the seaside – limpets, and sea-anemones, and rocks, and sands, and fishermen's boats, and lighthouses. I was impressed by the fact that limpets stick to the rock when one tries to pull them off, and I said to my Aunt Agatha, 'Aunty, do limpets think?' To which she answered, 'I don't know'. 'Then you must learn', I rejoined. I do not clearly remember the incident which first brought me into contact with my friend Whitehead. I had been told that the earth was round, and had refused to believe it. My people thereupon called in the vicar of the parish to persuade me, and it happened that he was Whitehead's father. Under clerical guidance, I adopted the orthodox view and began to dig a hole to the Antipodes. This incident, however, I know only from hearsay.

While at Broadstairs I was taken to see Sir Moses Montefiore, an old and much revered Jew who lived in the neighbourhood. (According to the Encyclopaedia, he had retired in 1824.) This was the first time I became aware of the existence of Jews outside the Bible. My people explained to me carefully, before taking me to see the old man, how much he deserved to be admired, and how abominable had been the former disabilities of Jews, which he and my grandfather had done much to remove. On this occasion the impression made by my grandmother's teaching was clear, but on other occasions I was puzzled. She was a fierce Little Englander, and disapproved strongly of Colonial wars. She told me that the Zulu War was very wicked, and that it was largely the fault of Sir Bartle Frere, the Governor of the Cape. Nevertheless, when Sir Bartle Frere came to live at Wimbledon, she took me to see him, and I observed that she did not treat him as a monster. I found this very difficult to understand.

My grandmother used to read aloud to me, chiefly the stories of Maria Edgeworth. There was one story in the book, called *The False Key*, which she said was not a very nice story, and she would therefore not read it to me. I read the whole story, a sentence at a time, in the course of bringing the book from the shelf to my grandmother. Her attempts to prevent me from knowing things were seldom successful. At a somewhat later date, during Sir Charles Dilke's very scandalous divorce case, she took the precaution of burning the newspapers every day, but I used to go to the Park gates to fetch them for her, and read every word of the divorce case before the papers reached her. The case interested me the more because I had once been to church with him, and I kept wondering what his feelings had been when he heard the Seventh Commandment. After I had learnt to read fluently I used to read to her, and I acquired in this way an extensive knowledge of standard English literature. I read with her Shakespeare, Milton, Dryden, Cowper's *Task*, Thomson's *Castle of Indolence*, Jane Austen, and hosts of other books.

There is a good description of the atmosphere of Pembroke Lodge in *A Victorian Childhood* by Amabel Huth Jackson (*née* Grant Duff). Her father was Sir Mountstuart Grant Duff, and the family lived in a large house at Twickenham. She and I were friends from the age of four until she died during the second world war. It was from her that I first heard of Verlaine, Dostoevsky, the German Romantics, and many other people of literary eminence. But it is of an earlier period that her reminiscences treat. She says:

'My only boy friend was Bertrand Russell, who with his grandmother old Lady Russell, Lord John's widow, lived at Pembroke Lodge, in Richmond Park. Bertie and I were great allies and I had an immense secret admiration for his beautiful and gifted elder brother Frank. Frank, I am sorry to say, sympathised with my brother's point of view about little girls and used to tie me up to trees by my hair. But Bertie, a solemn little boy in a blue velvet suit with an equally solemn governess, was always kind, and I greatly enjoyed going to tea at Pembroke Lodge. But even as a child I realised what an unsuitable place it was for children to be brought up in. Lady Russell always spoke in hushed tones and Lady Agatha always wore a white shawl and looked down-trodden. Rollo Russell never spoke at all. He gave one a handshake that nearly broke all the bones of one's fingers, but was quite friendly. They all drifted in and out of the rooms like ghosts and no one ever seemed to be hungry. It was a curious bringing up for two young and extraordinarily gifted boys.'

Throughout the greater part of my childhood, the most important hours of my day were those that I spent alone in the garden, and the most vivid part of my existence was solitary. I seldom mentioned my more serious thoughts to others, and when I did I regretted it. I knew each corner of the garden, and looked year by year for the white primroses in one place, the redstart's nest in another, the blossom of the acacia emerging from a tangle of ivy. I knew where the earliest blue-bells were to be found, and which of the oaks came into leaf soonest. I remember that in the year 1878 a certain oak tree was in leaf as early as the fourteenth of April. My window looked out upon two Lombardy poplars, each about a hundred feet high, and I used to watch the shadow of the house creeping up them as the sun set. In the morning I woke very early and sometimes saw Venus rise. On one occasion I mistook the planet for a lantern in the wood. I saw the sunrise on most mornings, and on bright April days I would sometimes slip out of the house for a long walk before breakfast. I watched the sunset turn the earth red and the clouds golden; I listened to the wind, and exulted in the lightning. Throughout my childhood I had an increasing sense of loneliness, and of despair of ever meeting anyone with whom I could talk. Nature and books and (later) mathematics saved me from complete despondency.

The early years of my childhood, however, were happy and it was only as adolescence approached that loneliness became oppressive. I had governesses, German and Swiss, whom I liked, and my intelligence was not yet sufficiently developed to suffer from the deficiency of my people in this respect. I must, however, have felt some kind of un-happiness, as I remember wishing that my parents had lived. Once, when I was six years old, I expressed this feeling to my grandmother, and she proceeded to tell me that it was very fortunate for me that they had died. At the time her remarks made a disagreeable impression upon me and I attributed them to jealousy. I did not, of course, know that from a Victorian point of view there was ample ground for them. My grandmother's face was very expressive, and in spite of all her experi-ence of the great world she never learned the art of concealing her emotions. I noticed that any allusion to insanity caused her a spasm of anguish, and I speculated much as to the reason. It was only many years later that I discovered she had a son in an asylum. He was in a smart regiment, and went mad after a few years of it. The story that I have been told, though I cannot vouch for its complete accuracy, is that his brother officers teased him because he was chaste. They kept a bear as a regimental pet, and one day, for sport, set the bear at him. He fled, lost his memory, and being found wandering about the country was put in a workhouse infirmary, his identity being unknown. In the middle of the night, he jumped up shouting 'the bear! – the bear!' and strangled a tramp in the next bed. He never recovered his memory, but lived till over eighty.

When I try to recall as much as I can of early childhood, I find that the first thing I remember after my arrival at Pembroke Lodge is walking in melting snow, in warm sunshine, on an occasion which must have been about a month later, and noticing a large fallen beech tree which was being sawn into logs. The next thing I remember is my fourth birthday, on which I was given a trumpet which I blew all day long, and had tea with a birthday cake in a summer-house. The next thing that I remember is my aunt's lessons on colours and reading, and then, very vividly, the kindergarten class which began just before I was five and continued for about a year and a half. That gave me very intense delight. The shop from which the apparatus came was stated on the lids to be in Berners Street, Oxford Street, and to this day, unless I pull myself together, I think of Berners Street as a sort of Aladdin's Palace. At the kindergarten class I got to know other children, most of whom I have lost sight of. But I met one of them, Jimmie Baillie, in 1929 at Vancouver as I stepped out of the train. I realise now that the good lady who taught us had had an orthodox Froebel training, and was at that time amazingly up-to-date. I can still remember almost all the lessons in detail, but I think what thrilled me most was the discovery that yellow and blue paints made green.

When I was just six my grandfather died, and shortly afterwards we went to St Fillans in Perthshire for the summer. I remember the funny old inn with knobbly wooden door-posts, the wooden bridge over the river, the rocky bays on the lake, and the mountain opposite. My recollection is that the time there was one of great happiness. My next recollection is less pleasant. It is that of a room in London at No. 8, Chesham Place, where my governess stormed at me while I endeavoured to learn the multiplication table but was continually impeded by tears. My grandmother took a house in London for some months when I was seven years old, and it was then that I began to see more of my mother's family. My mother's father was dead, but my mother's mother, Lady Stanley of Alderley, lived in a large house, No 40, Dover Street,[1] with her daughter Maude. I was frequently taken to lunch with her, and though the food was delicious, the pleasure was doubtful, as she had a caustic tongue, and spared neither age nor sex. I was always consumed with shyness while in her presence, and as none of the Stanleys were shy, this irritated her. I used to make desperate endeavours to produce a good impression, but they would fail in ways that I could not have foreseen. I remember telling her that I had grown $2\frac{1}{2}$ inches in the last seven months, and that at that rate I should grow $4\frac{2}{7}$ inches in a year. 'Don't you know', she said, 'that you should never talk about any fractions except halves and quarters? – it is pedantic!' 'I know it now', I replied. 'How like his father!' she said, turning to my Aunt Maude. Somehow or other, as in this incident, my best efforts always went astray. Once when I was about twelve years old, she had me before a roomful of visitors, and asked me whether I had read a whole string of books on popular science which she enumerated. I had

[1] Completely destroyed in the Blitz.

read none of them. At the end she sighed, and turning to the visitors, said: 'I have no intelligent grandchildren.' She was an eighteenth-century type, rationalistic and unimaginative, keen on enlightenment, and contemptuous of Victorian goody-goody priggery. She was one of the principal people concerned in the foundation of Girton College, and her portrait hangs in Girton Hall, but her policies were abandoned at her death. 'So long as I live', she used to say, 'there shall be no chapel at Girton.' The present chapel began to be built the day she died. As soon as I reached adolescence she began to try to counteract what she considered namby-pamby in my upbringing. She would say: 'Nobody can say anything against *me*, but I always say that it is not so bad to break the Seventh Commandment as the Sixth, because at any rate it requires the consent of the other party.' I pleased her greatly on one occasion by asking for *Tristram Shandy* as a birthday present. She said: 'I won't write in it, because people will say what an odd grandmother you have!' Nevertheless she did write in it. It was an autographed first edition. This is the only occasion I can remember on which I succeeded in pleasing her.

She had a considerable contempt for everything that she regarded as silly. On her birthday she always had a dinner-party of thirteen, and made the most superstitious member of the party go out first. I remember once an affected granddaughter of hers came to see her, bringing a lap dog which annoyed my grandmother by barking. Her granddaughter protested that the dog was an angel. 'Angel? – angel?' said my grandmother indignantly. 'What nonsense! Do you think he has a soul?' 'Yes, grandmama', replied the young woman pluckily. Throughout the rest of the afternoon, during which her granddaughter remained with her, she informed each visitor in turn: 'What do you think that silly girl Grisel says? She says dogs have souls.' It was her practice to sit in her large drawing-room every afternoon while streams of visitors, including the most eminent writers of the time, came to tea. When any of them left the room, she would turn to the others with a sigh and say: 'Fools are so fatiguin'.' She had been brought up as a Jacobite, her family being Irish Dillons, who fled to France after the Battle of the Boyne and had a private regiment of their own in the French army. The French Revolution reconciled them to Ireland, but my grandmother was brought up in Florence, where her father was Minister. In Florence she used to go once a week to visit the widow of the Young Pretender. She used to say that the only thing she regarded as stupid about her ancestors was their having been Jacobites. I never knew my maternal grandfather, but I heard it said that he used to brow-beat my grandmother, and felt that, if so, he must have been a very remarkable man.[1] She had an enormous family of sons and daughters, most of

[1] It was true. See *The Ladies of Alderley*, by Nancy Mitford, 1938.

whom came to lunch with her every Sunday. Her eldest son was a Mohammedan, and almost stone deaf. Her second son, Lyulph, was a free-thinker, and spent his time fighting the Church on the London School Board. Her third son, Algernon, was a Roman Catholic priest, a Papal Chamberlain and Bishop of Emmaus. Lyulph was witty, encyclopaedic, and caustic. Algernon was witty, fat, and greedy. Henry, the Mohammedan, was devoid of all the family merits, and was, I think, the greatest bore I have ever known. In spite of his deafness, he insisted upon hearing everything said to him. At the Sunday luncheons there would be vehement arguments, for among the daughters and sons-in-law there were representatives of the Church of England, Unitarianism, and Positivism, to be added to the religions represented by the sons. When the argument reached a certain pitch of ferocity, Henry would become aware that there was a noise, and would ask what it was about. His nearest neighbour would shout a biased version of the argument into his ear, whereupon all the others would shout 'No, no, Henry, it isn't that!' At this point the din became truly terrific. A favourite trick of my Uncle Lyulph at Sunday luncheons was to ask: 'Who is there here who believes in the literal truth of the story of Adam and Eve ?' His object in asking the question was to compel the Mohammedan and the priest to agree with each other, which they hated doing. I used to go to these luncheons in fear and trembling, since I never knew but what the whole pack would turn upon me. I had only one friend whom I could count on among them, and she was not a Stanley by birth. She was my Uncle Lyulph's wife, sister of Sir Hugh Bell. My grandmother always considered herself very broad-minded because she had not objected to Lyulph marrying into what she called 'trade', but as Sir Hugh was a multi-millionaire I was not very much impressed.

Formidable as my grandmother was, she had her limits. Once when Mr Gladstone was expected to tea, she told us all beforehand how she was going to explain to him exactly in what respects his Home Rule policy was mistaken. I was present throughout his visit, but not one word of criticism did she utter. His hawk's eye could quell even her. Her son-in-law, Lord Carlisle, told me of an even more humiliating episode which occurred at Naworth Castle on one occasion when she was staying there. Burne-Jones, who was also staying there, had a tobacco pouch which was made to look like a tortoise. There was also a real tortoise, which strayed one day by mistake into the library. This suggested a prank to the younger generation. During dinner, Burne-Jones's tobacco pouch was placed near the drawing-room fire, and when the ladies returned from dinner it was dramatically discovered that this time the tortoise had got into the drawing-room. On its being picked up, somebody exclaimed with astonishment that its back had grown soft. Lord Carlisle fetched from the library the appropriate volume of the Encyclopaedia, and read out a pretended passage saying that great heat sometimes had this effect. My grandmother expressed the greatest interest in this fact of natural history, and frequently alluded to it on subsequent occasions. Many years later, when she was quarrelling with Lady Carlisle about Home Rule, her daughter maliciously told her the truth of this incident. My grandmother retorted: 'I may be many things, but I am not a fool, and I refuse to believe you.'

My brother, who had the Stanley temperament, loved the Stanleys and hated the Russells. I loved the Russells and feared the Stanleys. As I have grown older, however, my feelings have changed. I owe to the Russells shyness, sensitiveness, and metaphysics; to the Stanleys vigour, good health, and good spirits. On the whole, the latter seems a better inheritance than the former.

Reverting to what I can remember of childhood, the next thing that is vivid in my memory is the winter of 1880–81, which we spent at Bournemouth. It was there that I first learned the name of Thomas Hardy, whose book *The Trumpet Major*, in three volumes, was lying on the drawing-room table. I think the only reason I remember it is that I wondered what a trumpet major might be, and that it was by the author of *Far from the Madding Crowd*, and I did not know either what a madding crowd was. While we were there, my German governess told me that one got no Christmas presents unless one believed in Father Christmas. This caused me to burst into tears, as I could not believe in such a personage. My only other recollections of the place are that there was an unprecedented snow-storm, and that I learned to skate – an amusement of which I was passionately fond throughout my boyhood. I never missed an opportunity of skating, even when the ice was unsafe. Once when I was staying in Dover Street I went skating in St James's Park and fell in. I had a feeling of disgrace in having to run through the streets dripping wet, but I nevertheless persisted in the practice of skating on thin ice. Of the following year I remember nothing whatever, but my tenth birthday is still as vivid to me as if it were yesterday. The weather was bright and warm, and I sat in a blossoming laburnum tree, but presently a Swiss lady, who had come to be interviewed, and subsequently became my governess, was sent out to play ball with me. She said she had 'catched' the ball, and I corrected her. When I had to cut my own birthday cake, I was much ashamed because I could not get the first slice to come out. But what stays most in my mind is the impression of sunshine.

At the age of eleven, I began Euclid, with my brother as my tutor. This was one of the great events of my life, as dazzling as first love. I had not imagined that there was anything so delicious in the world. After I had learned the fifth proposition, my brother told me that it was generally considered difficult, but I had found no difficulty whatever. This was the first time it had dawned upon me that I might have some intelligence. From that moment until Whitehead and I finished *Principia Mathematica*, when I was thirty-eight, mathematics was my chief interest, and my chief source of happiness. Like all happiness, however, it was not unalloyed. I had been told that Euclid proved things, and was much disappointed that he started with axioms. At first I refused to accept them unless my brother could offer me some reason for doing so, but he said: 'If you don't accept them we cannot go on', and as I wished to go on, I reluctantly admitted them *pro tem.* The doubt as to the premisses of mathematics which I felt at that moment remained with me, and determined the course of my subsequent work.

The beginnings of Algebra I found far more difficult, perhaps as a result of bad teaching. I was made to learn by heart: 'The square of the sum of two numbers is equal to the sum of their squares increased by twice their product.' I had not the vaguest idea what this meant, and when I could not remember the words, my tutor threw the book at my head, which did not stimulate my intellect in any way. After the first beginnings of Algebra, however, everything else went smoothly. I used to enjoy impressing a new tutor with my knowledge. Once, at the age of thirteen, when I had a new tutor, I spun a penny, and he said to me: 'Why does that penny spin?' and I replied: 'Because I make a couple with my fingers.' 'What do you know about couples?' he said. 'Oh, I know all about couples', I replied airily. My grandmother was always afraid that I should overwork, and kept my hours of lessons very short. The result was that I used to work in my bedroom on the sly with one candle, sitting at my desk in a night-shirt on cold evenings, ready to blow out the candle and pop into bed at the slightest sound. I hated Latin and Greek, and thought it merely foolish to learn a language that nobody speaks. I liked mathematics best, and next to mathematics I liked history. Having no one with whom to compare myself, I did not know for a long time whether I was better or worse than other boys, but I remember once hearing my Uncle Rollo saying goodbye to Jowett, the Master of Balliol, at the front door, and remarking: 'Yes, he's getting on very well indeed', and I knew, though how I cannot tell, that he was speaking of my work. As soon as I realised that I was intelligent, I determined to achieve something of intellectual importance if it should be at all possible, and throughout my youth I let nothing whatever stand in the way of this ambition.

It would be completely misleading to suggest that my childhood was all solemnity and seriousness. I got just as much fun out of life as I could, some of it I am afraid of a somewhat mischievous kind. The family doctor, an old Scotchman with mutton-chop whiskers, used to come in his brougham which waited at the front door while the man of healing spoke his piece. His coachman had an exquisite top-hat, calculated to advertise the excellence of the practice. I used to get on the roof above this splendid head-piece and drop rotten rosebuds out of the gutter on to its flat top. They spread all over with a delicious squish and I withdrew my head quickly enough for the coachman to suppose that they had fallen from heaven. Sometimes I did even worse. I threw snowballs at him when he was driving, thereby endangering the valuable lives of him and his employer. I had another amusement which I much enjoyed. On a Sunday, when the Park was crowded, I would climb to the very top of a large beech tree on the edge of our grounds. There I would hang upside down and scream and watch the crowd gravely discussing how a rescue should be effected. When I saw them nearing a decision I would get the right way up and quietly come down. During the time when Jimmie Baillie stayed with me I was led into even more desperate courses. The bath chair in which I remembered my grandfather being wheeled about had been lodged in a lumber room. We found it there and raced it down whatever hills we could find. When this was discovered it was considered blasphemy and we were reproached with melancholy gravity. Some of our doings, however, never came to the ears of the grown-ups. We tied a rope to a branch of a tree and learnt by long practice to swing in a complete circle and return to our starting point. It was only by great skill that one could avoid stopping half-way and bumping one's back painfully into the rough bark of the tree. When other boys came to visit us, we used to carry out the correct performance ourselves and when the others attempted to imitate us we maliciously exulted in their painful failure. My Uncle Rollo, with whom for a while we used to spend three months each year, had three cows and a donkey. The donkey was more intelligent than the cows and learnt to open the gates between the fields with his nose, but he was said to be unruly and useless. I did not believe this and, after some unsuccessful attempts, I learnt to ride him without saddle or bridle. He would kick and buck but he never got me off except when I had tied a can full of rattling stones to his tail. I used to ride him all round the country, even when I went to visit the daughter of Lord Wolseley who lived about three miles from my uncle's house.

Chapter 2

Adolescence

My childhood was, on the whole, happy and straightforward, and I felt affection for most of the grown-ups with whom I was brought in contact. I remember a very definite change when I reached what in modern child psychology is called the 'latency period'. At this stage, I began to enjoy using slang, pretending to have no feelings, and being generally 'manly'. I began to despise my people, chiefly because of their extreme horror of slang and their absurd notion that it was dangerous to climb trees. So many things were forbidden me that I acquired the habit of deceit, in which I persisted up to the age of twenty-one. It became second nature to me to think that whatever I was doing had better be kept to myself, and I have never quite overcome the impulse to concealment which was thus generated. I still have an impulse to hide what I am reading when anybody comes into the room, and to hold my tongue generally as to where I have been, and what I have done. It is only by a certain effort of will that I can overcome this impulse, which was generated by the years during which I had to find my way among a set of foolish prohibitions.

The years of adolescence were to me very lonely and very unhappy. Both in the life of the emotions and in the life of the intellect, I was obliged to preserve an impenetrable secrecy towards my people. My interests were divided between sex, religion, and mathematics. I find the recollection of my sexual preoccupation in adolescence unpleasant. I do not like to remember how I felt in those years, but I will do my best to relate things as they were and not as I could wish them to have been. The facts of sex first became known to me when I was twelve years old, through a boy named Ernest Logan who had been one of my kindergarten companions at an earlier age. He and I slept in the same room one night, and he explained the nature of copulation and its part in the generation of children, illustrating his remarks by funny stories. I found what he said extremely interesting, although I had as yet no physical response. It appeared to me at the time self-evident that free love was the only rational system, and that marriage was bound up with Christian superstition. (I am sure this reflection occurred to me only a very short time after I first knew the facts.) When I was fourteen, my tutor mentioned to me that I should shortly undergo an important physical change. By this time I was more or less able to understand what he meant. I had at that time another boy, Jimmie Baillie, staying with me, the same whom I met at Vancouver in 1929, and he and I used to talk things over, not only with each other, but with the page-boy, who was about our own age or perhaps a year older, and rather more knowing than we were. When it was discovered that we had spent a certain afternoon in doubtful conversation with the page-boy, we were spoken to in tones of deep sorrow, sent to bed, and kept on bread and water. Strange to say, this treatment did not destroy my interest in sex. We spent a great deal of time in the sort of conversation that is considered improper, and in endeavouring to find out things of which we were ignorant. For this purpose I found the medical dictionary very useful. At fifteen, I began to have sexual passions, of almost intolerable intensity. While I was sitting at work, endeavouring to concentrate, I would be continually distracted by erections, and I fell into the practice of masturbating, in which, however, I always remained moderate. I was much ashamed of this practice, and endeavoured to discontinue it. I persisted in it, nevertheless, until the age of twenty, when I dropped it suddenly because I was in love.

The same tutor who told me of the approach of puberty mentioned, some months later, that one speaks of a man's breast, but of a woman's breasts. This remark caused me such an intolerable intensity of feeling that I appeared to be shocked, and he rallied me on my prudery. Many hours every day were spent in desiring to see the female body, and I used to try to get glimpses through windows when the maids were dressing, always unsuccessfully, however. My friend and I spent a winter making an underground house, which consisted of a long tunnel, through which one crawled on hands and knees, and then of a room 6 foot cube. There was a housemaid whom I used to induce to accompany me to this underground house, where I kissed her and hugged her. Once I asked her whether she would like to spend a night with me, and she said she would die rather, which I believed. She also expressed surprise, saying that she had thought I was good. Consequently this affair proceeded no further. I had by this time quite lost the rationalist outlook on sex which I had had before puberty, and accepted entirely the conventional views as quite sound. I became morbid, and regarded myself as very wicked. At the same time, I took a considerable interest in my own psychology, which I studied carefully and not unintelligently, but I was told that all introspection is morbid, so that I regarded this interest in my own thoughts and feelings as another proof of mental aberration. After two or three years of introspection, however, I suddenly realised that, as it is the only method of obtaining a great deal of important knowledge, it ought not to be condemned as morbid. This relieved my feelings on this point.

Concurrently with this physical preoccupation with sex, went a great intensity of idealistic feeling, which I did not at that time recognise as sexual in origin. I became intensely interested in the beauty of sunsets and clouds, and trees in spring and autumn, but my interest was of a very sentimental kind, owing to the fact that it was an unconscious sublimation of sex, and an attempt to escape from reality. I read poetry widely, beginning with very bad poetry such as *In Memoriam*. While I was sixteen and seventeen, I read, as far as I can remember, the whole of Milton's poetry, most of Byron, a great deal of Shakespeare, large parts of Tennyson, and finally Shelley. I came upon Shelley by accident. One day I was waiting for my Aunt Maude in her sitting-room at Dover Street. I opened it at *Alastor*, which seemed to me the most beautiful poem I had ever read. Its unreality was, of course, the great element in my admiration for it. I had got about half-way through when my Aunt arrived, and I had to put the volume back in the shelf. I asked the grown-ups whether Shelley was not considered a great poet, but found that they thought ill of him. This, however, did not deter me, and I spent all my spare time reading him, and learning him by heart. Knowing no one to whom I could speak of what I thought or felt, I used to reflect how wonderful it would have been to know Shelley, and to wonder whether I should ever meet any live human being with whom I should feel so much in sympathy.

Alongside with my interest in poetry, went an intense interest in religion and philosophy. My grandfather was Anglican, my grandmother was a Scotch Presbyterian, but gradually became a Unitarian. I was taken on alternate Sundays to the (Episcopalian) Parish Church at Petersham and to the Presbyterian Church at Richmond, while at home I was taught the doctrines of Unitarianism. It was these last that I believed until about the age of fifteen. At this age I began a systematic investigation of the supposed rational arguments in favour of fundamental Christian beliefs. I spent endless hours in meditation upon this subject; I could not speak to anybody about it for fear of giving pain. I suffered acutely both from the gradual loss of faith and from the need of silence. I thought that if I ceased to believe in God, freedom and immortality, I should be very unhappy. I found, however, that the reasons given in favour of these dogmas were very unconvincing. I considered them one at a time with great seriousness. The first to go was free will. At the age of fifteen, I became convinced that the motions of matter, whether living or dead, proceeded entirely in accordance with the laws of dynamics, and therefore the will can have no influence upon the body. I used at this time to write down my reflections in English written in Greek letters in a book headed 'Greek Exercises'.[1] I did this for fear lest someone should find out what I was thinking. In this book

[1] Some portions of this book are included on pp. 42 to 52.

I recorded my conviction that the human body is a machine. I should have found intellectual satisfaction in becoming a materialist, but on grounds almost identical with those of Descartes (who was unknown to me except as the inventor of Cartesian co-ordinates), I came to the conclusion that consciousness is an undeniable datum, and therefore pure materialism is impossible. This was at the age of fifteen. About two years later, I became convinced that there is no life after death, but I still believed in God, because the 'First Cause' argument appeared to be irrefutable. At the age of eighteen, however, shortly before I went to Cambridge, I read Mill's *Autobiography*, where I found a sentence to the effect that his father taught him that the question 'Who made me ?' cannot be answered, since it immediately suggests the further question 'Who made God ?'. This led me to abandon the 'First Cause' argument, and to become an atheist. Throughout the long period of religious doubt, I had been rendered very unhappy by the gradual loss of belief, but when the process was completed, I found to my surprise that I was quite glad to be done with the whole subject.

Throughout this time, I read omnivorously. I taught myself enough Italian to read Dante and Machiavelli. I read Comte, of whom, however, I did not think much. I read Mill's *Political Economy* and *Logic*, and made elaborate abstracts of them. I read Carlyle with a good deal of interest, but with a complete repudiation of his purely sentimental arguments in favour of religion. For I took the view then, which I have taken ever since, that a theological proposition should not be accepted unless there is the same kind of evidence for it that would be required for a proposition in science. I read Gibbon, and Milman's *History of Christianity*, and *Gulliver's Travels* unexpurgated. The account of the Yahoos had a profound effect upon me, and I began to see human beings in that light.

It must be understood that the whole of this mental life was deeply buried; not a sign of it showed in my intercourse with other people. Socially I was shy, childish, awkward, well behaved, and good-natured. I used to watch with envy people who could manage social intercourse without anguished awkwardness. There was a young man called Cattermole who, I suppose, must have been a bit of a bounder; but I watched him walking with a smart young woman with easy familiarity and evidently pleasing her. And I would think that never, never, never should I learn to behave in a manner that could possibly please any woman in whom I might be interested. Until just before my sixteenth birthday, I was sometimes able to speak of some things to my tutors. Until that date I was educated at home, but my tutors seldom stayed more than three months. I did not know why this was, but I think it was because whenever a new tutor arrived, I used to induce him to enter into a conspiracy with me to deceive my people wherever their demands were absurd. One tutor I had was an agnostic, and used to allow me to discuss religion with him. I imagine that he was dismissed because this was discovered. The tutor whom my people liked best and who stayed the longest with me was a man dying of consumption whose breath stank intolerably. It never occurred to them that it was unwise, from a health point of view, to have me perpetually in his neighbourhood.

Just before my sixteenth birthday, I was sent to an Army crammer at Old Southgate, which was then in the country. I was not sent to him in order to cram for the Army, but in order to be prepared for the scholarship examination at Trinity College, Cambridge. Almost all of the other people there, however, were going into the Army, with the exception of one or two reprobates who were going to take Orders. Everybody, except myself, was seventeen or eighteen, or nineteen, so that I was much the youngest. They were all of an age to have just begun frequenting prostitutes, and this was their main topic of conversation. The most admired among them was a young man who asserted that he had had syphilis and got cured, which gave him great kudos. They would sit round telling bawdy stories. Every incident gave them opportunities for improper remarks. Once the crammer sent one of them with a note to a neighbouring house. On returning, he related to the others that he had rung the bell and a maid had appeared to whom he had said: 'I have brought a letter' (meaning a French letter) to which she replied: 'I am glad you have brought a letter.' When one day in church a hymn was sung containing the line: 'Here I'll raise my Ebenezer', they remarked: 'I never heard it called that before!'

In spite of my previous silent preoccupation with sex, contact with it in this brutal form deeply shocked me. I became very Puritanical in my views, and decided that sex without deep love is beastly. I retired into myself, and had as little to do with the others as possible. The others, however, found me suitable for teasing. They used to make me sit on a chair on a table and sing the only song I knew, which was:

> Old Abraham is dead and gone,
> We ne'er shall see him more,
> He used to wear an old great coat,
> All buttoned down before.
>
> He also had another coat,
> Which was of a different kind,
> Instead of buttoning down before,
> It buttoned up behind.

I soon realised that my only chance of escape from their attentions was to remain imperturbably good-humoured. After a term or two, another teasable boy arrived, who had the added merit of losing his temper. This caused them to let me alone. Gradually, also, I got used to their conversation and ceased to be shocked by it. I remained, however, profoundly unhappy. There was a footpath leading across fields to New Southgate, and I used to go there alone to watch the sunset and contemplate suicide. I did not, however, commit suicide, because I wished to know more of mathematics. My people would, of course, have been horrified if they had known of the sort of conversation that was habitual, but as I was getting on well with mathematics I wished on the whole to stay, and never told them a word as to the sort of place it was. At the end of the year and a half at the crammer's I was examined for scholarships in December 1889, and obtained a minor scholarship. During the ten months that intervened before my going to Cambridge, I lived at home, and coached with the man whom the crammer had hired to teach me.

For a time at the crammer's I had one friend – a man named Edward FitzGerald. His mother was American, and his father Canadian, and he became well known in later years as a great mountain climber, performing many exploits in the New Zealand Alps and the Andes. His people were very rich, and lived in a large house, No. 19 Rutland Gate.[1] He had a sister who wrote poetry and was a great friend of Robert Browning whom I frequently met at Rutland Gate.[2] She afterwards became first Lady Edmond Fitzmaurice, and then Signora de Philippi. His sister was considerably older than he was, and an accomplished classical scholar. I conceived a romantic admiration for her, though when I met her later she seemed an unmitigated bore. He had been brought up in America, and was exceedingly sophisticated. He was lazy and lackadaisical, but had remarkable ability in a great many directions, notably in mathematics. He could tell the year of any reputable wine or cigar. He could eat a spoonful of mixed mustard and Cayenne pepper. He was intimate with Continental brothels. His knowledge of literature was extensive, and while an undergraduate at Cambridge, he acquired a fine library of first editions. When he first came to the crammer's, I took to him at once, because he was at any rate a civilised being, which none of the others were. (Robert Browning died while I was there, and none of the others had ever heard of him.) We used both to go home for the weekend, and on the way he would

---

[1] It is now pulled down.

[2] I had met Robert Browning once before at the age of two when he came to lunch at Pembroke Lodge and talked unceasingly although everybody wished to hear the actor Salvini whom he had brought with him. At last I exclaimed in a piercing voice, 'I wish that man would stop talking'. And he did.

always take me first to lunch with his people and then to a matinée. My people made inquiries about the family, but were reassured by a testimonial from Robert Browning. Having been lonely so long, I devoted a somewhat absurd amount of affection to FitzGerald. To my great delight, I was invited to go abroad with him and his people in August. This was the first time I had been abroad since the age of two, and the prospect of seeing foreign countries excited me greatly. We went first to Paris, where the Exhibition of 1889 was in progress, and we went to the top of the Eiffel Tower, which was new that year. We then went to Switzerland, where we drove from place to place for about a week, ending up in the Engadine. He and I climbed two mountains, Piz Corvach, and Piz Palü. On both occasions there was a snow-storm. On the first I had mountain sickness, and on the second he did. The second occasion was quite exciting, as one of our guides fell over a precipice, and had to be hauled up by the rope. I was impressed by his *sang froid*, as he swore as he fell over.

Unfortunately, however, FitzGerald and I had a somewhat serious disagreement during this time. He spoke with what I thought unpardonable rudeness to his mother, and being young I reproached him for doing so. He was exceedingly angry, with a cold anger which lasted for months. When we returned to the crammer's, we shared lodgings, and he devoted himself to saying disagreeable things, in which he displayed great skill. I came to hate him with a violence which, in retrospect, I can hardly understand. On one occasion, in an access of fury, I got my hands on his throat and started to strangle him. I intended to kill him, but when he began to grow livid, I relented. I do not think he knew that I had intended murder. After this, we remained fairly good friends throughout his time at Cambridge, which, however, ended with his marriage at the end of his second year.

Throughout this time, I had been getting more and more out of sympathy with my people. I continued to agree with them in politics, but in nothing else. At first I sometimes tried to talk to them about things that I was considering, but they always laughed at me, and this caused me to hold my tongue. It appeared to me obvious that the happiness of mankind should be the aim of all action, and I discovered to my surprise that there were those who thought otherwise. Belief in happiness, I found, was called Utilitarianism, and was merely one among a number of ethical theories. I adhered to it after this discovery, and was rash enough to tell grandmother that I was a utilitarian. She covered me with ridicule, and ever after submitted ethical conundrums to me, telling me to solve them on utilitarian principles. I perceived that she had no good grounds for rejecting utilitarianism, and that her opposition to it was not intellectually respectable. When she discovered that I was interested in metaphysics, she told me that the whole subject could be summed up in the saying: 'What is mind? no matter; what is matter? never mind.' At the fifteenth or sixteenth repetition of this remark, it ceased to amuse me, but my grandmother's animus against metaphysics continued to the end of her life. Her attitude is expressed in the following verses:

> O Science metaphysical
> And very very quizzical,
> You only make this maze of life the mazier;
>   For boasting to illuminate
>   Such riddles dark as Will and Fate
> You muddle them to hazier and hazier.

> The cause of every action,
> You expound with satisfaction;
> Through the mind in all its corners and recesses
>   You say that you have travelled,
>   And all problems unravelled
> And axioms you call your learned guesses.

> Right and wrong you've so dissected,
> And their fragments so connected,
> That which we follow doesn't seem to matter;
>   But the cobwebs you have wrought,
>   And the silly flies they have caught,
> It needs no broom miraculous to shatter.

> You know no more than I,
> What is laughter, tear, or sigh,
> Or love, or hate, or anger, or compassion;
>   Metaphysics, then, adieu,
>   Without you I can do,
> And I think you'll very soon be out of fashion.

I remember her saying to me once after I was grown-up: 'I hear you are writing *another* book', in the tone of voice in which one might say: 'I hear you have another illegitimate child!' Mathematics she did not positively object to, though it was difficult for her to believe that it could serve any useful purpose. Her hope for me was that I should become a Unitarian minister. I held my tongue as to my religious opinions until I was twenty-one. Indeed, after the age of fourteen I found living at home only endurable at the cost of complete silence about everything that interested me. She practised a form of humour, which, though nominally amusing, was really full of animus. I did not at that time know how to reply in kind, and merely felt hurt and miserable. My Aunt Agatha was equally bad, and my Uncle Rollo at the time had withdrawn into himself through sorrow at his first wife's death. My brother, who was at Balliol, had become a Buddhist, and used to tell me that the soul could be contained in the smallest envelope. I remember thinking of all the smallest envelopes that I had seen, and I imagined the soul beating against them like a heart, but from what I could tell of esoteric Buddhism from my brother's conversation, it did not offer me anything that I found of service. After he came of age, I saw very little of him, as the family considered him wicked, and he therefore kept away from home. I was upheld by the determination to do something of importance in mathematics when I grew up, but I did not suppose that I should ever meet anybody with whom I could make friends, or to whom I could express any of my thoughts freely, nor did I expect that any part of my life would be free from great unhappiness.

Throughout my time at Southgate I was very much concerned with politics and economics. I read Mill's *Political Economy*, which I was inclined to accept completely; also Herbert Spencer, who seemed to me too doctrinaire in *The Man Versus The State*, although I was in broad agreement with his bias.

My Aunt Agatha introduced me to the books of Henry George, which she greatly admired. I became convinced that land national-isation would secure all the benefits that Socialists hoped to obtain from Socialism, and continued to hold this view until the war of 1914–18.

My grandmother Russell and my Aunt Agatha were passionate supporters of Gladstone's Home Rule policy, and many Irish M.P.s used to visit Pembroke Lodge. This was at a time when *The Times* professed to have documentary proof that Parnell was an accomplice in murder. Almost the whole upper class, including the great majority of those who had supported Gladstone till 1886, accepted this view, until, in 1889, it was dramatically disproved by the forger Piggot's inability to spell 'hesitancy'. My grandmother and aunt always vehemently rejected the view that Parnell's followers were in alliance with terror-ists. They admired Parnell, with whom I once shook hands. But when he became involved in scandal, they agreed with Gladstone in repudiat-ing him.

Twice I went with my Aunt Agatha to Ireland. I used to go for walks with Michael Davitt, the Irish patriot, and also by myself. The beauty of the scenery made a profound impression on me. I remember especially a small lake in County Wicklow, called Lugala. I have associated it ever since, though for no good reason, with the lines:

> Like as the waves make toward the pebbled shore,
> So do our minutes hasten to their end.

Fifty years later, when visiting my friend Crompton Davies in Dublin, I induced him to take me to Lugala. But he took me to a wood high above the lake, not to the 'pebbled shore' that I had remembered, and I went away convinced that one should not attempt to renew old memories.

In the year 1883 my Uncle Rollo bought a house on the slopes of Hindhead, where, for a long time, we all visited him for three months in every year. At that time there were no houses on Hindhead except two derelict coaching inns, the 'Royal Huts' and the 'Seven Thorns'. (They are not now derelict.) Tyndall's house, which started the fashion, was being built. I was frequently taken to see Tyndall, and he gave me one of his books, *The Forms of Water*. I admired him as an eminent Man of Science, and strongly desired to make some impression upon him. Twice I had some success. The first time was while he was talking to my Uncle Rollo, and I balanced on one finger two walking sticks with crooks. Tyndall asked me what I was doing, and I said I was thinking of a practical method of determining the centre of gravity. The second time, some years later, was when I told him that I had climbed the Piz Palü. He had been a pioneer Alpinist. I found inexpressible delight in walks through the heather, over Blackdown, down the Punchbowl, and as far as the Devil's Jumps at Churt. I particularly remember exploring a small road called 'Mother Bunch's Lane' (it is now full of houses, and has a sign saying 'Bunch Lane'). It continually diminished, and at last became a mere path leading to the crest of Hurt Hill. Quite suddenly, when I expected nothing, I came upon an enormous view, embracing half of Sussex and almost all of Surrey. Moments of this sort have been important in my life. In general, I find that things that have happened to me out of doors have made a deeper impression than things that have happened indoors.

APPENDIX: 'GREEK EXERCISES'

1888. March 3. I shall write about some subjects which now interest me. I have in consequence of a variety of circumstances come to look into the very foundations of the religion in which I have been brought up. On some points my conclusions have been to confirm my former creed, while on others I have been irresistibly led to such conclusions as would not only shock my people, but have given me much pain. I have arrived at certainty in few things, but my opinions, even where not convictions, are on some things nearly such. I have not the courage to tell my people that I scarcely believe in immortality. I used to speak freely to Mr Ewen on such matters, but now I cannot let out my thoughts to any one, and this is the only means I have of letting off steam. I intend to discuss some of my problems here.

19th. I mean today to put down my grounds for belief in God. I may say to begin with that I do believe in God and that I should call myself a theist if I had to give my creed a name. Now in finding reasons for believing in God I shall only take account of scientific arguments. This is a vow I have made which costs me much to keep, and to reject all sentiment. To find then scientific grounds for a belief in God we must go back to the beginning of all things. We know that the present laws of nature have always been in force. The exact quantity of matter and energy now in the universe must always have been in existence, but the nebular hypothesis points to no distant date for the time when the whole universe was filled with undifferentiated nebulous matter. Hence it is quite possible that the matter and force now in existence may have had a creation, which clearly could be only by divine power. But even granting that they have always been in existence, yet whence came the laws which regulate the action of force on matter ? I think they are only attributable to a divine controlling power, which I accordingly call God.

March 22. Now let us look into the reasonableness of the reasoning. Let us suppose that the universe we now see has, as some suppose, grown by mere chance. Should we then expect every atom to act in any given conditions precisely similarly to another atom ? I think if atoms be lifeless there is no reason to expect them to do anything without a controlling power. If on the other hand they be endowed with free will we are forced to the conclusion that all atoms in the universe have combined in the commonwealth and have made laws which none of them ever break. This is clearly an absurd hypothesis and therefore we are forced to believe in God. But this way of proving his existence at the same time disproves miracles and other supposed manifestations of divine power. It does not however disprove their possibility, for of course the maker of laws can also unmake them. We may arrive in another way at a disbelief in miracles. For if God is the maker of the laws, surely it would imply an imperfection in the law if it had to be altered occasionally, and such imperfection we can never impute to the divine nature, as in the Bible, God repented him of the work.

April 2. I now come to the subject which personally interests us poor mortals more perhaps than any other. I mean the question of immortality. This is the one in which I have been most disappointed and pained by thought. There are two ways of looking at it, first by evolution and comparing men to animals, second, by comparing men with God. The first is the more scientific, for we know all about the animals but not about God. Well, I hold that, taking free will first, to consider there is no clear dividing line between man and the protozoan, therefore if we give free will to men we must give it also the protozoan; this is rather hard to do. Therefore, unless we are willing to give free will to the protozoan we cannot give it to man. This however is possible but it is difficult to imagine, if, as seems to me probable, protoplasm only came together in the ordinary course of nature without any special providence from God; then we and all living things are simply kept going by chemical forces and are nothing more wonderful than a tree, which no one pretends has free will, and even if we had a good enough knowledge of the forces acting on anyone at any time, the motives pro and con, the constitution of his brain at any time, then we could tell exactly what he will do. Again from the religious point of view free will is a very arrogant thing for us to claim, for of course it is an interruption of God's laws, for by his ordinary laws all our actions would be fixed as the stars. I think we must leave to God the primary establishment of laws which are never broken and determine everybody's doings. And not having free will we cannot have immortality.

Monday, April 6. I do wish I believed in the life eternal, for it makes me quite miserable to think man is merely a kind of machine endowed, unhappily for himself, with consciousness. But no other theory is consistent with the complete omnipotence of God of which science, I think, gives ample manifestations. Thus I must either be an atheist or disbelieve in immortality. Finding the first impossible I adopt the second and let no one know. I think, however disappointing may be this view of men, it does give us a wonderful idea of God's greatness to think that He can in the beginning create laws which by acting on a mere mass of nebulous matter, perhaps merely ether diffused through this part of the universe, will produce creatures like ourselves, conscious not only of our existence but even able to fathom to a certain extent God's mysteries. All this with no more intervention on his part. Now let us think whether this doctrine of want of free will is so absurd. If we talk about it to anyone they kick their legs or something of that sort. But perhaps they cannot help it for they have something to prove and therefore that supplies a motive to them to do it. Thus in anything we do we always have motives which determine us. Also there is no line of demarcation between Shakespeare or Herbert Spencer and a Papuan. But between them and a Papuan there seems as much difference as between a Papuan and a monkey.

April 14th. Yet there are great difficulties in the way of this doctrine that man has not immortality nor free will nor a soul, in short that he is nothing more than a species of ingenious machine endowed with consciousness. For consciousness in itself is a quality quite distinguishing men from dead matter and if they have one thing different from dead matter why not have another, free will? By free will I mean that they do not for example obey the first law of motion, or at least that the direction in which the energy they contain is employed depends not entirely on external circumstances. Moreover it seems impossible to imagine that man, the Great Man, with his reason, his knowledge of the universe, and his ideas of right and wrong, Man with his emotions, his love and hate and his religion, that this Man should be a mere perishable chemical compound whose character and his influence for good or for evil depend solely and entirely on the particular motions of the molecules of his brain and that all the greatest men have been great by reason of some one molecule hitting up against some other a little oftener than in other men. Does not this seem utterly incredible and must not any one be mad who believes in such absurdity? But what is the alternative? That, accepting the evolution theory which is practically proved, apes having gradually increased in intelligence, God suddenly by a miracle endowed one with that wonderful reason which it is a mystery how we possess. Then is man, truly called the most glorious work of God, is man destined to perish utterly after he has been so many ages evolving? We cannot say, but I prefer that idea to God's having needed a miracle to produce man and now leaving him free to do as he likes.

April 18th. Accepting then the theory that man is mortal and destitute of free will, which is as much as ever a mere theory, as of course all these kinds of things are mere speculation, what idea can we form of right and wrong? Many say if you make any mention of such an absurd doctrine as predestination, which comes to much the same thing, though parsons don't think so, why what becomes of conscience, etc., which they think has been directly implanted in man by God. Now my idea is that our conscience is in the first place due to evolution, which would of course form instincts of self-preservation, and in the second place to education and civilisation, which introduces great refinements of the idea of self-preservation. Let us take for example the ten commandments as illustrative of primitive morality. Many of them are conducive to quiet living of the community which is best for the preservation of the species. Thus what is always considered the worst possible crime and the one for which most remorse is felt is murder, which is direct annihilation of the species. Again, as we know, among the Hebrews it was thought a mark of God's favour to have many children, while the childless were considered as cursed of God. Among the Romans also widows were hated and I believe forbidden to remain unmarried in Rome more than a year. Now why these peculiar ideas ? Were they not simply because these objects of pity or dislike did not bring forth fresh human beings ? We can well understand how such ideas might grow up when men became rather sensible, for if murder and suicide were common in a tribe that tribe would die out and hence one which held such acts in abhorrence would have a great advantage. Of course among more educated societies these ideas are rather modified. My own I mean to give next time.

April 20th. Thus I think that primitive morality always originates in the idea of the preservation of the species. But is this a rule which a civilised community ought to follow ? I think not. My rule of life, which I guide my conduct by, and a departure from which I consider as a sin, is to act in the manner which I believe to be most likely to produce the greatest happiness, considering both the intensity of the happiness and the number of people made happy. I know that Granny considers this an impractical rule of life and says that since you can never know the thing which will produce the greatest happiness you do much better in following the inner voice. The conscience, however, can easily be seen to depend mostly upon education, as for example common Irishmen do not consider lying wrong, which fact alone seems to me quite sufficient to disprove the divine value of conscience. And since, as I believe, conscience is merely the combined product of evolution and education, then obviously it is an absurdity to follow that rather than reason. And my reason tells me that it is better to act so as to produce maximum happiness than in any other way. For I have tried to see what other object I could set before me and I have failed. Not my own individual happiness in particular, but everybody's equally, making no distinction between myself, relations, friends, or perfect strangers. In real life it makes very little difference to me as long as others are not of my opinion, for obviously where there is any chance of being found out it is better to do what one's people consider right. My reason for this view: first that I can find no other, having been forced, as everybody must who seriously thinks about evolution, to give up the old idea of asking one's conscience, next that it seems to me that happiness is the great thing to seek after. As an application of the theory to practical life, I will say that in a case where nobody but myself was concerned, if indeed such a case exist, I should of course act entirely selfishly to please myself. Suppose for another instance that I had the chance of saving a man who would be better out of the world. Obviously I should consult my own happiness best by plunging in after him. For if I lost my life, that would be a very neat way of managing it, and if I saved him I should have the pleasure of no end of praise. But if I let him drown I should have lost an opportunity of death and should have the misery of much blame, but the world would be better for his loss and, as I have some slight hope, for my life.

April 29th. In all things I have made the vow to follow reason, not the instincts inherited partly from my ancestors and gained gradually by them, owing to a process of natural selection, and partly due to my education. How absurd it would be to follow these in the questions of right and wrong. For as I observed before, the inherited part can only be principles leading to the preservation of the species to which I belong, the part due to education is good or bad according to the individual education. Yet this inner voice, this God-given conscience which made Bloody Mary burn the Protestants, this is what we reasonable beings are to follow. I think this idea mad and I endeavour to go by reason as far as possible. What I take as my ideal is that which ultimately produces greatest happiness of greatest number. Then I can apply reason to find out the course most conducive to this end. In my individual case, however, I can also go more or less by conscience owing to the excellence of my education. But it is curious how people dislike the abandonment of brutish impulses for reason. I remember poor Ewen getting a whole dinner of argument, owing to his running down impulse. Today again at tea Miss Buhler and I had a long discussion because I said that I followed reason not conscience in matters of right and wrong. I do hate having such peculiar opinions because either I must keep them bottled up or else people are horrified at my scepticism, which is as bad with people one cares for as remaining bottled up. I shall be sorry when Miss Buhler goes because I can open my heart easier to her than to my own people, strange to say.

May 3rd. Miss Buhler is gone and I am left again to loneliness and reserve. Happily, however, it seems all but settled that I am going to Southgate and probably within the week. That will save me I feel sure from those morose cogitations during the week, owing to the amount of activity of my life, and novelty at first. I do not expect that I shall enjoy myself at first, but after a time I hope I shall. Certainly it will be good for my work, for my games and my manners, and my future happiness I expect. . . .

May 8th. What a much happier life mine would be but for these wretched ideas of mine about theology. Tomorrow I go, and tonight Granny prayed a beautiful prayer for me in my new life, in which

among other things she said: May he especially be taught to know
God's infinite love for him. Well that is a prayer to which I can
heartily say Amen, and moreover it is one of which I stand in the
greatest need. For according to my ideas of God we have no particular
reason to suppose he loves us. For he only set the machine in working
order to begin with and then left it to work out its own necessary
consequences. Now you may say his laws are such as afford the
greatest possible happiness to us mortals, but that is a statement of
which there can be no proof. Hence I see no reason to believe in
God's kindness towards me, and even the whole prayer was more or
less a solemn farce to me, though I was truly affected by the simple
beauty of prayer and her earnest way in saying it. What a thing it is
to have such people! What might I be had I been worse brought up!

By the way, to change to a more cheerful subject: Marshall[1] and
I had an awfully fine day of it. We went down to the river, marched
into Broom Hall,[2] bagged a boat of Frank's we found there, and rowed
up the river beyond Kingston Bridge without anybody at Broom Hall
having seen us except one old man who was lame. Who the dickens
he was I haven't the faintest idea. Marshall was awfully anxious to
have some tea and we came to an nth rate inn which he thought would
do. Having however like idiots left our jackets in the boat-house at
Teddington we had to march in without coats and were served by
the cheekiest of maids ever I saw who said she thought we were the
carpenters come to mend the house. Then we rowed back as hard as
possible and got home perspiring fearfully and twenty minutes late
which produced a small row.

May 20th. Here I am home again for the first time from Southgate.
It seems a pleasant place but it is sad really to see the kind of boys that
are common everywhere. No mind, no independent thought, no love
of good books nor of the higher refinements of morality. It is really
sad that the upper classes of a civilised and (supposed to be) moral
country can produce nothing better. I am glad I didn't go away from
home sooner as I should never have come to my present state had I
done so, but should have been merely like one of them. (By the way,
how terribly pharisaical I am getting.) I think the six months since
Baillie went have made a great alteration in me. I have become of a
calmer, thoughtfuller, poeticaller nature than I was. One little thing
I think illustrates this well. I never before thought much of the views
in spring, whereas this year I was so simply carried away by their
beauty that I asked Granny if they were not more beautiful than usual,
but she said not. I like poetry much better than I did and have read

[1] A former tutor.
[2] Where my brother was living.

all Shakespeare's historical plays with great delight, and long to read
In Memoriam.

May 27th. As I said last time, I attempt to work according to my
principles without the smallest expectations of reward, and even
without using the light of conscience blindly as an infallible guide . . .
It is very difficult for anyone to work aright with no aid from religion,
by his own internal guidance merely. I have tried and I may say
failed. But the sad thing is that I have no other resource. I have no
helpful religion. My doctrines, such as they are, help my daily life
no more than a formula in Algebra. But the great inducement to a
good life with me is Granny's love and the immense pain I know it
gives her when I go wrong. But she must I suppose die some day and
where then will be my stay? I have the very greatest fear that my life
hereafter be ruined by my having lost the support of religion. I desire
of all things that my religion should not spread, for I of all people
ought, owing to my education and the care taken of my moral well-
being, to be of all people the most moral. So I believe I might be
were it not for these unhappy ideas of mine, for how easy it is when
one is much tempted to convince oneself that only happiness will be
produced by yielding to temptation, when according to my ideas the
course one has been taught to abhor immediately becomes virtuous.
If ever I shall become an utter wreck of what I hope to be I think
I shall bring forward this book as an explanation. We stand in want of
a new Luther to renew faith and invigorate Christianity and to do
what the Unitarians would do if only they had a really great man such
as Luther to lead them. For religions grow old like trees unless reformed from time to time. Christianity of the existing kinds has had
its day. We want a new form in accordance with science and yet
helpful to a good life.

June 3rd. It is extraordinary how few principles or dogmas I have
been able to become convinced of. One after another I find my former
undoubted beliefs slipping from me into the region of doubt. For
example, I used never for a moment to doubt that truth was a good
thing to get hold of. But now I have the very greatest doubt and uncertainty. For the search for truth has led me to these results I have
put in this book, whereas had I been content to accept the teachings of
my youth I should have remained comfortable. The search for truth
has shattered most of my old beliefs and has made me commit what
are probably sins where otherwise I should have kept clear of them.
I do not think it has in any way made me happier. Of course it has
given me a deeper character, a contempt for trifles or mockery, but
at the same time it has taken away cheerfulness and made it much

harder to make bosom friends, and worst of all it has debarred me from free intercourse with my people, and thus made them strangers to some of my deepest thoughts, which, if by any mischance I do let them out, immediately become the subject for mockery, which is inexpressibly bitter to me though not unkindly meant. Thus in my individual case I should say the effects of a search for truth have been more bad than good. But the truth which I accept as such may be said not to be truth and I may be told that if I get at real truth I shall be made happier by it, but this is a very doubtful proposition. Hence I have great doubt of the unmixed advantage of truth. Certainly truth in biology lowers one's idea of man which must be painful. Moreoever, truth estranges former friends and prevents the making of new ones, which is also a bad thing. One ought perhaps to look upon all these things as a martyrdom, since very often truth attained by one man may lead to the increase in the happiness of many others though not to his own. On the whole I am inclined to continue to pursue truth, though truth of the kind in this book, if that indeed be truth, I have no desire to spread but rather to prevent from spreading.

July 15th. My holidays have begun about a week now and I am getting used to home and beginning to regard Southgate as an evil dream of the past. For although I tell people I like it very much, yet really, though better than I expected, life there has great trials and hardships. I don't suppose anybody hates disturbance as I do or can so ill stand mockery, though to outward appearance I keep my temper all right. Being made to sing, to climb on chairs, to get up for a sponging in the middle of the night, is to me fifty times more detestable than to others. I always have to go through in a moment a long train of reasoning as to the best thing to say or do, for I have sufficient self-control to do what I think best, and the excitement, which to others might seem small, leaves me trembling and exhausted. However, I think it is an excellent thing for me, as it increases my capacity for enjoyment and strengthens me morally to a very considerable extent. I shan't forget in a hurry their amazement that I had never said a 'damn', which with things like it goes near to making me a *fanfaron de crimes*. This, however, is a bad thing to be, when only too many real crimes are committed. ... I am glad I didn't go to school before. I should have wanted strength and have had no time for the original thought, which though it has caused me much pain, is yet my chief stay and support in troubles. I am always kept up by a feeling of contempt, erroneous though it may be, for all who despitefully use me and persecute me. I don't think contempt is misplaced when a chap's habitual language is about something like 'who put me on my cold, cold pot whether I would or not? My mother,' sung to the tune of

'Thy will be done'. Had my education, however, been the least bit less perfect than it is I should probably have been the same. But I feel I must enjoy myself at home much better than ever before, which with an imaginary feeling of heroism reconciles me to a great deal of unhappiness at Southgate.

July 20th. There are about three different, though converging ways of looking at this question of free will, first, from the omnipotence of God, second from the reign of law, and third, from the fact that all our actions, if looked into, show themselves as caused by motives. These three ways we see at once to be really identical, for God's omnipotence is the same thing as the reign of law, and the determination of actions by motives is the particular form which the reign of law takes in man. Let us now examine closely each of these ways.

First, from the omnipotence of God. What do we mean, in the first place, by free will? We mean that, where several courses are open to us, we can choose any one. But according to this definition, we are not ruled by God, and alone of created things, we are independent of him. That appears unlikely, but is by no means impossible, since his omnipotence is only an inference. Let us then pass on to the second, from the reign of law. Of all things we know, except perhaps the higher animals, it is obvious that law is completely the master. That man is also under its dominion appears from a fact such as Grimm's Law, and again from the fact that it is possible sometimes to predict human actions. If man, then, be subject to law, does not this mean, that his actions are predetermined, just as much as the motions of a planet or the growth of a plant? The Duke of Argyll, indeed, speaks of freedom within the bounds of law, but to me that's an unmeaning phrase, for subjection to law must mean a certain consequence always following in given conditions. No doubt different people in the same circumstances act differently, but that is only owing to difference of character, just as two comets in the same position move differently, because of differences in their eccentricities. The third, from the consideration of motives, is about the strongest. For if we examine any action whatsoever, we find always motives, over which we have no more control than matter over the forces acting on it, which produce our actions. The Duke of Argyll says we can present motives to ourselves, but is not that an action, determined by our character, and other unavoidable things? The argument for free will from the fact that we feel it, is worthless, for we do not feel motives which we find really exist, nor that mind depends on brain, etc. But I am not prepared dogmatically to deny free will, for I have often found that good arguments don't present themselves on one side of a question till they are told one. My nature may incline me to disbelieve free will, and there may be very excellent arguments for free will which either I have never thought of, or else have not had their full weight with me. ... It is difficult not to become reckless and commit suicide, which I believe I should do but for my people.

Chapter 3

Cambridge

My father had been at Cambridge, but my brother was at Oxford. I went to Cambridge because of my interest in mathematics. My first experience of the place was in December 1889 when I was examined for entrance scholarships. I stayed in rooms in the New Court, and I was too shy to enquire the way to the lavatory, so that I walked every morning to the station before the examination began. I saw the Backs through the gate of the New Court, but did not venture to go into them, feeling that they might be private. I was invited to dine with the Master, who had been Headmaster of Harrow in my father's time. I there, for the first time, met Charles and Bob Trevelyan. Bob characteristically had borrowed Charles's second best dress suit, and fainted during dinner because somebody mentioned a surgical operation. I was alarmed by so formidable a social occasion, but less alarmed than I had been a few months earlier when I was left *tête-à-tête* with Mr Gladstone. He came to stay at Pembroke Lodge, and nobody was asked to meet him. As I was the only male in the household, he and I were left alone together at the dinner table after the ladies retired. He made only one remark: 'This is very good port they have given me, but why have they given it me in a claret glass?' I did not know the answer, and wished the earth would swallow me up. Since then I have never again felt the full agony of terror.

I was very anxious to do well in the scholarship examination, and nervousness somewhat interfered with my work. Nevertheless, I got a minor scholarship, which gave me extreme happiness, as it was the first time I had been able to compare myself with able contemporaries.

From the moment that I went up to Cambridge at the beginning of October 1890 everything went well with me. All the people then in residence who subsequently became my intimate friends called on me during the first week of term. At the time I did not know why they did so, but I discovered afterwards that Whitehead, who had examined for scholarships, had told people to look out for Sanger and me. Sanger was a freshman like myself, also doing mathematics, and also a minor scholar. He and I both had rooms in Whewell's Court. Webb, our coach, had a practice of circulating MSS among his classes, and it fell to my lot to deliver a MS to Sanger after I had done with it. I had not

seen him before, but I was struck by the books on his shelves. I said:
'I see you have Draper's *Intellectual Development of Europe* which I
think a very good book.' He said: 'You are the first person I have ever
met who has heard of it!' From this point the conversation proceeded,
and at the end of half an hour we were lifelong friends. We compared
notes as to how much mathematics we had done. We agreed upon
theology and metaphysics. We disagreed upon politics (he was at the
time a Conservative, though in later life he belonged to the Labour
Party). He spoke of Shaw, whose name was until then unknown to me.
We used to work on mathematics together. He was incredibly quick,
and would be half-way through solving a problem before I had understood the question. We both devoted our fourth year to moral science,
but he did economics, and I did philosophy. We got our Fellowships
at the same moment. He was one of the kindest men that ever lived,
and in the last years of his life my children loved him as much as I
have done. I have never known anyone else with such a perfect
combination of penetrating intellect and warm affection. He became
a Chancery barrister, and was known in legal circles for his highly
erudite edition of Jarman *On Wills*. He used to lament that Jarman's
relatives had forbidden him to mention in the preface that Jarman died
intestate. He was also a very good economist, and he could read an
incredible number of languages, including such out-of-the-way items
as Magyar and Finnish. I used to go walking tours with him in Italy,
and he always made me do all the conversation with inn-keepers, but
when I was reading Italian, I found that his knowledge of the language
was vastly greater than mine. His death in the year 1930 was a great
sorrow to me.

The other friends whom I acquired during my first term I owed
chiefly to Whitehead's recommendation. I learned afterwards that in
the scholarship examination another man had obtained more marks
than I had, but Whitehead had the impression that I was the abler of
the two. He therefore burned the marks before the examiners' meeting,
and recommended me in preference to the other man. Two of my
closest friends were Crompton and Theodore Llewelyn Davies. Their
father was vicar of Kirkby Lonsdale, and translator of Plato's *Republic*
in the Golden Treasury edition, a distinguished scholar and a Broad
Churchman whose views were derived from F. D. Maurice. He had a
family of six sons and one daughter. It was said, and I believe with
truth, that throughout their education the six sons, of whom Crompton
and Theodore were the youngest, managed, by means of scholarships,
to go through school and university without expense to their father.
Most of them were also strikingly good-looking, including Crompton,
who had very fine blue eyes, which sometimes sparkled with fun and at
other times had a steady gaze that was deeply serious. The ablest and

one of the best loved of the family was the youngest, Theodore, with whom, when I first knew them, Crompton shared rooms in College. They both in due course became Fellows, but neither of them became resident. Afterwards the two lived together in a small house near Westminster Abbey, in a quiet out-of-the-way street. Both of them were able, high-minded and passionate, and shared, on the whole, the same ideals and opinions. Theodore had a somewhat more practical outlook on life than Crompton. He became Private Secretary to a series of Conservative Chancellors of the Exchequer, each of whom in turn he converted to Free Trade at a time when the rest of the Government wished them to think otherwise. He worked incredibly hard and yet always found time to give presents to the children of all his friends, and the presents were always exactly appropriate. He inspired the deepest affection in almost everybody who knew him. I never knew but one woman who would not have been delighted to marry him. She, of course, was the only woman he wished to marry. In the spring of 1905, when he was thirty-four, his dead body was found in a pool near Kirkby Lonsdale, where he had evidently bathed on his way to the station. It was supposed that he must have hit his head on a rock in diving. Crompton, who loved his brother above everyone, suffered almost unendurably. I spent the weeks after Theodore's death with him, but it was difficult to find anything to say.[1] The sight of his unhappiness was agonising. Ever since, the sound of Westminster chimes has brought back to me the nights I lay awake in misery at this time. On the Sunday after the accident, I was in church when his father, with determined stoicism, took the service as usual, and just succeeded in not breaking down. Gradually Crompton recovered, but not fully until his marriage. After that, for no reason that I could understand, I saw nothing of him for many years, until one evening, when I was living in Chelsea, I heard the front door bell, and found Crompton on the doorstep. He behaved as if we had met the day before, was as charming as ever, and insisted on seeing my children asleep. I think I had become so much associated with his suffering after Theodore's death, that for a long time he found my presence painful.

One of my earliest memories of Crompton is of meeting him in the darkest part of a winding College staircase and his suddenly quoting, without any previous word, the whole of 'Tyger, Tyger, burning bright'. I had never, till that moment, heard of Blake, and the poem affected me so much that I became dizzy and had to lean against the wall. Hardly a day passed without my remembering some incident connected with Crompton – sometimes a joke, sometimes a grimace of disgust at meanness or hypocrisy, most often his warm and generous

[1] See my letter to Lucy Donnelly, Appendix pp. 183–4; also Crompton Davies's letter on p. 203.

affection. If I were tempted at any time to any failure of honesty, the thought of his disapproval would still restrain me. He combined wit, passion, wisdom, scorn, gentleness, and integrity, in a degree that I have never known equalled. In addition to all these, his intense and unalterable affection gave to me and others, in later years, an anchor of stability in a disintegrating world.

His loyalties were usually peculiar to himself. He was incapable of following a multitude, either for good or evil. He would profess contempt and amusement for all the causes in which his friends excited themselves, laughing to scorn 'The Society for this' or 'The World League for Promoting that', while all the time he was a crusade in himself, for Ireland against England, for small business against big, for the have-nots against the haves, for competition against monopoly. His chief enthusiasm was for the taxation of land values.

Henry George is now an almost forgotten prophet, but in 1890, when I first knew Crompton, his doctrine that all rent should be paid to the State rather than to private landowners was still an active competitor with Socialism among those who were not satisfied with the economic *status quo*. Crompton, at this time, was already a fanatical adherent of Henry George. He had, as was to be expected, a strong dislike of Socialism, and a strong devotion to the principle of freedom for private enterprise. He had no dislike of the capitalist who made his money in industry, but regarded as a mere incubus the man who is able to levy toll on the industry of others because he owns the land that they need. I do not think he ever asked himself how the State could fail to become immensely powerful if it enjoyed all the revenue to be derived from landownership. In his mind, as in Henry George's, the reform was to be the completion of individualistic liberalism, setting free energies now throttled by monopoly power. In 1909, he believed that Henry George's principles were being carried out by Lloyd George, whose famous budget he helped to perfect.

At the beginning of the 1914–18 War he was solicitor to the Post Office, but his ardent agreement with the opinions of his wife, who was an Irish Nationalist and imprisoned as a Sinn Feiner, made his position untenable. He was dismissed at a moment's notice. In spite of the prejudice of the time he was almost immediately taken in as a partner by Messrs Coward, Chance & Co, one of the leading firms of City solicitors. In 1921, it was he who drafted the treaty of peace that established Irish self-government, though this was never publicly known. His unselfishness made any important worldly success impossible, since he never stood in the way of others acquiring credit for his work; and he did not care for public recognition and honours. But his ability, though it was not this that made him unforgettable, was very great. What made Crompton at the same time so admirable and so delightful, was not his ability, but his strong loves and hates, his fantastic humour, and his rock-like honesty. He was one of the wittiest men that I have ever known, with a great love of mankind combined with a contemptuous hatred for most individual men. He had by no means the ways of a saint. Once, when we were both young, I was walking with him in the country, and we trespassed over a corner of a farmer's land. The farmer came running out after us, shouting and red with fury. Crompton held his hand to his ear, and said with the utmost mildness: 'Would you mind speaking a little louder? I'm rather hard of hearing.' The farmer was reduced to speechlessness in the endeavour to make more noise than he was already making. Not long before his death I heard him tell this story, with great detail and exaggeration, attributing his part in it to me, while I interrupted, saying, 'Don't believe a word of it. It wasn't me, it was all Crompton,' until finally he dissolved in affectionate chuckles.

He was addicted to extreme shabbiness in his clothes, to such a degree that some of his friends expostulated. This had an unexpected result. When Western Australia attempted by litigation to secede from the Commonwealth of Australia, his law firm was employed, and it was decided that the case should be heard in the King's Robing Room. Crompton was overheard ringing up the King's Chamberlain and saying: 'The unsatisfactory state of my trousers has lately been brought to my notice. I understand that the case is to be heard in the King's Robing Room. Perhaps the King has left an old pair of trousers there that might be useful to me.'

His distastes – which were numerous and intense – were always expressed in a manner that made one laugh. Once, when he and I were staying with his father, a Bishop was also a guest – the mildest and most inoffensive type of cleric, the kind of whom it would be natural to say that he would not hurt a fly. Unfortunately his politics were somewhat reactionary. When at last we were alone, Crompton put on a manner that would have been appropriate to a fellow-captive on a pirate ship, and growled out: 'Seems a *desperate* character.'

When the Liberal Government came into office at the end of 1905, and Lord Haldane, fat, comfortable, and soothing, was put at the War Office, Crompton, very gravely, said he had been chosen to prevent the Generals from having apoplexy when Army reforms were suggested.

Motor traffic annoyed him by its imperiousness. He would cross London streets without paying attention to it, and when cars hooted indignantly he would look round with an air of fastidious vexation, and say, 'Don't make that noise!' Although he wandered about with an air of dreamy abstraction, wearing his hat on the back of his head, motorists became convinced that he must be someone of enormous importance, and waited patiently while he went his way.

He loved London as much as Lamb or Dr Johnson did. Once, when he was inveighing against Wordsworth for writing about the lesser celandine, I said, 'Do you like him better on Westminster Bridge?' 'Ah, yes,' he answered, 'if only he had treated it on the same scale.' In his last years we often walked together in London after dinner, he and my wife and I. Crompton would take our arms, if he were not holding them already, as we passed Wren's church of St Clement Danes, to remind us to look up at one of his favourite sights, the spire standing out dimly against the glowing blue of the evening sky. On these walks he would sometimes get into conversation with people that we met. I remember him engaging a park-keeper in an earnest discussion, perhaps of land values. The park-keeper was at first determined to remember both his class and his official position, and treated Crompton with respectful disapproval. Strangers ought not to be so ready to talk to strangers, gentlemen should not be so easy with workingmen, and no one should talk to officials on duty. But this stiffness soon melted. Crompton was truly democratic. He always spoke to his clerks or his servants with the same tone that he would have used to an important person such as one of the Indian Rajahs whose affairs he handled, and his manner in a two-roomed Irish cabin was exactly the same as in a party of celebrities. I remember with what grave courtesy he rose to bow and shake hands with our parlourmaid, on hearing that she came from the same district as his family.

By temperament he was inclined to anarchism; he hated system and organisation and uniformity. Once, when I was with him on Westminster Bridge, he pointed with delight to a tiny donkey-cart in the middle of the heavy traffic. 'That's what I like,' he said, 'freedom for all sorts.'

On another occasion, when I was walking with him in Ireland, we went to a bus station, where I, without thinking, made for the largest and most comfortable bus. His expression was quite shocked as he took me by the arm and hurried me away to a shabby little 'jalopie' of a bus, explaining gravely that it was pluckily defying the big combines.

His opinions were often somewhat wayward, and he had no objection to giving his prejudices free rein. He admired rebels rather more, perhaps, than was wholly rational. He had a horror of anything that seemed calculating, and I once shocked him deeply by saying that a war could not be justified unless there was a likelihood of victory. To him, heroic and almost hopeless defiance appeared splendid. Many of his prejudices were so consonant to my feelings that I never had the heart to argue with them – which in any case would have been a hopeless task.

With his temperament and opinions, it was natural that he should hate the Sidney Webbs. When they took up Poor Law Reform, he

would say that, since everyone else rejected their attempts at regula-
tion, they had at last been driven to organise the defenceless paupers.
He would allege, as one of their triumphs of organisation, that they
employed a pauper with a peg leg to drill holes for the potatoes.

He was my lawyer for many years – a somewhat thankless task which
he undertook out of friendship. Most of his practice consisted of affairs
of great importance, concerning Indian Princes, Dominion Governments, or leading Banks. He showed, in legal matters, unbending
straightforwardness, combined with skill and patience – this last truly
astonishing, since nature had made him one of the most impatient of
men. By these methods, which inspired confidence even in opponents,
he achieved results which ingenious trickery could never have
achieved. I remember the stony expression which came over his face
during the course of a legal consultation when someone suggested a
course that was not entirely straightforward.

With all his underlying seriousness, he was almost invariably gay.
At the end of a long day of exhausting and responsible work he would
arrive at a dinner party as jolly as if he had already enjoyed a good dose
of champagne, and would keep everybody laughing. It was in the
middle of a dinner party that he died, quite suddenly, of heart failure.
Probably he had known that this was liable to happen, but he had kept
the knowledge to himself. Afterwards, his friends remembered slight
indications that he had not expected to live long, but they had not been
sufficient to cause active anxiety among those who valued him.

In his last years he spent much of his leisure in writing a book on
philosophy, which he referred to disparagingly as his 'pie-dish' in
allusion to an old man in a play who had only one talent, the making
of pie-dishes, and only one ambition, to make a really good pie-dish
before he died. After Greek poetry, philosophy had been, when he
was young, his main intellectual preoccupation; when I first knew him,
we spent much time arguing about ethics and metaphysics. A busy
professional life had kept him, throughout his middle years, engaged in
practical affairs, but at last he was able to spare some time for purely
theoretical thinking, to which he returned with wholehearted joy.
When the book was nearly finished he lost it, as people do sometimes
lose the things they value most. He left it in a train. It was never recovered. Someone must have picked it up in the hope that it had
financial value. He mentioned the loss, sadly but briefly, said that there
was nothing for it but to begin all over again from the few notes he had,
and then changed the subject. We saw less of him during the few
months that were left before his death, though when we did see him
he was as gay and affectionate as ever. He was spending most of his
spare energy on trying to make up the work that was lost; but the
pie-dish was never finished.

Another friend of my Cambridge years was McTaggart, the philosopher, who was even shyer than I was. I heard a knock on my door one day – a very gentle knock. I said: 'Come in', but nothing happened. I said, 'Come in', louder. The door opened, and I saw McTaggart standing on the mat. He was already President of The Union, and about to become a Fellow, and inspired me with awe on account of his metaphysical reputation, but he was too shy to come in, and I was too shy to ask him to come in. I cannot remember how many minutes this situation lasted, but somehow or other he was at last in the room. After that I used frequently to go to his breakfasts, which were famous for their lack of food; in fact, anybody who had been once, brought an egg with him on every subsequent occasion. McTaggart was a Hegelian, and at that time still young and enthusiastic. He had a great intellectual influence upon my generation, though in retrospect I do not think it was a very good one. For two or three years, under his influence, I was a Hegelian. I remember the exact moment during my fourth year when I became one. I had gone out to buy a tin of tobacco, and was going back with it along Trinity Lane, when suddenly I threw it up in the air and exclaimed: 'Great God in boots! – the ontological argument is sound!' Although after 1898 I no longer accepted McTaggart's philosophy, I remained fond of him until an occasion during the first war, when he asked me no longer to come and see him because he could not bear my opinions. He followed this up by taking a leading part in having me turned out of my lectureship.

Two other friends whom I met in my early days in Cambridge and retained ever since, were Lowes Dickinson and Roger Fry. Dickinson was a man who inspired affection by his gentleness and pathos. When he was a Fellow and I was still an undergraduate, I became aware that I was liable to hurt him by my somewhat brutal statement of unpleasant truths, or what I thought to be such. States of the world which made me caustic only made him sad, and to the end of his days whenever I met him, I was afraid of increasing his unhappiness by too stark a realism. But perhaps realism is not quite the right word. What I really mean is the practice of describing things which one finds almost unendurable in such a repulsive manner as to cause others to share one's fury. He told me once that I resembled Cordelia, but it cannot be said that he resembled King Lear.

From my first moment at Cambridge, in spite of shyness, I was exceedingly sociable, and I never found that my having been educated at home was any impediment. Gradually, under the influence of congenial society, I became less and less solemn. At first the discovery that I could say things that I thought, and be answered with neither horror nor derision but as if I had said something quite sensible, was intoxicating. For a long time I supposed that somewhere in the university there were really clever people whom I had not yet met, and whom I should at once recognise as my intellectual superiors, but during my second year, I discovered that I already knew all the cleverest people in the university. This was a disappointment to me, but at the same time gave me increased self-confidence. In my third year, however, I met G. E. Moore, who was then a freshman, and for some years he fulfilled my ideal of genius. He was in those days beautiful and slim, with a look almost of inspiration, and with an intellect as deeply passionate as Spinoza's. He had a kind of exquisite purity. I have never but once succeeded in making him tell a lie, that was by a subterfuge, 'Moore,' I said, 'do you *always* speak the truth?' 'No', he replied. I believe this to be the only lie he had ever told. His people lived in Dulwich, where I once went to see them. His father was a retired medical man, his mother wore a large china brooch with a picture of the Colosseum on it. He had sisters and brothers in large numbers, of whom the most interesting was the poet, Sturge Moore. In the world of intellect, he was fearless and adventurous, but in the everyday world he was a child. During my fourth year I spent some days walking with him on the coast of Norfolk. We fell in by accident with a husky fellow, who began talking about Petronius with intense relish for his indecencies. I rather encouraged the man, who amused me as a type. Moore remained completely silent until the man was gone, and then turned upon me, saying: 'That man was horrible.' I do not believe that he has ever in all his life derived the faintest pleasure from improper stories or conversation. Moore, like me, was influenced by McTaggart, and was for a short time a Hegelian. But he emerged more quickly than I did, and it was largely his conversation that led me to abandon both Kant and Hegel. In spite of his being two years younger than me, he greatly influenced my philosophical outlook. One of the pet amusements of all Moore's friends was to watch him trying to light a pipe. He would light a match, and then begin to argue, and continue until the match burnt his fingers. Then he would light another, and so on, until the box was finished. This was no doubt fortunate for his health, as it provided moments during which he was not smoking.

Then there were the three brothers Trevelyan. Charles, the eldest, was considered the least able of the three by all of us. Bob, the second, was my special friend. He became a very scholarly, but not very inspired, poet, but when he was young he had a delicious whimsical humour. Once, when we were on a reading party in the Lakes, Eddie Marsh, having overslept himself, came down in his night-shirt to see if breakfast was ready, looking frozen and miserable. Bob christened him 'cold white shape', and this name stuck to him for a long time. George Trevelyan was considerably younger than Bob, but I got to know him well later on. He and Charles were terrific walkers. Once when I went a walking tour with George in Devonshire, I made him promise to be content with twenty-five miles a day. He kept his promise until the last day. Then he left me, saying that now he must have a little walking. On another occasion, when I was walking alone, I arrived at the Lizard one evening and asked if they could give me a bed. 'Is your name Mr Trevelyan?' they answered. 'No,' I said, 'are you expecting him?' 'Yes,' they said, 'and his wife is here already.' This surprised me, as I knew that it was his wedding day. I found her languishing alone, as he had left her at Truro, saying that he could not face the whole day without a little walk. He arrived about ten o'clock at night, completely exhausted, having accomplished the forty miles in record time, but it seemed to me a somewhat curious beginning for a honeymoon. On August 4, 1914, he and I walked together down the Strand quarrelling. Since then I saw him only once, until I returned to Trinity in 1944, after he had become Master. When he was still an undergraduate he explained to me once that the Trevelyans never make matrimonial mistakes. 'They wait', he said, 'until they are thirty, and then marry a girl who has both sense and money.' In spite of occasional bad times, I have never wished that I had followed this prescription.

Bob Trevelyan was, I think, the most bookish person that I have ever known. What is in books appeared to him interesting, whereas what is only real life was negligible. Like all the family, he had a minute knowledge of the strategy and tactics concerned in all the great battles of the world, so far as these appear in reputable books of history. But I was staying with him during the crisis of the battle of the Marne, and as it was Sunday we could only get a newspaper by walking two miles. He did not think the battle sufficiently interesting to be worth it, because battles in mere newspapers are vulgar. I once devised a test question which I put to many people to discover whether they were pessimists. The question was: 'If you had the power to destroy the world, would you do so?' I put the question to him in the presence of his wife and child, and he replied: 'What? Destroy my library? – Never!' He was always discovering new poets and reading their poems out aloud, but he always began deprecatingly: 'This is not one of his best poems.' Once when he mentioned a new poet to me, and said he would like to read me some of his things, I said: 'Yes, but don't read me a poem which is not one of his best.' This stumped him completely, and he put the volume away.

The dons contributed little to my enjoyment of Cambridge. The Master came straight out of Thackeray's *Book of Snobs.* He generally began his remarks with 'Just thirty years ago today . . .' or with, 'Do you by any chance remember what Mr Pitt was doing one hundred years ago today?', and he would then proceed to relate some very tedious historical anecdote to show how great and good were all the statesmen mentioned in history. His epistolary style is illustrated by the letter that he wrote me after the mathematical tripos in which I was bracketed seventh wrangler:

> Trinity Lodge,
> Cambridge,
> June 13th 1893

My dear B. Russell

I cannot tell you how happy this grand victory has made us. Just 33 years have passed since I placed the Fifth Form Prize for Latin Prose in the hands of your dear Father at Harrow, and now I am permitted to congratulate his son and his own Mother on a remarkable Mathematical success which will be much appreciated in the College.

We knew your Mathematical ability but we knew also that you had not given your whole mind to Mathematics but had bestowed large parts of it on other, possibly even greater, subjects. If this had seriously spoiled your Mathematical position I should of course have regretted it, but I should have understood that there were solid compensations.

Now there is happily nothing but congratulation, and you will look forward quietly to the Moral Science Tripos and the Fellowship without any misgiving that you have left behind you a Mathematical waste.

I must give myself the pleasure of writing just a few lines to Lady Russell and Lady Stanley. This will be a happy day for both of them.

> *Believe me to be,*
> *Most truly yours,*
> *H. Montagu Butler*
> (*Master of Trinity*)

I remember once going to breakfast at the Lodge, and it happened that the day was his sister-in-law's birthday. After wishing her many happy returns, he continued: 'Now, my dear, you have lasted just as long as the Peloponnesian War.' She did not know how long this might be, but feared it was longer than she could wish. His wife took to Christian Science, which had the effect of prolonging his life for some twenty years beyond what might otherwise have been expected. This happened through her lack of sympathy with his ailments. When he was ill, she would send word to the Council Meeting that the Master was in bed and refused to get up. It must be said, however, that the Vice-Master, Aldous Wright, and the Senior Fellow, Joey Prior, lasted almost equally long without the help of Christian Science. I remember when I was an undergraduate watching the three of them standing bare-headed at the Great Gate to receive the Empress Frederick. They were already very old men, but fifteen years later they seemed no older. Aldous Wright was a very dignified figure, standing always as straight as a ramrod, and never appearing out-of-doors without a top hat. Even once when he was roused from sleep at three in the morning by a fire the top hat was duly on his head. He stuck to the English pronunciation of Latin, while the Master adopted the Continental pronunciation. When they read grace in alternate verses, the effect was curious, especially as the Vice-Master gabbled it while the Master mouthed it with unction. While I was an undergraduate, I had regarded all these men merely as figures of fun, but when I became a Fellow and attended College meetings, I began to find that they were serious forces of evil. When the Junior Dean, a clergyman who raped his little daughter and became paralysed with syphilis, had to be got rid of in consequence, the Master went out of his way to state at College Meeting that those of us who did not attend chapel regularly had no idea how excellent this worthy's sermons had been. Next to these three the most important person in the College was the Senior Porter, a magnificent figure of a man, with such royal dignity that he was supposed by undergraduates to be a natural son of the future Edward the Seventh. After I was a Fellow I found that on one occasion the Council met on five successive days with the utmost secrecy. With great difficulty I discovered what their business had been. They had been engaged in establishing the painful fact that the Senior Porter had had improper relations with five bedmakers, in spite of the fact that all of them, by Statute, were '*nec juvenis, nec pulchra*'.

As an undergraduate I was persuaded that the Dons were a wholly unnecessary part of the university. I derived no benefits from lectures, and I made a vow to myself that when in due course I became a lecturer I would not suppose that lecturing did any good. I have kept this vow.

I had already been interested in philosophy before I went to Cambridge, but I had not read much except Mill. What I most desired was to find some reason for supposing mathematics true. The arguments in Mill's *Logic* on this subject already struck me as very inadequate. I read them at the age of eighteen. My mathematical tutors had never shown me any reason to suppose the Calculus anything but a tissue of fallacies. I had therefore two questions to trouble me, one philosophical, and one mathematical. The mathematical question had already in the main been solved on the Continent, though in England the Continental work was little known. It was only after I left Cambridge and began to live abroad that I discovered what I ought to have been taught during my three years as an undegraduate. Philosophy, however, was another matter. I knew in the country Harold Joachim, who taught philosophy at Merton, and was a friend of F. H. Bradley.

Joachim's sister had married my Uncle Rollo, and I used to meet him occasionally at tennis-parties and such occasions. I got him to give me a long list of philosophical books that I ought to read, and while I was still working at mathematics I embarked upon them. As soon as I was free to do so, I devoted myself to philosophy with great ardour. During my fourth year I read most of the great philosophers as well as masses of books on the philosophy of mathematics. James Ward was always giving me fresh books on this subject, and each time I returned them, saying that they were very bad books. I remember his disappointment, and his painstaking endeavours to find some book that would satisfy me. In the end, but after I had become a Fellow, I got from him two small books, neither of which he had read or supposed of any value. They were Georg Cantor's *Mannichfaltigkeitslehre*, and Frege's *Begriffsschrift*. These two books at last gave me the gist of what I wanted, but in the case of Frege I possessed the book for years before I could make out what it meant. Indeed, I did not understand it until I had myself independently discovered most of what it contained.

By this time, I had quite ceased to be the shy prig that I was when I first went to Cambridge. I remember a few months before I came into residence, going to see my tutor about rooms, and while I waited in the ante-room I turned over the pages of the *Granta* (the undergraduate newspaper). It was May Week, and I was shocked to read in the paper that during this week people's thoughts were not devoted to work. But by my fourth year I had become gay and flippant. Having been reading pantheism, I announced to my friends that I was God. They placed candles on each side of me and proceeded to acts of mock worship. Philosophy altogether seemed to me great fun, and I enjoyed the curious ways of conceiving the world that the great philosophers offer to the imagination.

The greatest happiness of my time at Cambridge was connected with a body whom its members knew as 'The Society', but which outsiders, if they knew of it, called 'The Apostles'. This was a small discussion society, containing one or two people from each year on the average, which met every Saturday night. It has existed since 1820, and has had as members most of the people of any intellectual eminence who have been at Cambridge since then. It is by way of being secret, in order that those who are being considered for election may be unaware of the fact. It was owing to the existence of The Society that I so soon got to know the people best worth knowing, for Whitehead was a member, and told the younger members to investigate Sanger and me on account of our scholarship papers. With rare exceptions, all the members at any one time were close personal friends. It was a principle in discussion that there were to be no *taboos*, no limitations, nothing considered shocking, no barriers to absolute freedom of speculation. We discussed all manner of things, no doubt with a certain immaturity, but with a detachment and interest scarcely possible in later life. The meetings would generally end about one o'clock at night, and after that I would pace up and down the cloisters of Nevile's Court for hours with one or two other members. We took ourselves perhaps rather seriously, for we considered that the virtue of intellectual honesty was in our keeping. Undoubtedly, we achieved more of this than is common in the world, and I am inclined to think that the best intelligence of Cambridge has been notable in this respect. I was elected in the middle of my second year, not having previously known that such a society existed, though the members were all intimately known to me already.

I was elected to The Society early in 1892. The following letters of congratulation require an explanation of some phrases which were adopted in The Society by way of making fun of German metaphysics. The Society was supposed to be The World of Reality; everything else was Appearance. People who were not members of The Society were called 'phenomena'. Since the metaphysicians maintained that Space and Time are unreal, it was assumed that those who were in The Society were exempted from bondage to Space and Time.

c/ Hon. Sir Charles Elliott, KCSI,
Lieut. Gov. of Bengal, India   Weds. March 9, 1892

Dear Russell

I have just heard by this morning's mail that you have joined us – Hurrah. It is good news indeed. I mustn't let the mail go off this afternoon without a few words to say how glad I am, and how sorry not to be at Cambridge now to give you a fraternal handshake. You will of course get your own impressions, but it was certainly a true new life to me, and a revelation of what Cambridge really was.

It is just time for letters to go, so I'm afraid I can't write just now to tell you of my experiences. Theodore will tell you how I am getting on. I was very sorry to hear that you had not been well. Get all right quick. Don't let Webb[1] kill you.

Excuse these hurried lines. Confound those absurd humbugs, space and time, which have the impudence to pretend that they are now separating us. Whereas we know that they have nothing to do with that true existence in the bonds of which I was in the beginning am now and ever shall be

> *fraternally and affectionately*
> *yours*
> *Crompton Ll. D.*

[1] My mathematical coach.

I haven't time to write to Sanger a proper letter, so would you mind handing him the enclosed scrawl?
Do write to me if you have time.

Devon St., New Plymouth,
Taranaki, New Zealand.   17th May, 1892

Dear Russell

Many congratulations on the delightful news of last February, which – with a bondage to space and time perfectly inexplicable in apostolic matters – has only just reached me via India.

I am most awfully glad. I hope you have been told of our brother Whitehead's penetration, who detected the apostolic nature of yourself and Sanger by your entrance scholarship essays, and put us on the watch for you.

I wish I could get back for a Saturday night or so, and have it out with Theodore about Xtianity being the religion of love – just the one thing which it isn't I should say. I don't see how the ideas of a personal God and real love can coexist with any vigour.

How about the Embryos?[1] I hear that the younger Trevelyan (Bob) is very promising, and Green of Kings.

I have innumerable more letters for the mail. I hope to see you in the middle of next January.

> *Yours fraternally,*
> *(Sgd.) Ellis McTaggart*

Some things became considerably different in the Society shortly after my time.

The tone of the generation some ten years junior to my own was set mainly by Lytton Strachey and Keynes. It is surprising how great a change in mental climate those ten years had brought. We were still Victorian; they were Edwardian. We believed in ordered progress by means of politics and free discussion. The more self-confident among us may have hoped to be leaders of the multitude, but none of us wished to be divorced from it. The generation of Keynes and Lytton did not seek to preserve any kinship with the Philistine. They aimed rather at a life of retirement among fine shades and nice feelings, and conceived of the good as consisting in the passionate mutual admirations of a clique of the élite. This doctrine, quite unfairly, they fathered upon G. E. Moore, whose disciples they professed to be. Keynes, in his memoir 'Early Beliefs' has told of their admiration for Moore, and, also, of their practice of ignoring large parts of Moore's doctrine.

[1] Our name for people we were thinking of electing.

Moore gave due weight to morals and by his doctrine of organic unities avoided the view that the good consists of a series of isolated passionate moments, but those who considered themselves his disciples ignored this aspect of his teaching and degraded his ethics into advocacy of a stuffy girls-school sentimentalising.

From this atmosphere Keynes escaped into the great world, but Strachey never escaped. Keynes's escape, however, was not complete. He went about the world carrying with him everywhere a feeling of the bishop *in partibus*. True salvation was elsewhere, among the faithful at Cambridge. When he concerned himself with politics and economics he left his soul at home. This is the reason for a certain hard, glittering, inhuman quality in most of his writing. There was one great exception, *The Economic Consequences of the Peace*, of which I shall have more to say in a moment.

I first knew Keynes through his father, and Lytton Strachey through his mother. When I was young, Keynes's father taught old-fashioned formal logic in Cambridge. I do not know how far the new developments in that subject altered his teaching. He was an earnest Nonconformist who put morality first and logic second. Something of the Nonconformist spirit remained in his son, but it was overlaid by the realisation that facts and arguments may lead to conclusions somewhat shocking to many people, and a strain of intellectual arrogance in his character made him find it not unpleasant to *épater les bourgeois*. In his *The Economic Consequences of the Peace* this strain was in abeyance. The profound conviction that the Treaty of Versailles spelt disaster so roused the earnest moralist in him that he forgot to be clever – without, however, ceasing to be so.

I had no contact with him in his economic and political work, but I was considerably concerned in his *Treatise on Probability*, many parts of which I discussed with him in detail. It was nearly finished in 1914, but had to be put aside for the duration.

He was always inclined to overwork, in fact it was overwork that caused his death. Once in the year 1904, when I was living in an isolated cottage in a vast moor without roads, he wrote and asked if I could promise him a restful week-end. I replied confidently in the affirmative, and he came. Within five minutes of his arrival the Vice Chancellor turned up full of University business. Other people came unexpectedly to every meal, including six to Sunday breakfast. By Monday morning we had had twenty-six unexpected guests, and Keynes, I fear, went away more tired than he came. On Sunday, August 2, 1914, I met him hurrying across the Great Court of Trinity. I asked him what the hurry was and he said he wanted to borrow his brother-in-law's motorcycle to go to London. 'Why don't you go by train', I said. 'Because there isn't time', he replied. I did not know what his business might be, but within a few days the bank rate, which panic-mongers had put up to ten per cent, was reduced to five per cent. This was his doing.

I do not know enough economics to have an expert opinion on Keynes's theories, but so far as I am able to judge it seems to me to be owing to him that Britain has not suffered from large-scale unemployment in recent years. I would go further and say that if his theories had been adopted by financial authorities throughout the world the great depression would not have occurred. There are still many people in America who regard depressions as acts of God. I think Keynes proved that the responsibility for these occurrences does not rest with Providence.

The last time that I saw him was in the House of Lords when he returned from negotiating a loan in America and made a masterly speech recommending it to their Lordships. Many of them had been doubtful beforehand, but when he had finished there remained hardly any doubters except Lord Beaverbrook and two cousins of mine with a passion for being in the minority. Having only just landed from the Atlantic, the effort he made must have been terrific, and it proved too much for him.

Keynes's intellect was the sharpest and clearest that I have ever known. When I argued with him, I felt that I took my life in my hands, and I seldom emerged without feeling something of a fool. I was sometimes inclined to feel that so much cleverness must be incompatible with depth, but I do not think this feeling was justified.

Lytton Strachey, as mentioned before, I first got to know through his mother. She and I were fellow members of a committee designed to secure votes for women. After some months she invited me to dinner. Her husband, Sir Richard Strachey, was a retired Indian official, and the British Raj was very much in the air. My first dinner with the family was a rather upsetting experience. The number of sons and daughters was almost beyond computation, and all the children were to my unpractised eyes exactly alike except in the somewhat superficial point that some were male and some were female. The family were not all assembled when I arrived, but dropped in one by one at intervals of twenty minutes. (One of them, I afterwards discovered, was Lytton.) I had to look round the room carefully to make sure that it was a new one that had appeared and not merely one of the previous ones that had changed his or her place. Towards the end of the evening I began to doubt my sanity, but kind friends afterwards assured me that things had really been as they seemed.

Lady Strachey was a woman of immense vigour, with a great desire that some at least of her children should distinguish themselves. She had an admirable sense of prose and used to read South's sermons aloud to her children, not for the matter (she was a free-thinker), but to give them a sense of rhythm in the writing of English. Lytton, who was too delicate to be sent to a conventional school, was seen by his mother to be brilliant, and was brought up to the career of a writer in an atmosphere of dedication. His writing appeared to me in those days hilariously amusing. I heard him read *Eminent Victorians* before it was published, and I read it again to myself in prison. It caused me to laugh so loud that the officer came round to my cell, saying I must remember that prison is a place of punishment.

Lytton was always eccentric and became gradually more so. When he was growing a beard he gave out that he had measles so as not to be seen by his friends until the hairs had reached a respectable length. He dressed very oddly. I knew a farmer's wife who let lodgings and she told me that Lytton had come to ask her if she could take him in. 'At first, Sir,' she said, 'I thought he was a tramp, and then I looked again and saw he was a gentleman, but a very queer one.' He talked always in a squeaky voice which sometimes contrasted ludicrously with the matter of what he was saying. One time when I was talking with him he objected first to one thing and then to another as not being what literature should aim at. At last I said, 'Well, Lytton, what should it aim at ?' And he replied in one word – 'Passion'. Nevertheless, he liked to appear lordly in his attitude towards human affairs. I heard someone maintain in his presence that young people are apt to think about Life. He objected, 'I can't believe people think about Life. There's nothing in it.' Perhaps it was this attitude which made him not a great man.

His style is unduly rhetorical, and sometimes, in malicious moments, I have thought it not unlike Macaulay's. He is indifferent to historical truth and will always touch up the picture to make the lights and shades more glaring and the folly or wickedness of famous people more obvious. These are grave charges, but I make them in all seriousness.

It was in The Society that I first became aware of Moore's excellence. I remember his reading a paper which began: 'In the beginning was matter, and matter begat the devil, and the devil begat God.' The paper ended with the death first of God and then of the devil, leaving matter alone as in the beginning. At the time when he read this paper, he was still a freshman, and an ardent disciple of Lucretius.

On Sunday it was our custom to breakfast late, and then spend the whole day till dinner-time walking. I got to know every road and footpath within ten miles of Cambridge, and many at much greater distances, in this way. In general I felt happy and comparatively calm while at Cambridge, but on moonlight nights I used to career round the country in a state of temporary lunacy. The reason, of course, was sexual desire, though at that time I did not know this.

After my time The Society changed in one respect. There was a long drawn out battle between George Trevelyan and Lytton Strachey, both members, in which Lytton Strachey was on the whole victorious. Since his time, homosexual relations among the members were for a time common, but in my day they were unknown.

Cambridge was important in my life through the fact that it gave me friends, and experience of intellectual discussion, but it was not important through the actual academic instruction. Of the mathematical teaching I have already spoken. Most of what I learned in philosophy has come to seem to me erroneous, and I spent many subsequent years in gradually unlearning the habits of thought which I had there acquired. The one habit of thought of real value that I acquired there was intellectual honesty. This virtue certainly existed not only among my friends, but among my teachers. I cannot remember any instance of a teacher resenting it when one of his pupils showed him to be in error, though I can remember quite a number of occasions on which pupils succeeded in performing this feat. Once during a lecture on hydrostatics, one of the young men interrupted to say: 'Have you not forgotten the centrifugal forces on the lid?' The lecturer gasped, and then said: 'I have been doing this example that way for twenty years, but you are right.' It was a blow to me during the War to find that, even at Cambridge, intellectual honesty had its limitations. Until then, wherever I lived, I felt that Cambridge was the only place on earth that I could regard as home.

Chapter 4

Engagement

In the summer of 1889, when I was living with my Uncle Rollo at his house on the slopes of Hindhead, he took me one Sunday for a long walk. As we were going down Friday's Hill, near Fernhurst, he said: 'Some new people have come to live at this house, and I think we will call upon them.' Shyness made me dislike the idea, and I implored him, whatever might happen, not to stay to supper. He said he would not, but he did, and I was glad he did. We found that the family were Americans, named Pearsall Smith, consisting of an elderly mother and father, a married daughter and her husband, named Costelloe, a younger daughter at Bryn Mawr home for the holidays, and a son at Balliol. The father and mother had been in their day famous evangelistic preachers, but the father had lost his faith as the result of a scandal which arose from his having been seen to kiss a young woman, and the mother had grown rather too old for such a wearing life. Costelloe, the son-in-law, was a clever man, a Radical, a member of the London County Council. He arrived fresh from London while we were at dinner, bringing the latest news of a great dock strike which was then in progress. This dock strike was of considerable interest and importance because it marked the penetration of Trade Unionism to a lower level than that previously reached. I listened open-mouthed while he related what was being done, and I felt that I was in touch with reality. The son from Balliol conversed in brilliant epigrams, and appeared to know everything with contemptuous ease. But it was the daughter from Bryn Mawr who especially interested me. She was very beautiful, as appears from the following extract from the *Bulletin*, Glasgow, May 10, 1921: 'I remember meeting Mrs Bertrand Russell at a civic reception or something of the kind (was it a reception to temperance delegates?) in Edinburgh twenty odd years ago. She was at that time one of the most beautiful women it is possible to imagine, and gifted with a sort of imperial stateliness, for all her Quaker stock. We who were present admired her so much that in a collected and dignified Edinburgh way we made her the heroine of the evening.' She was more emancipated than any young woman I had known, since she was at college and crossed the Atlantic alone, and was, as I soon discovered, an intimate friend of Walt Whitman. She asked me whether

I had ever read a certain German book called *Ekkehard,* and it happened that I had finished it that morning. I felt this was a stroke of luck. She was kind, and made me feel not shy. I fell in love with her at first sight. I did not see any of the family again that summer, but in subsequent years, during the three months that I spent annually with my Uncle Rollo, I used to walk the four miles to their house every Sunday, arriving to lunch and staying to supper. After supper they would make a camp fire in the woods, and sit round singing Negro spirituals, which were in those days unknown in England. To me, as to Goethe, America seemed a romantic land of freedom, and I found among them an absence of many prejudices which hampered me at home. Above all, I enjoyed their emancipation from good taste. It was at their house that I first met Sidney Webb, then still unmarried.

Sidney and Beatrice Webb, whom I knew intimately for a number of years, at times even sharing a house with them, were the most completely married couple that I have ever known. They were, however, very averse from any romantic view of love or marriage. Marriage was a social institution designed to fit instinct into a legal framework. During the first ten years of their marriage, Mrs Webb would remark at intervals, 'As Sidney always says, marriage is the waste-paper basket of the emotions'. In later years there was a slight change. They would generally have a couple to stay with them for the week-end, and on Sunday afternoon they would go for a brisk walk, Sidney with the lady and Beatrice with the gentleman. At a certain point, Sidney would remark, 'I know just what Beatrice is saying at this moment. She is saying, "As Sidney always says, marriage is the waste-paper basket of the emotions".' Whether Sidney ever really did say this is not known.

I knew Sidney before his marriage. But he was then much less than half of what the two of them afterwards became. Their collaboration was quite dove-tailed. I used to think, though, this was perhaps an undue simplification, that she had the ideas and he did the work. He was perhaps the most industrious man that I have ever known. When they were writing a book on local government, they would send circulars to all local government officials throughout the country asking questions and pointing out that the official in question could legally purchase their forthcoming book out of the rates. When I let my house to them, the postman, who was an ardent socialist, did not know whether to be more honoured by serving them or annoyed at having to deliver a thousand answers a day to their circulars. Webb was originally a second division clerk in the civil service, but by immense industry succeeded in rising into the first division. He was somewhat earnest and did not like jokes on sacred subjects such as political theory. On one occasion I remarked to him that democracy has at least one merit, namely, that a Member of Parliament cannot be stupider than his constituents, for the more stupid he is, the more stupid they were to elect him. Webb was seriously annoyed and said bitingly, 'That is the sort of argument I don't like'.

Mrs Webb had a wider range of interests than her husband. She took considerable interest in individual human beings, not only when they could be useful. She was deeply religious without belonging to any recognised brand of orthodoxy, though as a socialist she preferred the Church of England because it was a State institution. She was one of nine sisters, the daughters of a self-made man named Potter who acquired most of his fortune by building huts for the armies in the Crimea. He was a disciple of Herbert Spencer, and Mrs Webb was the most notable product of that philosopher's theories of education. I am sorry to say that my mother, who was her neighbour in the country, described her as a 'social butterfly', but one may hope that she would have modified this judgement if she had known Mrs Webb in later life. When she became interested in socialism she decided to sample the Fabians, especially the three most distinguished, who were Webb, Shaw and Graham Wallas. There was something like the Judgment of Paris with the sexes reversed, and it was Sidney who emerged as the counterpart of Aphrodite.

Webb had been entirely dependent upon his earnings, whereas Beatrice had inherited a competence from her father. Beatrice had the mentality of the governing class, which Sidney had not. Seeing that they had enough to live on without earning, they decided to devote their lives to research and to the higher branches of propaganda. In both they were amazingly successful. Their books are a tribute to their industry, and the School of Economics is a tribute to Sidney's skill. I do not think that Sidney's abilities would have been nearly as fruitful as they were if they had not been backed by Beatrice's self-confidence. I asked her once whether in her youth she had ever had any feeling of shyness. 'O no,' she said, 'if I ever felt inclined to be timid as I was going into a room full of people, I would say to myself, "You're the cleverest member of one of the cleverest families in the cleverest class of the cleverest nation in the world, why should you be frightened".'

I both liked and admired Mrs Webb, although I disagreed with her about many very important matters. I admired first and foremost her ability, which was very great. I admired next her integrity: she lived for public objects and was never deflected by personal ambition, although she was not devoid of it. I liked her because she was a warm and kind friend to those for whom she had a personal affection, but I disagreed with her about religion, about imperialism, and about the worship of the State. This last was of the essence of Fabianism. It led both the Webbs and also Shaw into what I thought an undue tolerance

of Mussolini and Hitler, and ultimately into a rather absurd adulation
of the Soviet Government.

But nobody is all of a piece, not even the Webbs. I once remarked to
Shaw that Webb seemed to me somewhat deficient in kindly feeling.
'No,' Shaw replied, 'you are quite mistaken.. Webb and I were once
in a tram-car in Holland eating biscuits out of a bag. A handcuffed
criminal was brought into the tram by policemen. All the other passengers shrank away in horror, but Webb went up to the prisoner and
offered him biscuits.' I remember this story whenever I find myself
becoming unduly critical of either Webb or Shaw.

There were people whom the Webbs hated. They hated Wells, both
because he offended Mrs Webb's rigid Victorian morality and because
he tried to dethrone Webb from his reign over the Fabian Society.
They hated Ramsay MacDonald from very early days. The least
hostile thing that I ever heard either of them say about him was at the
time of the formation of the first Labour Government, when Mrs
Webb said he was a very good substitute for a leader.

Their political history was rather curious. At first they co-operated
with the Conservatives because Mrs Webb was pleased with Arthur
Balfour for being willing to give more public money to Church Schools.
When the Conservatives fell in 1906, the Webbs made some slight
and ineffectual efforts to collaborate with the Liberals. But at last it
occurred to them that as socialists they might feel more at home in the
Labour Party, of which in their later years they were loyal members.

For a number of years Mrs Webb was addicted to fasting, from
motives partly hygienic and partly religious. She would have no breakfast and a very meagre dinner. Her only solid meal was lunch. She
almost always had a number of distinguished people to lunch, but she
would get so hungry that the moment it was announced she marched
in ahead of all her guests and started to eat. She nevertheless believed
that starvation made her more spiritual, and once told me that it gave
her exquisite visions. 'Yes,' I replied, 'if you eat too little, you see
visions; and if you drink too much, you see snakes.' I am afraid she
thought this remark inexcusably flippant. Webb did not share the
religious side of her nature, but was in no degree hostile to it, in spite
of the fact that it was sometimes inconvenient to him. When they and
I were staying at a hotel in Normandy, she used to stay upstairs in the
mornings since she could not bear the painful spectacle of us break-
fasting. Sidney, however, would come down for rolls and coffee. The
first morning Mrs Webb sent a message by the maid, 'We do not have
butter for Sidney's breakfast'. Her use of 'we' was one of the delights
of their friends.

Both of them were fundamentally undemocratic, and regarded it as
the function of a statesman to bamboozle or terrorise the populace. I

realised the origins of Mrs Webb's conceptions of government when she repeated to me her father's description of shareholders' meetings. It is the recognised function of directors to keep shareholders in their place, and she had a similar view about the relation of the Government to the electorate.

Her father's stories of his career had not given her any undue respect for the great. After he had built huts for the winter quarters of the French armies in the Crimea, he went to Paris to get paid. He had spent almost all his capital in putting up the huts, and payment became important to him. But, although everybody in Paris admitted the debt, the cheque did not come. At last he met Lord Brassey who had come on a similar errand. When Mr Potter explained his difficulties, Lord Brassey laughed at him and said, 'My dear fellow, you don't know the ropes. You must give fifty pounds to the Minister and five pounds to each of his underlings.' Mr Potter did so, and the cheque came next day.

Sidney had no hesitation in using wiles which some would think unscrupulous. He told me, for example, that when he wished to carry some point through a committee where the majority thought otherwise, he would draw up a resolution in which the contentious point occurred twice. He would have a long debate about its first occurrence and at last give way graciously. Nine times out of ten, so he concluded, no one would notice that the same point occurred later in the same resolution.

The Webbs did a great work in giving intellectual backbone to British socialism. They performed more or less the same function that the Benthamites at an earlier time had performed for the Radicals. The Webbs and the Benthamites shared a certain dryness and a certain coldness and a belief that the waste-paper basket is the place for the emotions. But the Benthamites and the Webbs alike taught their doctrines to enthusiasts. Bentham and Robert Owen could produce a well-balanced intellectual progeny and so could the Webbs and Keir Hardie. One should not demand of anybody all the things that add value to a human being. To have some of them is as much as should be demanded. The Webbs pass this test, and indubitably the British Labour Party would have been much more wild and woolly if they had never existed. Their mantle descended upon Mrs Webb's nephew, Sir Stafford Cripps, and but for them I doubt whether the British democracy would have endured with the same patience the arduous years through which we have been passing.

When I mentioned at home that I had met Sidney Webb, my grandmother replied that she had heard him lecture once in Richmond, and that he was 'not quite. . . .' 'Not quite what?' I persisted. 'Not quite a gentleman in mind or manners,' she finally said.

Among the Pearsall Smiths I escaped from this sort of thing. Among them I was happy and talkative and free from timidity. They would draw me out in such a way as to make me feel quite intelligent. I met interesting people at their house, for instance William James. Logan Pearsall Smith indoctrinated me with the culture of the nineties – Flaubert, Walter Pater, and the rest. He gave me rules for good writing, such as 'Put a comma every four words; never use "and" except at the beginning of a sentence'. I learned to make sentences full of parentheses in the style of Walter Pater. I learned the right thing to say about Manet, and Monet, and Degas, who were in those days what Matisse and Picasso were at a later date.

Logan Pearsall Smith was seven years older than I was, and gave me much moral advice. He was in a state of transition between the ethical outlook of Philadelphia Quakerism and that of Quartier-Latin Bohemia. Politically he was a socialist, having been converted by Graham Wallas, one of the founders of the Fabian Society (who, however, at a later date reverted to Liberalism). Logan tried to adapt the philanthropic practice of the Quakers to the socialist creed. In sexual morality he was at that time very ascetic, in fact almost Manichaean, but in religion he was agnostic. He wished to persuade free-thinking young people to preserve a high standard of personal discipline and self-denial. With this object, he created what he called humorously 'The Order of Prigs', which I joined, and whose rules I obeyed for several years.[1]

With each year that passed I became more devoted to Alys, the unmarried daughter. She was less flippant than her brother Logan, and less irresponsible than her sister, Mrs Costelloe. She seemed to me to possess all the simple kindness which I still cherished in spite of Pembroke Lodge, but to be devoid of priggery and prejudice. I wondered whether she would remain unmarried until I grew up, for she was five years older than I was. It seemed unlikely but, I became increasingly determined that, if she did, I would ask her to marry me. Once, I remember, I drove with her and her brother to Leith Hill to visit Judge Vaughan Williams, whose wife wore an Elizabethan ruff and was otherwise surprising. On the way they elicited from me that I believed in love at first sight, and chaffed me for being so sentimental. I felt deeply wounded, as the time had not yet come to say why I believed in it. I was aware that she was not what my grandmother would call a lady, but I considered that she resembled Jane Austen's Elizabeth Bennett. I think I was conscious of a certain pleasurable broadmindedness in this attitude.

I came of age in May 1893, and from this moment my relations with Alys began to be something more than distant admiration. In the

[1] I give the rules in the Appendix on p. 85, and these are followed by fragments of some of the letters received from L. P. S. during my years at Cambridge.

following month I was Seventh Wrangler in the mathematical Tripos, and acquired legal and financial independence. Alys came to Cambridge with a cousin of hers, and I had more opportunities of talking with her than I had ever had before. During the Long Vacation, she came again with the same cousin, but I persuaded her to stay for the inside of a day after the cousin was gone. We went on the river, and discussed divorce, to which she was more favourable than I was. She was in theory an advocate of free-love, which I considered admirable on her part, in spite of the fact that my own views were somewhat more strict. I was, however, a little puzzled to find that she was deeply ashamed of the fact that her sister had abandoned her husband for Berenson, the art critic. Indeed, it was not till after we were married that she consented to know Berenson. I was very much excited by her second visit to Cambridge, and began to correspond regularly with her. I was no longer spending the summers at Haslemere, because my grandmother and my Aunt Agatha did not get on with my Uncle Rollo's second wife. But on the 13th of September, I went to Friday's Hill for a two days' visit. The weather was warm and golden. There was not a breath of wind, and in the early morning there were mists in the valleys. I remember that Logan made fun of Shelley for speaking of 'golden mists', and I in turn made fun of Logan, saying there had been a golden mist that very morning, but before he was awake. For my part I was up and about early, having arranged with Alys to go for a walk before breakfast. We went and sat in a certain beech-wood on a hill, a place of extraordinary beauty looking like an early Gothic cathedral, and with a glimpse of distant views through the tree trunks in all directions. The morning was fresh and dewy, and I began to think that perhaps there might be happiness in human life. Shyness, however, prevented me from getting beyond feeling my way while we sat in the wood. It was only after breakfast, and then with infinite hesitation and alarm, that I arrived at a definite proposal, which was in those days the custom. I was neither accepted nor rejected. It did not occur to me to attempt to kiss her, or even take her hand. We agreed to go on seeing each other and corresponding, and to let time decide one way or the other. All this happened out-of-doors, but when we finally came in to lunch, she found a letter from Lady Henry Somerset, inviting her to the Chicago World's Fair to help in preaching temperance, a virtue of which in those days America was supposed not to have enough. Alys had inherited from her mother an ardent belief in total abstinence, and was much elated to get this invitation. She read it out triumphantly, and accepted it enthusiastically, which made me feel rather small, as it meant several months of absence, and possibly the beginning of an interesting career.

When I came home, I told my people what had occurred, and they reacted according to the stereotyped convention. They said she was no lady, a baby-snatcher, a low-class adventuress, a designing female taking advantage of my inexperience, a person incapable of all the finer feelings, a woman whose vulgarity would perpetually put me to shame. But I had a fortune of some £20,000 inherited from my father, and I paid no attention to what my people said. Relations became very strained, and remained so until after I was married.

At this time I kept a locked diary, which I very carefully concealed from everyone. In this diary I recorded my conversations with my grandmother about Alys and my feelings in regard to them. Not long afterwards a diary of my father's, written partly in shorthand (obviously for purposes of concealment), came into my hands. I found that he had proposed to my mother at just the same age at which I had proposed to Alys, that my grandmother had said almost exactly the same things to him as she had to me, and that he had recorded exactly the same reflections in his diary as I had recorded in mine. This gave me an uncanny feeling that I was not living my own life but my father's over again, and tended to produce a superstitious belief in heredity.[1]

Although I was deeply in love, I felt no conscious desire for any physical relations. Indeed, I felt that my love had been desecrated when one night I had a sexual dream, in which it took a less ethereal form. Gradually, however, nature took charge of this matter.

The next occasion of importance was on January 4, 1894, when I came up from Richmond for the day to visit Alys at her parents' house, 44 Grosvenor Road. It was a day on which there was a heavy snow-storm. All London was buried under about six inches of snow, and I had to wade through it on foot from Vauxhall. The snow brought a strange effect of isolation, making London almost as noiseless as a lonely hill top. It was on this occasion that I first kissed Alys. My only previous experience in this direction was with the housemaid mentioned in an earlier chapter, and I had not foreseen how great would be the ecstasy of kissing a woman whom I loved. Although she still said that she had not made up her mind whether to marry me or not, we spent the whole day, with the exception of meal-times, in kissing, with hardly a word spoken from morning till night, except for an interlude during which I read *Epipsychidion* aloud. I arrived home quite late, having walked the mile and a half from the station through a blizzard, tired but exultant.

Throughout my next term at Cambridge, there were alternations in

[1] In a letter to Alys, September 2, 1894, I wrote: 'My Aunt Georgy [the Lady Georgiana Peel, my grandmother's step-daughter] yesterday was very kind, but too inquisitive (as indeed most women are); she said even in old times at the slightest thought of a marriage my grandmother used to get into a sort of fever and be fussy and worried about it.'

her feelings. At some moments she seemed eager to marry me, and at other moments determined to retain her freedom. I had to work very hard during this time, as I was taking the second part of the Moral Sciences Tripos in one year, but I never found that love, either when it prospered or when it did not, interfered in the slightest with my intellectual concentration. When the Easter Vacation came, I went first with my Aunt Maude to Rome to stay with my uncle the Monsignor. And from there I went to Paris, where Logan had an apartment, and his mother and Alys were staying close by. It was my first experience of the life of American art students in Paris, and it all seemed to me very free and delightful. I remember a dance at which Alys appeared in a dress designed by Roger Fry. I remember, also, some rather unsuccessful attempts to instil culture into me by taking me to see Impressionist pictures in the Luxembourg. And I remember floating on the Seine at night near Fontainebleau with Alys beside me, while Logan filled the night with unbending cleverness. When I got back to Cambridge, James Ward spoke to me gravely about wasting my last vacation on the Continent when I ought to have been working. However, I did not take him seriously, and I got a First with distinction.

About the time that I finished with Triposes, Alys consented to become definitely engaged to me. At this, my people, who had never ceased from opposition, began to feel that something drastic must be done. They had no power to control my actions, and their strictures on her character had naturally remained without effect. Nevertheless, they found a weapon which very nearly gave them the victory. The old family doctor, a serious Scotsman with mutton-chop whiskers, began to tell me all the things that I had dimly suspected about my family history: how my Uncle William was mad, how my Aunt Agatha's engagement had had to be broken off because of her insane delusions, and how my father had suffered from epilepsy (from what medical authorities have told me since, I doubt whether this was a correct diagnosis). In those days, people who considered themselves scientific tended to have a somewhat superstitious attitude towards heredity, and of course it was not known how many mental disorders are the result of bad environment and unwise moral instruction. I began to feel as if I was doomed to a dark destiny. I read Ibsen's *Ghosts* and Björnson's *Heritage of the Kurts*. Alys had an uncle who was rather queer. By emphasising these facts until they rendered me nearly insane, my people persuaded us to take the best medical opinion as to whether, if we were married, our children were likely to be mad. The best medical opinion, primed by the family doctor, who was primed by the family, duly pronounced that from the point of view of heredity we ought not to have children. After receiving this verdict in the house of the family doctor at Richmond, Alys and I walked up and down

Richmond Green discussing it. I was for breaking off the engagement, as I believed what the doctors said and greatly desired children. Alys said she had no great wish for children, and would prefer to marry, while avoiding a family. After about half an hour's discussion, I came round to her point of view. We therefore announced that we intended to marry, but to have no children. Birth control was viewed in those days with the sort of horror which it now inspires only in Roman Catholics. My people and the family doctor tore their hair. The family doctor solemnly assured me that, as a result of his medical experience, he knew the use of contraceptives to be almost invariably gravely injurious to health. My people hinted that it was the use of contraceptives which had made my father epileptic. A thick atmosphere of sighs, tears, groans, and morbid horror was produced, in which it was scarcely possible to breathe. The discovery that my father had been epileptic, my aunt subject to delusions, and my uncle insane, caused me terror, for in those days everybody viewed the inheritance of mental disorders superstitiously. I had sensed something of the kind, though without definite knowledge. On July 21, 1893 (which I subsequently learnt to be Alys's birthday), I dreamed that I discovered my mother to be mad, not dead, and that, on this ground, I felt it my duty not to marry. After the facts had been told to me, I had great difficulty in shaking off fear, as appears from the following reflections, which I showed to nobody, not even Alys, until a much later date.

July 20–21 (1894). Midnight. This night is the anniversary of my dream about Alys, and also of her birth. Strange coincidence, which, combined with the fact that most of my dream has come true, very strongly impresses my imagination. I was always superstitious, and happiness has made me more so; it is terrifying to be so utterly absorbed in one person. Nothing has any worth to me except in reference to her. Even my own career, my efforts after virtue, my intellect (such as it is), everything I have or hope for, I value only as gifts to her, as means of shewing how unspeakably I value her love. And I am happy, divinely happy. Above all, I can still say, thank God, lust has absolutely no share in my passion. But just when I am happiest, when joy is purest, it seems to transcend itself and fall suddenly to haunting terrors of loss – it would be so easy to lose what rests on so slender and unstable a foundation! My dream on her birthday; my subsequent discovery that my people *had* deceived me as in that dream; their solemn and reiterated warnings; the gradual discovery, one by one, of the tragedies, hopeless and unalleviated, which have made up the lives of most of my family; above all, the perpetual gloom which hangs like a fate over PL,[1] and which, struggle as I will, invades

[1] Pembroke Lodge.

my inmost soul whenever I go there, taking all joy even out of Alys's love; all these, combined with the fear of heredity, cannot but oppress my mind. They make me feel as though a doom lay on the family and I were vainly battling against it to escape into the freedom which seems the natural birthright of others. Worst of all, this dread, of necessity, involves Alys too. I feel as tho' darkness were my native element, and a cruel destiny had compelled me, instead of myself attaining to the light, to drag her back with me into the gulf from which I have partially emerged. I cannot tell whether destiny will take the form of a sudden blow or of a long-drawn torture, sapping our energies and ruining our love; but I am haunted by the fear of the family ghost, which seems to seize on me with clammy invisible hands to avenge my desertion of its tradition of gloom.

All these feelings of course are folly, solely due to chocolate cake and sitting up late; but they are none the less real, and on the slightest pretence they assail me with tremendous force. Painful as it will necessarily be to them, I must for some time avoid seeing more than a very little of my people and of PL, otherwise I really shall begin to fear for my sanity. PL is to me like a family vault haunted by the ghosts of maniacs – especially in view of all that I have recently learnt from Dr Anderson. Here, thank heaven, all is bright and healthy, my Alys especially; and as long as I can forget PL and the ghastly heritage it bequeaths to me I have no forebodings, but only the pure joy of mutual love, a joy so great, so divine, that I have not yet ceased to wonder how such a thing can exist in this world which people abuse. But oh I *wish* I could know it would bring joy to her in the end, and not teach her further, what alas it has already begun to teach her, how terrible a thing life may be and what depths of misery it can contain.

The fears generated at that time have never ceased to trouble me subconsciously. Ever since, but not before, I have been subject to violent nightmares in which I dream that I am being murdered, usually by a lunatic. I scream out loud, and on one occasion, before waking, I nearly strangled my wife, thinking that I was defending myself against a murderous assault.

The same kind of fear caused me, for many years, to avoid all deep emotion, and live, as nearly as I could, a life of intellect tempered by flippancy. Happy marriage gradually gave me mental stability, and when, at a later date, I experienced new emotional storms, I found that I was able to remain sane. This banished the conscious fear of insanity, but the unconscious fear has persisted.

Whatever indecision I had felt as to what we ought to do was ended when Alys and I found another doctor, who assured me breezily that he had used contraceptives himself for many years, that no bad effects whatever were to be feared, and that we should be fools not to marry. So we went ahead, in spite of the shocked feelings of two generations. As a matter of fact, after we had been married two years we came to the conclusion that the medical authorities whom we had consulted had been talking nonsense, as indeed they obviously were, and we decided to have children if possible. But Alys proved to be barren, so the fuss had been all about nothing.

At the conclusion of this *fracas* I went to live at Friday's Hill with Alys's people, and there I settled down to work at a Fellowship dissertation, taking non-Euclidean Geometry as my subject. My people wrote almost daily letters to me about 'the life you are leading', but it was clear to me that they would drive me into insanity if I let them, and that I was getting mental health from Alys. We grew increasingly intimate.

My people, however, were not at the end of their attempts. In August they induced Lord Dufferin, who was then our Ambassador in Paris, to offer me the post of honorary attaché. I had no wish to take it, but my grandmother said that she was not much longer for this world, and that I owed it to her to see whether separation would lessen my infatuation. I did not wish to feel remorse whenever she came to die, so I agreed to go to Paris for a minimum of three months, on the understanding that if that produced no effect upon my feelings, my people would no longer actively oppose my marriage. My career in diplomacy, however, was brief and inglorious. I loathed the work, and the people, and the atmosphere of cynicism, and the separation from Alys. My brother came over to visit me, and although I did not know it at the time, he had been asked to come by my people, in order to form a judgement on the situation. He came down strongly on my side, and when the three months were up, which was on November 17th, I shook the dust of Paris off my feet, and returned to Alys. I had, however, first to make my peace with her, as she had grown jealous of her sister, of whom I saw a good deal during the latter part of my time in Paris. It must be said that making my peace only took about ten minutes.

The only thing of any permanent value that I derived from my time in Paris was the friendship of Jonathan Sturges, a man for whom I had a very great affection. Many years after his death, I went to see Henry James's house at Rye, which was kept at that time as a sort of museum. There I suddenly came upon Sturges's portrait hanging on the wall. It gave me so great a shock that I remember nothing else whatever about the place. He was a cripple, intensely sensitive, very literary, and belonging to what one must call the American aristocracy (he was a nephew of J. P. Morgan). He was a very witty man. I took him once into the Fellows' Garden at Trinity, and he said: 'Oh yes! This is where George Eliot told F. W. H. Myers that there is no God, and yet we must be good; and Myers decided that there is a God, and yet we need not be good.' I saw a great deal of him during my time in Paris, which laid the foundations of a friendship that ended only with his death.

LETTERS

15 rue du Sommerard
Paris
Oct. 25 '91

My dear Bertie

I have been meaning to write to you before, to tell you how much I enjoyed my visit to Cambridge, but I have been through such a season of woe in settling myself here! It is all due to that bothersome new order, for it is very hard to get rooms within the fixed margin, and I am much too proud to confess an excess so soon. So I have at last settled myself in the Latin Quarter, up seven flights of stairs, and I find that the spiritual pride that fills my breast more than amply compensates for all the bother. It *is* nice to feel better than one's neighbours! I met a friend yesterday who is living in cushioned ease across the river, and I felt so very superior, I am rather afraid that when I write to my adviser, I shall receive a hair shirt by return of post. Have you tried to observe the discipline? I do not speak evil, for I have no one to speak it to, though I think it of my landlady. And the other day, I was so reduced by the state of my things when I moved here that I could do nothing but eat a bun and read Tid-bits.

I have begun to write a novel, but be assured, it is not religious, and is not to be rejected by the publishers for a year or two yet.

My journey here after I left you was most amusing. On the steamer we sat in rows and glared at each other, after the pleasant English manner. There was a young married couple who stood out as a warning and a lesson to youth. He was a puzzled looking, beardless young man, and she was a limp figure of a woman, and there was a baby. The husband poured his wife into an armchair, and then walked up and down with the baby. Then he stood for a long while, looking at the watery horizon as if he were asking some question of it. But the dismal unwellness of his wife and baby soon put an end to his meditations. What a warning to youth! And I might have been in his place!

I hope you went to the debate to prove that the upper classes are un-educated – those broad generalisations are so stimulating – there is so much that one can say.

I hope you mean to join our order, and if you do, make me your adviser. I will set you nice penances, and then I shall be sure to hear from you – for there must be some rules that you will break – some rift in your integrity.

Give my regards to Sheldon Amos if you see him.

Yours ever,
Logan Pearsall Smith

15 Rue du Sommerard
Paris
Nov. 1891

Dear Bertie

I enclose the rules – the general outlines – we must have a meeting of the Order before long to settle them definitely. As for rule one, you had better fix a sum, and then keep to that. By the account you enclosed to me, you appear to be living on eggs and groceries – I should advise you to dine occasionally. Then at College one ought to entertain more or less – and that ought not to count as board and lodging. As to rule 4 – I should say at College it is perhaps better not to do too much at social work.

What you say about changing one's self denial is only too true and terrible – it went to my heart – one does form a habit, and then it is no bother. I will write to the Arch Prig about it.

Of course you must consider yourself a member, and you must confess to me, and I will write you back some excellent ghostly advice. And you must get other members. We shall expect to enroll half of Trinity.

I am living as quietly as an oyster, and I find it pleasant to untangle oneself for a while from all social ties, and look round a bit. And there is so much to look at here!

Yours ever,
Logan Pearsall Smith

Here are the rules of The Order of Prigs as Logan Pearsall Smith drew them up.

Maxims: Don't let anyone know you are a prig.
  1. Deny yourself in inconspicuous ways and don't speak of your economies.
  2. Avoid all vain and unkind criticism of others.[1]
  3. Always keep your company manners on – keep your coat brushed and your shoe-laces tied.
  4. Avoid the company of the rich and the tables of the luxurious – all those who do not regard their property as a trust.

[1] Logan was the most malicious scandal-monger I have ever known.

5. Don't be a Philistine! Don't let any opportunities of hearing good music, seeing good pictures or acting escape you.
6. Always let others profit as much as possible by your skill in these things.
7. Do what you can to spread the order.

Specific Rules:
1. Don't let your board and lodging exceed two pounds a week.
2. Keep a strict account of monies spent on clothes and pleasure.
3. If your income provides more than the necessities of Life, give at least a tenth of it in Charity.
4. Devote an evening a week, or an equivalent amount of time, to social work with the labouring Classes, or visiting the sick.
5. Set apart a certain time every day for examination of conscience.
6. Abstain entirely from all intoxicating liquors, except for the purposes of health.
7. Practise some slight self-denial every day, for instance – Getting up when called. No cake at tea, No butter at breakfast, No coffee after dinner.
8. Observe strictly the rules of diet and exercise prescribed by one's doctor, or approved by one's better reason.
9. Read some standard poetry or spiritual book every day, for at least half an hour.
10. Devote ½ hour every other day, or 1½ hours weekly, to the keeping fresh of learning already acquired – going over one's scientific or classical work.
11. Keep all your appointments punctually, and don't make any engagements or promises you are not likely to fulfil.

The Arch Prig[1] or the associate Prig is empowered to give temporary or permanent release from any of these rules, if he deem it expedient.
All neglect of the rules and maxims shall be avowed to the Arch Prig, or one's associate, who shall set a penance, if he think it expedient.

Suggested penances:
Pay a duty call.
Write a duty letter.
Learn some poetry or prose.
Translate English into another language.
Tidy up your room.
Extend your hospitality to a bore.
(Hair shirts can be had of the Arch Prig on application.)

[1] I don't know who the Arch Prig was, or even whether he existed outside Logan's imagination.

15 Rue du Sommerard
Paris
Dec. 3 1891

My dear Bertie

I think you make an excellent Prig, and you have lapses enough to make it interesting. I was shocked however by the price, 12/6 you paid for a stick. There seems an odour of sin about that. 2/6 I should think ought to be the limit, and if the morality of Cambridge is not much above that of Oxford, I should think that your 12/6 stick would not keep in your possession long.

I know nothing about tobacco and meerschaums, so I cannot follow you into these regions of luxury. I must ask some one who smokes pipes about it. Well, I think you'd better impose one of the penances out of the list on yourself and then if you continue in sin I shall become more severe.

I find Priggishness, like all forms of excellence, much more difficult than I had imagined – by-the-by – let me tell you that if one simply *thinks* one has read one's half hour, one has probably read only a quarter of an hour. Human nature, at least my nature, is invariably optimistic in regard to itself.

No, the rule as to 1½ hrs. a week need not apply to you – but you *ought* to go to concerts, unless you are too busy. As to charities – there are an infinite number that are good – but why not save what money you have for such purposes for the Prig fund? And then when we have a meeting we can decide what to do with it. It will be most interesting when we all meet, to compare experiences. I am afraid it may lead however to reflexions of a pessimistic tinge.

My adviser the Arch Prig, has failed me – if it were not speaking evil I should insinuate the suspicion that he had got into difficulties with the rules himself, which would be very terrible.

I live alone here with the greatest contentment. One inherits, when one comes here, such a wealth of tradition and civilisation! The achievements of three or four centuries of intelligence and taste – that is what one has at Paris. I was bewildered at first, and shivered on the brink, and was homesick for England, but now I have come to love Paris perfectly.

Do write again when you have collected more sins, and tell me whether the fear of penance acts on you in the cause of virtue. It does on a cowardly nature like mine.

Yours ever,
Logan Pearsall Smith

15 Rue du Sommerard
Paris
Jan. 11th 1892

My dear Bertie

I have just read through your letter again to see if I could not find
some excuse for imposing a penance on you, for having hurt my foot
this afternoon, I feel in a fierce mood. But I am not one of those who
see sin in a frock coat – if it be well fitting. But wait a bit – are you
sure you told me what you had read in order, as you say, to confound
my scepticism – was there not a slight infringement of maxim 1 lurking
in your mind? If upon severe self-examination you find there was, I
think you had better finish learning the 'Ode to the West Wind' which
you partly knew last summer.

So far I have written in my official capacity as your adviser. But as
your friend I was shocked and startled by your calm statement that you
indulge in 'all the vices not prohibited by the rules'. These I need not
point out are numerous, extending from Baccarat to biting one's finger
nails – I hesitate to believe that you have abandoned yourself to them
all. I think you must have meant that you read a great deal of Browning.

I am living in great quiet and contentment. A certain portion of the
day I devote to enriching the English language with tales and morali-
ties, the rest of the time I contemplate the mind of man as expressed
in art and literature. I am thirsting of course for that moment – and
without doubt the moment will come – when I shall hear my name
sounded by all Fame's tongues and trumpets, and see it misspelled in
all the newspapers. But I content myself in the meantime, by posing
as a poet in the drawing rooms of credulous American ladies.

As a novelist or 'fictionist' to use the Star expression, I make it my
aim to show up in my tales, in which truth is artistically mingled with
morality, 'Cupid and all his wanton snares'. I also wish to illustrate
some of the incidents of the eternal war between the sexes. What will
the whited sepulchres of America say? Je m'en fiche.

Well, it is pleasant thus to expatiate upon my own precious identity.

I suppose you are 'on the threshold' – as one says, when one wishes to
write high style – the threshold of another term – and so resuming my
character of moral adviser I will salt this letter with some sententious
phrase, if I can find one that is both true and fresh – but I cannot think
of any – the truth is always so banal – that is why the paradox has such
a pull over it.

Yours ever,
Logan Pearsall Smith

14 Rue de la Grande
Chaumière, Paris
March 19 '92

Dear Bertie

I think members ought to be admitted to the Order, who are moderate drinkers, if they are satisfactory in other ways. Good people are so rare. But on all these points we must debate when we meet. We are going to Haslemere sometime in Easter Week, I think, and I hope you will keep a few days free to pay us a visit then. But I will write to you again when I get to England. As you see by my address, I have moved again, and I am at last settled in a little apartment furnished by myself. I am in Bohemia, a most charming country, inhabited entirely by French Watchmen and American and English art students, young men and women, who live in simple elegance and deshabille. My £2.0.0 a week seems almost gross extravagance here, and one's eyes are never wounded by the sight of clean linen and new coats. Really you can't imagine how charming it is here – everybody young, poor and intelligent and hard at work.

When I came here first, I knew some 'society' people on the other side of the river, and used to go and take tea and talk platitudes with them, but now their lives seem so empty, their minds so waste and void of sense, that I cannot approach them without a headache of boredom. How dull and unintelligent people can make themselves if they but try.

> *Yours ever,*
> *L. P. Smith*

Friday's Hill
Haslemere
Nov. 24 '92

Ça va bien à Cambridge, Bertie ? I wish I could look in on you – only you would be startled at my aspect, as I have shaved my head till it is as bald as an egg, and dressed myself in rags, and retired to the solitude of Fernhurst, where I am living alone, in the Costelloe Cottage.[1] Stevens wrote to me, asking me to send something to the *Cambridge Observer*[2] and, prompted by Satan (as I believe) I promised I would. So I hurried up and wrote an article on Henry James, and when I had posted it last night, it suddenly came over me how stupid and bad it was. Well, I hope the good man won't print it.

[1] This was a cottage close to Friday's Hill, inhabited by the family of Logan's married sister Mrs Costelloe (afterwards Mrs Berenson).

[2] This was a high-brow undergraduate magazine, mainly promoted by Oswald Sickert (brother of the painter), who was a close friend of mine.

There are good things in the *Observer* he sent me. I was quite surprised – it certainly should be encouraged. Only I don't go with it in its enthusiasm for impurity – its jeers at what Milton calls 'The sage and serious doctrine of virginity'. It is dangerous for Englishmen to try to be French, they never catch the note – the accent. A Frenchman if he errs, does it 'dans un moment d'oubli', as they say – out of absent-mindedness, as it were – while the Englishman is much too serious and conscious. No, a civilisation must in the main develop on the lines and in the ways of feeling already laid down for it by those who founded and fostered it. I was struck with this at the 'New English Art Club' I went up to see. There are some nice things, but in the mass it bore the same relation to real art – French art – as A Church Congress does to real social movements.

So do show Sickert and his friends that a gospel of impurity, preached with an Exeter Hall zeal and denunciation, will do much to thicken the sombre fogs in which we live already.

I shall stay in England for a while longer – when does your vac. begin and where do you go ?

> *Yrs.*
> *L. P. Smith*

> 14 rue de la Grande
> Chaumière, Paris
> Feb. 14th '93

My dear Bertie

I was sorry that Musgrave and I could not get to Richmond, but I was only a short time in London. I shall hope to go at Easter, if I am back. Paris welcomed me as all her own, when I got here and I have been living in the charm of this delightful and terrible place. For it is pretty terrible in many ways, at least the part of Paris I live in. Perhaps it is the wickedness of Paris itself, perhaps the fact that people live in this quarter without conventions or disguises or perhaps – which I am inclined to believe – the life of artists is almost always tragical – or not wanting at least in elements of Tragedy – that gives me the sense of the wretchedness and the fineness of life here. Just think this very morning I discovered that a girl here I know had gone mad. She came in to see me, begged me to help her write a book to attack French immorality and now I am waiting to see the doctor I sent for, to see if we must shut her up.

As for 'morality', well – one finds plenty of the other thing, both in women and men. I met the other day one of the Young Davies' at Studd's studio – and my heart sank a little at the sight of another nice young Englishman come to live in Paris. But he I suppose can take care of himself.

But I must not abuse Paris too much, for after all this, and perhaps on account of it, Paris is beyond measure interesting. There are big stakes to be won or lost and everybody is playing for them.

Yours,
L. Pearsall Smith

44 Grosvenor Road
Westminster
Oct. 29 '93

My dear Bertie

You I suppose are watching the yellowing of the year at Cambridge, and indulging in the sentiments proper to the season. I am still kept unwillingly in London, and see no present prospect of getting away. I have tried to like London, for its grimy charms have never yet been adequately commended; – and charms it certainly has – but I have decided that if ever I 'do' London hatred and not love must be my inspiration, and for literary purposes hatred is an excellent theme. All French realism is rooted in hatred of life as it is, and according to Harold Joachim's rude but true remark, such pessimism must be based somehow on optimism. 'No shadow without light', and the bright dream of what London might be, and Paris already, to a small extent is – makes the present London seem ignoble and dark. Then I have been going a little into literary society – not the best literary society, but the London Bohemia of minor novelists, poets and journalists – and it does not win one to enthusiasm. No; the London Bohemia is wanting in just that quality which would redeem Bohemia – disinterestedness – it is a sordid, money-seeking Bohemia, conscious of its own meanness and determined to see nothing but meanness in the world at large. They sit about restaurant tables, these pale-faced little young men, and try to show that all the world is as mean and sordid as they themselves are – and indeed they do succeed for the moment in making the universe seem base.

How do you like your philosophy work? Don't turn Hegelian and lose yourself in perfumed dreams – the world will never get on unless a few people at least will limit themselves to believing what has been proved, and keep clear the distinction between what we really know and what we don't.

Yours ever,
Logan Pearsall Smith

Queen's Hotel
Barnsley
Nov. 16 1893

Dear Bertie

Thanks so much for your generous cheque[1] – the need here is very

[1] In support of a miners' strike.

great, but thanks to the money coming in, there is enough to keep the people going in some sort of way. They are splendid people certainly – and it is hard to believe they will ever give in. It seems pretty certain to me that the Masters brought on the strike very largely for the purpose of smashing the Federation. Of course the Federation is often annoying – and I daresay the owners have respectable grievances, but their profits are very great and no one seems to think that they could not afford the 'living wage'. Within the last year a good deal of money has been invested in collieries here, and several new pits started, showing that the business is profitable. Well, it does one good to see these people, and the way they stick by each other, men and women, notwithstanding their really dreadful privations.

> *Yrs.*
> *Logan Pearsall Smith*

> 44 Grosvenor Road
> Westminster Embankment
> S.W.
> Nov. 1893

Dear Bertie

You forgot to endorse this – write your name on the back, and send it to J. T. Drake, 41 Sheffield Road. It will be weeks before many of the Barnsley people will be able to get to work, and this money will come in most usefully. Every 10/– gives a meal to 240 children! I am very glad that I went to Barnsley, though I went with groans, but it does one good to see such a fine democracy. I wish you could have seen a meeting of miners I went to; a certain smart young Tory MP came with some courage, but very little sense to prove to the miners that they were wrong. They treated him with good-natured contempt and when he told them that their wages were quite sufficient they replied 'Try it lad yourself' – 'It wouldn't pay for your bloody starched clothes'. 'Lad, your belly's fool' and other playful remarks. 'Noo redooction' a woman shouted and everyone cheered. Then a miner spoke with a good deal of sense and sarcasm, and the young MP was in about as silly a position as one could be in – well-fed, well-dressed and rosy. The contrast between him and the man to whom he preached contentment was what you call striking. But he had to smile and look gracious, as only Tories can, and pretend he was enjoying it immensely.

> *Yrs.*
> *L. Pearsall Smith*

44 Grosvenor Road
Westminster Embankment
S.W.
Dec. 2nd (1893)

My dear Bertie

Of course I know how matters stand, and naturally being as fond of my sister as I am, I do not regard your way of feeling as folly. And if you remain of the same mind after several years, I can assure you that I don't know of anyone who I should like better as a brother-in-law – nor indeed do I think there is anyone who would make a better husband for Alys. But sincerely I think you would make a mistake by engaging yourself too soon – but I dare say you don't intend to do that. One never knows what one will develop into, and anyhow the first few years after 21 should be given to self education, and the search for one's work, and marriage, or even a settled engagement, interferes sadly with all that.

Yes I *do* believe in you, Bertie, though the faculty for belief is not one of those most developed in me – only I shall believe more in your decision when I see that after a few years of good work and experience of the world you still remain the same. Win your spurs, *mon cher* – let us see that you are good and sensible – as indeed we believe you are – your friends all have the highest ideas of your ability and promise, only keep yourself free and interested in your work. Love should be the servant, and not the master of life.

> *Yours affy.*
> *L. P. S.*

The following letters were written to Alys during our three-months' separation.

Pembroke Lodge
Richmond, Surrey
July 31st 1894

My darling Alys

As was to be expected there is nothing particular to be told, as nothing has happened. So far, however, it has not been particularly odious. When I arrived I found my Grandmother on a sofa in her sitting-room, looking very pale and sad; still, I was relieved to find her out of bed. Our meeting was *very* affectionate, though silent. We have talked only of indifferent subjects; she obviously realises that it is bad for her health to talk of anything agitating. The Doctor does not allow her to have any correspondence but what my Aunt thinks good for her (though she herself doesn't know this), however she was given my letter this morning and seems to have been pleased with it. My false conscience has been rather subdued by thee and the atmosphere of Friday's Hill, so that I find it far more endurable than last time in spite of my grandmother's illness; perhaps because of it too, in a way, because it sets everything in a kindlier and more natural key.

My aunt has been cross-questioning me about all my plans, but her comments, though *most* eloquent, have been silent. I told her about America, and she seemed to think it odd we should go unmarried: I said 'Well we thought it would be better than marrying before going out there', but to that she made no answer. All she said was 'I shan't tell Granny about that just yet'. She will probably have to go away for her health in September and she fished for me to offer to stay here with my grandmother; but I said I should be at Friday's Hill. I said I might in the following months come here every now and then, but should mainly live at Friday's Hill. She looked thunder, but said nothing. She has realised the uselessness of advice or criticism. She spoke about my grandmother seeing thee, but I said it would be better not without me.

My grandmother unfortunately is not so well this evening; she has to take sleeping-draughts and medicines for her digestion constantly and they are afraid both of stopping them and of her becoming dependent on them. She is very affecting in her illness, but having steeled my conscience I don't mind so much. She has been writing verses about Arthur to try and distract her mind from this one topic; she has also been reading a good deal with the same end in view; but apparently she has not succeeded very well.

But really it isn't half so bad here as it might be, so thee needn't make thyself unhappy about me or imagine I shall come back in the state of mind I was in yesterday fortnight. However I don't want – if I can help it, to make any promises as to when I shall come back. Goodnight Dearest. I am really happy but for being unutterably bored and I hope thee is enjoying the country even without me to force thee to do so.

> *Thine devotedly*
> *Bertie*

> Ramsbury Manor
> Wiltshire
> Aug. 30th 1894

My Darling

I am very much perplexed by this offer of a post in Paris. If I were sure it wouldn't last beyond Xmas, and then would not tie me down to the same sort of post in future, I should feel inclined to accept it: it would pass the time of our separation very enjoyably (for I should certainly enjoy being at the Paris Embassy immensely); it would give me about as much of the world as could well be crammed into the time; it would give me some knowledge of the inside of diplomacy, and would certainly be a valuable experience, if it could remain an isolated episode. I don't know whether it would necessarily postpone our meeting and marriage; I fear it would; and that would be an argument against it. Also I am afraid of the world and its tone, as they are very bad for me, especially when I enjoy them, and I am very much afraid that such a career, once entered on, would be very hard to leave. Besides it would mean a number of aristocratic ties, which would hamper our future activity. And hardly any home appointment could induce me to give up the year of travel we propose, as I am sure that would not only be *far* the pleasantest way of spending our first year of marriage, but would also have great educational value. I wish my grandmother had given me more particulars: all that is clear from her letter is that it would give her great satisfaction if I accepted it. I should probably offend Lord Dufferin if I refused it, though perhaps that could be avoided. I *do* wish we could meet to discuss it; and I should like to have Logan's opinion.

2 p.m. The more I think of it, the more it seems to me that it would be the first step in a career I wish to avoid; but I cannot be sure till I hear more. And if I refuse, it would of course definitely cut me off from Secretaryships etc., as people wouldn't want to offer things to so fastidious and apparently capricious a young man. That is an advantage or the reverse according as you look at it. My brain is in a whirl and it is too hot to think.

Pembroke Lodge
Richmond, Surrey
Sep. 1, 9 p.m. '94

My darling Alys

Now that I am home again I have time to write a really long letter, and I feel tonight as if I could write for ever: I am made sentimental and full of thoughts by the place. I am reminded so vividly of last September that it seems as if I had all my work still before me. I went out today and sat by the fountain and thought of the long solitary days I used to spend there, meditating, wishing, scarcely daring to hope; trying to read the minutest indications in the bare, dry little letters thee used to write me, and in the number of days thee waited before answering mine; miserable in a way, mad with impatience, and yet full of a new life and vigour, so that I used to start with surprise at finding I no longer wished to die, as I had done for 5 years, and had supposed I always should do. How I counted the hours till Dunrozel came to visit here, and I was free to leave my Grandmother! Being here alone again I feel as if the intervening year had been a dream; as if thee still were to me a distant, scarcely possible heaven; indifferent, as heaven must be, to mere earthly strugglers. But there is a strange weariness, like that of a troublesome dream, which forms an undercurrent to all my thoughts and makes the dream-feelings different in tone from those of last September; a weariness compounded of all the struggles and anxieties and pains of the past year, of all the strain and all the weary discussions and quarrels which winning thee has cost me. I am not unhappy, however, far from it; but for the moment it seems as if I had lived my life, and it had been good; it reached a climax, a supreme moment, and now there seems no more need to care about it: it can have nothing better in store, and therefore there would be no bitterness in death.

I suppose thee will think these feelings morbid, but I don't know that they are particularly so. I got into a dreamy mood from reading Pater: I was immensely impressed by it, indeed it seemed to me almost as beautiful as anything I had ever read (except here and there, where his want of humour allowed him to fall into a discordant note, as with the valetudinarian cat); especially I was struck by the poplars and another passage I can't find again. It recalled no definite childish memories, because since the age of definite memories I have not lived in a world of sensuous impressions like that of Florian; but rather in the manner of Wordsworth's Ode, I dimly feel again the very early time before my intellect had killed my senses. I have a vague confused picture of the warm patches of red ground where the setting summer sun shone on it, and of the rustling of the poplars in front of the house when I used to go to bed by daylight after hot days, and the shadow of the house crept slowly up them. I have a vague feeling of perpetual warm sunny weather, when I used to be taken driving and notice the speckled shadows moving across the carriage, before it occurred to me that they were caused by the leaves overhead. (As soon as I discovered this, the scientific interest killed the impression, and I began speculating as to why the patches of light were always circular and so on.) But very early indeed I lost the power of attending to impressions *per se*, and always abstracted from them and sought the scientific and intellectual and abstract that lay behind them, so that it wouldn't have occurred to me, as to Florian, to need a philosophy for them; they went bodily into my mental waste-paper basket. (That is why the book made me so dreamy, because it carried me back to my earliest childhood, where nothing seems really real.) I didn't begin to need such a philosophy till the age of puberty, when the sensuous and emotional reasserted itself more strongly than before or since, so that I felt carried back for a time to my infancy; then I made a sort of religion of beauty, such as Florian might have had; I had a passionate desire to find some link between the true and the beautiful, so strong that beauty gave me intense pain (tho' also a tingling sensuous thrill of

tremendous strength), for the constant sense of this unfulfilled require-
ment of harmony between it and fact. I read Alastor after I had lived
some time in this state, and there I found the exact mood I had
experienced, vividly described. It was only gradually, as I came to care
less and less for beauty, as I got through the natural period of morbidness (for in me so intense a passion for the beautiful was necessarily
abnormal), only as I became more purely intellectual again, that I
ceased to suffer from this conflict. Of course my taste of real life in the
Fitz episode got me out of such mere sentimentality, and since then it
has been only by moments I have suffered from it. If I could believe
in Bradley, as I do most days, I should never suffer from it again. . . .

Sunday morning Sep. 2

I sent thee a wire from Reading early yesterday morning to say
'Shan't come since Nov. 17 is unchanged', but I suppose thee was
already gone from Chichester before it arrived. Thee says thee will
come to Paris if I can't come to England, but I rather gather from my
Grandmother that I shall be able to chuck this post when I like. Will
thee send my hat in my hat-box, as I need both? And please write
by the 1st post tomorrow, otherwise I may be gone. I shall probably
go the day after hearing from Lord Kimberley. But I can't go and
see Edith and Bryson, as they surely are staying in Britanny till Nov?
Shall I send the Pater to Mariechen, or straight to Carey Thomas?
All these details are tiresome, and I am sorry not to have remembered
all the things I want sent in one batch, but my memory works that way
unavoidably.

I like the Tragic Muse immensely, it is such fun; besides it is
singularly appropriate to my present situation. – My Aunt Georgy
yesterday was very kind, but too inquisitive (as indeed most women
are); she said even in old times at the slightest thought of a marriage
my Grandmother used to get into a sort of fever and be fussy and
worried about it. . . .

. . . I am grown quite glad of the Paris plan, and shall make a great
effort not to hate my companions too much. At any rate I ought to be
able to write amusing letters from there. Give me literary criticisms
of my descriptions, so that I may make them as vivid as possible. – It
is sad thee should have grown bored with thy friend's talk, but it is
difficult to throw oneself into other people's petty concerns when
one's own are very absorbing and interesting. I am *not* sorry thee has
come to understand why I minded thy going right away to America
more than a separation with thee still in London. Thee thought it very
silly then, and so no doubt it is, but it is natural.

I hope this letter is long enough to satisfy thee: it has been a great
satisfaction to write it, and I shall expect a *very* long one in return.

If thee hears from Edith Thomas, thee will send me her letter, won't thee? I will wire as soon as I know when I'm going to Paris.

Goodbye my Darling. It was much better not to meet again and have the pain of a real parting.

Thine devotedly
Bertie

Pembroke Lodge
Richmond, Surrey
Sep. 3 '94, 10 a.m.

Dearest Alys

I got three letters from thee by the 1st post this morning, which was delightful; one of them forwarded from Ramsbury, a particularly charming one. I am returning the documents it contained, which amused me much.

I have quite settled to accept the Paris offer (owing to thy urging me to do so), and I fancy Lord Kimberley's confirmation of it is purely formal. I am only waiting here for another letter from Lord Dufferin, and then I shall be off immediately. But I am rather sorry thee makes so very light of the dangers and drawbacks of aristocracy; I begin to fear thee will never understand why I dread them, and that it is not a mere superstition. Thee and Logan could mix with aristocrats to any extent (before thy engagement at any rate) without ever coming across the stumbling-blocks they put in the way of one of their own class who wishes to 'escape'. Americans are liked in society just because they are for the most part queer specimens, and don't do the things other people do or abstain from the things other people abstain from; people expect a sort of spectacular amusement from them, and therefore tolerate anything, though all but a *very* small minority make up for it by bitterly abusing them behind their backs. It thus comes about that you would never see aristocrats as they are with one of themselves; rigid and stiff and conventional, and horrified at the minutest divergence from family tradition. Besides they are mostly my relations and my Grandmother's friends: unless I make a fool of myself in Paris, this offer will lead to others, at home; any refusal will give great pain to my Grandmother (whose death is by no means to be counted on) and will offend and annoy the whole set of them. Also being my relations they all feel they have a right to advise; when I am trying to work quietly and unobtrusively, in a way which seems to me honest, but is very unlikely to bring me the slightest fame or success till I'm 50 at least, they will come and badger me to go in for immediate success; from my many connections and the good will most of them unfortunately bear me, it will probably be easily within my reach, and

I shall be pestered and worried almost out of my life by their insist-ence. And (I must confess it) horrible as such a thought is, I do not *entirely* trust thee to back me up. I have a passion for experience, but if I am to make anything of the talents I have, I must eschew a vast deal of possible experience, shut myself up in my study, and live a quiet life in which I see only people who approve of such a life (as far as possible); I know myself well enough to be sure (though it is a confession of weakness) that if thee insists on my having a lot of experience, on my seeing a heterogeneous society and going out into the world, and perhaps having episodes of an utterly different, worldly sort of life, my nervous force will be unequal to the strain; I shall either have to give up the work my conscience approves of, or I shall be worn out and broken down by the time I'm 30. In short, [I] know my own needs, much better than thee does; and it is *very* important to me that thee should back me up in insisting on them. Casual experience of life is of very little use to a specialist, such as I aspire to be; good manners are *absolutely* useless. Thee has a sort of illogical kindness (not to call it weakness), which prevents thy seeing the application of a general rule to a particular case, if anybody is to derive a little pleasure from its infraction, so that thee is quite capable, while protesting that in general thee wishes me to lead a quiet student's life, of urging me in every particular case to accept offers, and go in for practical affairs, which really are hindrances to me. Both of us, too, are in danger of getting intoxicated by cheap success, which is the most damning thing on earth; if I waste these years, which ought to be given almost *entirely* to theoretic work and the acquisition of ideas by thought (since that is scarcely possible except when one is young), my conscience will reproach me throughout the rest of my life. Once for all, G. A. [God Almighty] has made me a theorist, not a practical man; a knowledge of the world is therefore of very little value to me. One hour spent in reading Wagner's statistics is probably of more value than 3 months in casual contact with society. *Do* be stern and consistent in accepting this view of myself, as otherwise (if I have to fight thee as well as my relations and the world) I shall certainly miss what I *hope* it lies in me to do. Thee may read what thee likes of this to Logan and see if he doesn't agree with me. The needs of a theorist are so utterly different from thine that it seems impossible for thee to realise how things of the greatest importance to thee may be utterly worthless to me. Beatrice Webb's case is very different, for she married a man whom all her smart relations hated, while thee with thy damnably friendly manner cannot help ingratiating thyself with them all! Besides I should imagine she was a person who feels it less than I do when she has to go against the wishes of those who are fond of her. And besides, all the early years of her life were wasted, so that she never can become first-rate,[1] or more than a shadow of her husband. – Excuse the tone of this letter: the fact is I have had the fear a long time that thee would ruin my career by wishing me to be too practical, and it has now at last come to a head. . . .

> Pembroke Lodge
> Richmond, Surrey
> Sep. 3 1894

Dearest Alys

. . . It was hardly in *early* boyhood I wished to harmonise the true and the beautiful, but rather when I was 16 and 17. I was peculiar chiefly because I was so constantly alone – when I had a spell of the society of other boys I soon became much more like them. I think when I was quite a child I was more thoughtful than rather later. I remember vividly a particular spot on the gravel walk outside the dining-room here, where a great uncle of mine told me one fine summer's afternoon at tea time that I should never enjoy future fine afternoons quite so much again. He was half in joke half in earnest, and went on to explain that one's enjoyments grow less and less intense and unmixed as one grows older. I was only 5 years old at the time, but, being a pessimistic theory about life, it impressed me profoundly; I remember arguing against it then, and almost weeping because I felt he probably knew better and was likely to be right; however I know now that he certainly wasn't, which is a consolation. Then as now, I hugged my enjoyments with a sort of personal affection, as tho' they were something outside of me. Little did he think what a profound impression his chance careless words had made! . . .

> Pembroke Lodge
> Richmond, Surrey
> Sunday morning
> September 9th 1894

Dearest Alys

. . . It is strange, but I'm really in some ways happier than during the month at Friday's Hill; I realise that thee and I together were trying to stamp out my affection for my Grandmother, and that the attempt was a failure. My conscience was bad, so that I dreamt about her every night, and always had an uneasy consciousness of her in the background of even the happiest moments. Now, if she dies, I shall have a good conscience towards her: otherwise I should have had, I believe for life, that worse sort of remorse, the remorse for cruelty to a person whom death has removed from one's longing to make up

---

[1] What a mistaken judgement!

for past deficiencies. My love for her is altogether too real to be ignored with impunity. . . .

> Victoria, 9 a.m.
> September 10th

Dearest Alys

I have got off after all today! I got thy two letters at breakfast: they will sustain me during the voyage. I feel too journeyfied to be sentimental or to have anything at all to say. I am very glad to be off, of course. But I was a little put off by my visit to the d'Estournelles yesterday. All the people were French except the Spanish Ambassador and the Italian Ambassadress, and I was not much impressed by their charms or even their manners: except the Spaniard, they were all oppressively and too restlessly polite for English taste: there was none of the repose and unobtrusiveness which constitutes good breeding to the British mind. I am to see three of them again in Paris, worse luck. It is very hard to live up to their incessant compliments and always have one ready to fire off in return. . . .

> British Embassy
> Paris
> Friday, October 12th, 1894
> 9.45 a.m.

My dearest Alys

. . . I had a perfectly delightful evening with Miss Belloc[1] last night – from 7 till 12 – as she stayed so late I suppose she enjoyed it too. I believe she was really very nice but to me she was surrounded by the halo of Friday's Hill and I should have thought her charming if she'd been the devil incarnate, or anything short of human perfection. We met at 7 at Neal's Library, Rue Rivoli – then we walked some time in the Tuilleries Gardens and elsewhere, and then dined at a queer quiet place in the Palais Royal. Then we walked about again for a long time, and both smoked an enormous number of cigarettes, and finally I left her at the door of her hotel at midnight, with hopes of another meeting today or tomorrow. We talked of thee and all the family, of French and English people, of Grant Allen, Stead and Mrs Amos, of the Embassy and its dreariness – of the various French poets who'd been in love with her and whom she'd been in love with – of her way of getting on with her French conventional relations and of their moral ideas (always incomprehensible and therefore interesting to me) – of Lady Henry and Pollen (whom we agreed to loathe) and Miss Willard – of vice in general and the difference between Parisian and London vice in particular and of her experiences in the way of being

[1] Afterwards Mrs Lowndes. She was a sister of Hilaire Belloc.

spoken to – and many other things. I found her talk very interesting and I think she enjoyed herself too – though not of course as much as I did, because she was the first congenial person I'd seen since I was at Vétheuil,[1] and the first to whom I could talk about thee. Her French sentiments come in very oddly – it is difficult to fit them in with her love of Stead – altogether being of two nations has made her not so much of a piece as she ought to be. But I *did* enjoy my evening – far more than anything since I left Friday's Hill – for the first time I was able to admire the Seine at night (which is *perfectly* lovely) without growing maudlin. . . .

> Monday, October 15th, 1894
> 12.30 a.m.

My Beloved

Don't say thee thinks of me from my letters as 'brains in the abstract', it does sound *so* cold and dry and lifeless. Letters *are* bad, but they ought to have more reality than that. To me too tonight five weeks seems a long time – that is because my brother is with me. I *shall* be glad when he goes. I hate him and half fear him – he dominates me when he is with me because I dread his comments if he should know me as I am. Thee hasn't made me less sensitive but more so – because I have had to embody one result of my real self in a form in which all the world can see it, which gives every one a hold for attacking me – I dread the moment when the Embassy people will discover it. Even the joy of getting away from all the people who annoy me would be enough by itself to be an intense source of joy. . . .

> British Embassy, Paris
> Wednesday, October 17th
> 1894
> 10 a.m.

My darling Alys

. . . I don't at all wish to alarm people – but my brother, of his own accord yesterday, while we were dining at La Perouse, said he could well imagine it, that *he* was afraid of me, though of hardly anyone else, because I never let myself go, and one felt me coldly critical inside. – Of course that *is* what I feel with my brother, but I'm sorry if I'm that way with people like Miss Belloc. He thinks himself

---

[1] I stayed a week-end at Vétheuil with three sisters named Kinsella, who were friends of the Pearsall Smiths. I there met Condor the painter, whose only remark was: 'Wouldn't it be odd if one were so poor that one had to give them shaving soap instead of cream with their tea?' It was there also that I made the acquaintance of Jonathan Sturges, who was in love with one of the sisters.

a person of universal Whitmaniac sympathy; but if you sympathise with *everybody* it comes to much the same as sympathising with none, or at any rate not with those who are hated! . . .

My brother won't want to come to Germany – I don't think he likes thee, which is a mercy – he thinks thee has the American hardness, by which he means not submitting completely to the husband and not being sensual. He says American women only love from the waist upwards. Thee can imagine I don't open my soul to him! It seems hard on thee to give thee a second objectionable brother-in-law called Frank. . . .

> British Embassy
> October 20th 1894
> 3 p.m.

My darling Alys

I think the real use of our separation is to give me a good conscience and to hasten our marriage. Thee doesn't think my good conscience will last, but I think it will if I don't see too much of my Grandmother. I feel no duties now, only a mild irritation when I think of her and Aunt Agatha, and it will be a good thing to continue to feel so. And all this separation is well worth while, for we should never have been really happy together without the knowledge we had really done something serious for my Grandmother. . . . I enclose Sanger's two letters – I have answered saying I would probably do two Dissertations – the second letter is much more encouraging than the first. I said I would make the Geometry the chief one my first shot and the Economics my second shot . . .

I have been reading more Mill and beginning an Essay on Axioms for the Moral Science Club at Cambridge, of which Trotter, the hard-working Scotsman I beat and despise, is Secretary. It will be an immense pleasure to go to Cambridge and read a paper and enjoy the Society again. The Society is a real passion to me – after thee, I know no greater joy. I shall read them a paper on controlling our passions, in which I shall point out that we can't, and that the greater they are the less we ought to though the more easily we can. – This sounds paradoxical but isn't. I take refuge in intellectual activity which has always been rather of the nature of a dissipation and opiate to me.

Goodbye my Darling, my Joy. I will write again tomorrow.

> *Thine heart and soul*
> *Bertie*

> British Embassy, Paris
> October 22nd 1894, 9 p.m.

My darling Alys

. . . I don't think thee'll be tempted to grow too dependent on me, because thee'll find I shall be bored if thee always agrees with me, and shall want an argument now and then to give my brain a little exercise. I feel a real and solid pleasure when anybody points out a fallacy in any of my views, because I care much less about my opinions than about their being true. But thee *Must* think for thyself instead of merely taking scraps from different people – that is what makes thy opinions so disjointed, because thee takes different opinions from different people, thinking the two subjects independent – but no two subjects are really independent, so that people with different Popes for different things have an extraordinary hotch-potch of views. Logan, thee and Mariechen all have that vice, Logan least, M. most.

Logan once told me thee had better taste in pictures than M., and yet thee seldom opens thy mouth, but leaves all the talking on such subjects to her dogmatising. This is an example how thee wastes thy mind, not from modesty, but from a combination of laziness and pride, the same pride that kept thee silent so long about thy real opinions. – What M. says about getting ideas from somewhere is true of herself but by no means of everybody – e.g. in my paper on space which I'm writing now, there is a whole section of close reasoning which I have seen nowhere, and which, for ought I know, may be quite original. It is like the rule of speak when you're spoken to – if everyone followed it, there could be no ideas in the world: they have to come from someone originally. And even when one's ideas are got from others, they have quite a different complexion when one has fought against them and wrestled with them and struggled to understand the process by which they are acquired than when one lazily accepts them because one thinks the man a good man. I fought every inch of the way against Idealism in Metaphysic and Ethics – and that is why I was forced to understand it thoroughly before accepting it, and why when I came to write it out, Ward used to be enchanted at my lucidity. But having lapsed into mere bragging, perhaps this homily had better stop! ...

British Embassy, Paris
Wednesday, October 31st
1894
9.30 p.m.

My darling Alys

... I shan't mind being 'run' in the unimportant details of practical things – where to dine, what to eat, etc. – in important practical matters, when I've had a little practice in them, I maintain that I'm not incompetent and I should sit on thee vigorously if thee tried to dictate to me! But Evelyn Nordhoff is right that thee wouldn't be likely to do so. As long as I remain a student or a theorist of any sort, I *shall* have no duties to the outside world. I remember saying to thee on the

Chelsea Embankment last November what Logan is always repeating, that that sort of person *ought* to lead a selfish life in small things, because it increases one's efficiency, and the work is so *vastly* more important than any good one does by little politenesses and so forth. Fortunately my needs are simple – tea and quiet are all I require. I enjoyed my lunch with the Dufferins very much. I was alone with Lord and Lady Dufferin and he was perfectly charming, though he appeared to have forgotten all about my engagement, at least nothing was said about it. He is really a delicious man – so perfect and well-rounded. He was very gracious – said it had been the greatest pleasure to him to find he could please my Grandmother by giving me this place – asked if there had been much work: so I said not so much lately, and he smiled and said there was always less with an Ambassador than a Minister. I told them Phipps was in raptures over Sarah's new play, and they smiled again and said they had no very high opinion of Phipps's taste. They seem to share the general contempt. He treated me so affectionately that my heart quite warmed to him, in spite of its being due to my Grandparents, not to myself. I was not the least shy, and did and said exactly what was proper. Thee will be glad to know that Lady Dufferin was *atrociously* dressed, in a sort of grey serge. Lord Dufferin had just come in from bicycling: he rides right up to the very Embassy door and wheels his machine in himself. The French used to be shocked but now, largely owing to him I believe, it has become far more fashionable for swells than it is in England. When he was in Petersburg there was quite a scandal because one night, by way of Duncrambo or some similar game, he acted a pig and hopped and grunted, and everyone thought it very shocking for an Ambassador. He treats his wife with a curious formal polite affection, which I believe is perfectly genuine, only that the habit of formal politeness has made that his only possible manner: but it sounds odd to hear 'my Love' and such terms in the tone in which he might say Your Majesty or Your Excellency. It was a glorious day and I went all round the Bois with Dodson, which I also enjoyed immensely – all the autumn tints were at their very finest, and I can't imagine more ideal weather. Coming back he was vastly impressed by my nerve in the traffic. I suppose it is mathematics or something, but I know I'm singularly good at riding through crowded streets! I quite won his respect, as he is of the type that worships 'nerve' in any form. He came lumbering on behind. He is a nice simple innocent youth, who thinks everybody else stupendously clever. Harford and I smile over him, but we both like him and I think he likes both of us.

I didn't mean to go on to a 2nd sheet but I'm not sleepy enough to go to bed, though it's 10.30, and I can't settle down to any other occupation than writing to thee – It's nice riding with Dodson,

because it makes him mad with envy to see me go without using my
hands on the handles! . . .[1]

Cambridge[2]
November 3rd, 1.30

My dearest Alys

. . . I have been wildly happy all morning: ever since I left King's
Cross I've felt as if we'd just parted and I were coming back as I did
so often by that train last winter. It's perfectly delightful seeing my
friends again – I never knew before how fond I am of them and how
infinitely nicer (and cleverer!) they are than the ordinary run of young
men. I've just been seeing Ward who says there's nothing philosophical for me to do in Economics but I might very well take some
mathematical job of pure theory, only then I should have to begin
specialising almost at once. He advised me to take in time and motion
too in my other Dissertation, and discuss Newton's 3 laws, which
would be interesting. It is lovely weather, and the yellow elms are
heavenly, and all the people are good and nice, and it is perfect paradise after the hell of Paris. I had a glorious long talk with Sanger and
revelled in his intellectual passion. . . . I will write again by Lion[3]
tomorrow, a longer letter telling all that happens. Ward is to be shewn
my paper on Space and I shall be wildly eager to hear what he says
about it. Short of love, his praise is about the most delightful thing in
the world to me. I got none today, but enjoyed seeing him, he's such
a delightful man. Now I must hunt up someone to lunch. Less than a
fortnight thank heaven! Fare thee well my Beloved.

Thine ever most devotedly
Bertie

In the train – Cambridge
Sunday, November 4th 1894
5.15 p.m.

My dearest Alys

It is a great pity all my letters come in a lump and I'm very sorry to
have addressed Friday's Hill. I hope it won't happen again. I'm *so*
glad thee's happy and busy too – if I were imagining thee unhappy it
would be unendurable not to see thee tonight – as it is, it gives me
pleasure to think thee is near. It has been *perfectly* delightful to be at

[1] I find myself shocked by the conceit and complacency of the above letter
and of some of the others written about the same time. I wonder that Alys
endured them.

[2] I went to Cambridge for the week-end, but did not see Alys as the three
months had not expired.

[3] Lion FitzPatrick – afterwards Mrs Phillimore.

Cambridge again. Moore and Sanger and Marsh were *so* nice to see again. I love them all far more than I supposed before. We had a large meeting last night. McT. and Dickinson and Wedd came, at which I could not help feeling flattered. Thee will be glad to hear that several of them thought my paper too theoretical, though McT. and I between us persuaded them in time that there was nothing definite to be said about practical conduct. I have left my paper behind as Marsh and Sanger want to read it over again. McT. spoke first and was excessively good, as I had hoped. I said in my paper I would probably accept anything he said, and so I did. For my sake he left out immortality, and reconciled my dilemma at the end without it. I can't put what he said in a letter, but I dare say I shall bring it out in conversation some day. We had a delightful dinner at Marsh's before the meeting, and I was *so* glad just to be with them again that I didn't talk a bit too much. Moore though he didn't say much looked and was as glorious as ever – I almost worship him as if he were a god. I have never felt such an extravagant admiration for anybody. I always speak the truth to Marsh, so I told·him we were separated three months to please my grandmother; the rest asked no inconvenient questions. Most of them were pleased with my paper, and were glad of my making Good and less good my terms instead of right and wrong. The beginning also amused them a good deal. I stayed up till 2 talking to Marsh and then slept till 10.30, when I went to breakfast with Sanger. I lunched with Marsh, and talked shop with Amos and saw my rooms. As he has furnished them – they're brighter but not *near* so nice. Sanger thought my bold idea in my Space paper 'colossal' – I hope Ward will think so too! Amos tells me Ward said I was so safe for a Fellowship that it didn't matter a bit what I wrote on – but this must be taken *cum grano salis* – it is slightly coloured by Amos's respect for me. They *all* urged me to do what I'm good at, rather than fly off to Economics, tho' all of them greatly respect Economics and would be delighted to have me do them ultimately. I have great respect for their judgments because they are honest and know me. So I shall do 2 Dissertations next year and only Space this – or Space and Motion, as Ward suggests. But of course I shall work at Economics at once. Sanger is working at Statistics, and explained several hideous difficulties in the theory, important for practice too, since the whole question of Bimetallism and many others turn on them. I had never suspected such difficulties before, and they inspired me with keen intellectual delight from the thought of obstacles to be overcome. My intellectual pleasures during the last years have been growing very rapidly keener, and I feel as if I might make a great deal out of them when we're married and all our difficulties are settled. I am convinced since reading Bradley that all knowledge is good, and therefore shouldn't need to bother

about immediate practical utility – though of course, when I come to
Economics, that will exist too. I'm very glad to find that passion
developing itself, for without it no one *can* accomplish good thinking
on abstract subjects – one can't think hard from a mere sense of duty.
Only I need little successes from time to time to keep it a source of
energy. My visit to Cambridge has put me in very good conceit with
myself and I feel very happy to think we are within our fortnight and
that Mariechen will make it fly. I laughed more than in all the time
since I left Friday's Hill and I talked well and made others laugh a
great deal too. ...

> Trinity College, Cambridge
> December 9th 1894, 2 a.m.

My dearest Alys

I will write a little letter tonight though it *is* late. Sanger met me
at the station and took me to tea with Marsh, where I found Crompton
who is as charming as ever and in better spirits than I ever saw him
before, delighted with the law and very glad to feel settled for life.
Moore read about lust and set forth exactly thy former ideal which
he got from me when we met the normal man on the walking-tour.
His paper did not give any good arguments, but was beautifully
written in parts, and made me very fond of him. A year ago I should
have agreed with every word – as it was, I spoke perfectly frankly
and said there need be nothing lustful in copulation where a spiritual
love was the predominant thing, but the spiritual love might seek it
as the highest expression of union. Everybody else agreed with me,
except McT. who came in after the discussion was over. Crompton
was very good indeed and quite worsted Moore, though Moore would
not admit it. I am going to see all the dons tomorrow. I have been
arguing with Amos, who is much incensed at my advocacy of hyper-
space, and is not coming to the wedding (not as a consequence of our
differences!) ...

> *Thine ever devotedly*
> *Bertie*

*I was at this time very intimate with Eddie Marsh (afterwards Sir
Edward Marsh), so I told him about Alys and got him to go and see her.
She was engaged in a crusade to induce daughters to rebel against their
parents. This is alluded to in Marsh's letter.*

> Cold Ash, Newbury
> March 25, '94

My dear Russell

I want to thank you for two very pleasant occasions last week. I
went on Sunday and found the room full of two American girls, one

of whom went away to write home and the other to do political economy. Then we had a delightful talk for an hour or two, about you and other matters. I think we shall be great friends. I'm very happy about you, still more so than I was before.

She wanted to make my sister revolt, and accordingly asked me to bring her to lunch last Wednesday wh. was exceedingly kind. My sister also seemed to make great friends, and was most enthusiastic when we went away. I don't know if she'll revolt or not. Mr Pearsall Smith is a dear old boy. I think he was very sarcastic to me but I'm not really sure if he was or not. Among other things he said I talked exactly like old Jowett, wh. I don't believe. What funny grammar they talk to one another.

It isn't much worth while telling you what you know already, I don't mean about the grammar, so perhaps this letter ought to come to an end here but it would be rather short so I'll go on with my own affairs. The most interesting thing is that I've been seeing a certain amount of Robert Bridges; he's a charming man, with thick dark hair which grows like thatch and a very attractive imped. in his sp. He reminded me curiously of Verrall, though he's much bigger all over and his face has funny bumps like Furness. I went for a walk with him on Friday; he talked in a very interesting way, tho' not quite as Coleridge talked to Hazlitt; after lunch he got a headache or something and seemed to get somehow much older (he's 49) and talked about his own plays a good deal. He had a perfect right to, as of course I was interested, but it was very funny how openly he praised them. He said 'I think I've given blank verse all the pliability it's capable of in the Humours of the Court, don't you ?' – 'The Feast of Bacchus is amusing from beginning to end: it's sure to find its way to the stage and when it gets there it'll keep there.'

This isn't vanity in the least, he's quite free from that. I'm just going over there to church, I hear he's trained the choir with remarkable success.

I suppose you're having an awfully good time in Rome. Don't bother to write till you come back. I thought you'd like to hear about Sunday. I should go on writing, except that I'm not sure how much goes for 2½d. Please remember me to Miss Stanley.

Yr. affectionate friend
Edward Marsh

Heidelberg
Neuenheimer Landstr. 52
Sept. 15

My dear Russell
I was just going comfortably to sleep over my Grammatik when I

unluckily fell to wondering whether the opposite to an icicle was called an isinglass or bicicle; and the shock of remembering that I was thinking about stalactite and stalagmite woke me up completely; but I'm not going to do any more Grammatik; so here is the answer to your letter, though it was so far from proper as to be quite shocking.

I should have thought Paris was a very good exchange for Dresden, as the separation would have taken place in either case wouldn't it? I'm very sorry not to see you, though in some ways it's a good thing, as I'm not in the least either solemn or suitable, and it's quite enough to have been seen by Sanger. I'm not going to give you an account of all my wickednesses, as I'm tired of doing that; I resolved to write to all my friends and see who'd be shocked first, beginning at the most likely end with Barran, G. Trevy, Conybeare; to my utter astonishment they contented themselves one after the other with telling me not to get fat, and the first person who thought of being horror-struck was Moore.

I'm getting on pretty well with German, though I haven't arrived at the stage of finding it a reasonable medium for the expression of thought. I think the original couple who spoke it must have died rather soon after the Tower of Babel, leaving a rather pedantically-minded baby, who had learnt all the words of one syllable, and had to make up the long ones with them – at least how else can you account for such words as Handschule and be-ab-sicht-igen? I never knew a language so little allusive – compare the coarseness of 'sich kleiden' with the elegance of 'se mettre' – English gains by having so many Latin words – their literalness is concealed – for instance independence is exactly the same as Unabhängigkeit, yet the one seems quite respectable, while the other is unspeakably crude. I can read pretty well by now, and can mostly find some way or other of expressing what I mean, but I can't understand when people talk at their natural pace. Unluckily all the plays they've done yet at Mannheim are too unattractive to go to; but I've seen more operas since I've been here than in my whole previous life, though that isn't saying much. The performances aren't quite satisfactory, as the actors are so dreadful to look at. I went to Fidelio yesterday. The heroine was played by a lady whom I mistook at first for Corney Grain – you know she is disguised as a page. Fat women are in a sad dilemma – either they must have their bodices all of the same stuff, in which case they look as if they were just going to burst, or they must have an interval of some other stuff, in which case they look as if they had. For instance Fidelio had a brown – jerkin? it was my idea of a jerkin – open in front, with something white showing underneath; and puffs of white in the sleeves, which had just that effect. I've seen innumerable sights since I've been here (anything does for a sight in Germany). I scandalised everybody the other day

by going to sleep in the middle of being driven slowly round Frankfort in a fly. I don't think even the Frenchmen find the sight quite so
funny as I do – but they're mostly rather young (I ought to explain
it's a big pension full of Frenchmen learning German and Germans
teaching them. I'm the only Englishman). They're mostly also very
delightful – I've made great friends with one German, who is a very
charming, but not Apostolic, and one Frenchman who is, very; I've
hardly ever seen a Frenchman who hadn't a charm of his own, quite
apart from his merits. . . .

Here came Mittagessen, after which I'm as learned to say I find
myself almost incapable of further exertion (by the way the Frau
Professor says I'm viel angenehmer in that respect than most Englishmen – I mean in respect of my general habit of 'eating what's set
before me', according to the nursery rule). So I've read through what
I've written already. I'm afraid it reads rather leichtsinnig – but
consider that it's an exquisite day and I'd spent the rest of the morning in the garden saying to myself 'behold how good and how pleasant
a thing it is for persons of different nationalities to sit together in
chairs' – with an interval for my German lesson, which was as usual
very funny, the Professor who talks English very badly, makes up
examples out of the rules; and I had to translate such sentences as
'Rid yourself of your whimps', 'Do you remember my?' and 'He
posted off all his wretches' – which, when I heard the German, I
recognised as 'He boasted of all his riches'.

Write me a postcard now and then when your brain is for the
moment off the boil – I'm here till the end of the month – I should
like very much to come back by Paris, but I'm debarred by 2 considerations, both insurmountable – I) I shan't have any money left –
II) I haven't any clothes in which I could come within a mile of an
Embassy, or be seen about with anyone connected with one – I hope
you're getting on all right.

> *Yrs. fraternally*
> *E. H. M.*

> Heidelberg
> (1894)

My dear Russell

I've got just ½ an hour before Abendessen, and I can think of 7
people on the spur of the moment whom I ought to write to rather
than you – however you seem to 'feel it more', as Mrs Gummidge
says. I'm awfully sorry you aren't enjoying yourself more in Paris.
I should have thought the mere feel of the place would be enough –
but your account of your people's letters is most depressing – the idea
of consoling oneself with a bad hymn when one might console oneself

with the Walrus and the Carpenter, say – however the 10th of December isn't very far off.

I don't quite understand your not liking Frenchmen – is it simply because they're unchaste? It is very disgusting – all the ones here for instance fornicate pretty regularly from 16 years old, and talk about it in a way that would sicken me in England – but it's merely a matter of education, and one can't object to individual people because they behave in the way they've been brought up to. ...

> *Yours fraternally*
> *Edward Marsh*

Heidelberg
Oct. 1 (1894)

Dear Russell

Barran sent me the enclosed letter for you today, and I accompany it with the greatest of all the treasures I found in 'Zion's Herald' – When one follows out the similitude in its details, it becomes too delightful especially the tact with which God has got over the little awkwardness caused by the 'Great superiority of his Social Station'. 'As is usual with lovers' is a good touch – and so is the coyness with which mankind is represented as 'wondering what God can see in us'. The whole thing is an 'Editorial'.

I got your letter this morning, and I'm very glad you're a little happier. I wondered for a long time if I could get in a day at Paris on my way back, but time, money and clothes were all inexorably against it.

The Frenchmen I've known here were nearly all too young to be repulsively bestial; some of them will become so no doubt, others, I think, will not. My chief friend for instance went to a brothel once to see what it was like and was so much sickened he could hardly 'baiser', as they call it.

I shall write you a very serious letter some day, for the sake of my character, but till then, I'll go on being frivolous if you like.

My last great adventure was meeting O. B.[1] accidentally at the station – he was on his way to Elfiel to buy German champagne (!) and had come here for German cigars. I brought him for a night to the Pension – he made a great impression on every one, and was very jolly. Almost the first thing he told me was that the Duchesses of York and Teck are going to pay him a visit at Cambridge next term – which, as he remarked, would give people a great deal to talk about, but it wasn't his fault, as they'd practically invited themselves.

What news of your brother?

> *Yours fraternally*
> *E. H. Marsh*

[1] Oscar Browning.

40 Dover Street, W
May 11 1894

Dearest Bertrand

I have been back[1] 3 weeks but have been overwhelmed with arrears of work and now I write because I have heard that a report is going about that you are probably going to be engaged to Miss Pearsall Smith. I hope this is not so, for if you thought you wd. be too young to enter Parliament before you were 29 I must think it would be a great pity for you to engage yr. self and take such an important step at 21 or 22. I forget which you are – It would stop you in so many things and you have seen so very little of the world 'of Young Women' as Lady Russell puts it, that I shall be very sorry if you have bound yr. self thus early. But all this may be idle gossip and you may be sure I shall not spread it, but could not help writing to say what a pity I think it wd. be at the very outset of life to enter on such an engagement and with a girl a good bit older than yourself. Do not answer my letter unless you wish it, but I shall hope that what I have is merely gossip founded perhaps on yr. having been at the Wild Duck with the young lady.

Yrs. afft.
Maude Stanley

Clandeboye
Co. Down
Septr. 5, '94

My dear Bertie

Lady Russell will have told you that everything has been arranged for your going to Paris. I am sure you will like it, and the climate is charming at this time of the year: and though perhaps there may be a certain amount of work, I hope it will not be too much to prevent you taking advantage of your stay to see all that is to be seen in Paris, for the autumn is the best time for that.

I think, if it could be arranged, that it would be very desirable from our official point of view that you should stay for at least three months, though I hope we shall tempt you to remain longer and to go out a little into Paris society, which would amuse you very much.

I have written to all the authorities at Paris to warn them of your arrival, and to tell them to do everything they can to make you feel at home.

Yours very sincerely
Dufferin and Ava

---

[1] From Rome, where I had accompanied her.

Hotel du Prince de Galles
Paris
Sep. 11, 1894

Dear Lord Dufferin

I have waited till I was established here to thank you warmly for
your two kind letters to me. It is very good of you to take so much
trouble about me, and I have indeed been most cordially received by
everybody. I arrived in Paris last night and spent this morning at the
Embassy. I am sure I shall like the work, and that the life generally
will be very agreeable.

I will certainly stay the three months which you speak of as officially
desirable, indeed under ordinary circumstances I should have been
glad to stay any length of time; but I am engaged to be married, and
had hoped that the wedding might be in December; so you will, I am
sure, understand that I should be glad to be free then, if that is
possible without any inconvenience. I hope you will not think this
wish ungracious on my part – no lesser inducement could have made
me wish to shorten my stay here, and I am deeply obliged to you for
having given me the appointment – but as I do not intend to take up
the diplomatic service as my career, it seemed perhaps needless to
postpone my wedding, for which I feel a natural impatience.

> *Yours gratefully and sincerely*
> *Bertrand Russell*

*The following letters have to do with a project, which I entertained for
a short time, of abandoning mathematical philosophy for economics, and
also with the affairs of The Society. It was the practice for one member,
in rotation, to read a short paper, chosen by the others the previous
Saturday out of four suggested subjects. In the subsequent discussion it
was a rule that everyone must say something.*

Trinity College, Cambridge
Oct. 18th, '94

Dear Russell

When I first read your letter I thought that you had gone raving
mad. I took it round to Marsh, and he did not take such a serious
view of the case. I will, of course, ask Ward about it directly. I don't
know how far it would be possible for you to do much good at the
subject, but I am fairly certain that the amount of economics which
you would have to read, would not be more than you could easily do.
But I expect that, as well as Psychology and Ethics that you would
have to learn some politics and law. I doubt whether you will really
find much life in trying to find out whether the word 'Utility' can have
any meaning and what is meant by a man's 'demand for tobacco'.

Surely you have a very excellent opportunity of being of some service to the Universe by writing about space whereas I doubt if you will quickly increase human happiness by doing the basis of economics. For, on the one hand, owing chiefly to the spread of democracy, it is distrusted and despised, and on the other hand the few people who, like myself, think that it is or ought to be a science naturally do not much mind whether it means anything or not. I expect McTaggart will have a fit if I tell him what you say. Trotter would like a paper from you (if it is possible) for the Moral Science Club. Last Saturday we chose subjects and Marsh is reading on Saturday on, I think, 'Why we like nature'. Please let someone know as soon as possible which day you are coming up on. It is splendid of you to come. We are thinking about George Trevvy but are not quite decided. I hear that Edward Carpenter has published yet another pamphlet on 'Marriage'. I will send you a copy as soon as I get one.

Have you got Erdmann's book on the Axioms of Geometry or do you know of anyone up here who has it; as I rather want to read it and can't find it in the 'Varsity library. Do you see the English papers? Some women have been raising hell about the prostitutes at the Empire and it is probably going to be closed. I wish they would protest against those in the streets instead.

I can't find anything to write about in Economics and I find law somewhat dull so I should be depressed if it were not that I am going to hear the 9th Symphony on the day after tomorrow.

> *Yours frat.*
> *Charles Percy Sanger*

Trinity College, Cambridge
Oct. 19th, '94

Dear Russell

I went to Ward and asked him about you. He said immediately that you had better do economics, if you thought that you would like it better. That the important thing was to work at what you liked and that though your dissertation would have to go in by August, yet you worked very fast and would probably have enough time. He also said that there was not the slightest objection to your sending in two or more dissertations, or that if you write an article on space in 'Mind' or elsewhere that you could count that in with your dissertation on Economics. But that, as one would expect, two moderate dissertations do not count as one good one. He said that he would not advise you about economics and suggested that you should write to Marshall. Have you read Keynes'[1] book on the Scope and Method of Economics?

[1] The Keynes in question was the father of Lord Keynes.

I think that that perhaps might interest you. Marsh tells me that McTaggart is rather horrified.

> *Your friend*
> *Charles Percy Sanger*

Trinity College, Cambridge
Oct. 23, '94

Dear Russell

I'm very glad you're coming soon and it's all your eye to say you don't want to write a paper.

Your first letter to Sanger was most subversive, the effect on us can only be compared (in its humble way) to that produced on Europe by the Cabinet Council last month – Sanger came rushing round here to say you were quite mad, and finding me unprepared with an opinion offered me his. Not being entirely satisfied with my attitude he proceeded to spoil McTaggart's appetite by telling him the dreadful news as he was marching up to the Fellows' table. He's since been more or less pacified by Ward – I don't know anything about the rights and wrongs of the case, but I can't refrain from appealing to your better nature to consider what o'clock it is, to consider what a long way you've got to go before July, to consider anything – before embarking on a rash project.

I was awfully glad to get your letter (the day before I left Heidelberg) and hear you were happier in Paris; I don't know how often I've nearly answered it since – I seem to be working very hard this term, as I do nothing else in the day except perhaps a game of 5's, 30 pages of Zola, and of course meals, but these very moderate and un-Heidelberg. Life affords few distractions. I know lamentably few people, yet the temptation to call on freshers is one which is easy to resist. The fact is I'm getting old and posé, even rheumatic, and almost respectable; parts of this letter are in my new Mary Bennet style. Z.B., the idea of life affording few distractions, though not perhaps wholly new, strikes me as well expressed.

I saw Miss Pearsall Smith on Saturday at the Richter Concert, and we discussed the comparative fascination of space and economics. She looked very well – and had such a pretty green cloak with fur trimmings. Sanger said he was going to tell you what had been happening in the Society. Last Sat. was rather a failure, as I had discovered that my paper was all nonsense on Friday; besides wh. Sanger and I were so completely done by the Concert that we hadn't an idea in our heads. I had 'brain stoppage' every time I was asked a question. We are thinking of little Trevy,[1] but Moore who knows him better than anyone else has scruples. I'm rather hoping that a young Babe at

---

[1] George Trevelyan, Master of Trinity, OM, etc., etc.

King's may turn out embryonic – He's infinitely the cleverest and most fascinating of the family.

I've done a fabulous amount of work today so I'd better leave off. esp. as I shall see you so soon and talking is better than writing (esp. my writing wh. has gone rather funny on this page).

> *Yrs. fraternally*
> *E. M.*
> (*Edward Marsh*)

> Trinity College, Cambridge
> Oct. 22nd, '94

Dear Russell

I am very glad that you can arrange to come up. I will see about the rooms. We should be very glad if you would read a paper as there are only four of us now.

Maggie Tulliver or Cleopatra sounds such a good subject that you had better read on it and thus don't trouble to send subjects for us to choose. Last week Marsh read an excellent paper on 'Do we like nature', but unfortunately the discussion was not so good as Marsh and I were quite stupid (we had heard the Choral Symphony in the afternoon) and there were only Moore and Dickinson besides. Dickinson was good and I expect that Moore was, but I couldn't understand him. In the letter that I wrote telling you what Ward had said, I don't know whether I sufficiently emphasised the fact that his great point was that you should work at what you like (in distinction I think to what you might think you ought to do). He was quite strong on the point that if Metageometry bored you, it was better that you should do something else. We are quite divided about George Trevey – that is to say Marsh and Wedgewood are in favour of him, and I am, on whole, neutral but Moore thinks that most of our discussions would not interest him. The spookical [psychical] society have got hold of a medium who does things that they can't explain. Myers is, of course, triumphant and Sidgwick is forced to admit that at the time he was convinced, but thinks that he isn't now.

> *Yours frat.*
> *Charles Percy Sanger*

> Trinity College, Cambridge
> Wednesday (1894)

Dear Russell

I'll send the paper off tomorrow; the end part is rather muddling to an uneducated person, but I'm glad I read it again.

I've just come back from a concert I was next an old lady who was exactly like the leg of mutton in Alice; the features were almost identical and she had a becoming pink paper frill on her head, which a closer inspection revealed as a dyed feather. I don't think she can have known the picture.

MacT.'s paper on Sunday was very interesting. Mackenzie remarked afterwards that Hegel's theory of punishment was quite different, and MacT. simply continued to smile – I don't know wh. was in the right, but I never saw MacT. shut up so easily. It was very funny to see Trotter follow him in the room, humble and imitative – he had an air of being 'also stark mad, in white cotton' (do you remember the Confidante in the Critic ?)

I had such a funny scene with my bedmaker the night you left. I was in my bedroom, and heard a timid voice calling me. 'Well', I said. 'Isn't this a sad affair, sir ?' she began in her plaintive voice. 'What ?' I asked (I thought Mrs Appleton must have had twins at least) – 'About your table, sir'. 'Well ?' 'Weren't you surprised to find the leaf still in ?' 'Very much, why was it ?' 'Didn't the gentleman tell you, sir ?' 'What gentleman ? What's happened ?' It turned out she'd broken a bit of the wood, just as Tommy Booth came in with a pipe of mine. Wasn't it extraordinary how she couldn't tell me straight out ? I hope when my wife dies, or anything like that, I shall always have someone to make my troubles ridiculous by their exaggerated concern. I never can mind when anything goes wrong in my room. I can't resist Mrs Roper's sympathy.

Oswald Sickert's book is out at last, he sent me a copy this morning. It is dedicated to me, which makes me very proud – it reads much better than it did in MS. I think it's splendid.

We're going to have another enormous meeting next Sat. Mayor, Trevy, Theo all coming to Moore's paper. I dare say I'll write to you about it. I think this is the end of my news for the present and it's near 12.

> *Goodnight*
> E. H. M. (*Marsh*)

> Trinity College Cambridge
> Nov. 21st '94

My dear Russell

I've just come back from such a funny concert – not that it was particularly funny, but I was put in a thoroughly unmusical frame of mind by the first performer who appeared – one of the wiry and businesslike kind (of monkeys, I mean – she is a monkey) – she played very much like a person, but not quite. Of course it was very creditable to the result of so recent an evolution to do it so well but it hindered one's appreciation of the music. The next person was a singer – one of those middle aged ladies who have an air of being caricatures of their former selves – she made one of those curious confessions which are only heard in Concert rooms about her behaviour once in a state of drink, when she enlaced a gentleman in her arms – Te souviens-tu de notre ivresse quand nos bras étaient enlacés ? Conybeare remarked that if she was in ivresse she was now in evening dress – her arch curtseys at the end were a sight to be seen.

When did I last write to you ? Have you heard about Moore's paper on Friendship ? There's not much to say about it, as it was a specification of one's own ideal more or less, without much practical bearing. Of course our poor old friend copulation came in for its usual slating, one wd. think from the way people talk about it in the Society that it was a kind of Home Rule Bill that has to be taken some notice of, but which everyone thinks a bore. The discussion was interesting. Trevy, Theo and Mayor were all up. Mayor gave Theo occasion to say he hadn't expected to find him such a middle aged phenomenon so soon. Mayor took wings – Wedd was there too, he and Theo talked well.[1] Last Sat. McT. read an old paper. Why are roseleaves crumpled ? on the origin of evil. – It wasn't quite satisfactory, as on the one hand MacT. has changed his position since he wrote it, and on the other it was rather a nuisance no one except him knowing the dialectic – one felt like the audience at an extension-lecture. Sanger reads on What is education ? on Sat. Crompton will be up.

Lady Trevy was up today. I always like her very much, she has such an essential gaiety. I met a lovely person on Sunday, Miss Stawell, whom Dickinson was nice enough to ask me to meet. I think she's very superior indeed – she seems to have quite a rare feeling for beauty in art, I hope we shall see more of her.[2] Mayor's sister was there too, she seemed rather common and flippant in comparison. It's great fun seeing so much of Verrall as I do now – (I go to him for composition again), the other day I asked him the meaning of something in the Shelley we had to translate – 'I'm sure I can't tell you my little dear', he answered, 'you pays yr money and you takes your choice.' That kind of thing makes me very cheerful.

The day's coming very near now, isn't it ? What a wonderful thought. Remember to tell me how your grandmother is when you write.

> *Yrs. fraternally*
> *Edward M.* (*Marsh*)

[1] Mayor and Theodore Davies were exact contemporaries, Mayor being the best and Theodore the second-best classical scholar of their year. To 'take wings' is to retire from habitual presence at meetings of The Society, which usually is done in the man's fifth or sixth year.

[2] Miss Stawell became a very distinguished classicist.

By the way thanks for the photograph, it's good on the whole, tho' you look rather bumptious.

Pembroke Lodge,
Richmond, Surrey
Sep. 16/'94

Dearest Bertie

I can't say I am much *disappointed* with your second letter – for 'I mean' to do so and so in yr first left little hope of yr considering any other course. Of course I am *very* sorry, as U.R.[1] and Auntie will be – she writes as if she cd not think you wd. wish to be out of the country this winter – but that is nothing.[2] You must do what you think best, and I must remember

> As one by one thy hopes depart
> Be resolute and calm—

They *have* been departing in rapid succession of late – but when I turn my mind to good and happy Dunrozel, to human perfection in Agatha, to the goodness and unceasing affection of my *old* children and *their* children, to other relations and to many faithful friends, I feel how much beauty there still is in life for wch in my old age I have to thank God. And for you, my too dear boy, I can only try to hope, though the way is not easy to find. Have you called on the people to whom the Baronne gave you letters? She asked me yesterday. The Warburtons are gone, and Lotty,[3] dear wonderful Lotty, come. You know what it is to her and me to be together. I'm glad you like Mr *Dodson* (no g) – I think there must be everythg. to like in Mr Hardinge or Ld. Dufferin wd. not call him 'a great friend' – I did not imagine Ld. Terence to be very nice – Ld. D's children seem to be rather disappointments. Of course one cannot find everybody with whom one has intercourse having the same interests as oneself, but one can often be the better for entering into theirs – I do hope that as time goes on and you know more people, you will enjoy Paris thoroughly – there is so much to enjoy there. Very good accounts of Auntie you'll be glad to hear but this is horrid letterless Sunday. Rollo proposes to come to me the 20th when Lotty goes – brings Arthur and Lisa – for 10 days – such a joy in prospect.

Goodbye and God bless you my dearest Child.

Yr. *ever loving*
Granny

---

[1] Uncle Rollo.
[2] On the ground that she was likely to die during the winter.
[3] Her sister, Lady Charlotte Portal.

My letters are for you alone – Remember I am more than willing to believe that you will profit by yr German experience, as regards yr studies.

Pembroke Lodge
Richmond, Surrey
Oct. 9, '94

Dearest Bertie

I am glad you have had more Embassy work to do. I guessed it would be so, owing to the 'tension' I think that's the diplomatic word – between England and France – it must also have been more interesting work I shd think ? I hope and trust that both countries will behave well, in wch case peace and goodwill will be preserved. I shd think the Govt of both likely to do so. I am also very glad Mr Austin Lee is back – he is a man well worth knowing. By this time, accordg to the D.E.'s (d'Estournelles), a good many of their friends are returning to Paris and I shall be anxious to hear how you get on with the scientific, the political, the musical and charming among them to whom you have letters. . . .

My dearest Child, you must not wish time to pass more quickly than it does! There is little enough of it for us to make the use of that we ought. Of course I understand as anybody would that you regret even this short separation – but perhaps you don't know how *very* much you would have suffered in the estimation of the many who wish you well in the highest sense and care for us and know what we had always thought and felt about you, had you remained in England leading the life you were leading – indeed you had already suffered greatly and so had she and I felt that having work to do abroad was the only chance to prevent increasing blame and if you are to marry her, before you have learned to know anybody else, I do most earnestly wish that there may be as little unfavourable impression as possible. You wrote to me once, dear boy, that you dreamed of me constantly by night and thought of me by day and wondered how you cd make me happier about you – and I have sometimes thought of puttg down on paper what has made me and yr Uncle and Aunt so unhappy – in regular order of events and incidents – to help you, even now, to make us happier. Shall I do so ? There is nothing I wish more ardently than to have good reason to love dearly the person you marry if I live to see you married. I am going on pretty well – only a very slow downward progress of the disease – so that I am still able to do pretty much as usual, except breathing in bed – I have discomfort but nothg worth callg pain.

If you write to Auntie only say about me that you hear I am going on very well.

Yr most loving
Granny

Pembroke Lodge
Richmond, Surrey
Oct. 23/'94

Dearest Bertie

We were glad of your letter to Tat,[1] but sorry that no notice had yet been taken of your cards. The cycling in the Bois de Boulogne must be great fun. I suppose you go with the others ? You don't mention Lord Dufferin having arrived; which according to newspapers ought I think to be the case. What a pity Frank's visit was no pleasure. I think he really went out of good nature to you on my telling him how lonely you felt, but we quite understand what you mean. I am better for the moment. I hope it may turn out for more than the moment – for Agatha's sake especially. She, poor darling, is far from well, and obliged to stay very late in bed. Dear good Isabel [Mrs Warburton] went yesterday – her visit has been touchingly delightful, in spite of or indeed partly because of my being very unwell most of the time – she is so simpatica, and we had much solemn conversation intermingled with pressing topics. – You have never answered my next to last letter, which I thought you would like but I will not enter upon the subject of you and Miss P. S. – writing is so unsatisfactory – except just to say her refusal to see me makes everything very difficult to me. It is the first time in my long life that such a thing has happened to me. I don't think it is doing her any good and tho' for her sake I put it as gently as I can. She was so good and thanked me when from my interest in her I several times told her where I thought she had been wrong – and on her various visits after that she was altogether nice, and I was growing happy and hopeful that we should find her deserving of the love we were more than ready to give. Then came the sudden and to us utterly unaccountable change – and I cannot but be saddened by the thought that the person you love is one who refuses to see me and whom therefore I can never know any better even if I live longer than is likely. However nothing can pain me much longer here below, and in the meantime I try as a duty not to think about all this, as it seems that mental troubles are particularly bad for my kind of illness. God bless you, my boy, and her too, is my most earnest prayer.

Yr ever loving
Granny

Pembroke Lodge
Richmond, Surrey
Oct. 30, 1894

Dearest Bertie

Granny is much less well again – bad nights, pains and weakness.

[1] Aunt Agatha.

She is quite kept to bed today – and yesterday. Of course she cannot see yr. letters. I have told her of them. She long ago saw Alys's letter to her and I think you will remember that in hers to Alys she said she wished *once* to say what she felt on that subject of yr proposed course – and never again. I suppose you will come here on yr way to Cambridge? *Let me know* at once. Granny I'm certain will be medically ordered never to touch on painful subjects and of course, I never shall, and she has once for all said what she felt and what was her duty to say if she cared for you and Alys. Dearest Bertie I cannot write more I am so disheartened seeing Granny suffer. It pains me beyond expression that you think I have been 'hard' and without sympathy. If my words have ever seemed so you must remember and will know some day that only love was in my heart and that nothing but love prevented absolute silence on my part for speaking was far more painful than you now understand.

> *Your loving*
> *Auntie*

> Pembroke Lodge
> Richmond, Surrey
> Nov. 19, 1894

My dear Alys

Rollo reminded us that Dec. 14th was the day of the death of Prince Albert and of Princess Alice – and considering our situation with regard to the Queen, we feel we could none of us like the Wedding being on that day. I am sure you will not mind our mentioning this. Would not the 15th do? We did not quite understand the reasons against that day. I hope you and Bertie had a pleasant visit to Dover Street.

> *Yours affectly.*
> *Agatha Russell*

> Pembroke Lodge
> Richmond, Surrey
> Dec. 10, 1894

My dearest Child

As my voice fails me whenever I try to speak of what is coming, although it is an event so full of happiness to you, it is natural that I should write you a few farewell words. More especially on this anniversary of a day once among the gladdest and most beloved of the year[1] – now as sad as it is sacred for me. For the memories it brings me of my dear, my gentle, my noble and deeply loving and hardly

---

[1] My father's birthday.

tried Johnny, naturally turn my thoughts to you, in whom we have always felt that something was still left to us of him – My memories of him are memories of unutterable joy, mingled with sorrow and anguish hard to bear even now, when *he* is past all sorrows.

When he and your mother, in the bloom of youth and health, asked me to look upon you as my own child in case of their death, I little thought that I should be called upon to fulfil the promise I gave them. But ere long the day came and your home was left empty. You came to us as an innocent, unconscious little comforter in our darkened home, and have been to us all three as our very own child. You were intertwined with our very being, our life was shaped and ordered with a view to your good; and as you grew in heart and mind you became our companion as well as our child. How thankfully I remember that all through your childhood and boyhood you would always cheerfully give up your own wishes for those of others, never attempt an excuse when you had done wrong, and never fail to receive warning or reproof as gratefully as praise. We trusted you, and you justified our trust, and all was happiness and affection.

Manhood came and brought with it fresh cause for thankfulness in your blameless and honourable University career. But manhood brings also severance and change. You are leaving us now for a new life, a new home, new ties and new affections. But your happiness and welfare must still be ours and our God will still be yours. May you take with you only that which has been best, and ask His forgiveness for what has been wrong, in the irrevocable past. May He inspire you to cherish holy thoughts and noble aims. May you remember that humble, loving hearts alone are dear to Him. May such a heart ever be yours, and hers who is to travel life's journey by your side.

God bless you both, and grant you light to find and to follow the heavenward path.

> *Ever, my dear, dear Child*
> *Your most loving*
> *Granny*

The following letter was my last contact with Edward Fitzgerald. He distinguished himself as a climber in New Zealand and the Andes, after escaping in this way from a period of despair brought about by his wife's death after only a few months of marriage. In the end he ran off with a married lady and made no attempt to keep up with old friends.

Colombo, Ceylon
Nov. 18th, '94

My dear Russell

Drop me a line occasionally to tell me how you are getting on and also when your marriage is coming off.

I have stopped here for a little while to look around. I went up country the other day to Anuradhapura and to Vauakarayankulam (don't try to pronounce that name, I find it worse than snakes) and got some big game shooting which I enjoyed. The country was however all under water and they said very feverish, but I did not feel that although I slept out several nights in the mists and got drenched through. I am off on a regular spree so to speak and am not coming home for three years at least. I have planned Japan and some climbing in South America before I return.

Drop me a line when you feel so inclined that I may know of your wandering. I will write occasionally when I feel so inclined, which you will say is not often. I suppose you have seen Austin's new apartment in the Avenue Hochell?

I will now draw this (letter?!) to a close.

Ever yours
Edw. A. Fitzgerald

Chapter 5

First Marriage

Alys and I were married on December 13, 1894. Her family had been Philadelphia Quakers for over two hundred years, and she was still a believing member of the Society of Friends. So we were married in Quaker Meeting in St Martin's Lane. I seem to remember that one of the Quakers present was moved by the Spirit to preach about the miracle of Cana, which hurt Alys's teetotal feelings. During our engagement we had frequently had arguments about Christianity, but I did not succeed in changing her opinions until a few months after we were married.

There were other matters upon which her opinions changed after marriage. She had been brought up, as American women always were in those days, to think that sex was beastly, that all women hated it, and that men's brutal lusts were the chief obstacle to happiness in marriage. She therefore thought that intercourse should only take place when children were desired. As we had decided to have no children, she had to modify her position on this point, but she still supposed that she would desire intercourse to be very rare. I did not argue the matter, and I did not find it necessary to do so.

Neither she nor I had any previous experience of sexual intercourse when we married. We found, as such couples apparently usually do, a certain amount of difficulty at the start. I have heard many people say that this caused their honeymoon to be a difficult time, but we had no such experience. The difficulties appeared to us merely comic, and were soon overcome. I remember, however, a day after three weeks of marriage, when, under the influence of sexual fatigue, I hated her and could not imagine why I had wished to marry her. This state of mind lasted just as long as the journey from Amsterdam to Berlin, after which I never again experienced a similar mood.

We had decided that during the early years of our married life, we would see a good deal of foreign countries, and accordingly we spent the first three months of 1895 in Berlin. I went to the university, where I chiefly studied economics. I continued to work at my Fellowship dissertation. We went to concerts three times a week, and we began to know the Social Democrats, who were at that time considered very wicked. Lady Ermyntrude Malet, the wife of the Ambassador, was my cousin, so we were asked to dinner at the Embassy. Everybody was friendly, and the attachés all said they would call. However, none of them came, and when we called at the Embassy, nobody was at home. For a long time we hardly noticed all this, but at last we discovered that it was due to Alys having mentioned to the Ambassador that we had been to a socialist meeting. We learned this from a letter of Lady Ermyntrude's to my grandmother. In spite of my grandmother's prejudice against Alys, she completely sided with her on this matter. The issue was a public one, and on all public political issues, both she and my Aunt Agatha could always be relied upon not to be liberal.

During this time my intellectual ambitions were taking shape. I resolved not to adopt a profession, but to devote myself to writing. I remember a cold, bright day in early spring when I walked by myself in the Tiergarten, and made projects of future work. I thought that I would write one series of books on the philosophy of the sciences from pure mathematics to physiology, and another series of books on social questions. I hoped that the two series might ultimately meet in a synthesis at once scientific and practical. My scheme was largely inspired by Hegelian ideas. Nevertheless, I have to some extent followed it in later years, as much at any rate as could have been expected. The moment was an important and formative one as regards my purposes.

When the spring came, we went to Fiesole and stayed with Alys's sister, who lived in a small villa, while Berenson lived next door in another small villa. After leaving her, we travelled down the Adriatic coast, staying at Pesaro, Urbino, Ravenna, Rimini, Ancona, and various other places. This remains in my memory as one of the happiest times of my life. Italy and the spring and first love all together should suffice to make the gloomiest person happy. We used to bathe naked in the sea, and lie on the sand to dry, but this was a somewhat perilous sport, as sooner or later a policeman would come along to see that no one got salt out of the sea in defiance of the salt tax. Fortunately we were never quite caught.

By this time, it was becoming necessary to think in earnest about my Fellowship dissertation, which had to be finished by August, so we settled down at Fernhurst, and I had my first experience of serious original work. There were days of hope alternating with days of despair, but at last, when my dissertation was finished, I fully believed that I had solved all philosophical questions connected with the foundations of geometry. I did not yet know that the hopes and despairs connected with original work are alike fallacious, that one's work is never so bad as it appears on bad days, nor so good as it appears on good days. My dissertation was read by Whitehead and James Ward, since it was in part mathematical and in part philosophical. Before the result was announced, Whitehead criticised it rather severely, though quite justly, and I came to the conclusion that it was worthless and that I would not wait for the result to be announced. However, as a matter of politeness I went to see James Ward, who said exactly the opposite, and praised it to the skies. Next day I learned that I had been elected a Fellow, and Whitehead informed me with a smile that he had thought it was the last chance anyone would get of finding serious fault with my work.

With my first marriage, I entered upon a period of great happiness and fruitful work. Having no emotional troubles, all my energy went in intellectual directions. Throughout the first years of my marriage, I read widely, both in mathematics and in philosophy. I achieved a certain amount of original work, and laid the foundations for other work later. I travelled abroad, and in my spare time I did a great deal of solid reading, chiefly history. After dinner, my wife and I used to read aloud in turns, and in this way we ploughed through large numbers of standard histories in many volumes. I think the last book that we read in this way was the *History of the City of Rome* by Gregorovius. This was intellectually the most fruitful period of my life, and I owe a debt of gratitude to my first wife for having made it possible. At first she disliked the idea of living quietly in the country, but I was determined to do so for the sake of my work. I derived sufficient happiness from her and my work to have no need of anything more, though as a matter of fact it was, as a rule, only about half the year that we spent quietly in the country. Even during that period, she would often be away making speeches on votes for women or total abstinence. I had become a pledged teetotaller in order to please her, and from habit I remained so after the original motive had ceased to move me. I did not take to drink until the King took the pledge during the first war. His motive was to facilitate the killing of Germans, and it therefore seemed as if there must be some connection between pacifism and alcohol.

In the autumn of 1895, after the Fellowship election, we went back to Berlin to study German Social Democracy. On this visit, we associated almost exclusively with socialists. We got to know Bebel and the elder Liebknecht. The younger Liebknecht, who was killed just after the first war, was at this time a boy. We must have met him when we dined at his father's house, although I have no recollection of him. In those days Social Democrats were fiery revolutionaries, and I was too young to realise what they would be like when they acquired power. At the beginning of 1896 I gave a course of lectures on them at the London School of Economics, which was at that time in John Adam Street, Adelphi. I was, I believe, their first lecturer. There I got to know W. A. S. Hewins, who considerably influenced me from that time until 1901. He came of a Catholic family, and had substituted the British Empire for the Church as an object of veneration.

I was, in those days, much more high-strung than I became later on. While I was lecturing at the School of Economics, my wife and I lived in a flat at 90 Ashley Gardens, but I could not work there because the noise of the lift disturbed me, so I used to walk every day to her parents' house in Grosvenor Road, where I spent the time reading Georg Cantor, and copying out the gist of him into a notebook. At that time I falsely supposed all his arguments to be fallacious, but I nevertheless went through them all in the minutest detail. This stood me in good stead when later on I discovered that all the fallacies were mine.

When the spring came, we took a small labourer's cottage at Fernhurst, called 'The Millhanger', to which we added a fair-sized sitting-room and two bedrooms. In this cottage many of the happiest times of my life were passed. I acquired a great deal of knowledge that interested me, and my original work was praised by experts more highly than I expected. While I was an undergraduate I did not think my abilities so good as they afterwards turned out to be. I remember wondering, as an almost unattainable ideal, whether I should ever do work as good as McTaggart's. During the early years of my first marriage Whitehead passed gradually from a teacher into a friend. In 1890 as a Freshman at Cambridge, I had attended his lectures on statics. He told the class to study article 35 in the text-book. Then he turned to me and said, 'You needn't study it, because you know it already'. I had quoted it by number in the scholarship examination ten months earlier. He won my heart by remembering this fact.

In England, Whitehead was regarded only as a mathematician, and it was left to America to discover him as a philosopher. He and I disagreed in philosophy, so that collaboration was no longer possible, and after he went to America I naturally saw much less of him. We began to drift apart during the first world war when he completely disagreed with my pacifist position. In our differences on this subject he was more tolerant than I was, and it was much more my fault than his that these differences caused a diminution in the closeness of our friendship.

In the last months of the war his younger son, who was only just eighteen, was killed. This was an appalling grief to him, and it was only by an immense effort of moral discipline that he was able to go on with his work. The pain of this loss had a great deal to do with turning his thoughts to philosophy and with causing him to seek ways of escaping from belief in a merely mechanistic universe. His philosophy was very obscure, and there was much in it that I never succeeded in understanding. He had always had a leaning towards Kant, of whom I thought ill, and when he began to develop his own philosophy he was considerably influenced by Bergson. He was impressed by the aspect of unity in the universe, and considered that it is only through this aspect that scientific inferences can be justified. My temperament led me in the opposite direction, but I doubt whether pure reason could have decided which of us was more nearly in the right. Those who prefer his outlook might say that while he aimed at bringing comfort to plain people I aimed at bringing discomfort to philosophers; one who favoured my outlook might retort that while he pleased the philosophers, I amused the plain people. However that may be, we went our separate ways, though affection survived to the last.

Whitehead was a man of extraordinarily wide interests, and his knowledge of history used to amaze me. At one time I discovered by chance that he was using that very serious and rather out-of-the-way work Paolo Sarpi's *History of the Council of Trent*, as a bed book. Whatever historical subjects came up he could always supply some illuminating fact, such, for example, as the connection of Burke's political opinions with his interests in the City, and the relation of the Hussite heresy to the Bohemian silver mines. He had delightful humour and great gentleness. When I was an undergraduate he was given the nick-name of 'the Cherub', which those who knew him in later life would think unduly disrespectful but which at the time suited him. His family came from Kent and had been clergymen ever since about the time of the landing of St Augustine in that county. He used to relate with amusement that my grandfather, who was much exercised by the spread of Roman Catholicism, adjured Whitehead's sister never to desert the Church of England. What amused him was that the contingency was so very improbable. Whitehead's theological opinions were not orthodox, but something of the vicarage atmosphere remained in his ways of feeling and came out in his later philosophical writings.

He was a very modest man, and his most extreme boast was that he did try to have the qualities of his defects. He never minded telling stories against himself. There were two old ladies in Cambridge who were sisters and whose manners suggested that they came straight out of *Cranford*. They were, in fact, advanced and even daring in their opinions, and were in the forefront of every movement of reform. Whitehead used to relate, somewhat ruefully, how when he first met them he was misled by their exterior and thought it would be fun to shock them a little. But when he advanced some slightly radical opinion they said, 'Oh, Mr Whitehead, we are so pleased to hear *you* say that', showing that they had hitherto viewed him as a pillar of reaction.

His capacity for concentration on work was quite extraordinary. One hot summer's day, when I was staying with him at Grantchester, our friend Crompton Davies arrived and I took him into the garden to say how-do-you-do to his host. Whitehead was sitting writing mathematics. Davies and I stood in front of him at a distance of no more than a yard and watched him covering page after page with symbols. He never saw us, and after a time we went away with a feeling of awe.

Those who knew Whitehead well became aware of many things in him which did not appear in more casual contacts. Socially he appeared kindly, rational and imperturbable, but he was not in fact imperturbable, and was certainly not that inhuman monster 'the rational man'. His devotion to his wife and his children was profound and passionate. He was at all times deeply aware of the importance of religion. As a young man, he was all but converted to Roman Catholicism by the influence of Cardinal Newman. His later philosophy gave him some part of what he wanted from religion. Like other men who lead extremely disciplined lives, he was liable to distressing soliloquies, and when he thought he was alone, he would mutter abuse of himself for his supposed shortcomings. The early years of his marriage were much clouded by financial anxieties, but, although he found this very difficult to bear, he never let it turn him aside from work that was important but not lucrative.

He had practical abilities which at the time when I knew him best did not find very much scope. He had a kind of shrewdness which was surprising and which enabled him to get his way on committees in a manner astonishing to those who thought of him as wholly abstract and unworldly. He might have been an able administrator but for one defect, which was a complete inability to answer letters. I once wrote a letter to him on a mathematical point, as to which I urgently needed an answer for an article I was writing against Poincaré. He did not answer, so I wrote again. He still did not answer, so I telegraphed. As he was still silent, I sent a reply-paid telegram. But in the end, I had to travel down to Broadstairs to get the answer. His friends gradually got to know this peculiarity, and on the rare occasions when any of them got a letter from him they would all assemble to congratulate the recipient. He justified himself by saying that if he answered letters, he would have no time for original work. I think the justification was complete and unanswerable.

Whitehead was extraordinarily perfect as a teacher. He took a personal interest in those with whom he had to deal and knew both their strong and their weak points. He would elicit from a pupil the best of which a pupil was capable. He was never repressive, or sarcastic, or superior, or any of the things that inferior teachers like to be. I think that in all the abler young men with whom he came in contact he inspired, as he did in me, a very real and lasting affection.

Whitehead and his wife used to stay with us in the country, and we used to stay with them in Cambridge. Once we stayed with the old

Master, Montagu Butler, in the Lodge, and slept in Queen Anne's bed, but this experience fortunately was not repeated.

My lectures on German Socialism were published in 1896. This was my first book, but I took no great interest in it, as I had determined to devote myself to mathematical philosophy. I re-wrote my Fellowship dissertation, and got it accepted by the Cambridge University Press, who published it in 1897 under the title *An Essay on the Foundations of Geometry*. I subsequently came to think this book much too Kantian, but it was fortunate for my reputation that my first philosophical work did not challenge the orthodoxy of the time. It was the custom in academic circles to dismiss all critics of Kant as persons who had failed to understand him, and in rebutting this criticism it was an advantage to have once agreed with him. The book was highly praised, far more highly in fact than it deserved. Since that time, academic reviewers have generally said of each successive book of mine that it showed a falling-off.

In the autumn of 1896, Alys and I went to America for three months, largely in order that I might make the acquaintance of her relations.[1] The first thing we did was to visit Walt Whitman's house in Camden, N.J. From there we went to a small manufacturing town called Millville, where a cousin of hers, named Bond Thomas, was the manager of a glass factory which had, for a long time, been the family business. His wife, Edith, was a great friend of Alys's. According to the Census, the town had 10,002 inhabitants, and they used to say that they were the two. He was a simple soul, but she had literary aspirations. She wrote bad plays in the style of Scribe, and imagined that if only she could get away from Millville and establish contact with the literary lights of Europe, her talent would be recognised. He was humbly devoted to her, but she had various flirtations with men whom she imagined to be of finer clay. In those days the country round about consisted of empty woodland, and she used to take me long drives over dirt tracks in a buggy. She always carried a revolver, saying one could never know when it would come in handy. Subsequent events led me to suspect that she had been reading *Hedda Gabler*. Two years later, they both came to stay with us in a palace in Venice, and we introduced her to various writers. It turned out that the work she had produced with such labour during the ten years' isolation in Millville was completely worthless. She went back to America profoundly discouraged, and the next we heard was that, after placing her husband's love letters over her heart, she had shot herself through them with the revolver. He subsequently married another woman who was said to be exactly like her.

[1] With us we took Bonté Amos, the sister of Maurice Sheldon Amos; see pp. 143 ff.

We went next to Bryn Mawr to stay with the President, Carey Thomas, sister of Bond Thomas. She was a lady who was treated almost with awe by all the family. She had immense energy, a belief in culture which she carried out with a business man's efficiency, and a profound contempt for the male sex. The first time I met her, which was at Friday's Hill, Logan said to me before her arrival: 'Prepare to meet thy Carey.' This expressed the family attitude. I was never able myself, however, to take her quite seriously, because she was so easily shocked. She had the wholly admirable view that a person who intends to write on an academic subject should first read up the literature, so I gravely informed her that all the advances in non-Euclidean geometry had been made in ignorance of the previous literature, and even because of that ignorance. This caused her ever afterwards to regard me as a mere *farceur*. Various incidents, however, confirmed me in my view of her. For instance, once in Paris we took her to see 'L'Aiglon', and I found from her remarks that she did not know there had been a Revolution in France in 1830. I gave her a little sketch of French history, and a few days later she told me that her secretary desired a handbook of French history, and asked me to recommend one. However, at Bryn Mawr she was Zeus, and everybody trembled before her. She lived with a friend, Miss Gwinn, who was in most respects the opposite of her. Miss Gwinn had very little will-power, was soft and lazy, but had a genuine though narrow feeling for literature. They had been friends from early youth, and had gone together to Germany to get the Ph.D degree, which, however, only Carey had succeeded in getting. At the time that we stayed with them, their friendship had become a little ragged. Miss Gwinn used to go home to her family for three days in every fortnight, and at the exact moment of her departure each fortnight, another lady, named Miss Garrett, used to arrive, to depart again at the exact moment of Miss Gwinn's return. Miss Gwinn, meantime, had fallen in love with a very brilliant young man, named Hodder, who was teaching at Bryn Mawr. This roused Carey to fury, and every night, as we were going to bed, we used to hear her angry voice scolding Miss Gwinn in the next room for hours together. Hodder had a wife and child, and was said to have affairs with the girls at the College. In spite of all these obstacles, however, Miss Gwinn finally married him. She insisted upon getting a very High Church clergyman to perform the ceremony, thereby making it clear that the wife whom he had had at Bryn Mawr was not his legal wife, since the clergyman in question refused to marry divorced persons. Hodder had given out that there had been a divorce, but Miss Gwinn's action showed that this had not been the case. He died soon after their marriage, worn out with riotous living. He had a very brilliant mind, and in the absence of women could talk very interestingly.

While at Bryn Mawr, I gave lectures on non-Euclidean geometry, and Alys gave addresses in favour of endowment of motherhood, combined with private talks to women in favour of free love. This caused a scandal, and we were practically hounded out of the college. From there we went to Baltimore, where I lectured on the same subject at the Johns Hopkins University. There we stayed with her uncle, Dr Thomas, the father of Carey. The Thomases were a curious family. There was a son at Johns Hopkins who was very brilliant in brain surgery; there was a daughter, Helen, at Bryn Mawr, who had the misfortune to be deaf. She was gentle and kind, and had very lovely red hair. I was very fond of her for a number of years, culminating in 1900. Once or twice I asked her to kiss me, but she refused. Ultimately she married Simon Flexner, the Head of the Rockefeller Institute of Preventive Medicine. I remained very good friends with her, although in the last years of her life I saw her seldom. There was another daughter who had remained a pious and very orthodox Quaker. She always alluded to those who were not Quakers as 'the world's people'. They all of them used 'thee' in conversation, and so did Alys and I when we talked to each other. Some of the Quaker doctrines seemed a little curious to those not accustomed to them. I remember my mother-in-law explaining that she was taught to consider the Lord's Prayer 'gay'. At first this remark caused bewilderment, but she explained that everything done by non-Quakers but not by Quakers was called 'gay', and this included the use of all fixed formulas, since prayer ought to be inspired by the Holy Spirit. The Lord's Prayer, being a fixed formula, was therefore 'gay'. On another occasion she informed the dinner-table that she had been brought up to have no respect for the Ten Commandments. They also were 'gay'. I do not know whether any Quakers remain who take the doctrine of the guidance of the Spirit so seriously as to have no respect for the Ten Commandments. Certainly I have not met any in recent years. It must not, of course, be supposed that the virtuous people who had this attitude ever, in fact, infringed any of the Commandments; the Holy Spirit saw to it that this should not occur. Outside the ranks of the Quakers, similar doctrines sometimes have more questionable consequences. I remember an account written by my mother-in-law of various cranks that she had known, in which there was one chapter entitled 'Divine Guidance'. On reading the chapter one discovered that this was a synonym for fornication.

My impression of the old families of Philadelphia Quakers was that they had all the effeteness of a small aristocracy. Old misers of ninety would sit brooding over their hoard while their children of sixty or seventy waited for their death with what patience they could command. Various forms of mental disorder appeared common. Those who must be accounted sane were apt to be very stupid. Alys had a maiden aunt in Philadelphia, a sister of her father, who was very rich and very absurd. She liked me well enough, but had a dark suspicion that I thought it was not *literally* the blood of Jesus that brought salvation. I do not know how she got this notion, as I never said anything to encourage it. We dined with her on Thanksgiving Day. She was a very greedy old lady, and had supplied a feast which required a gargantuan stomach. Just as we were about to eat the first mouthful, she said: 'Let us pause and think of the poor.' Apparently she found this thought an appetiser. She had two nephews who lived in her neighbourhood and came to see her every evening. They felt it would be unfair if the nephew and nieces in Europe got an equal share at her death. She, however, liked to boast about them, and respected them more than those whom she could bully as she chose. Consequently they lost nothing by their absence.

America in those days was a curiously innocent country. Numbers of men asked me to explain what it was that Oscar Wilde had done. In Boston we stayed in a boarding-house kept by two old Quaker ladies, and one of them at breakfast said to me in a loud voice across the table: 'Oscar Wilde has not been much before the public lately. What has he been doing?' 'He is in prison', I replied. Fortunately on this occasion I was not asked what he had done. I viewed America in those days with the conceited superiority of the insular Briton. Nevertheless, contact with academic Americans, especially mathematicians, led me to realise the superiority of Germany to England in almost all academic matters. Against my will, in the course of my travels, the belief that everything worth knowing was known at Cambridge gradually wore off. In this respect my travels were very useful to me.

Of the year 1897 I remember very little except that my *Foundations of Geometry* was published in that year. I remember also very great pleasure in receiving a letter of praise of this book from Louis Couturat, whom at that time I had never met, though I had reviewed his book *The Mathematical Infinite*. I had dreamed of receiving letters of praise from unknown foreigners, but this was the first time it had happened to me. He related how he had worked his way through my book 'armé d'un dictionnaire', for he knew no English. At a slightly later date I went to Caen to visit him, as he was at that time a professor there. He was surprised to find me so young, but in spite of that a friendship began which lasted until he was killed by a lorry during the mobilisation of 1914. In the last years I had lost contact with him, because he became absorbed in the question of an international language. He advocated Ido rather than Esperanto. According to his conversation, no human beings in the whole previous history of the human race had ever been quite so depraved as the Esperantists. He lamented that the word Ido did not lend itself to the formation of a word similar to Esperantist. I suggested 'idiot', but he was not quite pleased. I remember lunching with him in Paris in July 1900, when the heat was very oppressive. Mrs Whitehead, who had a weak heart, fainted, and while he was gone to fetch the *sal volatile* somebody opened the window. When he returned, he firmly shut it again, saying: 'De l'air, oui, mais pas de courant d'air.' I remember too his coming to see me in a hotel in Paris in 1905, while Mr Davies and his daughter Margaret (the father and sister of Crompton and Theodore) listened to his conversation. He talked without a moment's intermission for half an hour, and then remarked that 'the wise are those who hold their tongues'. At this point, Mr Davies, in spite of his eighty years, rushed from the room, and I could just hear the sound of his laughter as he disappeared. Couturat was for a time a very ardent advocate of my ideas on mathematical logic, but he was not always very prudent, and in my long duel with Poincaré I found it sometimes something of a burden to have to defend Couturat as well as myself. His most valuable work was on Leibniz's logic. Leibniz wished to be thought well of, so he published only his second-rate work. All his best work remained in manuscript. Subsequent editors, publishing only what *they* thought best, continued to leave his best work unprinted. Couturat was the first man who unearthed it. I was naturally pleased, as it afforded documentary evidence for the interpretation of Leibniz which I had adopted in my book about him on grounds that, without Couturat's work, would have remained inadequate. The first time I met Couturat he explained to me that he did not practise any branch of 'le sport'. When shortly afterwards I asked him if he rode a bicycle, he replied: 'But no, since I am not a sportsman.' I corresponded with him for many years, and during the early stages of the Boer War wrote him imperialistic letters which I now consider very regrettable.

In the year 1898 Alys and I began a practice, which we continued till 1902, of spending part of each year at Cambridge. I was at this time beginning to emerge from the bath of German idealism in which I had been plunged by McTaggart and Stout. I was very much assisted in this process by Moore, of whom at that time I saw a great deal. It was an intense excitement, after having supposed the sensible world unreal, to be able to believe again that there really were such things as tables and chairs. But the most interesting aspect of the matter to me was the logical aspect. I was glad to think that relations are real, and I was interested to discover the dire effect upon metaphysics of the belief that all propositions are of the subject-predicate form. Accident led me to read Leibniz, because he had to be lectured upon, and McTaggart wanted to go to New Zealand, so that the College asked me to take his place so far as this one course was concerned. In the study and criticism of Leibniz I found occasion to exemplify the new views on logic to which, largely under Moore's guidance, I had been led.

We spent two successive autumns in Venice, and I got to know almost every stone in the place. From the date of my first marriage down to the outbreak of the first war, I do not think any year passed without my going to Italy. Sometimes I went on foot, sometimes on a bicycle; once in a tramp steamer calling at every little port from Venice to Genoa. I loved especially the smaller and more out-of-the-way towns, and the mountain landscapes in the Apennines. After the outbreak of the war, I did not go back to Italy till 1949. I had the intention of going there to a Congress in the year 1922, but Mussolini, who had not yet accomplished his *coup d'état*, sent word to the organisers of the Congress that, while no harm should be done to me, any Italian who spoke to me should be assassinated. Having no wish to leave a trail of blood behind me, I avoided the country which he defiled, dearly as I loved it.

I remember the summer of 1899 as the last time that I saw Sally Fairchild until one afternoon in 1940, when we met as old people and wondered what we had seen in each other. She was an aristocratic Bostonian of somewhat diminished fortunes, whom I had first come to know in 1896 when we were staying in Boston. In the face she was not strikingly beautiful, but her movements were the most graceful that I have ever seen. Innumerable people fell in love with her. She used to say that you could always tell when an Englishman was going to propose, because he began: 'The governor's a rum sort of chap, but I think you'd get on with him.' The next time that I met her, she was staying with her mother at Rushmore, the country house of my Uncle, General Pitt-Rivers. With the exception of the General, most of the family were more or less mad. Mrs Pitt-Rivers, who was a Stanley, had become a miser, and if visitors left any of their bacon and egg she would put it back in the dish. The eldest son was a Guardsman, very smart and very correct. He always came down late for breakfast and rang the bell for fresh food. When he ordered it, my Aunt would scream at the footman, saying that there was no need of it as there was plenty left from the scrapings from the visitors' plates. The footman, however, paid no attention to her, but quietly obeyed the Guardsman. Then there was another son, who was a painter, mad and bad, but not sad. There was a third son who was a nice fellow, but incompetent. He had the good luck to marry Elspeth Phelps, the dressmaker, and thus escaped destitution. Then there was St George, the most interesting of the family. He was one of the first inventors of electric light, but he threw up all such things for esoteric Buddhism and spent his time travelling in Tibet to visit Mahatmas. When he returned, he found that Edison and Swan were making electric lights which he considered an infringement of his patent. He therefore entered upon a long series of lawsuits, which he always lost and which finally left him bankrupt. This confirmed him in the Buddhist faith that one should overcome mundane desires. My grandmother Stanley used to make him play whist, and when it came to his turn to deal, she used to say: 'I am glad it is your turn to deal, as it will take away your air of saintliness.' He combined saintliness and Company promoting in about equal proportions. He was in love with Sally Fairchild and had on that account invited her mother and her to Rushmore. There was as usual not enough food, and on one occasion at lunch there was a tug-of-war between Sally and the artist for the last plate of rice pudding, which I regret to say the artist won. On the day of her departure she wished to catch a certain train but Mrs Pitt-Rivers insisted that she should visit a certain ruin on the way to the station, and therefore catch a later train. She appealed to St George to support her, and at first he said he would, but when it came to the crisis, he preached instead the vanity of human wishes. This caused her to reject his proposal. (His subsequent marriage was annulled on the ground of his impotence.[1]) In the summer of 1899 she paid a long visit to Friday's Hill, and I became very fond of her. I did not consider myself in love with her, and I never so much as kissed her hand, but as years went by I realised that she had made a deep impression on me, and I remember as if it were yesterday our evening walks in the summer twilight while we were restrained by the strict code of those days from giving any expression whatever to our feelings.

In the autumn of 1899 the Boer War broke out. I was at that time a Liberal Imperialist, and at first by no means a pro-Boer. British defeats caused me much anxiety, and I could think of nothing else but the war news. We were living at The Millhanger, and I used most afternoons to walk the four miles to the station in order to get an evening paper. Alys, being American, did not have the same feelings in the matter, and was rather annoyed by my absorption in it. When the Boers began to be defeated, my interest grew less, and early in 1901 I became a pro-Boer.

In the year 1900, my book on the *Philosophy of Leibniz* was published. In July of that year I went to Paris, where a new chapter of my life began.

LETTERS

Pembroke Lodge
Richmond, Surrey
May 30, '95

Dearest Bertie
I hope yr Cambridge days had been useful though I don't exactly know in what way – I have asked you before, but forget yr answer,

[1] He married Lady Edith Douglas, sister of Lord Alfred.

what yr dissertation is called – how do you think you are succeeding with it? How vividly I remember the first tidings of yr first success, before you went to Cambridge – when you rushed upstairs to tell Auntie and me – the dear dear Bertie of that day – and then the last – oh the happy tears that start to eyes, at such moments in the old withered life to wch the young fresh life is bringing joy – Yet how I always felt 'these things wd not give me one moment's happiness if he were not loving and good and true'.

I came upon something of that kind yesty in a chance book I was reading – and am always coming upon passages in all kinds of books which seem written on purpose to answer to some experiences of my life – I suppose this is natural when life has been long. By the bye you have not yet said a word to Auntie about her little birthday letter – *she* has not said so, and she told me it was only a few lines, but such as they were she made an effort over illness to write them – the fact is that you take only the fag-end of the fragment of the shred of a minute or two for yr letters to us – and though it is pleasant now and then to look back to the full and talky ones you wrote in past days, they are not exactly substitutes for what those of the present might be! However as long as you have no *wish* for talkings on paper, wch at best is a poor affair, go on with yr scraps – I don't forget how very busy you are, but the very busy people are those who find most time for everything somehow – don't you think so? (What an ugly smudge!) As for talking off paper, you didn't intend as far as I cd make out when you went away, ever, within measurable distance to make that possible – Oh dear how many things I meant to say and have not said – about Quakers, of whose peculiar creed of rules we have been hearing things true or false – and about much besides. But it must all wait. What lovely skies and earth! and how glad you must have been to get back. Love and thanks to Alys.

Yr ever loving
Granny

I hope you found my untidy pencilled glossaries wch were loose inside the book – I thought they wd help to more pleasure in the book when you read it. How I wish we cd have read it together!

Pembroke Lodge
Richmond, Surrey
(1896)

Dearest Bertie

You say you have 'settled' yr plans – please mention them in case P.L. [Pembroke Lodge] comes into them – Gertrude[1] and bairns are

---

[1] Rollo's second wife.

to be here Sept. 1 to 16, I'm happy to say. U.R. in Scotland and elsewhere – so, that time wd not do – I can imagine the 'deeper Philosophy' and even 'L'Infini Mathematique' to be most interesting. It is rather painful dear Bertie, that knowing our love for Miss Walker, you still leave the death unmentioned. Nor do you say a word of dear Lady Tennyson's although so near you – Sir Henry Taylor called her 'very woman of very women' – no length of words could add to the praise of those five. I have sent for Green for Alys – a delightful history but not quite what I shd have liked as a gift to her.

> *Yr loving*
> *Granny*

Auntie has a *beautiful* note from poor Hallam.

> Pembroke Lodge
> Richmond, Surrey
> Aug. 11, 1896

Dearest Alys

We are delighted with the Bertie photo – It is perfect, such a natural, not photographic smile. As for you, we don't like you, and I hope Bertie doesn't, neither pose, nor dusky face, nor white humpy tippet – this is perhaps ungrateful of Agatha but she can't help it, nor can I. When is or was your birthday? I forget and only remember that I said I would give you a book. I will try to think of one and then ask you if you have it, but not Green I think – something less solid and instructive – have you Henriette Renan's letters? Agatha has just read them and says they are beautiful. Of course, my dear child I should never think of giving my health or want of it as an objection to your going to America. I felt it was for yourselves alone to decide whether 'to go or not to go'. I trust it may turn out for Bertie's good. It is sad that the last of the eminent group of authors, Holmes and Lowell, are gone – but no doubt there must be men well worth his knowing, whether authors or not. It is quite true that I have earnestly wished him to be thrown into a wider and more various set of men and women than has been the case – but this is most to be desired in his own country. Harold and Vita[1] came down – did I tell you? last week, such a nice natural pleasant girl. Thanks for your nice note. What a pity about your cold! Is it any fault in the cottage? What a horrible season for crossing and returning! Will sea air be good for your indigestion?

> *Your always affectionate*
> *Granny*

[1] My cousin Harold Russell and his wife.

Pembroke Lodge
Richmond, Surrey
May 17, '98

My dearest Bertie

I shall think of you very much tomorrow and of happy birthdays long ago when she was with us[1] to guide, counsel and inspire to all good and when you were still the child brightening our home and filling us with hope of what you might some day become. Dear dear Bertie has it been an upward growth since those days ? Have the joys of life which are now yours helped you to be not less but more loving, more helpful, more thoughtful, for those whose lives may be full of sorrow illness pain and loneliness. All of us who have known what it was to have Granny's love and prayers and wishes – and who have the blessed memory of her wonderful example must feel, at times almost despairingly, how terribly terribly far away we are from her ideal and her standard of life – but we must strive on and hope for more of her spirit. You cannot think how very lovely everything is here just now and though the aching longing for her is awful, yet I love to look upon it all and remember how she loved it.

Uncle Rollo is very unwell and has been for a long time. I was very anxious long ago about him when he was doing far too much, now he is ordered complete rest; – Perhaps you have been to Dunrozel. There has been an immense deal to do here and I have been quite overdone several times. Gwennie [Gwendoline Villiers] has saved me from a breakdown by working incessantly and helping in every possible way – It has been most painful to see the beautiful pictures go away and the house more and more dismantled and I shall be thankful when it is over. I am *most* glad that Uncle Rollo has several of the good pictures. They ought to be his and also I am grateful to Herbrand[2] for giving the Grant picture of your grandfather to the National Portrait Gallery. I am sorry I have no present for you just yet but it has been simply impossible during this unceasing business. Give Alys very best love.

God bless you dearest Bertie.

*Your very loving
Auntie*

To Graham Wallas

The Deanery
Bryn Mawr, Pa.
Nov. 13, 1896

Dear Wallas

I have been meaning to write to you ever since the Presidential

[1] My grandmother had lately died.
[2] The Duke of Bedford.

election, on account of a specimen ballot paper wh. I am sending you by book post. This document, I am told, is more complicated than in any other state: certainly it is a triumph. It seems to me to contain within it the whole 18th century theory of the free and intelligent demos, and the whole 19th century practice of bossism. Imagine using such a phrase as 'straight ticket' on a ballot-paper, and imagine the stupendous intellect of a man who votes anything else on such a ballot-paper. I have never seen a document more replete with theory of politics, or illustrating more neatly the short road from bad metaphysics to political corruption. The whole interest, in Philadelphia, centred about the election of the sheriff – Crow, the independent Republican, was making a stand against bossism, and strange to say, he got in, tho' by a very narrow majority.

I am sending you also some rather transparent boss's devices for allowing fictitious voters to vote. You will see that the vouchers I enclose enable a man to vote without being on the register. I was taken to a polling-booth in Philadelphia, and there stood, just outside, a sub-deputy boss, named Flanagan, instructing the ignorant how to vote, illegally watching them mark their ballot-paper, and when necessary vouching for the right to vote. A Republican and a Democrat sat inside to see that all was fair, it being supposed they would counteract each other; as a matter of fact, they make a deal, and agree to keep up their common friends the bosses, even if they have to admit fraudulent votes for the opposite party. Americans seem too fatalistic and pessimistic to do much against them: I was taken by a man appointed as official watcher by the Prohibitionists, but tho' he observed and pointed out the irregularities, he merely shrugged his shoulders when I asked why he did not interfere and make a row. The fact is, Americans are unspeakably lazy about everything but their business: to cover their laziness, they invent a pessimism, and say things can't be improved: tho' when I confront them, and ask for any single reform movement wh. has not succeeded, they are stumped, except one who mentioned the Consular service – naturally not a very soul-stirring cry. One of them, who prides himself on his virtue, frankly told me he found he could make more money in business than he could save in rates by fighting corruption – it never seemed to enter his head that one might think that a rather lame excuse. However, everything seems to be improving very fast, tho' nothing makes the lazy hypocritical Puritans so furious as to say so. They take a sort of pride in being the most corrupt place in the Union: everywhere you go they brag of the peculiar hopelessness of their own locality. The fall of Altgeld and the defeat of Tammany seem to irritate them: it might so easily have been otherwise, they say, and will be otherwise next election. Altogether I don't see that they deserve any better than they get. The Quakers and Puritans, so far as I have come across them, are the greatest liars and hypocrites I have ever seen and are as a rule totally destitute of vigour. Here's a Philadelphia story. Wanamaker is the local Whiteley, enormously rich and religious. The protective tariff is dear to his soul. In the election of 1888, when New York was the critical State, it was telegraphed to the Phila. Republican Committee that 80,000 dollars would win the election. Wanamaker planked down the sum, New York State was won by a majority of 500, and Wanamaker became Postmaster General. Here is a New York tale. Jay Gould, in 1884, offered a huge sum to the Republicans. This became known to the Democrats, who next day had a procession of several hours past his house shouting as they marched: 'Blood! Blood! Jay Gould's Blood!' He turned pale, and telegraphed any sum desired to the Democrats. Cleveland was elected. – However, individual Americans are delightful: but whether from lack of courage or from decentralisation, they do not form a society of frank people, and all in turn complain that they would be universally cut if they ever spoke their minds. I think this is largely due to the absence of a capital. A similar cause I think accounts for the religiosity and timidity of their Universities. Professor Ely was dismissed from the Johns Hopkins for being a Xtian Socialist! There are possibilities tho': everybody is far more anxious to be educated than in England, the level of intelligence is high, and thoughtful people admit – though only within the last few years, I am told, apparently since Bryce – that their form of government is not perfect. I think you will have, as we have, a very good time here. We probably sail December 30th, and strongly urge you to arrive before then. We shall be in New York, and want very much to see you, as also to introduce you to several nice people who will be there. If you have not yet written about the date of your arrival, please write soon. – This College is a fine place, immeasurably superior to Girton and Newnham; the Professor of Pol. Econ. oddly enough is a Socialist and a Free Silver man and has carried all his class with him tho' many of them are rich New Yorkers. Those I have met are intelligent and generous in their views of social questions.

> *Yours*
> *Bertrand Russell*

Maurice Sheldon Amos (afterwards Sir) was my only link between Cambridge and Friday's Hill. His father, who died in the 80s, was a theoretical lawyer of some eminence, and was the principal author of the Egyptian Constitution imposed by the English after their occupation of Egypt in 1881. His mother, as a widow, was devoted to Good Works, especially Purity. She was popularly supposed to have said: 'Since my dear husband's death I have devoted my life to prostitution.' It was also said that her husband, though a very hairy man, became as bald as an egg within six weeks of his marriage: but I cannot vouch for these stories. Mrs Amos, through her work, became a friend of Mrs Pearsall Smith. Accordingly Logan, when visiting me at Cambridge, took me to call on Maurice, then a freshman just beginning the study of moral science. He was an attractive youth, tall, enthusiastic, and awkward. He used to say: 'The world is an odd place: whenever I move about in it I bump into something.'

He became a barrister and went to Egypt, where his father was remembered. There he prospered, and after being a Judge for a long time retired, and stood for Cambridge as a Liberal. He was the only man I ever knew who read mathematics for pleasure, as other people read detective stories.

He had a sister named Bonté, with whom Alys and I were equally friends. Bonté suffered greatly from her mother's fanatical religiosity. She became a doctor, but a few weeks before her final examintion her mother developed the habit of waking her up in the night to pray for her, so we had to send her money to enable her to live away from home. Alys and I took her with us to America in 1896.

Bonté also went to Egypt, where she was at one time quarantine medical officer at Suez, whose duty (inter alia) it was to catch rats on ships declared by their captains to be free from such animals. She finally married an army officer who was at the head of the police force of Egypt. He had endured shipwrecks and mutinies and all kinds of 'hair-breadth 'scapes', but when I remarked to him, 'You seem to have had a very adventurous life', he replied, 'Oh no, of course I never missed my morning tea'.

Both brother and sister refused to continue to know me when I ceased to be respectable, but the brother relented in the end. The sister remained adamant.

c/o Miss Frigell
Cairo
November 6th, 1898

My dear Bertie

It is a great pleasure to hear from you and to be reminded that the right sort of people exist. Do you know that *Brunyate* has come out here to a law berth of £1200 a year? He is amiable, but a savage. He thinks apparently that no subject but mathematics can be of any difficulty to a really great mind. He sneered at Political Economy, in the person of Sanger, at Metaphysics in the person of McT. – and I fear did not spare yourself, telling me that Forsythe did not believe in your theories. I questioned Forsythe's competence; he said that F. was capable of judging any *logical* proposition. So I could only say that it took six months or a year to state any metaphysical proposition to a person who knew nothing about it. The beast seems to think that Trinity has fallen into the hands of mugs who give fellowships to political economists and metaphysicians for corrupt motives. However one ought to remember that some are predestined to damnation, and that instead of worrying oneself to set them right, one had better spend one's time lauding the G.A. for his inscrutable decrees, especially in the matter of one's own election. Sometimes I confess I have qualms that I also am a reprobate. What for instance Moore means by saying that the world consists of concepts alone, I do not know.

I should much like to discuss my own and your affairs with you. It seems to me that I at any rate fall further away as time goes on from the state of having definite and respectable ambitions. The worst of all is to feel flamboyant – as one does occasionally – and to see no opening for drilling – or even for being tried on.

I shall not really know what to think of this place till you and Alys and Bonté come and report on it to me from a dispassionate point of view. Meanwhile I think I am learning various useful things. I am only occupied at the Ministry in the mornings; and I have just arranged to spend my afternoons in the office of the leading lawyer here, a Belgian, where I think I shall pick up a lot. Meanwhile it is night, getting fairly cool, cheerful, and I have about enough to live on and come home in the summer. I also have plenty to do.

The plan of your book sounds splendid. Perhaps I shall be able to understand it when it comes out, but probably not. I think it possible that I may take up my mathematics again out here because – I wish I had said this to that b.f. Brunyate, there is no doubt that Mathematics is a less strain on the attention than any other branch of knowledge: you are borne up and carried along by the notation as by the Gulf Stream. On the other hand it is shiftless work, getting up a subject without any definite aim.

I am glad to hear that you are Jingo. But I think it is a good thing that we should win diplomatically, if possible, without a war – although the old Adam wants the latter.

This we now seem to have done, in the most triumphant manner. The Fashoda incident gives us a new position in Egypt; we now have it by right of Conquest, having offered fight to the French, which they have refused.

I very much wish I was doing anything of the same kind of work as you, so as to be able to write to you about it. I wonder if there is such a thing as mental paralysis, or if one is bound to emerge after all.

Your affectionate friend
M. S. Amos

Cairo
May 5, 1899

Dear Bertie

I have just got leave for three months and a half from the 9th of June. I shall be home about the 10th, and I am looking forward very much to seeing you and Alys. I shall unfortunately have to go to Paris during July for an examination, but I think I shall have long enough in England altogether to bore my friends. I hope you will give me a fair chance of doing so to you.

I was much struck by your lyrical letter about Moore. I have made it the text of more than one disquisition for the benefit of Frenchmen and other Barbarians, on the *real* state of spirits in England. I explain that our colonial and commercial activity is a mere pale reflection of the intense blaze of quintessential flame that consumes literary and philosophical circles. In fact that the true character of the present time in England is that of a Great Age, in which, under a perfect political system, administered by a liberal, respected and unenvied aristocracy teeming millions of a prosperous working class vie with the cultured and affluent orders of the middle rank in Imperial enthusiasm, loyalty to the Throne, and respect for learning – the same generous and stimulating atmosphere which has lent new life to trade, has had an even more stupendous and unprecedented effect on the intellectual life of the nation: this is especially seen in the Great Universities, which are not only, as heretofore, the nurseries of proconsuls of statesmen and of a territorial gentry of unrivalled liberality and elegance, but have within the last generation equalled and far surpassed all other seats of learning in Europe and America as centres of pure and abstract scientific inquiry. You should see the Frenchmen squirm. They can stand Spithead Reviews: they can just bear Fashoda, because they doubt where it is. But when it comes to new systems of Platonic philosophy, they tear their hair.

This is inexcusable frivolity. But it will be very nice to see you and Alys again and talk about all sorts of matters in all sorts of moods. Have you read *Les Déracinés* of Barrés?

Yours affectionately
M. Sheldon Amos

Chapter 6

'Principia Mathematica'

In July 1900, there was an International Congress of Philosophy in Paris in connection with the Exhibition of that year. Whitehead and I decided to go to this Congress, and I accepted an invitation to read a paper at it. Our arrival in Paris was signalised by a somewhat ferocious encounter with the eminent mathematician Borel. Carey Thomas had asked Alys to bring from England twelve empty trunks which she had left behind. Borel had asked the Whiteheads to bring his niece, who had a teaching post in England. There was a great crowd at the Gare du Nord, and we had only one luggage ticket for the whole party. Borel's niece's luggage turned up at once, our luggage turned up fairly soon, but of Carey's empty trunks only eleven appeared. While we were waiting for the twelfth, Borel lost patience, snatched the luggage ticket out of my hands, and went off with his niece and her one valise, leaving us unable to claim either Carey's trunks or our personal baggage. Whitehead and I seized the pieces one at a time, and used them as battering-rams to penetrate through the ring of officials. So surprised were they that the manoeuvre was successful.

The Congress was a turning point in my intellectual life, because I there met Peano. I already knew him by name and had seen some of his work, but had not taken the trouble to master his notation. In discussions at the Congress I observed that he was always more precise than anyone else, and that he invariably got the better of any argument upon which he embarked. As the days went by, I decided that this must be owing to his mathematical logic. I therefore got him to give me all his works, and as soon as the Congress was over I retired to Fernhurst to study quietly every word written by him and his disciples. It became clear to me that his notation afforded an instrument of logical analysis such as I had been seeking for years, and that by studying him I was acquiring a new and powerful technique for the work that I had long wanted to do. By the end of August I had become completely familiar with all the work of his school. I spent September in extending his methods to the logic of relations. It seems to me in retrospect that, through that month, every day was warm and sunny. The Whiteheads stayed with us at Fernhurst, and I explained my new ideas to him.

Every evening the discussion ended with some difficulty, and every morning I found that the difficulty of the previous evening had solved itself while I slept. The time was one of intellectual intoxication. My sensations resembled those one has after climbing a mountain in a mist, when, on reaching the summit, the mist suddenly clears, and the country becomes visible for forty miles in every direction. For years I had been endeavouring to analyse the fundamental notions of mathematics, such as order and cardinal numbers. Suddenly, in the space of a few weeks, I discovered what appeared to be definitive answers to the problems which had baffled me for years. And in the course of discovering these answers, I was introducing a new mathematical technique, by which regions formerly abandoned to the vaguenesses of philosophers were conquered for the precision of exact formulae. Intellectually, the month of September 1900 was the highest point of my life. I went about saying to myself that now at last I had done something worth doing, and I had the feeling that I must be careful not to be run over in the street before I had written it down. I sent a paper to Peano for his journal, embodying my new ideas. With the beginning of October I sat down to write *The Principles of Mathematics*, at which I had already made a number of unsuccessful attempts. Parts III, IV, V, and VI of the book as published were written that autumn. I wrote also Parts I, II, and VII at that time, but had to rewrite them later, so that the book was not finished in its final form until May 1902. Every day throughout October, November and December, I wrote my ten pages, and finished the MS on the last day of the century, in time to write a boastful letter to Helen Thomas about the 200,000 words that I had just completed.

Oddly enough, the end of the century marked the end of this sense of triumph, and from that moment onwards I began to be assailed simultaneously by intellectual and emotional problems which plunged me into the darkest despair that I have ever known.

During the Lent Term of 1901, we joined with the Whiteheads in taking Professor Maitland's house in Downing College. Professor Maitland had had to go to Madeira for his health. His housekeeper informed us that he had 'dried hisself up eating dry toast', but I imagine this was not the medical diagnosis. Mrs Whitehead was at this time becoming more and more of an invalid, and used to have intense pain owing to heart trouble. Whitehead and Alys and I were all filled with anxiety about her. He was not only deeply devoted to her but also very dependent upon her, and it seemed doubtful whether he would ever achieve any more good work if she were to die. One day, Gilbert Murray came to Newnham to read part of his translation of *The Hippolytus*, then unpublished. Alys and I went to hear him, and I was profoundly stirred by the beauty of the poetry.[1] When we came home, we found Mrs Whitehead undergoing an unusually severe bout of pain. She seemed cut off from everyone and everything by walls of agony, and the sense of the solitude of each human soul suddenly overwhelmed me. Ever since my marriage, my emotional life had been calm and superficial. I had forgotten all the deeper issues, and had been content with flippant cleverness. Suddenly the ground seemed to give way beneath me, and I found myself in quite another region. Within five minutes I went through some such reflections as the following: the loneliness of the human soul is unendurable; nothing can penetrate it except the highest intensity of the sort of love that religious teachers have preached; whatever does not spring from this motive is harmful, or at best useless; it follows that war is wrong, that a public school education is abominable, that the use of force is to be deprecated, and that in human relations one should penetrate to the core of loneliness in each person and speak to that. The Whitehead's youngest boy, aged three, was in the room. I had previously taken no notice of him, nor he of me. He had to be prevented from troubling his mother in the middle of her paroxysms of pain. I took his hand and led him away. He came willingly, and felt at home with me. From that day to his death in the War in 1918, we were close friends.

At the end of those five minutes, I had become a completely different person. For a time, a sort of mystic illumination possessed me. I felt that I knew the inmost thoughts of everybody that I met in the street, and though this was, no doubt, a delusion, I did in actual fact find myself in far closer touch than previously with all my friends, and many of my acquaintances. Having been an Imperialist, I became during those five minutes a pro-Boer and a Pacifist. Having for years cared only for exactness and analysis, I found myself filled with semi-mystical feelings about beauty, with an intense interest in children, and with a desire almost as profound as that of the Buddha to find some philosophy which should make human life endurable. A strange excitement possessed me, containing intense pain but also some element of triumph through the fact that I could dominate pain, and make it, as I thought, a gateway to wisdom. The mystic insight which I then imagined myself to possess has largely faded, and the habit of analysis has reasserted itself. But something of what I thought I saw in that moment has remained always with me, causing my attitude during the first war, my interest in children, my indifference to minor misfortunes, and a certain emotional tone in all my human relations.

At the end of the Lent Term, Alys and I went back to Fernhurst, where I set to work to write out the logical deduction of mathematics

[1] See letter to Gilbert Murray and his reply, p. 159. Also the subsequent letters relating to the *Bacchae*.

which afterwards became *Principia Mathematica*. I thought the work was nearly finished, but in the month of May I had an intellectual set-back almost as severe as the emotional set-back which I had had in February. Cantor had a proof that there is no greatest number, and it seemed to me that the number of all the things in the world ought to be the greatest possible. Accordingly, I examined his proof with some minuteness, and endeavoured to apply it to the class of all the things there are. This led me to consider those classes which are not members of themselves, and to ask whether the class of such classes is or is not a member of itself. I found that either answer implies its contradictory. At first I supposed that I should be able to overcome the contradiction quite easily, and that probably there was some trivial error in the reasoning. Gradually, however, it became clear that this was not the case. Burali-Forti had already discovered a similar contradiction, and it turned out on logical analysis that there was an affinity with the ancient Greek contradiction about Epimenides the Cretan, who said that all Cretans are liars. A contradiction essentially similar to that of Epimenides can be created by giving a person a piece of paper on which is written: 'The statement on the other side of this paper is false.' The person turns the paper over, and finds on the other side: 'The statement on the other side of this paper is true.' It seemed unworthy of a grown man to spend his time on such trivialities, but what was I to do? There was something wrong, since such contradictions were unavoidable on ordinary premisses. Trivial or not, the matter was a challenge. Throughout the latter half of 1901 I supposed the solution would be easy, but by the end of that time I had concluded that it was a big job. I therefore decided to finish *The Principles of Mathematics*, leaving the solution in abeyance. In the autumn Alys and I went back to Cambridge, as I had been invited to give two terms' lectures on mathematical logic. These lectures contained the outline of *Principia Mathematica*, but without any method of dealing with the contradictions.

About the time that these lectures finished, when we were living with the Whiteheads at the Mill House in Grantchester, a more serious blow fell than those that had preceded it. I went out bicycling one afternoon, and suddenly, as I was riding along a country road, I realised that I no longer loved Alys. I had had no idea until this moment that my love for her was even lessening. The problem presented by this discovery was very grave. We had lived ever since our marriage in the closest possible intimacy. We always shared a bed, and neither of us ever had a separate dressing-room. We talked over together everything that ever happened to either of us. She was five years older than I was, and I had been accustomed to regarding her as far more practical and far more full of worldly wisdom than myself, so that in many matters of daily life I left the initiative to her. I knew that she was still devoted to me. I had no wish to be unkind, but I believed in those days (what experience has taught me to think possibly open to doubt) that in intimate relations one should speak the truth. I did not see in any case how I could for any length of time successfully pretend to love her when I did not. I had no longer any instinctive impulse towards sex relations with her, and this alone would have been an insuperable barrier to concealment of my feelings. At this crisis my father's priggery came out in me, and I began to justify myself with moral criticisms of Alys. I did not at once tell her that I no longer loved her, but of course she perceived that something was amiss. She retired to a rest-cure for some months, and when she emerged from it I told her that I no longer wished to share a room, and in the end I confessed that my love was dead. I justified this attitude to her, as well as to myself, by criticisms of her character.

Although my self-righteousness at that time seems to me in retrospect repulsive, there were substantial grounds for my criticisms. She tried to be more impeccably virtuous than is possible to human beings, and was thus led into insincerity. Like her brother Logan, she was malicious, and liked to make people think ill of each other, but she was not aware of this, and was instinctively subtle in her methods. She would praise people in such a way as to cause others to admire her generosity, and think worse of the people praised than if she had criticised them. Often malice made her untruthful. She told Mrs Whitehead that I couldn't bear children, and that the Whitehead children must be kept out of my way as much as possible. At the same time she told me that Mrs Whitehead was a bad mother because she saw so little of her children. During my bicycle ride a host of such things occurred to me, and I became aware that she was not the saint I had always supposed her to be. But in the revulsion I went too far, and forgot the great virtues that she did in fact possess.

My change of feeling towards Alys was partly the result of perceiving, though in a milder form, traits in her which I disliked in her mother and brother. Alys had an unbounded admiration of her mother, whom she regarded as both a saint and a sage. This was a fairly common view; it was held, for example, by William James. I, on the contrary, came gradually to think her one of the wickedest people I had ever known. Her treatment of her husband, whom she despised, was humiliating in the highest degree. She never spoke to him or of him except in a tone that made her contempt obvious. It cannot be denied that he was a silly old man, but he did not deserve what she gave him, and no one capable of mercy could have given it. He had a mistress, and fondly supposed that his wife did not know of her. He used to tear up this woman's letters and throw the pieces into the waste-paper basket. His wife would fit the bits together, and read out the letters to Alys and Logan amid fits of laughter. When the old man died, she sold his false teeth and refused to carry out his death-bed request to give a present of £5 to the gardener. (The rest of us made up the sum without any contribution from her.) This was the only time that Logan felt critical of her: he was in tears because of her hardheartedness. But he soon reverted to his usual reverential attitude. In a letter written when he was 3½ months old, she writes:

'Logan and I had our first regular battle today, and he came off conqueror, though I don't think he knew it. I whipped him until he was actually black and blue, and until I really *could* not whip him any more, and he never gave up one single inch. However, I hope it was a lesson to him.[1]'

It was. She never had to whip him black and blue again. She taught her family that men are brutes and fools, but women are saints and hate sex. So Logan, as might have been expected, became homosexual. She carried feminism to such lengths that she found it hard to keep her respect for the Deity, since He was male. In passing a public house she would remark: 'Thy housekeeping, O Lord.' If the Creator had been female, there would have been no such thing as alcohol.

I found Alys's support of her mother difficult to bear. Once, when Friday's Hill was to be let, the prospective tenants wrote to inquire whether the drains had been passed by a sanitary inspector. She explained to us all at the tea-table that they had not, but she was going to say that they had. I protested, but both Logan and Alys said 'hush' as if I had been a naughty child who had interrupted Teacher. Sometimes I tried to discuss her mother with Alys, but this proved impossible. In the end, some of my horror of the old lady spread to all who admired her, not excluding Alys.

The most unhappy moments of my life were spent at Grantchester. My bedroom looked out upon the mill, and the noise of the millstream mingled inextricably with my despair. I lay awake through long nights, hearing first the nightingale, and then the chorus of birds at dawn, looking out upon sunrise and trying to find consolation in external beauty. I suffered in a very intense form the loneliness which I had perceived a year before to be the essential lot of man. I walked alone in the fields about Grantchester, feeling dimly that the whitening willows in the wind had some message from a land of peace. I read religious books such, as Taylor's *Holy Dying*, in the hope that there might be something independent of dogma in the comfort which their authors derived from their beliefs. I tried to take refuge in pure

[1] *A Religious Rebel*, by Logan Pearsall Smith, p. 8.

contemplation; I began to write *The Free Man's Worship*. The construction of prose rhythms was the only thing in which I found any real consolation.

Throughout the whole time of the writing of *Principia Mathematica* my relations with the Whiteheads were difficult and complex. Whitehead appeared to the world calm, reasonable, and judicious, but when one came to know him well one discovered that this was only a façade. Like many people possessed of great self-control, he suffered from impulses which were scarcely sane. Before he met Mrs Whitehead he had made up his mind to join the Catholic Church, and was only turned aside at the last minute by falling in love with her. He was obsessed by fear of lack of money, and he did not meet this fear in a reasonable way, but by spending recklessly in the hope of persuading himself that he could afford to do so. He used to frighten Mrs Whitehead and her servants by mutterings in which he addressed injurious objurgations to himself. At times he would be completely silent for some days, saying nothing whatever to anybody in the house. Mrs Whitehead was in perpetual fear that he would go mad. I think, in retrospect, that she exaggerated the danger, for she tended to be melodramatic in her outlook. But the danger was certainly real, even if not as great as she believed. She spoke of him to me with the utmost frankness, and I found myself in an alliance with her to keep him sane. Whatever happened his work never flagged, but one felt that he was exerting more self-control than a human being could be expected to stand and that at any moment a break-down was possible. Mrs Whitehead was always discovering that he had run up large bills with Cambridge tradesmen, and she did not dare to tell him that there was no money to pay them for fear of driving him over the edge. I used to supply the wherewithal surreptitiously. It was hateful to deceive Whitehead, who would have found the humiliation unbearable if he had known of it. But there was his family to be supported and *Principia Mathematica* to be written, and there seemed no other way by which these objects could be achieved. I contributed all that I could realise in the way of capital, and even that partly by borrowing. I hope the end justified the means. Until 1952 I never mentioned this to anyone.

Meanwhile Alys was more unhappy than I was, and her unhappiness was a great part of the cause of my own. We had in the past spent a great deal of time with her family, but I told her I could no longer endure her mother, and that we must therefore leave Fernhurst. We spent the summer near Broadway in Worcestershire. Pain made me sentimental, and I used to construct phrases such as 'Our hearts build precious shrines for the ashes of dead hopes'. I even descended to reading Maeterlinck. Before this time, at Grantchester, at the very height and crisis of misery, I finished *The Principles of Mathematics*.

The day on which I finished the manuscript was May 23rd. At Broadway I devoted myself to the mathematical elaboration which was to become *Principia Mathematica*. By this time I had secured Whitehead's co-operation in this task, but the unreal, insincere, and sentimental frame of mind into which I had allowed myself to fall affected even my mathematical work. I remember sending Whitehead a draft of the beginning, and his reply: 'Everything, even the object of the book, has been sacrificed to making proofs look short and neat.' This defect in my work was due to a moral defect in my state of mind.

When the autumn came we took a house for six months in Cheyne Walk, and life began to become more bearable. We saw a great many people, many of them amusing or agreeable, and we both gradually began to live a more external life, but this was always breaking down. So long as I lived in the same house with Alys she would every now and then come down to me in her dressing-gown after she had gone to bed, and beseech me to spend the night with her. Sometimes I did so, but the result was utterly unsatisfactory. For nine years this state of affairs continued. During all this time she hoped to win me back, and never became interested in any other man. During all this time I had no other sex relations. About twice a year I would attempt sex relations with her, in the hope of alleviating her misery, but she no longer attracted me, and the attempt was futile. Looking back over this stretch of years, I feel that I ought to have ceased much sooner to live in the same house with her, but she wished me to stay, and even threatened suicide if I left her. There was no other woman to whom I wished to go, and there seemed therefore no good reason for not doing as she wished.

The summers of 1903 and 1904 we spent at Churt and Tilford. I made a practice of wandering about the common every night from eleven till one, by which means I came to know the three different noises made by night-jars. (Most people only know one.) I was trying hard to solve the contradictions mentioned above. Every morning I would sit down before a blank sheet of paper. Throughout the day, with a brief interval for lunch, I would stare at the blank sheet. Often when evening came it was still empty. We spent our winters in London, and during the winters I did not attempt to work, but the two summers of 1903 and 1904 remain in my mind as a period of complete intellectual deadlock. It was clear to me that I could not get on without solving the contradictions, and I was determined that no difficulty should turn me aside from the completion of *Principia Mathematica*, but it seemed quite likely that the whole of the rest of my life might be consumed in looking at that blank sheet of paper. What made it the more annoying was that the contradictions were trivial, and that my time was spent in considering matters that seemed unworthy of serious attention.

It must not be supposed that all my time was consumed in despair and intellectual effort. I remember, for instance, the occasion mentioned earlier when Maynard Keynes came to spend Saturday to Monday with us at Tilford.

In 1905 things began to improve. Alys and I decided to live near Oxford, and built ourselves a house in Bagley Wood. (At that time there was no other house there.) We went to live there in the spring of 1905, and very shortly after we had moved in I discovered my Theory of Descriptions, which was the first step towards overcoming the difficulties which had baffled me for so long. Immediately after this came the death of Theodore Davies, of which I have spoken in an earlier chapter. In 1906 I discovered the Theory of Types. After this it only remained to write the book out. Whitehead's teaching work left him not enough leisure for this mechanical job. I worked at it from ten to twelve hours a day for about eight months in the year, from 1907 to 1910. The manuscript became more and more vast, and every time that I went out for a walk I used to be afraid that the house would catch fire and the manuscript get burnt up. It was not, of course, the sort of manuscript that could be typed, or even copied. When we finally took it to the University Press, it was so large that we had to hire an old four-wheeler for the purpose. Even then our difficulties were not at an end. The University Press estimated that there would be a loss of £600 on the book, and while the syndics were willing to bear a loss of £300, they did not feel that they could go above this figure. The Royal Society very generously contributed £200, and the remaining £100 we had to find ourselves. We thus earned minus £50 each by ten years' work. This beats the record of *Paradise Lost*.

The strain of unhappiness combined with very severe intellectual work, in the years from 1902 till 1910, was very great.[1] At the time I often wondered whether I should ever come out at the other end of the tunnel in which I seemed to be. I used to stand on the footbridge at Kennington, near Oxford, watching the trains go by, and determining that tomorrow I would place myself under one of them. But when the morrow came I always found myself hoping that perhaps *Principia Mathematica* would be finished some day. Moreover the difficulties appeared to me in the nature of a challenge, which it would be pusillanimous not to meet and overcome. So I persisted, and in the end the work was finished, but my intellect never quite recovered from the strain. I have been ever since definitely less capable of dealing with difficult abstractions than I was before. This is part, though by no means the whole, of the reason for the change in the nature of my work.

Throughout this period my winters were largely occupied with political questions. When Joseph Chamberlain began to advocate

[1] See my letters to Lucy on pp. 167 ff.

Protection, I found myself to be a passionate Free Trader. The influence which Hewins had exerted upon me in the direction of Imperialism and Imperialistic Zollverein had evaporated during the moments of crisis in 1901 which turned me into a Pacifist. Nevertheless in 1902 I became a member of a small dining club called 'The Coefficients', got up by Sidney Webb for the purpose of considering political questions from a more or less Imperialist point of view. It was in this club that I first became acquainted with H. G. Wells, of whom I had never heard until then. His point of view was more sympathetic to me than that of any other member. Most of the members, in fact, shocked me profoundly. I remember Amery's eyes gleaming with blood-lust at the thought of a war with America, in which, as he said with exultation, we should have to arm the whole adult male population. One evening Sir Edward Grey (not then in office) made a speech advocating the policy of the Entente, which had not yet been adopted by the Government. I stated my objections to the policy very forcibly, and pointed out the likelihood of its leading to war, but no one agreed with me, so I resigned from the club. It will be seen that I began my opposition to the first war at the earliest possible moment. After this I took to speaking in defence of Free Trade on behalf of the Free Trade Union. I had never before attempted public speaking, and was shy and nervous to such a degree as to make me at first wholly ineffective. Gradually, however, my nervousness got less. After the Election of 1906, when Protection ceased for the moment to be a burning question, I took to working for women's suffrage. On pacifist grounds I disliked the Militants, and worked always with the Constitutional party. In 1907 I even stood for Parliament at a by-election, on behalf of votes for women. The Wimbledon Campaign was short and arduous. It must be quite impossible for younger people to imagine the bitterness of the opposition to women's equality. When, in later years, I campaigned against the first world war, the popular opposition that I encountered was not comparable to that which the suffragists met in 1907. The whole subject was treated, by a great majority of the population, as one for mere hilarity. The crowd would shout derisive remarks: to women, 'Go home and mind the baby'; to men, 'Does your mother know you're out?' no matter what the man's age. Rotten eggs were aimed at me and hit my wife. At my first meeting rats were let loose to frighten the ladies, and ladies who were in the plot screamed in pretended terror with a view to disgracing their sex. An account of this is given in the following newspaper report:

Election Uproar
Rats let loose to scare women suffragists
Wimbledon fight

The Hon. Bertrand Russell, the suffragist candidate for the Wimble-don division, opened his campaign on Saturday night, when he ad-dressed a crowded and rather noisy meeting in Worple Hall. A mixed reception was given to the chairman, Mr O. H. Beatty, a member of the local Liberal Association executive council, and the platform party, which included the candidate, Mrs Russell, Mr St George Lane Fox-Pitt, the unsuccessful Liberal candidate at the General Election, Mrs Philip Snowden, Miss Alison Garland, and many others connected with the National Union of Women's Suffrage Societies.

From the outset it was apparent that a section of the audience – about 2,000 – was hostile to the promoters. The chairman often appealed in vain for silence. Within ten minutes of the start a free fight took place in one corner of the hall, and five minutes elapsed before peace was restored. People jumped on to the forms and chairs and encouraged the squabblers.

At another stage two large rats were let loose from a bag, and ran about the floor of the hall among a number of ladies sitting in the front seats. For a moment there was great commotion, the ladies jumping on the chairs, whilst a number of men hunted the rats about the seats, and at last managed to kill them. After the meeting one of the dead rats was taken to Victoria Crescent and flung into the candidate's committee room.

The rowdyism of the meeting, however, was confined to a large crowd of irresponsible young men and youths, who ought never to have been admitted, and it would therefore be unfair to blame the general body of Wimbledon electors for the blackguardly conduct of the political rabble.

Mr Russell was greeted with loud applause and general inter-ruptions, and, the latter being persisted in, the chairman remarked: 'Surely this is not the way that Wimbledon men and women greet a stranger.' (A Voice: 'Are we down-hearted?' and cries of 'No'.) A minute or so later the chairman again made an appeal to the rowdy section, and by asking them not to disgrace the name of Wimbledon he secured quietness for a time.

Mr Russell declared that he stood first and foremost for the suffrage for women on the same terms as men, and on the terms on which hereafter it might be granted to men. (A Voice: 'Do we want petti-coats?' and cries of 'No'.)

Proceeding, the candidate said he supported the present Govern-ment. (Cheers and uproar.) The most important of all the questions that divided the Liberal and Conservative parties was Free Trade, and a question closely associated with Free Trade was taxation of land values.

Mr Fox-Pitt rose, with a broad smile on his face. He wanted to tell them something about Mr Chaplin's history, but the meeting would have none of it, and he too gave up the task as hopeless.

Mrs Philip Snowden showed greater determination, and although at the start she was howled and jeered at, she was given a fairly good hearing. Mrs Arthur Webb, Miss Alison Garland, and Mr Walter MacLaren also spoke, and a resolution in support of Mr Russell was carried by an overwhelming majority.

The savagery of the males who were threatened with loss of supremacy was intelligible. But the determination of large numbers of women to prolong the contempt of the female sex was odd. I cannot recall any violent agitation of Negroes or Russian serfs against emancipation. The most prominent opponent of political rights for women was Queen Victoria.

I had been a passionate advocate of equality for women ever since in adolescence I read Mill on the subject. This was some years before I became aware of the fact that my mother used to campaign in favour of women's suffrage in the 'sixties. Few things are more surprising than the rapid and complete victory of this cause throughout the civilised world. I am glad to have had a part in anything so successful.

Gradually, however, I became convinced that the limited enfranchisement of women which was being demanded would be more difficult to obtain than a wider measure, since the latter would be more advantageous to the Liberals, who were in power. The professional suffragists objected to the wider measure, because, although it would enfranchise more women, it would not enfranchise them on exactly the same terms as men, and would therefore not, in their opinion, concede the principle of women's equality with men. On this point I finally left the orthodox suffragists, and joined a body which advocated adult suffrage. This body was got up by Margaret Davies (the sister of Crompton and Theodore), and had Arthur Henderson as its chairman. In those days I was still a Liberal, and tried to suppose that Arthur Henderson was somewhat of a fire-brand. In this effort, however, I was not very successful.

In spite of amusing and pleasant interludes, the years from 1902 to 1910 were very painful to me. They were, it is true, extremely fruitful in the way of work, but the pleasure to be derived from the writing of *Principia Mathematica* was all crammed into the latter months of 1900. After that time the difficulty and the labour were too great for any pleasure to be possible. The last years were better than the earlier ones because they were more fruitful, but the only really vivid delight connected with the whole matter was that which I felt in handing over the manuscript to the Cambridge University Press.

LETTERS

To and from Gilbert Murray:

Downing College
Cambridge
February 26, 1901

Dear Gilbert

I have now read the *Hippolytus*, and feel impelled to tell you how much it has affected me. Those of us who love poetry read the great masterpieces of modern literature before we have any experience of the passions they deal with. To come across a new masterpiece with a more mature mind is a wonderful experience, and one which I have found almost overwhelming.

It had not happened to me before, and I could not have believed how much it would affect me. Your tragedy fulfils perfectly – so it seems to me – the purpose of bringing out whatever is noble and beautiful in sorrow; and to those of us who are without a religion, this is the only consolation of which the spectacle of the world cannot deprive us.

The play itself was entirely new to me, and I have felt its power most keenly. But I feel that your poetry is completely worthy of its theme, and is to be placed in the very small list of truly great English poems. I like best of all the lyric with which you ended your reading at Newnham. I learnt it by heart immediately, and it has been in my head ever since. There is only one word in it which I do not wholly like, and that is the word *bird-droves*. Metrically it is excellent, but a drove seems to me to be something driven, which spoils the peacefulness of the idea to my mind.

Yours ever
Bertrand Russell

Barford, Churt,
Farnham, Surrey
March 2, 1901

My dear Bertie

I will not say that I feel pleased or delighted by your great enjoyment of my *Hippolytus*, because my feelings are quite different from that. It is rather that your strong praise makes a sort of epoch in my life and in my way of regarding my work. Of course I have felt great emotion in working at the *Hippolytus*; I have been entranced by it. And then the thought has always come to me, that there were dozens of translations of the Greek Tragedians in all the second-hand shops; and that I could not read any of them with the least interest; and that probably the authors of nearly all of them had felt exactly as I was feeling about the extraordinary beauty and power of the matter they were writing down. A translator, if he takes pains, naturally gets nearer to understanding his author than an ordinary reader does; and every now and again the poem means to him something approaching that which it meant to the poet.

Of course all authors – in different degrees, but all enormously – fail to convey their meaning. And translators, being less good writers and having a harder task, fail even more deplorably. That is the normal state of the case. But what seems to have happened in our case is that you have somehow or other understood and felt the whole of what I meant to convey.

I do not mean that I had anything mysterious or extraordinary to say; but merely that, even in the case of a bad poet or the Man-in-the-Street when in certain moods, if you could really understand what was in his mind it would be something astonishingly beautiful compared with what one ordinarily gets from reading a very good poem. When I am bored with poetry, I constantly have the feeling that I am simply not understanding the man or he is not expressing himself, and that probably something very fine indeed is going on inside him. And in some moment of special insight one might see inside him and get the fine thing.

I see what you mean about 'Bird-droves'. I will try to change it, but I cannot think of anything better so far. The MS arrived all right.

Yours ever
Gilbert Murray

Friday's Hill
April 3, 1902

Dear Gilbert

In all our discussions on ethical subjects, I observe a difference as to premisses, a real divergence as to moral axioms. As I am very anxious to be clear on the subject of immediate moral intuitions (upon which, as is evident, all morality must be based), and as a divergence upon fundamentals raises doubts, I should like to make an attempt to discover precisely what our differences are, and whether either of us holds at the same time mutually incompatible axioms.

Our differences seem to spring from the fact that you are a utilitarian, whereas I judge pleasure and pain to be of small importance compared to knowledge, the appreciation and contemplation of beauty, and a certain intrinsic excellence of mind which, apart from its practical effects, appears to me to deserve the name of virtue. What I want to discover is, whether you too do not hold moral principles not deducible from utilitarianism, and therefore inconsistent with it. (It is important to observe that the method of Sidgwick's *Ethics*, in which a number of commonly received moral axioms are shown to be roughly such as Utilitarianism would deduce as '*middle* axioms', is fallacious if, with Sidgwick, we accept the general basis of Intuitionism – i.e. the doctrine that immediate intuitions are the only source (for us) of moral premisses. For, if such axioms are immediate deliverances of moral consciousness, they are to be accepted even in those exceptional cases in which they are inconsistent with Utilitarianism; and thus any axiom not rigidly deducible from Utilitarianism is inconsistent with it.)

I may as well begin by confessing that for many years it seemed to me perfectly self-evident that pleasure is the only good and pain the only evil. Now, however, the opposite seems to me self-evident. This change has been brought about by what I may call moral experience. The ordinary *a priori* philosopher will tell you that experience has nothing to do with morals, since it tells us only what is, not what ought to be. This view seems to me philosophically and practically erroneous; it depends upon the sensational theory of knowledge, which, alas, is held in some form by many would be *a priori* philosophers. Having recognised that, in perception, our knowledge is not caused by the object perceived, it is plain that, if perception is experience, so is any other genesis in time, due to whatever cause, of knowledge not obtained by inference from other knowledge. Now circumstances are apt to generate perfectly concrete moral convictions: this or that, now present to me, is good or bad; and from a defect of imagination, it is often impossible to judge beforehand what our moral opinion of a fact will be. It seems to me that the genuine moral intuitions are of this very concrete kind; in fact that we see goodness or badness in things as we see their colours and shapes. The notion that general maxims are to be found in conscience seems to me to be a mistake fostered by the Decalogue. I should rather regard the true method of Ethics as inference from empirically ascertained facts, to be obtained in that moral laboratory which life offers to those whose eyes are open to it. Thus the principles I should now advocate are all inferences from such immediate concrete moral experiences.

What first turned me away from utilitarianism was the persuasion that I myself ought to pursue philosophy, although I had (and have still) no doubt that by doing economics and the theory of politics I could add more to human happiness. It appeared to me that the dignity of which human existence is capable is not attainable by devotion to the mechanism of life, and that unless the contemplation of eternal things is preserved, mankind will become no better than well-fed pigs. But I do not believe that such contemplation on the whole tends to happiness. It gives moments of delight, but these are outweighed by years of effort and depression. Also I reflected that the value of a work of art has no relation whatever to the pleasure it gives; indeed, the more I have dwelt upon the subject, the more I have come to prize austerity rather than luxuriance. It seems to me now that mathematics is capable of an artistic excellence as great as that of any music, perhaps greater; not because the pleasure it gives (although very pure) is comparable, either in intensity or in the number of people who feel it, to that of music, but because it gives in absolute perfection that combination, characteristic of great art, of godlike freedom, with the sense of inevitable destiny; because, in fact, it constructs an ideal world where everything is perfect and yet true. Again, in regard to actual human existence, I have found myself giving honour to those who feel its tragedy, who think truly about Death, who are oppressed by ignoble things even when they are inevitable; yet these qualities appear to me to militate against happiness, not only to the possessors, but to all whom they affect. And, generally, the best life seems to me one which thinks truly and feels greatly about human things, and which, in addition, contemplates the world of beauty and of abstract truths. This last is, perhaps, my most anti-utilitarian opinion: I hold all knowledge that is concerned with things that actually exist – all that is commonly called Science – to be of very slight value compared to the knowledge which, like philosophy and mathematics, is concerned with ideal and eternal objects, and is freed from this miserable world which God has made.

My point, in all this, is to suggest that my opinions would be shared by most moral people who are not biassed by a theory. Archimedes, I believe, was despised by contemporary geometers because he used geometry to make useful inventions. And utilitarians have been strangely anxious to prove that the life of the pig is not happier than that of the philosopher – a most dubious proposition, which, if they had considered the matter frankly, could hardly have been decided in the same way by all of them. In the matter of Art, too, I certainly have educated common sense on my side: anyone would hold it a paradox to regard Home Sweet Home as better than Bach. In this connection, too, it is necessary for the Utilitarian to hold that a beautiful object is not good *per se*, but only as a means; thus it becomes difficult to see why the contemplation of beauty should be specially good, since it is scarcely deniable that the same emotion which a person of taste obtains from a beautiful object may be obtained by another person from an ugly object. And a person of taste can only be defined as one who gets the emotion in question from beauty, not from ugliness. Yet all of us judge a person to be the better for the possession of taste, though only a blind theorist could maintain that taste increases happiness. Here is a hard nut for the Utilitarian!

All these arguments are at least as old as Plato; but I should like to know, when you have leisure, what answer a Utilitarian can make to them. The books contain only sophistries and lies – opinions possible, perhaps, to men who live only in the study, and have no knowledge of life whatever, but quite untenable by anyone who faces this ghastly world of ignoble degradation, in which only virtue is punished and vice lives and dies happy and respected.

Yours ever
Bertrand Russell

14 Cheyne Walk
Chelsea, S.W.
November 27, 1902

Dear Gilbert

I have been reading the *Bacchae* over again, and it seems to me now a much greater play than the *Hippolytus*, more marvellous, indeed, than any play I have ever read, unless perhaps *Hamlet* and *Lear*. It has been growing on me gradually ever since I read it first; like all great things, it is impossible to see the whole of it, but new points perpetually strike one.

The strange mystic exaltation of the chorus is very haunting, and the way that their world of frenzy and beauty supports itself till just the end against the everyday world is extraordinarily powerful. As a whole, I confess, the play does not strike me as at all puzzling: it is surely intelligible enough how those to whom such divine intoxication comes are filled with fury against the sceptics who try to drag them back to common life. And it is a commonplace that the worship of beauty makes for anarchy. It would have been absurd to make Pentheus a sympathetic character; I suppose he represents the British Public and Middle Class Respectability, and the respectable, though they are undoubtedly morally superior to the worshippers of Bacchus, are yet obviously unlovable in the conflict which they stir up.

I think your metres, now that I have mastered them, are exceedingly fine and wonderfully suited to the emotions they are meant to express: although there is perhaps no single chorus as good as some in the *Hippolytus*, I think you have shown more skill than you showed there; and altogether you are very much to be congratulated. Do you not think you would do well to make more translations? The two you have done have both been to me a really great help in trying times, helping me to support faith in the world of beauty, and in the ultimate dignity of life, when I was in danger of losing it: without them I should have often found the day much harder to get through. Surely there would be many who would feel the same, and as you have the power you have also the duty, have you not? Each of us is an Atlas to the world of his own ideals, and the poet, more than anyone else, lightens the burden for weary shoulders.

I wish I knew how to reconcile the world of beauty and the world of morals: some virtues, it is true, are beautiful, but many do not seem so.

I have been reading the *Republic*, and I agree with Plato that tragic poets ought to make us feel virtue to be beautiful, and ought (on the whole) to avoid the praises of vice. His austerity in matters of Art pleases me, for it does not seem to be the easy condemnation that comes from the Philistine.

> *Yours gratefully*
> *Bertrand Russell*

> 14 Cheyne Walk
> Chelsea, S.W.
> December 4, 1902

Dear Gilbert

I am glad my appreciation of your work is encouraging to you. Yes, an 'elegant leisure devoted to translating the classics' doesn't sound very nice as an epitaph! But one must choose more inspiring phrases to describe one's activity to oneself.

I have looked up again the chorus beginning 'O hounds raging and blind', and I still fail to find any difficulty in it. It seems very probable that the 'old bottles' is, as a matter of fact, the explanation of the savagery; but it is easy enough, if one wants such things, to find a psychological explanation. Have you never, when you were admiring the sunset, suddenly been jarred into 'Hell and Damnation, there are the so-and-so's come to call'? A country neighbour, under such circumstances, may easily be felt as a 'spy upon God's possessed'. And do you not know, when a Philistine breaks in upon a delicate imaginary world, the oscillation backwards and forwards between the exquisite mood one is loath to lose and rage against the wretch who is desecrating one's Holy of Holies? Do you know Blake's Defiled Sanctuary, beginning 'I saw a chapel all of gold', and ending 'So I turned into a sty, And laid me down among the swine'? This is from a worshipper of Bacchus who had been unable to combat his Pentheus. It was on account of the rapid alternation that I instanced Levine as a parallel. But I feel no doubt that it is the work of clarification that you have put into your translation that has made the *Bacchae* seem plain to me.

Yes, I know who the Storrs are and I can imagine that it is very hard for you to get away at present; it must make more of a burden on Mary when you are away. I am sorry you are sleepless and bedevilled. Sometimes sleepless nights are a time for thoughts that remain with one as a comfort through the day: I find darkness a help to isolating the essentials of things and fixing one's whole attention upon them. But I gather you do not find that compensation.

Alys is keeping well. The river shines like burnished bronze under the frosty sun, and the barges float dimly through the brightness like dream-memories of childhood.

Give my love to Mary, and write again when you can find time. I like to hear how domestic matters go – how Rosalind is, and so on.

Yours ever
Bertrand Russell

14 Cheyne Walk
Chelsea, S.W.
December 12, 1902

Dear Gilbert

It will suit us very well indeed to see you on Monday for luncheon and as early before it as you can manage to arrive. I shall expect you about 11-45. But it seems Miss Harrison will be gone; we have been urging her to stay, but she asserts (at present) that it is impossible. She begs you instead to go on to see her later, as soon after luncheon as you can manage, at an address which I do not know, but which she will no doubt divulge in due course. It will be perfectly delightful to see you, and I look forward to it very much; but I am sorry you will not find Miss Harrison. She has turned the tables on me by producing your poem in print; do bring me a copy on Monday. Could you not spend Monday night here? We shall be delighted to put you up, in case my Aunt Rosalind does not come to town; but we shall be dining out. London is a weary place, where it is quite impossible to think or feel anything worthy of a human being – I feel horribly lost here. Only the river and the gulls are my friends; they are not making money or acquiring power. Last night we made the acquaintance of the Mac-Cails, which we were very glad of. How beautiful she is! I had heard so much about his balance and judgment that I was surprised to find him a fanatic. But he is too democratic for me – he said his charwoman was more in contact with real things than anybody else he knew. But what can a charwoman know of the spirits of great men or the records of fallen empires or the haunting visions of art and reason? All this and much more I wished to say; but the words stuck in my throat. Let us not delude ourselves with the hope that the best is within the reach of all, or that emotion uniformed by thought can ever attain the highest level. All such optimisms seem to me dangerous to civilisation, and the outcome of a heart not yet sufficiently mortified. 'Die to Self' is an old maxim; 'Love thy neighbour as thyself' is new in this connexion, but also has an element of truth. From heaven we may return to our fellow-creatures, not try to make our heaven here among them; we ought to love our neighbour through the love of God, or else our love is too mundane. At least so it seems to me. But the coldness of my own doctrine is repellent to me; except at moments when the love of God glows brightly.

Modern life is very difficult; I wish I lived in a cloister wearing a hair shirt and sleeping on a crucifix. But now-a-days every impulse has to be kept within the bounds of black-coated Respectability, the living God.

> *Yours ever*
> *Bertrand Russell*

> I Tatti, Settignano
> Florence
> December 28th, 1902

Dear Gilbert

Our crossing and journey were uneventful and prosperous, and the beauty here is overwhelming. I do wish you had been able to come. We have had day after day of brilliant sunshine – hoar frosts in the morning, warmth that made sitting out agreeable in the day. Just behind the house is a hill-side covered with cypress and pine and little oaks that still have autumn leaves, and the air is full of deep-toned Italian bells. The house has been furnished by Berenson with exquisite taste; it has some very good pictures, and a most absorbing library. But the business of existing beautifully, except when it is hereditary, always slightly shocks my Puritan soul – thoughts of the East End, of intelligent women whose lives are sacrificed to the saving of pence, of young men driven to journalism or schoolmastering when they ought to do research, come up perpetually in my mind; but I do not justify the feeling, as someone ought to keep up the ideal of beautiful houses. But I think one makes great demands on the mental furniture where the outside is so elaborate, and one is shocked at lapses that one would otherwise tolerate. . . . I am glad you abandoned your plan of reading a mathematical book, for any book on the Calculus would have told you lies, and also my book is (I fear) not worth while for you to read, except a few bits. What general value it may have is so buried in technicalities and controversies that it is really only fit for those whose special business it is to go in for such things. The later mathematical volume, which will not be ready for two years or so, will I hope be a work of art; but that will be only for mathematicians. And this volume disgusts me on the whole. Although I denied it when Leonard Hobhouse said so, philosophy seems to me on the whole a rather hopeless business. I do not know how to state the value that at moments I am inclined to give it. If only one had lived in the days of Spinoza, when systems were still possible. . . .

> *Yours ever*
> *Bertrand Russell*

14 Cheyne Walk
Chelsea, S.W.
March 21st, 1903

Dear Gilbert

Your doctrine on beauty does not repel me in the least, indeed I agree with it strongly, except the slight sneer at specialists. Specialising is necessary to efficiency, which is a form of altruism, and however narrow the specialist becomes, we ought to pardon him if he does good work. This I feel strongly, because the temptation to be interesting rather than technically effective is a dangerous one.

I shall be more glad than I can say when you come back; though I shall have nothing to give you in the conversational way. I have been merely oppressed by the weariness and tedium and vanity of things lately: nothing stirs me, nothing seems worth doing or worth having done: the only thing that I strongly *feel* worth while would be to murder as many people as possible so as to diminish the amount of consciousness in the world. These times have to be lived through: there is nothing to be done with them.

Yours ever
B. Russell

To Lucy Martin Donnelly:

The Mill House
Grantchester, Cambridge
Telegrams, Trumpington
May 23, 1902

Dear Lucy

... You will wonder at my writing to you: the fact is, I finished today my magnum opus on the principles of Mathematics, on which I have been engaged since 1897. This has left me with leisure and liberty to remember that there are human beings in the world, which I have been strenuously striving to forget. I wonder whether you realise the degree of self-sacrifice (and too often sacrifice of others), of sheer effort of will, of stern austerity in repressing even what is intrinsically best, that goes into writing a book of any magnitude. Year after year, I found mistakes in what I had done, and had to re-write the whole from beginning to end: for in a logical system, one mistake will usually vitiate everything. The hardest part I left to the end: last summer I undertook it gaily, hoping to finish soon, when suddenly I came upon a greater difficulty than any I had known of before. So difficult it was, that to think of it at all required an all but superhuman effort. And long ago I got sick to nausea of the whole subject, so that I longed to think of anything else under the sun; and sheer fatigue has become almost incapacitating. But now at last all is finished, and as you may imagine, I feel a new man; for I had given up hope of ever coming to an end of the labour. Abstract work, if one wishes to do it well, must be allowed to destroy one's humanity; one raises a monument which is at the same time a tomb, in which, voluntarily, one slowly inters oneself. But the thankless muse will not share her favours – she is a jealous mistress. – Do not believe, if you wish to write, that the current doctrine of experience has any truth; there is a thousand times more experience in pain than in pleasure. Artists must have strong passions, but they deceive themselves in fancying it good to indulge their desires. The whole doctrine, too, that writing comes from technique, is quite mistaken; writing is the outlet to feelings which are all but overmastering, and are yet mastered. Two things are to be cultivated: loftiness of feeling, and control of feeling and everything else by the will. Neither of these are understood in America as in the old countries; indeed, loftiness of feeling seems to depend essentially upon a brooding consciousness of the past and its terrible power, a deep sense of the difference between the great eternal facts and the transient dross of merely personal feeling. If you tell these things to your fine-writing class, they will know less than if you hold your tongue.

Give my love to Helen. My advice to anyone who wishes to write is to know all the *very* best literature by heart, and ignore the rest as completely as possible.

> *Yours ever*
> *Bertrand Russell*

N.B. – This letter is not for Carey!

Trinity College, Cambridge
July 6, 1902

Dear Lucy

Many thanks for your very interesting letter, and for the excellent account of Harvard and Barrett Wendell. What a monstrous thing that a University should teach journalism! I thought that was only done at Oxford. This respect for the filthy multitude is ruining civilisation. A certain man had the impudence to maintain in my presence that every student ought to be made to expound his views to popular audiences, so I lifted up my voice and testified for a quarter of an hour, after which he treated me with the kind of respect accorded to wild beasts. – I suppose Wendell is better than his books: I was disappointed in his American literature. For, though I agree with him that America, like the Australian marsupials, is an interesting relic of a bygone age, I care little for the great truth that American writers have all been of good family, and that Harvard is vastly superior to Yale. And his failure to appreciate Walt Whitman to my mind is very damaging. He talks of Brooklyn ferry and so on, and quite forgets 'out of the cradle endlessly rocking', and 'when lilacs last in the door-yard bloomed'. This seems to me to show a deplorable convention-ality, both in taste generally, and in judgment of Whitman specially.

When my book was finished, I took ten days' holiday. Since then I have been working as usual, except during four days that I spent with my Aunt Agatha at Pembroke Lodge. A strange, melancholy, weird time it was: we talked of merriment long since turned to sad-ness, of tragedies in which all the actors are gone, of sorrows which have left nothing but a fading memory. All the life of the present grew to me dreamy and unreal, while the majestic Past, weighed down by age and filled with unspeakable wisdom, rose before me and dominated my whole being. The Past is an awful God, though he gives Life almost the whole of its haunting beauty. I believe those whose childhood has been spent in America can scarcely conceive the hold which the Past has on us of the Old World: the continuity of life, the weight of tradition, the great eternal procession of youth and age and death, seem to be lost in the bustling approach of the future which dominates American life. And that is one reason why great literature is not produced by your compatriots.

At present, I am staying in College by myself: none of my friends are up, and when work is over, I have a great deal of leisure left for meditation. I have been reading Maeterlinck's works straight through: alas, I have nearly come to the end of them. *Le Temple Enseveli* seems to me very admirable, both as literature and as morality. I am simple-minded enough, in spite of Miss Gwinn and Mr Hodder's grave man's world (being I suppose, not a grave man) to think it unnecessary for literature to have an immoral purpose. I hate this notion of being true to life! Life, thank God, is very largely what we choose to make of it, and ideals are unreal only to those who do not wish them to be otherwise. Tell Miss Gwinn, with my compliments, that every word of St Augustine's Confessions is true to life, and that Dante's love for Beatrice is a piece of unadulterated realism. If people will not realise this, they are sure to lose out of life its finest, rarest, most precious experiences. But this is too large a theme! ...

> *Yours very sincerely*
> *Bertrand Russell*

Friday's Hill
Haslemere
September 1, 1902

Dear Lucy

Vanity in regard to letter writing is not an emotion to encourage! One's friends are sure to be glad of one's news, even if it is not told in the most gorgeous diction. But as a matter of fact I found your letter very interesting. Yes, one's people are very trying: they are a living caricature of oneself, and have the same humiliating effect that is produced by the monkeys in the Zoo: one feels that here is the unvarnished truth at last. To most people, their family is real in a higher sense than any later acquaintance, husband or wife even. You may notice that with Carlyle – his people in Annandale existed for him in a way in which his wife never existed till she was dead. People are less cased in Self as children, and those associated with childhood have a vividness that becomes impossible later – they live in one's instinctive past. This is a frequent source of trouble in marriage. – I haven't read the Elizabethans since I was an undergraduate; as I remember them, their chief merit is a very rich and splendid diction. The old drama is not a gospel to regenerate you, its world is too hopelessly unreal. Your own life, naturally, is a paper life, as you say, a life in which experience comes through books, not directly. For this disease, more books are *not* the remedy. Only real life is the remedy – but that is hard to get. Real life means a life in some kind of intimate relation to other human beings – Hodder's life of passion has no reality at all. Or again, real life means the experience in one's own person of the emotions which make the material of religion and poetry. The road to it is the same as that recommended to the man who wanted to found a new religion: Be crucified, and rise again on the third day.

If you are prepared for both parts of this process, by all means take to real life. But in the modern world, the cross is usually self-inflicted and voluntary, and the rising again, to the hopes of new crucifixions, requires a considerable effort of will. It seems to me that your difficulty comes from the fact that there are no real people to speak of in your world. The young are never real, the unmarried very seldom. Also, if I may say so, the scale of emotion in America seems to me more frivolous, more superficial, more pusillanimous, than in Europe; there is a triviality of feeling which makes real people very rare – I find in England, that most women of 50 and upwards have gone through the experience of many years' voluntary endurance of torture, which has given a depth and a richness to their natures that your easy-going pleasure-loving women cannot imagine. On the whole, real life does not consist, as Hodder would have you believe, in intrigues with those who are already married. If one wants uncommon experiences, a little renunciation, a little performance of duty, will give one far more unusual sensations than all the fine free passion in the universe. But a life in books has great calm and peace – it is true that a terrible hunger for something less thin comes over one, but one is spared from remorse and horror and torture and the maddening poison of regret. For my part, I am constructing a mental cloister, in which my inner soul is to dwell in peace, while an outer simulacrum goes forth to meet the world. In this inner sanctuary I sit and think spectral thoughts. Yesterday, talking on the terrace, the ghosts of all former occasions there rose and walked before me in solemn procession – all dead, with their hopes and fears, their joys and sorrows, their aspirations and their golden youth – gone, gone into the great limbo of human folly. And as I talked, I felt myself and the others already faded into the Past and all seemed very small – struggles, pains, everything, mere fatuity, noise and fury signifying nothing. And so calm is achieved, and Fate's thunders become mere nursery-tales to frighten children. – Life here is always, in the summer, a strange phantasmagory: we had yesterday Grace, the Amos's, Miss Creighton, the Kinsellas, the Robinsons and J. M. Robertson, the man on whom Bradlaugh's mantle has fallen. Miss Creighton has to be rescued, because Robertson began to discuss whether God was made of green cheese or had whiskers – infinite for choice.

We have all been reading with great pleasure James on Religious Experience – everything good about the book except the conclusions. I have been re-reading the most exquisite of all bits of history, Carlyle's *Diamond Necklace*. He is the only author who knows the place of History among the Fine Arts.

Love to Helen.

> *Yours very sincerely*
> *Bertrand Russell*

> 14 Cheyne Walk
> Chelsea S.W.
> November 25, 1902

Dear Lucy

Many thanks for your letter. I am grateful to you for writing about yourself: after all, people can tell one nothing more interesting than their own feeling towards life. It is a great comfort that you are so much better, and able to enjoy life again. All that you write about the little most people get out of experience is most true: but I was not thinking when I wrote, of 'experiences', but of the inward knowledge of emotions. This, if one is rightly constituted, requires an absolute minimum of outward circumstances as its occasion; and this it is that is required for the development of character and for certain sorts of writing. But there is no profit in feeling unless one learns to dominate it and impersonalise it. – For people like you and me, whose main business is necessarily with books, I rather think experience of life should be as far as possible vicarious. If one has instinctive sympathy, one comes to know the true history of a certain number of people and from that one can more or less create one's world. But to plunge into life oneself takes a great deal of time and energy, and is, for most people, incompatible with preserving the attitude of a spectator. One needs, as the key to interpret alien experience, a personal knowledge of great unhappiness; but that is a thing which one need hardly set forth to seek, for it comes unasked. When once one possesses this key, the strange, tragic phantasmagoria of people hoping, suffering, and then dying, begins to suffice without one's desiring to take part, except occasionally to speak a word of encouragement where it is possible.

I have not been reading much lately: Fitzgerald's letters have interested me, also the new Cambridge Modern History, where one gets a connected view of things one has read before in a very fragmentary fashion. Gilbert Murray's translations of Euripides are out, and I recommend them to you (published by George Allen). I have been trying to be interested in Politics, but in vain: the British Empire is unreal to me, I visualise the Mother Country and the Colonies as an old hen clucking to her chickens, and the whole thing strikes me as laughable. I know that grave men take it seriously, but it all seems to me so unimportant compared to the great eternal facts. And London people, to whom the Eternal is represented by the Monthlies, to which they rise with difficulty from the daily papers, strike me as all puppets, blind embodiments of the forces of nature, never achieving the liberation that comes to man when he ceases to desire and learns at last to contemplate. Only in thought is man a God; in action and desire we are the slaves of circumstance.

> *Yours very sincerely*
> *Bertrand Russell*

Lucy Donnelly's life had for many years centred about her friendship for Helen Thomas. When Helen became engaged to Dr Simon Flexner, Lucy suffered profoundly. The following letter was an attempt to comfort her.

> 14 Cheyne Walk
> Chelsea, S.W.
> 7th February, 1903

Dear Lucy

I have just heard of Helen's engagement and for her sake I am glad – it has always seemed to me that she ought to marry and that College life was distinctly a second-best for her. But for you, I know, it must be hard, very hard. It is a dangerous thing to allow one's affections to centre too much in one person; for affection is always liable to be thwarted, and life itself is frail. One learns many things as year by year adds to the burden of one's life; and I think the chief of all is the power of making all one's loves purely contemplative. Do you know Walt Whitman's 'Out of the rolling ocean the crowd'? One learns to love all that is good with the same love – a love that knows of its existence, and feels warmed to the world by that knowledge, but asks for no possession, for no private gain except the contemplation itself. And there is no doubt that there are real advantages in loss: affection grows wider, and one learns insight into the lives of others. Everyone who realises at all what human life is must feel at some time the strange loneliness of every separate soul; and then the discovery in others of the same loneliness makes a new strange tie, and a growth of pity so warm as to be almost a compensation for what is lost.

Phrases, I know, do not mend matters; but it makes unhappiness far more bearable to think that some good will come of it; and indeed the facing of the world alone, without one's familiar refuge, is the beginning of wisdom and courage.

Forgive my writing so intimately; but the world is too serious a place, at times, for the barriers of reserve and good manners.

We shall hope to see a great deal of you when you come to England, as I hope you will do. And I shall be very glad to hear from you whenever you feel inclined to write.

Yours very sincerely
Bertrand Russell

Churt, Farnham
April 13, '03

Dear Lucy

It is impossible to tell you how like sunshine it was to me to hear that my letter had been a comfort. But alas! it is easier to see what is good than to practise it; and old as this observation is, I have not yet got used to it, or made up my mind that it really is true. Yet I have seen and known, at times, a life at a far higher level than my present one; and my precepts are very greatly superior to anything that I succeed in achieving.

Yes, the logic of life is a wonderful thing: sometimes I think of making up a set of aphorisms, to be called 'Satan's joys'; such as: Giving causes affection, receiving causes tedium; the reward of service is unrequited love. (This is the biography of all virtuous mothers, and of many wives.) Passions are smirched by indulgence and killed by restraint: the loss in either case is inevitable. And so on. But these bitter truths, though they deserve to be recognised so far as they are true, are not good to dwell upon. Wherever one finds oneself inclined to bitterness, it is a sign of emotional failure; a larger heart and a greater self-restraint, would put a calm autumnal sadness in the place of the instinctive outcry of pain. One of the things that makes literature so consoling is, that its tragedies are all in the past, and have the completeness and repose that comes of being beyond the reach of our endeavours. It is a most wholesome thing, when one's sorrow grows acute, to view it as having all happened long, long ago: to join in imagination, the mournful company of dim souls whose lives were sacrificed to the great machine that still grinds on. I see the past, like a sunny landscape, where the world's mourners mourn no longer. On the banks of the river of Time, the sad procession of human generations is marching slowly to the grave; but in the quiet country of the past, the tired wanderers rest, and all their weeping is hushed.

But as for me, I have felt no emotions of any kind, except on rare occasions, for some time now; and that is a state of things most convenient for work, though very dull. We are living a quiet country life: Alys is well, except now and then for a day or two. We read Montaigne aloud: he is pleasant and soothing, but very unexciting. To myself I am reading the history of Rome in the middle ages, by Gregorovius, a delightful book. Gilbert Murray, who is our near neighbour, has been telling me about Orphic tablets, and their directions to the soul after death: 'Thou wilt find a cypress, and by the cypress a spring, and by the spring two guardians, who will say to thee: who art thou? whence comest thou? And thou wilt reply: I am the child of earth and of the starry heaven; I am parched with thirst, I perish.' Then they tell him to drink of the fountain; sometimes the fountain itself speaks. Certainly a beautiful mysticism.

> *Yours very sincerely*
> *Bertrand Russell*

Friday's Hill
Haslemere
July 29, 1903

Dear Lucy

It is impossible to tell you how glad I am that our letters have been a help to you. It is *the* great reward of losing youth that one finds onseself able to be of use; and I cannot, without seeming to cant, say how great a reward I feel it. You need not mind bringing a budget of problems; I look forward to hearing them, and to thinking about them. . . .

Yes, the way people regard intimacy as a great opportunity for destroying happiness is most horrible. It is ghastly to watch, in most marriages, the competition as to which is to be torturer, which tortured; a few years, at most, settle it, and after it is settled, one has happiness and the other has virtue. And the torturer smirks and speaks of matrimonial bliss; and the victim, for fear of worse, smiles a ghastly assent. Marriage, and all such close relations, have quite infinite possibilities of pain; nevertheless, I believe it is good to be brought into close contact with people. Otherwise, one remains ignorant of much that it is good to know, merely because it is in the world, and because it increases human comradeship to suffer what others suffer. But it is hard not to long, in weak moments, for a simple life, a life with books and things, away from human sorrow. I am amazed at the number of people who are wretched almost beyond endurance. 'Truly the food man feeds upon is Pain.' One has to learn to regard happiness, for others as well as for oneself, as more or less unimportant – but though I keep on telling myself this, I do not yet fully and instinctively believe it.

I am glad to hear that Helen is getting rested. It has been no surprise not hearing from her; but tell her not to forget me, and to write again when she is able. Seeing Grace just before her departure, the other day, seemed to bring America nearer. Usually, when I write to you or Helen, I feel almost as if I were writing to dead people whom I have read about in books – the whole place seems so remote, so plunged in memories of an utterly different person who occupied my body seven years ago, that I can hardly believe it to be real or inhabited by real people. But when you come over in the autumn, I shall doubt whether you have really been in America all this time.

The last four months, I have been working like a horse, and have achieved almost nothing. I discovered in succession seven brand-new difficulties, of which I solved the first six. When the seventh turned up, I became discouraged, and decided to take a holiday before going on. Each in turn required a reconstruction of my whole edifice. Now I am staying with Dickinson; in a few days I shall go to town and plunge into the Free Trade question (as a student only). We are all wildly excited about Free Trade; it is to me the last piece of sane internationalism left, and if it went I should feel inclined to cut my throat. But there seems no chance whatever of Chamberlain's succeeding – all the brains are against him, in every class of society. . . .

> *Yours very sincerely*
> B. Russell

> 14 Cheyne Walk
> Chelsea, S.W.
> February 28, 1904

My dear Lucy

. . . Really the feeling of the worthlessness of one's work, where it is not justified, is the last refuge of self-love. It comes partly of too high an ideal of what one might hope to achieve, which is a form of pride; and partly of rebellion against one's private sufferings, which, one feels, can only be outweighed by some immense public good. But I know it is intolerably hard to drive self-love from this entrenchment, and I certainly have not yet succeeded. I do wish I could be with you, not only for the beauty of Sicily, but because it would be a great pleasure to see you, and because it would be so much easier to say just the things to build up in you the self-respect you deserve to have. You are really too modest altogether; but your friends' affection ought to persuade you that you have things to give which people value. I have not found myself, though, any way of banishing self except work; and while you are unable to work, it is very difficult for you.

I am glad Helen writes you nice letters. But I gather from what you say that her happiness is not great enough to exclude pains. That is a pity; yet perhaps it is a safeguard against greater pains in the future. This sounds a commonplace reflection, and I confess I think it better to have both pain and pleasure in an extreme degree than to have both soberly. But consolations are not to be rejected, even if they are commonplace . . .

There is not much news here. I have been very busy, but now my labours are practically ended. We go to Cambridge for two days this week, and Alys goes to visit Logan and look for sites at Oxford. I have been reading novels: *Diana*, and *Beauchamp's Career*, are the two I have read last. Meredith's psychology seems to me very good as a rule, though I didn't think Diana's betrayal was made credible. I fell in love with her at the Ball, and remained so through all her vagaries.

Last night I went to a remote part of London, to lecture to the local Branch of the Amalgamated Society of Engineers. They meet in a Public House, but permit no drinks during their meeting. They seemed excellent people, *very* respectable – indeed I shouldn't have guessed they were working men. They were of all shades of opinion, from Tory to Socialist. The Chairman, when I had finished, begged them not to follow their usual practice of flattering the lecturer; but even so I got not much criticism. The Secretary explained this to me on the way home by saying my arguments had 'bottled them up'. I liked them all, and felt an increased respect for the skilled workman, who seems usually an admirable person.

In a fortnight I shall have done with fiscal things, and then I shall go a walking-tour in Devonshire and Cornwall, before settling down to Philosophy. MacCarthy will go with me.

Write again as soon as you can. I feel there is much more to be said in answer to your letter, but Politics has rather scattered my thoughts. Try to keep up your spirits; and *please* don't imagine your life a useless one.

Yours affectionately
Bertrand Russell

Absender

(Postleitzahl) (Ort)

70761 Waldshut-Tiengen

Vermerke über Zusatzleistungen usw.

Entgelt		DM
Gewicht	3	kg

☐ Unfrei ☐ Eigenhändig ☐ Rückschein

☐ Sperrgut ☐ Eingeschriebene
Blindensendung-Schwer

☐ _____

☐ _____

☐ Besonderer Wert

_____ DM .

771177354743   10,00 DM
3,000 kg
84791780 6560 09.06.97

77.1477 35.474 3

(Id_____)

Empfänger   Vorausverfügungen

Forschungsgemeinschaft

Kennedyallee 40

(Straße und Hausnummer)

53175 Bonn

(Postleitzahl) (Bestimmungsort)

Einlieferungsschein

912-660-000

Wichtiger Hinweis

Sehr geehrte Kundin, sehr geehrter Kunde!

Für Anfragen zur Auslieferung Ihrer Sendung steht Ihnen unser Kundenservice Frachtpost gern zur Verfügung.

Service-Nummer: 01 80 - 2 30 22 00

Ihre
Deutsche Post AG

St Catherine's House
First Class Private Hotel
Fowey, Cornwall
March 29, 1904

My dear Lucy

... As for work, I have not thought at all, either with satisfaction or the reverse, about my fiscal career, now happily closed – that whole episode seems to have just faded away. Also I have not thought much about philosophy; though when I do think of it, the thought is rather pleasant. MacCarthy, who was an ideal companion, left me about 5 days ago. Since then I have been alone, and have found the time most valuable. A great sense of peace comes over me as I walk over green hills by the sea, with nobody to consult, and nobody to be careful of. In a quiet instinctive way (very uncommon with me) I think through practical difficulties that had seemed insoluble, and lay up a store of peace of mind to last through the agitations and fatigues of ordinary life. When I am not thinking of the way, or the scenery, I am mostly thinking about people's affairs; trying to get the facts straight, and to decide how much I can do to better the facts. It takes a good deal of time and thought to imagine oneself in a certain situation, and decide whether one could be sufficiently impressive to effect a great result. My Self comes in in being flattered by my knowledge of people's affairs, and anxious to have their confidence; but I try hard to make Self in this form subservient to good ends.

Then, when I reach an Inn, the people are all interesting owing to the solitude of my walks; I observe their little ways, compare land-ladies, and listen to the local gossip and the trials of innkeepers' lives. I could write at length on this subject, but it would be rather Pick-wickian. In this Hotel, we are a happy family party, and all dine to-gether. As I came downstairs, a middle-aged woman was giving herself some final touches before the Hall looking-glass; she looked round quickly, and when she saw I was not the man for whom she was doing it, she went on as before. Another middle-aged woman, with an earnest manner and a very small waist, was in great form, because *the* young man had given her a bunch of white violets, which she was wearing. Then there was the inevitable old lady who dined at a table apart, and only joined the conversation occasionally, throwing in a remark about how sweet the spring flowers are; and there was the pompous man, who was saying, 'Well, my opinion is that the directors have just thrown away £12,000 of the shareholders' money'. Then there was myself, much ashamed of having no change of clothes among all these respectable people, and much despised by them for the same reason; and like the man at the helm in the *Snark*, I spoke to no one and no one spoke to me; but I was well amused. Yesterday

I stayed at a place called Mevagissey, where there was a Parish Council Election going on. The landlady's daughter was laying my dinner when I asked her if it was a contest of Liberal and Tory.

'Oh no, Sir, it's only some of them wanted to put up a Doctor, and others said he wasn't a Mevagissey man, and had only lived 6 or 7 years in the place.'

'Disgraceful,' I said.

'Yes it is, Sir, ain't it? And they had a show of hands and he got the worst of it, but he demanded a poll and now the fishermen hope he'll be turned out.'

'Well,' I said, 'he doesn't seem to have much chance.'

'You see, Sir, the people who are backing him are powerful people, they're fish-buyers, and some of the fishermen get their nets from them. Then he's backed up by what they call the Christians, the people who are against us poor innkeepers.'

- Oho, I thought, now I'm getting it. 'Is he a Nonconformist?' I asked.

'Oh yes, Sir, he's not a churchman' – in a tone of great contempt.

Then I found his backers were also Nonconformists, that they had made their own money, were very kind to sober men, but very hard on drunkards; and that several pubs had been annoyed by them. I was interested to find that, in the common parlance of church-people 'Christian' is the antithesis to 'Churchman'. I found further from the Landlady that these monsters in human shape actually proposed a new drainage scheme and a new water supply, although the rates were already dreadfully high.

'How high?' I asked.

'I couldn't say, Sir, but I know they're dreadfully high.'

The Doctor was not elected; but I was consoled to learn that the parson had also been turned out. – These little distractions keep me from having a moment's boredom. ...

> *Yours affectionately*
> *Bertrand Russell*

Castle Howard
York
August 15, 1904

My dear Lucy

... This place is a large 18th century house, embodying family pride and the worship of reason in equal measure. It is a family party – the Murrays, whom you know; Cecilia and Roberts – she, devoted to all her family, especially her mother, placid usually, but capable of violent sudden rage, in which she utters magnificent invective, though at all other times she is a fat good-humoured saint and (oddly enough)

a Christian; Roberts (her husband) tall, thin, nervous, quivering like
a poplar in the wind, an idealist disillusioned and turned opportunist;
Oliver Howard, lately back from Nigeria, where he administered
brilliantly a lately-conquered district, containing a town of 500,000
inhabitants, in which he was almost the only white man. He is smart,
thin, delicate, conventional, with a soft manner concealing an oriental
cruelty and power of fury, of which his mother is the occasion and his
wife the victim – at least probably in the future. He is very beautiful
and his wife is very pretty: both are Christians; she too is very smart
and very conventional, but she has real good nature, and is on the
whole likeable. They are very openly affectionate; in him, one dimly
feels in the background the kind of jealousy that would lead to murder
if it saw cause. Being very like his mother in character, he differs from
her in every opinion, and relations are painfully strained. – Then there
is Dorothy, who seems to me just like my grandmother Stanley – crude,
sometimes cruel, plucky, very honourable, and full of instinctive
vitality and healthy animalism, oddly overlaid with her mother's
principles. Last there is Leif Jones,[1] Lady Carlisle's private secretary,
an infinitely lovable man: he does everything for everybody, has sunk
his own career, his own desires, the hope of a private life of any
personal kind: and all the family take him as a matter of course, and
no more expect him to make demands than they expect the stones to
call out for food.

Lady Carlisle conducts conversation in a way which makes it a game
of skill played for high stakes. It is always argument, in which, with
consummate art, she ignores relevancy and changes the issue until she
has the advantage, and then she charges down and scatters the enemy
like chaff before the wind. A large proportion of her remarks are
designed to cause pain to someone who has shown independence or
given ground for one of the thousand forms of jealousy. She has the
faults of Napoleonic women, with less mendacity and more deliberate
cruelty than in the case you know best, but with a desire to cause
quarrels and part friends which is really terrible. On the other hand,
she has really great public spirit, and devotes time and money to really
important objects. She has a just sense of values, and a kind of high-
mindedness – a most mixed and interesting character . . .

> *Yours affectionately*
> *Bertrand Russell*

Audierne, Finistère
October 3, 1904

My dear Lucy

This is not a real letter, but only a counter-irritant to my last. As

[1] Later Lord Rhayader.

soon as I got away I began to see things in their true proportions, and to be no longer oppressed by the complication of things. But on the whole, I think I shall have to avoid growing intimate with people I don't respect, or trying to help them: it seems to be a job for which I am not fitted.

Brittany is quite wonderful – it has a great deal of purely rural beauty, woods and streams and endless orchards of big red apples, scenting all the air; and besides all this, it has a combination of the beauties of Devonshire and Cornwall. We have been walking lately round the S.W. coast, places where the Atlantic rules as God. Every tiny village has a huge Gothic church, usually very beautiful; many churches stand quite by themselves, facing the sea as relics of ancient courage. At first I wondered how anyone could believe in God in the presence of something so much greater and more powerful as the sea; but very soon, the inhumanity and cruelty of the sea became so oppressive that I saw how God belongs to the human world, and is, in their minds, the Captain of an army in which they are the soldiers: God is the most vigorous assertion that the world is not all omnipotent Matter. And so the fishermen became and have remained the most religious population in the world. It is a strange, desolate, wind-swept region, where long ago great towns flourished, where Iseult of Brittany lived in a castle over the sea, and where ancient legends seem far more real than anything in the life of the present. The very children are old: they do not play or shout, like other children: they sit still, with folded hands and faces of weary resignation, waiting for the sorrows that time is sure to bring. The men are filled with melancholy; but they escape from it by drink. I have never imagined a population so utterly drunken; in every village we have seen men reeling into the gutter. Ordinary days here are as bad as Bank Holiday with us – except that I don't think the women drink much.

A very curious contrast to the Bretons was the proprietor of the last Inn we stayed at, at a place called St Guénolé, near the Pointe de Penmarc'h. He was tall and very erect, with a magnificent black beard, and quick, vigorous dramatic movements. We were wet, so we sat in the kitchen, where he was cooking the dinner with an energy and delight in his work which I have never seen surpassed. We soon found that he was a Parisian, that he had a sister married to a hotel-keeper in Lancaster, & another in the service of Lord Gerard (!) in Egypt; that he had been cook on a Far-Eastern liner, & that he had now at last saved up enough capital to start on a venture of his own. He told us that he was *really* a sculptor, not a cook, & that in winter, when no guests come, he devotes his time to statuary. He had a voice that would easily have filled the Albert Hall, & he used it as a dinner-gong. Indeed, at all sorts of times, from sheer good spirits, he would bellow some joke or some command through the Hotel, so that all the walls resounded. His cooking, needless to say, was perfect. We saw a poor fisherman come in & sell sardines to him for our dinner; a vast number were purchased for threepence, which, as far as I could discover, the miserable wretch immediately spent in the bar.

> *Yours affectionately*
> *Bertrand Russell*

4 Ralston Street
Tite Street, S.W.
February 8, 1905

My dear Lucy

... Now that we are back in Chelsea, I often wish you too were here again, and when I walk the Battersea Park round, I miss you very much. There is much too much of the Atlantic. This year, when I go walks, it is usually with MacCarthy, whom I find wonderfully soothing and restful, full of kindly humour, which makes the world seem gay. George Trevelyan also I walk with; but he, though he maintains that the world is better than I think, maintains it with an air of settled gloom, by comparison with which my jokes against optimism seem full of the joy of life! His wife, by the way, is one of the most simply lovable people I have ever met. She has not much to say, and I often find the talk flagging when I am with her; but she is filled full of generous loves and friendships, and honest and sincere in a very rare degree. She is ignorant of the world, as everyone is who has met with nothing but kindness and good fortune: she instinctively expects that everybody she meets will be nice. This gives her the pathos of very young people, and makes one long to keep sorrows away from her, well as one may know that that is impossible. I have liked and respected other people more, with almost no desire to shield them from pain; but towards her I feel as one does towards a child.

We see a great many people now that we are in town. Last night we dined at the Sidney Webbs, to meet

Lion Phillimore

Mackinder, whom you doubtless remember – the head Beast of the School of Economics

Granville Barker, the young and beautiful actor, who has been producing Shaw's and Murray's plays

Sir Oliver Lodge, Scientist and Spiritualist

Arthur Balfour; and, greatest of all,

Werner, of Werner Beit and Co, the chief of all the South African millionaires; a fat, good-natured, eupeptic German with an equally fat gold watch-chain and a strong German accent (characteristic of all the finest types of British Imperialists), bearing very lightly the load of blood, of nations destroyed and hatreds generated, of Chinese slavery and English corruption, which, by all the old rules, ought to weigh upon him like a cope of lead. It was an amusing occasion. When everyone had come except Balfour and Werner, Mrs Webb observed that we should see which of them thought himself the bigger swell, by which came last. Sure enough, Werner came last; for though Balfour governs the Empire, Werner governs Balfour. Balfour was most agreeable, absolutely free from the slightest sign of feeling himself a personage, sympathetic, anxious to listen rather than to talk. He puts his finger in his mouth, with the air of a small child deep in thought. He is quite obviously weak, obviously without strong feelings, apparently kindly, and not apparently able; at least I saw nothing I should have recognised as showing ability, except his tact, which probably is the main cause of his success. He professed not to know whether the Government would last another fortnight; said he could not arrange to see Shaw's play, for fear of a General Election intervening. All this I took to be blarney. He drew me out about Moore's philosophy, and then listened to a lecture from Mrs Webb on 'the first principles of Government, for beginners'; at least that would have been an appropriate title for her dinner-table discourse.

Sir Oliver Lodge, though I had a prejudice against him on account of theological differences, struck me as delightful: calm, philosophic, and disinterested. Poor Mackinder made a bee-line for Balfour, but got landed with me, much to my amusement. It was a sore trial to his politeness, from which he extricated himself indifferently.[1]

I am not working now, but merely seeing people and enjoying myself. I have fits of depression at times, but they don't last long. I have had a fair share of other people's tragedies lately; some in which intimate friends have behaved badly, which is always painful. Others, which vex me almost more, I only suspect and have to watch their disastrous effects in total impotence. Who was the heartless fool who said that loving other people made one happy? Still, with all its pains, it does help to make life tolerable. . . .

> *Yours affectionately*
> *Bertrand Russell*

> Lower Copse
> Bagley Wood, Oxford
> June 13, 1905

My dear Lucy

  . . . I did not remember (if I ever knew) that the *Spectator* had spoken of my writing; your allusion makes me curious to know what it said. I have not done any more of that sort of writing, but I have

[1] This dinner is also described by Mrs Webb in *Our Partnership*, p. 300.

been getting on very well with my work. For a long time I have been at intervals debating this conundrum: if two names or descriptions apply to the same object, whatever is true of the one is true of the other. Now George the Fourth wished to know whether Scott was the author of *Waverley*; and Scott was as a matter of fact the same person as the author of *Waverley*. Hence, putting 'Scott' in the place of 'the author of *Waverley*', we find that George the Fourth wished to know whether Scott was Scott, which implies more interest in the Laws of Thought than was possible for the First Gentleman of Europe. This little puzzle was quite hard to solve; the solution, which I have now found, throws a flood of light on the foundations of mathematics and on the whole problem of the relation of thought to things. It is a great thing to find a puzzle; because, so long as it is puzzling one knows one has not got to the bottom of things. I have hopes that I shall never again as long as I live have such difficult work as I had last year, and the year before; certainly this year, so far, my work has not been nearly so hard, and I have been reaping the harvest of previous work.

This place is a very great success. The house is pretty and comfortable, my study is so palatial that I am almost ashamed of it, and the country round has the typical English charm of fields and meadows and broad open views, with Oxford and the river besides. Alys seems to like the place thoroughly, and has been on the whole much better than in town. I find it a great advantage being in touch with Oxford people – it is easier to keep alive my interest in work when I can bring it into some relation with human interests. I have had to take myself in hand rather severely, and being here has made it much more feasible. . . .

Do write to me again as soon as you can, and tell me about yourself and also about Helen. Your letters are always a great pleasure to me. Just now I am in the middle of a fit of work; but though I shall do my best, it is likely to stop soon. Life would be delightfully simple if one could enjoy all one's duties, as some people do; it would be simpler than it is if one always did the duties one doesn't enjoy. Failing both, it is complicated to a frightful extent. But I live in hopes of becoming middle-aged, which, they tell me, makes everything easy.

> *Yours affectionately*
> *Bertrand Russell*

14 Barton Street
Westminster
August 3, 1905

My dear Lucy

You will probably have heard, by the time this reaches you, of the disaster which has befallen us all. Theodore Davies, bathing alone in a pool near Kirkby Lonsdale, was drowned; presumably by hitting his head against a rock in diving, and so getting stunned. It is a loss, to very many, which we shall feel as long as we live; and the loss to the public is beyond anything one can possibly estimate. But all other losses seem as nothing compared to Crompton's. They had been always together, they shared everything, and Theodore was as careful of Crompton and as tender with him as any mother could have been. Crompton bears it with wonderful courage; his mind endures it, but I doubt whether his body will. I am here to do what I can for him – there is little enough except to sit in silence with him and suffer as he suffers. As soon as he can get away, I am going abroad with him. This is Miss Sheepshanks's house; she and the other inmates are all away, and she has kindly lent it to me. Alys was very much upset by the news. When we got it, we were just starting for Ireland, to stay with the Monteagles. It seemed best for her not to be alone, so I went over with her, and then came back here. She will be there another 10 days or more. They are kind good people, who will take care of her. Crompton's sorrow is crushing, and I hardly know how to bear it. But it is a comfort to feel able to be of some help to him. Theodore had very many devoted friends, and all have done everything they could; their sympathy has pulled Crompton through the first shock, but there is a long anxious time to come.

... I have written an article[1] on George IV for '*Mind*', which will appear in due course; there you will find the 'answer' ...

I am too tired to write more now. I wanted to write to you about Theodore, but I have no thoughts for other things.

Yours affectionately
Bertrand Russell

Rozeldene, Grayshott
Haslemere, Surrey
September 3, 1905

My dear Lucy

Thank you very much for your kind letter. Crompton and I went to France for a fortnight, which was all the holiday he could get. I think it did him good. We stayed first with the Frys and then with the Whiteheads. I have not seen him since we got home 10 days ago. But I feel good hopes that he will avoid a complete collapse.

It has been, in a less degree, a rather terrible time for me too. It made everything seem uncertain and subject to chance, so that it was hard to keep any calm about all the goods whose loss one fears. And it brought up, as misfortunes do, all the memories of buried griefs which one had resolved to be done with. One after another, they burst

[1] The title was 'On Denoting'.

their tombs, and wailed in the desert spaces of one's mind. And the case was one which admitted of no philosophy at all – I could not see that there was anything to be said in mitigation of the disaster. But I have got myself in hand now, and tomorrow I go back to work, after a week's tour by myself. This Sunday I am with my Aunt Agatha. We talk of long-ago things, of people who are dead and old-world memories – it is very soothing. It is odd how family feeling is stirred by anything that makes one feel the universe one's enemy. . . .

> *Yours affectionately*
> *Bertrand Russell*

Lower Copse
Bagley Wood, Oxford
November 10, 1905

My dear Lucy

It was a great pleasure to hear from you again. I think letters *are* more important than one is apt to realise. If one doesn't write, one's doings and one's general state of mind cease to be known, and when a time comes for explaining, there are so many preliminaries that the task seems impossible in writing. So I do hope you will not be deterred by the fear of many words – it really doesn't do to wait till you are *in extremis*. What you say about Alys and 'my right living' rather makes me feel that there is something wrong – too much profession and talk about virtue; for I certainly know many people who live better lives than I do, and are more able to accomplish long and difficult duties without any moments of weakness. Only they make less fuss about it, and people do not know how difficult the duties are that they perform in silence.

I am grateful to you for writing about Helen. I understand very well the renewal of pain that comes when you see her, and the dread of entering the real life, with its tortures, after the numbness of routine. I am very sorry that it is still so bad. I wonder, though, whether any but trivial people could really find it otherwise. Life *is* a burden if those one loves best have others who come first, if there is no corner in the world where one's loneliness is at an end. I hardly know how it can be otherwise. Your problem is to face this with courage, and yet retain as much as possible of what is important to you. It would be easier to renounce everything once for all, and kill one's chief affection. But that leads to hardness, and in the long run to cruelty, the cruelty of the ascetic. The other course has its disadvantages too: it is physically and mentally exhausting, it destroys peace of mind, it keeps one's thoughts absorbed with the question of how much that one values one can hope to rescue without undue encroachment on the territory of others. It is horribly difficult. There is a temptation to let one's real life become wholly one of memory and imagination, where duty and facts do not fetter one, and to let one's present intercourse be a mere shadow and unreality; this has the advantage that it keeps the past unsmirched.

But to come to more practical things. I believe when one is not first in a person's life, it is necessary, however difficult, to make one's feelings towards that person purely receptive and passive. I mean, that one should not have an opinion about what such a person should do, unless one is asked; that one should watch their moods, and make oneself an echo, responding with affection in the measure in which it is given, repressing whatever goes further, ready to feel that one has no rights, and that whatever one gets is so much to the good. This must be, for example, the attitude of a good mother to a married son. Difficult as it is, it is a situation which is normal in the life of the affections, and a duty which one has to learn to perform without spiritual death. . . .

I have been seeing a good deal of Crompton Davies. . . . He is and will remain very profoundly unhappy, and I do not think that marriage or anything will heal the wound. But he is brave, and to the world he makes a good show. To his friends he is lovable in a very rare degree.

The Japanese alliance seems to me excellent – I am glad England should be ready to recognise the yellow man as a civilised being, and not wholly sorry at the quarrel with Australia which this recognition entails. Balfour's government has ceased to do any harm, having grown impotent. The general opinion is that Balfour will resign in February, trying to force the Liberals to take office before dissolving. Whatever happens, the Liberals are almost certain of an overwhelming majority in the next Parliament.

I am interested to hear that I have a disciple at Bryn Mawr. Two young men, Huntingdon at Harvard and Veblen at Princeton, have written works in which they make pleasing references to me. The latter, at least, is brilliantly able. . . .

Alys told me to say she had not time to write by this Saturday's mail – she is occupied with alternations of visitors and meetings, and rather tired. On the whole, however, she has been very well lately. She asked me also to tell you about Forster's 'Where angels fear to tread' – it seems to me a clever story, with a good deal of real merit, but too farcical in parts, and too sentimental at the end. He is one of our Cambridge set; his age, I suppose, about 26. He seems certainly to have talent.

Dickinson's new book is out, *A Modern Symposium*. It is quite excellent. He does the Tories with more sympathy than the Liberals, but all except Gladstone and the biologist are done with much sympathy. Besides Gladstone, there are Disraeli, Henry Sidgwick, and various private friends – Bob Trevelyan, Ferdinand Schiller (Audubon), a compound of Berenson and Santayana, Sidney Webb, and some characters who are nobody in particular. You must certainly read it.

My work has gone very well this summer, in spite of a long interruption caused by Theodore's death. I have made more solid and permanent progress than I usually do. But the end of Volume II is as far off as ever – the task grows and grows. For the rest, I have been much occupied with other people's tragedies – some unusually painful ones have come in my way lately. What rather adds to the oppression is the impossibility of speaking of them – Still, I could hardly endure life if I were not on those terms with people that make me necessarily share their sorrows; and if the sorrows exist, I would always rather know them than not. Only I feel increasingly helpless before misfortune; I used to be able to speak encouraging words, but now I feel too weary, and have too little faith in any remedy except endurance.

> *Yours affectionately*
> *Bertrand Russell*

> Lower Copse
> Bagley Wood, Oxford
> January 1, 1906

My dear Lucy

I am very glad your sense of values prevailed over your Puritan instinct, and I am sure your sense of values was right. Letters are important; I care about getting letters from you, and it is the only way not to meet as strangers when people only meet at intervals of some years. And generally, I am sure you are right not to give all your best hours to routine; people who do that infallibly become engrossed in routine, by which they both lose personally and do the routine less well. In this, at least, I practise what I preach: I spent the first hour and a half of the new year in an argument about ethics, with young Arthur Dakyns, who is supposed to be my only disciple up here, but is a very restive disciple, always going after the false gods of the Hegelians. (We were staying with his people at Haslemere.) His father is a delightful man, with a gift of friendliness and of generous admirations that I have seldom seen equalled; and Arthur has inherited a great deal of his father's charm. He is the only person up here (except the Murrays) that I feel as a real friend – the rest are rather alien, so far as I know them. ...

I am looking forward very much indeed to your visit, and I do hope nothing will happen to prevent it. I shall not be very busy at that time, as I shall have been working continuously all the spring. I am afraid you will find me grown more middle-aged, and with less power of throwing off the point of view of the daily round. The efforts of life and of work are great, and in the long run they tend to subdue one's spirit through sheer weariness. I get more and more into the way of filling my mind with the thoughts of what I have to do day by day, to the exclusion of things that have more real importance. It is perhaps inevitable, but it is a pity, and I feel it makes one a duller person. However, it suits work amazingly well. My work during 1905 was certainly better in quality and quantity than any I have done in a year before, unless perhaps in 1900. The difficulty which I came upon in 1901, and was worrying over all the time you were in Europe, has come out at last, completely and finally, so far as I can judge. It all came from considering whether the King of France is bald – a question which I decided in the same article in which I proved that George IV was interested in the Law of Identity. The result of this is that Whitehead and I expect to have a comparatively easy time from now to the publication of our book, which we may hope will happen within four or five years. Lately I have been working 10 hours a day, living in a dream, realising the actual world only dimly through a mist. Having to go first to my Aunt Agatha on Hindhead, then to the Dakyns's, I woke up suddenly from the dream; but now I must go back into it, until we go abroad with old Mr Ll. Davies and his daughter (on the 25th January). . . .

I found your kind present to Alys on my return today, but she has not had it yet, as she has gone to West Ham to canvass for Masterman. He is not the man I should have chosen, but she promised long ago, that she would help him when the election came on. The political outlook is good on the whole. The Liberals have done wisely, as well as rightly, in stopping the S. African Slave Trade in Chinamen. Campbell-Bannerman caused a flutter by declaring more or less for Home Rule; but today Redmond and the Duke of Devonshire both advise electors to vote Liberal, so Campbell-Bannerman has caught the Home Rule vote without losing the Free Trade Unionist vote. Exactly the opposite might just as well have happened, so it is a stroke of luck. But by the time you get this letter, the results will be coming in. The Cabinet is excellent. I am very glad John Burns is in it. But it may go to pieces later on the Irish question. However, I hope not. I breathe more freely every moment owing to those soundrels being no longer in office; but I wish I knew what majority we shall get. The question is: Will the Liberals be independent of the Irish ? It is bound to be a near thing one way or other.

I hope you will enjoy Dickinson's *Modern Symposium*. You will recognise Bob Trevylan and Sidney Webb. I like the book immensely.

Do write again soon. Your letters are a great pleasure to me.

Yours affectionately
Bertrand Russell

14 Barton Street
Westminster
February 18, 1906

My dear Lucy

... I have myself been horribly depressed lately. Margaret Davies is still in the depths of unhappiness, and needs a great deal of silent sympathy, which is much more tiring than the sort one can express. And I am as usual oppressed by a good many anxieties that I cannot speak about. I am looking forward to work, which is a refuge. But I tired myself out before starting for abroad, and I feel still rather slack, so I may find I need more holiday. Sometimes I think I should like never to stop work, if only I had the strength of body. Mathematics is a haven of peace without which I don't know how I should get on. So I am hardly the person to tell you how to avoid depression; because I can only give advice which I do not myself find effective. I have, however, two things which really make me happier – one is the result of the general election, which does mean that for the next few years at least public affairs in England will be more or less what one could wish; the other, more personal, is that my work has prospered amazingly, and that I have solved the most difficult problems I had to deal with, so that I have a prospect of some years of easy and rapid progress. I stayed a few days in Paris, and they got up a dinner of philosophers and mathematicians for me, which I found most agreeable – it was interesting to meet the people, and was sweet incense to my self-esteem. I was interested to observe, on a review of noses, that they were mostly Jews. They seemed most civilised people, with great public spirit and intense devotion to learning. One of them said he had read an English poem called 'le vieux matelot'; I couldn't think who had written anything called 'the old sailor' and began to think there might be something by Hood of that name, when the truth flashed upon me. I also saw Miss Minturn and Santayana in Paris, which I enjoyed. – I go back to Oxford the end of this week. Alys has been very well, not at all exhausted by her labours in West Ham. I shall hope for another letter from you soon.

Yours affectionately
Bertrand Russell

Providence House
Clovelly, near Bideford
April 22, 1906

My dear Lucy

... I am down here in absolute solitude for the best part of 2 months, and find it so far a very great success. The country is beautiful, beyond belief – tangled sleeping-beauty sort of woods, sloping steep down to the sea, and little valleys full of ferns and mosses and wild flowers of innumerable kinds. I take a long walk every afternoon, and all the rest of the day and evening I work, except at meals, when I re-read *War and Peace*, which I expect will last me most of my time. On my walks I stop and read little bits of Walton's *Lives*, or something else that is exquisite. My work goes ahead at a tremendous pace, and I get intense delight from it.[1] Being alone, I escape oppression of more things to think out, and more complicated decisions to make, than I have energy to accomplish; and so I am contented, and find enough to occupy me in work, and enough vigour to make work a pleasure instead of a torment.

As for fame, which you speak of, I have no consciousness of possessing it – certainly at Oxford they regard me as a conceited and soulless formalist. But I do not now care greatly what other people think of my work. I did care, until I had enough confidence that it was worth doing to be independent of praise. Now it gives me rather less pleasure than a fine day. I feel better able than anyone else to judge what my work is worth; besides, praise from the learned public is necessarily for things written some time ago, which probably now seem to me so full of imperfections that I hardly like to remember them. Work, when it goes well, is in itself a great delight; and after any considerable achievement I look back at it with the sort of placid satisfaction one has after climbing a mountain. What is absolutely vital to me is the self-respect I get from work – when (as often) I have done something for which I feel remorse, work restores me to a belief that it is better I should exist than not exist. And another thing I greatly value is the kind of communion with past and future discoverers. I often have imaginary conversations with Leibniz, in which I tell him how fruitful his ideas have proved, and how much more beautiful the result is than he could have foreseen; and in moments of self-confidence, I imagine students hereafter having similar thoughts about me. There is a 'communion of philosophers' as well as a 'communion of saints', and it is largely that that keeps me from feeling lonely.

Well, this disquisition shows how self-absorbed one grows when one is alone! . . .

I am glad your country girl has married the painter. All's well that ends well; which is the epitaph I should put on my tombstone if I were the last man left alive.

I am on the whole satisfied with Birrell. The Government have made some bad mistakes, but seem satisfactory in the main.

Write again when you can, and address here.

> *Yours affectionately*
> Bertrand Russell

[1] It turned out to be all nonsense.

To Lowes Dickinson:

Little Buckland
Nr. Broadway, Wors.
Aug. 2, '02

Dear Goldie

... This neighbourhood, which I didn't know before, is very charming; all the villages are built of a very good stone, and most of the houses are Jacobean or older. There is a great plain full of willows, into which the sun sets, and on the other side high hills. Our lodgings are in an old and very picturesque farm house. The place is bracing, and I have been getting through eight or nine hours of work a day, which has left me stupid at the end of it. My book, and Moore's too probably, will be out some time in the winter. The proofs come occasionally, and seem to me very worthless; I have a poor opinion of the stuff when I think of what it ought to be. Whitehead turned up in College, but I got little of his society, as he was terribly busy with exam-papers. It is a funny arrangement, by which the remuneration of dons is inversely proportional to the value of their work. I wish something better could be devised. – It would be most agreeable to live in Cambridge, and I daresay I shall do so some day; but at present it is out of the question. However, we shall be in town after September 15 for six months; I hope you will visit us during your weekly excursions to that haunt of purposeless activity and foolish locomotion. When I see people who desire money or fame or power, I find it hard to imagine what must be the emotional emptiness of their lives, that can leave room for such trivial things.

> *Yours ever*
> *Bertrand Russell*

Address: Friday's Hill
        Haslemere

Little Buckland
Nr. Broadway, Wors.
26 August, 1902

Dear Goldie

I was very glad of your letter, and I agree with all you said about the *Paradiso*, though it is many years since I read it. I feel also very strongly what you say about Italy and the North, though at bottom I disagree with you. I do not think, to begin with, that Dante can count as an Italian; Italy begins with the Renaissance, and the mediaeval mind is international. But there is to me about Italy a quality which the rest of Europe had in the 18th century, a complete lack of mystery. Sunshine is very agreeable, but fogs and mists have effects which sunshine can never attain to. Seriously, the unmystical, rationalistic view of life seems to me to omit all that is most important and most beautiful. It is true that among unmystical people there is no truth unperceived, which the mystic might reveal; but mysticism creates the truth it believes in, by the way in which it feels the fundamental facts – the helplessness of man before Time and Death, and the strange depths of feeling which lie dormant until some one of the Gods of life calls for our worship. Religion and art both, it seems to me, are attempts to humanise the universe – beginning, no doubt, with the humanising of man. If some of the stubborn facts refuse to leave one's consciousness, a religion or an art cannot appeal to one fully unless it takes account of those facts. And so all religion becomes an achievement, a victory, an assurance that although man may be powerless, his ideals are not so. The more facts a religion takes account of, the greater is its victory, and that is why thin religions appeal to Puritan temperaments. I should myself value a religion in proportion to its austerity – if it is not austere, it seems a mere childish toy, which the first touch of the real Gods would dispel. But I fear that, however austere, any religion must be less austere than the truth. And yet I could not bear to lose from the world a certain awed solemnity, a certain stern seriousness – for the mere fact of life and death, of desire and hope and aspiration and love in a world of matter which knows nothing of good and bad, which destroys carelessly the things it has produced by accident, in spite of all the passionate devotion that we may give – all this is not sunshine, or any peaceful landscapes seen through limpid air; yet life has the power to brand these things into one's soul so that all else seems triviality and vain babble. To have endowed only one minute portion of the universe with the knowledge and love of good, and to have made that portion the plaything of vast irresistible irrational forces, is a cruel jest on the part of God or Fate. The best Gospel, I suppose, is the Stoic one; yet even that is too optimistic, for matter can at any moment destroy our love of virtue.

After all this moping, you will be confirmed in your love of the South; and indeed I feel it too, but as a longing to have done with the burden of a serious life. 'Ye know, my friends, with what a gay carouse' – and no doubt there is much to be said for the Daughter of the Vine, as for any other of Satan's many forms. To Hell with unity, and artistic serenity, and the insight that perceives the good in other people's Pain – it sickens me. (And yet I know there is truth in it.)

Yes, one must learn to live in the Past, and so to dominate it that it is not a disquieting ghost or a horrible gibbering spectre stalking through the vast bare halls that once were full of life, but a gentle soothing companion, reminding one of the possibility of good things, and rebuking cynicism and cruelty – but those are temptations which I imagine you do not suffer from. For my part, I do not even wish to live rather with eternal things, though I often give them lip-service; but in my heart I believe that the best things are those that are fragile and temporary, and I find a magic in the Past which eternity cannot possess. Besides, nothing is more eternal than the Past – the present and future are still subject to Time, but the Past has escaped into immortality – Time has done his worst, and it yet lives.

I don't wonder you hate taking up your routine again. After one has had liberty of mind, and allowed one's thoughts and emotions to grow and expand, it is horrible to go back to prison, and enclose all feelings within the miserable compass of the prudent and desirable and practically useful – Pah! – But all good things must be left to the wicked – even virtue, which only remains spotless if it is kept under a glass case, for ornament and not for use.

I have been working nine hours a day until yesterday, living in a dream, thinking only of space; today I begin to realise the things that are in it, and on the whole they do not seem to me an improvement. But I hope we shall see you in town.

Yours ever
Bertrand Russell

Churt, Farnham
July 16, 1903

Dear Goldie

I enclose the translation, but I rather wish you would get someone with a better knowledge of French to look it over, as my French is not at all correct. And by the way, I expect *mémoire* would be better than *article*, but I am not sure.

I am glad you are writing on Religion. It is quite time to have things said that all of us know, but that are not generally known. It seems to me that our attitude on religious subjects is one which we ought as far as possible to preach, and which is not the same as that of any of the well-known opponents of Christianity. There is the Voltaire tradition, which makes fun of the whole thing from a common-sense, semi-historical, semi-literary point of view; this of course, is hopelessly inadequate, because it only gets hold of the accidents and excrescences of historical systems. Then there is the scientific, Darwin–Huxley attitude, which seems to me perfectly true, and quite fatal, if rightly carried out, to all the usual arguments for religion. But it is too external, too coldly critical, too remote from the emotions; moreover, it cannot get to the root of the matter without the help of philosophy. Then there are the philosophers, like Bradley, who keep a shadow of religion, too little for comfort, but quite enough to ruin their systems intellectually. But what we have to do, and what privately we do do, is to treat the religious instinct with profound respect, but to insist that there is no shred or particle of truth in any of the metaphysics it has suggested: to palliate this by trying to bring out the beauty of the world and of life, so far as it exists, and above all to insist upon preserving the seriousness of the religious attitude and its habit of asking ultimate questions. And if good lives are the best thing we know, the loss of religion gives new scope for courage and fortitude, and so may make good lives better than any that there was room for while religion afforded a drug in misfortune.

And often I feel that religion, like the sun, has extinguished the stars of less brilliancy but not less beauty, which shine upon us out of the darkness of a godless universe. The splendour of human life, I feel sure, is greater to those who are not dazzled by the divine radiance; and human comradeship seems to grow more intimate and more tender from the sense that we are all exiles on an inhospitable shore.

> *Yours ever*
> B. Russell

> Churt, Farnham
> July 19, 1903

Dear Goldie

Many thanks for sending me the three articles on Religion: they strike me as exceedingly good, and as saying things that much need saying. All your eloquent passages seem to me very successful; and the parable at the end I like quite immensely. I enclose a few remarks on some quite tiny points that struck me in reading – mostly verbal points.

The attack on Ecclesiasticism is, I think, much needed; you if anything underestimate, I should say, the danger of Ecclesiasticism in this country. Whenever I happen to meet Beatrice Creighton I feel the danger profoundly; and she illustrates one of the worst points from a practical point of view, that even when a man belonging to an ecclesiastical system happens to be broad-minded and liberal himself, he takes care to avoid such a state of mind in others whom he can influence.

Why should you suppose I think it foolish to wish to see the people one is fond of? What else is there to make life tolerable? We stand on the shore of an ocean, crying to the night and the emptiness; sometimes a voice answers out of the darkness. But it is a voice of one drowning; and in a moment the silence returns. The world seems to me quite dreadful; the unhappiness of most people is very great, and I often wonder how they all endure it. To know people well is to know their tragedy: it is usually the central thing about which their lives are built. And I suppose if they did not live most of the time in the things of the moment, they would not be able to go on.

> *Yours ever*
> B. Russell

Ivy Lodge
Tilford, Farnham
July 20, 1904

Dear Goldie

Yes, I think you would do well to republish your articles on Religion in a book. It is hard to say what one gathers from them in a constructive way, yet there certainly is something. I think it is chiefly, in the end, that one becomes persuaded of the truth of the passage you quote from Maeterlinck, i.e. that the emotion with which we contemplate the world may be religious, even if we have no definite theological beliefs. (Note that if Maeterlinck were not in French, he would be saying the same as In Memoriam, 'there lives more faith, etc.' This remark is linguistic.) You are likely to convince a certain number of people that the absence of a creed is no reason for not thinking in a religious way; and this is useful both to the person who insists on a creed in order to save his religious life, and to the person who ceases to think seriously because he has lost his creed.

Schiller, in his article, struck me as a pathetic fool, who had seized on Pragmatism as the drowning man's straw. I agree with you wholly that Philosophy cannot give religion, or indeed anything of more than intellectual interest. It seems to me increasingly that what gives one the beliefs by which one lives is of the nature of experience: it is a sudden realisation, or perhaps a gradual one, of ethical values which one had formerly doubted or taken on trust; and this realisation seems to be caused, as a rule, by a situation containing the things one realises to be good or bad. But although I do not think philosophy itself will give anything of human interest, I think a philosophical training enables one to get richer experiences, and to make more use of those that one does get. And I do not altogether wish mankind to become too firmly persuaded that there is no road from philosophy to religion, because I think the endeavour to find one is very useful, if only it does not destroy candour.

What is valuable in Tolstoi, to my mind, is his power of right ethical judgments, and his perception of concrete facts; his theorisings are of course worthless. It is the greatest misfortune to the human race that he has so little power of reasoning.

I have never read Lady Welby's writings, but she sent me some remarks on my book, from which I judged that she is interested in a good many questions that interest me. I doubt very much, all the same, how much she understood my book. I know too little of her to know whether I should understand her or not.

I think Shaw, on the whole, is more bounder than genius; and though of course I admit him to be 'forcible', I don't admit him to be 'moral'. I think envy plays a part in his philosophy in this sense, that if he allowed himself to admit the goodness of things which he lacks and others possess, he would feel such intolerable envy that he would find life unendurable. Also he hates self-control, and makes up theories with a view to proving that self-control is pernicious. I couldn't get on with Man and Superman: it disgusted me. I don't think he is a soul in Hell dancing on red-hot iron. I think his Hell is merely diseased vanity and a morbid fear of being laughed at.

Berenson is here. I shall be very curious to see what you say on Music. I have never made up my mind whether, if I were founding the Republic, I should admit Wagner or even Beethoven; but not because I do *not* like them.

I am working hard at Vol. II.[1] When it goes well, it is an intense delight, when I get stuck, it is equally intense torture.

> *Yours always*
> *Bertrand Russell*

> Ivy Lodge
> Tilford, Farnham
> Sep. 22, 1904

Dear Goldie

Thanks for sending me the enclosed, which I have read with interest. I think you state your position clearly and very well. It is not a position that I can myself agree with. I agree that 'faith in some form or other seems to be an almost necessary condition, if not of life, yet of the most fruitful and noble life'. But I do not agree that faith 'can be legitimate so long as it occupies a region not yet conquered by knowledge'. You admit that it is wrong to say: 'I believe, though truth testify against me.' I should go further, and hold it is wrong to say: 'I believe, though truth do not testify in my favour.' To my mind, truthfulness demands as imperatively that we should doubt what is doubtful as that we should disbelieve what is false. But here and in all arguments about beliefs for which there is no evidence, it is necessary to distinguish propositions which may be fairly allowed to be self-evident, and which therefore afford the basis of indirect evidence, from such as ought to have proofs if they are to be accepted. This is a difficult business, and probably can't be done exactly. As for faith, I hold (a) that there are certain propositions, an honest belief in which, apart from the badness of believing what is false, greatly improves the believer, (b) that many of these very propositions are false. But I think that faith has a legitimate sphere in the realm of ethical judgments, since these are of the sort that ought to be self-evident, and ought not to require proof. For practice, it seems to me that a very high degree of the utility of faith can be got by believing

[1] Which became *Principia Mathematica*.

passionately in the goodness of certain things which are good, and which, in a greater or less degree, our actions are capable of creating. I admit that the love of God, if there were a God, would make it possible for human beings to be better than is possible in a Godless world. But I think the ethical faith which *is* warranted yields *most* of what is necessary to the highest life conceivable, and all that is necessary to the highest life that is possible. Like every religion, it contains ethical judgments and judgments of fact, the latter asserting that our actions make a difference, though perhaps a small one, to the ethical value of the universe. I find this enough faith to live by, and I consider it warranted by knowledge; but anything more seems to me more or less *untruthful*, though not demonstrably *untrue*.

Let me know what you would reply. Address here, though I shall be away. I am going tomorrow to Brittany with Theodore for a fortnight. I hope your sciatica is better.

> Yours ever
> B. Russell

> I Tatti,
> Settignano, Florence
> March 22, 1903

Dear Bertie

I have read your essay three times, and liked it better and better. Perhaps the most flattering appreciation to be given of it is that the whole is neither out of tune with nor unworthy of the two splendid passages you wrote here – I see no objection to this essay form. I have no wish of my own with regard to the shape your writing is to take. I am eager that you shall express yourself sooner or later, and meanwhile you must write and write until you begin to feel that you are saying what you want to say, in the way that you wish others to understand it.

The really great event of the last few weeks has been Gilbert Murray. I fear I should fall into school-girlishness if I ventured to tell you how much I liked him. You will judge when I say that no woman in my earlier years made me talk more about myself than he has now. Conversation spread before us like an infinite thing, or rather like something opening out higher and greater with every talk. I found him so gentle, so sweetly reasonable – almost the ideal companion. Even I could forgive his liking Dickens, and Tennyson. – He has been responsible for the delay of this scrawl, for he absorbed my energies. What little was left went to my proofs. Happily they are nearly done.

I am so glad that Alys is coming out. It is very good of her. I shall enjoy her visit, and be much the better for it. Dickinson will I fear suffer from the contrast with Murray.

I am in the middle of the *Gespräche mit Goethe* all interesting. -
What have you done with your paper on mathematics?

> *Yours ever*
> *B. B. (Berenson)*

> Grayshott
> Haslemere, Surrey
> Ja. 10, 1904

My dearest Bertie

I was so very, very sorry to hear that you were not at Dora's[1]
funeral. I felt quite sure you would be present and can only think
that something very definite must have prevented you. - I know you
may feel that this last token of respect means little and is of no avail
- but I am *quite* sure after all she did for you in old days and all the
love she gave you that her sister and friends will have felt pained at
your absence - if you could have gone. - Many thanks to Alys for her
letter and the little Memorial Book she forwarded - I conclude you
have one. - Perhaps you have never heard it at the grave of one you
loved - but the Burial Service is about the most impressive and
solemn - and especially with music is sometimes a real help in hours
of awful sorrow in lifting one up above and beyond it. - I have had a
kind letter from Dora's sister to whom I wrote as I feel most deeply
for her - it is a terrible loss - she is alone and had hoped some day
Dora would live with her. - I hope you wrote to her.

Miss Sedgfield[2] is probably going on Tuesday to Highgate for a
week and very much hopes to be at your lecture next Friday. - Perhaps
you will see her but anyhow please ask Alys if she will look out for
her. She has written for tickets. She asks me to tell you that she
particularly hopes you are going to make it comprehensible to the
feeblest intelligence - no angles and squares and triangles no metaphysics or mathematics to be admitted!

Thank Alys very much for the enclosures which I was delighted to
see they are very interesting and I should like some to send to a few
who might be interested. But I don't like the sentence about Retaliation. The word alone is distasteful and I have just looked it out in
Johnson - To 'retaliate' (even when successful so-called) is not a
Tolstoyan or better a Christian maxim. - I hope your lectures will
contain some sentiment and some ideals! - even from the low point
of view of success they will be more effective if they do! - *How* I wish
I could come and hear you - I will read you in the *Edinburgh* but it

---

[1] 'Dora' was my former Swiss governess, Miss Bühler.
[2] My aunt's companion.

would be more interesting to hear and I never have heard you or Alys once!

With much love to you both and best wishes for your work in the good cause,[1]

> *Your loving*
> *Auntie*

> Ivy Lodge
> Tilford, Farnham
> May 17, 1904

My dearest Bertie

I hope thee will not mind my writing thee a real letter on thy birthday. I try very hard always to keep on the surface, as thee wishes, but I am sure thee will remember how some feelings long for expression.

I only want to tell thee again how very much I love thee, and how glad I am of thy existence. When I could share thy life and think myself of use to thee, it was the greatest happiness anyone has ever known. I am thankful for the memory of it, and thankful that I can still be near thee and watch thy development. When thee is well and happy and doing good work, I feel quite contented, and only wish that I were a better person and able to do more work and be more worthy of thee. I never wake in the night or think of thee in the daytime without wishing for blessings on my darling, and I shall always love thee, and I hope it will grow more and more unselfish.

> *Thine ever devotedly*
> *Alys*

> Cambo
> Northumberland
> (July, 1904)

Dear Bertie

I want to tell you how very fine the last part of your article is. If I could now and then write like that I should feel more certainly justified than I do in adopting writing as a business.

When I get south again at the beginning of August I should much like to talk to you. I have much to ask you now. Tolstoi's letter in *Times* has set me thinking very uncomfortably – or *feeling* rather. It fills me with (i) a new sense of doubt and responsibility as to my own manner of life (ii) as to this of war. I feel as if we were all living in the City of Destruction but I am not certain as to whether I ought to flee – or whither.

[1] The cause of Free Trade.

It may all come to nothing definite, but it ought at least to leave a different spirit.

I have for long been too happy and contented with everything including my work. Then the intense moral superiority of Tolstoi's recusant conscripts knocks all the breath out of one's fatuous Whig bladder of self contentment.

1. In ½ a sheet do you agree with Tolstoi about war?
2. Where will you be in August?

> *Yours*
> *George Trevelyan*

> Cambo
> Northumberland
> July 17, 1904

Dear Bertie

I am deeply grateful to you for having written me so long and carefully considered a letter. But it was not a waste of time. I am deeply interested in it and I think I agree with it altogether.

On the other hand I hold that though you are right in supposing the preparation of war to be a necessary function of modern states, in the spirit and under the restrictions you name, – *still* one of the principal means by which war will eventually be abolished is the passive resistance of conscripts in the conscription nations (to whose number we may be joined if things go badly). It will take hundreds of years to abolish war, and there will be a 'fiery roll of martyrdom', opening with these recusant convicts of Tolstoi's. It is these people, who will become an ever increasing number all over Europe, who will finally shame the peoples of Europe into viewing war and international hatred as you do, instead of viewing it as they do now. Great changes are generally effected in this way, but by a double process – gradual change in the general sentiment and practice, led and really inspired by the extreme opinion and action of people condemned by the mass of mankind, whom nevertheless they affect.

Three cheers for Tolstoi's letter all the same. Also I think that any proposal to introduce conscription into England must be resisted on this ground (among others) that govt. has not the right to coerce a person's conscience into fighting or training for war if he thinks it wrong.

I think I also agree with you as to the duty of living and working in the City of Destruction, rather than fleeing from it. But a duty that is also a pleasure, though it is none the less still a duty, brings dangers in the course of its performance. It is very difficult, in retaining the bulk of one's property and leisure at the disposal of one's own will, to live in the spirit of this maxim: 'One has only a right to that amount of property which will conduce most to the welfare of others in the long run.'

I enclose a letter and circular. Will you join ? I have done so, and I think we are probably going to elect Goldie Dickinson who expressed a willingness to join. There will certainly be perfectly free discussion and the people will be worth getting to know. There is no obligation, as of reading papers, incumbent on any member. I think the various points of view of the really religious who are also really free seekers after truth (a meagre band) is worth while our getting to know. They have expressed great hopes that you will join.

> *Yours ever*
> George Trevelyan

> 8 Cheyne Gardens
> Tuesday
> Oct. 11, '04

My dear Russell

It did me much good to see you again. I had a tale of woe and desperation to pour out – vague enough and yet not enough so it seemed while I was revolving it this morning; but when I had been with you a little while I did not feel – well, magnificently wretched enough to use desperate language. I was reminded of so many things I had well worth having. And my trouble seemed nothing that rational fortitude and very ordinary precepts properly obeyed could not surmount.

I look to you to help me more than anybody else just now. I feel that all those refinements which you suspect often are half weaknesses and I too, help me. It is everything to me to feel that you have no cut and dried rules of what one man ought and ought not to say to another, yet I know how you hate a spiritual indelicacy.

Do not answer this letter unless you want to or unless you have anything you want to say. We can talk of so many things right to the bottom which is the blessing of blessings.

I want to stop in London for a fortnight or so and get some work done. Then I shall be better able to tell you how it is with [*sic*]. I must begin to hope a little before I can talk about my despair.

> *Your affectionate*
> Desmond MacCarthy

> 41 Grosvenor Road
> Westminster Embankment
> Oct. 16, 1904

My dear Bertie

It was kind of you to write to me your opinion of L. H. [Leonard

Hobhouse] pamphlet and I am glad that it coincides so exactly with my own. I quite agree with you in thinking that the fact that a 'mood' (such, for instance, as the instinctive faith in a 'Law of Righteousness', and my instinctive faith in prayer) is felt to be 'compelling and recurrent' has no relevance, as Proof of its correspondence 'with our order of things'.

I make an absolute distinction between the realm of proof (Knowledge of Processes) and the realm of aspiration or Faith – (the choice of Purposes.) All I ask for this latter World, is tolerance – a 'Let live' policy. In my interpretation of this 'Let live' policy, I should probably differ with you and L. H. – since I would permit each local community to teach its particular form of 'aspiration' or 'Faith' out of common funds. I should even myself desire this for my own children – since I have found that my own existence would have been more degraded without it – and as I 'desire' what we call nobility of Purpose, I wish for the means to bring it about. I know no other way of discovering these means but actual experience or experiment, and so far my own experience and experiment leads me to the working Hypothesis of persistent Prayer. I do not in the least wish to force this practice on other people and should be equally glad to pay for a school in which the experiment of complete secularisation (viz. nothing but the knowledge of Processes) was tried or for an Anglican or Catholic or Christian Science Establishment. All I desire is that each section or locality should, as far as possible, be free to teach its own kind of aspirations or absence of Aspirations.

Can you and Alys come to lunch on *Thursday 10th* and meet Mr Balfour ? I am taking him to Bernard Shaw's play. Could you not take tickets for that afternoon ? It will be well for you to know Mr Balfour – in case of Regius Professorships and the like!

> Ever
> B. Webb

Private   Rozeldene, Grayshott
                                            Haslemere, Surrey
                                            March 20, 1905

My dearest Bertie

I am only writing today on one subject which I wish now to tell you about. – I have had and kept carefully ever since his death, your Grandfather's gold watch and chain – I need not tell you how *very very* precious it is to me as of course I so well remember his always wearing it.

But I should like very much now to give it to you – only with one condition that you will leave it to Arthur, – or failing Arthur to Johnny – as I am anxious it should remain a Russell possession. I do not remember whether you have and wear now any watch which has any past association – if so of course do not hesitate to tell me and I will keep this, for Arthur later on. But if not you could of course give (or keep if you prefer) your present watch away – as I should like to feel you will wear and use this one – not put it away. – However this you will tell me about.

Dear dear Bertie I should like to feel that you will always try to be worthy – you *will* try I know – of being his grandson for he was indeed one of the very best men the world has known – courageous – gentle – true – and with a most beautiful childlike simplicity and straight-forwardness of nature which is most rare – I like to think that you remember him – and that his last words to you 'Good little boy', spoken from his deathbed with loving gentleness, – can remain with you as an inspiration to goodness through life; – but of course you cannot remember and cannot know all that he was. – But if you will have it I should like you to wear and treasure this watch in memory of him – and of the long ago days in the dear home of our childhood.[1]

God bless you.

> *Your loving*
> *Auntie*

I have just had the watch seen to in London – it is in perfect condition. I could give it you on the 28th. – Thanks for your welcome letter last week.

> Vicarage
> Kirkby Lonsdale
> 27 July, 1905

Bertie

Theodore is dead, drowned while bathing alone on Tuesday in a pool in the Fells, stunned as I have no doubt by striking his head in taking a header and then drowned.

I shall be back in London on Monday. Let me see you some time soon.

> *Crompton*

(Oct. 31 ?, '05)

Dear Bertie

I enclose photo which I trust will do.

I have some more of Theo which I want to shew you. When will you come for a night?

I have failed with —.[2] She says she thought she could have done

---

[1] I have worn this watch and chain ever since 1949.

[2] The woman whom Theodore loved, and whom, after Theodore's death, Crompton wished to marry.

anything for me but resolutely declines to marry me so the matter is at an end.

Harry and I are going to Grantchester next Saturday. I haven't managed a visit to Bedales yet.

I have prepared your will but think I will keep it till I see you and can go thro' it with you.

The loss of Theodore seems still a mere phantasy and the strange mixture of dream and waking thoughts and recollection and fact leave me in bewilderment but slowly the consciousness of a maimed existence remaining for me makes itself felt, as of a body that has lost its limbs and strength and has to go on with made-up supports and medical regimen and resignation to the loss of possibilities of achievement and hopes of sunny days.

I cling to you with all my heart and bless you for loving and helping me.

Crompton

Stocks Cottage
Tring
23rd May, 1907

Dear Bertie

So now you have 'fought a contested election', which Teufelsdröck puts with the state of being in love, as being the second great experience of human life. I am the greater coward that I have never done the same, and probably never shall. I don't suppose a pair of more oddly contrasted candidates will be in the field again for another 100 years, as you and Chaplin.

What a sporting cove you are! Next time the Austrians conquer Italy you and I will go in a couple of red shirts, together, and get comfortably killed in an Alpine pass. I hardly thought you were such an adventurer, and had so much of the fine old Adam in you, till I came home (like old mother Hubbard) and found you conducting an election!!

I am very grateful to you for the article in the *Edinburgh*.[1] It did the book a lot of good, and helped to pull up the sale, which began badly and is now doing well. It was, I gather from Elliot, a disappointment to you not to be able to do it at more leisure, and I want to tell you that I appreciate this sacrifice to friendship, and that it was a real service to me to have the review out in April.

I was very much interested in several things you said, especially the sentence at the top of p. 507 about the special function of the Revolutionaries. I did not guess who had written it till Alys told us, tho' I

[1] A review of George Trevelyan's *Garibaldi's Defence of the Roman Republic*.

might have guessed it from your favourite story of Jowett's remark on Mazzini.

I hope you are both back in the academic pheasant preserve and that the quiet of Oxford is pleasant after such turmoil.

> *Yours fraternally*
> George Trevy

> 67 Belsize Park Gardens
> Hampstead, N.W.
> 23 October, 1907

Dear Russell

I have just read your article on Mathematics (in proof) and can't resist writing to say how much I was carried away by it. Really it's magnificent – one's carried upwards into sublime heights – perhaps the sublimest of all! Your statement of the great thing about it seems to me absolutely clear and absolutely convincing; it gives one a new conception of the glories of the human mind. The simile of the Italian Castle struck me as particularly fine, and the simplicity of the expression added tremendously to the effect. What scoundrels the *Independent* editors were![1] And what fools!

I could go on writing for pages – such is my excitement and enthusiasm. It's terrific to reflect that I know you, and can speak to you, and even contradict you. Oh! – I shall have this engraved on my tombstone –

HE KNEW MOORE AND RUSSELL

and nothing more.

> *Yours ever*
> G. L. Strachey

> 57 Gordon Square
> London W.C.
> 3rd March, 1908

My dear Bertie

I see in the papers that you are to be made an FRS! What an honour! at your age too. Ever since I saw it I have have been strutting about swelling with reflected glory. It's the first sensible thing I ever heard of philosophy doing. One can understand that if one can't your books.

Seriously though I do congratulate you most heartily. I have always looked on an FRS as superior to any position on earth, even Archbishop or Prime Minister and the feeling still survives though I know a good many personally.

> *Yours affectionately*
> Russell

[1] They had refused to print the article.

Charing Cross Hotel
October 4, 1908

Dear Russell

I was at Oxford for three days last week, and hoped until the last day, when I found it was going to be quite impossible, to drive out and see you and Mrs Russell. It was squeezed out by other necessities. I saw Schiller and spent a night at McDougall's most pleasantly. I would fain have spent a night with you, to make up for the rather blunt way in which I declined your invitation last June. I was done-up then, and am comparatively fresh now, but a daughter and a son have come over since then and, as normal, their needs have seemed more urgent than their parent's, so the time has proved too short for many things that I should have liked to accomplish. The son remains at Oxford, in A. L. Smith's family (tutor at Balliol). The rest of us sail in the *Saxonia* on Tuesday.

One of the first things I am going to do after I get back to my own library is to re-read the Chapter on Truth in your Phil. of M., which I haven't looked at since it appeared. I want to get a better grasp of it than you have of my theory! Your remarks on Dewey (sharp as your formulation is!) in the last Hibbert shows that you haven't yet grasped the thing broadly enough. My dying words to you are 'Say good-by to mathematical logic if you wish to preserve your relations with concrete realities!' I have just had this morning a three-hour conversation with Bergson which possibly may account for this ejaculation! Best regards to you both, in which my wife would join were she here.

Truly yours
Wm. James

8 Grosvenor Crescent
S.W.
26th April, 1909

Dear Bertrand Russell

It is a great pleasure to know that you are elected at the Athenaeum. My own balloting – in 1877 – was sufficiently anxious to make me always feel glad when any friend, however certain of success, is through the ordeal. I was not wanting on the occasion and spent a solid part of the afternoon there while your ballot was on.

Your membership will sensibly increase to me, and many others, the interest and pleasure of the Club.[1]

I remain
Yours very sincerely
George O. Trevelyan

[1] I can't think why. I never saw Sir George Trevelyan there.

Eleven, Cranmer Road
Cambridge
May 27/10

Dear Bertie

The College Council decided today to offer you a lectureship in Logic and the Principles of Mathematics to continue for five years, the duties being

  (i) to give a course (24 lectures) of lectures in each term,

 (ii) to reside in Cambridge during term time –

Also provided that you are willing to satisfy certain conditions as to the number of hours during which you will be present in College (15 hours per week during term time, I think) they offer rooms in College and dinner (i.e. *free* dinner). The stipend is £200 per year.

All this is of course entirely unofficial – I need not tell you how delighted I am about it – It will give you a splendid opportunity to 'expose' the subject – just what is wanted.

By the bye, I ought to mention that there is no implication that the lectureship will be continued after five years. – Of course the whole difficulty in this respect comes from the extremely few students who, as far as it can be *foreseen*, will be taught by you directly in lectures – I confess to a hope that there may be much more to be done – now that we know our own subject – than any of us can guarantee at present. – But the offer is for 5 years and no more, directly or indirectly.

The Council has been very spirited, for at the same time we elected a 'prelector' in Biochemistry.

No more news at present.

> *Yours affectionately*
> *A. N. W.*

Trinity Lodge
Cambridge
June 3, 1910

My dear B. Russell

We are delighted to hear that there is now more than a hope of having you among us for some time to come. Not a shred of credit can *I* claim for the step which we have so wisely taken, but I rejoice to have given the heartiest assent to the advice of your scientific friends. I can hardly hope to last out during the whole of your happy Quinquennium, but I may at least look forward to giving you an early and a hearty greeting.

With our united kindest regards to Mrs Russell.

> *Believe me to be most truly yours*
> *H. Montagu Butler*

There cannot be many living who, like myself, saw Lord John Russell starting from the Hotel at Callender in 1850, through a good Scotch Rain, for 'Rest and be Thankful'. I wonder if you know those delightful regions.

Merton College
Oxford
April 11/10

Dear Mr Russell

Many thanks for your letter. I have no doubt that in what I wrote I have misinterpreted you more or less. And that makes me unwilling to write at all, only no one else seemed doing it. I shall look forward to reading the off prints of the article from the *Revue* and I will attend to what you have written in your letter.

I feel, I confess, some alarm at the prospect of you being occupied with politics, if that means that you will have no time for philosophy. Will it not be possible to combine them? If not it is not for me to venture to judge in what direction you feel the greater 'call'. The only thing I feel clear about is this that no one else will do your work in philosophy so far as human probability goes. And more than this I don't feel I have any right to say.

If you are able to write something for 'Mind' I am sure that it will be welcome to the readers thereof and not least to myself.

Yours truly
F. H. Bradley

I have no idea as to who will get this Professorship. I hear that Webb's chances are thought good on the ground that the two clerics are likely to vote for him and Warren also. But nothing is really known.

Merton College
Oxford
April 20/10

Dear Mr Russell

I am really glad to hear that you have no intention of going permanently into politics which of course are very absorbing. It is quite another thing to get a temporary change of occupation and you must have worked very hard at philosophy now for some years.

Certainly in the study of philosophy, &, I presume, in many other studies, the having to work alone so much is inhuman & trying. And I do not see any remedy for it. The amount to which one can collaborate with another is so small. My health has always been too bad for me to get a change by way of another occupation, but I am afraid that I have been driven to take a great deal of holidays instead. Another occupation might have been better.

I am too stupid now to read your article even if I had it but I shall look forward to seeing it.

I have always had a high opinion of your work from the first, & I feel no doubt whatever that philosophy would lose greatly by your permanent withdrawal. I don't see who else is going to do the work there, which you would, &, I hope, will do.

> *Yours truly*
> *F. H. Bradley*

Chapter 7

Cambridge Again

Principia Mathematica being finished, I felt somewhat at a loose end. The feeling was delightful, but bewildering, like coming out of prison. Being at the time very much interested in the struggle between the Liberals and the Lords about the Budget and the Parliament Act, I felt an inclination to go into politics. I applied to Liberal Head-quarters for a constituency, and was recommended to Bedford. I went down and gave an address to the Liberal Association, which was received with enthusiasm. Before the address, however, I had been taken into a small back room, where I was subjected to a regular catechism, as nearly as I remember in the following terms:

Q. Are you a member of the Church of England?
A. No, I was brought up as a Nonconformist.
Q. And have remained so?
A. No, I have not remained so.
Q. Are we to understand that you are an agnostic?
A. Yes, that is what you must understand.
Q. Would you be willing to attend church occasionally?
A. No, I should not.
Q. Would your wife be willing to attend church occasionally?
A. No, she would not.
Q. Would it come out that you are an agnostic?
A. Yes, it probably would come out.

In consequence of these answers, they selected as their candidate Mr Kellaway, who became Postmaster General, and held correct opinions during the War. They must have felt that they had had a lucky escape.

I also felt that I had had a lucky escape, for while Bedford was deliberating, I received an invitation from Trinity College to become a lecturer in the principles of mathematics. This was much more attractive to me than politics, but if Bedford had accepted me I should have had to reject Cambridge. I took up my residence at the beginning of the October term in 1910. Alys and I had lodgings in Bridge Street, and I had rooms in letter I, Nevile's Court. I became very fond of these rooms, which were the first place exclusively my own that I possessed since leaving Cambridge in 1894. We sold our house at Bagley Wood, and it seemed as if life were going to be settled in a new groove.

This, however, was not the case. In the Election of January, 1910, while I was still living at Bagley Wood, I decided that I ought to help the Liberals as much as I could, but I did not want to help the Member for the constituency in which I was living, as he had broken some pledges which I considered important. I therefore decided to help the Member for the neighbouring constituency across the river. This Member was Philip Morrell, a man who had been at Oxford with my brother-in-law, Logan, who had been passionately attached to him. Philip Morrell had married Lady Ottoline Cavendish-Bentinck, sister of the Duke of Portland. I had known her slightly since we were both children, as she had an aunt named Mrs Scott,[1] who lived at Ham Common. I had two vivid memories connected with Mrs Scott's house, but neither of them concern Ottoline. The first of these memories was of a children's party at which I first tasted ice-cream. I thought it was an ordinary pudding, and took a large spoonful. The shock caused me to burst into tears, to the dismay of the elders, who could not make out what had happened. The other experience was even more unpleasant. In getting out of a carriage at her door, I fell on the paving-stones, and hurt my penis. After this I had to sit twice a day in a hot bath and sponge it carefully. As I had always hitherto been taught to ignore it, this puzzled me. When Philip first became engaged to Ottoline, Logan was filled with jealous rage, and made unkind fun of her. Later, however, he became reconciled. I used to see her and Philip occasionally, but I had never had any high opinion of him, and she offended my Puritan prejudices by what I considered an excessive use of scent and powder. Crompton Davies first led me to revise my opinion of her, because she worked for his Land Values Organisation in a way that commanded his admiration.

During the Election of January 1910, I addressed meetings in support of Philip Morrell most nights, and spent most days in canvassing. I remember canvassing a retired Colonel at Iffley, who came rushing out into the hall exclaiming: 'Do you think I'd vote for a scoundrel like that? Get out of the house, or I'll put the dogs on you!' I spoke in almost every village between Oxford and Caversham. In the course of this campaign I had many opportunities of getting to know Ottoline. I discovered that she was extraordinarily kind to all sorts of people, and that she was very much in earnest about public life. But Philip, in common with all the other Liberal Members in the neighbourhood, lost his seat, and was offered a new constituency at Burnley, for which he was Member from December 1910 until the 'Hang-the-Kaiser' Election. The result was that for some time I did not see much

[1] Grandmother of the Queen-Mother, Elizabeth.

of the Morrells. However, in March 1911 I received an invitation to
give three lectures in Paris, one at the Sorbonne and two elsewhere. It
was convenient to spend the night in London on the way, and I asked
the Morrells to put me up at their house, 44 Bedford Square. Ottoline
had very exquisite though rather startling taste, and her house was
very beautiful. In Alys there was a conflict between Quaker asceticism
and her brother's aestheticism. She considered it right to follow the
best artistic canons in the more public part of one's life, such as
drawing-rooms and dresses for the platform. But in her instincts, and
where she alone was concerned, Quaker plainness held sway; for
example, she always wore flannel night-gowns. I have always liked
beautiful things, but been incapable of providing them for myself.
The atmosphere of Ottoline's house fed something in me that had
been starved throughout the years of my first marriage. As soon as I
entered it, I felt rested from the rasping difficulties of the outer world.
When I arrived there on March 19th, on my way to Paris, I found that
Philip had unexpectedly had to go to Burnley, so that I was left
tête-à-tête with Ottoline. During dinner we made conversation about
Burnley, and politics, and the sins of the Government. After dinner
the conversation gradually became more intimate. Making timid
approaches, I found them to my surprise not repulsed. It had not,
until this moment, occurred to me that Ottoline was a woman who
would allow me to make love to her, but gradually, as the evening
progressed, the desire to make love to her became more and more
insistent. At last it conquered, and I found to my amazement that I
loved her deeply, and that she returned my feeling. Until this moment
I had never had complete relations with any woman except Alys. For
external and accidental reasons, I did not have full relations with
Ottoline that evening, but we agreed to become lovers as soon as
possible. My feeling was overwhelmingly strong, and I did not care
what might be involved. I wanted to leave Alys, and to have her leave
Philip. What Philip might think or feel was a matter of indifference
to me. If I had known that he would murder us both (as Mrs Whitehead assured me he would) I should have been willing to pay that
price for one night. The nine years of tense self-denial had come to
an end, and for the time being I was done with self-denial. However,
there was not time to settle future plans during that one evening. It
was already late when we first kissed, and after that, though we stayed
up till four in the morning, the conversation was intermittent. Early
the next day I had to go to Paris, where I had to lecture in French to
highly critical audiences. It was difficult to bring my mind to bear
upon what I had to do, and I suspect that I must have lectured very
badly. I was living in a dream, and my surroundings appeared quite
unreal. Ottoline was going to Studland (in those days quite a tiny

place), and we arranged that I should join her there for three days. Before going, I spent the weekend with Alys at Fernhurst. I began the weekend by a visit to the dentist, who told me that he thought I had cancer, and recommended a specialist, whom, however, I could not see for three weeks, as he had gone away for his Easter holiday. I then told Alys about Ottoline. She flew into a rage, and said that she would insist upon a divorce, bringing in Ottoline's name. Ottoline, on account of her child, and also on account of a very genuine affection for Philip, did not wish for a divorce from him. I therefore had to keep her name out of it. I told Alys that she could have the divorce whenever she liked, but that she must not bring Ottoline's name into it. She nevertheless persisted that she would bring Ottoline's name in. Thereupon I told her quietly but firmly that she would find that impossible, since if she ever took steps to that end, I should commit suicide in order to circumvent her. I meant this, and she saw that I did. Thereupon her rage became unbearable. After she had stormed for some hours, I gave a lesson in Locke's philosophy to her niece, Karin Costelloe, who was about to take her Tripos. I then rode away on my bicycle, and with that my first marriage came to an end. I did not see Alys again till 1950, when we met as friendly acquaintances.[1]

From this scene I went straight to Studland, still believing that I had cancer. At Swanage, I obtained an old-fashioned fly with an incredibly slow horse. During his leisurely progress up and down the hills, my impatience became almost unendurable. At last, however, I saw Ottoline sitting in a pine-wood beside the road, so I got out, and let the fly go on with my luggage. The three days and nights that I spent at Studland remain in my memory as among the few moments when life seemed all that it might be, but hardly ever is. I did not, of course, tell Ottoline that I had reason to fear that I had cancer, but the thought of this possibility heightened my happiness by giving it greater intensity, and by the sense that it had been wrenched from the jaws of destruction. When the dentist told me, my first reaction was to congratulate the Deity on having got me after all just as happiness seemed in sight. I suppose that in some underground part of me I believed in a Deity whose pleasure consists of ingenious torture. But throughout the three days at Studland, I felt that this malignant Deity had after all been not wholly successful. When finally I did see the specialist, it turned out that there was nothing the matter.

Ottoline was very tall, with a long thin face something like a horse, and very beautiful hair of an unusual colour, more or less like that of marmalade, but rather darker. Kind ladies supposed it to be dyed, but in this they were mistaken. She had a very beautiful, gentle, vibrant voice, indomitable courage, and a will of iron. She was very shy, and,

[1] Alys died on January 21, 1951.

at first, we were both timid of each other, but we loved profoundly, and the gradual disappearance of the timidity was an added delight. We were both earnest and unconventional, both aristocratic by tradition but deliberately not so in our present environment, both hating the cruelty, the caste insolence, and the narrow-mindedness of aristocrats, and yet both a little alien in the world in which we chose to live, which regarded us with suspicion and lack of understanding because we were alien. All the complicated feelings resulting from this situation we shared. There was a deep sympathy between us which never ceased as long as she lived. Although we ceased to be lovers in 1916, we remained always close friends.

Ottoline had a great influence upon me, which was almost wholly beneficial. She laughed at me when I behaved like a don or a prig, and when I was dictatorial in conversation. She gradually cured me of the belief that I was seething with appalling wickedness which could only be kept under by an iron self-control. She made me less self-centred, and less self-righteous. Her sense of humour was very great, and I became aware of the danger of rousing it unintentionally. She made me much less of a Puritan, and much less censorious than I had been. And of course the mere fact of happy love after the empty years made everything easier. Many men are afraid of being influenced by women, but as far as my experience goes, this is a foolish fear. It seems to me that men need women, and women need men, mentally as much as physically. For my part, I owe a great deal to women whom I have loved, and without them I should have been far more narrow-minded.

After Studland various difficulties began to cause trouble. Alys was still raging, and Logan was quite as furious as she was. The White-heads, who showed great kindness at this time, finally persuaded them to abandon the idea of a divorce involving Ottoline, and Alys decided that in that case a divorce was not worth having. I had wished Ottoline to leave Philip, but I soon saw that this was out of the question. Meanwhile, Logan went to Philip, and imposed conditions, which Philip in turn had to impose upon Ottoline. These conditions were onerous, and interfered seriously with the happiness of our love. The worst of them was that we should never spend a night together. I raged and stormed, along with Philip and Logan and Alys. Ottoline found all this very trying, and it produced an atmosphere in which it was difficult to recapture the first ecstasy. I became aware of the solidity of Ottoline's life, of the fact that her husband and her child and her possessions were important to her. To me nothing was important in comparison with her, and this inequality led me to become jealous and exacting. At first, however, the mere strength of our mutual passion overcame all these obstacles. She had a small house at Peppard in the Chilterns, where she spent the month of July. I stayed at Ipsden, six miles from Peppard, and bicycled over every day, arriving about noon, and leaving about midnight. The summer was extraordinarily hot, reaching on one occasion 97° in the shade. We used to take our lunch out into the beech-woods, and come home to late tea. That month was one of great happiness, though Ottoline's health was bad. Finally, she had to go to Marienbad, where I joined her after a while, staying, however, at a different hotel. With the autumn she returned to London, and I took a flat in Bury Street, near the Museum, so that she could come and see me. I was lecturing at Cambridge all the time, but used to come up in the morning, and get back in time for my lecture, which was at 5.30. She used to suffer from terrible headaches, which often made our meetings disappointing, and on these occasions I was less considerate than I ought to have been. Nevertheless, we got through the winter with only one serious disagreement, arising out of the fact that I denounced her for being religious. Gradually, however, I became increasingly turbulent, because I felt that she did not care for me as much as I cared for her. There were moments when this feeling disappeared entirely, and I think that often what was really ill-health appeared to me as indifference, but this was certainly not always the case. I was suffering from pyorrhoea although I did not know it, and this caused my breath to be offensive, which also I did not know. She could not bring herself to mention it, and it was only after I had discovered the trouble and had it cured, that she let me know how much it had affected her.

At the end of 1913 I went to Rome to see her, but Philip was there, and the visit was very unsatisfactory. I made friends with a German lady whom I had met in the summer on the Lake of Garda. Sanger and I had spent a month walking from Innsbruck over the Alps, and had arrived at Punto San Vigilio, where we joined a party of friends, consisting of Miss Silcox, the mistress of St Felix School, Melian Stawell, and the latter's protegée, whose name I have forgotten. We observed a young woman sitting at a table by herself, and discussed whether she was married or single. I suggested that she was divorced. In order to settle the point, I made her acquaintance, and found that I was right. Her husband was a psychoanalyst, and apparently professional etiquette required that he should not get on with his wife. Consequently, at the time when I knew her, she was divorced. But as soon as honour was satisfied, they remarried, and lived happily ever after. She was young and charming, and had two small children. At that time my dominant passion was desire for children, and I could not see even a child playing in the street without an almost unbearable ache. I made friends with the lady and we made an expedition into the country. I wished to make love to her, but thought that I ought first to explain about Ottoline. Until I spoke about Ottoline, she was acquiescent, but afterwards she ceased to be so. She decided, however, that for that one day her objections could be ignored. I have never seen her since, though I still heard from her at intervals for some years.

An event of importance to me in 1913 was the beginning of my friendship with Joseph Conrad, which I owed to our common friendship with Ottoline. I had been for many years an admirer of his books, but should not have ventured to seek acquaintance without an introduction. I travelled down to his house near Ashford in Kent in a state of somewhat anxious expectation. My first impression was one of surprise. He spoke English with a very strong foreign accent, and nothing in his demeanour in any way suggested the sea. He was an aristocratic Polish gentleman to his fingertips. His feeling for the sea, and for England, was one of romantic love – love from a certain distance, sufficient to leave the romance untarnished. His love for the sea began at a very early age. When he told his parents that he wished for a career as a sailor, they urged him to go into the Austrian navy, but he wanted adventure and tropical seas and strange rivers surrounded by dark forests; and the Austrian navy offered him no scope for these desires. His family were horrified at his seeking a career in the English merchant marine, but his determination was inflexible.

He was, as anyone may see from his books, a very rigid moralist and by no means politically sympathetic with revolutionaries. He and I were in most of our opinions by no means in agreement, but in something very fundamental we were extraordinarily at one.

My relation to Joseph Conrad was unlike any other that I have ever had. I saw him seldom, and not over a long period of years. In the out-works of our lives, we were almost strangers, but we shared a certain outlook on human life and human destiny, which, from the very first, made a bond of extreme strength. I may perhaps be pardoned for quoting a sentence from a letter that he wrote to me very soon after we had become acquainted. I should feel that modesty forbids the quotation except for the fact that it expresses so exactly what I felt about him. What he expressed and I equally felt was, in his words, 'A deep admiring affection which, if you were never to see me again and forgot my existence tomorrow, would be unalterably yours *usque ad finem*'.

Of all that he had written I admired most the terrible story called *The Heart of Darkness*, in which a rather weak idealist is driven mad by horror of the tropical forest and loneliness among savages. This story expresses, I think, most completely his philosophy of life. I felt, though I do not know whether he would have accepted such an image, that he thought of civilised and morally tolerable human life as a dangerous walk on a thin crust of barely cooled lava which at any moment might break and let the unwary sink into fiery depths. He was very conscious of the various forms of passionate madness to which men are prone, and it was this that gave him such a profound belief in the importance of discipline. His point of view, one might perhaps say, was the antithesis of Rousseau's: 'Man is born in chains, but he can become free.' He becomes free, so I believe Conrad would have said, not by letting loose his impulses, not by being casual and uncontrolled, but by subduing wayward impulse to a dominant purpose.

He was not much interested in political systems, though he had some strong political feelings. The strongest of these were love of England and hatred of Russia, of which both are expressed in *The Secret Agent*; and the hatred of Russia, both Czarist and revolutionary, is set forth with great power in *Under Western Eyes*. His dislike of Russia was that which was traditional in Poland. It went so far that he would not allow merit to either Tolstoy or Dostoievsky. Turgeniev, he told me once, was the only Russian novelist whom he admired.

Except for love of England and hatred of Russia, politics did not much concern him. What interested him was the individual human soul faced with the indifference of nature, and often with the hostility of man, and subject to·inner struggles with passions both good and bad that led towards destruction. Tragedies of loneliness occupied a great part of his thought and feeling. One of his most typical stories is *Typhoon*. In this story the Captain, who is a simple soul, pulls his ship through by unshakeable courage and grim determination. When the storm is over, he writes a long letter to his wife, telling about it. In his account his own part is, to him, perfectly simple. He has merely performed his Captain's duty as, of course, anyone would expect. But the reader, through his narrative, becomes aware of all that he has done and dared and endured. The letter, before he sends it off, is read surreptitiously by his steward, but is never read by anyone else at all because his wife finds it boring and throws it away unread.

The two things that seem most to occupy Conrad's imagination are loneliness and fear of what is strange. *An Outcast of the Islands* like *The Heart of Darkness* is concerned with fear of what is strange. Both come together in the extraordinarily moving story called *Amy Foster*. In this story a South-Slav peasant, on his way to America, is the sole survivor of the wreck of his ship, and is cast away in a Kentish village. All the village fears and ill-treats him, except Amy Foster, a dull, plain girl who brings him bread when he is starving and finally marries him. But she, too, when, in fever, he reverts to his native language, is seized with a fear of his strangeness, snatches up their child and abandons him. He dies alone and hopeless. I have wondered at times how much of this man's loneliness Conrad had felt among the English and had suppressed by a stern effort of will.

Conrad's point of view was far from modern. In the modern world there are two philosophies: the one which stems from Rousseau, and sweeps aside discipline as unnecessary, the other, which finds its fullest expression in totalitarianism, which thinks of discipline as essentially imposed from without. Conrad adhered to the older tradition, that discipline should come from within. He despised indiscipline and hated discipline that was merely external.

In all this I found myself closely in agreement with him. At our very first meeting, we talked with continually increasing intimacy. We seemed to sink through layer after layer of what was superficial, till gradually both reached the central fire. It was an experience unlike any other that I have known. We looked into each other's eyes, half appalled and half intoxicated to find ourselves together in such a region. The emotion was as intense as passionate love, and at the same time all-embracing. I came away bewildered, and hardly able to find my way among ordinary affairs.

I saw nothing of Conrad during the war or after it until my return from China in 1921. When my first son was born in that year I wished Conrad to be as nearly his godfather as was possible without a formal ceremony. I wrote to Conrad saying: 'I wish, with your permission, to call my son John Conrad. My father was called John, my grandfather was called John, and my great grandfather was called John; and Conrad is a name in which I see merits.' He accepted the position and duly presented my son with the cup which is usual on such occasions.

I did not see much of him, as I lived most of the year in Cornwall, and his health was failing. But I had some charming letters from him, especially one about my book on China. He wrote: 'I have always liked the Chinese, even those that tried to kill me (and some other people) in the yard of a private house in Chantabun, even (but not so much) the fellow who stole all my money one night in Bankok, but brushed and folded my clothes neatly for me to dress in the morning, before vanishing into the depths of Siam. I also received many kindnesses at the hands of various Chinese. This with the addition of an evening's conversation with the secretary of His Excellency Tseng on the verandah of an hotel and a perfunctory study of a poem, "The Heathen Chinee", is all I know about the Chinese. But after reading your extremely interesting view of the Chinese Problem I take a gloomy view of the future of their country.' He went on to say that my views of the future of China 'strike a chill into one's soul', the more so, he said, as I pinned my hopes on international socialism – 'The sort of thing', he commented, 'to which I cannot attach any sort of definite meaning. I have never been able to find in any man's book or any man's talk anything convincing enough to stand up for a moment against my deep-seated sense of fatality governing this man-inhabited world.' He went on to say that although man has taken to flying, 'he doesn't fly like an eagle, he flies like a beetle. And you must have noticed how ugly, ridiculous and fatuous is the flight of a beetle.' In these pessimistic remarks, I felt that he was showing a deeper wisdom than I had shown in my somewhat artificial hopes for a happy issue in China. It must be said that so far events have proved him right.

This letter was my last contact with him. I never again saw him to speak to. Once I saw him across the street, in earnest conversation with a man I did not know, standing outside the door of what had been my grandmother's house, but after her death had become the Arts Club. I did not like to interrupt what seemed a serious conversation, and I went away. When he died, shortly afterwards, I was sorry I had not been bolder. The house is gone, demolished by Hitler. Conrad, I suppose, is in process of being forgotten, but his intense and passionate nobility shines in my memory like a star seen from the bottom of a well. I wish I could make his light shine for others as it shone for me.

I was invited to give the Lowell lectures in Boston during the spring of 1914, and concurrently to act as temporary professor of philosophy at Harvard. I announced the subject of my Lowell lectures, but could not think of anything to say. I used to sit in the parlour of 'The Beetle and Wedge' at Moulsford, wondering what there was to say about our knowledge of the external world, on which before long I had to deliver a course of lectures. I got back to Cambridge from Rome on New Year's Day 1914, and, thinking that the time had come when I really must get my lectures prepared, I arranged for a shorthand typist to come next day, though I had not the vaguest idea what I should say to her when she came. As she entered the room, my ideas fell into place, and I dictated in a completely orderly sequence from that moment until the work was finished. What I dictated to her was subsequently published as a book with the title *Our Knowledge of the External World as a Field for Scientific Method in Philosophy*.

I sailed on the *Mauretania* on March 7th. Sir Hugh Bell was on the ship. His wife spent the whole voyage looking for him, or finding him with a pretty girl. Whenever I met him after the sinking of the *Lusitania*, I found him asserting that it was on the *Lusitania* he had sailed.

I travelled straight from New York to Boston, and was made to feel at home in the train by the fact that my two neighbours were talking to each other about George Trevelyan. At Harvard I met all the professors. I am proud to say that I took a violent dislike to Professor Lowell, who subsequently assisted in the murder of Sacco and Vanzetti. I had at that time no reason to dislike him, but the feeling was just as strong as it was in later years, when his qualities as a saviour of society had been manifested. Every professor to whom I was introduced in Harvard made me the following speech: 'Our philosophical faculty, Dr Russell, as doubtless you are aware, has lately suffered three great losses. We have lost our esteemed colleague, Professor William James, through his lamented death; Professor Santayana, for reasons which doubtless appear to him to be sufficient, has taken up his residence in Europe; last, *but* not least, Professor Royce, who, I am happy to say, is still with us, has had a stroke.' This speech was delivered slowly, seriously, and pompously. The time came when I felt that I must do something about it. So the next time that I was introduced to a professor, I rattled off the speech myself at top speed. This device, however, proved worthless. 'Yes, Dr Russell,' the professor replied: 'As you very justly observe, our philosophical faculty. . . .' and so the speech went on to its inexorable conclusion. I do not know whether this is a fact about professors or a fact about Americans. I think, however, that it is the former. I noticed another fact about Harvard professors: that when I dined with them, they would always tell me the way home, although I had had to find their house without this assistance. There were limitations to Harvard culture. Schofield, the professor of Fine Arts, considered Alfred Noyes a very good poet.

On the other hand, the students, especially the post-graduates, made a great impression upon me. The Harvard school of philosophy, until the three great losses mentioned above, had been the best in the world. I had stayed with William James at Harvard in 1896, and I had admired Royce's determination to introduce mathematical logic into the philosophical curriculum. Santayana, who had a great friendship for my brother, had been known to me since 1893, and I admired him as much as I disagreed with him. The tradition of these men was still strong. Ralph Barton Perry was doing his best to take their place, and was inspired with the full vigour of what was called 'the new realism'. He had married Berenson's sister. He already displayed, however, something of that New England moralism which caused him to be intellectually ruined by the first War. On one occasion he met, in my rooms, Rupert Brooke, of whom he had not then heard. Rupert was on his way back from the South Sea Islands, and discoursed at length about the decay of manhood in these regions produced by the cessation of cannibalism. Professor Perry was pained, for is not cannibalism a sin ? I have no doubt that when Rupert died, Professor Perry joined in his apotheosis, and I do not suppose he ever realised that the flippant young man he had met in my rooms was identical with the golden-haired god who had given his life for his country.

The students, however, as I said before, were admirable. I had a post-graduate class of twelve, who used to come to tea with me once a week. One of them was T. S. Eliot, who subsequently wrote a poem about it, called 'Mr Apollinax'. I did not know at the time that Eliot wrote poetry. He had, I think, already written 'A Portrait of a Lady', and 'Prufrock', but he did not see fit to mention the fact. He was extraordinarily silent, and only once made a remark which struck me. I was praising Heraclitus, and he observed: 'Yes, he always reminds me of Villon.' I thought this remark so good that I always wished he would make another. Another pupil who interested me was a man called Demos. He was a Greek whose father, having been converted by the missionaries, was an evangelical minister. Demos had been brought up in Asia Minor, and has risen to be librarian of some small library there, but when he had read all the books in that library he felt that Asia Minor had nothing further to offer him. He therefore saved up until he could afford a passage, steerage, to Boston. Having arrived there, he first got a job as a waiter in a restaurant, and then entered Harvard. He worked hard, and had considerable ability. In the course of nature he ultimately became a professor. His intellect was not free from the usual limitations. He explained to me in 1917 that while he could see through the case made by the other belligerents for their participation in the war, and perceived clearly that their arguments were humbug, the matter was quite different in the case of Greece, which was coming in on a genuine moral issue.

When the Harvard term came to an end, I gave single lectures in a few other universities. Among others I went to Ann Arbor, where the president showed me all the new buildings, more especially the library, of which he was very proud. It appeared that the library had the most scientific card-index in the world, and that its method of central heating was extraordinarily up-to-date. While he was explaining all this, we were standing in the middle of a large room with admirable desks. 'And does anybody ever read the books?' I asked. He seemed surprised, but answered: 'Why yes, there is a man over there now reading.' We went to look, and found that he was reading a novel.

From Ann Arbor I went to Chicago, where I stayed with an eminent gynaecologist and his family. This gynaecologist had written a book on the diseases of women containing a coloured frontispiece of the uterus. He presented this book to me, but I found it somewhat embarrassing, and ultimately gave it to a medical friend. In theology he was a free-thinker, but in morals a frigid Puritan. He was obviously a man of very strong sexual passions, and his face was ravaged by the effort of self-control. His wife was a charming old lady, rather shrewd within her limitations, but something of a trial to the younger generation. They had four daughters and a son, but the son, who died shortly after the war, I never met. One of their daughters came to Oxford to work at Greek under Gilbert Murray, while I was living at Bagley Wood, and brought an introduction to Alys and me from her teacher of English literature at Bryn Mawr. I only saw the girl a few times at Oxford, but I found her very interesting, and wished to know her better. When I was coming to Chicago, she wrote and invited me to

stay at her parents' house. She met me at the station, and I at once felt
more at home with her than I had with anybody else that I had met in
America. I found that she wrote rather good poetry, and that her feeling
for literature was remarkable and unusual. I spent two nights under
her parents' roof, and the second I spent with her. Her three sisters
mounted guard to give warning if either of the parents approached.
She was very delightful, not beautiful in the conventional sense, but
passionate, poetic, and strange. Her youth had been lonely and unhappy, and it seemed that I could give her what she wanted. We agreed
that she should come to England as soon as possible and that we would
live together openly, perhaps marrying later on if a divorce could be
obtained. Immediately after this I returned to England. On the boat I
wrote to Ottoline telling her what had occurred. My letter crossed one
from her, saying that she wished our relations henceforth to be platonic. My news and the fact that in America I had been cured of
pyorrhoea caused her to change her mind. Ottoline could still, when
she chose, be a lover so delightful that to leave her seemed impossible,
but for a long time past she had seldom been at her best with me. I
returned to England in June, and found her in London. We took to
going to Burnham Beeches every Tuesday for the day. The last of these
expeditions was on the day on which Austria declared war on Serbia.
Ottoline was at her best. Meanwhile, the girl in Chicago had induced
her father, who remained in ignorance, to take her to Europe. They
sailed on August 3rd. When she arrived I could think of nothing but
the war, and as I had determined to come out publicly against it, I did
not wish to complicate my position with a private scandal, which
would have made anything that I might say of no account. I felt it
therefore impossible to carry out what we had planned. She stayed in
England and I had relations with her from time to time, but the shock
of the war killed my passion for her, and I broke her heart. Ultimately
she fell a victim to a rare disease, which first paralysed her, and then
made her insane. In her insanity she told her father all that had
happened. The last time I saw her was in 1924. At that time paralysis
made her incapable of walking, but she was enjoying a lucid interval.
When I talked with her, however, I could feel dark, insane thoughts
lurking in the background. I understand that since then she had no
lucid intervals. Before insanity attacked her, she had a rare and
remarkable mind, and a disposition as lovable as it was unusual. If the
war had not intervened, the plan which we formed in Chicago might
have brought great happiness to us both. I feel still the sorrow of this
tragedy.

LETTERS

Jan. 15, 1911
Colonial Club
Cambridge, Mass.

Dear Russell

It is rather late to thank you for your *Philosophical Essays*, but you may soon see unmistakable evidence of the great interest I have taken in them, as I am writing an elaborate review – in three articles – for the Whited Sepulchre – which is what we call the Columbia *Journal of Philosophy*, etc. You will not expect me to agree with you in everything, but, whatever you may think of my ideas, I always feel that yours, and Moore's too, make for the sort of reconstruction in philosophy which I should welcome. It is a great bond to dislike the same things, and dislike is perhaps a deeper indication of our real nature than explicit affections, since the latter may be effects of circumstances, while dislike is a reaction against them.

I had hoped to go to Cambridge in June, but now it is arranged that I shall go instead to California, where I have never been. I am both glad and sorry for this, but it seemed as well to see the Far West once in one's life, especially as I hope soon to turn my face resolutely in the opposite direction.

Thank you again very much for sending me the book.

Yours sincerely
G. Santayana

(June 1911)
Newnham College
Cambridge

Dear Bertie

I have heard from Alys. I cannot help saying how sad I am for you as well as her – you have been thro' hell I know – that is written in your face.

May I say just this? You have always stood to me for goodness and asceticism – I shall always think of you – till you tell me not – as doing the straight hard thing.

Yours always
Jane E. Harrison

This needs no answer, forgive my writing it. You have been thro' too much these last days to want to see people, but I am always glad when you come.

Telegraph House
Chichester
6 June, 1911

My dear Bertie

Mollie and I have both received your news with much regret. We had as you say an idea, but only an idea, that the original devotion had rather passed away, and that you found each other trying, but we hoped nothing so definite as a separation would result. People of good manners can often manage to get on in the same house, once they have agreed to differ, and I hope for the comfort of both of you, and your friends, that this may still be the case. But of that of course you are the only possible judges.

In the meantime we can only regret the annoyance any such re-arrangement causes, and the break up of a union which seemed to promise well at the beginning. A broken marriage is always a tragedy.

Yours affectionately
Russell

Trinity College
Cambridge
June 11th, 1911

My dear Gilbert

Thank you very much indeed for your kind letter. The decision[1] as you know, is not sudden or hasty; and though the present is painful, I feel no doubt that *both* will in the long run be happier.

It is true that I have seen less of you than formerly – I wish it were not. But business and work seem to overwhelm one more and more. During the time I lived at Oxford I never could shake off work except by going away. I suppose that is the essence of middle age. But I do not find, on that account, that my affections grow less – it is only the outward show that suffers.

Please give my love to Mary.

Yours ever
Bertrand Russell

June 17, 1911
I Tatti
Settignano (Florence)

My dear Bertie

I have just received a telegram, telling me of Karin's success in her Tripos, and I cannot help writing to express my gratitude to you for

[1] To leave Alys.

your overwhelming share in bringing this about. I feel most sincerely grateful. I cannot but hope further work of the same nature may be temptingly put in her way, for she seems to have a capacity to do it well, and it might 'make a man of her', so to speak. So I beg of you to continue to bear the child in mind, and suggest her doing any work that you may think it worth while for her to do.

I won't say anything about the decision you and Alys have come to, except to send you my love and sympathy in all you have certainly suffered over it, and to assure you of B. B.'s and my continued friendliness and good wishes.

Yours always affectionately
Mary Berenson

(From Gilbert Murray, on
  Problems of Philosophy)

The Home University Library
14 Henrietta Street
Covent Garden, W.C.
August 10, 1911

Messrs Williams and Norgate[1] will be glad to meet Mr Russell's wishes as far as practicable, but have some difficulty in understanding his point of view. About the earwig, for instance, they are ready, if Mr Russell is inconvenienced by his suspicions of its presence in his room, to pay a rat-catcher (who is also accustomed to earwigs) two-shillings an hour to look for it and make sure, provided the total payment does not exceed Ten Shillings. (10s.) The animal, if caught, shall be regarded as Mr Russell's property, but in no case shall its capture, or the failure to capture it, be held as exonerating Mr Russell from his contract with Messrs W & N. Mr Russell's further complaint that he has not the acquaintance of the Emperor of China cannot be regarded by Messrs W & N as due in any way to any oversight or neglect of theirs. Mr R should have stipulated for an introduction before signing his contract. As to Mr Russell's memory of his breakfast and his constantly returning alarm lest his next meal should poison him, Messrs W & N express their fullest sympathy with Mr R in his trying situation, but would point out that remonstrances should be addressed not to them but to the Head Cook at Trinity College. In the meantime they trust that they do not exceed their duty in remind-ing Mr Russell that, in his own words, a philosopher should not always have his mind centred upon such subjects. They would observe further that their senior editor is much gratified by Mr Russell's frank admission that a bald man is, nevertheless, a man, while his next

[1] Publishers of The Home University Library of which Gilbert Murray was one of the editors.

sentence has caused some little trouble among the staff. All three editors have rather good figures; at least there is no one among them who could be called conspicuously 'plain' in that respect. Perhaps Mr Russell referred to Mr Perris ?[1] If so, however, we do not quite understand who is meant by the poet. We would almost venture to suggest the omission of all these personalities. When gratifying to one individual, they nearly always give pain to others.

> The Mischief Inn,
> Madingley Road
> 26. VIII. 11

Dear Russell

I send you all I can find of the notes Frege sent me on my account of his work.

Hardy told me of your translation into symbolism of the Deceased Wife's Sister Bill. If you have time would you send it to me to include in the 'Philosophy of Mr B — R —'.[2] Also Hardy told me of your proof of the existence of God by an infinite complex of false propositions.[3] May I have this too ?

> *Yrs. ever*
> *Philip Jourdain*

Georg Cantor, the subject of the following letter, was, in my opinion, one of the greatest intellects of the nineteenth century. The controversy with Poincaré which he mentions is still (1949) raging, though the original protagonists are long since dead. After reading the following letter, no one will be surprised to learn that he spent a large part of his life in a lunatic asylum, but his lucid intervals were devoted to creating the theory of infinite numbers.

He gave me a book on the Bacon–Shakespeare question, and wrote on the cover: 'I see your motto is "Kant or Cantor" and described Kant as "yonder sophistical Philistine who knew so little mathematics." ' Unfortunately I never met him.

> 75 Victoria Street
> S.W.
> 16. 9. 11

Dear Mr Russell

By accident I met to-day Professor Georg Cantor, professor of Mathematics at Halle University, and his chief wish during his stay in

---

[1] Assistant Editor.

[2] A humorous résumé of my conversations with Jourdain.

[3] Most unfortunately I have forgotten this proof, and have no note of it, so this rather important matter must remain in doubt.

England is to meet you and talk about your books. He was overcome
with pleasure when he learnt on talking of Cambridge that I knew you
a little – you must forgive my boasting of my acquaintance with an
English 'Mathematiker' and I had to promise I would try to find out
if he could see you. He proposes to visit Cambridge on Tuesday and
Oxford on Thursday, and meanwhile is staying for a week at 62
Nevern Square, South Kensington.

It was a great pleasure to meet him though if you are kind enough to
see him you will sympathise with my feeling worn out with nearly four
hours conversation. He was like a fog horn discoursing on Mathematics – to me! – and the Bacon theory.[1]

Could you send a line to him or to me at Woodgate, Danehill,
Sussex. He is a Geheimrath & so forth. I could relate his whole family
history to you!

> *Yours sincerely and with many*
> *apologies*
> *Margery I. Corbett Ashby*

To the Hon. Bertrand Russell   19 Sept. 1911
  Trinity College, Cambridge   62 Nevern Square
                                   South Kensington
                                   London

Sir and dear Colleague!

From Mrs Margaret Corbett Ashby I have to present you with the
ensuing letter. I am now staying here for a week about, with my
daughter Mary, probably unto Sunday 24 Sept. on which day I will
depart perhaps to Paris also for a week about, or to go at home. It
would give me much pleasure if you could accompany us to Paris.
There we could meet perhaps Monsieur Poincaré together, which
would be a fine jolly 'Trio'.

As for myself you do know perhaps, that I am a great heretic upon
many scientific, but also in many literary matters, as, to pronounce
but two of them: I am Baconian in the Bacon–Shakespeare question
and I am *quite an adversary* of *Old Kant*, who, in my eyes has done
much harm and mischief to philosophy, even to mankind; as you easily
see by the most perverted development of metaphysics in Germany
in all that followed him, as in Fichte, Schelling, Hegel, Herbart,
Schopenhauer, Hartmann, Nietzsche, etc. etc. on to this very day. I
never could understand that and why such reasonable and enobled
peoples as the Italiens, the English and the French are, could follow
yonder *sophistical philistine*, who was *so bad a mathematician*.

[1] He thought that Bacon wrote Shakespeare and that Christ was the
natural son of Joseph of Arimathea.

And now it is that in just this abominable mummy, as Kant is, Monsieur Poincaré felt quite enamoured, if he is not bewitched by him. So I understand quite well the opposition of Mons. Poincaré, by which I felt myself honoured, though he never had in his mind to honour me, as I am sure. If he perhaps expect, that I will answer him for defending myself, he is certainly in great a mistake.

I think he is about ten years younger than I, but I have learned to wait in all things and I foresee now clearly, that in this quarrel *I will not be the succumbent*. I let him do at his pleasure.

But I feel no forcing to enter myself into the battle; others will him precipitate and I allowed to do with greater and more important things. As for the little differences between you and me, I am sure, that they will disappear soon after an oral discourse.

I intend to pay a visit today to Major Macmahon.

I hope to see you in these days in Cambridge or in London, and so I am, Sir,

> *Your very faithfull*
> *Georg Cantor*

On Thursday to Friday we are to follow an invitation of Mrs Constance Pott, an old friend and correspondent of mine, of London, staying now in Folkestone, 15 Clifton Crescent.

As to Kant and his successors I see, and will show you the real cause of his standing upon so *seeming*-fermly ground of success, honour, veneration, idolatry. *This cause is*, that the German Protestantism in his development to 'Liberalism' *needs* himself a *fundament* on which to build his *seeming*-Christianity, so Kant or one of his successors are picked out, by the protestant Theologians of divers scools, to be their *Atlas*. One hand washes the other, one depends on the other and *one has to fall with the other !*

I never did harm to Monsieur Poincaré; au contraire, je l'honorait fortement dans mes 'grundlagen einer allgemeinen-M. lehre'.

To the Hon. Bertrand Russell	London
Trinity College, Cambridge	19 Sept. 1911

Dear Sir

My first letter to you was just finished as I received your despatch. If I would be free and would not depend upon the freewill of two young German Ladies, my daughter Mary and my niece Fräulein Alice Guttmann of Berlin, I would come *this just* day to meet you in Ipsden Wallingford. So probably I can generally not come to you!

> *Yours faithfully*
> *Georg Cantor*

This second letter being finished, just I receive the following despatch from my dear wife at home.

'Erich erkrankt – sofort Halle kommen.'

You see, dear Sir, destiny playing upon me. The two young ladies I spoke of, are just departed to see Westminster.

It is my *only* son Erich, *quite healthy* when I left him; he is the Doctor of one division of a large Hospital of alienates in Bunzlau (Silesia). He is 32 years old.

I will hope that the worst has not happened.

He had been married three months ago and we assisted at his wedding with a very amiabel good and clever young girl, daughter of a tanner in the little Saxonia town Nossen in the Kingdom of Saxony.

My address in Halle a.d. Saale is: Handelstr. 13. We depart this evening. I hope to be here in the last half of August 1912 to the international Congress.

I had been also just writing a short description of my journey to and sojourning at Saint Andrews, and I intented to offer it to the editor of 'Review of Reviews'.

I could not go to Major Macmahon as had been my intention to do; you will see it in my first letter.

In Saint Andrews I have seen with great pleasure my very good friend Mr Hobson of Cambridge, who was going to Mailand to a congress of Mr Felix Klein, the great field-marshall of all german Mathematicians. Neither my father nor my mother were of german blood, the first being a Dane, borne in Kopenhagen, my mother of Austrian Hungar descension. You must know, Sir, that I am not a *regular just Germain*, for I am born 3 March 1845 at Saint Peterborough, Capital of Russia, but I went with my father and mother and brothers and sister, eleven years old in the year 1856, into Germany, first sojourning at Wiesbaden, then at Frankfort a/Main, then at Darmstadt, four years, then at Zürich, Berlin and Göttingen, coming then as 'Privat Dozent' Easter of the year 1869 to Halle a.d. Saale where I stay now *forty two* years and more.

Dear Sir

The last word of mine to you is *a good one*, just I receive from my wife the second telegram: 'Erich besser.' But you will understand that we must return this evening at home.

41 Grosvenor Road
Westminster Embankment
October 11th (1912)

My dear Bertrand

I was so sorry not to see you when you called the other day, and I feel that I cannot let your visit pass in silence.

Now don't be angry with me, if I ask you to put yourself in our place. Supposing you and Alys were living in absolute happiness in complete comradship [*sic*], and you became aware that Sidney had repudiated me, and that I was 'living on in a state of dark despair'. Would you not, both of you, feel rather sore with Sidney?

I know nothing of the cause of your estrangement – all I know is that Alys wants us to be friends with you. And that is also my own instinct. I have always admired your very great intelligence, and tho' I have sometimes had my doubts about the strength of your character, I have always felt its peculiar charm.

So don't think that I have withdrawn my friendship; and if, at any time, I can be of use to you, with or without your complete confidence let me know and come and see me. And now that I have expressed quite frankly what is in my mind come and see us, if you feel inclined, and talk about the world's affairs without reference to your and Alys' troubles.

We had a delightful time in the Far East and India – there are wonderful new outlooks in Human Purpose and Human Destiny, both in Japan and among the Hindus in India. We were wholly unable to appreciate China and found ourselves unsympathetic to Mohamedan India.

Now we are again immersed in British problems: but the memory of our travels is a constant refreshment. Why don't you go for a long holiday and complete change of thought?

> *Ever your friend*
> *Beatrice Webb*

> 37 Alfred Place W
> South Kensington, S.W.
> 13 October 1912

Dear Mr Russell

Thanks for your kind letter. I will ask Dr Seal to pay you a visit at Cambridge, when you will have an opportunity to know him.

I read your article on the Essence of Religion in the last issue of the *Hibbert Journal* with very great interest. It reminded me of a verse in the Upanishad which runs thus –

'Yato vácho nivartanté aprápya manasá saha

Ánandam Brahmano Vidván na vibhéti Kutushchana.'

'From him words, as well as mind, come back baffled. Yet he who knows the joy of Brahman (the Infinite) is free from all fear.'

Through knowledge you cannot apprehend him; yet when you live the life of the Infinite and are not bound within the limits of the finite self you realise that great joy which is above all the pleasures and pains of our selfish life and so you are free from all fear.

This joy itself is the positive perception of Brahman. It is not a creed which authority imposes on us but an absolute realisation of the Infinite which we can only attain by breaking through the bonds of the narrow self and setting our will and love free.

> *Yours sincerely*
> *Rabindranath Tagore*

Trinity College
13th Feb. 1913

My dear Goldie

It was very nice to see your handwriting, and such parts of your letter as I could decipher interested me very much! (In fact, there was very little I didn't make out in the end.) I am interested to see that India is *too* religious for you. Religion and daily bread – superstition and the belly – it doesn't sound attractive. I expect you will find China much more interesting – much more civilised, and more aware of the subtler values – at least if you could get in touch with the educated people.

I haven't much news. I suppose you have become aware that the Tories have dropped food taxes, and are on the move about protection in general; also that the Germans are accepting a 16 to 10 naval proportion, so that the public world is rather cheerful. Here in Cambridge things go on as usual. There is another agitation against Little-Go Greek being got up, and everybody is saying what they have always said. It all seems rather remote from anything of real importance. My friend Wittgenstein was elected to the Society, but thought it a waste of time, so he imitated henry john roby[1] and was cursed. I think he did quite right, though I tried to dissuade him. He is much the most apostolic and the ablest person I have come across since Moore.

I have done nothing to my Discourse. All the later summer I tried in vain to recapture the mood in which I had written it, but winter in England being in any case hopeless for that sort of writing I gave up for the present, and have been working at the philosophy of matter, in which I seem to see an opening for something important. The whole question of our knowledge of the external world is involved. In the spring of next year, I am going to Harvard for three months to lecture. I doubt if the people there are much good, but it will be

---

[1] Henry John Roby was elected a member of the Society, but wrote to say that he was far too busy to attend the meetings and was therefore ritualistically cursed and his name was spelt thenceforth without capitals. Ever after when a new member was elected the curse was solemnly read out.

interesting. Santayana has brought out a new book, *Winds of Doctrine*, mostly on Bergson and me. I have only looked it through so far – it has his usual qualities. Karin read a paper in praise of Bergson to the Aristotelian the other day – Moore and I attacked her with all imaginable ferocity, but she displayed undaunted courage. – Frank Darwin is going to marry Mrs Maitland, as I suppose you have heard. – There – that is all the news I can think of – it all seems curiously trivial. We here in Cambridge all keep each other going by the unquestioned assumption that what we do is important, but I often wonder if it really is. What is important I wonder? Scott and his companions dying in the blizzard seem to me impervious to doubt – and his record of it has a really great simplicity. But intellect, except at white heat, is very apt to be trivial.

I feel as if one would only discover on one's death-bed what one ought to have lived for, and realise too late that one's life had been wasted. Any passionate and courageous life seems good in itself, yet one feels that some element of delusion is involved in giving so much passion to any humanly attainable object. And so irony creeps into the very springs of one's being. Are you finding the Great Secret in the East? I doubt it. There is none – there is not even an enigma. There is science and sober daylight and the business of the day – the rest is mere phantoms of the dusk. Yet I know that when the summer comes I shall think differently.

I wish I were with you, or you with me. Give my love to Bob.[1]

> *Yours ever*
> B. *Russell*

The Doves Press
April 1913

My dear Bertie

At last, at last the Miltons are bound and I am sending them to your address at Trinity. I also was at Trinity this year just half a century ago and this same year just the same long time ago first saw your mother then Kate Stanley. I am not sorry then to have so long delayed as to make my little offering in this same year of grace.

In a little while this will be closed and I shall be printing no more books – did I send you my swan-song? I forget. But before I close I shall have printed the letters in their year of anniversary, 1914, and that will make a fitting end.

Let me hear of you and see you when next you come to Town.

> *Affectionately always*
> T. *J. Cobden-Sanderson*

[1] Trevelyan.

Hon. B. A. W. Russell   29 Sparks Street
Trinity College   Cambridge, Mass.
Cambridge, Eng.   June 15, 1913
Esteemed Colleague

My son, Norbert Wiener, will this week receive his degree of Ph.D. at Harvard University, his thesis being 'A comparative Study of the Algebra of Relatives of Schroeder and that of Whitehead and Russell'. He had expected to be here next year and have the privilege of being your student in the second semester, but as he has received a travelling fellowship, he is obliged to pass the whole of the year in Europe, and so he wishes to enjoy the advantage of studying under you at Trinity during the first half of the academic year. He intended to write to you about this matter, but his great youth, – he is only eighteen years old and his consequent inexperience with what might be essential for him to know in his European sojourn, leads me to do this service for him and ask your advice.

Norbert graduated from College, receiving his A.B., at the age of fourteen, not as the result of premature development or of unusual precocity, but chiefly as the result of careful home training, free from useless waste, which I am applying to all of my children. He is physically strong (weighing 170 lbs.), perfectly balanced morally and mentally, and shows no traits generally associated with early precocity. I mention all this to you that you may not assume that you are to deal with an exceptional or freakish boy, but with a normal student whose energies have not been mis-directed. Outside of a broad, and liberal classical education, which includes Greek, Latin, and the modern languages, he has had a thorough course in the sciences, and in Mathematics has studied the Differential and integral Calculus, Differential Equations, the Galois Theory of Equations, and some branches of Modern Algebra (under Prof. Huntington). In philosophy he has pursued studies under Professors Royce, Perry, Palmer, Münsterberg, Schmidt, Holt, etc., at Harvard and Cornell Universities.[1] His predilection is entirely for Modern Logic, and he wishes during his one or two years' stay in Europe to be benefited from those who have done distinguished work in that direction.

Will he be able to study under you, or be directed by you, if he comes to Cambridge in September or early October? What should he do in order to enjoy that privilege? I have before me The Student's Handbook to Cambridge for 1908, but I am unable to ascertain from it that any provisions are made for graduate students wishing to obtain such special instruction or advice. Nor am I able to find out anything about his residence there, whether he would have to matriculate in

[1] Nevertheless he turned out well.

234 *The Autobiography of Bertrand Russell*

Trinity College or could take rooms in the city. This is rather an important point to him as he is anxious, as far as possible, to get along on his rather small stipend. For any such information, which would smooth his first appearance in a rather strange world to him I shall be extremely obliged to you.

I shall take great pleasure to thank you in person for any kindness that thus may be shown to my son, when, next year, you come to our American Cambridge to deliver lectures in the Department of Philosophy.

> *Sincerely Yours*
> *Leo Wiener*
> *Professor of Slavic Languages*
> *and Literatures at Harvard*
> *University*

> Capel House
> Orlestone
> Nr. Ashford, Kent
> 4 Sept. 1913

Dear Sir

Why bring a bicycle in this windy, uncertain weather? The true solution is to take a ticket (by the 11 a.m. train from Charing Cross I presume) to Hamstreet (*change* in Ashford after a few minutes' wait) where my boy will meet you with our ancient puffer and bring you to the door before half past one. Then there is a decent train at 5.48 from Ashford to get back to town a few minutes after seven.

Whether there's anything in me to make up for you the grind of the journey I don't know. What's certain is that you will give me the very greatest pleasure by coming. So you may look upon the expedition as something in the nature of 'good works'. I would suggest Wednesday, since, as far as I know, there is no Act of Parliament as yet to stop the running of trains on that day of the week – our new secular Sunday.

> *Believe me very faithfully yours*
> *Joseph Conrad*

> Capel House
> Orlestone, Nr. Ashford
> 13 Sept. 1913

My dear Russell

Your letter has comforted me greatly. It seems to me that I talked all the time with fatuous egotism. Yet somewhere at the back of my brain I had the conviction that you would understand my unusual talkativeness. Generally I don't know what to say to people. But your personality drew me out. My instinct told me I would not be misread.

Let me thank you most heartily for the pleasure of your visit and for the letter you had the friendly thought to write.

> *Believe me sincerely yours*
> *Joseph Conrad*

Capel House
Orlestone, Nr. Ashford
22 Dec. 1913

My dear Russell

Just a word of warmest good wishes from us all.

I am glad I read the little book before coming to your essays. If in reading the first I felt moving step by step, with delight, on the firmest ground, the other gave me the sense of an enlarged vision in the clearest, the purest atmosphere. Your significant words so significantly assembled, seemed to wake a new faculty within me. A wonderful experience for which one cannot even express one's thanks – one can only accept it silently like a gift from the Gods. You have reduced to order the inchoate thoughts of a life-time and given a direction to those obscure *mouvements d'ame* which, unguided, bring only trouble to one's weary days on this earth. For the marvellous pages on the Worship of a free man the only return one can make is that of a deep admiring affection, which, if you were never to see me again and forgot my existence tomorrow, will be unalterably yours *usque ad finem.*

> *Yours ever*
> *J. Conrad*

P.S. – I have been reading you yesterday and today and I have received too many different kinds of delight (I am speaking soberly) to be able to write more today.

3 Claremont Crescent
Weston-super-Mare
Jan. 31, '14

Dear Mr Russell

Many thanks for your letter which has come on here where I am, I hope, getting over a short period of illness and incapacity. I am sure that I need not tell you that my expressions of admiration for your work were not mere words. I am not able to agree with your views in some points (at least as I understand them) but I don't feel the smallest doubt about their great value. And I am full of hope and expectation that you will go on to do still better and better, though I am afraid that I can't hope for much longer to be able to appreciate and enjoy any speculation.

I think I understand what you say as to the way in which you philosophise. I imagine that it is the right way and that its promises are never illusions, though they may not be kept to the letter. There is something perhaps in the whole of things that one feels is wanting when one considers the doctrines before one, and (as happens elsewhere) one feels that one knows what one wants and that what one wants is there – if only one could find it. And for my part I believe that one does find it more or less. And yet still I must believe that one never does or can find the whole in all its aspects, and that there never after all will be a philosopher who did not reach his truth, after all, except by some partiality and one-sidedness – and that, far from mattering, this is the right and the only way. This is however only faith and I could not offer to prove it.

I am sure that in my own work, such as it is, I have illustrated the partiality – if nothing else. I am afraid that I always write too confidently – perhaps because otherwise I might not write at all. Still I don't see that in doing so one can do much harm, or run the risk of imposing on anyone whose judgment is of any value.

If I have helped you in any way by my objections, that I feel will justify their existence more or less – even where they are quite mistaken – and it will be a very great satisfaction to me always to have had your good opinion of my work.

Perhaps I may add that I am getting the impression that I have been tending more and more to take refuge in the unknown and unknowable – in a way which I maintain is right, but which still is not what I quite like.

Wishing you all success with your work and venturing to express the hope that you will not allow yourself to be hurried.

> *I am*
> *Yours truly*
> *F. H. Bradley*

1914–1944

The Defiled Sanctuary

by William Blake

I saw a chapel all of gold
    That none did dare to enter in,
And many weeping stood without,
    Weeping, mourning, worshipping.

I saw a serpent rise between
    The white pillars of the door,
And he forced and forced and forced
    Till down the golden hinges tore:

And along the pavement sweet,
    Set with pearls and rubies bright,
All his shining length he drew, –
    Till upon the altar white

Vomited his poison out
    On the bread and on the wine.
So I turned into a sty,
    And laid me down among the swine.

Chapter 8

The First War

The period from 1910 to 1914 was a time of transition. My life before 1910 and my life after 1914 were as sharply separated as Faust's life before and after he met Mephistopheles. I underwent a process of rejuvenation, inaugurated by Ottoline Morrell and continued by the War. It may seem curious that the War should rejuvenate anybody, but in fact it shook me out of my prejudices and made me think afresh on a number of fundamental questions. It also provided me with a new kind of activity, for which I did not feel the staleness that beset me whenever I tried to return to mathematical logic. I have therefore got into the habit of thinking of myself as a non-supernatural Faust for whom Mephistopheles was represented by the Great War.

During the hot days at the end of July, I was at Cambridge, discussing the situation with all and sundry. I found it impossible to believe that Europe would be so mad as to plunge into war, but I was persuaded that, if there was war, England would be involved. I felt strongly that England ought to remain neutral, and I collected the signatures of a large number of professors and Fellows to a statement which appeared in the *Manchester Guardian* to that effect. The day War was declared, almost all of them changed their minds. Looking back, it seems extraordinary that one did not realise more clearly what was coming. On Sunday, August 2nd, as mentioned in the earlier volume of this autobiography, I met Keynes hurrying across the Great Court of Trinity to borrow his brother-in-law's motor-bicycle to go up to London.[1] I presently discovered that the Government had sent for him to give them financial advice. This made me realise the imminence of our participation in the War. On the Monday morning I decided to go to London. I lunched with the Morrells at Bedford Square, and found Ottoline entirely of my way of thinking. She agreed with Philip's determination to make a pacifist speech in the House. I went down to the House in the hope of hearing Sir Edward Grey's famous statement, but the crowd was too great, and I failed to get in. I learned, however, that Philip had duly made his speech. I spent the evening walking round the streets, especially in the neighbourhood of

[1] His brother-in-law was A. V. Hill, eminent in scientific medicine. He had rooms on the next staircase to mine.

Trafalgar Square, noticing cheering crowds, and making myself sensitive to the emotions of passers-by. During this and the following days I discovered to my amazement that average men and women were delighted at the prospect of war. I had fondly imagined, what most pacifists contended, that wars were forced upon a reluctant population by despotic and Machiavellian governments. I had noticed during previous years how carefully Sir Edward Grey lied in order to prevent the public from knowing the methods by which he was committing us to the support of France in the event of war. I naïvely imagined that when the public discovered how he had lied to them, they would be annoyed; instead of which, they were grateful to him for having spared them the moral responsibility.

On the morning of August 4th, I walked with Ottoline up and down the empty streets behind the British Museum, where now there are University buildings. We discussed the future in gloomy terms. When we spoke to others of the evils we foresaw, they thought us mad; yet it turned out that we were twittering optimists compared to the truth. On the evening of the 4th, after quarrelling with George Trevelyan along the whole length of the Strand, I attended the last meeting of a neutrality committee of which Graham Wallas was chairman. During the meeting there was a loud clap of thunder, which all the older members of the committee took to be a German bomb. This dissipated their last lingering feeling in favour of neutrality. The first days of the War were to me utterly amazing. My best friends, such as the Whiteheads, were savagely warlike. Men like J. L. Hammond, who had been writing for years against participation in a European War, were swept off their feet by Belgium. As I had long known from a military friend at the Staff College that Belgium would inevitably be involved, I had not supposed important publicists so frivolous as to be ignorant on this vital matter. The *Nation* newspaper used to have a staff luncheon every Tuesday, and I attended the luncheon on August 4th. I found Massingham, the editor, vehemently opposed to our participation in the war. He welcomed enthusiastically my offer to write for his newspaper in that sense. Next day I got a letter from him, beginning: 'Today is not yesterday . . .', and stating that his opinion had completely changed. Nevertheless, he printed a long letter from me protesting against the War in his next issue.[1] What changed his opinion I do not know. I know that one of Asquith's daughters saw him descending the steps of the German Embassy late on the afternoon of August 4th, and I have some suspicion that he was consequently warned of the unwisdom of a lack of patriotism in such a crisis. For the first year or so of the War he remained patriotic, but as time went on he began to forget that he had ever been so. A few pacifist MPs, together with two or three

[1] The full text is reproduced on page 264.

sympathisers, began to have meetings at the Morrells' house in Bedford Square. I used to attend these meetings, which gave rise to the Union of Democratic Control. I was interested to observe that many of the pacifist politicians were more concerned with the question which of them should lead the anti-war movement than with the actual work against the War. Nevertheless, they were all there was to work with, and I did my best to think well of them.

Meanwhile, I was living at the highest possible emotional tension. Although I did not foresee anything like the full disaster of the War, I foresaw a great deal more than most people did. The prospect filled me with horror, but what filled me with even more horror was the fact that the anticipation of carnage was delightful to something like ninety per cent of the population. I had to revise my views on human nature. At that time I was wholly ignorant of psycho-analysis, but I arrived for myself at a view of human passions not unlike that of the psycho-analysts. I arrived at this view in an endeavour to understand popular feeling about the War. I had supposed until that time that it was quite common for parents to love their children, but the War persuaded me that it is a rare exception. I had supposed that most people liked money better than almost anything else, but I discovered that they liked destruction even better. I had supposed that intellectuals frequently loved truth, but I found here again that not ten per cent of them prefer truth to popularity. Gilbert Murray, who had been a close friend of mine since 1902, was a pro-Boer when I was not. I therefore naturally expected that he would again be on the side of peace; yet he went out of his way to write about the wickedness of the Germans, and the super-human virtue of Sir Edward Grey. I became filled with despairing tenderness towards the young men who were to be slaughtered, and with rage against all the statesmen of Europe. For several weeks I felt that if I should happen to meet Asquith or Grey I should be unable to refrain from murder. Gradually, however, these personal feelings disappeared. They were swallowed up by the magnitude of the tragedy, and by the realisation of the popular forces which the statesmen merely let loose.

In the midst of this, I was myself tortured by patriotism. The successes of the Germans before the Battle of the Marne were horrible to me. I desired the defeat of Germany as ardently as any retired colonel. Love of England is very nearly the strongest emotion I possess, and in appearing to set it aside at such a moment, I was making a very difficult renunciation. Nevertheless, I never had a moment's doubt as to what I must do. I have at times been paralysed by scepticism, at times I have been cynical, at other times indifferent, but when the War came I felt as if I heard the voice of God. I knew that it was my business to protest, however futile protest might be. My whole nature was involved. As a lover of truth, the national propaganda of all the belligerent nations sickened me. As a lover of civilisation, the return to barbarism appalled me. As a man of thwarted parental feeling, the massacre of the young wrung my heart. I hardly supposed that much good would come of opposing the War, but I felt that for the honour of human nature those who were not swept off their feet should show that they stood firm. After seeing troop trains departing from Waterloo, I used to have strange visions of London as a place of unreality. I used in imagination to see the bridges collapse and sink, and the whole great city vanish like a morning mist. Its inhabitants began to seem like hallucinations, and I would wonder whether the world in which I thought I had lived was a mere product of my own febrile nightmares.[1] Such moods, however, were brief, and were put an end to by the need of work.

Throughout the earlier phases of the War, Ottoline was a very great help and strength to me. But for her, I should have been at first completely solitary, but she never wavered either in her hatred of war, or in her refusal to accept the myths and falsehoods with which the world was inundated.

I found a minor degree of comfort in the conversation of Santayana, who was at Cambridge at that time. He was a neutral, and in any case he had not enough respect for the human race to care whether it destroyed itself or not. His calm, philosophical detachment, though I had no wish to imitate it, was soothing to me. Just before the Battle of the Marne, when it looked as if the Germans must soon take Paris, he remarked in a dreamy tone of voice: 'I think I must go over to Paris. My winter underclothes are there, and I should not like the Germans to get them. I have also another, though less important, reason, which is that I have there a manuscript of a book on which I have been working for the last ten years, but I do not care so much about that as about the underclothes.' He did not, however, go to Paris, because the Battle of the Marne saved him the trouble. Instead, he remarked to me one day: 'I am going to Seville tomorrow because I wish to be in a place where people do not restrain their passions.'

With the beginning of the October Term, I had to start again lecturing on mathematical logic, but I felt it a somewhat futile occupation. So I took to organising a branch of the Union of Democratic Control among the dons, of whom at Trinity quite a number were at first sympathetic. I also addressed meetings of undergraduates who were quite willing to listen to me. I remember in the course of a speech, saying: 'It is all nonsense to pretend the Germans are wicked', and to my surprise the whole room applauded. But with the sinking of the *Lusitania*, a fiercer spirit began to prevail. It seemed to be supposed that I was in some way responsible for this disaster. Of the dons who had belonged

[1] I spoke of this to T. S. Eliot, who put it into *The Waste Land*.

to the Union of Democratic Control, many had by this time got commissions. Barnes (afterwards Bishop of Birmingham) left to become Master of the Temple. The older dons got more and more hysterical, and I began to find myself avoided at the high table.

Every Christmas throughout the War I had a fit of black despair, such complete despair that I could do nothing except sit idle in my chair and wonder whether the human race served any purpose. At Christmas time in 1914, by Ottoline's advice, I found a way of making despair not unendurable. I took to visiting destitute Germans on behalf of a charitable committee to investigate their circumstances and to relieve their distress if they deserved it. In the course of this work, I came upon remarkable instances of kindness in the middle of the fury of war. Not infrequently in the poor neighbourhoods landladies, themselves poor, had allowed Germans to stay on without paying any rent, because they knew it was impossible for Germans to find work. This problem ceased to exist soon afterwards, as the Germans were all interned, but during the first months of the War their condition was pitiable.

One day in October 1914 I met T. S. Eliot in New Oxford Street. I did not know he was in Europe, but I found he had come to England from Berlin. I naturally asked him what he thought of the War. 'I don't know,' he replied, 'I only know that I am not a pacifist.' That is to say, he considered any excuse good enough for homicide. I became great friends with him, and subsequently with his wife, whom he married early in 1915. As they were desperately poor, I lent them one of the two bedrooms in my flat, with the result that I saw a great deal of them.[1] I was fond of them both, and endeavoured to help them in their troubles until I discovered that their troubles were what they enjoyed. I held some debentures nominally worth £3,000, in an engineering firm, which during the War naturally took to making munitions. I was much puzzled in my conscience as to what to do with these debentures, and at last I gave them to Eliot. Years afterwards, when the War was finished and he was no longer poor, he gave them back to me.

During the summer of 1915 I wrote *Principles of Social Reconstruction*, or *Why Men Fight* as it was called in America without my consent. I had had no intention of writing such a book, and it was totally unlike anything I had previously written, but it came out in a spontaneous manner. In fact I did not discover what it was all about until I had finished it. It has a framework and a formula, but I only discovered both when I had written all except the first and last words. In it I suggested a philosophy of politics based upon the belief that impulse has more effect than conscious purpose in moulding men's lives. I

[1] The suggestion sometimes made, however, that one of us influenced the other is without foundation.

divided impulses into two groups, the possessive and the creative, considering the best life that which is most built on creative impulses. I took, as examples of embodiments of the possessive impulses, the State, war and poverty; and of the creative impulses, education, marriage and religion. Liberation of creativeness, I was convinced, should be the principle of reform. I first gave the book as lectures, and then published it. To my surprise, it had an immediate success. I had written it with no expectation of its being read, merely as a profession of faith, but it brought me in a great deal of money, and laid the foundation for all my future earnings.

These lectures were in certain ways connected with my short friendship with D. H. Lawrence. We both imagined that there was something important to be said about the reform of human relations, and we did not at first realise that we took diametrically opposite views as to the kind of reform that was needed. My acquaintance with Lawrence was brief and hectic, lasting altogether about a year. We were brought together by Ottoline, who admired us both and made us think that we ought to admire each other. Pacifism had produced in me a mood of bitter rebellion, and I found Lawrence equally full of rebellion. This made us think, at first, that there was a considerable measure of agreement between us, and it was only gradually that we discovered that we differed from each other more than either differed from the Kaiser.

There were in Lawrence at that time two attitudes to the war: on the one hand, he could not be whole-heartedly patriotic, because his wife was German; but on the other hand, he had such a hatred of mankind that he tended to think both sides must be right in so far as they hated each other. As I came to know these attitudes, I realised that neither was one with which I could sympathise. Awareness of our differences, however, was gradual on both sides, and at first all went merry as a marriage bell. I invited him to visit me at Cambridge and introduced him to Keynes and a number of other people. He hated them all with a passionate hatred and said they were 'dead, dead, dead'. For a time I thought he might be right. I liked Lawrence's fire, I liked the energy and passion of his feelings, I liked his belief that something very fundamental was needed to put the world right. I agreed with him in thinking that politics could not be divorced from individual psychology. I felt him to be a man of a certain imaginative genius, and, at first, when I felt inclined to disagree with him, I thought that perhaps his insight into human nature was deeper than mine. It was only gradually that I came to feel him a positive force for evil and that he came to have the same feeling about me.

I was at this time preparing the courses of lectures which was afterwards published as *Principles of Social Reconstruction*. He, also, wanted to lecture, and for a time it seemed possible that there might be some sort of loose collaboration between us. We exchanged a number of letters, of which mine are lost but his have been published. In his letters the gradual awareness of the consciousness of our fundamental disagreements can be traced. I was a firm believer in democracy, whereas he had developed the whole philosophy of Fascism before the politicians had thought of it. 'I don't believe', he wrote, 'in democratic control. I think the working man is fit to elect governors or overseers for his immediate circumstances, but for no more. You must utterly revise the electorate. The working man shall elect superiors for the things that concern him immediately, no more. From the other classes, as they rise, shall be elected the higher governors. The thing must culminate in one real head, as every organic thing must – no foolish republic with foolish presidents, but an elected King, something like Julius Caesar.' He, of course, in his imagination, supposed that when a dictatorship was established he would be the Julius Caesar. This was part of the dream-like quality of all his thinking. He never let himself bump into reality. He would go into long tirades about how one must proclaim 'the Truth' to the multitude, and he seemed to have no doubt that the multitude would listen. I asked him what method he was going to adopt. Would he put his political philosophy into a book ? No: in our corrupt society the written word is always a lie. Would he go into Hyde Park and proclaim 'the Truth' from a soap box ? No: that would be far too dangerous (odd streaks of prudence emerged in him from time to time). Well, I said, what would you do ? At this point he would change the subject.

Gradually I discovered that he had no real wish to make the world better, but only to indulge in eloquent soliloquy about how bad it was. If anybody overheard the soliloquies, so much the better, but they were designed at most to produce a little faithful band of disciples who could sit in the deserts of New Mexico and feel holy. All this was conveyed to me in the language of a Fascist dictator as what I *must* preach, the 'must' having thirteen underlinings.

His letters grew gradually more hostile. He wrote, 'What's the good of living as you do anyway ? I don't believe your lectures *are* good. They are nearly over, aren't they ? What's the good of sticking in the damned ship and haranguing the merchant pilgrims in their own language ? Why don't you drop overboard ? Why don't you clear out of the whole show ? One must be an outlaw these days, not a teacher or preacher.' This seemed to me mere rhetoric. I was becoming more of an outlaw than he ever was and I could not quite see his ground of complaint against me. He phrased his complaint in different ways at different times. On another occasion he wrote: 'Do stop working and writing altogether and become a creature instead of a mechanical instrument. Do clear out of the whole social ship. Do for your very pride's sake become a mere nothing, a mole, a creature that feels its way and doesn't think. Do for heavens sake be a baby, and not a savant any more. Don't *do* anything more – but for heavens sake begin to *be* – Start at the very beginning and be a perfect baby: in the name of courage.

'Oh, and I want to ask you, when you make your will, do leave me enough to live on. I want you to live for ever. But I want you to make me in some part your heir.'

The only difficulty with this programme was that if I adopted it I should have nothing to leave.

He had a mystical philosophy of 'blood' which I disliked. 'There is', he said, 'another seat of consciousness than the brain and nerves. There is a blood-consciousness which exists in us independently of the ordinary mental consciousness. One lives, knows and has one's being in the blood, without any reference to nerves and brain. This is one half of life belonging to the darkness. When I take a woman, then the blood-percept is supreme. My blood-knowing is overwhelming. We should realise that we have a blood-being, a blood-consciousness, a blood-soul complete and apart from a mental and nerve consciousness.' This seemed to me frankly rubbish, and I rejected it vehemently, though I did not then know that it led straight to Auschwitz.

He always got into a fury if one suggested that anybody could possibly have kindly feelings towards anybody else, and when I objected to war because of the suffering that it causes, he accused me of hypocrisy. 'It isn't in the least true that you, your basic self, want ultimate peace. You are satisfying in an indirect, false way your lust to jab and strike. Either satisfy it in a direct and honourable way, saying "I hate you all, liars and swine, and am out to set upon you", or stick to mathematics, where you can be true – But to come as the angel of peace – no, I prefer Tirpitz a thousand times in that role.'

I find it difficult now to understand the devastating effect that this letter had upon me. I was inclined to believe that he had some insight denied to me, and when he said that my pacifism was rooted in blood-lust I supposed he must be right. For twenty-four hours I thought that I was not fit to live and contemplated suicide. But at the end of that time, a healthier reaction set in, and I decided to have done with such morbidness. When he said that I *must* preach his doctrines and not mine I rebelled, and told him to remember that he was no longer a school-master and I was not his pupil. He had written, 'the enemy of all mankind you are, full of the lust of enmity. It is *not* a hatred of falsehood which inspires you, it is the hatred of people of flesh and blood, it is a perverted mental blood-lust. Why don't you own it? Let us become strangers again. I think it is better.' I thought so too. But he found a pleasure in denouncing me and continued for some months to write letters containing sufficient friendliness to keep the correspondence alive. In the end, it faded away without any dramatic termination.

Lawrence, though most people did not realise it, was his wife's mouthpiece. He had the eloquence, but she had the ideas. She used to spend part of every summer in a colony of Austrian Freudians at a time when psycho-analysis was little known in England. Somehow, she imbibed prematurely the ideas afterwards developed by Mussolini and Hitler, and these ideas she transmitted to Lawrence, shall we say, by blood-consciousness. Lawrence was an essentially timid man who tried to conceal his timidity by bluster. His wife was not timid, and her denunciations have the character of thunder, not of bluster. Under her wing he felt comparatively safe. Like Marx, he had a snobbish pride in having married a German aristocrat, and in *Lady Chatterley* he dressed her up marvellously. His thought was a mass of self-deception masquerading as stark realism. His descriptive powers were remarkable, but his ideas cannot be too soon forgotten.

What at first attracted me to Lawrence was a certain dynamic quality and a habit of challenging assumptions that one is apt to take for granted. I was already accustomed to being accused of undue slavery to reason, and I thought perhaps that he could give me a vivifying dose of unreason. I did in fact acquire a certain stimulus from him, and I think the book that I wrote in spite of his blasts of denunciation was better than it would have been if I had not known him.

But this is not to say that there was anything good in his ideas. I do not think in retrospect that they had any merit whatever. They were the ideas of a sensitive would-be despot who got angry with the world because it would not instantly obey. When he realised that other people existed, he hated them. But most of the time he lived in a solitary world of his own imaginings, peopled by phantoms as fierce as he wished them to be. His excessive emphasis on sex was due to the fact that in sex alone he was compelled to admit that he was not the only human being in the universe. But it was so painful that he conceived of sex relations as a perpetual fight in which each is attempting to destroy the other.

The world between the wars was attracted to madness. Of this attraction Nazism was the most emphatic expression. Lawrence was a suitable exponent of this cult of insanity. I am not sure whether the cold inhuman sanity of Stalin's Kremlin was any improvement.[1]

With the coming of 1916, the War took on a fiercer form, and the position of pacifists at home became more difficult. My relations with Asquith had never become unfriendly. He was an admirer of Ottoline's before she married, and I used to meet him every now and then at Garsington, where she lived. Once when I had been bathing stark

[1] See also my letters to Ottoline with reference to Lawrence on pages 277–8.

naked in a pond, I found him on the bank as I came out. The quality of
dignity which should have characterised a meeting between the Prime
Minister and a pacifist was somewhat lacking on this occasion. But at
any rate, I had the feeling that he was not likely to lock me up. At the
time of the Easter Rebellion in Dublin, thirty-seven conscientious
objectors were condemned to death and several of us went on a deputation to Asquith to get their sentences reduced. Although he was just
starting for Dublin, he listened to us courteously, and took the necessary action. It had been generally supposed, even by the Government,
that conscientious objectors were not legally liable to the death penalty,
but this turned out to be a mistake, and but for Asquith a number of
them would have been shot.

Lloyd George, however, was a tougher proposition. I went once with
Clifford Allen (chairman of the No Conscription Fellowship) and Miss
Catherine Marshall, to interview him about the conscientious objectors who were being kept in prison. The only time that he could see
us was at lunch at Walton Heath. I disliked having to receive his hospitality, but it seemed unavoidable. His manner to us was pleasant and
easy, but he offered no satisfaction of any kind. At the end, as we were
leaving, I made him a speech of denunciation in an almost Biblical
style, telling him his name would go down to history with infamy. I
had not the pleasure of meeting him thereafter.

With the coming of conscription, I gave practically my whole time
and energies to the affairs of the conscientious objectors. The No
Conscription Fellowship consisted entirely of men of military age, but
it accepted women and older men as associates. After all the original
committee had gone to prison, a substitute committee was formed, of
which I became the acting chairman. There was a great deal of work to
do, partly in looking after the interests of individuals, partly in keeping
a watch upon the military authorities to see that they did not send conscientious objectors to France, for it was only after they had been sent
to France that they became liable to the death penalty. Then there was
a great deal of speaking to be done up and down the country. I spent
three weeks in the mining areas of Wales, speaking sometimes in halls,
sometimes out-of-doors. I never had an interrupted meeting, and
always found the majority of the audience sympathetic so long as I
confined myself to industrial areas. In London, however, the matter
was different.

Clifford Allen,[1] the chairman of the No Conscription Fellowship,
was a young man of great ability and astuteness. He was a Socialist, and
not a Christian. There was always a certain difficulty in keeping harmonious relations between Christian and Socialist pacifists, and in this
respect he showed admirable impartiality. In the summer of 1916,

[1] Afterwards Lord Allen of Hurtwood.

however, he was court-martialled and sent to prison. After that, throughout the duration of the War, I only saw him during the occasional days between sentences. He was released on grounds of health (being, in fact, on the point of death) early in 1918, but shortly after that I went to prison myself.

It was at Clifford Allen's police court case when he was first called up that I first met Lady Constance Malleson, generally known by her stage name of Colette O'Niel. Her mother, Lady Annesley, had a friendship with Prince Henry of Prussia which began before the War and was resumed when the War was over. This, no doubt, gave her some bias in favour of a neutral attitude, but Colette and her sister, Lady Clare Annesley, were both genuine pacifists, and threw themselves into the work of the No Conscription Fellowship. Colette was married to Miles Malleson, the actor and playwright. He had enlisted in 1914, but had had the good luck to be discharged on account of a slight weakness in one foot. The advantageous position which he thus secured, he used most generously on behalf of the conscientious objectors, having after his enlistment become persuaded of the truth of the pacifist position. I noticed Colette in the police court, and was introduced to her. I found that she was one of Allen's friends and learned from him that she was generous with her time, free in her opinions, and whole-hearted in her pacifism. That she was young and very beautiful, I had seen for myself. She was on the stage, and had had a rapid success with two leading parts in succession, but when the War came she spent the whole of the daytime in addressing envelopes in the office of the No Conscription Fellowship. On these data, I naturally took steps to get to know her better.

My relations with Ottoline had been in the meantime growing less intimate. In 1915, she left London and went to live at the Manor House at Garsington, near Oxford. It was a beautiful old house which had been used as a farm, and she became absorbed in restoring all its potentialities. I used to go down to Garsington fairly frequently, but found her comparatively indifferent to me.[1] I sought about for some other woman to relieve my unhappiness, but without success until I met Colette. After the police court proceedings I met Colette next at a dinner of a group of pacifists. I walked back from the restaurant with her and others to the place where she lived, which was 43 Bernard Street, near Russell Square. I felt strongly attracted, but had no chance to do much about it beyond mentioning that a few days later I was to make a speech in the Portman Rooms, Baker Street. When I came to make the speech, I saw her on one of the front seats, so I asked her after

[1] Some of my letters to Lady Ottoline, written during the early years of the War and reflecting the state of my mind at that time, are to be found on pages 276–82, 285–8 and 293–4.

the meeting to come to supper at a restaurant, and then walked back with her. This time I came in, which I had not done before. She was very young, but I found her possessed of a degree of calm courage as great as Ottoline's (courage is a quality that I find essential in any woman whom I am to love seriously). We talked half the night, and in the middle of talk became lovers. There are those who say that one should be prudent, but I do not agree with them. We scarcely knew each other, and yet in that moment there began for both of us a relation profoundly serious and profoundly important, sometimes happy, sometimes painful, but never trivial and never unworthy to be placed alongside of the great public emotions connected with the War. Indeed, the War was bound into the texture of this love from first to last. The first time that I was ever in bed with her (we did not go to bed the first time we were lovers, as there was too much to say), we heard suddenly a shout of bestial triumph in the street. I leapt out of bed and saw a Zeppelin falling in flames. The thought of brave men dying in agony was what caused the triumph in the street. Colette's love was in that moment a refuge to me, not from cruelty itself, which was unescapable, but from the agonising pain of realising that that is what men are. I remember a Sunday which we spent walking on the South Downs. At evening we came to Lewes Station to take the train back to London. The station was crowded with soldiers, most of them going back to the Front, almost all of them drunk, half of them accompanied by drunken prostitutes, the other half by wives or sweethearts, all despairing, all reckless, all mad. The harshness and horror of the war world overcame me, but I clung to Colette. In a world of hate, she preserved love, love in every sense of the word from the most ordinary to the most profound, and she had a quality of rock-like immovability, which in those days was invaluable.

After the night in which the Zeppelin fell I left her in the early morning to return to my brother's house in Gordon Square where I was living. I met on the way an old man selling flowers, who was calling out: 'Sweet lovely roses!' I bought a bunch of roses, paid him for them, and told him to deliver them in Bernard Street. Everyone would suppose that he would have kept the money and not delivered the roses, but it was not so, and I knew it would not be so. The words, 'Sweet lovely roses', were ever since a sort of refrain to all my thoughts of Colette.

We went for a three days' honeymoon (I could not spare more from work) to the 'Cat and Fiddle' on the moors above Buxton. It was bitterly cold and the water in my jug was frozen in the morning. But the bleak moors suited our mood. They were stark, but gave a sense of vast freedom. We spent our days in long walks and our nights in an emotion that held all the pain of the world in solution, but distilled from it an ecstasy that seemed almost more than human.

I did not know in the first days how serious was my love for Colette. I had got used to thinking that all my serious feelings were given to Ottoline. Colette was so much younger, so much less of a personage, so much more capable of frivolous pleasures, that I could not believe in my own feelings, and half supposed that I was having a light affair with her. At Christmas I went to stay at Garsington, where there was a large party. Keynes was there, and read the marriage service over two dogs, ending, 'Whom man hath joined, let not dog put asunder.' Lytton Strachey was there and read us the manuscript of *Eminent Victorians*. Katherine Mansfield and Middleton Murry were also there. I had just met them before, but it was at this time that I got to know her well. I do not know whether my impression of her was just, but it was quite different from other people's. Her talk was marvellous, much better than her writing, especially when she was telling of things that she was going to write, but when she spoke about people she was envious, dark, and full of alarming penetration in discovering what they least wished known and whatever was bad in their characteristics.[1] She hated Ottoline because Murry did not. It had become clear to me that I must get over the feeling that I had had for Ottoline, as she no longer returned it sufficiently to give me any happiness. I listened to all that Katherine Mansfield had to say against her; in the end I believed very little of it, but I had become able to think of Ottoline as a friend rather than a lover. After this I saw no more of Katherine, but was able to allow my feeling for Colette free scope.

The time during which I listened to Katherine was a time of dangerous transition. The War had brought me to the verge of utter cynicism, and I was having the greatest difficulty in believing that anything at all was worth doing. Sometimes I would have fits of such despair as to spend a number of successive days sitting completely idle in my chair with no occupation except to read Ecclesiastes occasionally. But at the end of this time the spring came, and I found myself free of the doubts and hesitations that had troubled me in relation to Colette. At the height of my winter despair, however, I had found one thing to do, which turned out as useless as everything else, but seemed to me at the moment not without value. America being still neutral, I wrote an open letter to President Wilson, appealing to him to save the world. In this letter I said:

Sir,

You have an opportunity of performing a signal service to mankind, surpassing even the service of Abraham Lincoln, great as that was. It is in your power to bring the war to an end by a just peace, which shall do all that could possibly be done to allay the fear of new wars in the

[1] See also my letter to Lady Ottoline on page 277.

near future. It is not yet too late to save European civilisation from destruction; but it may be too late if the war is allowed to continue for the further two or three years with which our militarists threaten us.

The military situation has now developed to the point where the ultimate issue is clear, in its broad outlines, to all who are capable of thought. It must be obvious to the authorities in all the belligerent countries that no victory for either side is possible. In Europe, the Germans have the advantage; outside Europe, and at sea, the Allies have the advantage. Neither side is able to win such a crushing victory as to compel the other to sue for peace. The war inflicts untold injuries upon the nations, but not such injuries as to make a continuance of fighting impossible. It is evident that however the war may be prolonged, negotiations will ultimately have to take place on the basis of what will be substantially the present balance of gains and losses, and will result in terms not very different from those which might be obtained now. The German Government has recognised this fact, and has expressed its willingness for peace on terms which ought to be regarded at least as affording a basis for discussion, since they concede the points which involve the honour of the Allies. The Allied Governments have not had the courage to acknowledge publicly what they cannot deny in private, that the hope of a sweeping victory is one which can now scarcely be entertained. For want of this courage, they are prepared to involve Europe in the horrors of a continuance of the war, possibly for another two or three years. This situation is intolerable to every humane man. You, Sir, can put an end to it. Your power constitutes an opportunity and a responsibility; and from your previous actions I feel confident that you will use your power with a degree of wisdom and humanity rarely to be found among statesmen.

The harm which has already been done in this war is immeasurable. Not only have millions of valuable lives been lost, not only have an even greater number of men been maimed or shattered in health, but the whole standard of civilisation has been lowered. Fear has invaded men's inmost being, and with fear has come the ferocity that always attends it. Hatred has become the rule of life, and injury to others is more desired than benefit to ourselves. The hopes of peaceful progress in which our earlier years were passed are dead, and can never be revived. Terror and savagery have become the very air we breathe. The liberties which our ancestors won by centuries of struggle were sacrificed in a day, and all the nations are regimented to the one ghastly end of mutual destruction.

But all this is as nothing in comparison with what the future has in store for us if the war continues as long as the announcements of some of our leading men would make us expect. As the stress increases, and weariness of the war makes average men more restive, the severity of repression has to be continually augmented. In all the belligerent countries, soldiers who are wounded or home on leave express an utter loathing of the trenches, a despair of ever achieving a military decision, and a terrible longing for peace. Our militarists have successfully opposed the granting of votes to soldiers; yet in all the countries an attempt is made to persuade the civilian population that war-weariness is confined to the enemy soldiers. The daily toll of young lives destroyed becomes a horror almost too terrible to be borne; yet everywhere, advocacy of peace is rebuked as treachery to the soldiers, though the soldiers above all men desire peace. Everywhere, friends of peace are met with the diabolical argument that the brave men who have died must not have shed their blood in vain. And so every impulse of mercy towards the soldiers who are still living is dried up and withered by a false and barren loyalty to those who are past our help. Even the men hitherto retained for making munitions, for dock labour, and for other purposes essential to the prosecution of the war, are gradually being drafted into the armies and replaced by women, with the sinister threat of coloured labour in the background. There is a very real danger that, if nothing is done to check the fury of national passion, European civilisation as we have known it will perish as completely as it perished when Rome fell before the Barbarians.

It may be thought strange that public opinion should appear to support all that is being done by the authorities for the prosecution of the war. But this appearance is very largely deceptive. The continuance of the war is actively advocated by influential persons, and by the Press, which is everywhere under the control of the Government. In other sections of Society feeling is quite different from that expressed by the newspapers, but public opinion remains silent and uninformed, since those who might give guidance are subject to such severe penalties that few dare to protest openly, and those few cannot obtain a wide publicity. From considerable personal experience, reinforced by all that I can learn from others, I believe that the desire for peace is almost universal, not only among the soldiers, but throughout the wage-earning classes, and especially in industrial districts, in spite of high wages and steady employment. If a plebiscite of the nation were taken on the question whether negotiations should be initiated, I am confident that an overwhelming majority would be in favour of this course, and that the same is true of France, Germany, and Austria-Hungary.

Such acquiescence as there is in continued hostilities is due entirely to fear. Every nation believes that its enemies were the aggressors, and may make war again in a few years unless they are utterly defeated. The United States Government has the power, not only to compel the European Governments to make peace, but also to reassure the populations by making itself the guarantor of the peace. Such action, even if it were resented by the Governments, would be hailed with joy by the populations. If the German Government, as now seems likely, would not only restore conquered territory, but also give its adherence to the League to Enforce Peace or some similar method of settling disputes without war, fear would be allayed, and it is almost certain that an offer of mediation from you would give rise to an irresistible movement in favour of negotiations. But the deadlock is such that no near end to the war is likely except through the mediation of an outside Power, and such mediation can only come from you.

Some may ask by what right I address you. I have no formal title; I am not any part of the machinery of government. I speak only because I must; because others, who should have remembered civilisation and human brotherhood, have allowed themselves to be swept away by national passion; because I am compelled by their apostasy to speak in the name of reason and mercy, lest it should be thought that no one in Europe remembers the work which Europe has done and ought still to do for mankind. It is to the European races, in Europe and out of it, that the world owes most of what it possesses in thought, in science, in art, in ideals of government, in hope for the future. If they are allowed to destroy each other in futile carnage, something will be lost which is more precious than diplomatic prestige, incomparably more valuable than a sterile victory which leaves the victors themselves perishing. Like the rest of my countrymen I have desired ardently the victory of the Allies; like them, I have suffered when victory has been delayed. But I remember always that Europe has common tasks to fulfil; that a war among European nations is in essence a civil war; that the ill which we think of our enemies they equally think of us; and that it is difficult in time of war for a belligerent to see facts truly. Above all, I see that none of the issues in the war are as important as peace; the harm done by a peace which does not concede all that we desire is as nothing in comparison to the harm done by the continuance of the fighting. While all who have power in Europe speak for what they falsely believe to be the interests of their separate nations, I am compelled by a profound conviction to speak for all the nations in the name of Europe. In the name of Europe I appeal to you to bring us peace.

The censorship in those days made it difficult to transmit a document of this sort, but Helen Dudley's sister, Katherine, who had been visiting her, undertook to take it back with her to America. She found an ingenious method of concealing it, and duly delivered it to a committee of American pacifists through whom it was published in almost every newspaper in America. As will be seen in this account, I thought, as most people did at that time, that the War could not end in a victory for either party. This would no doubt have been true if America had remained neutral.

From the middle of 1916 until I went to prison in May 1918, I was very busy indeed with the affairs of the No Conscription Fellowship. My times with Colette were such as could be snatched from pacifist work, and were largely connected with the work itself. Clifford Allen would be periodically let out of prison for a few days, to be court-martialled again as soon as it became clear that he still refused to obey military orders. We used to go together to his courts-martial.

When the Kerensky Revolution came, a great meeting of sympathisers with it was held in Leeds. I spoke at this meeting, and Colette and her husband were at it. We travelled up in the train with Ramsay MacDonald, who spent the time telling long stories of pawky Scotch humour so dull that it was almost impossible to be aware when the point had been reached. It was decided at Leeds to attempt to form organisations in the various districts of England and Scotland with a view to promoting workers' and soldiers' councils on the Russian model. In London a meeting for this purpose was held at the Brotherhood Church in Southgate Road. Patriotic newspapers distributed leaflets in all the neighbouring public houses (the district is a very poor one) saying that we were in communication with the Germans and signalled to their aeroplanes as to where to drop bombs. This made us somewhat unpopular in the neighbourhood, and a mob presently besieged the church. Most of us believed that resistance would be either wicked or unwise, since some of us were complete non-resisters, and others realised that we were too few to resist the whole surrounding slum population. A few people, among them Francis Meynell, attempted resistance, and I remember his returning from the door with his face streaming with blood. The mob burst in led by a few officers; all except the officers were more or less drunk. The fiercest were viragos who used wooden boards full of rusty nails. An attempt was made by the officers to induce the women among us to retire first so that they might deal as they thought fit with the pacifist men, whom they supposed to be all cowards. Mrs Snowden behaved on this occasion in a very admirable manner. She refused point-blank to leave the hall unless the men were allowed to leave at the same time. The other women present agreed with her. This rather upset the officers in charge of the roughs, as they did not particularly wish to assault women. But by this time the mob had its blood up, and pandemonium broke loose. Everybody had to escape as best they could while the police looked on calmly. Two of the drunken viragos began to attack me with their boards full of nails. While I was wondering how one defended oneself against this type of attack, one of the ladies among us went up to the police and suggested that they should defend me. The police, however, merely shrugged their shoulders. 'But he is an eminent philosopher', said the lady, and the police still shrugged. 'But he is famous all over the world as a man of learning', she continued. The police remained unmoved. 'But he is the brother of an earl', she finally cried. At this, the police rushed to my assistance. They were, however, too late to be of any service, and I owe my life to a young woman whom I did not know, who interposed herself between me and the viragos long enough for me to make my escape. She, I am happy to say, was not attacked. But quite a number of people, including several women, had their clothes torn off their backs as they left the building. Colette was present on this occasion, but there was a heaving mob between me and her, and I was unable to reach her until we were both outside. We went home together in a mood of deep dejection.

The clergyman to whom the Brotherhood Church belonged was a pacifist of remarkable courage. In spite of this experience, he invited me on a subsequent occasion to give an address in his church. On this occasion, however, the mob set fire to the pulpit and the address was not delivered. These were the only occasions on which I came across personal violence; all my other meetings were undisturbed. But such is the power of Press propaganda that my non-pacifist friends came to me and said: 'Why do you go on trying to address meetings when all of them are broken up by the mob ?'

By this time my relations with the Government had become very bad. In 1916, I wrote a leaflet[1] which was published by the No Conscription Fellowship about a conscientious objector who had been sentenced to imprisonment in defiance of the conscience clause. The leaflet appeared without my name on it, and I found rather to my surprise, that those who distributed it were sent to prison. I therefore wrote to *The Times* to state that I was the author of it. I was prosecuted at the Mansion House before the Lord Mayor, and made a long speech in my own defence. On this occasion I was fined £100. I did not pay the sum, so that my goods at Cambridge were sold to a sufficient amount to realise the fine. Kind friends, however, bought them in and gave them back to me, so that I felt my protest had been somewhat futile. At Trinity, meanwhile, all the younger Fellows had obtained commissions, and the older men naturally wished to do their bit. They therefore deprived me of my lectureship. When the younger men came back at the end of the War I was invited to return, but by this time I had no longer any wish to do so.

Munition workers, oddly enough, tended to be pacifists. My speeches to munition workers in South Wales, all of which were inaccurately reported by detectives, caused the War Office to issue an

[1] The full text will be found on pages 289–90.

256 *The Autobiography of Bertrand Russell*

order that I should not be allowed in any prohibited area.[1] The prohibited areas were those into which it was particularly desired that no spies should penetrate. They included the whole sea-coast. Representations induced the War Office to state that they did not suppose me to be a German spy, but nevertheless I was not allowed to go anywhere near the sea for fear I should signal to the submarines. At the moment when the order was issued I had gone up to London for the day from Bosham in Sussex, where I was staying with the Eliots. I had to get them to bring up my brush and comb and tooth-brush, because the Government objected to my fetching them myself. But for these various compliments on the part of the Government, I should have thrown up pacifist work, as I had become persuaded that it was entirely futile. Perceiving, however, that the Government thought otherwise, I supposed I might be mistaken, and continued. Apart from the question whether I was doing any good, I could not well stop when fear of consequences might have seemed to be my motive.

At the time, however, of the crime for which I went to prison, I had finally decided that there was nothing further to be done, and my brother had caused the Government to know my decision. There was a little weekly newspaper called *The Tribunal*, issued by the No Conscription Fellowship, and I used to write weekly articles for it. After I had ceased to be editor, the new editor, being ill one week, asked me at the last moment to write the weekly article. I did so, and in it I said that American soldiers would be employed as strike-breakers in England, an occupation to which they were accustomed when in their own country.[2] This statement was supported by a Senate Report which I quoted. I was sentenced for this to six months' imprisonment. All this, however, was by no means unpleasant. It kept my self-respect alive, and gave me something to think about less painful than the universal destruction. By the intervention of Arthur Balfour, I was placed in the first division, so that while in prison I was able to read and write as much as I liked, provided I did no pacifist propaganda. I found prison in many ways quite agreeable. I had no engagements, no difficult decisions to make, no fear of callers, no interruptions to my work. I read enormously; I wrote a book, *Introduction to Mathematical Philosophy*, a semi-popular version of *The Principles of Mathematics*, and began the work for *Analysis of Mind.* I was rather interested in my fellow-prisoners, who seemed to me in no way morally inferior to the rest of the population, though they were on the whole slightly below the usual level of intelligence, as was shown by their having been caught. For anybody not in the first division, especially for a person accustomed to reading and

[1] See my statement concerning my meeting with General Cockerill of the War Office on page 300.
[2] The full text is reproduced on pages 308–10.

writing, prison is a severe and terrible punishment; but for me, thanks to Arthur Balfour, this was not so. I owe him gratitude for his intervention although I was bitterly opposed to all his policies. I was much cheered, on my arrival, by the warder at the gate, who had to take particulars about me. He asked my religion and I replied 'agnostic'. He asked how to spell it, and remarked with a sigh: 'Well, there are many religions, but I suppose they all worship the same God.' This remark kept me cheerful for about a week. One time, when I was reading Strachey's *Eminent Victorians*, I laughed so loud that the warder came round to stop me, saying I must remember that prison was a place of punishment. On another occasion Arthur Waley, the translator of Chinese poetry, sent me a translated poem that he had not yet published called 'The Red Cockatoo'.[1] It is as follows:

> Sent as a present from Annam –
> A red cockatoo.
> Coloured like the peach-tree blossom,
> Speaking with the speech of men.
> And they did to it what is always done
> To the learned and eloquent
> They took a cage with stout bars
> And shut it up inside.

I had visits once a week, always of course in the presence of a warder, but nevertheless very cheering. Ottoline and Colette used to come alternately, bringing two other people with them. I discovered a method of smuggling out letters by enclosing them in the uncut pages of books. I could not, of course, explain the method in the presence of the warder, so I practised it first by giving Ottoline the *Proceedings of the London Mathematical Society*, and telling her that it was more interesting than it seemed. Before I invented this device, I found another by which I could incorporate love-letters to Colette into letters which were read by the Governor of the prison. I professed to be reading French Revolutionary Memoirs, and to have discovered letters from the Girondin Buzot to Madame Roland. I concocted letters in French, saying that I had copied them out of a book. His circumstances were sufficiently similar to my own to make it possible to give verisimilitude to these letters. In any case, I suspect that the Governor did not know French, but would not confess ignorance.

The prison was full of Germans, some of them very intelligent. When I once published a review of a book about Kant, several of them came up to me and argued warmly about my interpretation of that philosopher. During part of my time, Litvinov was in the same prison,

[1] Now included in *Chinese Poems* (London, George Allen & Unwin Ltd).

but I was not allowed any opportunity of speaking to him, though I used to see him in the distance.

Some of my moods in prison are illustrated by the following extracts from letters to my brother, all of which had to be such as to be passed by the Governor of the prison:

(May 6, 1918) . . . 'Life here is just like life on an Ocean Liner; one is cooped up with a number of average human beings, unable to escape except into one's own state-room. I see no sign that they are worse than the average, except that they probably have less will-power, if one can judge by their faces, which is all I have to go by. That applies to debtors chiefly. The only real hardship of life here is not seeing one's friends. It was a great delight seeing you the other day. Next time you come, I hope you will bring two others – I think you and Elizabeth both have the list. I am anxious to see as much of my friends as possible. You seemed to think I should grow indifferent on that point but I am certain you were wrong. Seeing the people I am fond of is not a thing I should grow indifferent to, though thinking of them is a great satisfaction. I find it comforting to go over in my mind all sorts of occasions when things have been to my liking.

'Impatience and lack of tobacco do not as yet trouble me as much as I expected, but no doubt they will later. The holiday from responsibility is really delightful, so delightful that it almost outweighs everything else. Here I have not a care in the world: the rest to nerves and will is heavenly. One is free from the torturing question: What more might I be doing? Is there any effective action that I haven't thought of? Have I a right to let the whole thing go and return to philosophy? Here, I *have* to let the whole thing go, which is far more restful than choosing to let it go and doubting if one's choice is justified. Prison has some of the advantages of the Catholic Church . . .'

(May 27, 1918) . . . 'Tell Lady Ottoline I have been reading the two books on the Amazon: Tomlinson I *loved*; Bates bores me while I am reading him, but leaves pictures in my mind which I am glad of afterwards. Tomlinson owes much to *Heart of Darkness*. The contrast with Bates is remarkable: one sees how our generation, in comparison, is a little mad, because it has allowed itself glimpses of the truth, and the truth is spectral, insane, ghastly: the more men see of it, the less mental health they retain. The Victorians (dear souls) were sane and successful because they never came anywhere near truth. But for my part I would rather be mad with truth than sane with lies . . .'

(June 10, 1918) . . . 'Being here in these conditions is not as disagreeable as the time I spent as attaché at the Paris Embassy, and not in the same world of horror as the year and a half I spent at a crammer's. The young men there were almost all going into the Army or the Church, so they were at a much lower moral level than the average . . .

(July 8, 1918) . . . 'I am not fretting at all, on the contrary. At first I thought a good deal about my own concerns, but not (I think) more than was reasonable; now I hardly ever think about them, as I have done all I can. I read a great deal, and think about philosophy quite fruitfully. It is odd and irrational, but the fact is my spirits depend on the military situation as much as anything: when the Allies do well I feel cheerful, when they do badly, I worry over all sorts of things that seem quite remote from the War . . .'

(July 22, 1918) . . . 'I have been reading about Mirabeau. His death is amusing. As he was dying he said "*Ah ! si j'eusse vécu, que j'eusse donné de chagrin à ce Pitt !*" which I prefer to Pitt's words (except in Dizzy's version). They were not however quite the *last* words Mirabeau uttered. He went on: "*Il ne reste plus qu'une chose à faire: c'est de se parfumer, de se couronner de fleurs et de s'environner de musique, afin d'entrer agréablement dans ce sommeil dont on ne se réveille plus. Legrain, qu'on se prépare à me raser, à faire ma toilette toute entière.*" Then, turning to a friend who was sobbing, "*Eh bien ! êtes-vous content, mon cher connaisseur en belles morts ?*" At last, hearing some guns fired, "*Sont-ce déjà les funérailles d'Achille ?*" After that, apparently, he held his tongue, thinking, I suppose, that any further remark would be an anticlimax. He illustrates the thesis I was maintaining to you last Wednesday, that all unusual energy is inspired by an unusual degree of vanity. There is just one other motive: love of power. Philip II of Spain and Sidney Webb of Grosvenor Road are not remarkable for vanity.'

There was only one thing that made me mind being in prison, and that was connected with Colette. Exactly a year after I had fallen in love with her, she fell in love with someone else, though she did not wish it to make any difference in her relations with me. I, however, was bitterly jealous.[1] I had the worst opinion of him, not wholly without reason. We had violent quarrels, and things were never again quite the same between us. While I was in prison, I was tormented by jealousy the whole time, and driven wild by the sense of impotence. I did not think myself justified in feeling jealousy, which I regarded as an abominable

[1] Later I recognised the fact that my feeling sprang not only from jealousy, but also, as is often the case in so deeply serious a relationship as I felt ours to be, from a sense both of collaboration broken and, as happened so often and in so many ways during these years, of the sanctuary defiled.

emotion, but none the less it consumed me. When I first had occasion
to feel it, it kept me awake almost the whole of every night for a fortnight, and at the end I only got sleep by getting a doctor to prescribe
sleeping-draughts. I recognise now that the emotion was wholly
foolish, and that Colette's feeling for me was sufficiently serious to persist through any number of minor affairs. But I suspect that the philosophical attitude which I am now able to maintain in such matters is
due less to philosophy than to physiological decay. The fact was, of
course, that she was very young, and could not live continually in the
atmosphere of high seriousness in which I lived in those days. But
although I know this now, I allowed jealousy to lead me to denounce
her with great violence, with the natural result that her feelings towards
me were considerably chilled. We remained lovers until 1920, but we
never recaptured the perfection of the first year.

I came out of prison in September 1918, when it was already clear
that the War was ending. During the last weeks, in common with most
other people, I based my hopes upon Woodrow Wilson. The end of the
War was so swift and dramatic that no one had time to adjust feelings
to changed circumstances. I learned on the morning of November 11th,
a few hours in advance of the general public, that the Armistice was
coming. I went out into the street, and told a Belgian soldier, who said:
'*Tiens, c'est chic!*' I went into a tobacconist's and told the lady who
served me. 'I am glad of that', she said, 'because now we shall be able to
get rid of the interned Germans.' At eleven o'clock, when the Armistice
was announced, I was in Tottenham Court Road. Within two minutes
everybody in all the shops and offices had come into the street. They
commandeered the buses, and made them go where they liked. I saw a
man and woman, complete strangers to each other, meet in the middle
of the road and kiss as they passed.

Late into the night I stayed alone in the streets, watching the temper
of the crowd, as I had done in the August days four years before. The
crowd was frivolous still, and had learned nothing during the period of
horror, except to snatch at pleasure more recklessly than before. I felt
strangely solitary amid the rejoicings, like a ghost dropped by accident
from some other planet. True, I rejoiced also, but I could find nothing
in common between my rejoicing and that of the crowd. Throughout
my life I have longed to feel that oneness with large bodies of human
beings that is experienced by the members of enthusiastic crowds. The
longing has often been strong enough to lead me into self-deception. I
have imagined myself in turn a Liberal, a Socialist, or a Pacifist, but I
have never been any of these things, in any profound sense. Always the
sceptical intellect, when I have most wished it silent, has whispered
doubts to me, has cut me off from the facile enthusiasms of others, and
has transported me into a desolate solitude. During the War, while I

worked with Quakers, non-resisters, and socialists, while I was willing to accept the unpopularity and the inconvenience belonging to unpopular opinions, I would tell the Quakers that I thought many wars in history had been justified, and the socialists that I dreaded the tyranny of the State. They would look askance at me, and while continuing to accept my help would feel that I was not one of them. Underlying all occupations and all pleasures I have felt since early youth the pain of solitude. I have escaped it most nearly in moments of love, yet even there, on reflection, I have found that the escape depended partly upon illusion.[1] I have known no woman to whom the claims of intellect were as absolute as they are to me, and wherever intellect intervened, I have found that the sympathy I sought in love was apt to fail. What Spinoza calls 'the intellectual love of God' has seemed to me the best thing to live by, but I have not had even the somewhat abstract God that Spinoza allowed himself to whom to attach my intellectual love. I have loved a ghost, and in loving a ghost my inmost self has itself become spectral. I have therefore buried it deeper and deeper beneath layers of cheerfulness, affection, and joy of life. But my most profound feelings have remained always solitary and have found in human things no companionship. The sea, the stars, the night wind in waste places, mean more to me than even the human beings I love best, and I am conscious that human affection is to me at bottom an attempt to escape from the vain search for God.

The War of 1914–18 changed everything for me. I ceased to be academic and took to writing a new kind of books. I changed my whole conception of human nature. I became for the first time deeply convinced that Puritanism does not make for human happiness. Through the spectacle of death I acquired a new love for what is living. I became convinced that most human beings are possessed by a profound unhappiness venting itself in destructive rages, and that only through the diffusion of instinctive joy can a good world be brought into being. I saw that reformers and reactionaries alike in our present world have become distorted by cruelties. I grew suspicious of all purposes demanding stern discipline. Being in opposition to the whole purpose of the community, and finding all the everyday virtues used as means for the slaughter of Germans, I experienced great difficulty in not becoming a complete Antinomian. But I was saved from this by the profound compassion which I felt for the sorrows of the world. I lost old friends and made new ones. I came to know some few people whom I could deeply admire, first among whom I should place E. D. Morel. I got to know him in the first days of the War, and saw him frequently until he and I were in prison. He had single-minded devotion to the truthful presentation of facts. Having begun by exposing the iniquities

[1] This and what follows is no longer true (1967).

of the Belgians in the Congo, he had difficulty in accepting the myth of 'gallant little Belgium'. Having studied minutely the diplomacy of the French and Sir Edward Grey in regard to Morocco, he could not view the Germans as the sole sinners. With untiring energy and immense ability in the face of all the obstacles of propaganda and censorship, he did what he could to enlighten the British nation as to the true purposes for which the Government was driving the young men to the shambles. More than any other opponent of the War, he was attacked by politicians and the press, and of those who had heard his name ninety-nine per cent believed him to be in the pay of the Kaiser. At last he was sent to prison for the purely technical offence of having employed Miss Sidgwick, instead of the post, for the purpose of sending a letter and some documents to Romain Rolland. He was not, like me, in the first division, and he suffered an injury to his health from which he never recovered. In spite of all this, his courage never failed. He often stayed up late at night to comfort Ramsay MacDonald, who frequently got 'cold feet', but when MacDonald came to form a government, he could not think of including anyone so tainted with pro-Germanism as Morel. Morel felt his ingratitude deeply, and shortly afterwards died of heart disease, acquired from the hardships of prison life.

There were some among the Quakers whom I admired very greatly, in spite of a very different outlook. I might take as typical of these the treasurer of the No Conscription Fellowship, Mr Grubb. He was, when I first knew him, a man of seventy, very quiet, very averse from publicity, and very immovable. He took what came without any visible sign of emotion. He acted on behalf of the young men in prison with a complete absence of even the faintest trace of self-seeking. When he and a number of others were being prosecuted for a pacifist publication, my brother was in court listening to his cross-examination. My brother, though not a pacifist, was impressed by the man's character and integrity. He was sitting next to Matthews, the Public Prosecutor, who was a friend of his. When the Public Prosecutor sat down at the end of his cross-examination of Mr Grubb, my brother whispered to him: 'Really, Matthews, the role of Torquemada does not suit you!' My brother's remark so angered Matthews that he would never speak to him again.

One of the most curious incidents of the War, so far as I was concerned, was a summons to the War Office to be kindly reasoned with. Several Red Tabs with the most charming manners and the most friendly attitude, besought me to acquire a sense of humour, for they held that no one with a sense of humour would give utterance to unpopular opinions. They failed, however, and afterwards I regretted that I had not replied that I held my sides with laughter every morning as I read the casualty figures.

When the War was over, I saw that all I had done had been totally useless except to myself. I had not saved a single life or shortened the War by a minute. I had not succeeded in doing anything to diminish the bitterness which caused the Treaty of Versailles. But at any rate I had not been an accomplice in the crime of all the belligerent nations, and for myself I had acquired a new philosophy and a new youth. I had got rid of the don and the Puritan. I had learned an understanding of instinctive processes which I had not possessed before, and I had acquired a certain poise from having stood so long alone. In the days of the Armistice men had high hopes of Wilson. Other men found their inspiration in Bolshevik Russia. But when I found that neither of these sources of optimism was available for me, I was nevertheless able not to despair. It is my deliberate expectation that the worst is to come,[1] but I do not on that account cease to believe that men and women will ultimately learn the simple secret of instinctive joy.

LETTERS

From Norbert Wiener

> Bühlstr. 28
> Göttingen
> Germany
> [*c.* June or July, 1914]

My dear Mr Russell

At present I am studying here in Göttingen, following your advice. I am hearing a course on the Theory of Groups with Landau, a course on Differential Equations with Hilbert (I know it has precious little to do with Philosophy but I wanted to hear Hilbert), and three courses with Husserl, one on Kant's ethical writings, one on the principles of Ethics, and the seminary on Phenomenology. I must confess that the intellectual contortions through which one must go before one finds oneself in the true Phenomenological attitude are utterly beyond me. The applications of Phenomenology to Mathematics, and the claims of Husserl that no adequate account can be given of the foundations of Mathematics without starting out from Phenomenology seem to me absurd.

Symbolic logic stands in little favour in Göttingen. As usual, the Mathematicians will have nothing to do with anything so philosophical as logic, while the philosophers will have nothing to do with anything so mathematical as symbols. For this reason, I have not done much

---

[1] This passage was written in 1931.

original work this term: it is disheartening to try to do original work where you know that not a person with whom you talk about it will understand a word you say.

During the Pfingsten holidays, I called on Frege up at Brunns-haupten in Mecklenburg, where he spends his holidays. I had several interesting talks with him about your work.

A topic which has interested me of late is the question whether one can obtain a simpler set of postulates for Geometry by taking the convex solid & relations between convex solids as indefinable, and defining points as you define instants. I have obtained five or six sets of *definitions* of the fundamental Geometrical concepts in this manner, but I am utterly at a loss for a method to simplify the postulates of Geometry in this manner: e.g. the triangle-transversal postulate offers almost insuperable difficulties if one attempts to simplify it by resolving it into a proposition about arbitrary convex surfaces.

I thank you very much for your interest in my article & discovery. I have some material now that might go with my work on sensation-intensities to make a new article: I would like to ask you what I should do with it. It is an extension of my work on time to polyadic relations having some of the properties of series: for example, to the 'between' relation among the points of a given straight line . . .[1]

I herewith send you my reprints, and offer my apologies to you for not having sent them sooner. The reason is this: I sent all of my articles destined for distribution in America to father, with directions to 'sow them where they would take root'. Father probably imagined that I had sent your copies to you direct.

I am very glad to hear that you had such an enjoyable time with us, and I shall certainly spend next year studying under you in Cambridge. I am just beginning to realise what my work under you there has ment [*sic*] for me.

> *Yours very respectfully*
> *Norbert Wiener*

To the London *Nation* for August 15, 1914
Sir

Against the vast majority of my countrymen, even at this moment, in the name of humanity and civilisation, I protest against our share in the destruction of Germany.

A month ago Europe was a peaceful comity of nations; if an Englishman killed a German, he was hanged. Now, if an Englishman kills a German, or if a German kills an Englishman, he is a patriot, who has deserved well of his country. We scan the newspapers with greedy

[1] The central part of this letter has been omitted as being too technical for general interest.

eyes for news of slaughter, and rejoice when we read of innocent young men, blindly obedient to the word of command, mown down in thousands by the machine-guns of Liège. Those who saw the London crowds, during the nights leading up to the Declaration of War, saw a whole population, hitherto peaceable and humane, precipitated in a few days down the steep slope to primitive barbarism, letting loose, in a moment, the instincts of hatred and blood lust against which the whole fabric of society has been raised. 'Patriots' in all countries acclaim this brutal orgy as a noble determination to vindicate the right; reason and mercy are swept away in one great flood of hatred; dim abstractions of unimaginable wickedness – Germany to us and the French, Russia to the Germans – conceal the simple fact that the enemy are men, like ourselves, neither better nor worse – men who love their homes and the sunshine, and all the simple pleasures of common lives; men now mad with terror in the thought of their wives, their sisters, their children, exposed, with our help, to the tender mercies of the conquering Cossack.

And all this madness, all this rage, all this flaming death of our civilisation and our hopes, has been brought about because a set of official gentlemen, living luxurious lives, mostly stupid, and all without imagination or heart, have chosen that it should occur rather than that any one of them should suffer some infinitesimal rebuff to his country's pride. No literary tragedy can approach the futile horror of the White Paper. The diplomatists, seeing from the first the inevitable end, mostly wishing to avoid it, yet drifted from hour to hour of the swift crisis, restrained by punctilio from making or accepting the small concessions that might have saved the world, hurried on at last by blind fear to loose the armies for the work of mutual butchery.

And behind the diplomatists, dimly heard in the official documents, stand vast forces of national greed and national hatred – atavistic instincts, harmful to mankind at its present level, but transmitted from savage and half-animal ancestors, concentrated and directed by Governments and the Press, fostered by the upper class as a distraction from social discontent, artificially nourished by the sinister influence of the makers of armaments, encouraged by a whole foul literature of 'glory', and by every text-book of history with which the minds of children are polluted.

England, no more than other nations which participate in this war, can be absolved either as regards its national passions or as regards its diplomacy.

For the past ten years, under the fostering care of the Government and a portion of the Press, a hatred of Germany has been cultivated and a fear of the German Navy. I do not suggest that Germany has been guiltless; I do not deny that the crimes of Germany have been greater than our own. But I do say that whatever defensive measures were necessary should have been taken in a spirit of calm foresight, not in a wholly needless turmoil of panic and suspicion. It is this deliberately created panic and suspicion that produced the public opinion by which our participation in the war has been rendered possible.

Our diplomacy, also, has not been guiltless. Secret arrangements, concealed from Parliament and even (at first) from almost all the Cabinet, created, in spite of reiterated denials, an obligation suddenly revealed when the war fever had reached the point which rendered public opinion tolerant of the discovery that the lives of many, and the livelihood of all, had been pledged by one man's irresponsible decisions. Yet, though France knew our obligations, Sir E. Grey refused, down to the last moment, to inform Germany of the conditions of our neutrality or of our intervention. On August 1st he reports as follows a conversation with the German Ambassador (No. 123):

'He asked me whether, if Germany gave a promise not to violate Belgian neutrality, we would engage to remain neutral. I replied that I could not say that; our hands were still free, and we were considering what our attitude should be. All I could say was that our attitude would be determined largely by public opinion here, and that the neutrality of Belgium would appeal very strongly to public opinion here. I did not think that we could give a promise of neutrality on that condition alone. The Ambassador pressed me as to whether I could not formulate conditions on which we would remain neutral. He even suggested that the integrity of France and her colonies might be guaranteed. I said I felt obliged to refuse definitely any promise to remain neutral on similar terms, and I could only say that we must keep our hands free.'

It thus appears that the neutrality of Belgium, the integrity of France and her colonies, and the naval defence of the northern and western coasts of France, were all mere pretexts. If Germany had agreed to our demands in all these respects, we should still not have promised neutrality.

I cannot resist the conclusion that the Government has failed in its duty to the nation by not revealing long-standing arrangements with the French, until, at the last moment, it made them the basis of an appeal to honour; that it has failed in its duty to Europe by not declaring its attitude at the beginning of the crisis; and that it has failed in its duty to humanity by not informing Germany of conditions which would insure its non-participation in a war which, whatever its outcome, must cause untold hardship and the loss of many thousands of our bravest and noblest citizens.

Yours, etc.

August 12, 1914   *Bertrand Russell*

From Lord Morley[1]   Flowermead
                                        Princes Road
                                        Wimbledon Park, S.W.
                                        Aug. 7. 16 ['14]

Dear Mr Russell

Thank you for telling me that you and I are in accord on this breakdown of right and political wisdom. The approval of a man like you is of real value, and I value it sincerely.

                                        Yours
                                        M
                                        [Morley]

From C. P. Sanger   Cote Bank
                                        Westbury-on-Trym
                                        Bristol
                                        Friday 7th Aug. 1914

Dear Bertie

It was very kind of you to write. I feel overwhelmed by the horror of the whole thing. As you know I have always regarded Grey as one of the most wicked and dangerous criminals that has ever disgraced civilisation, but it is awful that a liberal Cabinet should have been parties to engineering a war to destroy Teutonic civilisation in favour of Servians and the Russian autocracy. I pray that the economic disturbance may be so great as to compel peace fairly soon, but it looks as bad as can be.

                                        Yours fraternally
                                        C. P. Sanger

From F. C. S. Schiller   Esher House
                                        Esher, Surrey
                                        19/8/14

Dear Russell

I have just read first your admirable letter in the *Nation* and then the White Book, with special attention to the sequence of events which culminated in the passage you quote from No. 123. As a result I must express to you not only my entire agreement with your sentiments (which are those of every civilised man) but also with your argument. It seems to me clear on his own evidence that Sir E. Grey must bear a large share of the catastrophe, whether he acted as he did consciously or stupidly. He steadily refused to give Germany any assurance of neutrality on any conditions, until he produced a belief that he meant

---

[1] I wrote to congratulate him on having resigned from the Government on the outbreak of war.

England to fight, and Germany thereupon ran 'amok'. But the evidence shows that she was willing to bid high for our neutrality.

First (No. 85) she promised the integrity of France proper and of Belgium (tho leaving her neutrality contingent). When Grey said that wasn't enough (No. 101) and demanded a pledge about Belgian neutrality (No. 114), the German Secretary of State explained, stupidly but apparently honestly, what the difficulty was (No. 122), and said he must consult the Chancellor and Kaiser. This the papers have represented as a refusal to give the pledge, whereas it is obvious that Lichnowsky's conversation with Grey (No. 123) next day *was* the answer. And I don't see how anything more could have been conceded. Belgian neutrality and the integrity of France and her colonies, with a hint of acceptance of any conditions Grey would impose if only he would state them. Of course, that would have reduced the war with France to a farce, and meant presumably that France would not be (seriously) attacked at all, but only contained. One gets the impression throughout that Germany really wanted to fight *Russia* and had to take on France because of the system of alliances. Also that Russia had been goading Austria into desperation, (No. 118 s.f.), was willing to fight, (109, 139), was lying, or suspected of lying by Germany (112, 121, 139 p. 72 top of 144). It is sickening to think that this deluge of blood has been let loose all in order that the tyranny of the Tsar shall be extended over all the world. As regards the question of Grey's good faith, have you noted that the abstract of the despatches gives no hint of the important contents of No. 123 ? That was presumably the reason why none of the papers at first noticed it. As for the *Nation* Editor's reply to you, he simply distorts the time order. Lichnowsky's offer to respect Belgian neutrality came *after* Grey's inquiry and answered it. Grey's answers seem mere 'fencing', and if he had really wanted to be neutral he would surely have said to L's. offers 'are these firm pledges ?'. But he did not respond at all.

However it is no use crying over spilt milk, and not much to consider as yet how European civilisation can be saved; I fear this horror will go on long enough to ruin it completely. But I suspect that not much will be left of the potentates, statesmen and diplomats who have brought about this catastrophy, when the suffering millions have borne it 6 months.

> *Ever sincerely yours*
> *F. C. S. Schiller*

To and from J. L. Hammond　　　　5 Sept. 1914
Dear Hammond

I am glad Norman Angell is replying and am very satisfied to be displaced by him.

As regards Belgium, there are some questions I should like to ask you, not in a controversial spirit, but because I wish, if possible, to continue to feel some degree of political respect for the *Nation*, with which in the past I have been in close agreement.

I. Were the *Nation* ignorant of the fact, known to all who took any interest in military matters, that the Germans, for many years past, had made no secret of their intention to attack France through Belgium in the next war?

II. Did the *Nation* in former years regard the violation of Belgium, if it should occur, as a just ground for war with Germany?

III. If so, why did they never give the slightest hint of this opinion, or ask the Government to make this view clear to Germany? If the object was to save Belgium, this was an obvious duty.

IV. Why did the *Nation* in the past protest against Continental entanglements, when the alleged duty of protecting Belgium already involved all the trouble that could arise from an alliance with France and Russia?

It seems to me that in the past, as in the present, the policy of the *Nation* has been sentimental, in the sense that it has refused to face facts which went against its policy. I do not see, at any rate, how it can be absolved from the charge of either having been thoughtless in the past, or being hysterical now.

If there is an answer, I should be very grateful for it.

Yours sincerely
Bertrand Russell

Oatfield
19 Oct. 1914

Dear Russell

Your letter – accusing my handwriting of a certain obscurity – was a great shock, but less than it would have been had I not already received a similar intimation, less tactfully conveyed, from the printers. I had therefore already addressed myself to the painful task of reform, with the result that you see.

My letter was in answer to one from you asking why if the *Nation* thought we should fight over Belgium it had not let its readers know that this was its opinion, and why if it took this view, it objected to foreign entanglements. (I send your letter as the simplest way.) First of all I must ask you – in justice to the *Nation* – to distinguish between the *Nation* and me. I have had no responsibility for the paper's line on foreign policy (or on Armaments) with which I have not associated myself. I agreed with the *N.* entirely on Persia. I am therefore not quite the right person to answer your questions; but I think the *Nation* could clear itself of inconsistency.

1. I don't know whether the *Nation* was aware of this or not. (Per-

sonally I was not. I always thought Germany might develop designs on
Belgium and Holland and in the last article on Foreign Policy that I
wrote in the *Speaker* I said we could not look idly on if she attacked
them.)

2. The *Nation* drew attention to our obligation to Belgium in April
1912, March 1913, and the week before the war.

3. I imagine that they did not call upon the Government to impress
this on Germany because they imagined that it was generally known
that an English Government would consider the obligation binding.

4. The *Nation* argued that the entente with France and Russia made
a general war more probable, and that if we were quite independent we
could more easily protect Belgium. 'Germany would not violate the
neutrality of Belgium for the sake of some small military advantage if
she might otherwise reckon on our neutrality' (March 1.1913). They
may have been wrong, their general criticisms of Grey may have been
right or wrong and their idea that it was possible to build up an Anglo-
French-German entente may have been impracticable, but there seems
to be no inconsistency in working for that policy for some years and in
thinking that it is Germany that has wrecked it. Massingham's view is
that Germany 1) would make no concessions during the last fortnight
for the Peace of Europe 2) insisted on invading Belgium.

If you say that you think the *Nation* has not allowed enough for the
warlike forces in Germany in the past I agree. I think that has been the
mistake of all the Peace people. In his book – in many respects admirable – on *The War of Steel and Gold* Brailsford was entirely
sceptical, predicting that there would never be a great war in Europe
again.

> *Yours*
> *J. L. Hammond*

From Helen Dudley   [1914]

Thank you so much for the flowers. They are a great comfort to me
and your letter also – I have read it many times. It was terrible the
other evening – yet if we had not seen each other it might have been
infinitely more terrible – I might have come to feel that I could never
see you again. That is all past now – I do understand how it is with you
and I feel more than ever that a profound and lasting friendship will be
possible – I hope very soon – as soon as I get back my strength. Nothing
that has happened makes any difference finally – it was and still is of
the very best.

Goodbye now and if one may speak of peace in this distracted world
– peace be with you.

> *H.*
> [Helen Dudley]

To Geo. Turner, Esq.   Trinity College
                                        Cambridge
                                        26 April 1915

Dear Sir

I am sorry to say I cannot renew my subscription to the Cambridge
Liberal Association, and I do not wish any longer to be a member of it.
One of my chief reasons for supporting the Liberal Party was that I
thought them less likely than the Unionists to engage in a European
war. It turns out that ever since they have been in office they have been
engaged in deceiving their supporters, and in secretly pursuing a policy
of which the outcome is abhorrent to me. Under these circumstances I
can do nothing directly or indirectly to support the present Government.

                                        Yours faithfully
                                        Bertrand Russell

*The writer of the following letter was a distinguished explorer and soldier.
He was in command of the British Expedition to Tibet in 1903–4. He was a
very delightful and liberal-minded man, for whom I had a great regard.
We travelled together on the 'Mauretania' in 1914.*

From Sir Francis Younghusband   London
                                        May 11 1915

My dear Russell

I am so distressed at what you say about feeling a sense of isolation
because of your views regarding the war. It should be all the other way
round. You ought to be feeling the pride your friends feel in you for
your independence and honesty of thought. Vain and conceited cranks
may well be abominated by their friends. But unfortunately it is not
they who have the sense of isolation which you feel. They are too
satisfied with themselves to have any such feelings. It is only men like
you would have the feeling.

But do please remember this that your friends admire and are helped
by you even though they may not agree. It is everything that at such a
time as this you should have said what you thought. For you know
more about the Germans and other continental countries than most of
us and you have also made a special study of the first principles of
action. And in these times it is of the utmost importance and value that
there should be men like you by whom the rest of us can test themselves. I knew scarcely anything of Germany until the war came on.
And I am by heredity inclined to take the soldier's view. So I approached this question from quite a different standpoint to what you
did. I was all the more interested in knowing what you thought, and
tried to get my ideas straight and just by yours.

From my own experience of Government action and of military attitudes I should say that it was almost impossible for any one outside the inner Government circle to get a true view at the first start off. The crisis came so suddenly to the outside public. Underneath the surface it had been brewing up but we knew nothing of it – or very little. Then suddenly it breaks and we have to form the best opinion we can. And as regards the military attitude I know from experience how frightfully dangerous it is when you have the physical means of enforcing your own point of view – how apt you are to disregard any one else's. I have seen that with military commanders on campaign and probably I have been pretty bad myself. This it seems to me is what Germany is suffering from. She certainly had accumulated tremendous power and this made her utterly inconsiderate of the feelings and rights of others. And what I take it we have to drive into her is the elementary fact that it does not pay to disregard these rights and feelings – that she *must* regard them.

> *Yours very sincerely*
> *Francis Younghusband*

A specimen typical of many: Ryde
                                  Sept. 20 '15

It may be perfectly true, and happily so, that you are not a Fellow of Trinity, – but your best friends, if you have any, would not deny that you are a silly ass. And not only a silly ass, – but a mean-spirited and lying one at that, – for you have the sublime impertinence and untruthfulness to talk about 'no doubt atrocities have occurred on both sides'. You, together with your friends (?) Pigou, Marshall, Walter G. Bell, A. R. Waller, Conybeare, etc. know perfectly well that to charge the British Army with atrocities is a pernicious lie of which only an English Boche traitor could be guilty, – and your paltry attempt to introduce the Russians stamps you for what you are!

> *Yours*
> *J. Bull*

The occasion of the following letter was my taking the chair for Shaw at a meeting to discuss the War:

From G. B. Shaw   10 Adelphi Terrace
                                  [London] W.C.
                                  16th October. 1915

Dear Bertrand Russell

You had better talk it over with the Webbs. As far as I am concerned, do exactly as the spirit moves you. If you wish to reserve your fire, it is quite easy to open the meeting by simply stating that it is a Fabian meeting, and that the business of the Fabian Society is, within human limits, the dispassionate investigation of social problems, and the search for remedies for social evils; that war is a social problem like other social problems and needs such investigation side by side with recruiting demonstrations and patriotic revivals; that the subject of this evenings lecture is the psychological side of war; and that you have pleasure in calling upon etc etc etc etc.

I am certainly not going to be obviously politic, conciliatory and bland. I mean to get listened to, and to make the lecture a success; and I also mean to *encourage* the audience if I can; but I shall do it with as much ostensible defiance of the lightning as possible. The important thing is that the meeting should be good humoured and plucky; for what is really the matter with everybody is funk. In the right key one can say anything: in the wrong key, nothing: the only delicate part of the job is the establishment of the key.

I have no objection on earth to the lines you indicate; and before or after my speech is the same to me. Our job is to make people serious about the war. It is the monstrous triviality of the damned thing, and the vulgar frivolity of what we imagine to be patriotism, that gets at my temper.

> *Yours ever*
> G.B.S.

P.S. As this will not be delivered until late afternoon (if then) I send it to Webb's.

The occasion of the following letter was my pamphlet on the policy of the Entente, in which I criticised Gilbert Murray's defence of Grey.

To Gilbert Murray   34, Russell Chambers
                                            Bury Street, W.C.
                                            28th December 1915

Dear Gilbert

Thank you for your letter. I am very sorry I gave a wrong impression about your connection with the F.O. I certainly thought you had had more to do with them.

I agree with all you say about the future. I have no wish to quarrel with those who stand for liberal ideas, however I may disagree about the war. I thought it necessary to answer you, just as you thought it necessary to write your pamphlet, but I did not mean that there should be anything offensive in my answer; if there was, I am sorry. I feel our friendship still lives in the eternal world, whatever may happen to it here and now. And I too can say God bless you.

Yours ever

B. Russell

The following letter should have been included in Volume I [Part I of this edition] had it been available at the time of the publication of Volume I. As it was not, I add it here to other letters from Santayana.

From George Santayana

Queen's Acre
Windsor
Feb. 8. 1912

Dear Russell

Many thanks for your message, which came this morning in a letter from your brother. I am going to spend Sunday with him at Telegraph House, but expect to go up to Cambridge on Monday or Tuesday of next week, and count on seeing you. Meantime I have a proposal to make, or rather to renew, to you on behalf of Harvard College. Would it be possible for you to go there next year, from October 1912 to June 1913, in the capacity of professor of philosophy ? Royce is to be taking a holiday, I shall be away, and Palmer will be there only for the first half of the academic year. Perry, Münsterberg, and two or three young psychologists will be alone on hand. What they have in mind is that you should give a course – three hours a week, of which one may be delegated to the assistant which would be provided for you, to read papers, etc. – in logic, and what we call a 'Seminary' or 'Seminar' in anything you liked. It would also be possible for you to give some more popular lectures if you liked, either at Harvard, or at the Lowell Institute in Boston. For the latter there are separate fees, and the salary of a professor is usually $4000 (£800). We hope you will consider this proposal favourably, as there is no one whom the younger school of philosophers in America are more eager to learn of than of you. You would bring new standards of precision and independence of thought which would open their eyes, and probably have the greatest influence on the rising generation of professional philosophers in that country.

There is no particular urgency in receiving your answer, so that you needn't write to me at all, but wait until I see you next week, unless your decision is absolutely clear and unalterable, in which case you might send me a line to Telegraph House. My permanent address is

c/o Brown Shipley & Co.
123 Pall Mall, S.W.

Yours sincerely

G. Santayana

P.S. I didn't mean to decline your kind offer to put me up, when I go to Cambridge, but as I am going in the middle of the week, I don't know whether it would be equally convenient for you to do so.

Oxford, May 5th [1915]

I read this about 'war babies' in a Spanish newspaper: 'Kitchener, in creating an army, has created love. This is a great change in a country where only marriage was known before.'

G. Santayana

[Dec. '17]

The situation is certainly bad from a military point of view, or for those who are angry because the war interferes with their private or political machinations. It may last a long time yet; or else be renewed after a mock peace. But, looking at it all calmly, like a philosopher, I find nothing to be pessimistic about. When I go to Sandford to lunch, which is often, it does my heart good to see so many freshly ploughed fields: England is becoming a cultivated country, instead of being a land of moors and fens, like barbarous North Germany. That alone seems to me more than a compensation for all losses: it is setting the *foundations* right. As for Russia, I rather like Lenin, (not that fatuous Kerensky!); he has an ideal he is willing to fight for, and it is a profoundly anti-German ideal. If he remains in power, he may yet have to fight the Germans, and it will be with very poisonous gas indeed. Besides, I think their plans at Berlin have profoundly miscarried, and that the Prussian educational-industrial-military domination we were threatened with is undermined at home. Military victory would not now do, because the more peoples they rope in, the more explosives they will be exploding under their own establishment.

As for deaths and loss of capital, I don't much care. The young men killed would grow older if they lived, and then they would be good for nothing; and after being good for nothing for a number of years they would die of catarrh or a bad kidney or the halter or old age – and would that be less horrible? I am willing, almost glad, that the world should be poorer: I only wish the population too could become more sparse: and I am perfectly willing to live on a bread-ticket and a lodging-ticket and be known only by a number instead of a baptismal name, provided all this made an end of living on lies, and really cleared the political air. But I am afraid the catastrophe won't be great enough for that, and that some false arrangement will be patched up – in spite of Lenin – so that we shall be very much as we were before. People are not intelligent. It is very unreasonable to expect them to be so, and that is a fate my philosophy reconciled me to long ago. How else could I have lived for forty years in America?

All this won't interest you, but since it is written I will let it go.
[*G. Santayana*]

To Ottoline Morrell   [Cambridge]
                                        1915
Did you see in to-day's *Morning Post* a letter from an American,
dated 'Ritz Hotel', expressing his horrified bewilderment to find, in
New College Chapel, a tablet inscribed 'Pro Patria', on which are
being inscribed the names of New College men who have been killed in
the war, among the rest *three Germans*! He expressed his horror to the
verger, who replied 'They died for *their* country. I knew them – they
were very fine men.' It is creditable to New College. The worthy
American thinks it necessary to give us a lesson in how to be patriots.
    'Elizabeth' [my sister-in-law] expressed regret at the fact that her 5
German nephews in the war are all still alive. She is a true patriot. The
American would like her.
    I could come to you Tues. & Wed. 15th and 16th, if it suited you. I
should like to see [D. H.] Lawrence ...

                                        [Cambridge]
                                        Sunday evg.
                                        [Postmark 10 May '15]
    I am feeling the weight of the war much more since I came back
here – one is made so terribly aware of the waste when one is here.
And Rupert Brooke's death brought it home to me. It is deadly to be
here now, with all the usual life stopped. There will be other generations – yet I keep fearing that something of civilisation will be lost for
good, as something was lost when Greece perished in just this way.
Strange how one values civilisation – more than all one's friends or
anything – the slow achievement of men emerging from the brute – it
seems the ultimate thing one lives for. I don't live for human *happiness*,
but for some kind of struggling emergence of mind. And here, at most
times, that is being helped on – and what has been done is given to new
generations, who travel on from where we have stopped. And now it is
all arrested, and no one knows if it will start again at anything like the
point where it stopped. And all the elderly apostates are overjoyed.

                                        34 Russell Chambers
                                        Wed. night
                                        [Postmark 27 My. '15]
    I am only just realising how Cambridge oppressed me. I feel far
more alive here, and far better able to face whatever horrors the time
may bring. Cambridge has ceased to be a home and a refuge to me

since the war began. I find it unspeakably painful being thought a traitor. Every casual meeting in the Court makes me quiver with sensitive apprehension. One ought to be more hardened.

My Dearest, forgive me that I have been so horrid lately. But really I have had rather a bad time, and I have been haunted by horrors, and I didn't want to speak all that was in my mind until it had subsided, because it was excessive and mad. So I got stiff and dull.

Friday
[Postmark 11 Ju '15]

I think I will make friends with the No-Conscription people. The U.D.C. is too mild and troubled with irrelevancies. It will be all right after the war, but not now. I wish good people were not so mild. The non-resistance people I know here are so Sunday-schooly – one feels they don't know the volcanic side of human nature, they have little humour, no intensity of will, nothing of what makes men effective. They would never have denounced the Pharisees or turned out the money-changers. How passionately I long that one could break through the prison walls in one's own nature. I feel now-a-days so much as if some great force for good were imprisoned within me by scepticism and cynicism and lack of faith. But those who have no such restraint always seem ignorant and a little foolish. It all makes one feel very lonely.

I can't make head or tail of Lawrence's philosophy. I dread talking to him about it. It is not sympathetic to me.

July 1915

Lawrence took up my time from morning till 10.30, so I couldn't write yesterday. We had a terrific argument but not a disastrous one. He attacks me for various things that I don't feel to blame about – chiefly, in effect, for having a scientific temper and a respect for fact. I will send you his written comments on my syllabus. I shall be glad to know what you think of them. He took me to see a Russian Jew, Kotiliansky, and [Middleton] Murry and Mrs Murry [Katherine Mansfield] – they were all sitting together in a bare office high up next door to the Holborn Restaurant, with the windows shut, smoking Russian cigarettes without a moment's intermission, idle and cynical. I thought Murry *beastly* and the whole atmosphere of the three dead and putrefying.

Then we went to the Zoo – the baboon gave me much cynical satisfaction: he looked long and deliberately at everybody, and then slowly showed his teeth and snarled, with inconceivable hatred and disgust. Swift would have loved him. Then we went up to Hampstead, to the

Radfords, where Mrs Lawrence was staying. I was dead tired after the first hour, as we began arguing at once. I told Lawrence that I thought we ought to be independent of each other, at any rate at first, and not try to start a school. When he talks politics he seems to me so wild that I could not formally work with him. I hope he won't be hurt. He did not seem to be, as I put it very carefully. He is undisciplined in thought, and mistakes his wishes for facts. He is also muddle-headed. He says 'facts' are quite unimportant, only 'truths' matter. London is a 'fact' not a 'truth'. But he wants London pulled down. I tried to make him see that that would be absurd if London were unimportant, but he kept reiterating that London doesn't really exist, and that he could easily make people see it doesn't, and then they would pull it down. He was so confident of his powers of persuasion that I challenged him to come to Trafalgar Square at once and begin preaching. That brought him to earth and he began to shuffle. His attitude is a little mad and not quite honest, or at least very muddled. He has not learnt the lesson of individual impotence. And he regards all my attempts to make him acknowledge facts as mere timidity, lack of courage to think boldly, self-indulgence in pessimism. When one gets a glimmer of the facts into his head, as I did at last, he gets discouraged, and says he will go to the South Sea Islands, and bask in the sun with 6 native wives. He is tough work. The trouble with him is a tendency to mad exaggeration.

July 1915
Tuesday

Yes, the day Lawrence was with me was horrid. I got filled with despair, and just counting the moments till it was ended. Partly that was due to liver, but not wholly. Lawrence is very like Shelley – just as fine, but with a similar impatience of fact. The revolution he hopes for is just like Shelley's prophecy of banded anarchs fleeing while the people celebrate a feast of love. His psychology of people is amazingly good up to a point, but at a certain point he gets misled by love of violent colouring.

Friday evg. I dined with my Harvard pupil, [T. S.] Eliot, and his bride. I expected her to be terrible, from his mysteriousness; but she was not so bad. She is light, a little vulgar, adventurous, full of life – an artist I think he said, but I should have thought her an actress. He is exquisite and listless; she says she married him to stimulate him, but finds she can't do it. Obviously he married in order to be stimulated. I think she will soon be tired of him. She refuses to go to America to see his people, for fear of submarines. He is ashamed of his marriage, and very grateful if one is kind to her. He is the Miss Sands type of American. [Miss Sands was a highly-cultivated New Englander, a painter and a friend of Henry James and Logan Pearsall Smith.]

Hatch
Kingsley Green
Haslemere
Thurs. mg.
[Postmark 9 Sp. '15]

My Darling

I was very glad of your letter this morning – such a dear letter. I wish I could avoid getting unhappy. I can, if I have interests away from you and do not stay on and on in the family atmosphere – but otherwise the feeling of being a mere superfluous ghost, looking on but not participating, grows too strong to be borne. By spending some days in town each week it will be all right. The Lady[1] has been explaining the situation to me, and is going to do so further today, as she is taking me out for a picnic, while Mrs Waterlow [her sister] goes to town. She says – and I believe her – that she was unguarded with my brother at first, because she looked upon him as safely married, and therefore suitable as a lover. Suddenly, without consulting her, he wrote and said he was getting divorced. It took her breath away, and rather flattered her; she drifted, said nothing definite, but allowed him tacitly to assume everything. Now she is feeling very worried, because the inexorable moment is coming when his divorce will be absolute and she will have to decide. Her objections to him are the following:

(a) He sleeps with 7 dogs on his bed. She couldn't sleep a wink in such circumstances.[2]

(b) He reads Kipling aloud.

(c) He loves Telegraph House, which is hideous.

I daresay other objections might be found if one searched long enough, they are all three well chosen to appeal to me. She is a flatterer, and has evidently set herself to the task of getting me to be not against her if she breaks with him. But it is an impossible task. I am too fond of my brother, and shall mind his suffering too much, to forgive her inwardly even if she has a perfectly good case. She says she is still in great uncertainty, but I don't think she will marry him. She would be *delighted* to go on having him for a lover, but I feel sure he will never agree to that.

I must finish, as this must be posted in a moment.

Don't worry about me. It will be all right as long as I don't let my thoughts get too concentrated on what I can't have. I *loved* the children's picnic, because for once I was not a ghost. I can't enter into the

---

[1] 'Elizabeth', my brother's third wife.

[2] I told her about Josephine's dog biting Napoleon. What Emperors have borne, she may. [Josephine's dog bit Napoleon in the calf on their wedding-night.]

family life when you are present, partly because you absorb my attention, partly because in your presence I am always paralysed with terror, stiff and awkward from the sense of your criticism. I know that some things I do or don't do annoy you, for reasons I don't understand, and it makes it impossible for me to be natural before you, though sometimes it makes me exaggerate the things you hate. But when I am not tired, I can surmount all those things. Owing to being constrained and frightened when I am with you, my vitality doesn't last long at Garsington, and when it is gone I become defenceless against thoughts I want to keep at a distance.

> Thursday night
> [Postmark London,
> 29 October '15]

My Darling

I *was* glad to get your letter. I had begun to feel anxious. I am glad Lawrence was so wonderful. I have no doubt he is right to go, but I couldn't desert England. I simply *cannot bear* to think that England is entering on its autumn of life – it is too much anguish. I will not believe it, and I will believe there is health and vigour in the nation somewhere. It is all hell now, and shame – but I believe the very shame will in the end wake a new spirit. The more England goes down and down, the more profoundly I want to help, and the more I feel tied to England for good or ill. I cannot write of other things, they seem so small in comparison.

> *Your*
> B.

> Wednesday
> [Postmark Nov. 10, '15]

Eliot had a half holiday yesterday and got home at 3.30. It is quite funny how I have come to love him, as if he were my son. He is becoming much more of a man. He has a profound and quite unselfish devotion to his wife, and she is really very fond of him, but has impulses of cruelty to him from time to time. It is a Dostojevsky type of cruelty, not a straightforward every-day kind. I am every day getting things more right between them, but I can't let them alone at present, and of course I myself get very much interested. She is a person who lives on a knife-edge, and will end as a criminal or a saint – I don't know which yet. She has a perfect capacity for both.

> [1915] Wed.

My Darling

I don't know what has come over me lately but I have sunk again into the state of lethargy that I have had at intervals since the war began. I am sure I ought to live differently, but I have utterly lost all will-power. I want someone to take me in hand and order me about, telling me where to live and what to do and leaving me no self-direction at all. I have never felt quite like that before. It is all mental fatigue I am sure, but it is very intense, and it leaves me with no interest in anything, and not enough energy to get into a better frame of mind by my own efforts. In fact I should fight against anything that might be suggested to do me good. My impulse is just to sit still and brood.

I can't do much till my lectures are over but that won't be long now. If I could get some one like Desmond [MacCarthy] to come to the country with me then and make me walk a lot, I should get better. But everyone is busy and I haven't the energy to arrange things. I don't do any work. I shall have to get to work for Harvard some time but the thought of work is a nightmare. I am sure something ought to be done or I shall go to pieces.

Irene [Cooper Willis] has just been here scolding me about Helen [Dudley] – someone told her the whole story lately – that hasn't made me any more cheerful than I was before. Sense of Sin is one of the things that trouble me at these times. The state of the world is at the bottom of it I think, and the terrible feeling of impotence. I thought I had got over it but it has come back worse than ever. Can you think of anything that would help me? I *should* be grateful if you could. My existence just now is really too dreadful.

I know now that it is just an illness and it doesn't any longer make me critical of you or of anybody. It is my will that is gone. I have used it too much and it has snapped.

You have enough burdens already – but if you know anyone who could look after me for a while and order me about it would make a difference.

Your
B.

Sat. [1916]

I enclose a letter from Captain White. You will see that he feels the same sort of hostility or antagonism to me that Lawrence feels – I think it is a feeling that seems to exist in most of the people with whom I feel in sympathy on the spiritual side – probably the very same thing which has prevented you from caring for me as much as you thought you would at first. I wish you could find out and tell me what it is. It makes one feel very isolated. People with whom I have intellectual sympathy hardly ever have any spiritual life, or at any rate have very little; and the others seem to find the intellectual side of me unbearable. You will think I am lapsing into morbidness again, but that is not so; I simply want to get to the bottom of it so as to understand it; if I can't get over it, it makes it difficult to achieve much.

I had told White I was troubled by the fact that my audiences grow, and that people who ought to be made uncomfortable by my lectures[1] are not – notably Mrs Acland [whose husband was in the Government], who sits enjoying herself, with no feeling that what I say is a condemnation of the Government. I thought after my last lecture I would point the moral practically.

I feel I know very little of what you have been thinking and feeling lately. I have been so busy that my letters have been dull, so I can't complain. But it will be a relief to see you and to find out something of what has been going on in you. Ever since the time when I was at Garsington last, I have been quite happy as far as personal things are concerned. Do you remember that at the time when you were seeing Vittoz [a Swiss physician who treated her] I wrote a lot of stuff about Theory of Knowledge, which Wittgenstein criticised with the greatest severity? His criticism, tho' I don't think you realised it at the time, was an event of first-rate importance in my life, and affected everything I have done since. I saw he was right, and I saw that I could not hope ever again to do fundamental work in philosophy. My impulse was shattered, like a wave dashed to pieces against a breakwater. I became filled with utter despair,[2] and tried to turn to you for consolation. But you were occupied with Vittoz and could not give me time. So I took to casual philandering, and that increased my despair. I *had* to produce lectures for America, but I took a metaphysical subject although I was and am convinced that all fundamental work in philosophy is logical. My reason was that Wittgenstein persuaded me that what wanted doing in logic was too difficult for me. So there was no really vital satisfaction of my philosophical impulse in that work, and philosophy lost its hold on me. That was due to Wittgenstein more than to the war. What the war has done is to give me a new and less difficult ambition, which seems to me quite as good as the old one. My lectures have persuaded me that there is a possible life and activity in the new ambition. So I want to work quietly, and I feel more at peace as regards work than I have ever done since Wittgenstein's onslaught.

From Stanley Unwin
40, Museum Street
London, W.C.
November 29th, 1915

Dear Sir

I notice with very great interest in the current number of *The*

---

[1] These lectures afterwards became *Principles of Social Reconstruction*.
[2] I soon got over this mood.

Cambridge Magazine that you are planning to give a Course of Lectures on 'The Principles of Social Reconstruction'.

If it is your intention that the Lectures should subsequently be published in book form, I hope we may have the pleasure of issuing them for you.

We enclose a prospectus of *Towards a Lasting Settlement*, a volume in which we know you are interested. We hope to publish the book on December 6th.

> *Yours faithfully*
> *Stanley Unwin*

[*This was the beginning of my connection with Allen & Unwin.*]

From T. S. Eliot
Tuesday
[Jan. 1916.]

Dear Bertie

This is wonderfully kind of you – really the last straw (so to speak) of generosity. I am very sorry you have to come back – and Vivien says you have been an angel to her – but of course I shall jump at the opportunity with the utmost gratitude. I am sure you have done *everything* possible and handled her in the very best way – better than I – I often wonder how things would have turned out but for you – I believe we shall owe her life to you, even.

I shall take the 10.30, and look forward to a talk with you before you go. Mrs Saich[1] is expecting you. She has made me very comfortable here.

> *Affectionately*
> *Tom*

From Charlotte C. Eliot
4446 Westminster Place
May 23rd, 1916

Dear Mr Russell

Your letter relative to a cablegram sent us, was received some little time ago. I write now to thank you for the affection that inspired it. It was natural you should feel as you did with the awful tragedy of the Sussex of such recent occurrence. Mr Eliot did not believe it possible that even the Germans, (a synonym for all that is most frightful,) would attack an American liner. It would be manifestly against their

[1] The charwoman at my flat. She said I was 'a very percentric gentleman'. Once when the gasman came and turned out to be a socialist, she said 'he talked just like a gentleman'. She had supposed only 'gentlemen' were socialists.
Mrs Eliot was ill and needed a holiday. Eliot at first could not leave London, so I went first with her to Torquay, and Eliot replaced me after a few days.

interest. Yet I am aware there is still a possibility of war between Germany and America. The more we learn of German methods, open and *secret*, the greater is the moral indignation of many Americans. I am glad all our ancestors are English with a French ancestry far back on one line. I am sending Tom copy of a letter written by his Great-great-grandfather in 1811, giving an account of his grandfather (*one* of them) who was born about 1676 – in the county of Devon, England – Christopher Pearse.

I am sure your influence in every way will confirm my son in his choice of Philosophy as a life work. Professor Wood speaks of his thesis as being of exceptional value. I had hoped he would seek a University appointment next year. If he does not I shall feel regret. I have absolute faith in his Philosophy but not in the vers libres.

Tom is very grateful to you for your sympathy and kindness. This gratitude I share.

> Sincerely yours
> *Charlotte C. Eliot*
> [T. S. Eliot's mother]

To Lucy Martin Donnelly,
Professor of English at Bryn Mawr College

> 34 Russell Chambers
> Bury St., W.C.
> 10 Feb. 1916

My dear Lucy

I was glad to hear from you at Kyoto – as for Continents, there are so far only 3 in which I have written to you – it is your plain duty to go to Africa & Australia in order to complete your collection.

I *do* hope you will manage to come to England by the Siberian Railway. It would be a great pleasure to see you, & I am sure that I could make you sympathise with the point of view which I & most of my friends take about the war.

You needn't have been afraid about my lectures. Helen [Flexner] wrote me quite a serious remonstrance, which amused me. I should have thought she would have known by this time that social caution in the expression of opinion is not my strong point. If she had known Christ before he delivered the Sermon on the Mount she would have begged him to keep silence for fear of injuring his social position in Nazareth. People who count in the world are oblivious of such things. As a matter of fact, my lectures are a great success – they are a rallying-ground for the intellectuals, who are coming daily more to my way of thinking not only as regards the war but also as regards general politics. All sorts of literary & artistic people who formerly despised politics are being driven to action, as they were in France by the

Dreyfus case. In the long run, their action will have a profound effect. It is primarily to them that I am speaking. – I have given up writing on the war because I have said my say & there is nothing new to say. – My ambitions are more vast & less immediate than my friends' ambitions for me. I don't care for the applause one gets by saying what others are thinking; I want actually to *change* people's thoughts. Power over people's minds is the main personal desire of my life; & this sort of power is not acquired by saying popular things. In philosophy, when I was young, my views were as unpopular & strange as they could be; yet I have had a very great measure of success. Now I have started on a new career, & if I live & keep my faculties, I shall probably be equally successful. Harvard has invited me to give a course of lectures 12 months hence on the sort of things I am now lecturing on, & I have agreed to go. As soon as the war is over, people here will want just that sort of thing. When you once understand what my ambitions are, you will see that I go the right way about to realise them. In any large undertaking, there are rough times to go through, & of course success may not come till after one is dead – but those things don't matter if one is in earnest. I have something important to say on the philosophy of life & politics, something appropriate to the times. People's general outlook here has changed with extraordinary rapidity during the last 10 years; their beliefs are disintegrated, & they want a new doctrine. But those who will mould the future won't *listen* to anything that retains old superstitions & conventions. There is a sharp cleavage between old & young; after a gradual development, I have come down on the side of the young. And because I am on their side, I can contribute something of experience which they are willing to respect when it is not merely criticism. – Let me hear again soon – I am interested by your impressions of the Far East.

> *Yrs affly*
> *B Russell*

Have you read Romain Rolland's Life of Michel Angelo ? It is a wonderful book.

To Ottoline Morrell   Sunday aft.
                                       [Postmark London 30 Jan. '16.]
I have read a good deal of Havelock Ellis on sex. It is full of things that everyone ought to know, very scientific and objective, most valuable and interesting. What a folly it is the way people are kept in ignorance on sexual matters, even when they think they know everything. I think almost all civilised people are in some way what would be thought abnormal, and they suffer because they don't know that really ever so many people are just like them. One so constantly hears of things going wrong when people marry, merely through not know-

ing the sort of things that are likely to happen, and through being afraid to talk frankly. It seems clear to me that marriage ought to be constituted by children, and relations not involving children ought to be ignored by the law and treated as indifferent by public opinion. It is only through children that relations cease to be a purely private matter. The whole traditional morality I am sure is superstitious. It is not true that the very best things are more likely to come to those who are very restrained – they either grow incapable of letting themselves go, or when they do, they become too violent and headlong. Do you agree?

Goodbye my darling. I am as happy as one can be in these times, and very full of love. It *will* be a joy to see you again if you come up.

> *Your*
> *B.*

Trin. Coll.
Feb. 27 1916

My Darling

I believe I forgot to tell you I was coming here for the week-end. I came to speak to the 'Indian Majliss' a Club of Indian students here. They were having their annual dinner, about 100 of them, and they asked me to propose the toast of 'India'. Your friend Professor Shaheed Suhrawardy was there, and spoke extraordinarily well. They had asked me because of the line I have taken about the war – at least I suppose so. But when I came to speak an odd sense of responsibility came over me. I remembered that after all I don't want the Germans to win, and I don't want India to rebel at this moment. I said that if I were a native of India I did not think I should desire a German victory. This was received in dead silence, and subsequent speeches said that was the only thing in my speech that they disagreed with. Their nationalism was impressive. They spoke of unity between Moslems and Hindoos, of the oppressiveness of England, of sharp defeat as the only way of checking tyrants. Many of them were able, very earnest, quite civilised. The man who spoke last was a biologist, full of passion for science, just going to return to India. 'I am going', he said, 'from this land of prosperity to the land of plague and famine, from this land of freedom to the land where if I am truthful I am disloyal, if I am honest I am seditious; from this land of enlightenment to the land of religious bigotry, the land that I love, my country. A man must be more than human to love such a country; but those who would serve it have become more than human.' What a waste to make such men fight political battles! In a happier world, he would probably discover preventives for cholera; as it is, his life will be full of strife and bitterness, resisting evil, not creating good. All of them were fearless and thoughtful; most of them were very bitter. Mixed in with it all was an odd

strain of undergraduate fun and banter, jibes about the relative merits
of Oxford and Cambridge, and such talk as amuses the English youth
in quiet times. The mixture, which was in each separate speech, was
very curious.

Tonight I meet them again, or some of them, and give them my
lecture on education. I am very glad indeed to have got to know their
point of view and their character. It must be appallingly tragic to be
civilised and educated and belong to such a country as India.

Helen [Dudley] is coming to lunch. I hope I shall see Nicod; also
Armstrong[1]. Yesterday I lunched with Waterlow[2] which was dull.

I spoke to the Indians for half an hour, entirely without preparation
or any scrap of notes. I believe I speak better that way, more spon-
taneously and less monotonously.

> Trinity College
> Sunday evening 19 Mar. '16

My Darling

The melancholy of this place now-a-days is beyond endurance – the
Colleges are dead, except for a few Indians and a few pale pacifists and
bloodthirsty old men hobbling along victorious in the absence of
youth. Soldiers are billeted in the courts and drill on the grass;
bellicose parsons preach to them in stentorian tones from the steps of
the Hall. The town at night is plunged in a darkness compared to
which London is a blaze of light. All that one has cared for is dead, at
least for the present; and it is hard to believe that it will ever revive.
No one thinks about learning or feels it of any importance. And from
the outer deadness my thoughts travel to the deadness in myself – I
look round my shelves at the books of mathematics and philosophy
that used to seem full of hope and interest, and now leave me utterly
cold. The work I have done seems so little, so irrelevant to this world
in which we find we are living. And in everything except work I have
failed so utterly. All the hopes of five years ago come before me like
ghosts. I struggle to banish them from my mind but I can't. All our
happy times are in my memory, though I know it is better not to think
of them. I know I must work and think and learn to be interested in
mental things, but utter weariness overwhelms me in the thought. It is
no use to keep on running away from spectres. I must let them catch
me up and then face them. When I have learnt to work properly again,
I shall feel more inward independence, and things will be better. Ever

[1] Armstrong was a man whom I came to know as an under-graduate at
Cambridge. He enlisted at the beginning of the war, lost a leg and became a
pacifist.

[2] Afterwards Sir Sidney. He was a nephew of Elizabeth, and in the Foreign
Office. We had many common friends at Cambridge.

since I knew you, I have tried to get from you what one ought to get out of oneself.

> 46 Gordon Square
> Bloomsbury
> Tuesday night
> [1916]

My Darling

I have not heard from you since the letter you wrote on Friday, but as I only get my letters once a day now (when I call for them, in the morning) it is not surprising.

I had a queer adventure today. Lloyd George was led to think he might as well find out at first hand about the conscientious objectors, so he had Clifford Allen and Miss Marshall and me to lunch at his place near Reigate, fetching us and sending us back in his own motor. He was very unsatisfactory, and I think only wanted to exercise his skill in trying to start a process of bargaining. Still, it was worth something that he should see Allen and know the actual man. It will make him more reluctant to have him shot.

I feel convinced the men will have to suffer a good deal before public opinion and Government will cease to wish to persecute them. I got the impression that Ll. George expects the war to go on for a long time yet; also that he thinks the whole situation very black. He seemed *quite* heartless. Afterwards I saw Anderson [a Labour MP] at the House: he is an oily humbug.

It is quite private about L. G. I suppose.

The first thing that wants doing is to overhaul the whole of the decisions of the Tribunals and have all conscience cases re-heard. No doubt a good many are cowards: people are unspeakably cruel about cowardice – some have gone mad, some have committed suicide, and people merely shrug their shoulders and remark that they had no pluck. Nine-tenths of the human race are incredibly hateful.

From Bernard Shaw   10 Adelphi Terrace. W.C.
                                     18th April 1916

Dear Bertrand Russell

Yeats wrote to me about Chappelow, enclosing a letter from a lady, a cousin of his. But I really don't see what is to be done. The Act has been passed; and he must either serve or go through with his martyrdom. There is no ground on which exemption can be demanded for him: he seems to have just let things slide, like a child unable to conceive that the law had anything to do with him personally, instead of appealing or taking advice. I have no private influence; and exfluence, which I probably have, would not help him.

His letter is not that of a man made of martyr-stuff. He seems to be, like many literary people, helpless in practical affairs and the army is in some ways the very place for him; for he will be trained to face the inevitable, and yet have no responsibilities. He will be fed and clothed and exercised and told what to do; and he will have unlimited opportunities for thinking about other things. He will not be asked to kill anybody for a year to come; and if he finds his conscience insuperably averse, he can throw down his arms and take his two years hard labour then if he must, and be in much better condition for it. But by that time he will either have been discharged as unfit for service or else have realised that a man living in society must act according to the collective conscience under whatever protest his individual conscience may impel him to make. I think that is what we are bound to tell all the pacific young men who apply to us. Martyrdom is a matter for the individual soul: you can't advise a man to undertake it.

I do not blame any intelligent man for trying to dodge the atrocious boredom of soldiering if it can be dodged; but Chappelow seems to have been too helpless to make any attempt to dodge it: he simply stood gaping in the path of the steamroller. I am sorry for him; but I can only advise him to serve. Can you suggest anything better?

Yours ever
G. Bernard Shaw

Postscript

It would hardly help him to say 'I don't mind being bound by the conscience of England, or by my own conscience; but I don't feel at home with the conscience of Lord Northcliffe, Sir Edward Carson, and General Robertson, who naturally thinks there is nothing like leather'.
P.P.S.

Influence can work only in the direction of letting the prisoner out after he is sentenced on some pretext or other.

The following is the leaflet for which I, in common with those who distributed it, was prosecuted:

TWO YEARS' HARD LABOUR FOR
REFUSING TO DISOBEY THE
DICTATES OF CONSCIENCE.

This was the sentence passed on Ernest F. Everett, of 222, Denton's Green Lane, St Helens, by a Court Martial held on April 10th [1916].

Everett was a teacher at St Helens, and had been opposed to all war since the age of 16. He appealed as a Conscientious Objector before the Local and Appeal Tribunals, both of which treated him very unfairly, going out of their way to recommend his dismissal from school. They recognised his conscientious claim only so far as to award him non-combatant service. But as the purpose of such service is to further the prosecution of the war, and to release others for the trenches, it was impossible for him to accept the decision of the Tribunals.

On March 31st he was arrested as an absentee, brought before the magistrates, fined £2, and handed over to the Military Authorities. By them he was taken under escort to Warrington Barracks, where he was compelled to put on uniform. On April 1st he was taken to Abergele, where he was placed in the Non-Combatant Corps, which is part of the Army.

He adopted consistently a policy of passive resistance to all military orders. The first morning, April 2, when the men were ordered to fall in for fatigue duty, he refused, saying: 'I refuse to obey any order given by any military authority.' According to the Corporal, who gave the order, Everett 'said it in quite a nice way'.

The Corporal informed the Lieutenant, who repeated the order, and warned Everett of the seriousness of his conduct. Everett still answered politely, but explained why he could not obey. The Lieutenant ordered the Conscientious Objector to the guard-room, where he remained all night.

The Captain visited the prisoner, who stated that 'he was not going to take orders'. The Captain ordered him to be brought before the Commanding Officer on a charge of disobedience.

Everett was next brought before the Colonel, who read aloud to him Section 9 of the Army Act, and explained the serious consequences of disobedience. But Everett remained firm, saying 'He could not and would not obey any military order'.

The result was that he was tried by Court Martial on April 10th. He stated in evidence in his own defence: 'I am prepared to do work of national importance which does not include military service, so long as I do not thereby release some other man to do what I am not prepared to do myself.'

The sentence was two years' hard labour. Everett is now suffering this savage punishment solely for refusal to go against his conscience. He is fighting the old fight for liberty and against religious persecution in the same spirit in which martyrs suffered in the past. Will you join the persecutors? Or will you stand for those who are defending conscience at the cost of obloquy and pain of mind and body?

Forty other men are suffering persecution for conscience sake in the same way as Mr Everett. Can you remain silent whilst this goes on?

Issued by the No-Conscription Fellowship, 8, Merton House, Salisbury Court, Fleet Street, London, E.C.

From *The Times* of May 17th, 1916

ADSUM QUI FECI.[1]

To the editor of *The Times*

Sir, A leaflet was lately issued by the No-Conscription Fellowship dealing with the case of Mr Everett, a conscientious objector, who was sentenced to two years' hard labour by Court-martial for disobedience to the military authorities. Six men have been condemned to varying terms of imprisonment with hard labour for distributing this leaflet. I wish to make it known that I am the author of this leaflet, and that if anyone is to be prosecuted I am the person primarily responsible.

> *Yours faithfully*
> *Bertrand Russell*

From A. N. Whitehead   June 4th [1916]

Dearest Bertie

Good luck to you in every way. Let me know if and how I can help or shew any office of friendship. You know well enough that the mere fact that I think your views of state policy and of private duty in relation to it to be mistaken, do not diminish affection.

> *Yours affectionately*
> *A. N. Whitehead*

I am just going to commence my address for Section A at Newcastle in September – I will shew it you in ms.

From Cecil Spring Rice   British Embassy
[British Ambassador in   Washington
Washington]   8 June 1916

My dear Mr President[2]

I am sorry to say that Russell has been convicted under 'defence of the realm act' for writing an undesirable pamphlet. Under these circumstances it would be impossible to issue a passport to him to leave the country.

I am sorry, and Sir Edward Grey is sorry, that it is impossible to meet your wishes but I trust that you will understand the necessity in which my government is placed.

Oddly enough I was at the Berlin Embassy when we got into trouble

---

[1] The heading to this letter was added by *The Times*.
[2] The President of Harvard University.

owing to Russell's attitude when on a visit to Berlin as the German government strongly objected to his language.[1]

> *Yours sincerely*
> *Cecil Spring Rice*

To Professor James H. Woods,
of the Harvard Department of
Philosophy

34 Russell Chambers
30 July 1916

Dear Professor Woods

Your letter and the Ambassador's were not wholly a surprise to me. I cabled to you on receiving them, but I doubt if the cable ever reached you. Your letter was most kind. The allusion to my doings in Berlin was misleading. I was there in 1895 for the purpose of writing a book on German Socialism; this led me to associate with Socialists, and therefore to be excluded from the Embassy. I did nothing publicly all the time I was there. The Kaiser was having Socialists imprisoned in large numbers for their opinions, which gave me a hatred for him that I retain to this day. But unless in quite private conversations I never expressed my feelings all the time I was there. I have never been in Berlin since 1895.

I should be glad to know whether you have seen or received the verbatim report of my trial. It has been sent you, but may have been stopped by the Censor, who is anxious that America should not know the nature of my crime. You will have heard that I have been turned out of Trinity for the same offence. The sum-total of my crime was that I said two years' hard labour in prison was an excessive punishment for the offence of having a conscientious objection to participation in war. Since then, the same offence has been punished by the death-sentence, commuted to 10 years' penal servitude. Anyone who thinks that I can be made to hold my tongue when such things are being done is grossly mistaken. And the Government only advertises its own errors by trying ineffectually to punish those of us who won't be silent. Working men are sent to prison when they commit the crime that I committed. And when they come out, no one will employ them, so that they are reduced to living on charity. This is a war for liberty.

This letter will no doubt never reach you, but it may be found interesting by the Censor. If it does reach you, please let me know by return of post. It is a matter of some public interest to know what is allowed to pass, and if I don't hear from you within 6 weeks I shall assume that this letter has been stopped.

These are fierce times. But there is a new spirit abroad, and good will

[1] It was not my language, but my attending Socialist meetings, that was objected to.

come out of it all in the end. I wish your country had not embarked upon the career of militarism.

> *Yours ever gratefully*
> *B.R.*

To Ottoline Morrell

[June 1916]

My Darling

A 1000 thanks for your dear dear letter which I have just got. I am grateful for it.

This prosecution is the very thing I wanted. I have a very good case morally – as good as possible. I think myself that the legal case is good tho' no doubt they will convict, and I rather hope they will. I have seen the solicitor (George Baker) and arranged to defend myself without a barrister in the 1st Court on Monday. Then I shall appeal,[1] and employ a barrister the 2nd time. The 2nd time is not till the autumn, so I shall be able to go round the country in the summer as I had planned. That is not at all a wild scheme – apart from any good it may do, I shall learn a lot that I want to know.

I saw Miss Marshall and Allen and a number of the others – they were all delighted and hoping I should get a savage sentence. It is all great fun, as well as a magnificent opportunity. The sort of opportunity I have longed for – and I have come by it legitimately, without going out of my way. I am going back to Cambridge now, coming up again Friday and staying here till Monday. Think of me Monday 11.30. I hope I shall be worthy of the occasion.

Goodbye my Darling Love. Your love and sympathy do help far more than you know.

> *Your*
> *B.*

Monday evg. [1916]

Today I had lunch and a country walk with the Rev. Morgan Jones, a prominent pacifist here [in South Wales] and a real saint. Then I went to a neighbouring town for a meeting – it was to have been in the school, but that was refused at the last moment, so we had it in the open air. A Unitarian Minister spoke who has a son a CO. It is wonderful what the COs. have done for the cause of peace – the heroism is no longer all on the side of war.

I ought to have gone into more hostile districts. Here it is merely a picnic and I feel I should be better employed in town. After the 23rd I shall be back in town – by then most of our Nat. Committee will be gone.

[1] I appealed and was again convicted.

I am *longing* to know how Allen's visit went off. I am so terribly afraid it will have been a failure.

Speaking is a great nervous strain. I feel very slack all the rest of the time. But I sleep well and my mind is at peace so I don't get really tired. I never have any fundamental worries now-a-days.

I shall be very poor, having lost America and probably Trinity. I shall have to find some other way of making money. I think if Trinity turns me out I shall advertise academic lectures in London on philosophical subjects. It would be delightful if they succeeded, as they wouldn't interfere with political work. I have often dreamt of having an independent school like Abelard. It might lead to great things. I feel I am only on the threshold of life – the rest has been preparation – I mean as far as work is concerned. Quite lately I have somehow found myself – I have poise and sanity – I no longer have the feeling of powers unrealised within me, which used to be a perpetual torture. I don't care what the authorities do to me, they can't stop me long. Before I have felt either wicked or passively resigned – now I feel fully active and contented with my activity – I have no inward discords any more – and nothing ever really troubles me.

I realise that as soon as the worst of the stress is over I shall want some more intellectual occupation. But I see room for endless work on political theory. And it will have the advantage that it will involve seeing all sorts of people and getting to know all sorts of human facts – it won't leave half of me unsatisfied as abstract work does. The only doubt is whether I shan't some day be suddenly overwhelmed by the passion for the things that are eternal and perfect, like mathematics. Even the most abstract political theory is terribly mundane and temporary. But that must be left to the future.

It is very sad seeing you so seldom. I feel as if we should lose intimacy and get out of the way of speaking of personal things – it would be a great loss if that happened. I know extraordinarily little of your inner life now-a-days, and I wish I knew more, but I don't know how to elicit it. My own existence has become so objective that I hardly have an inner life any more for the present – but I should have if I had leisure.

My Dearest, I am full of love to you – visions are always in my mind of happy days after the war, when we shall get back to poetry and beauty and summer woods, and the vision of things outside this earth. But the war keeps one tied to earth. And sometimes I wonder if we have both grown so impersonal that it has become difficult to give oneself to personal love – it always was difficult for you. It is a great loss if it is so. I hope it isn't. Do write a full letter when you can, and tell me something of your inward life.

From the Trinity College Council Trinity College
            Cambridge
            11 July 1916

Dear Russell

It is my duty to inform you that the following resolution was unanimously passed by the College Council today:

'That, since Mr Russell has been convicted under the Defence of the Realm Act, and the conviction has been affirmed on appeal, he be removed from his Lectureship in the College.'

            Yours sincerely
            H. McLeod Innes

From S. Alexander   24, Brunswick Road
            Withington
            M/C
            16.7.16

Dear Russell

I feel indignant about the action of Trinity, which disgraces them (as well as making them ridiculous). I don't share your views about War (as I think you may know) and I can't well judge the effect of your action – though I have hated the bungling and injustice of the treatment of Conscientious Objectors. But sensible people, even if they don't know and admire you personally, respect honest convictions; and Trinity's action is both intolerant and impertinent. It matters to all of us at Universities (and elsewhere) more perhaps than it matters to you.

            Yours sincerely
            S. Alexander
         [The distinguished philosopher]

I have only the Trinity address, and must send that way.

From my brother Frank   Telegraph House
            Chichester
            16 July 1916

My dear ,Bertie

I have seen the Trinity announcement in the paper, and whatever you may say, I very much regret it. No doubt these stuffy old dons were very uncongenial to you, and were also unfriendly on account of your views, but still, I always thought you well suited to an academic life, and a personality of great value to the young – in stirring their ideas. I think as time goes on you will miss it more than you realise and probably regret it.

I can't attempt to shape your career for you – you must be the only guide and the only judge of your own actions – but don't finally cut yourself off too rashly and above all beware of popular audiences. The average [man] is such a fool that any able man who can talk can sway him for a time. What the world wants of first class intellects like yours is not action – for which the ordinary politician or demagogue is good enough – but thought, a much more rare quality. Think out our problems, embody the result in writing, and let it slowly percolate through the teachers of the next generation. And don't suppose the people you meet are as earnest, as deep or as sincere as you are.

As mere experience and learning about human beings what you are doing now may have its value, but you see what I am trying to say is that you are *wasting* yourself. You are not making the best use for the world of your talents. As soon as you come to see that you will change your activities.

Well – I don't preach to you often, because as a rule you don't need it, but at the moment I think you are a little (or rather, a great deal) carried away.

It's a long time to Feb. 1 – why not go to America sooner ? – they ought to be glad to get rid of you!

Come and see us when you are in London and try and spend a few placid days here with us in August.

> Yours affectionately
> F

From F. M. Cornford[1]

> Burrows Hill
> Gomshall
> Surrey
> 23 July 1916

Dear Russell

I have only today received an account of the College Council's action and a report of your trial before the Mayor.

I must tell you that I think your case was as unanswerable as it was unanswered, and the decision, so far as I can see, was utterly unwarranted by the evidence.

I was glad you said you could respect your friends who are not pacifists in quite the same sense that you are. What you think of me I don't know: but I have admired the fight you have put up.

As for the College Council, you know too much to confuse it with the College. The older dons, last time I saw them, seemed to me to be in various stages of insanity. Something will have to be done when the younger ones come back. I am sure there would have been a majority of the whole body against the Council, if it had come before a full College meeting.

[1] Cornford was a Fellow of Trinity, and a distinguished writer on ancient philosophy. His wife was Frances Cornford the poet. His son was killed in the Spanish Civil War. I was very fond of both him and his wife.

I feel very bitterly that the Council has disgraced us. When you and Moore came back,[1] I was delighted that we had recovered you both, and now we have lost one of you, it is a real grief and humiliation.

> *Yours sincerely*
> *F. M. Cornford*

To G. Lowes Dickinson

34 Russell Chambers
Bury Street, W.C.
Sunday [1916]

Dear Goldie

Thank you very much for your letter in the *Nation*,[2] which I read with gratitude. One has a little the sense of reading one's own obituaries,[3] a thing I have always wished to be able to do! The Whiteheads are *very* decent about this. I think McT.[4] and Lawrence were the prime movers. I have been sold up, but owing to kind friends I have lost nothing. I don't know who they are – whoever they are, I am most grateful and touched.

Clifford Allen is to be taken tomorrow. Casement[5] is to be shot. I am ashamed to be at large.

> *Yours ever*
> *B.R.*

From C. P. Sanger

Finches
Aston Tirrold
22 Aug. 1916

Dear Bertie

You will have realised how I feel about all this persecution. Did you ever meet Constable – a young economist who was going to the bar – at our house. He's a Major now and in writing to me from the front says 'I was very glad to see that there have been protests against the action of Trinity with regard to Bertrand Russell. I must say that men I have met out here nearly all agree with me that the College has merely stultified itself' . . .

Masefield writing up the Dardanelles – has been allowed to see some official documents and so on. It is most disheartening that literary men

[1] Moore had been invited back from Edinburgh where he had had a post.
[2] Of July 29th, 1916.
[3] I was able to in 1921. The allusion is to my being turned out of Trinity.
[4] McTaggart.
[5] Sir Roger Casement, who first became known for his protests against atrocities in the Congo, was an Irish rebel who sided with the Germans. He was captured, tried and executed.

of standing should try to make a mere calamity 'epic' for American consumption.

> *Yours fraternally*
> *Charles Percy Sanger*

From James Ward

> 6, Selwyn Gardens
> Cambridge
> 3.ix.16

Dear Russell

I am amazed and grieved to see how you are being badgered and hounded about. It is most outrageous, and what the motive for it all may be I am quite at a loss to surmise. Are they afraid that you will sneak off to America or is there some rabid fanatic trying to persuade them that you are what the McTaggarts call us – pro-Germans? I see you are announced to lecture in Manchester: is there no danger of your lectures being prohibited? Well you have just got to compose yourself with dignity and patience and there will be voices in your favour to speak out before long.

Since I saw you I have been trying to draw up a statement to justify your action and to serve as a separate preamble to accompany an invitation to protest against the action of the College Council to be sent to all the fellows of the College (exclusive of the Council)[1] . . .

> *Yours ever*
> *James Ward*

The writer of the following letter was killed not long afterwards. I never met him, but I came to know his fiancée, Dorothy Mackenzie, who, on the news of his death, became blind for three weeks.

From Lieut. A. Graeme West

> 9th Batt. Oxfordshire &
> Buckinghamshire Light
> Infantry
> Bovington Camp
> Wareham
> Dorset
> Sunday, Sept. 3. 1916

Dear Mr Russell

Seeing the new scene that has been added to this amazing farce of which you are the unfortunate protagonist, I could not help writing to you. Of course you know that such sane men as still live, or have kept their sanity, have nothing but admiration for you, and therefore you

[1] Nothing came of this.

may cry that this note is impertinent. Literally, I suppose it is; but not to me.

I cannot resist the joy of communicating directly with one whom I admired so much before the war, as the writer of the clearest and finest philosophical English prose, and whom I admire so much more now when all the intellectuals, except, thank god, Shaw, have lost the use of their reason.

I think there may be some shade of excuse for this liberty at a time when reason and thought are in danger and when you, their ablest champion, are the victim of incompetence and derision: at such a time those who love Justice should speak.

I know you must have many friends in the army, and are aware that it, too, contains men of good-will, though it is through it and its domination that England finds herself as she is; yet one more assurance of complete understanding and sympathy may not annoy you.

Were I back in the Ranks again – and I wish I were – I could have picked half-a-dozen men of our platoon to have signed with me: here, it is not so.

Thank you, then, for all you are and all you have written, for 'A Free Man's Worship' and *Justice in War Time* and *The Policy of the Entente* and many others; and I hope that I (and you, of course, for we don't know what they mayn't do to you) may live to see you.

> *Yours sincerely*
> *A. Graeme West*
> *2nd Lieut.*

From H. G. Wells
[to Miles Malleson]

52, St James's Court
Buckingham Gate, S.W.
[1916]

My dear Sir

I think that a small minority of the CO's are sincerely honest men but I believe that unless the path of the CO is made difficult it will supply a stampede track for every variety of shirker. Naturally a lot of the work of control falls on the hands of clumsy and rough minded men. I really don't feel very much sympathy for these 'martyrs'. I don't feel so sure as you do that all CO's base the objection on love rather than hate. I have never heard either Cannan or Norman speak lovingly of any human being. Their normal attitude has always been one of opposition – to anything. Enthusiasm makes them liverish. And the *Labour Leader* group I believe to be thoroughly dishonest, Ramsey MacDonald, I mean, Morel and the editor. I may be wrong but that is my slow and simple conviction.

> *Very sincerely yours*
> *H. G. Wells*

My statement concerning my meeting with General Cockerill on September 5th, 1916:

I called at the War Office with Sir Francis Younghusband by appointment at 3.15 to see General Cockerill. He had beside him a report of my speeches in S. Wales and drew special attention to a sentence in a speech I made at Cardiff saying there was no good reason why this war should continue another day. He said that such a statement made to miners or munition workers was calculated to diminish their ardour. He said also that I was encouraging men to refuse to fight for their country. He said he would withdraw the order forbidding me to enter prohibited areas if I would abandon political propaganda and return to mathematics. I said I could not conscientiously give such an undertaking.

He said:

'You and I probably regard conscience differently. I regard it as a still small voice, but when it becomes blatant and strident I suspect it of no longer being a conscience.'

I replied:

'You do not apply this principle to those who write and speak in favour of the war; you do not consider that if they hold their opinions in secret they are conscientious men, but if they give utterance to them in the Press or on the platform they are mere propagandists. There seems some lack of justice in this differentiation.'

He remained silent a long while and then replied:

'Yes, that is true. But', he said, 'you have said your say, can you not rest content with having said it and return to those other pursuits in which' – so he was pleased to add – 'you have achieved so much distinction? Do you not think there is some lack of a sense of humour in going on reiterating the same thing?'

I failed to reply that I had observed this lack – if it were one – in *The Times*, the *Morning Post* and other patriotic organs, which appeared to me to be somewhat addicted to reiteration, and that if it would not serve any purpose to repeat myself I failed to see why he was so anxious to prevent me from doing so. But what I did say was that new issues are constantly arising and I could not barter away my right to speak on such issues. I said:

'I appeal to you as a man, would you not feel less respect for me if I agreed to this bargain which you propose ?'

After a long hesitation he replied:

'No, I should respect you more; I should think better of your sense of humour if you realised the uselessness of saying the same thing over and over again.'

I told him that I was thinking of delivering lectures on the general principles of politics in Glasgow, Edinburgh and Newcastle. He asked whether these would involve the propaganda he objected to. I said no, not directly, but they would state the general principles out of which the propaganda has grown, and no doubt men with sufficient logical acumen would be able to draw inferences. He then gave it to be understood that such lectures could not be permitted. He wound up with an earnest appeal to me not to make the task of the soldiers more difficult when they were engaged in a life and death struggle.

I told him that he flattered me in supposing my influence sufficient to have any such result, but that I could not possibly cease my propaganda as the result of a threat and that if he had wished his appeal to have weight he ought not to have accompanied it by a threat. I said I was most sincerely sorry to be compelled to do anything which the authorities considered embarrassing, but that I had no choice in the matter.

We parted with mutual respect, and on my side at least, without the faintest feeling of hostility. Nevertheless it was perfectly clear that he meant to proceed to extremities if I did not abandon political propaganda.

To Ottoline Morrell   [September 1916]
                                        Monday night

My Darling

There seems a good chance that the authorities will relent towards me – I am half sorry! I shall soon have come to the end of the readjustment with Mrs E. [Mrs T. S. Eliot] I think it will all be all right, on a better basis. As soon as it is settled, I will come to Garsington. I long to come.

I have been realising various things during this time. It is odd how one finds out what one really wants, and how very selfish it always is. What I want permanently – not consciously, but deep down – is stimulus, the sort of thing that keeps my brain active and exuberant. I suppose that is what makes me a vampire. I get a stimulus most from the instinctive feeling of success. Failure makes me collapse. Odd things give me a sense of failure – for instance, the way the cos all take alternative service, except a handful. Wittgenstein's criticism gave me a sense of failure. The real trouble between you and me has always been that you gave me a sense of failure – at first, because you were not happy; then, in other ways. To be *really* happy with you, not only momentarily, I should have to lose that sense of failure. I had a sense of success with Mrs E. because I achieved what I meant to achieve (which was not so very difficult), but now I have lost that, not by your fault in the least. The sense of success helps my work: when I lose it, my writing grows dull and lifeless. I often feel success quite apart from happiness: it depends upon what one puts one's will into. Instinctively, I turn to things in which success is possible, just for the stimulus.

I have always cared for you in yourself, and not as a stimulus or for any self-centred reason; but when I have felt that through caring for you and feeling unsuccessful I have lost energy, it has produced a sort of instinctive resentment. That has been at the bottom of everything – and now that I have at last got to the bottom of it, it won't be a trouble any longer. But unless I can cease to have a sense of failure with you, I am bound to go on looking for stimulus elsewhere from time to time. That would only cease if I ceased to care about work – I am sure all this is the exact truth.

I would set my will in a different direction as regards you, if I knew of any direction in which I *could* succeed. But I don't think it can be done in that way.

The rare moments of mystic insight that I have had have been when I was free from the will to succeed. But they have brought a new kind of success, which I have at once noticed and wanted, and so my will has drifted back into the old ways. And I don't believe I should do anything worth doing without that sort of will. It is very tangled.

To Constance Malleson (Colette)   Gordon Square
                                   September 29, 1916

You are already where I have struggled to be, and without the weariness of long effort. I have hated many people in the past. The language of hate still comes to me easily, but I don't really hate anyone now. It is defeat that makes one hate people – and now I have no sense of defeat anywhere. No one need ever be defeated – it rests with oneself to make oneself invincible. Quite lately I have had a sense of freedom I never had before . . . I don't like the spirit of socialism – I think freedom is the basis of everything.

*   *   *

'The keys to an endless peace' –

I am not so great as that, *really* not – I know where peace is – I have seen it, and felt it at times – but I can still imagine misfortunes that would rob me of peace. But there is a world of peace, and one can live in it and yet be active still over all that is bad in the world. Do you know how sometimes all the barriers of personality fall away, and one is free for all the world to come in – the stars and the night and the wind, and all the passions and hopes of men, and all the slow centuries of growth – and even the cold abysses of space grow friendly – '*E il naufragar m'e dolce in questo mare*'. And from that moment some quality of ultimate peace enters into all one feels – even when one feels most passionately. I felt it the other night by the river – I thought you were going to withdraw yourself – I felt that if you did I should lose the most wonderful thing that had ever come to me – and yet an ultimate fundamental peace remained – if it hadn't, I believe I should have lost you then. I cannot bear the littleness and enclosing walls of *purely* personal things – I want to live always open to the world, I want personal love to be like a beacon *fire* lighting up the darkness, not a timid refuge from the cold as it is very often.

London under the stars is strangely moving. The momentariness of the separate lives seems so strange –

In some way I can't put into words, I feel that some of our thoughts and feelings are just of the moment, but others are part of the eternal world, like the stars – even if their actual existence is passing, something – some spirit or essence – seems to last on, to be part of the real history of the universe, not only of the separate person. Somehow, that is how I want to live, so that as much of life as possible may have that quality of eternity. I can't explain what I mean – you will have to know – of course I don't succeed in living that way – but that is 'the shining key to peace'.

Oh, I am happy, happy, happy –

B.

Gordon Square
October 23, 1916

I have meant to tell you many things about my life, and every time the moment has conquered me. I am strangely unhappy because the pattern of my life is complicated, because my nature is hopelessly complicated; a mass of contradictory impulses; and out of all this, to my intense sorrow, pain to you must grow. The centre of me is always and eternally a terrible pain – a curious wild pain – a searching for something beyond what the world contains, something transfigured and infinite – the beatific vision – God – I do not find it, I do not think it is to be found – but the love of it is my life – it's like passionate love for a ghost. At times it fills me with rage, at times with wild despair, it is the source of gentleness and cruelty and work, it fills every passion that I have – it is the actual spring of life within me.

I can't explain it or make it seem anything but foolishness – but whether foolish or not, it is the source of whatever is any good in me. I have known others who had it – Conrad especially – but it is rare – it sets one oddly apart and gives a sense of great isolation – it makes people's gospels often seem thin. At most times, now, I am not conscious of it, only when I am strongly stirred, either happily or unhappily. I seek escape from it, though I don't believe I ought to. In that moment with you by the river I felt it most intensely.

'Windows always open to the world' I told you once, but through one's windows one sees not only the joy and beauty of the world, but also its pain and cruelty and ugliness, and the one is as well worth seeing as the other, and one must look into hell before one has any right to speak of heaven.

B.

From Lieut. A. Graeme West   Wednesday night
                                      Dec. 27. 1916

Dear Mr Russell

To-night here on the Somme I have just finished your *Principles of Social Reconstruction* which I found waiting for me when I came out of the line. I had seen a couple of Reviews of it, one in the *Nation*, one in *Land and Water* and from the praise of the former and the thinly veiled contempt of the latter I augured a good book. It encouraged me all the more as the state of opinion in England seems to fall to lower and lower depths of undignified hatred. It is only on account of such thoughts as yours, on account of the existence of men and women like yourself that it seems worth while surviving the war – if one should haply survive. Outside the small circle of that cool light I can discern nothing but a scorching desert.

Do not fear though that the life of the spirit is dying in us, nor that hope or energy will be spent; to some few of us at any rate the hope of helping to found some 'city of God' carries us away from these present horrors and beyond the grayer intolerance of thought as we see in it our papers. We shall not faint and the energy and endurance we have used here on an odious task we shall be able to redouble in the creative work that peace will bring to do. We are too young to be permanently damaged in body or spirit, even by these sufferings.

Rather what we feared until your book came was that we would find no one left in England who would build with us. Remember, then, that we are to be relied on to do twice as much afterwards as we have done during the war, and after reading your book that determination grew intenser than ever; it is for you that we would wish to live on.

I have written to you before and should perhaps apologise for writing again, but that seems to me rather absurd: you cannot mind knowing that you are understood and admired and that those exist who would be glad to work with you.

> *Yours sincerely*
> *A. Graeme West.* 2nd Lt.
> 6th Oxford & Bucks. L.I.
> B.E.F.

From the Press:
SECOND LIEUTENANT ARTHUR GRAEME WEST, Oxford and Bucks Light Infantry, whose death is officially announced to-day, was the eldest son of Arthur Birt West, 4 Holly Terrace, Highgate. He fell on April 3 [1917], aged 25.

To Colette   Guildford
                              December 28, 1916

How can love blossom among explosions and falling Zeppelins and all the surroundings of our love? It has to grow jagged and painful before it can live in such a world. I long for it to be otherwise – but soft things die in this horror, and our love has to have pain for its life blood.

I hate the world and almost all the people in it. I hate the Labour Congress and the journalists who send men to be slaughtered, and the fathers who feel a smug pride when their sons are killed, and even the pacifists who keep saying human nature is essentially good, in spite of all the daily proofs to the contrary. I hate the planet and the human race – I am ashamed to belong to such a species – And what is the good of me in that mood?

> *B.*

From Dorothy Mackenzie   77, Lady Margaret Road
                              Highgate. N.W.5
                              June 5th. [1917]

Dear Mr Russel

I am glad you sent Graeme West's letters to the *Cambridge Magazine*, for I am very sure he speaks for a great many, some of whom *will* survive.

When I had read your *Principles of Social Reconstruction*, being a young woman instead of a young man, I had the joy of being able to come and hear you speak at the Nursery of the Fabian Society. And I dared to say you were too gloomy, and that the world was not so spoilt as you thought. It was because West was in my thoughts that I was able to do that, and kindly you smiled at the optimism of youth, but the sadness of your smiling set me fearing.

Now I know that you were right and I was wrong. But I assure you Mr Russel, that we women want to build, and we unhappily do survive.

And I can end my letter as he ended his and say very truly 'it is for you that we would wish to live on'.

It is very difficult to know what to do. I am an elementary teacher, and every class in the school but mine is disciplined by a military method. I have to work as it were by stealth, disguising my ideas as much as possible. Children, as you are aware, do not develop themselves, in our elementary schools. Your chapter on education encouraged me more than anything I have read or heard since I started teaching. I thank you for that encouragement. It is most sad to teach in these days; underpaid, overworked, the man I loved most killed for a cause in which he no longer believed, out of sympathy with most of my friends and relations, I find strength and comfort in you through your book. I feel indeed that you understand.

Dorothy Mackenzie

From A. N. Whitehead

Twelve
Elm Park Gardens
Chelsea. S.W.
Jan. 8th, 17

Dear Bertie

I am awfully sorry, but you do not seem to appreciate my point.

I don't want my ideas propagated *at present* either under my name or anybody else's – that is to say, as far as they are at present on paper. The result will be an incomplete misleading exposition which will inevitably queer the pitch for the final exposition when I want to put it out.

My ideas and methods grow in a different way to yours and the period of incubation is long and the result attains its intelligible form in the final stage, – I do not want you to have my notes which in chapters are lucid, to precipitate them into what I should consider as a series of half-truths. I have worked at these ideas off and on for all my life, and should be left quite bare on one side of my speculative existence if I handed them over to some one else to elaborate. Now that I begin to see day-light, I do not feel justified or necessitated by any view of scientific advantage in so doing.

I am sorry that you do not feel able to get to work except by the help of these notes – but I am sure that you must be mistaken in this, and that there must be the whole of the remaining field of thought for you to get to work on – though naturally it would be easier for you to get into harness with some formed notes to go on. But my reasons are conclusive. I will send the work round to you naturally, when I have got it into the form which expresses my ideas.

Yours affectly
Alfred N. Whitehead

*Before the war started, Whitehead had made some notes on our know-
ledge of the external world and I had written a book on this subject in which
I made use with due acknowledgement of ideas that Whitehead had passed
on to me. The above letter shows that this had vexed him. In fact, it put an
end to our collaboration.*

To Lady Emily Lutyens   57, Gordon Square
                                 W.C. (1)
                                 21.III.17

Dear Lady Emily

I have shortened my article by seven lines, which was what seemed
needed – six lines close to the end and one in the middle of the last
column.

Is it really necessary to say that I am 'heir-presumptive to the present
Earl Russell'? I cannot see that my brother's having no children makes
my opinions more worthy of respect.

I have corrected a few inaccuracies in the biography.

'Critical detachment' is hardly my attitude to the war. My attitude is
one of intense and passionate protest – I consider it a horror, an infamy,
an overwhelming and unmitigated disaster, making the whole of life
ghastly.

> *Yours very sincerely*
> *Bertrand Russell*

To Colette   Gordon Square
                                 March 27, 1917

I cannot express a thousandth part of what is in my heart – our day
in the country was so marvellous. All through Sunday it grew and
grew, and at night it seemed to pass beyond the bounds of human
things. I feel no longer all alone in the world. Your love brings warmth
into all the recesses of my being. You used to speak of a wall of
separation between us. That no longer exists. The winter is ending,
we shall have sunshine and the song of birds, and wild flowers,
primroses, bluebells, and then the scent of the may. We will keep joy
alive in us. You are strong and brave and free, and filled with passion
and love – the very substance of all my dreams come to life.

> Gordon Square
> September 23, 1917

The whole region in my mind where you lived, seems burnt out.
There is nothing for us both but to try and forget each other.
Goodbye –

> B.

From Colette   Mecklenburgh Square
                                      September 26, 1917

I thought, until last night, that our love would grow and grow until it was strong as loneliness itself.

I have gazed down Eternity with you. I have held reins of glory in my two hands – Now, though I will still believe in the beauty of eternal things, they will not be for me. You will put the crown on your work. You still stand on the heights of impersonal greatness. I worship you, but our souls are strangers – I pray that I may soon be worn out and this torture ended.

C.

To Colette   Gordon Square
                                      October 25, 1917

I have known real happiness with you – If I could live by my creed, I should know it still. I feel imprisoned in egotism – weary of effort, too tired to break through into love.

How can I bridge the gulf?

B.

From *The Tribunal*. Thursday, January 3rd, 1918

THE GERMAN PEACE OFFER

by Bertrand Russell

The more we hear about the Bolsheviks, the more the legend of our patriotic press becomes exploded. We were told that they were incompetent, visionary and corrupt, that they must fall shortly, that the mass of Russians were against them, and that they dared not permit the Constituent Assembly to meet. All these statements have turned out completely false, as anyone may see by reading the very interesting despatch from Arthur Ransome in the *Daily News* of December 31st.

Lenin, whom we have been invited to regard as a German Jew, is really a Russian aristocrat who has suffered many years of persecution for his opinions. The social revolutionaries who were represented as enemies of the Bolsheviks have formed a connection with them. The Constituent Assembly is to meet as soon as half its members have reached Petrograd, and very nearly half have already arrived. All charges of German money remain entirely unsupported by one thread of evidence.

The most noteworthy and astonishing triumph of the Bolsheviks is in their negotiations with the Germans. In a military sense Russia is defenceless, and we all supposed it a proof that they were mere visionaries when they started negotiations by insisting upon not surrendering any Russian territory to the Germans. We were told that the Germans would infallibly insist upon annexing the Baltic Provinces and establishing a suzerainty over Poland. So far from this being the case, the German and Austrian Governments have officially announced that they are prepared to conclude a Peace on the Russian basis of no annexations and no indemnities, provided that it is a general Peace, and they have invited the Western Powers to agree to these terms.

This action has placed the Governments of the Western Powers in a most cruel dilemma. If they refuse the German offer, they are unmasked before the world and before their own Labour and Socialist Parties: they make it clear to all that they are continuing the war for purposes of territorial aggrandisement. If they accept the offer, they afford a triumph to the hated Bolsheviks and an object lesson to democratic revolutionaries everywhere as to the way to treat with capitalists, Imperialists and war-mongers. They know that from the patriotic point of view they cannot hope for a better peace by continuing the war, but from the point of view of preventing liberty and universal peace, there is something to be hoped from continuation. It is known that unless peace comes soon there will be starvation throughout Europe. Mothers will be maddened by the spectacle of their children dying. Men will fight each other for possession of the bare necessaries of life. Under such conditions the sane constructive effort required for a successful revolution will be impossible. The American Garrison which will by that time be occupying England and France, whether or not they will prove efficient against the Germans, will no doubt be capable of intimidating strikers, an occupation to which the American Army is accustomed when at home. I do not say that these thoughts are in the mind of the Government. All the evidence tends to show that there are no thoughts whatever in their mind, and that they live from hand to mouth consoling themselves with ignorance and sentimental twaddle. I say only that if they were capable of thought, it would be along such lines as I have suggested that they would have to attempt to justify a refusal to make Peace on the basis of the German offer, if indeed they do decide to refuse.

Some democrats and Socialists are perhaps not unwilling that the war should continue, since it is clear that if it does it must lead to universal revolution. I think it is true that this consequence must follow, but I do not think that we ought on that account to acquiesce in the refusal to negotiate should that be the decision at which our Governments arrive. The kind of revolution with which we shall in that case be threatened will be far too serious and terrible to be a source of good. It would be a revolution full of violence, hatred and bloodshed, driven by hunger, terror and suspicion, – a revolution in which all that is best in Western civilisation is bound to perish. It is this prospect that our rulers ought to be facing. It is this risk that they run for such paltry objects as the annexation of African Colonies and Mesopotamia. Labour's war aims accepted almost unanimously on December 28th are on the whole very sane, and might easily form the basis for the immediate initiation of negotiations. Labour at the moment has enormous power. Is it too much to hope that it will use this power to compel some glimmer of sanity on the part of the blinded and maddened rulers of the Western Powers? Labour holds the key. It can if it chooses secure a just and lasting peace within a month, but if this opportunity is allowed to pass by, all that we hold dear will be swallowed up in universal ruin.

The above article was that for which I was sentenced to prison.

To Professor Gilbert Murray   57, Gordon Square
                                   London, W.C.1
                                   15th February 1918

My dear Gilbert

I am very much touched by the kindness of your letter. It really is good of you to act when our views are so different. Of course if I had known the blaze of publicity that was going to be directed upon that one sentence of the *Tribunal*, I should have phrased it very much more carefully, in such a way as to prevent misunderstanding by a public not used to the tone of exasperated and pugnacious pacifists. Unless the Government had prosecuted, no-one but pacifists would ever have seen the sentence. Certainly it is a thousand to one that no American would ever have seen it. I wrote for the *Tribunal* once a week for a year, generally in great haste in the middle of other work. In the course of this time it was almost unavoidable that I should emit at least one careless sentence – careless that is as to form, for as regards the matter I adhere to it.

So far as I can discover, the immediate cause of the prosecution was the fact that I had ceased to write these articles, or indeed to take any part in pacifist work beyond attending an occasional Committee. I made up my mind to this course last autumn, but it was impossible to carry it out instantly without inconvenience to colleagues. I therefore informed the NCF that I would cease to be their Acting Chairman at the New Year. Accordingly, the last article I wrote for the *Tribunal* appeared on January 10, a week after the article for which I am prosecuted. It seems that the authorities realised that if they wished to punish me they must act at once, as I should not be committing any further crimes. All my plans were made for going back entirely to writing and philosophical lecturing, but whether I shall now be able to resume these plans when I come out of prison is of course doubtful. I do not much dislike the prospect of prison, provided I am allowed plenty of books to read. I think the freedom from responsibility will be rather restful. I cannot imagine anything that there could be to do for me, unless the American Embassy were to take the view that the matter is too trumpery to be worth a prosecution, but I cannot say that I have any great desire to see the prosecution quashed. I think those of us who live in luxury on money which is secured to us by the Criminal Law ought to have some idea of the mechanism by which our happiness is secured, and for this reason I shall be glad to know the inside of a prison.

With my very warmest thanks,

> *Yours ever affectionately*
> *Bertrand Russell*

57 Gordon Square W.C.1
27.3.18

Dear Gilbert

You have been so very kind that I feel I ought to write to you in regard to what is being done in my case. Assuming that the sentence is confirmed, it seems it will be the thing to ask for 1st Division. This will need preparing soon, as things move slowly. Hirst is willing to approach Morley, Loreburn, Buckmaster, & Lansdowne, asking them to write to Cave. It seems to me that Asquith & Grey might be willing to; also a certain number of un-political learned men. If you were willing, you could do this better than any one else. If private representations fail (as they probably will) letters to the Press will be necessary. All this will have to be done quickly if it is to be effective.

I saw E. D. Morel yesterday for the first time since he came out, & was impressed by the seriousness of a six months' sentence. His hair is completely white (there was hardly a tinge of white before) – when he first came out, he collapsed completely, physically & mentally, largely as the result of insufficient food. He says one only gets three quarters of an hour for reading in the whole day – the rest of the time is spent on prison work etc. It seems highly probable that if the sentence is not mitigated my mind will not remain as competent as it has been. I should regret this, as I still have a lot of philosophy that I wish to do.

> *Yrs ever*
> *Bertrand Russell*

From E. M. Forster   Alexandria
                            12-2-18

Dear Russell,

In the middle of a six course dinner at the Club last night I was told that you were in prison. This is to send you my love. I suppose they will let you have it when you come out.

Here all is comfort and calm. One will become very queer indeed if it, and the war, last much longer.

> *Yours fraternally*
> *E. M. Forster*

From Lancelot Hogben   London April 10th. 18

Dear Mr Russell

I am only writing a little note to tell you how splendid I think your stand has been. Being an ex convict, I understand a little at what cost you have been true. It is inspiring to us who are younger men and who see so many of our own friends succumbing to cynical indifference or academic preoccupation to know that there is at least one of the Intellectuals of Europe who have not allowed the life of the mind to kill the life of the spirit ... This is rather ineffective, but well,

> *Good luck*
> *Yours very sincerely*
> *Lancelot Hogben*

From G. Lowes Dickinson   11 Edwardes Square
                                          W. 8. Ap. 19, [1918]

Dear Bertie

I wish I could have seen you, but I haven't been able to fit it in, and I go away today for the rest of April. I hope to be there on May 1st. It is difficult to have any hope. I suppose the best thing that could happen now would be for you to get first-class imprisonment. If they fine you, you will I suppose be called up at once, and have to go through the mill as a CO. The only chance is that the brute [Lord] Derby has gone from the War Office and I understand that Milner is more sympathetic to the COs. We are governed by men as base as they are incompetent, and the country, maddened by fear and hate, continues to will it so. I blush all over to be English, sometimes. Yet one knows that the individual Englishman is a decent, kindly well-meaning chap. Its the pack, and its leaders, that are so vile. But what use in words ? One can alter nothing; and human speech seems to have lost all meaning. To change the subject, I am reading Aristotle on the Soul. Its refreshing to be back at a time when the questions were being examined freshly by first-class minds. Aristotle's method of approach might be yours. One sees however, I think, that the conception of 'substance' has already fixed thought in a certain unconscious rut. In my old age, owing I suppose to you and others, I find my mind more disencumbered and active than it was in youth. But the packs of wolves will not be satisfied until they have killed off every free mind and brave soul. That's the secret object of the war. So long.

G.L.D.
[Lowes Dickinson]

From C. P. Sanger

58 Oakley Street
Chelsea, S.W.3
28th April 1918

Dear Bertie

Although we haven't met much lately, you are constantly in my thoughts. Its difficult to say what one feels – you have always been so very much to me and I can't bear the thought that you may go to prison, though I know that your fortitude and self control will bring you safely through the ordeal. Its a mad world – a nightmare. I sometimes think I shall wake up and find that it was a dream after all. I hope that reality will prove to be better than appearance – if there is anything besides this absurd world of blood and explosives.

But if things can be improved, it is you and those like you who will do it and the younger men – if any of them survive – will look to you.

Yours fraternally
C. P. Sanger

P.S. Daphne[1] directs me to send her love.

From G. B. Shaw

Ayot St Lawrence
Welwyn, Herts.
18th March 1918

Dear Miss Mackenzie

I am naturally a good deal concerned about Russell; but I can do nothing: he must help himself, and that vigorously, if he is to win his appeal. At his trial there seems to have been no adequate defence: he, or his counsel, should have talked for a week and clamoured to the heavens against tyranny and injustice and destruction of popular rights and deuce knows what else in order to make the authorities as sorry as possible that they had stirred up these questions, even if they had obtained the sentence all the same. Russell is not an imbecile who cannot defend himself. He is not a poor man who cannot afford a strong bar. He is practically a nobleman with a tremendous family record on the Whig side as a hereditary defender of popular liberties. Yet the impression left on the public is that he has been disposed of in ten minutes like an ordinary pickpocket. That must be to some extent the fault of himself and his friends. It seems like a repetition of the monstrous mistake of Morell's plea of guilty, which must have been

[1] His daughter.

made under silly advice under the impression that guilt is a question of fact, and not of the ethical character of the action in question.

The only matter that is really in doubt is whether Russell should conduct his own case or employ counsel. In his place I should unhesitatingly do the job myself. A barrister will put up some superficially ingenious plea which will give him a good professional chance of shewing off before the Court of Appeal, one which will not compromise him by any suspicion of sympathy with Russell's views, and the failure of which will be a foregone conclusion. Russell will have no preoccupations of that sort; and he can, as an amateur, take liberties with court procedure which a barrister cannot. He is accustomed to public speaking, and therefore not under the necessity of getting another man to speak for him simply through nervousness and inexperience.

His case is not by any means a weak one. To begin with, he can point out that he is being prosecuted for a hypothetical prophecy occupying half a dozen lines in an article containing several positive statements which have since turned out to be entirely wrong and might even have been dangerously misleading. He was wrong about the Bolsheviks, about the Constituent Assembly, about the German and Austrian Governments. Yet no exception is taken to these errors.

But when he got on to the solider ground taken by Lord Lansdowne, and argued that a continuation of the war must lead inevitably to starvation throughout Europe, a ridiculous pretext is found for attacking him. The war is full of ironies: the belligerents claiming to be the defenders of liberties which they have all been engaged at one time or another in vigorously suppressing. The Germans forget their oppression of Prussian Poland, and denounce England as the oppressor of Ireland, Egypt and India. The French forget Tonquin, Morocco, Algeria and Tunisia, and the Bonapartist regime, and revile the Germans as conquerors and annexationists. Italy forgets Abyssinia and the Tripolitaine, and claims Dalmatia and part of the Austrian Tyrol, whilst driving Austria from the Trentino on nationalist grounds. Finally, America, which has been engaged in conflicts with her own workers which in Colorado and some other States have almost approached the proportions of a civil war, assumes the mission of redeeming the German proletariat from slavery. All these ironies have been pointed out again and again in the bitterest terms by philosophic journalists, except the last which Russell was the first to hint at very mildly in *The Tribunal*. Immediately some foolish censor, knowing nothing about irony or history or anything else except the rule of thumb of his department, pounces on the allusion as something that has not been passed before, and therefore must be challenged.

But the main point is that if Russell, in spite of his social and academic position, is to be savagely punished for writing about the war as a Pacifist and a philosopher, the intimidation of the Press will be carried thereby to a point in England which it has not yet attained in Germany or Austria; and if it be really an advantage to be a free country, that advantage will go to Germany. We are claiming the support of the world in this war solely on the ground that we represent Liberal institutions, and that our enemies represent despotic ones. The enemy retorts that we are the most formidable and arbitary Empire on the face of the earth; and there is so much to be said for this view in consequence of our former conquests that American and Russian public opinion is sorely perplexed about us. Russell can say, 'If you like to persecute me for my Liberal opinions, persecute away and be damned: I am not the first of my family to suffer in that good cause; but if you have any regard for the solidarity of the Alliance, you will take care to proclaim to the world that England is still the place where a man can say the thing he will &c. (peroration ad lib.).

This is the best advice I can give in the matter as Russell's friend.

Yours faithfully
G. Bernard Shaw

10 Adelphi Terrace W.C.2
29th April 1917 [1918]

Dear Bertrand Russell

I have an uneasy feeling that you will take legal advice on Wednesday, and go into prison for six months for the sake of allowing your advocate to make a favourable impression on the bench by advancing some ingenious defence, long since worn out in the service of innumerable pickpockets, which they will be able to dismiss (with a compliment to the bar) with owl-like gravity.

I see nothing for it but to make a scene by refusing indignantly to offer any defence at all of a statement that any man in a free country has a perfect right to make, and declaring that as you are not an unknown person, and your case will be reported in every capital from San Francisco east to Tokyo, and will be taken as the measure of England's notion of the liberty she professes to be fighting for, you leave it to the good sense of the bench to save the reputation of the country from the folly of its discredited and panic striken Government. Or words to that effect. You will gain nothing by being considerate, and (unlike a barrister) lose nothing by remembering that a cat may look at a king, and, *a fortiori*, a philosopher at a judge.

ever
G.B.S.

To my brother Frank

Brixton
June 3, 1918

Existence here is not disagreeable, but for the fact that one can't see one's friends. The one fact does make it, to me, very disagreeable – but if I were devoid of affection, like many middle aged men, I should find nothing to dislike. One has no responsibilities, and infinite leisure. My time passes very fruitfully. In a normal day, I do four hours philosophical writing, four hours philosophical reading, and four hours general reading – so you can understand my wanting a lot of books. I have been reading Madame Roland's memoirs and have come to the conclusion that she was a very over-rated woman: snobbish, vain, sentimental, envious – rather a German type. Her last days before her execution were spent in chronicling petty social snubs or triumphs of many years back. She was a democrat chiefly from envy of the *noblesse*. Prisons in her day were more cheerful than now: she says if she were not writing her memoirs she would be painting flowers or playing an air. Pianos are not provided in Brixton. On the other hand, one is not guillotined on leaving, which is in some ways an advantage. – During my two hours' exercise I reflect upon all manner of things. It is good to have a time of leisure for reflection and altogether it is a godsend being here. But I don't want too much godsend!

I am quite happy and my mind is very active. I enjoy the sense that the time is fruitful – after giving out all these last years, reading almost nothing and writing very little and having no opportunity for anything civilised, it is a real delight to get back to a civilised existence. But oh I *shall* be glad when it is over! I have given up the bad habit of imagining the war may be over some day. One must compare the time with that of the Barbarian invasion. I feel like Appolinaris Sidonius – The best one could be would be to be like St Augustine. For the next 1000 years people will look back to the time before 1914 as they did in the Dark Ages to the time before the Gauls sacked Rome. Queer animal, man !

> *Your loving brother*
> *Bertrand Russell*

To Colette   5th July 1918
Beloved I do long for you – I keep thinking of all the wonderful things we will do together – I think of what we will do when we can go abroad after the war – I long to go with you to Spain: to see the great Cathedral of Burgos, the Velasquez in Madrid – the gloomy Escorial, from which madmen used to spread ruin over the world in the days before madness was universal – Seville in dancing sunlight, all orange groves and fountains – Granada, where the Moors lingered till Ferdinand and Isabella drove them out – Then we could cross the straits, as the Moors did, into Morocco – and come back by Naples and Rome and Siena and Florence and Pisa – Imagine the unspeakable joy of it – the riot of colour and beauty – freedom – the sound of Italian bells – the strange cries, rich, full-throated, and melancholy with all

the weight of the ages – the great masses of flowers, inconceivably bright – men with all the beauty of wild animals, very erect, with bright swiftly-glancing eyes – and to step out into the morning sunshine, with blue sea and blue hills – it is all theré for us, some day. I long for the madness of the South with you.

The other thing I long for with you – which we can get sooner – is the Atlantic – the Connemara coast – driving mist – rain – waves that moan on the rocks – flocks of sea-birds with wild notes that seem the very soul of the restless sadness of the sea – and gleams of sun, unreal, like glimpses into another world – and wild wild wind, free and strong and fierce – There, there is life – and there, I feel, I could stand with you and let our love commune with the western storm – for the same spirit is in both. My Colette, my Soul, I feel the breath of greatness inspiring me through our love – I want to put the spirit of the Atlantic into words – I must, *I must*, before I die, fine *some* way to say the essential thing that is in me, that I have never said yet – a thing that is not love or hate or pity or scorn, but the very breath of life, fierce, and coming from far away, bringing into human life the vastness and the fearful passionless force of non-human things.

10th August [1918]

If I had been in Gladstone's place I would never have let Gordon go to Khartoum, but having let him go I think it was foolish not to back him up, because it was bound to incense people. It started the movement of imperialism which led on to the Boer War and thence to the present horror. It is useless in politics to apply a policy people won't understand. I remember a talk we had in the woods once about what Allen would do if he were Prime Minister, in which this came up.

I didn't realise that the film job you refused was the life of Lloyd George. Certainly you *had* to refuse that. One might as well have expected St John to take employment under Pontius Pilate as official biographer of Judas Iscariot.

What a queer work the Bible is. Abraham (who is a pattern of all the virtues) twice over, when he is going abroad, says to his wife: 'Sarah my dear, you are a very good-looking person, and the King is very likely to fall in love with you. If he thinks I am your husband, he will put me to death, so as to be able to marry you; so you shall travel as my sister, which you are, by the way.' On each occasion the King does fall in love with her, takes her into his harem, and gets diseased in consequence, so he returns her to Abraham. Meanwhile Abraham has a child by the maidservant, whom Sarah dismisses into the wilderness with the new-born infant, without Abraham objecting. Rum tale.

And God has talks with Abraham at intervals, giving shrewd worldly advice. Then later, when Moses begs to see God, God allows him to see his 'hind parts'. There is a terrible fuss, thunder and whirlwind and all the paraphernalia, and then all God has to say is that he wants the Jews to eat *un*leavened bread at the Passover – he says this over and over again, like an old gentleman in his dotage. Queer book.

Some texts are *very* funny. Deut. XXIV, 5: 'When a man hath taken a new wife, he shall not go out to war, neither shall he be charged with any business: but he shall be free at home one year, and shall cheer up his wife which he hath taken.' I should never have guessed 'cheer up' was a Biblical expression. Here is another really inspiring text: 'Cursed be he that lieth with his mother-in-law. And all the people shall say, Amen.' St Paul on marriage: 'I say therefore to the unmarried and widows, It is good for them if they abide even as I. But if they cannot contain, let them marry: for it is better to marry than to burn.' This has remained the doctrine of the Church to this day. It is clear that the Divine purpose in the text 'it is better to marry than to burn' is to make us all feel how *very* dreadful the torments of Hell must be.

Thursday 16th [August 1918]

Dear one, will you be very patient and kind with me the seven weeks that remain, and bear with me if I grow horrid? It has been difficult after the hopes of release. I am very tired, very weary. I am of course tortured by jealousy; I knew I should be. I know so little of your doings that I probably imagine more than the truth. I have grown so nervy from confinement and dwelling on the future that I feel a sort of vertigo, an impulse to destroy the happiness in prospect. *Will you please quite calmly ignore anything I do these next weeks in obedience to this impulse.* As yet, I am just able to see that it is mad, but soon it will seem the only sanity. I shall set to work to hurt you, to make you break with me; I shall say I won't see you when I first come out; I shall pretend to have lost all affection for you. All this is madness – the effect of jealousy and impatience combined. The pain of wanting a thing very much at last grows so great that one has to try not to want it any longer – Now here it is: *I want everything as we planned it – Ashford, then Winchelsea if you can. If later I say I don't want this, please pay no attention.*

To Miss Rinder[1]   30th July, 1918

Many thanks for *Spectator* review. Is it not odd that people can in the same breath praise 'the free man's worship' and find fault with my views on the war? The free man's worship is merely the expression of the pacifist outlook when it was new to me. So many people enjoy rhetorical expressions of fine feelings, but hate to see people perform the actions that must go with the feelings if they are genuine. How

[1] Miss Rinder worked at the No Conscription Fellowship, and was chiefly concerned with details in the treatment of pacifist prisoners.

could any one, approving the free man's worship, expect me to join in the trivial self-righteous moral condemnation of the Germans ? All moral condemnation is utterly against the whole view of life that was then new to me but is now more and more a part of my being. I am naturally pugnacious, and am only restrained (when I am restrained) by a realisation of the tragedy of human existence, and the absurdity of spending our little moment in strife and heat. That I, a funny little gesticulating animal on two legs, should stand beneath the stars and declaim in a passion about *my* rights – it seems so laughable, so out of all proportion. Much better, like Archimedes, to be killed because of absorption in eternal things. And when once men get away from their rights, from the struggle to take up more room in the world than is their due, there is such a capacity of greatness in them. All the loneliness and the pain and the eternal pathetic hope – the power of love and the appreciation of beauty – the concentration of many ages and spaces in the mirror of a single mind – these are not things one would wish to destroy wantonly, for any of the national ambitions that politicians praise. There is a possibility in human minds of something mysterious as the night-wind, deep as the sea, calm as the stars, and strong as Death, a mystic contemplation, the 'intellectual love of God'. Those who have known it cannot *believe* in wars any longer, or in any kind of hot struggle. If I could give to others what has come to me in this way, I could make them too feel the futility of fighting. But I do not know how to communicate it: when I speak, they stare, applaud, or smile, but do not understand.

To Ottoline Morrell   August 8th, 1918

All you write about S.S. [Siegfried Sassoon] is interesting and poignant. I know so well the indignation he suffers from – I have lived in it for months, and on the edge of it for years. I think that one way of getting over it is to perceive that others might judge oneself in the same way, unjustly, but with just as good grounds. Those of us who are rich are just like the young women whose sex flourishes on the blood of soldiers. Every motor-tyre is made out of the blood of negroes under the lash, yet motorists are not all heartless villains. When we buy wax matches, we buy a painful and lingering death for those who make them . . . War is only the final flower of the capitalist system, but with an unusual proletariat. S.S. sees war, not peace, from the point of view of the proletariat. But this is only politics. The fundamental mistake lies in wrong expectations, leading to cynicism when they are not realised. Conventional morality leads us to expect unselfishness in decent people. This is an error. Man is an animal bent on securing food and propagating the species. One way of succeeding in these objects is to persuade others that one is after *their* welfare – but to be really after any welfare but one's own and one's children's is unnatural. It occurs like sadism and sodomy, but is equally against nature. A good social system is not to be secured by making people unselfish, but by making their own vital impulses fit in with other people's. This is feasible. Our present system makes self-preservation only possible at the expense of others. The system is at fault; but it is a weakness to be disgusted with people because they aim at self-preservation. One's idealism needs to be too robust for such weaknesses. It doesn't do to forget or deny the animal in man. The God in man will not be visible, as a rule, while the animal is thwarted. Those who have produced stoic philosophies have all had enough to eat and drink. The sum total of the matter is that one's idealism must be *robust* and must fit in with the facts of nature; and that which is horrible in the actual world is mainly due to a bad system. Spinoza, always, is right in all these things, to my mind.

11th August, 1918

It is quite true what you say, that you have never expressed yourself – but who has, that has anything to express ? The things one says are all unsuccessful attempts to say something else – something that perhaps by its very nature cannot be said. I know that I have struggled all my life to say something that I never shall learn how to say. And it is the same with you. It is so with all who spend their lives in the quest of something elusive, and yet omnipresent, and at once subtle and infinite. One seeks it in music, and the sea, and sunsets; at times I have seemed very near it in crowds when I have been feeling strongly what they were feeling; one seeks it in love above all. But if one lets oneself imagine one has found it, some cruel irony is sure to come and show one that it is not really found. (I have come nearest to expressing myself in the chapter on Education in *Social Reconstruction*. But it is a very long way from a really full self-expression. You are hindered by timidity.)

The outcome is that one is a ghost, floating through the world without any real contact. Even when one feels nearest to other people, something in one seems obstinately to belong to God and to refuse to enter into any earthly communion – at least that is how I should express it if I thought there was a God. It is odd isn't it ? I care passionately for this world, and many things and people in it, and yet . . . what is it all ? There *must* be something more important, one feels, though I don't *believe* there is. I am haunted – some ghost, from some extramundane region, seems always trying to tell me something that I am to repeat to the world, but I cannot understand the message. But it is from listening to the ghost that one comes to feel oneself a ghost. I feel I shall find the truth on my deathbed and be surrounded by people too stupid to understand – fussing about medicines instead of searching for wisdom. Love and imagination mingled; that seems the main thing so far.

Your B.

27th August, 1918

I have been reading Marsh[1] on Rupert [Brooke]. It makes me very sad and very indignant. It hurts reading of all that young world now swept away – Rupert and his brother and Keeling and lots of others – in whom one foolishly thought at the time that there was hope for the world – they were full of life and energy and truth – Rupert himself loved life and the world – his hatreds were very concrete, resulting from some quite specific vanity or jealousy, but in the main he found the world lovable and interesting. There was nothing of humbug in him. I feel that after the war-mongers had killed his body in the Dardanelles they have done their best to kill his spirit by ——'s lies ... When will people learn the robustness of truth ? I do not know who my biographer may be, but I should like him to report 'with what flourish his nature will' something like this: 'I was not a solemn stained glass saint, existing only for purposes of edification; I existed from my own centre, many things that I did were regrettable, I did not respect respectable people, and when I pretended to do so it was humbug. I lied and practised hypocrisy, because if I had not I should not have been allowed to do my work; but there is no need to continue the hypocrisy after my death. I hated hypocrisy and lies: I loved life and real people, and wished to get rid of the shams that prevent us from loving real people as they really are. I believed in laughter and spontaneity, and trusted to nature to bring out the genuine good in people, if once genuineness could come to be tolerated.' Marsh goes building up the respectable legend, making the part of youth harder in the future, so far as lies in his power – I try so hard not to hate, but I do hate respectable liars and oppressors and corruptors of youth – I hate them with all my soul, and the war has given them a new lease of power. The young were shaking them off, but they have secured themselves by setting the young to kill each other. But rage is useless; what is wanted is to carry over into the new time something of the gaiety and civilised outlook and genial expansive love that was growing when the war came. It is useless to add one's quota to the sum of hate – and so I try to forget those whom I cannot but hate when I remember them.

Friday, 30 Aug. 18

My dearest O

It was a *delight* seeing you – tho' you do not seem in very good health

---

[1] Afterwards Sir Edward. He had been a close friend of mine when we were undergraduates, but became a civil servant, an admirer of Winston Churchill and then a high Tory.

– and those times are difficult for talking – letters are really more satisfactory – your letters are the *very greatest joy* to me – To begin with personal things: I do trust my *friends* to do everything possible – no one ever had such kind and devoted friends – I am wonderfully touched by what all of you have done; the people I don't trust are the philosophers (including Whitehead). They are cautious and constitutionally timid; nine out of ten hate me personally (not without reason); they consider philosophical research a foolish pursuit, only excusable when there is money in it. Before the war I fancied that quite a lot of them thought philosophy important; now I know that most of them resemble Professors Hanky and Panky in *Erewhon Revisited*.

I trust G. Murray, on the whole, over this business. If he gets me a post, I hope it will be not *very* far from London – not further than Birmingham say. I don't the least desire a post except as a way of getting round Geddes: what I desire is to do original work in philosophy, but apparently no one in Government circles considers that worth doing. Of course a post will interfere to some extent with research tho' it need not interfere very much. I *must* have *some* complete holiday when I first come out of prison. I do not want *residence* away from London: I would *almost* as soon face another term of imprisonment, for reasons which can't be explained to G. Murray. But I am *most* grateful to him for all the trouble he is taking. I am not *worrying* in the least.

How delightful of you to think of Lulworth too. It was the very place I had been thinking of, because I came upon it in R. Brooke. I was only there once for a moment on a walking-tour (1912) and have always wanted to go back. *Do* stick to the plan – latish October. We can settle exactly when, later. It will be *glorious*.

I wonder whether you quite get at Brett. I am sure her deafness is the main cause of all that you regret in her. She wrote a terrible account of what it means to her the other day in a letter you sent me – I don't know whether you read it. If not I will show it you. I am *very* sorry about Burnley. It is a blow. There will be no revival of pacifism; the war will go on till the Germans admit themselves beaten, which I put end of next year. Then we shall have the League to *Enforce* Peace, which will require conscription everywhere. – Much interested about S.S. and munition factory; all experience may be useful. It would never occur to me to think of it as an 'attitude'.

I was sorry to refuse so many books, and also to give you the trouble of taking so many away. I believe in future I shall be able to send them by Carter Paterson. My cell is small and I *must* keep down the number of books. Between books and earwigs I have hardly had room to turn round.

Please thank Miss Bentinck most warmly for the lovely peaches. I think it *very* kind of her to send them when she thinks me so wicked. – I don't know how long you are staying at Kirkby Lonsdale – All that region is so associated in my mind with Theodore's death.

Oh won't it be glorious to be able to walk across fields and see the horizon and talk freely and be with friends – It is near enough now to believe it will come – I am settled into this existence, and fairly placid, but only because it will end soon. All kinds of delights float before my mind – above all talk, *talk*, TALK. I never knew how one can hunger for it – The time here has done me good, I have read a lot and thought a lot and grown *collected*, I am bursting with energy – but I do long for civilisation and civilised talk – And I long for the SEA and wildness and wind – I hate being all tidy like a book in a library where no one reads – Prison is horribly like that – Imagine if you knew you were a delicious book, and some Jew millionaire bought you and bound you uniform with a lot of others and stuck you up in a shelf behind glass, where you merely illustrated the completeness of his System – and no anarchist was allowed to read you – That is what one feels like – but soon now one will be able to insist of being read. – Goodbye – Much much love – and endless thanks for your endless kindness. *Do* stick to Lulworth –

Your B.

P.S. Letter to Brett elsewhere. Please return commonplace books – Wednesday will do. But I run short of them unless they are returned.

To Dorothy Brett   30. 8 18

My dear Brett

Thank you for your letter. It is a kindness writing letters to me when I am here, as they are the only unhampered contact I can have with other people. I think prison, if it lasted, would be worse than your fate, but as mine is so brief it is nothing like as bad as what you have to endure. I do realise how terrible it is. But I believe there are things you could do that would make it less trying, small things mostly. To begin with a *big* thing: practise the mental discipline of not thinking how great a misfortune it is; when your mind begins to run in that direction, stop it violently by reciting a poem to yourself or thinking of the multiplication-table or some such plan. For smaller things: try, as far as possible, not to sit about with people who are having a general conversation; get in a corner with a tête-à-tête; make yourself interesting in the first place by being interested in whoever you are talking with, until things become easy and natural. I suppose you have practised lip-reading? Take care of your inner attitude to people: let it not be satirical or aloof, set yourself to try and get inside their skins and feel the passions that move them and the seriousness of the things that matter to them. Don't judge people morally: however just one's judgment, that is a barren attitude. Most people have a key, fairly simple; if you find it, you can unlock their hearts. Your deafness need not prevent this, if you make a point of tête-à-tête. It has always seemed to me fearfully trying for you at Garsington to spend so much time in the middle of talk and laughter that you cannot understand. Don't do more of that than you must. You *can* be 'included in human life'. But it wants effort, and it wants that you should *give* something that people will value. Though your deafness may make that harder, it doesn't make it impossible. Please don't think all this very impertinent. I have only written it because I can't bear to think how you suffer.

Poor Mr Green! Tell him to consult me when he wants to make a conquest; I will give him sage advice, which he evidently needs. – Your picture of the 3 women sounds most exciting. I do hope it will be glorious. I hope I shall see you when you return from destroying your fellow-creatures in Scotland – I sympathise with the Chinese philosopher who fished without bait, because he liked fishing but did not like catching fish. When the Emperor found him so employed, he made him Prime Minister. But I fear that won't happen to me.

> Yrs.
> B.R.

The lady to whom the above letter is addressed was a daughter of Lord Esher but was known to all her friends by her family name of Brett. At the time when I wrote the above letter, she was spending most of her time at Garsington with the Morrells. She went later to New Mexico in the wake of D. H. Lawrence.

To Ottoline Morrell   31/8/18
(For any one whom it may interest)

There never was such a place as prison for crowding images – one after another they come upon me – early morning in the Alps, with the smell of aromatic pines and high pastures glistening with dew – the lake of Garda as one first sees it coming down out of the mountains, just a glimpse far below, dancing and gleaming in the sunlight like the eyes of a laughing, mad, Spanish gypsy – thunderstorm in the Mediterranean, with a dark violet sea, and the mountains of Corsica in sunshine far beyond – the Scilly Isles in the setting sun, enchanted and unreal, so that you think they must have vanished before you can reach them, looking like the Islands of the Blest, not to be achieved during this mortal life – the smell of the bog myrtle in Skye – memories of sunsets long ago, all the way back into childhood – I can hear now as if it were yesterday the street-cry of a man in Paris selling 'artichaux verts et beaux' 24 years ago almost to a day. Quite from childhood I member a certain row of larches after rain, with a raindrop at the end of every twig – and I can hear the wind in the tree-tops in midnight woods on summer nights – everything free or beautiful comes into my thoughts sooner or later. What is the use of shutting up the body, seeing that the mind remains free ? And outside my own life, I have lived, while I have been here, in Brazil and China and Tibet, in the French Revolution, in the souls of animals and even of the lowest animals. In such adventures I have forgotten the prison in which the world is keeping itself at the moment: I am free, and the world shall be.

September 4th, 1918

Dearest O

It is *dreadful* the killing of the people who might have made a better future. As for me: I am *sure* it is a 'sure firm growth'. It is two quite distinct things: some quite good technical ideas, which have come simply because they were due, like cuckoos in April; and a way of feeling towards life and the world, which I have been groping after especially since the war started, but also since a certain moment in a churchyard near Broughton, when you told me to make a place for wildness in my morality, and I asked you what you meant, and you explained. It has been very difficult: my instinctive morality was so much that of self-repression. I used to be afraid of myself and the darker side of my instincts; now I am not. You began that, and the war completed it.

Chapter 9

Russia

The ending of the war enabled me to avoid several unpleasant things which would otherwise have happened to me. The military age was raised in 1918, and for the first time I became liable to military service, which I should of course have had to refuse. They called me up for medical examination, but the Government with its utmost efforts was unable to find out where I was, having forgotten that it had put me in prison. If the War had continued I should very soon have found myself in prison again as a conscientious objector. From a financial point of view also the ending of the War was very advantageous to me. While I was writing *Principia Mathematica* I felt justified in living on inherited money, though I did not feel justified in keeping an additional sum of capital that I inherited from my grandmother. I gave away this sum in its entirety, some to the University of Cambridge, some to Newnham College, and the rest to various educational objects. After parting with the debentures that I gave to Eliot, I was left with only about £100 a year of unearned money, which I could not get rid of as it was in my marriage settlement. This did not seem to matter, as I had become capable of earning money by my books. In prison, however, while I was allowed to write about mathematics, I was not allowed to write the sort of book by which I could make money. I should therefore have been nearly penniless when I came out but for the fact that Sanger and some other friends got up a philosophical lectureship for me in London. With the end of the War I was again able to earn money by writing, and I have never since been in serious financial difficulties except at times in America.

The ending of the War made a difference in my relations with Colette. During the War we had many things to do in common, and we shared all the very powerful emotions connected with the War. After the War things became more difficult and more strained. From time to time we would part for ever, but repeatedly these partings proved unexpectedly temporary. During the three summer months of 1919, Littlewood (the mathematician) and I rented a farmhouse on a hill about a mile outside Lulworth. There were a good many rooms in this farmhouse, and we had a series of visitors throughout the whole summer. The place was extraordinarily beautiful, with wide views along the coast. The bathing was good, and there were places where Littlewood could exhibit his prowess as a climber, an art in which he was very expert. Meantime I had been becoming interested in my second wife. I met her first in 1916 through her friend Dorothy Wrinch. Both were at Girton, and Dorothy Wrinch was a pupil of mine. She arranged in the summer of 1916 a two days' walk with herself, Dora Black, Jean Nicod, and me. Jean Nicod was a young French philosopher, also a pupil of mine, who had escaped the War through being consumptive. (He died of phthisis in 1924.) He was one of the most delightful people that I have ever known, at once very gentle and immensely clever. He had a type of whimsical humour that delighted me. Once I was saying to him that people who learned philosophy should be trying to understand the world, and not only, as in universities, the systems of previous philosophers. 'Yes,' he replied, 'but the systems are so much more interesting than the world.' Dora Black, whom I had not seen before, interested me at once. We spent the evening at Shere, and to beguile the time after dinner, I started by asking everybody what they most desired in life. I cannot remember what Dorothy and Nicod said; I said that I should like to disappear like the man in Arnold Bennett's *Buried Alive*, provided I could be sure of discovering a widow in Putney as he did. Dora, to my surprise, said that she wanted to marry and have children. Until that moment I had supposed that no clever young woman would confess to so simple a desire, and I concluded that she must possess exceptional sincerity. Unlike the rest of us she was not, at that time, a thorough-going objector to the War.

In June 1919, at Dorothy Wrinch's suggestion, I invited her to come to tea with Allen and me at the flat that I shared with him in Battersea. She came, and we embarked on a heated argument as to the rights of fathers. She said that, for her part, if she had children she would consider them entirely her own, and would not be disposed to recognise the father's rights. I replied hotly: 'Well, whoever I have children by, it won't be you!' As a result of this argument, I dined with her next evening, and at the end of the evening we arranged that she should come to Lulworth for a long visit. I had on that day had a more than usually definitive parting from Colette, and I did not suppose that I should ever see her again. However, the day after Littlewood and I got to Lulworth I had a telegram from Colette to say that she was on her way down in a hired car, as there was no train for several hours. Fortunately, Dora was not due for some days, but throughout the summer I had difficulties and awkwardnesses in preventing their times from overlapping.

I wrote the above passage in 1931, and in 1949 I showed it to Colette. Colette wrote to me, enclosing two letters that I had written to her in 1919, which showed me how much I had forgotten. After reading them I remembered that throughout the time at Lulworth my feelings underwent violent fluctuations, caused by fluctuations in Colette's behaviour. She had three distinct moods: one of ardent devotion, one of resigned determination to part for ever, and one of mild indifference. Each of these produced its own echo in me, but the letters that she enclosed showed me that the echo had been more resounding than I had remembered. Her letter and mine show the emotional unreliability of memory. Each knew about the other, but questions of tact arose which were by no means easy. Dora and I became lovers when she came to Lulworth, and the parts of the summer during which she was there were extraordinarily delightful. The chief difficulty with Colette had been that she was unwilling to have children, and that I felt if I was ever to have children I could not put it off any longer. Dora was entirely willing to have children, with or without marriage, and from the first we used no precautions. She was a little disappointed to find that almost immediately our relations took on all the character of marriage, and when I told her that I should be glad to get a divorce and marry her, she burst into tears, feeling, I think, that it meant the end of independence and light-heartedness. But the feeling we had for each other seemed to have that kind of stability that made any less serious relation impossible. Those who have known her only in her public capacity would scarcely credit the quality of elfin charm which she possessed whenever the sense of responsibility did not weigh her down. Bathing by moonlight, or running with bare feet on the dewy grass, she won my imagination as completely as on her serious side she appealed to my desire for parenthood and my sense of social responsibility.

Our days at Lulworth were a balance of delicious outdoor activities, especially swimming, and general conversations as good as any that I have ever had. The general theory of relativity was in those days rather new, and Littlewood and I used to discuss it endlessly. We used to debate whether the distance from us to the post-office was or was not the same as the distance from the post-office to us, though on this matter we never reached a conclusion. The eclipse expedition which confirmed Einstein's prediction as to the bending of light occurred during this time, and Littlewood got a telegram from Eddington telling him that the result was what Einstein said it should be.

As always happens when a party of people who know each other well is assembled in the country, we came to have collective jokes from which casual visitors were excluded. Sometimes the claims of politeness made these jokes quite painful. There was a lady called Mrs Fiske Warren whom I had known when I lived at Bagley Wood, rich and beautiful and intellectual, highly intellectual in fact. It was for her unofficial benefit that Modern Greats were first invented. Carefully selected dons taught her Greek philosophy without demanding a knowledge of Greek. She was a lady of deep mystical intuitions, and an admirer of Blake. I had stayed at her country house in Massachusetts in 1914, and had done my best to live up to her somewhat rarefied atmosphere. Her husband, whom I had never met, was a fanatical believer in Single Tax, and was in the habit of buying small republics, such as Andorra, with a view to putting Henry George's principles into practice. While we were at Lulworth, she sent me a book of her poems and a book of her husband's on his hobby. At the same time a letter came from her husband, who was in London, saying that he wished to see me. I replied that it was impossible as I was not in London. He telegraphed back to say that he would come to lunch Monday, Tuesday, Wednesday, Thursday, or Friday, whichever suited me, although to do so he had to leave London at six in the morning. I chose Friday, and began hastily cutting the pages of his wife's poems. I found a poem headed 'To One who Sleeps by my Side', in which occurred the line: 'Thou art too full of this world's meat and wine.' I read the poem to the company, and called up the housekeeper, giving orders that the meal should be plentiful and that there should be no deficiency of alcohol. He turned out to be a lean, ascetic, anxious character, too earnest to waste any of the moments of life here below in jokes or frivolities. When we were all assembled at lunch, and I began to offer him food and drink, he replied in a sad voice: 'No, thank you. I am a vegetarian and a teetotaller.' Littlewood hastily made a very feeble joke at which we all laughed much more than its merits warranted.

Summer, the sea, beautiful country, and pleasant company, combined with love and the ending of the War to produce almost ideally perfect circumstances. At the end of the summer I went back to Clifford Allen's flat in Battersea, and Dora went to Paris to pursue the researches which she was making, in her capacity of Fellow of Girton, into the beginnings of French free-thinking philosophy in the seventeenth and eighteenth centuries. I still saw her occasionally, sometimes in London, sometimes in Paris. I was still seeing Colette, and was in a mood of indecision.

At Christmas Dora and I met at the Hague, to which place I went to see my friend Wittgenstein. I knew Wittgenstein first at Cambridge before the War. He was an Austrian, and his father was enormously rich. Wittgenstein had intended to become an engineer, and for that purpose had gone to Manchester. Through reading mathematics he became interested in the principles of mathematics, and asked at Manchester who there was who worked at this subject. Somebody mentioned my name, and he took up his residence at Trinity. He was perhaps the most perfect example I have ever known of genius as traditionally conceived, passionate, profound, intense, and dominating.

He had a kind of purity which I have never known equalled except by G. E. Moore. I remember taking him once to a meeting of the Aristotelian Society, at which there were various fools whom I treated politely. When we came away he raged and stormed against my moral degradation in not telling these men what fools they were. His life was turbulent and troubled, and his personal force was extraordinary. He lived on milk and vegetables, and I used to feel as Mrs Patrick Campbell did about Shaw: 'God help us if he should ever eat a beef-steak.' He used to come to see me every evening at midnight, and pace up and down my room like a wild beast for three hours in agitated silence. Once I said to him: 'Are you thinking about logic or about your sins ?' 'Both', he replied, and continued his pacing. I did not like to suggest that it was time for bed, as it seemed probable both to him and me that on leaving me he would commit suicide. At the end of his first term at Trinity, he came to me and said: 'Do you think I am an ab-solute idiot ?' I said: 'Why do you want to know ?' He replied: 'Because if I am I shall become an aeronaut, but if I am not I shall become a philosopher.' I said to him: 'My dear fellow, I don't know whether you are an absolute idiot or not, but if you will write me an essay during the vacation upon any philosophical topic that interests you, I will read it and tell you.' He did so, and brought it to me at the beginning of the next term. As soon as I read the first sentence, I became persuaded that he was a man of genius, and assured him that he should on no account become an aeronaut. At the beginning of 1914 he came to me in a state of great agitation and said: 'I am leaving Cambridge, I am leaving Cambridge at once.' 'Why ?' I asked. 'Because my brother-in-law has come to live in London, and I can't bear to be so near him.' So he spent the rest of the winter in the far north of Norway. In early days I once asked G. E. Moore what he thought of Wittgenstein. 'I think very well of him', he said. I asked why, and he replied: 'Because at my lectures he looks puzzled, and nobody else ever looks puzzled.'

When the War came, Wittgenstein, who was very patriotic, became an officer in the Austrian Army. For the first few months it was still possible to write to him and to hear from him, but before long this became impossible, and I knew nothing of him until about a month after the Armistice, when I got a letter from him written from Monte Cassino, saying that a few days after the Armistice he had been taken prisoner by the Italians, but fortunately with his manuscript. It ap-peared that he had written a book in the trenches, and wished me to read it. He was the kind of man who would never have noticed such small matters as bursting shells when he was thinking about logic. He sent me the manuscript of his book, which I discussed with Nicod and Dorothy Wrinch at Lulworth. It was the book which was sub-sequently published under the title *Tractatus Logico-Philosophicus*. It was obviously important to see him and discuss it by word of mouth, and it seemed best to meet in a neutral country. We therefore decided upon the Hague. At this point, however, a surprising difficulty arose. His father, just before the outbreak of the War, had transferred his whole fortune to Holland, and was therefore just as rich at the end as at the beginning. Just about at the time of the Armistice his father had died, and Wittgenstein inherited the bulk of his fortune. He came to the conclusion, however, that money is a nuisance to a philosopher, so he gave every penny of it to his brother and sisters. Consequently he was unable to pay the fare from Vienna to the Hague, and was far too proud to accept it from me. At last a solution of this difficulty was found. The furniture and books which he had had at Cambridge were stored there, and he expressed a willingness to sell them to me. I took the advice of the Cambridge furniture dealer in whose care they were as to their value, and bought them at the figure he suggested. They were in fact worth far more than he supposed, and it was the best bargain I ever made. This transaction made it possible for Wittgenstein to come to the Hague, where we spent a week arguing his book line by line, while Dora went to the Public Library to read the invectives of Salmatius against Milton.

Wittgenstein, though a logician, was at once a patriot and a pacifist. He had a very high opinion of the Russians, with whom he had fraternised at the Front. He told me that once in a village in Galicia, where for the moment he had nothing to do, he found a book-shop, and it occurred to him that there might be a book in it. There was just one, which was Tolstoy on the Gospels. He therefore bought it, and was much impressed by it. He became for a time very religious, so much so that he began to consider me too wicked to associate with. In order to make a living he became an elementary school-master in a country village in Austria, called Trattenbach. He would write to me saying: 'The people of Trattenbach are very wicked.' I would reply: 'Yes, all men are very wicked.' He would reply: 'True, but the men of Trattenbach are more wicked than the men of other places.' I replied that my logical sense revolted against such a proposition. But he had some justification for his opinion. The peasants refused to supply him with milk because he taught their children sums that were not about money. He must have suffered during this time hunger and considerable privation, though it was very seldom that he could be induced to say anything about it, as he had the pride of Lucifer. At last his sister decided to build a house, and employed him as architect. This gave him enough to eat for several years, at the end of which time he returned to Cambridge as a don, where Clive Bell's son wrote poems in heroic couplets against him. He was not always easy to fit into a social occasion. Whitehead described to me the first time that Wittgenstein came to see him.

He was shown into the drawing-room during afternoon tea. He appeared scarcely aware of the presence of Mrs Whitehead, but marched up and down the room for some time in silence, and at last said explosively: 'A proposition has two poles. It is *apb*.' Whitehead, in telling me, said: 'I naturally asked what are *a* and *b*, but I found that I had said quite the wrong thing. "*a* and *b* are indefinable," Wittgenstein answered in a voice of thunder.'

Like all great men he had his weaknesses. At the height of his mystic ardour in 1922, at a time when he assured me with great earnestness that it is better to be good than clever, I found him terrified of wasps, and, because of bugs, unable to stay another night in lodgings we had found in Innsbruck. After my travels in Russia and China, I was inured to small matters of that sort, but not all his conviction that the things of this world are of no account could enable him to endure insects with patience. In spite of such slight foibles, however, he was an impressive human being.

I spent almost the whole of the year 1920 in travelling. At Easter, I was invited to lecture at Barcelona at the Catalan University there. From Barcelona I went to Majorca, where I stayed at Soller. The old inn-keeper (the only one in the place) informed me that, as he was a widower, he could not give me any food, but I was at liberty to walk in his garden and pluck his oranges whenever I pleased. He said this with such a courteous air that I felt constrained to express my profound gratitude. In Majorca, I began a great quarrel which raged for many months through many changes of latitude and longitude.

I was planning to go to Russia, and Dora wanted to go with me. I maintained that, as she had never taken much interest in politics, there was no good reason why she should go, and, as typhus was raging, I should not feel justified in exposing her to the risk. We were both adamant, and it was an issue upon which compromise was impossible. I still think I was right, and she still thinks she was right.

Soon after returning from Majorca, my opportunity came. A Labour deputation was going to Russia, and was willing that I should accompany it. The Government considered my application, and after causing me to be interviewed by H. A. L. Fisher, they decided to let me go. The Soviet Government was more difficult to persuade, and when I was already in Stockholm on the way, Litvinov was still refusing permission, in spite of our having been fellow prisoners in Brixton. However, the objections of the Soviet Government were at last overcome. We were a curious party, Mrs Snowden, Clifford Allen, Robert Williams, Tom Shaw, an enormously fat old Trade Unionist named Ben Turner, who was very helpless without his wife and used to get Clifford Allen to take his boots off for him, Haden Guest as medical attendant, and several Trade Union officials. In Petrograd, where they put the imperial motor-car at our disposal, Mrs Snowden used to drive about enjoying its luxury and expressing pity for the 'poor Czar'. Haden Guest was a theosophist with a fiery temper and a considerable libido. He and Mrs Snowden were very anti-Bolshevik. Robert Williams, I found, was very happy in Russia, and was the only one of our party who made speeches pleasing to the Soviet Government. He always told them that revolution was imminent in England, and they made much of him. I told Lenin that he was not to be trusted, and the very next year, on Black Friday, he ratted. Then there was Charlie Buxton, whose pacifism had led him to become a Quaker. When I shared a cabin with him, he would beg me to stop in the middle of a sentence in order that he might practise silent prayer. To my surprise, his pacifism did not lead him to think ill of the Bolsheviks.

For my part, the time I spent in Russia was one of continually increasing nightmare. I have said in print what, on reflection, appeared to me to be the truth, but I have not expressed the sense of utter horror which overwhelmed me while I was there. Cruelty, poverty, suspicion, persecution, formed the very air we breathed. Our conversations were continually spied upon. In the middle of the night one would hear shots, and know that idealists were being killed in prison. There was a hypocritical pretence of equality, and everybody was called 'tovarisch', but it was amazing how differently this word could be pronounced according as the person addressed was Lenin or a lazy servant. On one occasion in Petrograd (as it was called) four scarecrows came to see me, dressed in rags, with a fortnight's beard, filthy nails, and tangled hair. They were the four most eminent poets of Russia. One of them was allowed by the Government to make his living by lecturing on rhythmics, but he complained that they insisted upon his teaching this subject from a Marxian point of view, and that for the life of him he could not see how Marx came into the matter.

Equally ragged were the Mathematical Society of Petrograd. I went to a meeting of this society at which a man read a paper on non-Euclidean geometry. I could not understand anything of it except the formulae which he wrote on the blackboard, but these were quite the right sort of formulae, so that one may assume the paper to have been competent. Never, in England, have I seen tramps who looked so abject as the mathematicians of Petrograd. I was not allowed to see Kropotkin, who not long afterwards died. The governing classes had a self-confidence quite as great as that produced by Eton and Oxford. They believed that their formulae would solve all difficulties. A few of the more intelligent knew that this was not the case, but did not dare to say so. Once, in a *tête-à-tête* conversation with a scientific physician named Zalkind, he began to say that climate has a great effect upon character, but instantly he pulled himself up short, and said: 'Of course that is not really the case; only economic circumstances affect character.' I felt that everything that I valued in human life was being destroyed in the interests of a glib and narrow philosophy, and that in the process untold misery was being inflicted upon many millions of people. With every day that I spent in Russia my horror increased, until I lost all power of balanced judgement.

From Petrograd we went to Moscow, which is a very beautiful city, and architecturally more interesting than Petrograd because of the Oriental influence. I was amused by various small ways in which Bolshevik love of mass-production showed itself. The main meal of the day occurred at about four o'clock in the afternoon, and contained among other ingredients the heads of fishes. I never discovered what happened to their bodies, though I suppose they were eaten by the peoples' Komissars. The river Moskwa was chock full of fish, but people were not allowed to catch them, as no up-to-date mechanical method had yet been found to supersede the rod and line. The city was almost starving, but it was felt that fishes' heads, caught by trawlers, were better than fishes' bodies caught by primitive methods.

We went down the Volga on a steamer, and Clifford Allen became extremely ill with pneumonia, which revived the tuberculosis from which he had previously suffered. We were all to leave the boat at Saratov, but Allen was too ill to be moved, so Haden Guest, Mrs Snowden and I remained on the boat to look after him, while it travelled on to Astrakan. He had a very small cabin, and the heat was inconceivable. The windows had to be kept tight shut on account of the malarial mosquitoes, and Allen suffered from violent diarrhoea. We had to take turns nursing him, for although there was a Russian nurse on board, she was afraid to sit with him at night for fear that he might die and his ghost might seize her.

Astrakan seemed to me more like hell than anything I had ever imagined. The town water-supply was taken from the same part of the river into which ships shot their refuse. Every street had stagnant water which bred millions of mosquitoes; every year one third of the inhabitants had malaria. There was no drainage system, but a vast mountain of excrement at a prominent place in the middle of the town. Plague was endemic. There had recently been fighting in the civil war against Denikin. The flies were so numerous that at meal-time a table-cloth had to be put over the food, and one had to insert one's hand underneath and snatch a mouthful quickly. The instant the table-cloth was put down, it became completely black with flies, so that nothing of it remained visible. The place is a great deal below sea-level, and the temperature was 120 degrees in the shade. The leading doctors of the place were ordered by the Soviet officials who accompanied us to hear what Haden Guest had to say about combating malaria, a matter on which he had been engaged for the British Army in Palestine. He gave them an admirable lecture on the subject, at the end of which they said: 'Yes, we know all that, but it is very hot.' I fancy that the next time the Soviet officials came that way those doctors were probably put to death, but of this I have no knowledge. The most eminent of the doctors in question examined Clifford Allen and informed me that he could not possibly live two days. When about a fortnight later we got him out to Reval, the doctor who examined him there again told me that he could not live two days, but by this time I had come to know something of Allen's determination to live, and I was less alarmed. He survived for many years, and became an ornament of the House of Lords.

After I returned to England I endeavoured to express my changing moods, before starting and while in Russia, in the shape of antedated letters to Colette, the last of which I subsequently published in my book about China. As they express my moods at that time better than I can do by anything written now, I will insert them here:

I

London,
April 24, 1920

The day of my departure comes near. I have a thousand things to do, yet I sit here idle, thinking useless thoughts, the irrelevant, rebellious thoughts that well-regulated people never think, the thoughts that one hopes to banish by work, but that themselves banish work instead. How I envy those who *always* believe what they believe, who are not troubled by deadness and indifference to all that makes the framework of their lives. I have had the ambition to be of some use in the world, to achieve something notable, to give mankind new hopes. And now that the opportunity is near, it all seems dust and ashes. As I look into the future, my disillusioned gaze sees only strife and still more strife, rasping cruelty, tyranny, terror and slavish submission. The men of my dreams, erect, fearless and generous, will they ever exist on earth? Or will men go on fighting, killing and torturing to the end of time, till the earth grows cold and the dying sun can no longer quicken their futile frenzy? I cannot tell. But I do know the despair in my soul. I know the great loneliness, as I wander through the world like a ghost, speaking in tones that are not heard, lost as if I had fallen from some other planet.

The old struggle goes on, the struggle between little pleasures and the great pain. I know that the little pleasures are death and yet – I am so tired, so very tired. Reason and emotion fight a deadly war within me, and leave me no energy for outward action. I know that no good thing is achieved without fighting, without ruthlessness and organisation and discipline. I know that for collective action the individual must be turned into a machine. But in these things, though my reason may force me to believe them, I can find no inspiration. It is the individual human soul that I love – in its loneliness, its hopes and fears, its quick impulses and sudden devotions. It is such a long journey from this to armies and States and officials; and yet it is only by making this long journey that one can avoid a useless sentimentalism.

All through the rugged years of the War, I dreamed of a happy day after its end, when I should sit with you in a sunny garden by the Mediterranean, filled with the scent of heliotrope, surrounded by cypresses and sacred groves of ilex – and there, at last, I should be able to tell you of my love, and to touch the joy that is as real as pain. The time is come, but I have other tasks, and you have other desires; and to me, as I sit brooding, all tasks seem vain and all desires foolish.

Yet it is not upon these thoughts that I shall act.

2

Petrograd,
May 12, 1920

I am here at last, in this city which has filled the world with history, which has inspired the most deadly hatreds and the most poignant hopes. Will it yield me up its secret ? Shall I learn to know its inmost soul ? Or shall I acquire only statistics and official facts ? Shall I understand what I see, or will it remain an external bewildering show ? In the dead of night we reached the empty station, and our noisy motors panted through the sleeping streets. From my window, when I arrived, I looked out across the Neva to the fortress of Peter and Paul. The river gleamed in the early northern dawn; the scene was beautiful beyond all words, magical, eternal, suggestive of ancient wisdom. 'It is wonderful', I said to the Bolshevik who stood beside me. 'Yes,' he replied, 'Peter and Paul is now not a prison, but the Army Headquarters.'

I shook myself. 'Come, my friend,' I thought, 'you are not here as a tourist, to sentimentalise over sunrises and sunsets and buildings starred by Baedeker; you are here as a social investigator, to study economic and political facts. Come out of your dream, forget the eternal things. The men you have come among would tell you they are only the fancies of a bourgeois with too much leisure, and can you be sure they are anything more ?' So I came back into the conversation, and tried to learn the mechanism for buying an umbrella at the Soviet Stores, which proved as difficult as fathoming the ultimate mysteries.

The twelve hours that I have so far spent on Russian soil have chiefly afforded material for the imp of irony. I came prepared for physical hardship, discomfort, dirt, and hunger, to be made bearable by an atmosphere of splendid hope for mankind. Our communist comrades, no doubt rightly, have not judged us worthy of such treatment. Since crossing the frontier yesterday afternoon, I have made two feasts and a good breakfast, several first-class cigars, and a night in a sumptuous bedroom of a palace where all the luxury of the *ancien régime* has been preserved. At the stations on the way, regiments of soldiers filled the platform, and the plebs was kept carefully out of sight. It seems I am to live amid the pomp surrounding the government of a great military Empire. So I must readjust my mood. Cynicism is called for, but I am strongly moved, and find cynicism difficult. I come back eternally to the same question: What is the secret of this passionate country? Do the Bolsheviks know its secret? Do they even suspect that it has a secret? I wonder.

3

Petrograd,
May 13, 1920

This is a strange world into which I have come, a world of dying beauty and harsh life. I am troubled at every moment by fundamental questions, the terrible insoluble questions that wise men never ask. Empty palaces and full eating-houses, ancient splendours destroyed, or mummified in museums, while the sprawling self-confidence of re-turned Americanised refugees spreads throughout the city. Everything is to be systematic: there is to be organisation and distributive justice. The same education for all, the same clothes for all, the same kind of houses for all, the same books for all, and the same creed for all – it is very just, and leaves no room for envy, except for the fortunate victims of injustice in other countries.

And then I begin upon the other side of the argument. I remember Dostoevski's *Crime and Punishment*, Gorki's *In the World*, Tolstoy's *Resurrection*. I reflect upon the destruction and cruelty upon which the ancient splendour was built: the poverty, drunkenness, prostitution, in which life and health were uselessly wasted; I think of all the lovers of freedom who suffered in Peter and Paul; I remember the knoutings and pogroms and massacres. By hatred of the old, I become tolerant of the new, but I cannot like the new on its own account.

Yet I reproach myself for not liking it. It has all the characteristics of vigorous beginnings. It is ugly and brutal, but full of constructive energy and faith in the value of what it is creating. In creating a new machinery for social life, it has no time to think of anything beyond machinery. When the body of the new society has been built, there will be time enough to think about giving it a soul – at least, so I am as-sured. 'We have no time for a new art or a new religion', they tell me with a certain impatience. I wonder whether it is possible to build a body first, and then afterwards inject the requisite amount of soul. Perhaps – but I doubt it.

I do not find any theoretical answer to these questions, but my feelings answer with terrible insistence. I am infinitely unhappy in this atmosphere – stifled by its utilitarianism, its indifference to love and beauty and the life of impulse. I cannot give that importance to man's merely animal needs that is given here by those in power. No doubt that is because I have not spent half my life in hunger and want, as many of them have. But do hunger and want necessarily bring wisdom ? Do they make men more, or less, capable of conceiving the ideal society that should be the inspiration of every reformer ? I cannot avoid the belief that they narrow the horizon more than they enlarge it. But an uneasy doubt remains, and I am torn in two . . .

4

On the Volga,
June 2, 1920.

Our boat travels on, day after day, through an unknown and mysterious land. Our company are noisy, gay, quarrelsome, full of facile theories, with glib explanations of everything, persuaded that there is nothing they cannot understand and no human destiny outside the purview of their system. One of us lies at death's door,[1] fighting a grim battle with weakness and terror and the indifference of the strong, assailed day and night by the sounds of loud-voiced love-making and trivial laughter. And all around us lies a great silence, strong as Death, unfathomable as the heavens. It seems that none have leisure to hear the silence, yet it calls to me so insistently that I grow deaf to the harangues of propagandists and the endless information of the well-informed.

Last night, very late, our boat stopped in a desolate spot where there were no houses, but only a great sandbank, and beyond it a row of poplars with the rising moon behind them. In silence I went ashore, and found on the sand a strange assemblage of human beings, half-nomads, wandering from some remote region of famine, each family huddled together surrounded by all its belongings, some sleeping, others silently making small fires of twigs. The flickering flames lighted up gnarled bearded faces of wild men, strong patient primitive women, and children as sedate and slow as their parents. Human beings they undoubtedly were, and yet it would have been far easier for me to grow intimate with a dog or a cat or a horse than with one of them. I knew that they would wait there day after day, perhaps for weeks, until a boat came in which they could go to some distant place where they had heard – falsely perhaps – that the earth was more generous than in the country they had left. Some would die by the way, all would suffer hunger and thirst and the scorching midday sun, but their sufferings would be dumb. To me they seemed to typify the very soul of Russia, unexpressive, inactive from despair, unheeded by the little set of westernisers who make up all the parties of progress or reaction. Russia is so vast that the articulate few are lost in it as man and his planet are lost in interstellar space. It is possible, I thought, that the theorists may increase the misery of the many by trying to force them into actions contrary to their primeval instincts, but I could not believe that happiness was to be brought to them by a gospel of industrialism and forced labour.

Nevertheless, when morning came, I resumed the interminable discussions of the materialistic conception of history and the merits of a truly popular government. Those with whom I discussed had not seen the sleeping wanderers, and would not have been interested if they had seen them, since they were not material for propaganda. But something of that patient silence had communicated itself to me, something lonely and unspoken remained in my heart through all the comfortable familiar intellectual talk. And at last I began to feel that all politics are inspired by a grinning devil, teaching the energetic and quick-witted to torture submissive populations for the profit of pocket or power or theory. As we journeyed on, fed by food extracted from the peasants, protected by an army recruited from among their sons, I wondered what we had to give them in return. But I found no answer. From time to time I heard their sad songs or the haunting music of the balalaika; but the sound mingled with the great silence of the steppes, and left me with a terrible questioning pain in which occidental hopefulness grew pale.

Sverdlov, the Minister of Transport (as we should call him), who was with us on the steamer on the Volga, was extraordinarily kind and helpful about Allen's illness. We came back on the boat as far as Saratov, and from there to Reval, we travelled all the way in the carriage that had belonged to the Czar's daughters, so that Allen did not have to be moved at any stage. If one might judge from the carriage, some of their habits must have been curious. There was a luxurious sofa of which the seat lifted up, and one then discovered three holes in a row suitable for sanitary purposes. At Moscow on the way home Haden Guest and I had a furious quarrel with Chicherin because he would not allow Allen to leave Moscow until he had been examined by two Soviet doctors, and at first he said that he could not get the Soviet doctors to see him for another two days. At the height of the quarrel, on a staircase, I indulged in a shouting match because Chicherin had been a friend of my Uncle Rollo and I had hopes of him. I shouted that I should denounce him as a murderer. It seemed to us and to Allen vital to get him out of

Russia as soon as possible, and we felt that this order to wait for Soviet doctors would endanger his life. At last a compromise was effected by which the doctors saw him at once. One of them was called Popoff; the name of the other I have forgotten. The Soviet Government thought that Allen was friendly to them and that Guest and Mrs Snowden and I were anxious he should die so as to suppress his testimony in their favour.

At Reval I met by accident Mrs Stan Harding, whom I had not known before. She was going into Russia filled with enthusiasm for the Bolsheviks. I did what I could to disenchant her, but without success. As soon as she arrived they clapped her into gaol, and kept her there for eight months. She was finally liberated on the insistent demand of the British Government. The fault, however, lay not so much with the Soviet Government as with a certain Mrs Harrison. Mrs Harrison was an American lady of good family who was with us on the Volga. She was in obvious terror and longing to escape from Russia, but the Bolsheviks kept her under very close observation. There was a spy named Axionev, whom they had taken over from the *ancien régime*, who watched her every movement and listened to her every word. He had a long beard and a melancholy expression, and wrote decadent French verse with great skill. On the night-train he shared a compartment with her; on the boat whenever anybody spoke with her he would creep behind silently. He had extraordinary skill in the art of creeping. I felt sorry for the poor lady, but my sorrow was misplaced. She was an American spy, employed also by the British. The Russians discovered that she was a spy, and spared her life on condition that she became a spy for them. But she sabotaged her work for them, denouncing their friends and letting their enemies go free. Mrs Harding knew that she was a spy, and therefore had to be put away quickly. This was the reason of her denouncing Mrs Harding to the Soviet authorities. Nevertheless, she was a charming woman, and nursed Allen during his illness with more skill and devotion than was shown by his old friends. When the facts about her subsequently came to light, Allen steadfastly refused to hear a word against her.

Lenin, with whom I had an hour's conversation, rather disappointed me. I do not think that I should have guessed him to be a great man, but in the course of our conversation I was chiefly conscious of his intellectual limitations, and his rather narrow Marxian orthodoxy, as well as a distinct vein of impish cruelty. I have told of this interview, as well as of my adventures in Russia, in my book *Practice and Theory of Bolshevism*.

There was at that time no communication with Russia either by letter or telegram, owing to the blockade. But as soon as I reached Reval I began telegraphing to Dora. To my surprise, I got no reply.

At last, when I was in Stockholm, I telegraphed to friends of hers in Paris, asking where she was, and received the answer that when last heard of she was in Stockholm. I supposed she had come to meet me, but after waiting twenty-four hours in the expectation of seeing her, I met by chance a Finn who informed me that she had gone to Russia, via the North Cape. I realised that this was a move in our long-drawn-out quarrel on the subject of Russia, but I was desperately worried for fear they would put her in prison, as they would not know why she had come. There was nothing one could do about it, so I came back to England, where I endeavoured to recover some kind of sanity, the shock of Russia having been almost more than I could bear. After a time, I began to get letters from Dora, brought out of Russia by friends, and to my great surprise she liked Russia just as much as I had hated it. I wondered whether we should ever be able to overcome this difference. However, among the letters which I found waiting for me when I got back to England, was one from China inviting me to go there for a year to lecture on behalf of the Chinese Lecture Association, a purely Chinese body which aimed at importing one eminent foreigner each year, and had in the previous year imported Dr Dewey. I decided that I would accept if Dora would come with me, but not otherwise. The difficulty was to put the matter before her, in view of the blockade. I knew a Quaker at Reval, named Arthur Watts, who frequently had to go into Russia in connection with Quaker relief, so I sent him a telegram costing several pounds, explaining the circumstances and asking him to find Dora if he could, and put the matter before her. By a stroke of luck this all worked out. If we were to go, it was necessary that she should return at once, and the Bolsheviks at first supposed that I was playing a practical joke. In the end, however, she managed.

We met at Fenchurch Street on a Sunday, and at first we were almost hostile strangers to each other. She regarded my objections to the Bolsheviks as bourgeois and senile and sentimental. I regarded her love of them with bewildered horror. She had met men in Russia whose attitude seemed to her in every way superior to mine. I had been finding the same consolation with Colette as I used to find during the War. In spite of all this, we found ourselves taking all the necessary steps required for going off together for a year in China. Some force stronger than words, or even than our conscious thoughts, kept us together, so that in action neither of us wavered for a moment. We had to work literally night and day. From the time of her arrival to the time of our departure for China was only five days. It was necessary to buy clothes, to get passports in order, to say goodbye to friends and relations, in addition to all the usual bustle of a long journey; and as I wished to be divorced while in China, it was necessary to spend the nights in official adultery. The detectives were so stupid that this had to be done again and again. At last, however, everything was in order. Dora, with her usual skill, had so won over her parents that they came to Victoria to see us off just as if we had been married. This in spite of the fact that they were completely and entirely conventional. As the train began to move out of Victoria, the nightmares and complications and troubles of recent months dropped off, and a completely new chapter began.

LETTERS

From J. E. Littlewood

> Trinity College
> Cambridge
> [1919]

Dear Russell

Einstein's theory is completely confirmed. The predicted displacement was $1''·72$ and the observed $1''·75 ± ·06$.

> *Yours*
> *J.E.L.*

From Harold J. Laski

> Harvard University
> Cambridge
> August 29, 1919

Dear Mr Russell

I wish I knew how to thank you at all adequately for your letter. When I had finished that book I felt that I cared more for what you and Mr Justice Holmes thought about it than for the opinion of any two living men; and to have you not merely think it worth while, but agree with it is a very big thing to me. So that if I merely thank you abruptly you will realise that it is not from any want of warmth.

I have ventured to send you my first book, which has probably all the vices of the book one writes at twenty-three; but you may be interested in the first chapter and the appendices. And if you'll allow me to, I'd like to send you some more technical papers of mine. But I don't want you to be bothered by their presence, and allow them to interfere with your work.

My interest in liberal Catholicism really dates from 1913 when I read Figgis' *Churches in the Modern State* at Oxford; and while I was writing my first book I came to see that, historically, the church and the State have changed places since the Reformation and that all the evils of unified ecclesiastical control are slowly becoming the technique of the modern State – if they have not already become so: it then struck me that the evil of this sovereignty could be shown fairly easily in the sphere of religion in its state-connection where men might still hesitate to admit it in the economic sphere. The second book tried to bridge the gap; and the book I'm trying now to write is really an attempt to explain the general problem of freedom in institutional terms. If by any lucky chance you have time to write I'd greatly like to send you its plan and have your opinion on it.

There is a more private thing about which I would like you to know in case you think there is a chance that you can help. I know from your *Introduction to Mathematical Logic* that you think well of Sheffer who is at present in the Philosophy Department here. I don't know if you have any personal acquaintance with him. He is a jew and he has married someone of whom the University does not approve; moreover he hasn't the social qualities that Harvard so highly prizes. The result is that most of his department is engaged on a determined effort to bring his career here to an end. Hoernle, who is at present its chairman, is certain that if someone can explain that Sheffer is worth while the talk against him would cease; and he's finished a paper on some aspect of mathematical logic that he himself feels will give him a big standing when it can get published. Myself I think that the whole thing is a combination of anti-semitism and that curious university worship of social prestige which plays so large a part over here. Do you know anyone at Harvard well enough to say (if you so think) that Sheffer ought to have a chance? Of course I write this entirely on my own responsibility but I'm very certain that if Lowell could know your opinion of Sheffer it would make a big difference to his future. And if he left here I think he would find it very difficult to get another post. Please forgive me for bothering you with these details.

I shall wait with immense eagerness for the *Nation*. I owe Massingham many debts; but none so great as this.

> *Believe me*
> *Yours very sincerely*
> *Harold J. Laski*

From this time onward I used to send periodical cables to President Lowell, explaining that Sheffer was a man of the highest ability and that Harvard would be eternally disgraced if it dismissed him either because he was a Jew or because it disliked his wife. Fortunately these cables just succeeded in their object.

Harvard University
Cambridge
September 29, 1919

Dear Mr Russell
Thank you heartily for your letter. I am sending you some semi-

344 The Autobiography of Bertrand Russell

legal papers and a more general one on administration. The book I
ventured to send you earlier. I am very grateful for your kindness in
wanting them.

And I am still more grateful for your word on Sheffer. I have given
it to Hoernle who will show it to the members of the Philosophy Department and, if necessary, to Lowell. And I have sent copies to two
members of the Corporation who will fight if there is need. I don't
think there is anything further to be done at the moment. It would do
no good to write to Perry. These last years, particularly twelve months
in the War Department of the US have made him very conservative
and an eager adherent of 'correct form'. He is the head and centre of
the enemy forces and I see no good in trying to move him directly. He
wants respectable neo-Christians in the Department who will explain
the necessity of ecclesiastical sanctions; or, if they are not religious, at
least they must be materially successful. I don't think universities are
ever destined to be homes of liberalism; and the American system is in
the hands of big business and dominated by its grosser ideals. Did you
ever read Veblen's *Higher Learning in America*?

You may be interested to know that I have a graduate class at Yale
this term reading *Roads to Freedom*. I've never met Yale men before;
but it was absorbingly interesting to see their amazement that Marx
and Bakunin and the rest could be written of without abuse. Which
reminds me that in any new edition of that book I wish you would say a
good word for Proudhon! I think his *Du Principe Fédératif* and his
Justice Dans La Révolution are two very great books.

And may I have a photograph with your name on it to hang in my
study. That would be an act of genuine nobility on your part.

> Yours very sincerely
> Harold J. Laski

Harvard University
Cambridge
November 2 1919

Dear Mr Russell

Many thanks for the photograph. Even if it is bad, it gives a basis to
the imagination and that's what I wanted.

The matter with Perry is the war. He got converted to conscription,
was at Washington with the educational(!) section of the War Office
and became officialised. The result is that he looks aslant at all outside
the 'correct' things much as a staff major who saw life from Whitehall
and the Army and Navy Club. He still means well – all New
Englanders do; but he has lost hold of Plato's distinction between willing what is right and knowing what it is right to will. I think he might
be turned on Sheffer's side if Sheffer would get his paper out amid the

applause of you and Whitehead and Lewis; but Sheffer is a finnicky little fellow and publication halts on his whims and fancies. I haven't given up hope, but I don't dare to hope greatly.

Yale is really interesting, or perhaps all youth, when one is twenty-six, is interesting. I find that when one presents the student-mind with syndicalism or socialism namelessly they take it as reasonable and obvious; attach the name and they whisper to the parents that name-less abominations are being perpetrated. I spoke for the striking police here the other day – one of those strikes which makes one equally wonder at the endurance of the men and the unimaginative stupidity of the officials. Within a week two papers and two hundred alumni de-manded my dismissal – teaching sovietism was what urging that men who get $1100 and work 73 hours are justified in striking after 13 years agitation was called. As it happens Lowell does believe in freedom of speech, so that I stay; but you get some index to the present American state of mind.

> *Yours very sincerely*
> *Harold J. Laski*

Harvard University
Cambridge
December 4 1919

Dear Mr Russell

Hoernle tells me that Sheffer's paper is on its way to you. May I tell you how the position stands? Hocking and Hoernle definitely fight for his reappointment. Perry wavers on account of Huntingdon's em-phatic praise of Sheffer's work and says his decision will depend most largely on what you and Moore of Chicago feel. So if you do approve of it, the more emphatic your telegram the more helpful it will be. There is a real fighting chance at the moment.

Things here are in a terrible mess. Injunctions violating specific government promises; arrest of the miners' leaders because the men refused to go back; recommendation of stringent legislation against 'reds'; arrest of men in the West for simple possession of an IWW card; argument by even moderates like Eliot that the issue is a straight fight between labor and constitutional government; all these are in the ordinary course of events. And neither Pound nor I think the crest of the wave has been reached. Some papers have actually demanded that the Yale University Press withdraw my books from circulation because they preach 'anarchy'. On the other hand Holmes and Brandeis wrote (through Holmes) a magnificent dissent in defence of freedom of speech in an espionage act case. I've sent the two opinions to Massing-ham and suggested that he show them to you.

This sounds very gloomy; but since America exported Lady Astor to England there's an entire absence of political comedy.

> *Yours very sincerely*
> *Harold J. Laski*

[*Plus ça change.*]

> Harvard University
> Cambridge
> January 5, 1919 [1920]

Dear Mr Russell

It was splendid to have your telegram about Sheffer's paper. I am afraid we are fighting a lost battle as it looks as if Hoernle will go to Yale, which means the withdrawal of our main support. Harvard is determined to be socially respectable at all costs. I have recently been interviewed by the Board of Overseers to know (a) whether I believe in a revolution with blood (b) whether I believe in the Soviet form of government (c) whether I do not believe that the American form of government is superior to any other (d) whether I believe in the right of revolution.

In the last three days they have arrested five thousand socialists with a view to deportation. I feel glad that Graham Wallas is going to try and get me home!

> *Yours very sincerely*
> *Harold J. Laski*

> Harvard University
> Cambridge
> February 18th, 1920

Dear Mr Russell

Above all, warm congratulations on your return to Cambridge. That sounds like a real return of general sanity. I hope you will not confine your lectures to mathematical logic . . .

I sent you the other day a volume of Duguit's my wife and I translated last year; I hope you will find time to glance at it. I am very eager to get away from this country, as you guessed, but rather baffled as to how to do it. I see no hope in Oxford and I know no one at all in Cambridge. Wallas is trying to do something for me in London, but I don't know with what success. I am heartily sick of America and I would like to have an atmosphere again where an ox does not tread upon the tongue.

> *Yours very sincerely*
> *Harold Laski*

16, Warwick Gardens
[London] W.14
2.1.22

Dear Russell

This enclosure formally. Informally let me quote from Rivers: We asked him to stand as the labour candidate for London. This is part of his reply. 'I think that a distinct factor in my decision has been *The Analysis of Mind* which I have now read really carefully. It is a great book, and makes me marvel at his intellect. It has raised all kinds of problems with which I should like to deal, and I certainly should not be able to do so if I entered on a political life. κτ λ.'

What about Rivers, Joad, Delisle Burns, Clifford Allen as the nucleus of our new utilitarians?

Yours
H. J. Laski

From Ludwig Wittgenstein
[a postcard]

Cassino
Provincia Caserta
Italy
9.2.19

Dear Russell

I don't know your precise address but hope these lines will reach you somehow. I am prisoner in Italy since November and hope I may communicàte with you after a three years interruption. I have done lots of logikal work which I am dying to let you know before publishing it.

Ever yours
Ludwig Wittgenstein

[Postcard]

Cassino
10.3.19

You cann't immagine how glad I was to get your cards! I am affraid though there is no hope that we may meet before long. Unless you came to see me here, but this would be too much joy for me. I cann't write on Logic as I'm not allowed to write more than 2 Cards (15 lines each) a week. I've written a book which will be published as soon as I get home. I think I have solved our problems finaly. Write to me often. It will shorten my prison. God bless you.

Ever yours
Wittgenstein

13.3.19

Dear Russell

Thanks so much for your postcards dated 2nd and 3rd of March. I've had a *very* bad time, not knowing wether you were dead or alive! I cann't write on Logic as I'm not allowed to write more than two p.cs. a week (15 lines each). This letter is an ecception, it's posted by an Austrian medical student who goes home tomorrow. I've written a book called *Logisch-Philosophische Abhandlung* containing all my work of the last 6 years. I believe I've solved our problems finally. This may sound arrogant but I cann't help believing it. I finished the book in August 1918 and two months after was made Prigioniere. I've got the manuscript here with me. I wish I could copy it out for you; but it's pretty long and I would have no safe way of sending it to you. In fact you would not understand it without a previous explanation as it's written in quite short remarks. (This of cours means that *nobody* will understand it; allthough I believe it's all as clear as crystall. But it upsets all our theory of truth, of classes, of numbers and all the rest.) I will publish it as soon as I get home. Now I'm affraid this *won't* be 'before long'. And consequently it will be a long time yet till we can meet. I can hardly immagine seeing you again! It will be too much! I supose it would be impossible for you to come and see me here? Or perhaps you think it's collossal cheek of me even to think of such a thing. But if you were on the other end of the world and I *could* come to you I would do it.

Please write to me how you are, remember me to Dr Whitehead. Is old Johnson still alive? Think of me often!

Ever yours
Ludwig Wittgenstein

[Cassino
12.6.19]

Lieber Russell!

Vor einigen Tagen schickte ich Dir mein Manuskript durch Keynes's Vermittelung. Ich schrieb damals nur ein paar Zeilen fuer Dich hinein. Seither ist nun Dein Buch ganz in meine Haende gelangt und nun haette ich ein grosses Beduerfnis Dir einiges zu schreiben. – Ich haette nicht geglaubt, dass das, was ich vor 6 Jahren in Norwegen dem Moore diktierte an Dir so spurlos voruebergehen wuerde. Kurz ich fuerchte jetzt, es moechte sehr schwer fuer mich sein mich mit Dir zu verstaendigen. Und der geringe Rest von Hoffnung mein Manuskript koenne Dir etwas sagen, ist ganz verschwunden. Einen Komentar zu meinem Buch zu schreiben, bin ich wie Du Dir denken kannst, nicht im Stande. Nur muendlich koennte ich Dir einen geben. Ist Dir irgend an dem Verstaendnis der Sache etwas gelegen und kannst Du ein Zusammentreffen mit mir bewerk-

stelligen, so, bitte, tue es. – Ist dies nicht moeglich, so sei so gut und schicke das Manuskript so bald Du es gelesen hast auf sicherem Wege nach Wien zurueck. Es ist das einzige korrigierte Exemplar, welches ich besitze und die Arbeit meines Lebens! Mehr als je brenne ich jetzt *darauf es gedruckt zu sehen. Es ist bitter, das vollendete Werk in der Gefangenschaft herumschleppen zu muessen und zu sehen, wir der Unsinn draussen sein Spiel treibt! Und ebenso bitter ist es zu denken dass niemand es verstehen wird, auch wenn es gedruckt sein wird! – Hast Du mir jemals seit Deinen zwei ersten Karten geschrieben? Ich habe nichts erhalten.*

Sei herzlichst gegruesst und glaube nicht, dass alles Dummheit ist was Du nicht verstehen wirst.

Dein treuer
Ludwig Wittgenstein

[This and the following translations of Wittgenstein's letters in German are by B. F. McGuinness.]

[Cassino
12.6.19]

Dear Russell

Some days ago I sent you my manuscript, through Keynes's good offices. I enclosed only a couple of lines for you at the time. Since then your book has arrived here safely and I now feel a great need to write you a number of things. – I should never have believed that what I dictated to Moore in Norway six years ago would pass over you so completely without trace. In short, I am afraid it might be very difficult for me to reach an understanding with you. And my small remaining hope that my manuscript would convey something to you has now quite vanished. Writing a commentary on my book is out of the question for me, as you can imagine. I could only give you an oral one. If you attach any importance whatsoever to understanding the thing, and if you can arrange a meeting with me, please do so. – If that is impossible, then be so good as to send the manuscript back to Vienna by a safe route as soon as you have read it. It is the only corrected copy I possess and it is my life's work! I long to see it in print, *now* more than ever. It is bitter to have to lug the completed work around with me in captivity and to see nonsense rampant in the world outside. And it is just as bitter to think that no one will understand it even if it is printed! – Have you written to me at all since your first two cards? I have received nothing. Kindest regards, and *don't suppose that everything that you won't be able to understand is a piece of stupidity!*

Yours ever
Ludwig Wittgenstein

Cassino
19.8.1919

Dear Russell

Thanks so much for your letter dated 13 August. As to your queries, I cann't answer them *now*. For firstly I don't know allways what the numbers refer to, having no copy of the M S here. Secondly some of your questions want a very lengthy answer and you know how difficult it is for me to write on logic. That's also the reason why my book is so short, and consequently so obscure. But that I cann't help. – Now I'm affraid you haven't realy got hold of my main contention, to which the whole business of logical props is only a corolary. The main point is the theory of what can be expressed (*gesagt*) by props – i.e. by linguage – (and, which comes to the same, what can be *thought*) and what can not be expressed by props, but only shown (*gezeigt*); which, I believe, is the cardinal problem of philosophy. –

I also sent my M S to Frege. He wrote to me a week ago and I gather that he doesn't understand a word of it all. So my only hope is to see *you* soon and explain all to you, for it is *very* hard not to be understood by a single sole!

Now the day after tomorrow we shall probably leave the campo concentramento and go home. Thank God! – But how can we meet as soon as possible. I should like to come to England, but you can imagine that it's rather awkward for a German to travel to England now. (By far more so, than for an Englishman to travel to Germany.) But in fact I didn't think of asking you to come to Vienna now, but it would seem to me the best thing to meet in Holland or Svitserland. Of cors, if you cann't come abroad I will do my best to get to England. Please write to me as soon as possible about this point, letting me know when you are likely to get the permission of coming abroad. Please write to Vienna IV Alleegasse 16. As to my M S, please send it to the same address; but only if there is an absolutely safe way of sending it. Otherwise please keep it. I should be very glad though, to get it soon, as it's the only corrected coppy I've got. – My mother wrote to me, she was very sorry not to have got your letter, but glad that you tried to write to her at all.

Now write soon. Best wishes.

Ever *yours*
Ludwig Wittgenstein

P.S. After having finished my letter I feel tempted after all to answer some of your simpler points . . .[1]

20.9.20

Lieber Russell!

Dank' Dir fuer Deinen lieben Brief! Ich habe jetzt eine Anstellung bekommen; und zwar als Volksschullehrer in einem der kleinsten Doerfer; es heisst Trattenbach und liegt 4 Stunden suedlich von Wien im Gebirge. Es duerfte wohl das erste mal sein, dass der Volksschullehrer von

[1] The postscript to this letter has been omitted because of its technical nature. It can be found in Wittgenstein's *Notebooks 1914–1916*, pp. 129–30.

Trattenbach mit einem Universitaetsprofessor in Peking korrespondiert.
Wie geht es Dir und was traegst Du vor? Philosophie? Dann wollte ich,
ich koennte zuhoeren und dann mit Dir streiten. Ich war bis vor kurzem
schrecklich bedrueckt *und lebensmuede, jetzt aber bin ich etwas*
hoffnungsvoller und jetzt hoffe ich auch, dass wir uns wiedersehen werden.

Gott mit Dir! Und sei herzlichst gegruesst

> *von Deinem treuen*
> *Ludwig Wittgenstein*

20.9.20

Dear Russell

Thank you for your kind letter. I have now obtained a position: I am
to be an elementary-school teacher in a tiny village called Trattenbach.
It's in the mountains, about four hours' journey south of Vienna. It must
be the first time that the schoolmaster at Trattenbach has ever corresponded with a professor in Peking. How are you? And what are you
lecturing on? Philosophy? If so, I wish I could be there and could argue
with you afterwards. A short while ago I was *terribly* depressed and tired
of living, but now I am slightly more hopeful, and one of the things I
hope is that we'll meet again.

God be with you! Kindest regards.

> Yours ever
> *Ludwig Wittgenstein*

[Trattenbach]
23.10.21

Lieber Russell!

Verzeih, dass ich Dir erst jetzt auf Deinen Brief aus China antworte.
Ich habe ihn sehr verspaetet erhalten. Er traf mich nicht in Trattenbach
und wurde mir an verschiedene Orte nachgeschickt, ohne mich zu
erreichen. – Es tut mir sehr leid, dass Du krank warst; und gar schwer!
Wie geht es denn jetzt?! *Bei mir hat sich nichts veraendert. Ich bin*
noch immer in Trattenbach und bin nach wie vor von Gehaessigkeit und
Gemeinheit umgeben. Es ist wahr, dass die Menschen im Durchschnitt
nirgends sehr viel wert sind; aber hier sind sie viel mehr als anderswo
nichtsnutzig und unverantwortlich. Ich werde vielleicht noch dieses Jahr in
Trattenbach bleiben, aber laenger wohl nicht, da ich mich hier auch mit den
uebrigen Lehrern nicht gut vertrage. (Vielleicht wird das wo anders auch
nicht besser sein.) Ja, das waere schoen, wenn Du mich einmal besuchen
wolltest! Ich bin froh zu hoeren, dass mein Manuskript in Sicherheit ist.
Wenn es gedruckt wird, wird's mir auch recht sein. –

Schreib mir bald ein paar Zeilen, wie es Dir geht, etc. etc.

Sei herzlich gegruesst

> *von Deinem treuen*
> *Ludwig Wittgenstein*

Empfiehl mich der Miss Black.

[Trattenbach]
23.10.21

Dear Russell

Forgive me for only now answering your letter from China. I got it after a very long delay. I wasn't in Trattenbach when it arrived and it was forwarded to several places before it reached me. — I am very sorry that you have been ill — and seriously ill! *How are you now, then?* As regards me, nothing has changed. I am still at Trattenbach, surrounded, as ever, by odiousness and baseness. I know that human beings on the average are not worth much anywhere, but here they are much more good-for-nothing and irresponsible than elsewhere. I will perhaps stay on in Trattenbach for the present year but probably not any longer, because I don't get on well here even with the other teachers (perhaps that won't be any better in another place). Yes, it would be nice indeed, if you would visit me sometime. I am glad to hear that my manuscript is in safety. And if it's printed, that will suit me too. —

Write me a few lines soon, to say how you are, etc. etc.

Kindest regards
Yours ever
Ludwig Wittgenstein

Remember me to Miss Black.

[Trattenbach]
28.11.21

Lieber Russell!

Dank Dir vielmals fuer Deinen lieben Brief. Ehrlich gestanden: es freut mich, dass mein Zeug gedruckt wird. Wenn auch der Ostwald ein Erzscharlatan ist! Wenn er es nur nicht verstuemmelt! Liest Du die Korrekturen? Dann bitte sei so lieb und gib acht, dass er es genau so druckt, wie es bei mir steht. Ich traue dem Ostwald zu, dass er die Arbeit nach seinem Geschmack, etwa nach seiner bloedsinnigen Orthographie, varaendert. Am liebsten ist es mir, dass die Sache in England erscheint. Moege sie der vielen Muehe die Du und andere mit ihr hatten wuerdig sein! —

Du hast recht: nicht die Trattenbacher allein sind schlechter, als alle uebrigen Menschen; wohl aber ist Trattenbach ein besonders minderwertiger Ort in Oesterreich und die Oesterreicher sind — seit dem Kreig — bodenlos tief gesunken, dass es zu traurig ist, davon zu reden! So ist es. — Wenn Du diese Zeilen kriegst, ist vielleicht schon Dein Kind auf dieser merkwuerdigen Welt. Also: ich gratuliere Dir und Deiner Frau herzlichst. Verzeih, dass ich so lange nicht geschrieben habe; auch ich bin etwas kraenklich und riesig beschaeftift. Bitte schreibe wieder einmal wenn Du Zeit hast. Von Ostwald habe ich keinen Brief erhalten. Wenn alles gut geht werde ich Dich mit tausend Freuden besuchen!

Herzlichste Gruesse
Dein
Ludwig Wittgenstein

[Trattenbach]
28.11.21

Dear Russell

Many thanks for your kind letter! I must admit I am pleased that my stuff is going to be printed. Even though Ostwald[1] is an utter charlatan. As long as he doesn't tamper with it! Are you going to read the proofs? If so, please take care that he prints it exactly as I have it. He is quite capable of altering the work to suit his own tastes – putting it into his idiotic spelling, for example. What pleases me most is that the whole thing is going to appear in England. I hope it may be worth all the trouble that you and others have taken with it.

You are right: the Trattenbachers are not uniquely worse than the rest of the human race. But Trattenbach is a particularly insignificant place in Austria and the *Austrians* have sunk so miserably low since the war that it's too dismal to talk about. That's what it is.

By the time you get this letter your child will perhaps already have come into this remarkable world. So: warmest congratulations to you and your wife! Forgive me for not having written to you for so long. I too haven't been very well and I've been tremendously busy. Please write again when you have time. I have not had a letter from Ostwald. If all goes well, I will come and visit you with the greatest of pleasure.

> *Kindest regards*
> *Yours*
> *Ludwig Wittgenstein*

From C. K. Ogden

The International Library of
Psychology
Nov. 5, 1921

Dear Russell

Kegan Paul ask me to give them some formal note for their files with regard to the Wittgenstein rights.

I enclose, with envelope for your convenience, the sort of thing I should like. As they can't drop less than £50 on doing it I think it very satisfactory to have got it accepted – though of course if they did a second edition soon and the price of printing went suddenly down they might get their costs back. I am still a little uneasy about the title and don't want to feel that we decided in a hurry on *Philosophical Logic*. If on second thoughts you are satisfied with it, we can go ahead with that. But you might be able to excogitate alternatives that I could submit.

Moore's Spinoza title which he thought obvious and ideal is no use if you feel Wittgenstein wouldn't like it. I suppose his *sub specie aeterni* in the last sentences of the book made Moore think the contrary, and

---

[1] Wilhelm Ostwald, editor of *Annalen der Naturphilosophie*, where the *Tractatus* with my Introduction first appeared in 1921.

several Latin quotes. But as a selling title *Philosophical Logic* is better, if it conveys the right impression.

Looking rapidly over the off print in the train last night, I was amazed that Nicod and Miss Wrinch had both seemed to make so very little of it. The main lines seem so reasonable and intelligible – apart from the Types puzzles. I know you are frightfully busy just at present, but I should very much like to know why all this account of signs and symbols cannot best be understood in relation to a thoroughgoing causal theory. I mean the sort of thing in the enclosed: – on 'Sign Situations' (= Chapter II of the early Synopsis attached). The whole book which the publishers want to call *The Meaning of Meaning* is now passing through the press; and before it is too late we should like to have discussed it with someone who has seriously considered Watson. Folk here still don't think there is a problem of *Meaning* at all, and though your *Analysis of Mind* has disturbed them, everything still remains rather astrological.

With best wishes for, and love to the family,

> *Yours sincerely*
> C. K. Ogden

P.S. On second thoughts, I think that as you would prefer Wittgenstein's German to appear as well as the English, it might help if you added the P.S. I have stuck in, and I will press them further if I can.[1]

To Ottoline Morrell

> Hotel Continental
> Stockholm
> 25th June 1920

Dearest O

I have got thus far on my return, but boats are very full and it may be a week before I reach England. I left Allen in a nursing home in Reval, no longer in danger, tho' twice he had been given up by the Doctors. Partly owing to his illness, but more because I loathed the Bolsheviks, the time in Russia was infinitely painful to me, in spite of being one of the most interesting things I have ever done. Bolshevism is a close tyrannical bureaucracy, with a spy system more elaborate and terrible than the Tsar's, and an aristocracy as insolent and unfeeling, composed of Americanised Jews. No vestige of liberty remains, in thought or speech or action. I was stifled and oppressed by the weight of the machine as by a cope of lead. Yet I think it the right government for Russia at this moment. If you ask yourself how Dostoevsky's characters should be governed, you will understand. Yet it is terrible. They are a nation of artists, down to the simplest peasant; the aim of

---

[1] This note now appears at the beginning of the *Tractatus*.

the Bolsheviks is to make them industrial and as Yankee as possible. Imagine yourself governed in every detail by a mixture of Sidney Webb and Rufus Isaacs, and you will have a picture of modern Russia. I went hoping to find the promised land.

All love – I hope I shall see you soon.

Your B.

From Emma Goldman

Mrs E. G. Kerschner
Bei Von Futtkamer
Rudesheimerstr. 3
Wilmersdorf, Berlin
July 8th [1922]

My dear Mr Russell

My niece forwarded your kind letter to her of June 17th. I should have replied earlier, but I was waiting for her arrival, as I wanted to talk the matter over with her.

Thank you very much for your willingness to assist me. I daresay you will meet with very great difficulties. I understand that the British Foreign Office refused visés to such people as Max Eastman of the *Liberator*, and Lincoln Steffens, the journalist. It is not likely that the Government will be more gracious to me.

I was rather amused at your phrase 'that she will **not** engage in the more violent forms of Anarchism?' I know, of course, that it has been my reputation that I indulged in such forms, but it has never been borne out by the facts. However, I should not want to gain my right of asylum in England or any country by pledging to abstain from the expression of my ideas, or the right to protest against injustice. The Austrian Government offered me asylum if I would sign such a pledge. Naturally, I refused. Life as we live it today is not worth much. I would not feel it was worth anything if I had to forswear what I believe and stand for.

Under these conditions, if it is not too great a burden, I would appreciate any efforts made in my behalf which would give me the right to come to England. For the present I will probably get an extension of my visé in Germany because I have had an offer to write a book on Russia from Harper Bros. of New York.

No, the Bolsheviki did not compel me to leave Russia. Much to my surprise they gave me passports. They have however made it difficult for me to obtain visés from other countries. Naturally they can not endure the criticism contained in the ten articles I wrote for the *New York World*, in April last, after leaving Russia.

Very sincerely yours
Emma Goldman

Emma Goldman did at last acquire permission to come to England. A dinner was given in her honour at which I was present. When she rose to speak, she was welcomed enthusiastically; but when she sat down, there was dead silence. This was because almost the whole of her speech was against the Bolsheviks.

Chapter 10

China

We travelled to China from Marseilles in a French boat called *Portos*. Just before we left London, we learned that, owing to a case of plague on board, the sailing would be delayed for three weeks. We did not feel, however, that we could go through all the business of saying good-bye a second time, so we went to Paris and spent the three weeks there. During this time I finished my book on Russia, and decided, after much hesitation, that I would publish it. To say anything against Bolshevism was, of course, to play into the hands of reaction, and most of my friends took the view that one ought not to say what one thought about Russia unless what one thought was favourable. I had, however, been impervious to similar arguments from patriots during the War, and it seemed to me that in the long run no good purpose would be served by holding one's tongue. The matter was, of course, much complicated for me by the question of my personal relations with Dora. One hot summer night, after she had gone to sleep, I got up and sat on the balcony of our room and contemplated the stars. I tried to see the question without the heat of party passion and imagined myself holding a conversation with Cassiopeia. It seemed to me that I should be more in harmony with the stars if I published what I thought about Bolshevism than if I did not. So I went on with the work and finished the book on the night before we started for Marseilles.

The bulk of our time in Paris, however, was spent in a more frivolous manner, buying frocks suitable for the Red Sea, and the rest of the trousseau required for unofficial marriage. After a few days in Paris, all the appearance of estrangement which had existed between us ceased, and we became gay and light-hearted. There were, however, moments on the boat when things were difficult. I was sensitive because of the contempt that Dora had poured on my head for not liking Russia. I suggested to her that we had made a mistake in coming away together, and that the best way out would be to jump into the sea. This mood, however, which was largely induced by the heat, soon passed.

The voyage lasted five or six weeks, so that one got to know one's fellow-passengers pretty well. The French people mostly belonged to the official classes. They were much superior to the English, who were rubber planters and business men. There were rows between the

English and the French, in which we had to act as mediators. On one occasion the English asked me to give an address about Soviet Russia. In view of the sort of people that they were, I said only favourable things about the Soviet Government, so there was nearly a riot, and when we reached Shanghai our English fellow-passengers sent a telegram to the Consulate General in Peking, urging that we should not be allowed to land. We consoled ourselves with the thought of what had befallen the ring-leader among our enemies at Saigon. There was at Saigon an elephant whose keeper sold bananas which the visitors gave to the elephant. We each gave him a banana, and he made us a very elegant bow, but our enemy refused, whereupon the elephant squirted dirty water all over his immaculate clothes, which also the keeper had taught him to do. Perhaps our amusement at this incident did not increase his love of us.

When we arrived at Shanghai there was at first no one to meet us. I had had from the first a dark suspicion that the invitation might be a practical joke, and in order to test its genuineness I had got the Chinese to pay my passage money before I started. I thought that few people would spend £125 on a joke, but when nobody appeared at Shanghai our fears revived, and we began to think we might have to creep home with our tails between our legs. It turned out, however, that our friends had only made a little mistake as to the time of the boat's arrival. They soon appeared on board and took us to a Chinese hotel, where we passed three of the most bewildering days that I have ever experienced. There was at first some difficulty in explaining about Dora. They got the impression that she was my wife, and when we said that this was not the case, they were afraid that I should be annoyed about their previous misconception. I told them that I wished her treated as my wife, and they published a statement to that effect in the Chinese papers. From the first moment to the last of our stay in China, every Chinese with whom we came in contact treated her with the most complete and perfect courtesy, and with exactly the same deference as would have been paid to her if she had been in fact my wife. They did this in spite of the fact that we insisted upon her always being called 'Miss Black'.

Our time in Shanghai was spent in seeing endless people, Europeans, Americans, Japanese, and Koreans, as well as Chinese. In general the various people who came to see us were not on speaking terms with each other; for instance, there could be no social relations between the Japanese and the Korean Christians who had been exiled for bomb-throwing. (In Korea at that a time a Christian was practically synonymous with a bomb-thrower.) So we had to put our guests at separate tables in the public room, and move round from table to table throughout the day. We had also to attend an enormous banquet, at which various Chinese made after-dinner speeches in the best English style, with exactly the type of joke which is demanded of such an occasion. It was our first experience of the Chinese, and we were somewhat surprised by their wit and fluency. I had not realised until then that a civilised Chinese is the most civilised person in the world. Sun Yat-sen invited me to dinner, but to my lasting regret the evening he suggested was after my departure, and I had to refuse. Shortly after this he went to Canton to inaugurate the nationalist movement which afterwards conquered the whole country, and as I was unable to go to Canton, I never met him.

Our Chinese friends took us for two days to Hangchow to see the Western Lane. The first day we went round it by boat, and the second day in chairs. It was marvellously beautiful, with the beauty of ancient civilisation, surpassing even that of Italy. From there we went to Nanking, and from Nanking by boat to Hankow. The days on the Yangtse were as delightful as the days on the Volga had been horrible. From Hankow we went to Changsha, where an educational conference was in progress. They wished us to stay there for a week, and give addresses every day, but we were both exhausted and anxious for a chance to rest, which made us eager to reach Peking. So we refused to stay more than twenty-four hours, in spite of the fact that the Governor of Hunan in person held out every imaginable inducement, including a special train in all the way to Wuchang.

However, in order to do my best to conciliate the people of Changsha, I gave four lectures, two after-dinner speeches, and an after-lunch speech, during the twenty-four hours. Changsha was a place without modern hotels, and the missionaries very kindly offered to put us up, but they made it clear that Dora was to stay with one set of missionaries, and I with another. We therefore thought it best to decline their invitation, and stayed at a Chinese hotel. The experience was not altogether pleasant. Armies of bugs walked across the bed all through the night.

The Tuchun[1] gave a magnificent banquet, at which we first met the Deweys, who behaved with great kindness, and later, when I became ill, John Dewey treated us both with singular helpfulness. I was told that when he came to see me in the hospital, he was much touched by my saying, 'We must make a plan for peace' at a time when everything else that I said was delirium. There were about a hundred guests at the Tuchun's banquet. We assembled in one vast hall and then moved into another for the feast, which was sumptuous beyond belief. In the middle of it the Tuchun apologised for the extreme simplicity of the fare, saying that he thought we should like to see how they lived in everyday

---

[1] The military Governor of the Province.

life rather than to be treated with any pomp. To my intense chagrin, I was unable to think of a retort in kind, but I hope the interpreter made up for my lack of wit. We left Changsha in the middle of a lunar eclipse, and saw bonfires being lit and heard gongs beaten to frighten off the Heavenly Dog, according to the traditional ritual of China on such occasions. From Changsha, we travelled straight through to Peking, where we enjoyed our first wash for ten days.

Our first months in Peking were a time of absolute and complete happiness. All the difficulties and disagreements that we had had were completely forgotten. Our Chinese friends were delightful. The work was interesting, and Peking itself inconceivably beautiful.

We had a house boy, a male cook and a rickshaw boy. The house boy spoke some English and it was through him that we made ourselves intelligible to the others. This process succeeded better than it would have done in England. We engaged the cook sometime before we came to live in our house and told him that the first meal we should want would be dinner some days hence. Sure enough, when the time came, dinner was ready. The house boy knew everything. One day we were in need of change and we had hidden what we believed to be a dollar in an old table. We described its whereabouts to the house boy and asked him to fetch it. He replied imperturbably, 'No, Madam. He bad.' We also had the occasional services of a sewing woman. We engaged her in the winter and dispensed with her services in the summer. We were amused to observe that while, in winter, she had been very fat, as the weather grew warm, she became gradually very thin, having re-placed the thick garments of winter gradually by the elegant garments of summer. We had to furnish our house which we did from the very excellent second-hand furniture shops which abounded in Peking. Our Chinese friends could not understand our preferring old Chinese things to modern furniture from Birmingham. We had an official interpreter assigned to look after us. His English was very good and he was especi-ally proud of his ability to make puns in English. His name was Mr Chao and, when I showed him an article that I had written called 'Causes of the Present Chaos', he remarked, 'Well, I suppose, the causes of the present Chaos are the previous Chaos.' I became a close friend of his in the course of our journeys. He was engaged to a Chinese girl and I was able to remove some difficulties that had impeded his marriage. I still hear from him occasionally and once or twice he and his wife have come to see me in England.

I was very busy lecturing, and I also had a seminar of the more advanced students. All of them were Bolsheviks except one, who was the nephew of the Emperor. They used to slip off to Moscow one by one. They were charming youths, ingenuous and intelligent at the same time, eager to know the world and to escape from the trammels of

Chinese tradition. Most of them had been betrothed in infancy to old-fashioned girls, and were troubled by the ethical question whether they would be justified in breaking the betrothal to marry some girl of modern education. The gulf between the old China and the new was vast, and family bonds were extraordinarily irksome for the modern-minded young man. Dora used to go to the Girls' Normal School, where those who were to be teachers were being trained. They would put to her every kind of question about marriage, free love, contraception, etc., and she answered all their questions with complete frankness. Nothing of the sort would have been possible in any similar European institution. In spite of their freedom of thought, traditional habits of behaviour had a great hold upon them. We occasionally gave parties to the young men of my seminar and the girls at the Normal School. The girls at first would take refuge in a room to which they supposed no men would penetrate, and they had to be fetched out and encouraged to associate with males. It must be said that when once the ice was broken, no further encouragement was needed.

The National University of Peking for which I lectured was a very remarkable institution. The Chancellor and the Vice-Chancellor were men passionately devoted to the modernising of China. The Vice-Chancellor was one of the most whole-hearted idealists that I have ever known. The funds which should have gone to pay salaries were always being appropriated by Tuchuns, so that the teaching was mainly a labour of love. The students deserved what their professors had to give them. They were ardently desirous of knowledge, and there was no limit to the sacrifices that they were prepared to make for their country. The atmosphere was electric with the hope of a great awakening. After centuries of slumber, China was becoming aware of the modern world, and at that time the sordidnesses and compromises that go with governmental responsibility had not yet descended upon the reformers. The English sneered at the reformers, and said that China would always be China. They assured me that it was silly to listen to the frothy talk of half-baked young men; yet within a few years those half-baked young men had conquered China and deprived the English of many of their most cherished privileges.

Since the advent of the Communists to power in China, the policy of the British towards that country has been somewhat more enlightened than that of the United States, but until that time the exact opposite was the case. In 1926, on three separate occasions, British troops fired on unarmed crowds of Chinese students, killing and wounding many. I wrote a fierce denunciation of these outrages, which was published first in England and then throughout China. An American missionary in China, with whom I corresponded, came to England shortly after this time, and told me that indignation in China had been such as to endanger the lives of all Englishmen living in that country. He even said – though I found this scarcely credible – that the English in China owed their preservation to me, since I had caused infuriated Chinese to conclude that not all Englishmen are vile. However that may be, I incurred the hostility, not only of the English in China, but of the British Government.

White men in China were ignorant of many things that were common knowledge among the Chinese. On one occasion my bank (which was American) gave me notes issued by a French bank, and I found that Chinese tradesmen refused to accept them. My bank expressed astonishment, and gave me other notes instead. Three months later, the French bank went bankrupt, to the surprise of all other white banks in China.

The Englishman in the East, as far as I was able to judge of him, is a man completely out of touch with his environment. He plays polo and goes to his club. He derives his ideas of native culture from the works of eighteenth-century missionaries, and he regards intelligence in the East with the same contempt which he feels for intelligence in his own country. Unfortunately for our political sagacity, he overlooks the fact that in the East intelligence is respected, so that enlightened Radicals have an influence upon affairs which is denied to their English counterparts. MacDonald went to Windsor in knee-breeches, but the Chinese reformers showed no such respect to their Emperor, although our monarchy is a mushroom growth of yesterday compared to that of China.

My views as to what should be done in China I put into my book *The Problem of China* and so shall not repeat them here.

In spite of the fact that China was in a ferment, it appeared to us, as compared with Europe, to be a country filled with philosophic calm. Once a week the mail would arrive from England, and the letters and newspapers that came from there seemed to breathe upon us a hot blast of insanity like the fiery heat that comes from a furnace door suddenly opened. As we had to work on Sundays, we made a practice of taking a holiday on Mondays, and we usually spent the whole day in the Temple of Heaven, the most beautiful building that it has ever been my good fortune to see. We would sit in the winter sunshine saying little, gradually absorbing peace, and would come away prepared to face the madness and passion of our own distracted continent with poise and calm. At other times, we used to walk on the walls of Peking. I remember with particular vividness a walk one evening starting at sunset and continuing through the rise of the full moon.

The Chinese have (or had) a sense of humour which I found very congenial. Perhaps communism has killed it, but when I was there they constantly reminded me of the people in their ancient books. One hot day two fat middle-aged business men invited me to motor into the country to see a certain very famous half-ruined pagoda. When we reached it, I climbed the spiral staircase, expecting them to follow, but on arriving at the top I saw them still on the ground. I asked why they had not come up, and with portentous gravity they replied:

'We thought of coming up, and debated whether we should do so. Many weighty arguments were advanced on both sides, but at last there was one which decided us. The pagoda might crumble at any moment, and we felt that, if it did, it would be well there should be those who could bear witness as to how the philosopher died.'

What they meant was that it was hot and they were fat.

Many Chinese have that refinement of humour which consists in enjoying a joke more when the other person cannot see it. As I was leaving Peking a Chinese friend gave me a long classical passage microscopically engraved by hand on a very small surface; he also gave me the same passage written out in exquisite calligraphy. When I asked what it said, he replied: 'Ask Professor Giles when you get home.' I took his advice, and found that it was 'The Consultation of the Wizard', in which the wizard merely advises his clients to do whatever they like. He was poking fun at me because I always refused to give advice to the Chinese as to their immediate political difficulties.

The climate of Peking in winter is very cold. The wind blows almost always from the north, bringing an icy breath from the Mongolian mountains. I got bronchitis, but paid no attention to it. It seemed to get better, and one day, at the invitation of some Chinese friends, we went to a place about two hours by motorcar from Peking, where there were hot springs. The hotel provided a very good tea, and someone suggested that it was unwise to eat too much tea as it would spoil one's dinner. I objected to such prudence on the ground that the Day of Judgement might intervene. I was right, as it was three months before I ate another square meal. After tea, I suddenly began to shiver, and after I had been shivering for an hour or so, we decided that we had better get back to Peking at once. On the way home, our car had a puncture, and by the time the puncture was mended, the engine was cold. By this time, I was nearly delirious, but the Chinese servants and Dora pushed the car to the top of a hill, and on the descent the engine gradually began to work. Owing to the delay, the gates of Peking were shut when we reached them, and it took an hour of telephoning to get them open. By the time we finally got home, I was very ill indeed. Before I had time to realise what was happening, I was delirious. I was moved into a German hospital, where Dora nursed me by day, and the only English professional nurse in Peking nursed me by night. For a fortnight the doctors thought every evening that I should be dead before morning. I remember nothing of this time except a few dreams.

When I came out of delirium, I did not know where I was, and did not recognise the nurse. Dora told me that I had been very ill and nearly died, to which I replied: 'How interesting', but I was so weak that I forgot it in five minutes, and she had to tell me again. I could not even remember my own name. But although for about a month after my delirium had ceased they kept telling me I might die at any moment, I never believed a word of it. The nurse whom they had found was rather distinguished in her profession, and had been the Sister in charge of a hospital in Serbia during the War. The whole hospital had been captured by the Germans, and the nurses removed to Bulgaria. She was never tired of telling me how intimate she had become with the Queen of Bulgaria. She was a deeply religious woman, and told me when I began to get better that she had seriously considered whether it was not her duty to let me die. Fortunately, professional training was too strong for her moral sense.

All through the time of my convalescence, in spite of weakness and great physical discomfort, I was exceedingly happy. Dora was very devoted, and her devotion made me forget everything unpleasant. At an early stage of my convalescence Dora discovered that she was pregnant, and this was a source of immense happiness to us both. Ever since the moment when I walked on Richmond Green with Alys, the desire for children had been growing stronger and stronger within me, until at last it had become a consuming passion. When I discovered that I was not only to survive myself, but to have a child, I became completely indifferent to the circumstances of convalescence, although, during convalescence, I had a whole series of minor diseases. The main trouble had been double pneumonia, but in addition to that I had heart disease, kidney disease, dysentery, and phlebitis. None of these, however, prevented me from feeling perfectly happy, and in spite of all gloomy prognostications, no ill effects whatever remained after my recovery.

Lying in my bed feeling that I was not going to die was surprisingly delightful. I had always imagined until then that I was fundamentally pessimistic and did not greatly value being alive. I discovered that in this I had been completely mistaken, and that life was infinitely sweet to me. Rain in Peking is rare, but during my convalescence there came heavy rains bringing the delicious smell of damp earth through the windows, and I used to think how dreadful it would have been to have never smelt that smell again. I had the same feeling about the light of the sun, and the sound of the wind. Just outside my windows were some very beautiful acacia trees, which came into blossom at the first moment when I was well enough to enjoy them. I have known ever since that at bottom I am glad to be alive. Most people, no doubt, always know this, but I did not.

I was told that the Chinese said that they would bury me by the

Western Lake and build a shrine to my memory. I have some slight regret that this did not happen, as I might have become a god, which would have been very *chic* for an atheist.

There was in Peking at that time a Soviet diplomatic mission, whose members showed great kindness. They had the only good champagne in Peking, and supplied it liberally for my use, champagne being apparently the only proper beverage for pneumonia patients. They used to take first Dora, and later Dora and me, for motor drives in the neighbourhood of Peking. This was a pleasure, but a somewhat exciting one, as they were as bold in driving as they were in revolutions.

I probably owe my life to the Rockefeller Institute in Peking which provided a serum that killed the *pneumococci*. I owe them the more gratitude on this point, as both before and after I was strongly opposed to them politically, and they regarded me with as much horror as was felt by my nurse.

The Japanese journalists were continually worrying Dora to give them interviews when she wanted to be nursing me. At last she became a little curt with them, so they caused the Japanese newspapers to say that I was dead. This news was forwarded by mail from Japan to America and from America to England. It appeared in the English newspapers on the same day as the news of my divorce. Fortunately, the Court did not believe it, or the divorce might have been postponed. It provided me with the pleasure of reading my obituary notices, which I had always desired without expecting my wishes to be fulfilled. One missionary paper, I remember, had an obituary notice of one sentence: 'Missionaries may be pardoned for heaving a sigh of relief at the news of Mr Bertrand Russell's death.' I fear they must have heaved a sigh of a different sort when they found that I was not dead after all. The report caused some pain to friends in England. We in Peking knew nothing about it until a telegram came from my brother enquiring whether I was still alive. He had been remarking meanwhile that to die in Peking was not the sort of thing I would do.

The most tedious stage of my convalescence was when I had phlebitis, and had to lie motionless on my back for six weeks. We were very anxious to return home for the confinement, and as time went on it began to seem doubtful whether we should be able to do so. In these circumstances it was difficult not to feel impatience, the more so as the doctors said there was nothing to do but wait. However, the trouble cleared up just in time, and on July 10th we were able to leave Peking, though I was still very weak and could only hobble about with the help of a stick.

Shortly after my return from China, the British Government decided to deal with the question of the Boxer indemnity. When the Boxers had been defeated, the subsequent treaty of peace provided that the

Chinese Government should pay an annual sum to all those European Powers which had been injured by it. The Americans very wisely decided to forgo any payment on this account. Friends of China in England urged England in vain to do likewise. At last it was decided that, instead of a punitive payment, the Chinese should make some payment which should be profitable to both China and Britain. What form this payment should take was left to be determined by a Committee on which there should be two Chinese `members. While MacDonald was Prime Minister he invited Lowes Dickinson and me to be members of the Committee, and consented to our recommendation of V. K. Ting and Hu Shih as the Chinese members. When, shortly afterwards, MacDonald's Government fell, the succeeding Conservative Government informed Lowes Dickinson and myself that our services would not be wanted on the Committee, and they would not accept either V. K. Ting or Hu Shih as Chinese members of it, on the ground that we knew nothing about China. The Chinese Government replied that it desired the two Chinese whom I had recommended and would not have anyone else. This put an end to the very feeble efforts at securing Chinese friendship. The only thing that had been secured during the Labour period of friendship was that Shantung should become a golf course for the British Navy and should no longer be open for Chinese trading.

Before I became ill I had undertaken to do a lecture tour in Japan after leaving China. I had to cut this down to one lecture, and visits to various people. We spent twelve hectic days in Japan, days which were far from pleasant, though very interesting. Unlike the Chinese, the Japanese proved to be destitute of good manners, and incapable of avoiding intrusiveness. Owing to my being still very feeble, we were anxious to avoid all unnecessary fatigues, but the journalists proved a very difficult matter. At the first port at which our boat touched, some thirty journalists were lying in wait, although we had done our best to travel secretly, and they only discovered our movements through the police. As the Japanese papers had refused to contradict the news of my death, Dora gave each of them a type-written slip saying that as I was dead I could not be interviewed. They drew in their breath through their teeth and said: 'Ah! veree funnee!'

We went first to Kobe to visit Robert Young, the editor of the *Japan Chronicle*. As the boat approached the quay, we saw vast processions with banners marching along, and to the surprise of those who knew Japanese, some of the banners were expressing a welcome to me. It turned out that there was a great strike going on in the dock-yards, and that the police would not tolerate processions except in honour of distinguished foreigners, so that this was their only way of making a demonstration. The strikers were being led by a Christian pacifist called Kagawa, who took me to strike meetings, at one of which I made a speech. Robert Young was a delightful man, who, having left England in the eighties, had not shared in the subsequent deterioration of ideas. He had in his study a large picture of Bradlaugh, for whom he had a devoted admiration. His was, I think, the best newspaper I have ever known, and he had started it with a capital of £10, saved out of his wages as a compositor. He took me to Nara, a place of exquisite beauty, where Old Japan was still to be seen. We then fell into the hands of the enterprising editors of an up-to-date magazine called *Kaizo*, who conducted us around Kyoto and Tokyo, taking care always to let the journalists know when we were coming, so that we were perpetually pursued by flashlights and photographed even in our sleep. In both places they invited large numbers of professors to visit us. In both places we were treated with the utmost obsequiousness and dogged by police-spies. The room next to ours in the hotel would be occupied by a collection of policemen with a typewriter. The waiters treated us as if we were royalty, and walked backwards out of the room. We would say: 'Damn this waiter', and immediately hear the police typewriter clicking. At the parties of professors which were given in our honour, as soon as I got into at all animated conversation with anyone, a flashlight photograph would be taken, with the result that the conversation was of course interrupted.

The Japanese attitude towards women is somewhat primitive. In Kyoto we both had mosquito nets with holes in them, so that we were kept awake half the night by mosquitoes. I complained of this in the morning. Next evening my mosquito net was mended, but not Dora's. When I complained again the next day, they said: 'But we did not know it mattered about the lady.' Once, when we were in a suburban train with the historian Eileen Power, who was also travelling in Japan, no seats were available, but a Japanese kindly got up and offered his seat to me. I gave it to Dora. Another Japanese then offered me *his* seat. I gave this to Eileen Power. By this time the Japanese were so disgusted by my unmanly conduct that there was nearly a riot.

We met only one Japanese whom we really liked, a Miss Ito. She was young and beautiful, and lived with a well-known anarchist, by whom she had a son. Dora said to her: 'Are you not afraid that the authorities will do something to you?' She drew her hand across her throat, and said: 'I know they will do that sooner or later.' At the time of the earthquake, the police came to the house where she lived with the anarchist, and found him and her and a little nephew whom they believed to be the son, and informed them that they were wanted at the police station. When they arrived at the police station, the three were put in separate rooms and strangled by the police, who boasted that they had not had much trouble with the child, as they had managed to make friends with him on the way to the police station. The police in question became national heroes, and school children were set to write essays in their praise.

We made a ten hours' journey in great heat from Kyoto to Yokohama. We arrived there just after dark, and were received by a series of magnesium explosions, each of which made Dora jump, and increased my fear of a miscarriage. I became blind with rage, the only time I have been so since I tried to strangle Fitzgerald.[1] I pursued the boys with the flashlights, but being lame, was unable to catch them, which was fortunate, as I should certainly have committed murder. An enterprising photographer succeeded in photographing me with my eyes blazing. I should not have known that I could have looked so completely insane. This photograph was my introduction to Tokyo. I felt at that moment the same type of passion as must have been felt by Anglo-Indians during the Mutiny, or by white men surrounded by a rebel coloured population. I realised then that the desire to protect one's family from injury at the hands of an alien race is probably the wildest and most passionate feeling of which man is capable. My last experience of Japan was the publication in a patriotic journal of what purported to be my farewell message to the Japanese nation, urging them to be more Chauvinistic. I had not sent either this or any other farewell message to that or any other newspaper.

We sailed from Yokohama by the Canadian Pacific, and were seen off by the anarchist, Ozuki, and Miss Ito. On the *Empress of Asia* we experienced a sudden change in the social atmosphere. Dora's condition was not yet visible to ordinary eyes, but we saw the ship's doctor cast a professional eye upon her, and we learned that he had communicated his observations to the passengers. Consequently, almost nobody would speak to us, though everybody was anxious to photograph us. The only people willing to speak to us were Mischa Elman, the violinist, and his party. As everybody else on the ship wished to speak to him, they were considerably annoyed by the fact that he was always in our company. After an uneventful journey, we arrived in Liverpool at the end of August. It was raining hard, and everybody complained of the drought, so we felt we had reached home. Dora's mother was on the dock, partly to welcome us, but partly to give Dora wise advise, which she was almost too shy to do. On September 27th we were married, having succeeded in hurrying up the King's Proctor, though this required that I should swear by Almighty God on Charing Cross platform that Dora was the woman with whom I had committed the official adultery. On November 16th, my son John was born, and from that moment my children were for many years my main interest in life.

[1] Cf. p. 39.

LETTERS

From Johnson Yuan

6 Yu Yang Li
Avenue Joffre
Shanghai, China
6th Oct. [? Nov.] 1920

Dear Sir

We are very glad to have the greatest social philosopher of world to arrive here in China, so as to salve the Chronic deseases of the thought of Chinese Students. Since 1919, the student's circle seems to be the greatest hope of the future of China; as they are ready to welcome to have revolutionary era in the society of China. In that year, Dr John Dewey had influenced the intellectual class with great success.

But I dare to represent most of the Chinese Students to say a few words to you:

Although Dr Dewey is successful here, but most of our students are not satisfied with his conservative theory. Because most of us want to acquire the knowledge of Anarchism, Syndicalism, Socialism, etc.; in a word, we are anxious to get the knowledge of the social revolutionary philosophy. We are the followers of Mr Kropotkin, and our aim is to have anarchical society in China. We hope you, Sir, to give us fundamentally the thorough Social philosophy, base on Anarchism. Moreover, we want you to recorrect the theory of Dr Dewey, the American Philosopher. We hope you have the absolute freedom in China, not the same as in England. So we hope you to have a greater success than Dr Dewey here.

I myself am old member of the Peking Govt. University, and met you in Shanghai many times, the first time is in 'The Great Oriental Hotel', the first time of your reception here, in the evening.

The motto, you often used, of Lao-Tzu ought to be changed in the first word, as 'Creation without Possession ...' is better than the former translative; and it is more correctly according to what you have said 'the creative impulsive and the possessive impulse'. Do you think it is right?

Your Fraternally Comrade
Johnson Yuan
(Secretary of the Chinese Anarchist-Communist Association)

From The General Educational Association of Hunan

Changsha
October 11th, 1920

Dear Sir

We beg to inform you that the educational system of our province is just at infancy and is unfortunately further weakened by the fearful disturbances of the civil war of late years, so that the guidance and assistances must be sought to sagacious scholars.

The extent to which your moral and intellectual power has reached is so high that all the people of this country are paying the greatest regard to you. We, Hunanese, eagerly desire to hear your powerful instructions as a compass.

A few days ago, through Mr Lee-Shuh-Tseng, our representative at Shanghai, we requested you to visit Hunan and are very grateful to have your kind acceptance. A general meeting will therefore be summoned on the 25th instant in order to receive your instructive advices. Now we appoint Mr Kun-Chao-Shuh to represent us all to welcome you sincerely. Please come as soon as possible.

We are, Sir
Your obedient servants
The General Educational
Association of Hunan
(Seal)

I wrote the following account on the Yiangtse:
To Ottoline Morrel[1]

28th October, 1920

Since landing in China we have had a most curious and interesting time, spent, so far, entirely among Chinese students and journalists, who are more or less Europeanised. I have delivered innumerable lectures – on Einstein, education and social questions. The eagerness for knowledge on the part of students is quite extraordinary. When one begins to speak, their eyes have the look of starving men beginning a feast. Everywhere they treat me with a most embarrassing respect. The day after I landed in Shanghai they gave a vast dinner to us, at which they welcomed me as Confucius the Second. All the Chinese newspapers that day in Shanghai had my photograph. Both Miss Black and I had to speak to innumerable schools, teachers' conferences, congresses, etc. It is a country of curious contrasts. Most of Shanghai is quite European, almost American; the names of streets, and notices and advertisements are in English (as well as Chinese). The buildings are magnificent offices and banks; everything looks very opulent. But the side streets are still quite Chinese. It is a vast city about the size of Glasgow. The Europeans almost all look villainous and ill. One of the leading Chinese newspapers invited us to lunch, in a modern building, completed in 1917, with all the latest plant (except linotype, which can't be used for Chinese characters). The editorial staff gave us a

[1] Published in *The Nation*, January 8th, 1921.

Chinese meal at the top of the house with Chinese wine made of rice, and innumerable dishes which we ate with chopsticks. When we had finished eating they remarked that one of their number was fond of old Chinese music, and would like to play to us. So he produced an instrument with seven strings, made by himself on the ancient model, out of black wood two thousand years old, which he had taken from a temple. The instrument is played with the finger, like a guitar, but is laid flat on a table, not held in the hand. They assured us that the music he played was four thousand years old, but that I imagine must be an overstatement. In any case, it was exquisitely beautiful, very delicate, easier for a European ear than more recent music (of which I have heard a good deal). When the music was over they became again a staff of bustling journalists.

From Shanghai our Chinese friends took us for three nights to Hangchow on the Western Lake, said to be the most beautiful scenery in China. This was merely holiday. The Western Lake is not large – about the size of Grasmere – it is surrounded by wooded hills, on which there are innumerable pagodas and temples. It has been beautified by poets and emperors for thousands of years. (Apparently poets in ancient China were as rich as financiers in modern Europe.) We spent one day in the hills – a twelve hour expedition in Sedan chairs – and the next in seeing country houses, monasteries, etc. on islands in the lake.

Chinese religion is curiously cheerful. When one arrives at a temple, they give one a cigarette and a cup of delicately fragrant tea. Then they show one round. Buddhism, which one thinks of as ascetic, is here quite gay. The saints have fat stomachs, and are depicted as people who thoroughly enjoy life. No one seems to believe the religion, not even the priests. Nevertheless, one sees many rich new temples.

The country houses are equally hospitable – one is shewn round and given tea. They are just like Chinese pictures, with many arbours where one can sit, with everything made for beauty and nothing for comfort – except in the grandest rooms, where there will be a little hideous European furniture.

The most delicious place we saw on the Western Lake was a retreat for scholars, built about eight hundred years ago on the lake. Scholars certainly had a pleasant life in the old China.

Apart from the influence of Europeans, China makes the impression of what Europe would have become if the eighteenth century had gone on till now without industrialism or the French Revolution. People seem to be rational hedonists, knowing very well how to obtain happiness, exquisite through intense cultivation of their artistic sensibilities, differing from Europeans through the fact that they prefer enjoyment to power. People laugh a great deal in all classes, even the lowest.

The Chinese cannot pronounce my name, or write it in their characters. They call me 'Luo-Su' which is the nearest they can manage. This, they can both pronounce and print.

From Hangchow we went back to Shanghai, thence by rail to Nanking, an almost deserted city. The wall is twenty-three miles in circumference, but most of what it encloses is country. The city was destroyed at the end of the Taiping rebellion, and again injured in the Revolution of 1911, but it is an active educational centre, eager for news of Einstein and Bolshevism.

From Nanking we went up the Yiangtse to Hangkow, about three days' journey, through very lovely scenery – thence by train to Cheng-Sha, the capital of Hu-Nan, where a great educational conference was taking place. There are about three hundred Europeans in Cheng-Sha, but Europeanisation has not gone at all far. The town is just like a mediaeval town – narrow streets, every house a shop with a gay sign hung out, no traffic possible except Sedan chairs and a few rickshaws. The Europeans have a few factories, a few banks, a few missions and a hospital – the whole gamut of damaging and repairing body and soul by western methods. The Governor of Hu-Nan is the most virtuous of all the Governors of Chinese provinces, and entertained us last night at a magnificent banquet. Professor and Mrs Dewey were present; it was the first time I had met them. The Governor cannot talk any European language, so, though I sat next to him, I could only exchange compliments through an interpreter. But I got a good impression of him; he is certainly very anxious to promote education, which seems the most crying need of China. Without it, it is hard to see how better government can be introduced. It must be said that bad government seems somewhat less disastrous in China than it would be in a European nation, but this is perhaps a superficial impression which time may correct.

We are now on our way to Pekin, which we hope to reach on October 31st.

Bertrand Russell

From S. Yamamoto

Tokyo, Japan
December 25, 1920

Dear Sir

We heartily thank you for your esteemed favour of the latest date and also for the manuscript on 'The Prospects of Bolshevik Russia', which has just arrived.

When a translation of your article on 'Patriotism' appeared in our

New Year issue of the *Kaizo* now already on sale, the blood of the young Japanese was boiled with enthusiasm to read it. All the conversations everywhere among gentlemen classes, students and laborers centered upon your article, so great was the attraction of your thoughts to them.

The only regret was that the government has requested us to omit references you made to Japan in your article as much as possible, and we were obliged to cut out some of your valuable sentences. We trust that you will generously sympathise with us in the position in which we are placed and that you will excuse us for complying with the government's request.

Hereafter, however, we shall publish your articles in the original as well as in a translation according the dictate of our principle.

The admiration for you of the millions of our young men here is something extraordinary.

Your principle is identical with that of ourselves, so that as long as we live we wish to be with you. But that our country is still caught in the obstinate conventional mesh of 3,000 years standing, so that reforms cannot be carried out, is a cause of great regret. We have to advance step by step. Your publications have served as one of the most important factors to move our promising young men of Japan in their steadfast advancement.

In the past thirty odd years, physical and medical sciences have especially advanced in Japan. But it is a question how much progress we have made in the way of original inventions. Yet we are confident that in pure science we are by no means behind America in advancement. Only the majority of our country men are still enslaved by the ideas of class distinctions and other backward thoughts, of which we are greatly ashamed. The Japanese military clique and the gentlemen clique have been anxious to lead Japan in the path of aggression, thereby only inviting the antipathy of the nation. The present Japanese world of thought has been subject to an undercurrent of struggle. We will be very much grieved if our country were regarded as an aggressive nation because of that.

One half of our government officials and almost eighty per cent of the army men have been caught in dreams of aggression, it is true. But recently there has been much awakening from that.

We have confidence in our young men who have begun to awaken, so that they may advance in the path of civilisation not to disappoint the world. We trust that you will write your articles with the object in view to encourage our young men in their efforts for advancement.

Please give our regards to Miss Black.

> *Yours respectfully*
> S. *Yamamoto*

[*Humbug is international*]

To Ottoline Morrell

[1921]

The other day Dora and I went to a Chinese feast given by the Chinese Students here. They made speeches full of delicate wit, in the style of 18th century France, with a mastery of English that quite amazed me. The Chinese Chargé d'Affaires said he had been asked to speak on Chinese Politics – he said the urgent questions were the General Election, economy and limitation of armaments – he spoke quite a long time, saying only things that might have been said in a political speech about England, and which yet were quite all right for China – when he sat down he had not committed himself to anything at all, but had suggested (without ever saying) that China's problems were worse than ours. The Chinese constantly remind me of Oscar Wilde in his first trial when he thought wit would pull one through anything, and found himself in the grip of a great machine that cared nothing for human values. I read of a Chinese General the other day, whose troops had ventured to resist a Japanese attack, so the Japanese insisted that he should apologise to their Consul. He replied that he had no uniform grand enough for such an august occasion, and therefore to his profound sorrow he must forego the pleasure of visiting a man for whom he had so high an esteem. When they nevertheless insisted, he called the same day on all the other Consuls, so that it appeared as if he were paying a mere visit of ceremony. Then all Japan raised a howl that he had insulted the Japanese nation.

I would do anything in the world to help the Chinese, but it is difficult. They are like a nation of artists, with all their good and bad points. Imagine Gertler and [Augustus] John and Lytton set to govern the British Empire, and you will have some idea how China has been governed for 2,000 years. Lytton is very like an old fashioned Chinaman, not at all like the modern westernised type.

I must stop. All my love.

Your B.

From my brother Frank

Telegraph House
Chichester
27 January 1921

Dear Bertie

The Bank to which I have rashly given a Guarantee is threatening to sell me up, so that by the time you return I shall probably be a pauper walking the streets. It is not an alluring prospect for my old age but I dare say it will afford great joy to Elizabeth.

I have not seen the elusive little Wrinch again although she seems to spend as much time in London as at Girton. I did not know a don had so much freedom of movement in term time.

Did you know that our disagreeable Aunt Gertrude was running the Punch Bowl Inn at Hindhead? I feel tempted to go and stay there for a week end but perhaps she would not take me in. The Aunt Agatha was very bitter about it when I last saw her and said the horrible woman was running all over Hindhead poisoning people's minds against her by saying the most shocking things – we can guess what about. I think when one reflects on the P.L. [Pembroke Lodge] atmosphere it is amusing to think of the Aunt Agatha becoming an object of scandal in her old age.[1] Naturally she feels that something must be seriously wrong with the world for such a thing to be possible. She was quite amusingly and refreshingly bitter about Gertrude and next time I see her I will draw her out a bit.

I am afraid I have no more news to tell you: my mind is entirely occupied with thoughts of what it is like to be a bankrupt – and how – and where – to live on nothing a year. The problem is a novel one and I dislike all its solutions.

> *Yours affectionately*
> *Russell*

From Robert Young

> *The Japan Chronicle*
> P.O. Box No. 91 Sannomiya
> Kobe, Japan
> January 18, 1921

Dear Mr Russell

Your books have always been so helpful to me that when I heard you were coming out here I ventured to send you a copy of the *Chronicle* in the hope that you might find something of interest in it from time to time. Please do not trouble about the subscription; I am very glad if the paper has been of service.

When I was in England a year ago I hoped to have the opportunity of a talk with you, and Francis Hirst tried to arrange it but found you were away from London at the time. Do you intend to visit Japan before you return to England? If so I shall hope to have a chance of meeting you, and if I can do anything here in connection with such a visit please let me know.

I shall be glad to read your new book on Bolshevism. Since you wrote you will perhaps have noticed a review of *Bolshevism in Theory and Practice*. It may perhaps be interesting to you to know that I can re-

[1] She was suspiciously friendly with her chauffeur. The Duke of Bedford gave her a car, which she was too nervous ever to use, but she kept the chauffeur.

member your father's will being upset in the Courts, and that as a result I have followed your career with interest.

Sincerely Yours
Robert Young

The Japan Chronicle
P.O. Box No. 91 Sannomiya
Kobe, Japan
Kobe, January 2, 1922

Dear Mr Russell

It is a long time since August, when you wrote to me from the *Empress of Asia*, and I ought to have acknowledged your letter earlier, but with my small staff I am always kept very busy, and my correspondence tends to accumulate.

I have just heard from Mrs Russell of the birth of an heir, and I congratulate you in no formal sense, for it has given us great pleasure and much relief to learn that Mrs Russell did not suffer from her experiences in Japan. I published the letter you sent me, and I think some good has been done by the protest. So few people have courage to protest against an evil of this character, lest worse things may befall them in the way of criticism.

What a farce the Washington Conference is. From the first I doubted the sincerity of this enthusiasm for peace on the part of those who made the war. Perhaps it is the head rather than the heart that is at fault. The statesmen do not seem to realise that so long as the old policies are pursued, we shall have the same results, and that a limitation of armaments to the point they have reached during the war puts us in a worse position regarding the burden carried and the danger of explosion than in 1914. Japan has sulkily accepted the ratio proposed by America, but is supporting the French demand for more submarines. France is showing herself a greater danger to Europe than Germany ever was. China has been betrayed at the Washington Conference, as we expected. The Anglo–Japanese Alliance has been scrapped, to be replaced by a Four-Power agreement which is still more dangerous to China. Her salvation, unhappily, lies in the jealousies of the Powers. United, the pressure on her will be increased. But I doubt whether the Senate will endorse the treaty, once its full implications are understood.

You are very busy, I note, and I hope that you will be able to make people think. But it is a wicked and perverse generation, I am afraid. Sometimes I despair. It looks as if all the ideals with which I started life had been overthrown. But I suppose when one is well into the sixties, the resilience of youth has disappeared.

By the way, I have suggested to the Conway Memorial Committee that you be asked to deliver the annual lecture. If you are asked, I hope you will see your way to consent. Moncure Conway was a fine character, always prepared to champion the oppressed and defend free speech. He stood by Bradlaugh and Mrs Besant when they were prosecuted for the publication of the *Fruits of Philosophy*, as he stood by Foote when prosecuted on account of the *Freethinker*, though personally objecting to that style of propaganda.

I have given Mrs Russell some Japan news in a letter I have just written to her, so I will not repeat here. I hope you are receiving the *Japan Weekly Chronicle* regularly, so that you can keep in touch with news in this part of the world. It has been sent to you care of George Allen & Unwin. Now I have your Chelsea address I will have it sent there. For some years our Weekly has been steadily increasing in circulation, going all over the world. But from the 1st of this year the Japanese Post Office has doubled the foreign postage rates, which makes 6 yen for postage alone per annum on a copy of the Weekly, and I am afraid our circulation will suffer accordingly.

It is very good to hear that you are completely restored to health. Mrs Russell says you would scarcely be recognised by those who only saw you in Japan. Your visit was a great pleasure to me. For years I had admired your writings and been encouraged by the stand you had taken in public affairs when even the stoutest seemed to waver. It therefore meant much to me to make your acquaintance and I hope your friendship.

With our united good wishes,

> *Sincerely yours*
> *Robert Young*

From C. P. Sanger

> 5 New Square
> Lincolns Inn, W.C.2
> 2 June 1921

My dear Bertie

How kind of you to write; and to say such kind things. Until there was a false rumour of your death I never really knew how *very* fond I am of you. I didn't believe the rumour, but the mere idea that I might never see you again had never come into my mind; and it was an intense relief when the Chinese Embassy ascertained that the rumour was false. You will take care of your health now, won't you?

The Political situation is, as always, damnable – millions of unemployed – soldiers camping in the parks – but an excellent day yesterday for the Derby which is all that anyone apparently cares about.

Einstein lectures at King's College in 10 days time, but I can't get a ticket. I've been reading some of Einstein's actual papers and they give me a most tremendous impression of the clearness of his thoughts.

We spent a delightful Whitsuntide at the Shiffolds: Tovey[1] was there and talked endlessly and played Beethoven Sonatas and Bach, so I was very happy.

I enclose a letter for Miss Black – I'm afraid its a little inadequate but it's so difficult to write to a person one has never seen. I hope this experience with her and her devoted nursing of you will form an eternal basis for you both.

Dora sends her love.

> *Yours fraternally and*
> *affectionately*
> C. P. Sanger

From Joseph Conrad

Oswalds
Bishopsbourne, Kent
2. Nov. 1921

My Dear Russell

We were glad to hear that your wife feels none the worse for the exertions and agitations of the move.[2] Please give her our love and assure her that she is frequently in our thoughts.

As to yourself I have been dwelling with you mentally for several days between the covers of your book[3] – an habitation of great charm and most fascinatingly furnished; not to speak of the wonderful quality of light that reigns in there. Also all the windows (I am trying to write in images) are, one feels, standing wide open. Nothing less stuffy – of the Mansions of the mind – could be conceived! I am sorry for the philosophers (p. 212 – end) who (like the rest of us) cannot have their cake and eat it. There's no exactitude in the vision or in the words. I have a notion that we are condemned in all things to the *à-peu-près*, which no scientific passion for weighing and measuring will ever do away with.

It is very possible that I haven't understood your pages – but the good try I have had was a delightful experience. I suppose you are enough of a philosopher not to have expected more from a common mortal.

I don't believe that Charles I was executed (pp. 245–246 et seq.) but there is not enough paper left here to explain why. Next time perhaps. For I certainly intend to meet you amongst your Chinoiseries at the very earliest fitting time.

> *Always affectly yours*
> *J. Conrad*

[1] The music critic.
[2] The move from one abode to another in London after we returned from China.
[3] *The Analysis of Mind.*

Oswalds
Bishopsbourne, Kent
18th Nov. 1921

My Dear Russell

Jessie must have sent yesterday our congratulations and words of welcome to the 'comparative stranger' who has come to stay with you (and take charge of the household as you will soon discover). Yes! Paternity is a great experience of which the least that can be said is that it is eminently worth having – if only for the deepened sense of fellowship with all men it gives one. It is the only experience perhaps whose universality does not make it common but invests it with a sort of grandeur on that very account. My affection goes out to you both, to him who is without speech and thought as yet and to you who have spoken to men profoundly with effect and authority about the nature of the mind. For your relation to each other will have its poignant moments arising out of the very love and loyalty binding you to each other.

Of all the incredible things that come to pass this – that there should be one day a Russell bearing mine for one of his names is surely the most marvellous. Not even my horoscope could have disclosed that for I verily believe that all the sensible stars would have refused to combine in that extravagant manner over my cradle. However it has come to pass (to the surprise of the Universe) and all I can say is that I am profoundly touched – more than I can express – that I should have been present to your mind in that way and at such a time.

Please kiss your wife's hand for me and tell her that in the obscure bewildered masculine way (which is not quite unintelligent however) I take part in her gladness. Since your delightful visit here she was much in our thoughts – and I will confess we felt very optimistic. She has justified it fully and it is a great joy to think of her with two men in the house. She will have her hands full presently. I can only hope that John Conrad has been born with a disposition towards indulgence which he will consistently exercise towards his parents. I don't think that I can wish you anything better and so with my dear love to all three of you, I am

always yours
Joseph Conrad

P.S. I am dreadfully offended at your associating me with some undesirable acquaintance of yours[1] who obviously should not have been allowed inside the B. Museum reading-room. I wish you to understand that my attitude towards [the] King Charles question is not

[1] Who did not agree that Julius Caesar is dead, and when I asked why, replied: 'Because I am Julius Caesar.'

phantastic but philosophical and I shall try to make it clear to you later when you will be more in a state to follow my reasoning closely. Knowing from my own experience I imagine that it's no use talking to you seriously just now.

From Eileen Power

184 Ebury Street
S.W.1
Saturday, [December, 1921]

Dear Bertie

The book is *The Invention of a New Religion* by Professor Chamberlain. If you want to consult it, here it is and perhaps you would let me have it back anon.

I am so glad that you and Dora can come to luncheon to meet Dr Wise on Wednesday and tell Dora that 1.30 will do beautifully. I am also asking B. K. Martin, a very intelligent young man who is now teaching history at Magdalene, having got his BA last year. He wrote to me three days ago and said 'if you would introduce me to Bertrand Russell I should be forever in your debt. I'd rather meet him than any other living (or dead) creature.' I felt that in view of this pre-eminence over the shades of Plato, Julius Caesar, Cleopatra, Descartes, Ninon de l'Enclos and Napoleon the Great, you would consent to shine upon him! Also he is extremely clever and a nice boy.

> *Yours ever*
> *Eileen Power*

I was asked to dine with the Webbs the other day, but I don't think I ever shall be again for we nearly came to blows over the relative merits of China and Japan!

From Claud Russell

Sept. 22. 1923
British Legation
Adis Ababa

Dear Bertie

I have just read with great pleasure your *Problem of China*, where I spent some years. It is a fact that the Treaty of Versailles (article 131) provided for the restoration of the astronomical instruments to China, but I am under the impression that the obligation has not been carried out. If so, I fear you cannot count it among the 'important benefits' secured to the world by that treaty. Perhaps you might suggest to your friends in China the occupation of Swabia or Oldenburg to secure its enforcement. I must say, however, in fairness to the Treaty of Versailles, that you do it less than justice. You have overlooked article 246, under which 'Germany will hand over to H.B.M.'s Government the skull of the Sultan Mkwawa . . .'

I think, if I may say so, that on page 24 (top) 'animal' should be 'annual'. I feel sure the Temple of Heaven was never the scene of the sort of sacrifice that pleased the God of Abel.

Your affec cousin
Claud Russell

From J. Ramsay MacDonald

Foreign Office
S.W.1
31st May, 1924

My dear Russell

For some time past, His Majesty's Government have been considering the best means of allocating and administering the British share of the China Boxer Indemnity, which, it has been decided, should be devoted to purposes mutually beneficial to British and Chinese interests.

In order to obtain the best results from the policy thus indicated, it has been decided to appoint a committee to advise His Majesty's Government; and I am approaching you in the hope that you may be able to serve on this Committee, feeling confident that your experience would be of the greatest assistance in this matter, which will so deeply and permanently affect our relations with China.

The terms of reference will probably be as follows: –

'In view of the decision of His Majesty's Government to devote future payments of the British share of the Boxer Indemnity to purposes mutually beneficial to British and Chinese interests.

'To investigate the different objects to which these payments should be allocated, and the best means of securing the satisfactory administration of the funds, to hear witnesses and to make such recommendations as may seem desirable.'

For the sake of efficiency, the Committee will be kept as small as possible, especially at the outset of its proceedings. But it will of course be possible to appoint 'ad hoc' additional members for special subjects, if such a course should recommend itself later on. The following are now being approached, as representing the essential elements which should go to the composition of the Committee:

Chairman: Lord Phillimore.
Foreign Office: Sir John Jordan and Mr S. P. Waterlow.
Department of Overseas Trade: Sir William Clark.
House of Commons: Mr H. A. L. Fisher, MP.
Finance: Sir Charles Addis.
Education: Mr Lowes Dickinson and The Honourable Bertrand Russell.
Women: Dame Adelaide Anderson.
China: A suitable Chinese.

It will be understood that the above list is of a tentative character and should be regarded as confidential.

I enclose a brief memorandum which shows the present position with regard to the Indemnity, and to the legislation which has now been introduced into the House. I trust that you will be able to see your way to undertake this work, to which I attach the highest importance.

Yours very sincerely
J. Ramsay MacDonald

Note on a scrap of paper:
'It is desired that the Committee should consist wholly of men with an extensive knowledge of China and its affairs.'

MEMORANDUM ON THE BOXER INDEMNITY
by
Bertrand Russell

The Boxer Indemnity Bill, now in Committee, provides that what remains unpaid of the Boxer Indemnity shall be spent on purposes to the mutual advantage of Great Britain & China. It does not state that these purposes are to be educational. In the opinion of all who know China (except solely as a field for capitalist exploitation), it is of the utmost importance that an Amendment should be adopted specifying Chinese education as the sole purpose to which the money should be devoted. The following are the chief grounds in favour of such an Amendment:

(1) That this would be the expenditure most useful to China.

(2) That no other course would produce a good effect on influential Chinese opinion.

(3) That the interests of Great Britain, which are to be considered, can only be secured by winning the good will of the Chinese.

(4) That any other course would contrast altogether too unfavourably with the action of America, which long ago devoted all that remained of the American share of the Boxer indemnity to Chinese education.

(5) That the arguments alleged in favour of other courses all have a corrupt motive, i.e. are designed for the purpose of securing private profit through Government action.

For these reasons, it is profoundly desirable that Labour Members of Parliament should take action to secure the necessary Amendment before it is too late.

The China Indemnity Bill, in its present form, provides that the remainder of the Boxer Indemnity shall be applied to 'purposes, educational or other', which are mutually beneficial to Great Britain and China.

Sir Walter de Frece proposed in Committee that the words 'connected with education' should be substituted for 'educational or other'.

It is much to be hoped that the House of Commons will carry this Amendment on the Report stage. Certain interests are opposed to the Amendment for reasons with which Labour can have no sympathy. The Government thinks it necessary to placate these interests, but maintains that the Committee to be appointed will be free to decide in favour of education only. The Committee, however, is appointed by Parliament, and one third of its members are to retire every two years; there is therefore no guarantee against its domination by private interests in the future.

The Bill in its present form opens the door to corruption, is not calculated to please Chinese public opinion, displays Great Britain as less enlightened than America and Japan, and therefore fails altogether to achieve its nominal objects. The Labour Party ought to make at least an attempt to prevent the possibility of the misapplication of public money to purposes of private enrichment. This will be secured by the insertion of the words 'connected with education' in Clause 1, after the word 'purposes'.

Bertrand Russell

From Y. R. Chao   Berlin August 22 '24

Dear Russell

Here is an abbreviated translation of C. L. Lo's letter to me (Lo & S. N. Fu being S. Hu [Hu Shih]'s chief disciples, both in Berlin).

'Heard from China that Wu pei fu advised Ch. Governm. to use funds for railways. *Morning Post* said (4 weeks ago) that Brit. Gov't cabled Ch. Gov't to send a delegate. If so, it would be terrible. Already wrote to London Ch. stud. Club to inquire Chu. If report true, try to cancel action by asking Tsai to mount horse with his prestige. In any case, Brit. Gov't still has full power. We have written trying to influence Chu, but on the other hand you please write to Lo Su [Russell] to influence Brit. For. Office, asking him to recommend Tsai if nothing else is possible. There is already a panic in Peking educ'l world. There was a cable to Brit. Gov't, and another to Tsai asking him to go to London . . .'

Another letter, from Chu, came to me last night:

'I did give my consent (?) to the nomination (?) of Mr Ting. I quite agree (?) with you Ting is the most desirable man for the post, but recently I learnt that Peking (For. Office ?) is in favor of (?) Dr C. H. Wang, who is not in Europe. I doubt whether the latter would accept the appt'm't . . . I will talk over this question with Mr Russell when he returns to town.'

I know Wang (brother of C. T. Wang of Kuo Ming Tang (National People Party) fame), C. H. Wang is a fine gentle fellow, recently worked in business and a Christian. One should emphasise the personal attractiveness and goodness but do the opposite to his suitability to this in-its-nature roughneck tussle of a job.

My noodles are getting cold and my Kleines helles bier is getting warm 200 meters away where my wife is waiting.

Excuse me 1000 times for not reading this letter over again.

Yrs ever
Y. R. Chao

Chapter 11

Second Marriage

With my return from China in September 1921, my life entered upon a less dramatic phase, with a new emotional centre. From adolescence until the completion of *Principia Mathematica*, my fundamental pre-occupation had been intellectual. I wanted to understand and to make others understand; also I wished to raise a monument by which I might be remembered, and on account of which I might feel that I had not lived in vain. From the outbreak of the First World War until my return from China, social questions occupied the centre of my emotions: the War and Soviet Russia alike gave me a sense of tragedy, and I had hopes that mankind might learn to live in some less painful way. I tried to discover some secret of wisdom, and to proclaim it with such persuasiveness that the world should listen and agree. But, gradually, the ardour cooled and the hope grew less; I did not change my views as to how men should live, but I held them with less of prophetic ardour and with less expectation of success in my campaigns.

Ever since the day, in the summer of 1894, when I walked with Alys on Richmond Green after hearing the medical verdict, I had tried to suppress my desire for children. It had, however, grown continually stronger, until it had become almost insupportable. When my first child was born, in November 1921, I felt an immense release of pent-up emotion, and during the next ten years my main purposes were parental. Parental feeling, as I have experienced it, is very complex. There is, first and foremost, sheer animal affection, and delight in watching what is charming in the ways of the young. Next, there is the sense of inescapable responsibility, providing a purpose for daily activities which scepticism does not easily question. Then there is an egoistic element, which is very dangerous: the hope that one's children may succeed where one has failed, that they may carry on one's work when death or senility puts an end to one's own efforts, and, in any case, that they will supply a biological escape from death, making one's own life part of the whole stream, and not a mere stagnant puddle without any overflow into the future. All this I experienced, and for some years it filled my life with happiness and peace.

The first thing was to find somewhere to live. I tried to rent a flat, but I was both politically and morally undesirable, and landlords refused to have me as a tenant. So I bought a freehold house in Chelsea, No. 31 Sydney Street, where my two older children were born. But it did not seem good for children to live all the year in London, so in the spring of 1922 we acquired a house in Cornwall, at Porthcurno, about four miles from Land's End. From then until 1927 we divided our time about equally between London and Cornwall; after that year, we spent no time in London and less in Cornwall.

The beauty of the Cornish coast is inextricably mixed in my memories with the ecstasy of watching two healthy happy children learning the joys of sea and rocks and sun and storm. I spent a great deal more time with them than is possible for most fathers. During the six months of the year we spent in Cornwall we had a fixed and leisurely routine. During the morning my wife and I worked while the children were in the care of a nurse, and later a governess. After lunch we all went to one or other of the many beaches that were within a walk of our house. The children played naked, bathing or climbing or making sand castles as the spirit moved them, and we, of course, shared in these activities. We came home very hungry to a very late and a very large tea; then the children were put to bed and the adults reverted to their grown-up pursuits. In my memory, which is of course fallacious, it was always sunny, and always warm after April. But in April the winds were cold. One April day, when Kate's age was two years three and a half months, I heard her talking to herself and wrote down what she said:

> The North wind blows over the North Pole.
> The daisies hit the grass.
> The wind blows the bluebells down.
> The North wind blows to the wind in the South.

She did not know that any one was listening, and she certainly did not know what 'North Pole' means.

In the circumstances it was natural that I should become interested in education. I had already written briefly on the subject in *Principles of Social Reconstruction*, but now it occupied a large part of my mind. I wrote a book, *On Education, especially in early childhood*, which was published in 1926 and had a very large sale. It seems to me now somewhat unduly optimistic in its psychology, but as regards values I find nothing in it to recant, although I think now that the methods I proposed with very young children were unduly harsh.

It must not be supposed that life during these six years from the autumn of 1921 to the autumn of 1927 was all one long summer idyll. Parenthood had made it imperative to earn money. The purchase of two houses had exhausted almost all the capital that remained to me. When I returned from China I had no obvious means of making money, and at first I suffered considerable anxiety. I took whatever odd journalistic jobs were offered me: while my son John was being born, I wrote an article on Chinese pleasure in fireworks, although concentration on so remote a topic was difficult in the circumstances. In 1922 I published a book on China, and in 1923 (with my wife Dora) a book on *The Prospects of Industrial Civilization*, but neither of these brought much money. I did better with two small books, *The A.B.C. of Atoms* (1923) and *The A.B.C. of Relativity* (1925), and with two other small books, *Icarus or The Future of Science* (1924) and *What I Believe* (1925). In 1924 I earned a good deal by a lecture tour in America. But I remained rather poor until the book on education in 1926. After that, until 1933, I prospered financially, especially with *Marriage and Morals* (1929) and *The Conquest of Happiness* (1930). Most of my work during these years was popular, and was done in order to make money, but I did also some more technical work. There was a new edition of *Principia Mathematica* in 1925, to which I made various additions; and in 1927 I published *The Analysis of Matter*, which is in some sense a companion volume to *The Analysis of Mind*, begun in prison and published in 1921. I also stood for Parliament in Chelsea in 1922 and 1923, and Dora stood in 1924.

In 1927, Dora and I came to a decision, for which we were equally responsible, to found a school of our own in order that our children might be educated as we thought best. We believed, perhaps mistakenly, that children need the companionship of a group of other children, and that, therefore, we ought no longer to be content to bring up our children without others. But we did not know of any existing school that seemed to us in any way satisfactory. We wanted an unusual combination: on the one hand, we disliked prudery and religious instruction and a great many restraints on freedom which are taken for granted in conventional schools; on the other hand, we could not agree with most 'modern' educationists on thinking scholastic instruction unimportant, or in advocating a *complete* absence of discipline. We therefore endeavoured to collect a group of about twenty children, of roughly the same ages as John and Kate, with a view to keeping these same children throughout their school years.

For the purposes of the school we rented my brother's house, Telegraph House, on the South Downs, between Chichester and Petersfield. This owed its name to having been a semaphore station in the time of George III, one of a string of such stations by which messages were flashed between Portsmouth and London. Probably the news of Trafalgar reached London in this way.

The original house was quite small, but my brother gradually added to it. He was passionately devoted to the place, and wrote about it at length in his autobiography, which he called *My Life and Adventures*.

The house was ugly and rather absurd, but the situation was superb. There were enormous views to East and South and West; in one direction one saw the Sussex Weald to Leith Hill, in another one saw the Isle of Wight and the liners approaching Southampton. There was a tower with large windows on all four sides. Here I made my study, and I have never known one with a more beautiful outlook.

With the house went two hundred and thirty acres of wild downland, partly heather and bracken, but mostly virgin forest – magnificent beech trees, and yews of vast age and unusual size. The woods were full of every kind of wild life, including deer. The nearest houses were a few scattered farms about a mile away. For fifty miles, going eastward, one could walk on footpaths over unenclosed bare downs.

It is no wonder that my brother loved the place. But he had speculated unwisely, and lost every penny that he possessed. I offered him a much higher rent than he could have obtained from anyone else, and he was compelled by poverty to accept my offer. But he hated it, and ever after bore me a grudge for inhabiting his paradise.

The house must, however, have had for him some associations not wholly pleasant. He had acquired it originally as a discreet retreat where he could enjoy the society of Miss Morris, whom, for many years, he hoped to marry if he could ever get free from his first wife. Miss Morris, however, was ousted from his affections by Molly, the lady who became his second wife, for whose sake he suffered imprisonment after being condemned by his Peers for bigamy. For Molly's sake he had been divorced from his first wife. He became divorced in Reno and immediately thereupon married Molly, again at Reno. He returned to England and found that British law considered his marriage to Molly bigamous on the ground that British law acknowledges the validity of Reno marriages, but not of Reno divorces. His second wife, who was very fat, used to wear green corduroy knickerbockers; the view of her from behind when she was bending over a flower-bed at Telegraph House used to make one wonder that he had thought her worth what he had gone through for her sake.

Her day, like Miss Morris's, came to an end, and he fell in love with Elizabeth. Molly, from whom he wished to be divorced, demanded £400 a year for life as her price; after his death, I had to pay this. She died at about the age of ninety.

Elizabeth, in her turn, left him and wrote an intolerably cruel novel about him, called *Vera*. In this novel, Vera is already dead; she had been his wife, and he is supposed to be heartbroken at the loss of her. She died by falling out of one of the windows of the tower of Telegraph House. As the novel proceeds, the reader gradually gathers that her death was not an accident, but suicide brought on by my brother's cruelty. It was this that caused me to give my children an emphatic piece of advice: 'Do not marry a novelist.'

In this house of many memories we established the school. In managing the school we experienced a number of difficulties which we ought to have foreseen. There was, first, the problem of finance. It became obvious that there must be an enormous pecuniary loss. We could only have prevented this by making the school large and the food inadequate, and we could not make the school large except by altering its character so as to appeal to conventional parents. Fortunately I was at this time making a great deal of money from books and from lecture tours in America. I made four such tours altogether – during 1924 (already mentioned), 1927, 1929, and 1931. The one in 1927 was during the first term of the school, so that I had no part in its beginnings. During the second term, Dora went on a lecture tour in America. Thus throughout the first two terms there was never more than one of us in charge. When I was not in America, I had to write books to make the necessary money. Consequently, I was never able to give my whole time to the school.

A second difficulty was that some of the staff, however often and however meticulously our principles were explained to them, could never be brought to act in accordance with them unless one of us was present.

A third trouble, and that perhaps the most serious, was that we got an undue proportion of problem children. We ought to have been on the look-out for this pit-fall, but at first we were glad to take almost any child. The parents who were most inclined to try new methods were those who had difficulties with their children. As a rule, these difficulties were the fault of the parents, and the ill effects of their unwisdom were renewed in each holiday. Whatever may have been the cause, many of the children were cruel and destructive. To let the children go free was to establish a reign of terror, in which the strong kept the weak trembling and miserable. A school is like the world: only government can prevent brutal violence. And so I found myself, when the children were not at lessons, obliged to supervise them continually to stop cruelty. We divided them into three groups, bigs, middles, and smalls. One of the middles was perpetually ill-treating the smalls, so I asked him why he did it. His answer was: 'The bigs hit me, so I hit the smalls; that's fair.' And he really thought it was.

Sometimes really sinister impulses came to light. There were among the pupils a brother and sister who had a very sentimental mother, and had been taught by her to profess a completely fantastic degree of affection for each other. One day the teacher who was superintending the midday meal found part of a hatpin in the soup that was about to be ladled out. On inquiry, it turned out that the supposedly affectionate

sister had put it in. 'Didn't you know it might kill you if you swallowed
it?' we said. 'Oh yes,' she replied, 'but I don't take soup.' Further
investigation made it fairly evident that she had hoped her brother
would be the victim. On another occasion, when a pair of rabbits had
been given to a child that was unpopular, two other children made an
attempt to burn them to death, and in the attempt, made a vast fire
which blackened several acres, and, but for a change of wind, might
have burnt the house down.

For us personally, and for our two children, there were special
worries. The other boys naturally thought that our boy was unduly
favoured, whereas we, in order not to favour him or his sister, had to
keep an unnatural distance between them and us except during the
holidays. They, in turn, suffered from a divided loyalty: they had either
to be sneaks or to practise deceit towards their parents. The complete
happiness that had existed in our relations to John and Kate was thus
destroyed, and was replaced by awkwardness and embarrassment. I
think that something of the sort is bound to happen whenever parents
and children are at the same school.

In retrospect, I feel that several things were mistaken in the
principles upon which the school was conducted. Young children in a
group cannot be happy without a certain amount of order and routine.
Left to amuse themselves, they are bored, and turn to bullying or
destruction. In their free time, there should always be an adult to suggest some agreeable game or amusement, and to supply an initiative
which is hardly to be expected of young children.

Another thing that was wrong was that there was a pretence of more
freedom than in fact existed. There was very little freedom where
health and cleanliness were concerned. The children had to wash, to
clean their teeth, and to go to bed at the right time. True, we had never
professed that there should be freedom in such matters, but foolish
people, and especially journalists in search of a sensation, had said or
believed that we advocated a complete absence of all restraints and
compulsions. The older children, when told to brush their teeth, would
sometimes say sarcastically: 'Call this a free school!' Those who had
heard their parents talking about the freedom to be expected in the
school would test it by seeing how far they could go in naughtiness
without being stopped. As we only forbade things that were obviously
harmful, such experiments were apt to be very inconvenient.

In 1929, I published *Marriage and Morals*, which I dictated while
recovering from whooping-cough. (Owing to my age, my trouble was
not diagnosed until I had infected most of the children in the school.)
It was this book chiefly which, in 1940, supplied material for the attack
on me in New York. In it, I developed the view that complete fidelity
was not to be expected in most marriages, but that a husband and wife

ought to be able to remain good friends in spite of affairs. I did not maintain, however, that a marriage could with advantage be prolonged if the wife had a child or children of whom the husband was not the father; in that case, I thought, divorce was desirable. I do not know what I think now about the subject of marriage. There seem to be insuperable objections to every general theory about it. Perhaps easy divorce causes less unhappiness than any other system, but I am no longer capable of being dogmatic on the subject of marriage.

In the following year, 1930, I published *The Conquest of Happiness*, a book consisting of common-sense advice as to what an individual can do to overcome temperamental causes of unhappiness, as opposed to what can be done by changes in social and economic systems. This book was differently estimated by readers of three different levels. Unsophisticated readers, for whom it was intended, liked it, with the result that it had a very large sale. Highbrows, on the contrary, regarded it as a contemptible pot-boiler, an escapist book, bolstering up the pretence that there were useful things to be done and said outside politics. But at yet another level, that of professional psychiatrists, the book won very high praise. I do not know which estimate was right; what I do know is that the book was written at a time when I needed much self-command and much that I had learned by painful experience if I was to maintain any endurable level of happiness.

I was profoundly unhappy during the next few years and some things which I wrote at the time give a more exact picture of my mood than anything I can now write in somewhat pale reminiscence.

At that time I used to write an article once a week for the Hearst Press. I spent Christmas Day, 1931, on the Atlantic, returning from one of my American lecture tours. So I chose for that week's article the subject of 'Christmas at Sea'. This is the article I wrote:

CHRISTMAS AT SEA

For the second time in my life, I am spending Christmas Day on the Atlantic. The previous occasion when I had this experience was thirty-five years ago, and by contrasting what I feel now with what I remember of my feelings then, I am learning much about growing old.

Thirty-five years ago I was lately married, childless, very happy, and beginning to taste the joys of success. Family appeared to me as an external power hampering to freedom: the world, to me, was a world of individual adventure. I wanted to think my own thoughts, find my own friends, and choose my own abode, without regard to tradition or elders or anything but my own tastes. I felt strong enough to stand alone, without the need of buttresses.

Now, I realise, what I did not know then, that this attitude was dependent upon a superabundant vitality. I found Christmas at sea a pleasant amusement, and enjoyed the efforts of the ship's officers to make the occasion as festive as possible. The ship rolled prodigiously, and with each roll all the steamer trunks slid from side to side of all the state-rooms with a noise like thunder. The louder the noise became, the more it made me laugh: everything was great fun.

Time, they say, makes a man mellow. I do not believe it. Time makes a man afraid, and fear makes him conciliatory, and being conciliatory he endeavours to appear to others what they will think mellow. And with fear comes the need of affection, of some human warmth to keep away the chill of the cold universe. When I speak of fear, I do not mean merely or mainly personal fear: the fear of death or decrepitude or penury or any such merely mundane misfortune. I am thinking of a more metaphysical fear. I am thinking of the fear that enters the soul through experience of the major evils to which life is subject: the treachery of friends, the death of those whom we love, the discovery of the cruelty that lurks in average human nature.

During the thirty-five years since my last Christmas on the Atlantic, experience of these major evils has changed the character of my unconscious attitude to life. To stand alone may still be possible as a moral effort, but is no longer pleasant as an adventure. I want the companionship of my children, the warmth of the family fire-side, the support of historic continuity and of membership of a great nation. These are very ordinary human joys, which most middle-aged persons enjoy at Christmas. There is nothing about them to distinguish the philosopher from other men; on the contrary, their very ordinariness makes them the more effective in mitigating the sense of sombre solitude.

And so Christmas at sea, which was once a pleasant adventure, has become painful. It seems to symbolise the loneliness of the man who chooses to stand alone, using his own judgment rather than the judgment of the herd. A mood of melancholy is, in these circumstances, inevitable, and should not be shirked.

But there is something also to be said on the other side. Domestic joys, like all the softer pleasures, may sap the will and destroy courage. The indoor warmth of the traditional Christmas is good, but so is the South wind, and the sun rising out of the sea, and the freedom of the watery horizon. The beauty of these things is undiminished by human folly and wickedness, and remains to give strength to the faltering idealism of middle age.

December 25, 1931.

As is natural when one is trying to ignore a profound cause of unhappiness, I found impersonal reasons for gloom. I had been very full of personal misery in the early years of the century, but at that time I had a more or less Platonic philosophy which enabled me to see beauty in the extra-human universe. Mathematics and the stars consoled me when the human world seemed empty of comfort. But changes in my philosophy have robbed me of such consolations. Solipsism oppressed me, particularly after studying such interpretations of physics as that of Eddington. It seemed that what we had thought of as laws of nature were only linguistic conventions, and that physics was not really concerned with an external world. I do not mean that I quite believed this, but that it became a haunting nightmare, increasingly invading my imagination. One foggy night, sitting in my tower at Telegraph House after everyone else was asleep, I expressed this mood in a pessimistic meditation:

MODERN PHYSICS

Alone in my tower at midnight, I remember the woods and downs, the sea and sky, that daylight showed. Now, as I look through each of the four windows, north, south, east and west, I see only myself dimly reflected, or shadowed in monstrous opacity upon the fog. What matter? Tomorrow's sunrise will give me back the beauty of the outer world as I wake from sleep.

But the mental night that has descended upon me is less brief, and promises no awakening after sleep. Formerly, the cruelty, the meanness, the dusty fretful passion of human life seemed to me a little thing, set, like some resolved discord in music, amid the splendour of the stars and the stately procession of geological ages. What if the universe was to end in universal death? It was none the less unruffled and magnificent. But now all this has shrunk to be no more than my own reflection in the windows of the soul through which I look out upon the night of nothingness. The revolutions of nebulae, the birth and death of stars, are no more than convenient fictions in the trivial work of linking together my own sensations, and perhaps those of other men not much better than myself. No dungeon was ever constructed so dark and narrow as that in which the shadow physics of our time imprisons us, for every prisoner has believed that outside his walls a free world existed; but now the prison has become the whole universe. There is darkness without, and when I die there will be darkness within. There is no splendour, no vastness, anywhere; only triviality for a moment, and then nothing.

Why live in such a world? Why even die?

In May and June, 1931, I dictated to my then secretary, Peg Adams, who had formerly been secretary to a Rajah and Ranee, a short autobiography, which has formed the basis of the present book down to 1921. I ended it with an epilogue, in which, as will be seen, I did not admit private unhappiness, but only political and metaphysical disillusionment. I insert it here, not because it expressed what I now feel, but because it shows the great difficulty I experienced in adjusting myself to a changing world and a very sober philosophy.

EPILOGUE

My personal life since I returned from China has been happy and peaceful. I have derived from my children at least as much instinctive satisfaction as I anticipated, and have in the main regulated my life with reference to them. But while my personal life has been satisfying, my impersonal outlook has become increasingly sombre, and I have found it more and more difficult to believe that the hopes which I formerly cherished will be realised in any measurable future. I have endeavoured, by concerning myself with the education of my children and with making money for their benefit, to shut out from my thoughts the impersonal despairs which tend to settle upon me. Ever since puberty I have believed in the value of two things: kindness and clear thinking. At first these two remained more or less distinct; when I felt triumphant I believed most in clear thinking, and in the opposite mood I believed most in kindness. Gradually, the two have come more and more together in my feelings. I find that much unclear thought exists as an excuse for cruelty, and that much cruelty is prompted by superstitious beliefs. The War made me vividly aware of the cruelty in human nature, but I hoped for a reaction when the War was over. Russia made me feel that little was to be hoped from revolt against existing governments in the way of an increase of kindness in the world, except possibly in regard to children. The cruelty to children involved in conventional methods of education is appalling, and I have been amazed at the horror which is felt against those who propose a kinder system.

As a patriot I am depressed by the downfall of England, as yet only partial, but likely to be far more complete before long. The history of England for the last four hundred years is in my blood, and I should have wished to hand on to my son the tradition of public spirit which has in the past been valuable. In the world that I foresee there will be no place for this tradition, and he will be lucky if he escapes with his life. The feeling of impending doom gives a kind of futility to all activities whose field is in England.

In the world at large, if civilisation survives, I foresee the domination of either America or Russia, and in either case of a system where a tight organisation subjects the individual to the State so completely that splendid individuals will be no longer possible.

And what of philosophy ? The best years of my life were given to the Principles of Mathematics, in the hope of finding somewhere some certain knowledge. The whole of this effort, in spite of three big volumes, ended inwardly in doubt and bewilderment. As regards metaphysics, when, under the influence of Moore, I first threw off the belief in German idealism, I experienced the delight of believing that the sensible world is real. Bit by bit, chiefly under the influence of physics, this delight has faded, and I have been driven to a position not unlike that of Berkeley, without his God and his Anglican complacency.

When I survey my life, it seems to me to be a useless one, devoted to impossible ideals. I have not found in the post-war world any attainable ideals to replace those which I have come to think unattainable. So far as the things I have cared for are concerned, the world seems to me to be entering upon a period of darkness. When Rome fell, St Augustine, a Bolshevik of the period, could console himself with a new hope, but my outlook upon my own time is less like his than like that of the unfortunate Pagan philosophers of the time of Justinian, whom Gibbon describes as seeking asylum in Persia, but so disgusted by what they saw there that they returned to Athens, in spite of the Christian bigotry which forbade them to teach. Even they were more fortunate than I am in one respect, for they had an intellectual faith which remained firm. They entertained no doubt as to the greatness of Plato. For my part, I find in the most modern thought a corrosive solvent of the great systems of even the recent past, and I do not believe that the constructive efforts of present-day philosophers and men of science have anything approaching the validity that attaches to their destructive criticism.

My activities continue from force of habit, and in the company of others I forget the despair which underlies my daily pursuits and pleasure. But when I am alone and idle, I cannot conceal for myself that my life had no purpose, and that I know of no new purpose to which to devote my remaining years. I find myself involved in a vast mist of solitude both emotional and metaphysical, from which I can find no issue.

[June 11, 1931.]

LETTERS

From Joseph Conrad

Oswalds
Bishopsbourne, Kent
Oct. 23rd. 1922

My Dear Russell
When your book[1] arrived we were away for a few days. Perhaps *les*

[1] *The Problem of China.*

convenances demanded that I should have acknowledged the receipt at once. But I preferred to read it before I wrote. Unluckily a very unpleasant affair was sprung on me and absorbed all my thinking energies for a fortnight. I simply did not attempt to open the book till all the worry and flurry was over, and I could give it two clear days.

I have always liked the Chinese, even those that tried to kill me (and some other people) in the yard of a private house in Chantabun, even (but not so much) the fellow who stole all my money one night in Bankok, but brushed and folded my clothes neatly for me to dress in the morning, before vanishing into the depths of Siam. I also received many kindnesses at the hands of various Chinese. This with the addition of an evening's conversation with the secretary of His Excellency Tseng on the verandah of an hotel and a perfunctory study of a poem, *The Heathen Chinee*, is all I know about Chinese. But after reading your extremely interesting view of the Chinese Problem I take a gloomy view of the future of their country.

He who does not see the truth of your deductions can only be he who does not want to see. They strike a chill into one's soul especially when you deal with the American element. That would indeed be a dreadful fate for China or any other country. I feel your book the more because the only ray of hope you allow is the advent of international socialism, the sort of thing to which I cannot attach any sort of definite meaning. I have never been able to find in any man's book or any man's talk anything convincing enough to stand up for a moment against my deep-seated sense of fatality governing this man-inhabited world. After all it is but a system, not very recondite and not very plausible. As a mere reverie it is not of a very high order and wears a strange resemblance to a hungry man's dream of a gorgeous feast guarded by a lot of beadles in cocked hats. But I know you wouldn't expect me to put faith in *any* system. The only remedy for Chinamen and for the rest of us is the change of hearts, but looking at the history of the last 2000 years there is not much reason to expect that thing, even if man has taken to flying – a great 'uplift', no doubt, but no great change. He doesn't fly like an eagle; he flies like a beetle. And you must have noticed how ugly, ridiculous and fatuous is the flight of a beetle.

Your chapter on Chinese character is the sort of marvellous achievement that one would expect from you. It may not be complete. That I don't know. But as it stands, in its light touch and profound insight, it seems to me flawless. I have no difficulty in accepting it, because I do believe in amenity allied to barbarism, in compassion co-existing with complete brutality, and in essential rectitude underlying the most obvious corruption. And on this last point I would offer for your reflection that we ought not to attach too much importance to that trait of character – just because it is *not* a trait of character! At any rate no more than in other races of mankind. Chinese corruption is, I suspect, institutional: a mere method of paying salaries. Of course it was very dangerous. And in that respect the Imperial Edicts recommending honesty failed to affect the agents of the Government. But Chinese, essentially, are creatures of Edicts and in every other sphere their characteristic is, I should say, scrupulous honesty.

There is another suggestion of yours which terrifies me, and arouses my compassion for the Chinese, even more than the prospect of an Americanised China. It is your idea of some sort of selected council, the strongly disciplined society arriving at decisions etc. etc. (p. 244). If a constitution proclaimed in the light of day, with at least a chance of being understood by the people is not to be relied on, then what trust could one put in a self-appointed and probably secret association (which from the nature of things must be above the law) to commend or condemn individuals or institutions? As it is unthinkable that you should be a slave to formulas or a victim of self-delusion, it is with the greatest diffidence that I raise my protest against your contrivance which must *par la force des choses* and by the very manner of its inception become but an association of mere swelled-heads of the most dangerous kind. There is not enough honour, virtue and selflessness *in the world* to make any such council other than the greatest danger to every kind of moral, mental and political independence. It would become a centre of delation, intrigue and jealousy of the most debased kind. No freedom of thought, no peace of heart, no genius, no virtue, no individuality trying to raise its head above the subservient mass, would be safe before the domination of such a council, and the unavoidable demoralisation of the instruments of its power. For, I must suppose that you mean it to have power and to have agents to exercise that power – or else it would become as little substantial as if composed of angels of whom ten thousand can sit on the point of a needle. But I wouldn't trust a society of that kind even if composed of angels ... More! I would not, my dear friend, (to address you in Salvation Army style) trust that society if Bertrand Russell himself were, after 40 days of meditation and fasting, to undertake the selection of the members. After saying this I may just as well resume my wonted calm; for, indeed, I could not think of any stronger way of expressing my utter dislike and mistrust of such an expedient for working out the salvation of China.

I see in this morning's *Times* (this letter was begun yesterday) a leader on your *Problem of China* which I hope will comfort and sustain you in the face of my savage attack. I meant it to be deadly; but I perceive that on account of my age and infirmities there was never any need for you to fly the country or ask for police protection. You will no doubt be glad to hear that my body is disabled by a racking cough and

398 The Autobiography of Bertrand Russell

my enterprising spirit irretrievably tamed by an unaccountable depression. Thus are the impious stricken, and things of the order that
'passeth understanding' brought home to one! . . . But I will not treat
you to a meditation on my depression. That way madness lies.

Your – truly Christian in its mansuetude – note has just reached me.
I admire your capacity for forgiving sinners, and I am warmed by the
glow of your friendliness. But I protest against your credulity in the
matter of newspaper pars. I did not know I was to stay in town to
attend rehearsals. Which is the rag that decreed it I wonder ? The fact
is I came up for just 4 hours and 20 min. last Wednesday; and that I
may have to pay another visit to the theatre (the whole thing is like an
absurd dream) one day this week. You can not doubt *mon Compère*
that I *do* want to see the child whose advent has brought about this
intimate relation between us. But I shrink from staying the night in
town. In fact I am afraid of it. This is no joke. Neither is it a fact that
I would shout on housetops. I am confiding it to you as a sad truth.
However – this cannot last; and before long I'll make a special trip to
see you all on an agreed day. Meantime my love to him – special and
exclusive. Please give my duty to your wife as politeness dictates and –
as my true feelings demand – remember me most affectionately to *ma
très honorée Commère*. And pray go on cultivating forgiveness towards
this insignificant and unworthy person who dares to subscribe himself

> *Always yours*
> *Joseph Conrad*

From Wm. F. Philpott   Chelsea, S.W.
                                        14.11.22

Dear Sir
    Herewith I return some of the literature you have sent for my
perusal.
    One of the papers says 'Why do thinking people vote Labor'.
    Thinking people don't vote Labor at all, it is only those who cannot
see beyond their nose who vote Labor.
    According to your Photo it does not look as though it is very long
since you left your cradle so I think you would be wise to go home and
suck your titty. The Electors of Chelsea want a man of experience to
represent them. Take my advice and leave Politics to men of riper
years. If you cannot remember the Franco Prussian War of 1870 or the
Russo Turkish War of 1876/7 then you are not old enough to be a
Politician.
    I can remember both those Wars and also the War of –/66 when the
Battle of Sadowa was fought.
    England had men of experience to represent them then.

I am afraid we shall never get anyone like Lord Derby (The Rupert of Debate) and Dizzy to lead us again.

Yours obedy
Wm. F. Philpott

Parliamentary General Election, 15th November, 1922

To the Electors of Chelsea

Dear Sir or Madam

At the invitation of the Executive Committee of the Chelsea Labour Party, I come before you as Labour candidate at the forthcoming General Election. I have been for many years a member of the Independent Labour Party, and I am in complete agreement with the programme of the Labour Party as published on October 26.

The Government which has been in power ever since the Armistice has done nothing during the past four years to restore normal life to Europe. Our trade suffers because our customers are ruined. This is the chief cause of the unemployment and destitution, unparalleled in our previous history, from which our country has suffered during the past two years. If we are to regain any measure of prosperity, the first necessity is a wise and firm foreign policy, leading to the revival of Eastern and Central Europe, and avoiding such ignorant and ill-considered adventures as nearly plunged us into war with the Turks. The Labour Party is the only one whose foreign policy is sane and reasonable, the only one which is likely to save Britain from even worse disasters than those already suffered. The new Government, according to the statement of its own supporters, does not differ from the old one on any point of policy. The country had become aware of the incompetence of the Coalition Government, and the major part of its supporters hope to avert the wrath of the electors by pretending to be quite a different firm. It is an old device – a little too old to be practised with success at this time of day. Those who see the need of new policies must support new men, not the same men under a new label.

There is need of drastic economy, but not at the expense of the least fortunate members of the community, and above all not at the expense of education and the care of children, upon which depends the nation's future. What has been thrown away in Irak and Chanak and such places has been wasted utterly, and it is in these directions that we must look for a reduction in our expenditure.

I am a strong supporter of the capital levy, and of the nationalisation of mines and railways, with a great measure of control by the workers in those industries. I hope to see similar measures adopted, in the course of time, in other industries.

The housing problem is one which must be dealt with at the earliest possible moment. Something would be done to alleviate the situation by the taxation of land values, which would hinder the holding up of vacant land while the owner waits for a good price. Much could be done if public bodies were to eliminate capitalists' profits by employing the Building Guild. By these methods, or by whatever methods prove available, houses must be provided to meet the imperative need.

The main cure for unemployment must be the improvement of our trade by the restoration of normal conditions on the Continent. In the meantime, it is unjust that those who are out of work through no fault of their own should suffer destitution; for the present, therefore, I am in favour of the continuation of unemployed benefit.

I am in favour of the removal of all inequalities in the law as between men and women. In particular, I hold that every adult citizen, male or female, ought to be entitled to a vote.

As a result of mismanagement since the armistice, our country and the world are faced with terrible dangers. The Labour Party has a clear and sane policy for dealing with these dangers. I am strongly opposed to all suggestions of violent revolution, and I am persuaded that only by constitutional methods can a better state of affairs be brought about. But I see no hope of improvement from parties which advocate a continuation of the muddled vindictiveness which has brought Europe to the brink of ruin. For the world at large, for our own country, and for every man, woman and child in our country, the victory of Labour is essential. On these grounds I appeal for your votes.

Bertrand Russell

From G. B. Shaw

10 Adelphi Terrace, W.C.2
[1922]

Dear Russell

I should say yes with pleasure if the matter were in my hands; but, as you may imagine, I have so many calls that I must leave it to the Labor Party, acting through the Fabian Society as far as I am concerned, to settle where I shall go. You had better therefore send in a request at once to the Fabian Society, 25 Tothill Street, Westminster, S.W.1. for a speech from me.

I must warn you, however, that though, when I speak, the hall is generally full, and the meeting is apparently very successful, the people who run after and applaud me are just as likely to vote for the enemy, or not vote at all, on polling day. I addressed 13 gorgeous meetings at the last election; but not one of my candidates got in.

Faithfully
G. Bernard Shaw

P.S. As you will see, this is a circular letter, which I send only because it explains the situation. Nothing is settled yet except that I am positively engaged on the 2nd, 3rd and 10th.

I suppose it is too late to urge you not to waste any of your own money on Chelsea, where no Progressive has a dog's chance. In Dilke's day it was Radical; but Lord Cadogan rebuilt it fashionably and drove all the Radicals across the bridges to Battersea. It is exasperating that a reasonably winnable seat has not been found for you. I would not spend a farthing on it myself, even if I could finance the 400 or so Labor candidates who would like to touch me for at least a fiver apiece.

| From and to Jean Nicod | France |
| | 15 June [1919] |

Dear Mr Russell

We shall come with joy. We are both so happy to see you. How nice of you to ask us!

I have not written to you all this time because I was doing nothing good, and was in consequence a little ashamed.

Your *Justice in War Time* is slowly appearing in *La Forge*, and is intended to be published in book-form afterwards. I ought to have done better, I think.

And I have done no work, only studied some physics. I have been thinking a tremendous time on the External World, with no really clear results. Also, I have been yearning in vain to help it *à faire peau neuve*.

So you will see us coming at the beginning of September at Lulworth. We feel quite elated at the thought of being some time with you.

> *Yours very sincerely*
> *Jean Nicod*

> 53 rue Gazan
> Paris XIV*e*
> 28th September 1919

Dear Mr Russell

I could not see Romain Rolland, who is not in Paris now. I shall write to him and send him your letter with mine.

We are not going to Rumania. I am going to Cahors to-morrow, and Thérèse is staying here. There is now a prospect of going to Brazil in eighteen months. Of course I am ceasing to believe in any of these things; but we are learning a great deal of geography.

I have definitely arranged to write a thesis on the external world. Part of it will be ready at Christmas, as I am being assured that I shall find very little work at Cahors.

We hope to hear that you are back in Cambridge now.
You know how glad we both are to have seen you again.

> Yours
> *Jean Nicod*

> 1, rue Pot Trinquat, Cahors
> 20 April [1920]

Dear Mr Russell

Here is the geometry of the fish, as you said you liked it. It will appear in the *Revue du Métaphysique,* but I cannot refrain from sending it to you now as a prolongation of our talk. I hope you will look through it, but please do not feel bound to write to me about it. I know you are very busy.

It was so nice of you to stop. When I heard that you were to come, it seemed like the realisation of a dream. This day with you has been a great joy to me.

> Yours very sincerely
> *Jean*

I do not want the MS. back.

> Campagne Saunex
> Prégny, Genève
> 22 Sept. 1921

Dear Mr Russell

Do you know that your death was announced in a Japanese paper ? I sent a telegram to the University of Peking, who answered 'Recovered' – but we were terribly anxious. We hope you are quite well again now.

I shall leave this office in February or March, with some money, and do nothing till next October at the very least. I do hope that I shall see you.

> Yours affectionately
> *Jean Nicod*

> 70, Overstrand Mansions
> Prince of Wales Road
> Battersea, S.W.11
> 2.10.21

Dear Nicod

I have sent your query to Whitehead, as I have forgotten his theory and never knew it very thoroughly. I will let you know his answer as soon as I get it. I *am* glad your book is so nearly done. *Please* let me see it when it is. – I know about the announcement of my death – it was a fearful nuisance. It was in the English and American papers too. I am practically well now but I came as near dying as one can without going over the edge – Pneumonia it was. I was delirious for three weeks, and I have no recollection of the time whatever, except a few dreams of negroes singing in deserts, and of learned bodies that I thought I had to address. The Doctor said to me afterwards: 'When you were ill you behaved like a true philosopher; every time that you came to yourself you made a joke.' I never had a compliment that pleased me more.

Dora and I are now married, but just as happy as we were before. We both send our love to you both. It *will* be delightful to see you when you leave Geneva. We shall be in London.

Yours aff.
Bertrand Russell

31 Sydney Street
London, S.W.3
13.9.23

Dear Nicod

I have been meaning to write to you for the last eight months, but have somehow never done so. Did Keynes ever answer your letter? He is now so busy with politics and money-making that I doubt if he ever thinks about probability. He has become enormously rich, and has acquired *The Nation*. He is Liberal, not Labour.

Principia Mathematica is being reprinted, and I am writing a new introduction, abolishing axiom of reducibility, and assuming that functions of props are always truth-functions, and functions of functions only occur through values of the functions and are always extensional. I don't know if these assumptions are true, but it seems worth while to work out their consequences.

What do you think of the enclosed proposal? I have undertaken to try to get articles. I asked if they would admit Frenchmen, and they say yes, if they write in German or English. Will you send me an article for them? I want to help them as much as I can. *Do*.

All goes well with us. Dora expects another child about Xmas time, and unfortunately I have to go to America to lecture for three months at the New Year.

The world gets more and more dreadful. What a misfortune not to have lived fifty years sooner. And now God has taken a hand at Tokyo. As yet, he beats human war-mongers, but they will equal him before long.

Yours ever
Bertrand Russell

From Moritz Schlick, founder of the Vienna Circle

> Philosophisches
> Institut der Universität
> in Wien
> Vienna, Sep. 9th 1923

Dear Mr Russell

Thank you most heartily for your kind letter. I was overjoyed to receive your affirmative answer. I feel convinced that the future of the magazine is safe since you have consented to lend your help by being one of the editors. It is a pity, of course, that you cannot send an article of your own immediately and that you have not much hope of getting contributions from your English and American friends during the next months, but we must be patient and shall be glad to wait till you have more time. I am sure that the scheme will work very well later on. It already means a great deal to know that we have your support, that your name will in some way be identified with the spirit of the magazine.

Thank you for your further suggestions. In my opinion contributions by M. Nicod would be most welcome, and I have no doubt that none of the editors would object to French articles, but unfortunately the publisher (who of course takes the business standpoint) has declared that at present he cannot possibly print anything in French, but I hope he will have nothing against publishing articles by French authors in the German or English language.

I have written to Reichenbach about your suggestion concerning the Polish logicians at Warsaw; I do not think there will be any political difficulties in approaching them. I believe we must be careful not to have too many articles dealing with mathematical logic or written in symbolic form in the first issues, as they might frighten away many readers, they must get used to the new forms gradually.

I have asked Reichenbach to send you some offprints of his chief papers; I hope you have received them by the time these lines reach you.

I should like to ask you some philosophical questions, but I am extremely busy just now. Our 'Internationale Hochschulkurse' are beginning this week, with lecturers and students from many countries. It would be splendid if you would be willing to come to Vienna on a similar occasion next year.

Thanking you again I remain

> *yours very sincerely*
> M. Schlick

From Jean Nicod

Chemin des Coudriers
Petit Saconnex, Genève
17 September, 1923

Dear Mr Russell

I should like very much to dedicate my book *La Géométrie dans le Monde sensible* to you. It is not very good; but I still hope that bits of it may be worth something. Will you accept it, such as it is? I have thought of the following inscription:

A mon maître
L'Honorable Bertrand Russell
Membre de la Société Royale d'Angleterre
en témoignage de reconnaissante affection

Can I let it go like that? The book is the chief one of my theses. The other one is *Le Problème logique de l'Induction*, which is a criticism of Keynes. I think I prove there that two instances differing only numerically (or in respects assumed to be immaterial) *do* count for more than one only; also, that Keynes' Limitation of Variety does *not* do what he thinks it does. Both books will be printed in three weeks or so (although they cannot be published till after their discussion en Sorbonne some time next winter).

I've sent my ms. to Keynes, offering to print his answer along with it. But he says he is too absorbed by other things; and altogether, I fear that he does not take me seriously – which is sad, because I am sure my objections well deserve to be considered.

Physically, I am settling down to a state which is not health, but which allows some measure of life, and may improve with time.

We hope you three are flourishing, and send you our love.

Jean Nicod

Chemin des Coudriers
Petit Saconnex, Genève
19 Sept. 1923

Dear Mr Russell

I got your letter the very morning I had posted mine to you.

I should love to write an article for this new review. But I have just sent one to the *Revue de Métaphysique* (on relations of values (i.e. truth values) and relations of meanings in Logic) and have nothing even half ready. I have been thinking of a sequel to my book, dealing with a universe of perspectives where objects are in motion (uniform) and Restricted Relativity applies, everything being as simple as possible. I would set forth what the observer (more like an angel than a man) would observe, and the order of his sensible world. What attracts me to that sort of thing is its quality of freshness of vision – to take stock of a world as of something entirely new. But it may well be rather childish, and I don't propose to go on with it until you have seen the book itself and tell me it is worth while.

Since you are re-publishing *Principia*, I may remind you that I have proved *both* Permutation *and* Association by help of the other three primitive props (Tautology, Addition, and the syllogistic prop.), where I only changed the order of some letters. It is in a Memoir I wrote for the BA degree. I have entirely forgotten how it is done, but I daresay I could find it again for you, if you wished to reduce your 5 prim. props to those three (observe there is one with one letter, one with two letters, and one with three letters).

Keynes did answer the letter I sent you. His answer convinced me I was right on both points; so I went on with my small book. It is a pity he will not do anything more for the theory of Induction.

Your son does look pleased with the stones he holds. His appearance is splendid.

We send our love.

> *Yours ever*
> *Jean Nicod*

From and to Thérèse Nicod

le 18 *février* [1924]

Dear Mr Russell

Jean has died on Saturday last after a short illness.

Je veux vous l'écrire pendant qu'il repose encore près de moi dans cette maison où il a tant travaillé, tant espéré guérir – et où nous avons été si heureux.

Vous savez combien il vous aimait – quelle lumière vous avez été pour lui – vous savez aussi l'être délicieux et noble qu'il était. C'est absolument déchirant.

Je voudrais avoir des nouvelles de Dora.

Affectueusement à vous deux.

> *Thérèse Nicod*

Genève 22 Juillet 1924

Dear Mr Russell

Please pardon me for not having thanked you sooner for the Preface (or introduction, we shall call it what you think best). I do not tell you how grateful I am to you because I know you did it for Jean.

I shall translate it as soon as I get some free time. We are absolutely loaded with things to do.

Of course your preface is everything and more that we could want it to be. I mean to say that it is very beautiful – How could I suggest a single alteration to it.

I remember that last winter I wrote to Jean that he was the most beautiful type of humanity I knew. (I do not recollect what about – We had outbreaks like that from time to time) and he answered immediately: '*Moi le plus beau type d'humanity que je connais c'est Russell.*'

Thank you again most deeply.

> *Yours very sincerely*
> *Thérèse Nicod*

> 12 *Chemin Thury*
> *Genève*
> *le* 19 *octobre* 1960

Cher Lord Russell

Permettez-moi de m'adresser à vous à travers toutes ces années. J'ai toujours eu l'intention de faire une réédition des thèses de Jean Nicod et je sais qu'aujourd'hui encore, sa pensée n'est pas oubliée. J'ai eu l'occasion de rencontrer dernièrement M. Jean Hyppolite, Directeur de l'Ecole normale supérieure qui m'a vivement conseillée de rééditer en premier Le problème logique de l'induction *dont il avait gardé un souvenir tout à fait précis et qu'il recommande aux jeunes philosophes.*

Parmi ceux qui m'ont donné le même conseil je citerai le Professeur Gonseth de Zurich, M. Gaston Bachelard, Jean Lacroix, etc. J'ai même trouvé, l'autre jour, par hasard, dans un manuel paru en 1959 un passage intitulé: 'Axiome de Nicod'.

L'ouvrage réédité paraîtrait à Paris, aux Presses universitaires de France, qui en assureront la diffusion.

Je viens vous demander, si vous jugez cette réédition opportune, de bien vouloir accepter d'écrire quelques lignes qui s'ajouteraient à la première préface de M. Lalande. Qui mieux que vous pourrait donner à ce tardif hommage le poids et l'envol ?

Veuillez, cher Lord Russell, recevoir l'assurance de ma profonde admiration et de mes sentiments respectueux.

> *Thérèse Nicod*

Je vous écris à une adresse qu'j'ai trouvée par hasard dans un magazine et dont je suis si peu sûre que je me permets de recommander le pli.

> Plas Penrhyn
> 1 November, 1960

Dear Thérèse Nicod

Thank you for your letter of October 19. I was very glad to have news of you. I entirely agree with you that it is very desirable to bring out a new edition of Nicod's work on induction which I think is very important and which has not received adequate recognition. I am quite willing to make a short addition to the preface by Monsieur Lalande. I suppose that you are in communication with Sir Roy Harrod (Christ Church, Oxford) who has been for some time concerned in obtaining a better English translation of Nicod's work than the one made long ago.

I was very sorry to hear of the death of your son.

If ever you are in England it would be a very great pleasure to see you.

> *Yours very sincerely*
> *Bertrand Russell*

From G. B. Shaw[1]

> Hotel Metropole
> Minehead, Somerset
> 11 April 1923

My dear Russell

The other day I read your laudably unapologetic *Apologia* from cover to cover with unflagging interest. I gather from your *Au Revoir* that it is to be continued in your next.

I was brought up – or left to bring myself up – on your father's plan all through. I can imagine nothing more damnable than the position of a boy started that way, and then, when he had acquired an adult free-thinking habit of mind and character, being thrust back into the P.L. sort of tutelage. You say you had a bad temper; but the fact that you neither burnt the lodge nor murdered Uncle Rollo is your eternal testimonial to the contrary.

No doubt Winchester saved Rollo and his shrine. Your description of the school is the only really descriptive description of one of the great boys farms I have ever read.

> *ever*
> *G. Bernard Shaw*

Extract from *Unity*, Chicago   19 Jun. 1924

Bertrand Russell has returned to England, and one of the most impressive tours ever made in this country by a distinguished foreigner has thus come to an end. Everywhere Professor Russell spoke, he was greeted by great audiences with rapturous enthusiasm, and listened to with a touching interest and reverence. At most of his meetings, admission was charged, frequently at regular theater rates, but this seemed to make no difference in the attendance. Throngs of eager men and women crowded the auditoriums where he appeared, and vied with one another in paying homage to the distinguished man whom they

[1] This letter was addressed to my brother and is about his *My Life and Adventures*, published 1923.

so honored. From this point of view, Bertrand Russell's visit was a triumph. From another and quite different point of view, it was a failure and disgrace! What was the great public at large allowed to know about this famous Englishman and the message which he brought across the seas to us Americans? Nothing! The silence of our newspapers was wellnigh complete. Only when Mr Russell got into a controversy with President Lowell, of Harvard, which gave opportunity to make the eagle scream, did his name or words appear in any conspicuous fashion in our public prints. The same journals which publish columns of stuff about millionaires, actors, singers, prizefighters and soldiers from abroad, and blazen forth their most casual comments about anything from women to the weather, reported almost nothing about this one of the most eminent Europeans of the day. But this is not the worst. Turn from the newspapers to the colleges and universities! Here is Mr Russell, the ablest and most famous mathematical philosopher of modern times – for long an honored Fellow of Cambridge, England – author of learned essays and treatises which are the standard authorities in their field – at the least, a great scholar, at the most, one of the greatest of scholars! But how many colleges in America officially invited him to their halls? How many gave him degrees of honor? So far as we know, Smith College was the only institution which officially received him as a lecturer, though we understand that he appeared also at the Harvard Union. Practically speaking, Professor Russell was ignored. A better measure of the ignorance, cowardice and Pharisaism of American academic life we have never seen!

From T. S. Eliot

> 9, Clarence Gate Gardens
> N.W.1
> 15.X.23

Dear Bertie

I was delighted to get your letter. It gives me very great pleasure to know that you like the *Waste Land*, and especially Part V which in my opinion is not only the best part, but the only part that justifies the whole, at all. It means a great deal to me that you like it.

I must tell you that 18 months ago, before it was published anywhere, Vivien wanted me to send you the MS. to read, because she was sure that you were one of the very few persons who might possibly see anything in it. But we felt that *you* might prefer to have nothing to do with *us*: It is absurd to say that we wished to drop you.

Vivien has had a frightful illness, and nearly died, in the spring – as Ottoline has probably told you. And that she has been in the country ever since. She has not yet come back.

Dinner is rather difficult for me at present. But might I come to tea with you on Saturday ? I should like to see you very much – there have been *many times* when I have thought that.

> *Yours ever*
> *T.S.E.*

> 9, Clarence Gate Gardens
> N.W.1
> 21 April. [1925]

Dear Bertie

If you are still in London I should very much like to see you.

My times and places are very restricted, but it is unnecessary to mention them unless I hear from you.

I want words from you which only you can give. But if you have now ceased to care at all about either of us, just write on a slip 'I do not care to see you' or 'I do not care to see either of you' – and I will understand.

In case of that, I will tell you now that everything has turned out as you predicted 10 years ago. You are a great psychologist.

> *Yours*
> *T.S.E.*

> *The Criterion*
> 17, Thavies Inn
> London, E.C.1
> 7 May [1925]

My dear Bertie

Thank you very much indeed for your letter. As you say, it is very difficult for you to make suggestions until I can see you. For instance, I don't know to what extent the changes which have taken place, since we were in touch with you, would seem to you material. What you suggest seems to me of course what should have been done years ago. Since then her[1] health is a thousand times worse. Her only alternative would be to live quite alone – if she could. And the fact that living with me has done her so much damage does not help me to come to any decision. I need the help of someone who understands her – I find her still perpetually baffling and deceptive. She seems to me like a child of 6 with an immensely clever and precocious mind. She writes *extremely* well (stories, etc.) and great originality. And I can never escape from the spell of her persuasive (even coercive) gift of argument.

Well, thank you very much, Bertie – I feel quite desperate. I hope to see you in the Autumn.

> *Yours ever*
> *T.S.E.*

[1] This refers to his first wife.

From my brother Frank

50 Cleveland Square
London, W.2
8 June, 1925

Dear Bertie

I lunched with the Aunt Agatha on Friday, and she was even more tedious than usual. In fact, she gave me the treatment that I think she generally reserves for you. She began by being very sighful and P.L.y about Alys, and said how she still loved you and how determined you had been to marry her. She infuriated me so that I reminded her at last that at the time the P.L. view, which she had fully shared, was that you were an innocent young man pursued by a designing woman, and that the one view was not any truer than the other. Then she went on to Birth Control, with a sniff at Dora, and aggravated me to such an extent that I was bound to tell her that I did not think old women of seventy-three were entitled to legislate for young ones of twenty-five. Thereupon she assured me that she had been twenty-five herself once, but I unfortunately lacked the courage to say Never! You can gather how provoking she must have been from the fact that I was driven to reply, which I don't generally do. She then went on to try and make mischief about you and Elizabeth, by telling me how much you were in love with Elizabeth and how regularly you saw her.[1] She really is a villainous old cat.

In order to take the taste of her out of my mouth when I got home I read, or at any rate looked through, three books I had not seen before: *Daedalus, Icarus* and *Hypatia.* Haldane's 'Test Tube Mothers' gave me the shivers: I prefer the way of the music-hall song! I liked what I read of Dora's book, and intend to read it more carefully.

Will you tell Dora that I am not the least anxious to go to the Fabian people, as it would bore me to tears, and would only have done it to back her up, so I hope she won't put anyone else on to me. Dora says you are fat, and something that at first I thought was 'beneath consideration', which gave me a faint hope that you had ceased to be a philosopher, but on looking at it again I see that it is 'writing about education'.

Dorothy Wrinch said that she was coming down to see you early in August, and I suggested driving her down, but I suppose that means taking old Heavyweight too. The time she suggested, shortly after the August Bank Holiday, would suit me if you could have me then. You will no doubt be surprised to hear that I am going to the British Ass. this year, as it is held at Southampton, quite convenient.

Damn that acid old spinster.

Yours affectionately
Russell

[1] This, of course, was quite untrue.

50 Cleveland Square
London, W.2
15 June, 1925

Dear Bertie

Thanks for your amusing letter. I was going to write to you anyhow, because I have been reading your delightful *What I believe*. My word! You have compressed it, and succeeded in saying a good many things calculated to be thoroughly annoying and disconcerting to the virtuous in the space. I am so delighted with it that I am going to get half-a-dozen copies and give them away where I think they will be appreciated. I like your conclusive proof that bishops are much more brutal than Aztecs who go in for human sacrifices. I don't think I shall try a copy on my tame bishop because, although I am very fond of him, intellect is not his strong point.

I am going to write to Dorothy and make your suggestion.

Yours affectionately
Russell

From Gertrude Beasly

8 Woburn Place, W.C.1
Gresham Hotel, London
June 21. 1925

Dear Mr Russell

Shortly after you left in March I found a publisher for my book, a semi-private company in Paris. Several weeks ago a few of the proofs reached me. Yesterday morning I found myself before the Magistrate at Bow Street after a night in prison.

In the afternoon of June 19 an officer from Scotland Yard called to see me bringing with him a bundle of the proofs of my book which he described as 'grossly obscene'. He said I would have to appear before the Magistrate on the charge of sending improper matter through the post. He examined my passport and found it had not been registered. I was arrested and escorted to Bow Street to register my passport, and detained over night. The Alien Officer brought a charge of failure to register my passport to which I pleaded guilty before the Magistrate and offered explanation of my negligence. The Scotland Yard agent brought a charge of sending obscene literature by post and asked the Magistrate to punish (I believe he said) and make arrangement for my deportation. The punishment, I believe, refers to a heavy fine or imprisonment.

I am on bail, 10 pounds, and the case is to be tried on Saturday June 27 at about 11 o'clock, I shall find out definitely tomorrow as to the hour.

Mr Ewer thinks he can find an attorney to take my case. I shall go to the American Consul tomorrow and talk with others here who know me. Shall probably see Dr Ellis tomorrow.

If you can offer any advice I shall be glad.

Sincerely yours
Gertrude Beasly

Miss Beasly was a schoolteacher from Texas, who wrote an autobiography. It was truthful, which is illegal.

To Max Newman, the distinguished mathematician

24th April 1928

Dear Newman

Many thanks for sending me the off-print of your article about me in *Mind*. I read it with great interest and some dismay. You make it entirely obvious that my statements to the effect that nothing is known about the physical world except its structure are either false or trivial, and I am somewhat ashamed at not having noticed the point for myself.

It is of course obvious, as you point out, that the only effective assertion about the physical world involved in saying that it is susceptible to such and such a structure is an assertion about its cardinal number. (This by the way is not quite so trivial an assertion as it would seem to be, if, as is not improbable, the cardinal number involved is finite. This, however, is not a point upon which I wish to lay stress.) It was quite clear to me, as I read your article, that I had not really intended to say what in fact I did say, that *nothing* is known about the physical world except its structure. I had always assumed spacio-temporal continuity with the world of percepts, that is to say, I had assumed that there might be co-punctuality between percepts and non-percepts, and even that one could pass by a finite number of steps from one event to another compresent with it, from one end of the universe to the other. And co-punctuality I regarded as a relation which might exist among percepts and is itself perceptible.

I have not yet had time to think out how far the admission of co-punctuality alone in addition to structure would protect me from your criticisms, nor yet how far it would weaken the plausibility of my metaphysic. What I did realise was that spacio-temporal continuity of percepts and non-percepts was so axiomatic in my thought that I failed to notice that my statements appeared to deny it.

I am at the moment much too busy to give the matter proper thought, but I should be grateful if you could find time to let me know whether you have any ideas on the matter which are not merely negative, since it does not appear from your article what your own position is. I gathered in talking with you that you favoured phenomenalism, but I do not quite know how definitely you do so.

Yours sincerely
Bertrand Russell

To Harold Laski

12th May 1928

My dear Laski

I am afraid it is quite impossible for me to speak to the Socratic Society this term, much as I should like to do so. But the fact is I am too busy to have any ideas worth having, like Mrs Eddy who told a friend of mine that she was too busy to become the second incarnation.

I am not at all surprised that Bentham suggests companionate marriage; in fact one could almost have inferred it. I discovered accidentally from an old envelope used as a bookmark that at the moment of my birth my father was reading Bentham's *Table of the Springs of Action*. Evidently this caused me to be Benthamitically 'conditioned', as he has always seemed to me a most sensible fellow. But as a schoolmaster, I am gradually being driven to more radical proposals, such as those of Plato. If there were an international government I should seriously be in favour of the root and branch abolition of the family, but as things are, I am afraid it would make people more patriotic.

Yours ever
Bertrand Russell

To Mr Gardner Jackson

28th May 1929

Dear Mr Jackson

I am sorry I shall not be in America at the time of your meeting on August 23rd, the more so as I shall be there not so very long after that. I think you are quite right to do everything possible to keep alive the memory of Sacco and Vanzetti. It must, I think, be clear to any unprejudiced person that there was not such evidence against them as to warrant a conviction, and I have no doubt in my own mind that they were wholly innocent. I am forced to conclude that they were condemned on account of their political opinions and that men who ought to have known better allowed themselves to express misleading views as to the evidence because they held that men with such opinions have no right to live. A view of this sort is one which is very dangerous, since it transfers from the theological to the political sphere a form of persecution which it was thought that civilised countries had outgrown. One is not so surprised at occurrences of this sort in Hungary or

Lithuania, but in America they must be matters of grave concern to all who care for freedom of opinion.

Yours sincerely
Bertrand Russell

P.S. I hope that out of the above you can make a message for the meeting; if you do not think it suitable, please let me know, and I will concoct another.

From and to Mr C. L. Aiken

8, Plympton St.
Cambridge, Mass.
March 2, 1930

My Dear Mr Russell

I am preparing a free-lance article on the subject of parasitic nuisances who bedevil authors: autograph and photograph hunters, those thoughtless myriads who expect free criticism, poems, speeches, lectures, jobs, and who in general impose on the literary professional. (I suppose you will place me in the same category, but hope you can feel that the end justifies the means in this case.)

Would you be so good as to send me an account of your grievances, the length and nature of which of course I leave to you?

Very truly yours
Clarice Lorenz Aiken

19th March 1930

Dear Mr Aiken

In common with other authors, I suffer a good deal from persons who think that an author ought to do their work for them. Apart from autograph hunters, I get large numbers of letters from persons who wish me to copy out for them the appropriate entry in *Who's Who*, or ask me my opinion on points which I have fully discussed in print.

I get many letters from Hindus, beseeching me to adopt some form of mysticism, from young Americans, asking me where I think the line should be drawn in petting, and from Poles, urging me to admit that while all other nationalism may be bad that of Poland is wholly noble.

I get letters from engineers who cannot understand Einstein, and from parsons who think that I cannot understand Genesis, from husbands whose wives have deserted them – not (they say) that that would matter, but the wives have taken the furniture with them, and what in these circumstances should an enlightened male do?

I get letters from Jews to say that Solomon was not a polygamist, and from Catholics to say that Torquemada was not a persecutor. I get letters (concerning whose genuineness I am suspicious) trying to get me to advocate abortion, and I get letters from young mothers asking my opinion of bottle-feeding.

I am sorry to say that most of the subjects dealt with by my correspondents have escaped my memory at the moment, but the few that I have mentioned may serve as a sample.

> *Yours very truly*
> *Bertrand Russell*

To Miss Brooks[1]

5th May 1930

Dear Miss Brooks

I am not sure whether you are right in saying that the problem of America is greater than that of China. It is likely that America will be more important during the next century or two, but after that it may well be the turn of China. I think America is very worrying. There is something incredibly wrong with human relations in your country. We have a number of American children at our school, and I am amazed at their mothers' instinctive incompetence. The fount of affection seems to have dried up. I suppose all Western civilisation is going to go the same way, and I expect all our Western races to die out, with the possible exception of the Spaniards and Portuguese. Alternatively the State may take to breeding the necessary citizens and educating them as Janissaries without family ties. Read John B. Watson on mothers. I used to think him mad; now I only think him American; that is to say, the mothers that he has known have been American mothers. The result of this physical aloofness is that the child grows up filled with hatred against the world and anxious to distinguish himself as a criminal, like Leopold and Loeb.

> *Yours sincerely*
> *Bertrand Russell*

Here is part of the preface I wrote:

In view of the aggression of Western nations, the Chinese who were in many respects more civilised than ourselves and at a higher ethical level, were faced with the necessity of developing a policy with more military efficacy than could be derived from the Confucian teaching. Social life in Old China was based upon the family. Sun Yat Sen justly perceived that if China was to resist successfully the onslaughts of military nations, it would be necessary to substitute the state for the family; and patriotism for filial piety – in a word, the Chinese had to choose whether they would die as saints or live as sinners. Under Christian influence they chose the latter alternative.

[1] Who became the Rev. Rachel Gleason Brooks, for whose still unpublished book on China I in 1931 wrote a preface.

Assuming the nationalist (Chiang Kai Shek) government to be successful, the outcome must be to add another and very important member to the ruthless militaristic governments which compete in everything except the destruction of civilisation on which task alone they are prepared to cooperate. All the intellect, all the heroism, all the martyrdoms, and agonising disillusionments of Chinese history since 1911, will have led up only to this: to create a new force for evil and a new obstacle to the peace of the world. The history of Japan should have taught the West caution. But Western civilisation with all its intelligence is as blind in its operation as an avalanche, and must take its course to what dire conclusion, I dare not guess.

In her book This is Your Inheritance: A History of the Chemung County, N.Y. Branch of the Brooks Family *(p. 167, published by Century House, Watkins Glen, New York, U.S.A., 1963) she wrote: 'Bertrand Russell's preface (omitting the laudatory remarks about the author) sums up what happened during our lifetime in China ... This preface was taken down by me in the parlor of the Mayflower hotel in Akron, Ohio on the morning of Dec. 1st, 1931 as Mr Russell paced the floor smoking his pipe. Then he signed it and we went to the railroad station; he to go to another lecturing appointment and I to return to Oberlin.'*

To H. G. Wells

24th May '28

My dear H.G.

Thank you very much for sending me your book on *The Open Conspiracy*. I have read it with the most complete sympathy, and I do not know of anything with which I agree more entirely. I enjoyed immensely your fable about Provinder Island. I am, I think, somewhat less optimistic than you are, probably owing to the fact that I was in opposition to the mass of mankind during the war, and thus acquired the habit of feeling helpless.

You speak for example, of getting men of science to join the Open Conspiracy, but I should think there is hardly a single one who would do so, with the exception of Einstein – a not unimportant exception I admit. The rest in this country would desire knighthoods, in France to become *membres de l'institut*, and so on. Even among younger men, I believe your support would be very meagre. Julian Huxley would not be willing to give up his flirtations with the episcopate; Haldane would not forego the pleasure to be derived from the next war.

I was interested to read what you say about schools and education generally, and that you advocate 'a certain sectarianism of domestic and social life in the interests of its children' and 'grouping of its families and the establishment of its own schools'. It was the feeling of this necessity which led us to found Beacon Hill School, and I am every day more convinced that people who have the sort of ideas that we have ought not to expose their children to obscurantist influence, more especially during their early years when these influences can operate upon what will be their unconscious in adult life.

This brings me to a matter which I approach with some hesitation, but which I had decided to write to you about before I read your book. This school is costing me about £2000 a year, that is to say very nearly the whole of my income. I do not think that this is due to any incompetence in management; in fact all experimental schools that I have ever heard of have been expensive propositions. My income is precarious since it depends upon the tastes of American readers who are notoriously fickle, and I am therefore very uncertain as to whether I shall be able to keep the school going. In order to be able to do so I should need donations amounting to about £1000 a year. I have been wondering whether you would be willing to help in any way towards the obtaining of this sum, either directly or by writing an appeal which might influence progressive Americans. I should be very grateful if you would let me know whether you would consider anything of the sort. You will see of course that an appeal written by Dora and me is less effective than one from an impartial pen, especially if that pen were yours.

I believe profoundly in the importance of what we are doing here. If I were to put into one single phrase our educational objects, I should say that we aim at training initiative without diminishing its strength. I have long held that stupidity is very largely the result of fear leading to mental inhibitions, and the experience that we are having with our children confirms me in this view. Their interest in science is at once passionate and intelligent, and their desire to understand the world in which they live exceeds enormously that of children brought up with the usual taboos upon curiosity. What we are doing is of course only an experiment on a small scale, but I confidently expect its results to be very important indeed. You will realise that hardly any other educational reformers lay much stress upon intelligence. A. S. Neill, for example, who is in many ways an admirable man, allows such complete liberty that his children fail to get the necessary training and are always going to the cinema, when they might otherwise be interested in things of more value. Absence of opportunity for exciting pleasures at this place is, I think, an important factor in the development of the children's intellectual interests. I note what you say in your book on the subject of amusements, and I agree with it very strongly.

I hope that if you are back in England you will pay a visit to this school and see what we are doing.

Yours very sincerely
Bertrand Russell

From and to A. S. Neill, the progressive schoolmaster

Summerhill,
Lyme Regis, Dorset
23.3.26

Dear Mr Russell

I marvel that two men, working from different angles, should arrive at essentially the same conclusions. Your book and mine are complementary. It may be that the only difference between us comes from our respective complexes. I observe that you say little or nothing about handwork in education. My hobby has always been handwork, and where your child asks you about stars my pupils ask me about steels and screw threads. Possibly also I attach more importance to emotion in education than you do.

I read your book with great interest and with very little disagreement. Your method of overcoming your boy's fear of the sea I disagreed with heartily! An introverted boy might react with the thought: 'Daddy wants to drown me.' My complex again . . . arising from my dealing with neurotics mostly.

I have no first-hand knowledge of early childhood, for I am so far unmarried, but your advices about early childhood seem to me to be excellent. Your attitude to sex instruction and masturbation is splendid and you put it in a way that will not shock and offend. (I have not that art!)

I do not share your enthusiasm for Montessori. I cannot agree with a system set up by a strong churchwoman with a strict moral aim. Her orderliness to me is a counterblast against original sin. Besides I see no virtue in orderliness at all. My workshop is always in a mess but my handwork isn't. My pupils have no interest in orderliness until they come to puberty or thereabouts. You may find that at the age of five your children will have no use for Montessori apparatus. Why *not* use the apparatus to make a train with? I argued this out with Madame Macaroni, Montessori's chief lieutenant a few years ago. Is it not our awful attitude to learning that warps our outlook? After all a train is a reality, while an inset frame is purely artificial. I never use artificial apparatus. My apparatus in the school is books, tools, test tubes, compasses. Montessori wants to direct a child. I don't.

By the way, to go back to the sea fear, I have two boys who never enter the water. My nephew age nine (the watch-breaker of the book) and an introverted boy of eleven who is full of fears. I have advised the other children to make no mention of the sea, never to sneer at the two, never to try and persuade them to bathe. If they do not come to bathing from their own inner *Drang* . . . well, it does not much matter. One of my best friends, old Dauvit in my native village, is 89 and he never had a bath in his life.

You will be interested to know Homer Lane's theory about time-table sucking. He used to advocate giving a child the breast whenever it demanded it. He held that in sucking there are two components . . . pleasure and nutrition. The timetable child accumulates both components, and when the sucking begins the pleasure component goes away with a rush and is satisfied in a sort of orgasm. But the nutrition element is unsatisfied, and he held that many cases of mal-nutrition were due to this factor, that the child stopped sucking before the nutrition urge was satisfied.

To me the most interesting thing about your book is that it is scholarly (nasty word) in the sense that it is written by a man who knows history and science. I am ignorant of both and I think that my own conclusions come partly from a blind intuition. I say again that it is marvellous that we should reach very much the same philosophy of education. It is the only possible philosophy today, but we cannot hope to do much in the attack against schools from Eton to the LCC. Our only hope is the individual parent.

My chief difficulty is the parent, for my pupils are products of ignorant and savage parents. I have much fear that one or two of them, shocked by my book, may withdraw their children. That would be tragedy.

Well, thank you ever so much for the book. It is the only book on education that I have read that does not make me swear. All the others are morals disguised as education.

One warning however . . . there is always the chance that your son may want to join the Primrose League one day! One in ten million chance, but we must face the fact that human nature has not yet fitted into any cause and effect scheme; and never will fit in.

If you ever motor to your Cornwall home do stop and see us here.

Yours very truly
A. S. Neill

Summerhill School
Leiston, Suffolk
18.12.30

Dear Russell

Have you any political influence? The Labour Ministry are refusing to let me employ a Frenchman to teach French. The chap I want is with me now, has been analysed and is a tiptop man to deal with my bunch of problem kids. Other schools have natives to teach their languages ... and I naturally ask why the hell a damned department should dictate to me about my educational ways. I have given the dept a full account of the man and why he is necessary to me and the fools reply: 'But the Dept is not satisfied that a British subject could not be trained in the special methods of teaching in operation in your school.'

Have you any political bigbug friend who would or could get behind the bloody idiots who control our departments ? I am wild as hell.

Cheerio, help me if you can. I know George Lansbury but hesitate to approach him as he will have enough to do in his own dept.

> *Yours*
> *A. S. Neill*

20th Dec. 30

Dear Neill

What you tell me is quite outrageous. I have written to Charles Trevelyan and Miss Bondfield, and I enclose copies of my letters to them.

I wonder whether you make the mistake of mentioning psycho-analysis in your application. You know, of course, from Homer Lane's case that policemen regard psycho-analysis as merely a cloak for crime. The only ground to put before the department is that Frenchmen are apt to know French better than Englishmen do. The more the department enquires into your methods, the more it will wish to hamper you. Nobody is allowed to do any good in this country except by means of trickery and deceit.

> *Yours ever*
> *Bertrand Russell*

To Charles Trevelyan

20th Dec. 30

Dear Trevelyan

A. S. Neill, of Summerhill School, Leiston, Suffolk, who is, as you probably know, very distinguished in the educational world, having developed from a conventional school dominie into one of the most original and successful innovators of our time, writes to me to say that the Ministry of Labour is refusing to allow him to continue to employ Frenchmen to teach French. He has at present a French master whose services he wishes to retain, but the Ministry of Labour has officially informed him that Englishmen speak French just as well as Frenchmen do, and that his present master is not to be allowed to stay.

I think you will agree with me that this sort of thing is intolerable. I know that many of the most important questions in education do not come under your department but are decided by policemen whose judgment is taken on the question whether a foreigner is needed in an educational post. If the principles upon which the Alien Act is administered had been applied in Italy in the 15th century, the Western world would never have acquired a knowledge of Greek and the Renaissance could not have taken place.

Although the matter is outside your department, I cannot doubt that the slightest word from you would cause the Ministry of Labour to alter its decision. A. S. Neill is a man of international reputation, and I hate the thought of what he may do to hold up British Bumbledom to ridicule throughout the civilised world. If you could do anything to set the matter right, you will greatly relieve my anxiety on this score.

> *Yours very sincerely*
> *Bertrand Russell*

P.S. I have also written to Miss Bondfield on this matter.

From and to A. S. Neill

> Summerhill School
> Leiston, Suffolk
> 22.12.30

Dear Russell

Good man! That's the stuff to give the troops. Whatever the result accept my thanks. I didn't mention psychoanalysis to them. I applied on the usual form and they wrote asking me what precise steps I had taken 'to find a teacher of French who was British or an alien already resident in this country'. Then I told them that I wanted a Frenchman but that any blinking Frenchie wouldn't do ... that mine was a psychological school and any teacher had to be not only an expert in his subject but also in handling neurotic kids.

Apart from this display of what you call Bumbledom I guess that there will be some battle when Trevelyan's Committee on Private Schools issues its report. You and I will have to fight like hell against having a few stupid inspectors mucking about demanding why Tommy can't read. Any inspector coming to me now would certainly be greeted by Colin (aged 6) with the friendly words, 'Who the fucking hell are you?' So that we must fight to keep Whitehall out of our schools.

I'll let you know what happens.

Many thanks,

> *Yours*
> *A. S. Neill*

About time that you and I met again and compared notes.

> Leiston. 31.12.30

Dear Russell

You have done the deed. The letter [from the Ministry of Labour] is a nasty one but I guess that the bloke as wrote it was in a nasty position. Sounds to me like a good prose Hymn of Hate.

I have agreed to his conditions . . . feeling like slapping the blighter in the eye at the same time. It is my first experience with the bureaucracy and I am apt to forget that I am dealing with a machine.

Many thanks for your ready help. My next approach to you may be when the Committee on Private Schools gets busy. They will call in all the respectable old deadheads of education as expert witnesses (Badley and Co) and unless men of moment like you make a fight for it we (the out and outer Bolshies of education) will be ignored. Then we'll have to put up with the nice rules advocated by the diehards. Can't we get up a league of heretical dominies called the 'Anal'-ists?

> *Yours with much gratitude*
> *A. S. Neill*

5th Jan. 31

Dear Neill

Thank you for your letter and for the information about your French teacher. I am sorry you accepted the Ministry of Labour's terms, as they were on the run and could, I think, have been induced to grant unconditional permission.

I suppose you do not mind if I express to Miss Bondfield my low opinion of her officials, and to Trevelyan my ditto of Miss Bondfield? It is quite possible that the Ministry may still decide to let you keep your present master indefinitely. I am going away for a short holiday, and I am therefore dictating these letters now to my secretary who will not send them until she hears from you that you are willing they should go. Will you therefore be so kind as to send a line to her (Mrs O. Harrington), and not to me, as to whether you are willing the letters should go.

> *Yours ever*
> *Bertrand Russell*

Neill agreed to my sending the following letters:

To Miss Bondfield

12th Jan. 31

Dear Miss Bondfield

I am much obliged to you for looking into the matter of Mr A. S. Neill's French teacher. I doubt whether you are aware that in granting him permission to retain his present teacher for one year your office made it a condition that he should not even ask to retain his present teacher after the end of that year.

I do not believe that you have at any time been in charge of a school, but if you had, you would know that to change one's teachers once a year is to increase enormously the difficulty of achieving any kind of success. What would the headmaster of one of our great public schools say to your office if it were to insist that he should change his teachers once a year? Mr Neill is attempting an experiment which everybody interested in modern education considers very important, and it seems a pity that the activities of the Government in regard to him should be confined to making a fair trial of the experiment impossible. I have no doubt whatever that you will agree with me in this, and that some subordinate has failed to carry out your wishes in this matter.

With apologies for troubling you,

> *I remain*
> *Yours sincerely*
> *Bertrand Russell*

To Charles Trevelyan

12th Jan. 31

Dear Charles

Thank you very much for the trouble you have taken in regard to the French teacher at A. S. Neill's school. The Ministry of Labour have granted him permission to stay for one year, but on condition that Neill does not ask to have his leave extended beyond that time. You will, I think, agree with me that this is an extraordinary condition to have made. Neill has accepted it, as he has to yield to *force majeure*, but there cannot be any conceivable justification for it. Anybody who has ever run a school knows that perpetual change of masters is intolerable. What would the Headmaster of Harrow think if the Ministry of Labour obliged him to change his masters once a year?

Neill is trying an experiment which everybody interested in education considers most important, and Whitehall is doing what it can to make it a failure. I do not myself feel bound by Neill's undertaking, and I see no reason why intelligent people who are doing important work should submit tamely to the dictation of ignorant busybodies, such as the officials in the Ministry of Labour appear to be. I am quite sure that you agree with me in this.

Thanking you again,

> *Yours very sincerely*
> *Bertrand Russell*

To and from A. S. Neill

27th Jan. 31

Dear Neill

As you will see from the enclosed, there is nothing to be got out of the Ministry of Labour.

I have written a reply which I enclose, but I have not sent it. If you think it will further your case, you are at liberty to send it; but remember Miss Bondfield is celibate.

Yours ever
Bertrand Russell

The enclosed reply to the Ministry of Labour:

27th Jan. 31

Dear Sir

Thank you very much for your letter of January 26th. I quite understand the principle of confining employment as far as possible to the British without regard for efficiency. I think, however, that the Ministry is not applying the principle sufficiently widely. I know many Englishmen who have married foreigners, and many English potential wives who are out of a job. Would not a year be long enough to train an English wife to replace the existing foreign one in such cases?

Yours faithfully
Bertrand Russell

Summerhill School
Leiston, Suffolk
28.1.31

Dear Russell

No, there is no point in replying to the people. Very likely the chief aim in govt offices is to save the face of the officials. If my man wants to stay on later I may wangle it by getting him to invest some cash in the school and teach on AS AN EMPLOYER of labour. Anyway you accomplished a lot as it is. Many thanks. I think I'll vote Tory next time!

Today I have a letter from the widow of Norman MacMunn. She seems to be penniless and asks me for a job as matron. I can't give her one and don't suppose you can either. I have advised her to apply to our millionaire friends in Dartington Hall. I am always sending on the needy to them . . . hating them all the time for their affluence. When Elmhirst needs a new wing he writes out a cheque to Heals . . . Heals! And here am I absolutely gravelled to raise cash for a pottery shed. Pioneering is a wash out, man. I am getting weary of cleaning up the mess that parents make. At present I have a lad of six who shits his pants six times daily . . . his dear mamma 'cured' him by making him eat the shit. I get no gratitude at all . . . when after years of labour I cure this lad the mother will send him to a 'nice' school. It ain't good enough . . . official indifference or potential enmity, parental jealousy

... the only joy is in the kids themselves. One day I'll chuck it all and start a nice hotel round about Salzburg.

You'll gather that I am rather fed this morning. I'd like to meet you again and have a yarn. Today my *Stimmung* is partly due to news of another debt ... £150 this last year all told. All parents whose problems I bettered.

> *Yours*
> *A. S. Neill*

I wonder what Margaret Bondfield's views would be on my views on Onanie!

31st Jan. 31

Dear Neill

I am sorry you are feeling so fed up. It is a normal mood with me so far as the school is concerned. Parents owe me altogether about £500 which I shall certainly never see. I have my doubts as to whether you would find hotel keeping much better. You would find penniless pregnant unmarried women left on your hands, and would undertake the care of them and their children for the rest of their natural lives. You might find this scarcely more lucrative than a modern school. Nobody can make a living, except by dishonesty or cruelty, at no matter what trade.

It is all very sad about Elmhirst. However, I always think that a man who marries money has to work for his living. I have no room for a Matron at the moment, having at last obtained one who is completely satisfactory.

I have sometimes attempted in a mild way to get a little financial support from people who think they believe in modern education, but I have found the thing that stood most in my way was the fact which leaked out, that I do not absolutely insist upon strict sexual virtue on the part of the staff. I found that even people who think themselves quite advanced believe that only the sexually starved can exert a wholesome moral influence.

Your story about the boy who shits in his pants is horrible. I have not had any cases as bad as that to deal with.

I should very much like to see you again. Perhaps we could meet in London at some time or other ...

> *Yours*
> *Bertrand Russell*

From Mrs Bernard Shaw   Ayot St Lawrence
                                          Welwyn, Herts.
                                          28 Oct. 1928

Dear Bertrand Russell

I was grateful and *honoured* by your splendidness in sending me your MS. of your lecture and saying I may keep it. It's wonderful of you. I have read it once, and shall keep it as you permit until I have time for another good, quiet go at it.

You know you have a humble, but convinced admirer in me. I have a very strong mystical turn in me, which does not appear in public, and I find your stuff the best corrective and *steadier* I ever came across!

My best remembrances to you both. I hope the school is flourishing.

                                Yours gratefully
                                C. F. Shaw

To C. P. Sanger   Telegraph House
                                            Harting, Petersfield
                                          23 Dec. 1929

My dear Charlie

I am very sorry indeed to hear that you are so ill. I do hope you will soon be better. Whenever the Doctors will let me I will come and see you. It is a year today since Kate's operation, when you were so kind – I remember how Kate loved your visits. Dear Charlie, I don't think I have ever expressed the deep affection I have for you, but I suppose you have known of it.

I got home three days ago and found everything here satisfactory. The children are flourishing, and it is delicious to be at home. One feels very far off in California and such places. I went to Salt Lake City and the Mormons tried to convert me, but when I found they forbade tea and tobacco I thought it was no religion for me.

My warmest good wishes for a speedy recovery,

                              Yours very affectionately
                              Bertrand Russell

From Lord Rutherford

                                        Newnham Cottage
                                        Queen's Road
                                        Cambridge
                                          March 9, 1931

Dear Bertrand Russell

I have just been reading with much interest and profit your book *The Conquest of Happiness* & I would like to thank you for a most stimulating and I think valuable analysis of the factors concerned. The chief point where I could not altogether agree was in your treatment of the factors of envy & jealousy. Even in the simple -- and I agree with you -- fundamentally happy life of the scientific man, one has naturally sometimes encountered examples of this failing but either I have been unusually fortunate or it may be too obtuse to notice it in the great majority of my friends. I have known a number of men leading simple lives whether on the land or in the laboratory who seemed to me singularly free from this failing. I quite agree with you that it is most obtrusive in those who are unduly class-conscious. These remarks are not in criticism but a mere personal statement of my own observations in these directions.

I was very sorry to hear of the sudden death of your brother whom I knew only slightly, and I sympathise with you in your loss. I hope, however, you will be interested enough to take some part in debates in the House of Lords in the future.

> *Yours sincerely*
> *Rutherford*

Chapter 12

Later Years of Telegraph House

When I left Dora, she continued the school until after the beginning of the Second War, though after 1934 it was no longer at Telegraph House. John and Kate were made wards in Chancery and were sent to Dartington school where they were very happy.

I spent a summer at Hendaye and for part of another summer took the Gerald Brenans' house near Malaga. I had not known either of the Brenans before this and I found them interesting and delightful. Gamel Brenan surprised me by turning out to be a scholar of great erudition and wide interests, full of all sorts of scraps of out-of-the-way knowledge and a poet of haunting and learned rhythms. We have kept up our friendship and she visits us sometimes – a lovely autumnal person.

I spent the summer of 1932 at Carn Voel, which I later gave to Dora. While there, I wrote *Education and the Social Order*. After this, having no longer the financial burden of the school, I gave up writing potboilers. And having failed as a parent, I found that my ambition to write books that might be important revived.

During my lecture tour in America in 1931, I had contracted with W. W. Norton, the publisher, to write the book which was published in 1934 under the title *Freedom and Organization, 1814–1914*. I worked at this book in collaboration with Patricia Spence, commonly known as Peter Spence, first at a flat in Emperor's Gate (where John and Kate were disappointed to find neither an Emperor nor a gate), and then at Deudraeth Castle in North Wales, which was at that time an annex of Portmeirion Hotel. I very much enjoyed this work, and I found the life at Portmeirion pleasant. The hotel was owned by my friends Clough Williams-Ellis, the architect, and his wife, Amabel, the writer, whose company was delightful.

When the writing of *Freedom and Organization* was finished, I decided to return to Telegraph House and tell Dora she must live elsewhere. My reasons were financial. I was under a legal obligation to pay a rent of £400 a year for Telegraph House, the proceeds being due to my brother's second wife as alimony. I was also obliged to pay alimony to Dora, as well as all the expenses of John and Kate. Meanwhile my income had diminished catastrophically. This was due partly to the depression, which caused people to buy much fewer books, partly to the fact that I was no longer writing popular books, and partly to my having refused to stay with Hearst in 1931 at his castle in California. My weekly articles in the Hearst newspapers had brought me £1000 a year, but after my refusal the pay was halved, and very soon I was told the articles were no longer required. Telegraph House was large, and was only approachable by two private drives, each about a mile long. I wished to sell it, but could not put it on the market while the school was there. The only hope was to live there, and try to make it attractive to possible purchasers.

After settling again at Telegraph House, without the school, I went for a holiday to the Canary Islands. On returning, I found myself, though sane, quite devoid of creative impulse, and at a loss to know what work to do. For about two months, purely to afford myself distraction, I worked on the problem of the twenty-seven straight lines on a cubic surface. But this would never do, as it was totally useless and I was living on capital saved during the successful years that ended in 1932. I decided to write a book on the daily increasing menace of war. I called this book *Which Way to Peace?* and maintained in it the pacifist position that I had taken up during the First War. I did, it is true, make an exception: I held that, if ever a world government were established, it would be desirable to support it by force against rebels. But as regards the war to be feared in the immediate future, I urged conscientious objection.

This attitude, however, had become unconsciously insincere. I had been able to view with reluctant acquiescence the possibility of the supremacy of the Kaiser's Germany; I thought that, although this would be an evil, it would not be so great an evil as a world war and its aftermath. But Hitler's Germany was a different matter. I found the Nazis utterly revolting – cruel, bigoted, and stupid. Morally and intellectually they were alike odious to me. Although I clung to my pacifist convictions, I did so with increasing difficulty. When, in 1940, England was threatened with invasion, I realised that, throughout the First War, I had never seriously envisaged the possibility of utter defeat. I found this possibility unbearable, and at last consciously and definitely decided that I must support what was necessary for victory in the Second War, however difficult victory might be to achieve, and however painful in its consequences.

This was the last stage in the slow abandonment of many of the beliefs that had come to me in the moment of 'conversion' in 1901. I had never been a complete adherent of the doctrine of non-resistance;

I had always recognised the necessity of the police and the criminal law, and even during the First War I had maintained publicly that some wars are justifiable. But I had allowed a larger sphere to the method of non-resistance – or, rather, non-violent resistance – than later experience seemed to warrant. It certainly has an important sphere; as against the British in India, Gandhi led it to triumph. But it depends upon the existence of certain virtues in those against whom it is employed. When Indians lay down on railways, and challenged the authorities to crush them under trains, the British found such cruelty intolerable. But the Nazis had no scruples in analogous situations. The doctrine which Tolstoy preached with great persuasive force, that the holders of power could be morally regenerated if met by non-resistance, was obviously untrue in Germany after 1933. Clearly Tolstoy was right only when the holders of power were not ruthless beyond a point, and clearly the Nazis went beyond this point.

But private experience had almost as much to do with changing my beliefs as had the state of the world. In the school, I found a very definite and forceful exercise of authority necessary if the weak were not to be oppressed. Such instances as the hatpin in the soup could not be left to the slow operation of a good environment, since the need for action was immediate and imperative. In my second marriage, I had tried to preserve that respect for my wife's liberty which I thought that my creed enjoined. I found, however, that my capacity for forgiveness and what may be called Christian love was not equal to the demands that I was making on it, and that persistence in a hopeless endeavour would do much harm to me, while not achieving the intended good to others. Anybody else could have told me this in advance, but I was blinded by theory.

I do not wish to exaggerate. The gradual change in my views, from 1932 to 1940, was not a revolution; it was only a quantitative change and a shift of emphasis. I had never held the non-resistance creed absolutely, and I did not now reject it absolutely. But the practical difference, between opposing the First War and supporting the Second, was so great as to mask the considerable degree of theoretical consistency that in fact existed.

Although my reason was wholly convinced, my emotions followed with reluctance. My whole nature had been involved in my opposition to the First War, whereas it was a divided self that favoured the Second. I have never since 1940 recovered the same degree of unity between opinion and emotion as I had possessed from 1914 to 1918. I think that, in permitting myself that unity, I had allowed myself more of a creed than scientific intelligence can justify. To follow scientific intelligence wherever it may lead me had always seemed to me the most imperative of moral precepts for me, and I have followed this precept even when it has involved a loss of what I myself had taken for deep spiritual insight.

About a year and a half was spent by Peter Spence, with whom for some time I had been in love, and me on *The Amberley Papers*, a record of the brief life of my parents. There was something of the ivory tower in this work. My parents had not been faced with our modern problems; their radicalism was confident, and throughout their lives the world was moving in directions that to them seemed good. And although they opposed aristocratic privilege, it survived intact, and they, however involuntarily, profited by it. They lived in a comfortable, spacious, hopeful world, yet in spite of this I could wholly approve of them. This was restful, and in raising a monument to them my feelings of filial piety were assuaged. But I could not pretend that the work was really important. I had had a period of uncreative barrenness, but it had ended, and it was time to turn to something less remote.

My next piece of work was *Power, a new social analysis*. In this book I maintained that a sphere of freedom is still desirable even in a socialist state, but this sphere has to be defined afresh and not in liberal terms. This doctrine I still hold. The thesis of this book seems to me important, and I hoped that it would attract more attention than it has done. It was intended as a refutation both of Marx and of the classical economists, not on a point of detail, but on the fundamental assumptions that they shared. I argued that power, rather than wealth, should be the basic concept in social theory, and that social justice should consist in equalisation of power to the greatest practicable degree. It followed that State ownership of land and capital was no advance unless the State was democratic, and even then only if methods were devised for curbing the power of officials. A part of my thesis was taken up and popularised in Burnham's *Managerial Revolution*, but otherwise the book fell rather flat. I still hold, however, that what it has to say is of very great importance if the evils of totalitarianism are to be avoided, particularly under a Socialist régime.

In 1936, I married Peter Spence and my youngest child, Conrad, was born in 1937. This was a great happiness. A few months after his birth, I at last succeeded in selling Telegraph House. For years I had had no offers, but suddenly I had two: one from a Polish Prince, the other from an English business man. In twenty-four hours, owing to their competition, I succeeded in increasing the price they offered by £1000. At last the business man won, and I was rid of the incubus, which had been threatening me with ruin since I had to spend capital so long as it was not disposed of, and very little capital remained.

Although, for financial reasons, I had to be glad to be rid of Telegraph House, the parting was painful. I loved the downs and the woods and my tower room with its views in all four directions. I had known the place for forty years or more, and had watched it grow in my brother's day. It represented continuity, of which, apart from work, my life has had far less than I could have wished. When I sold it, I could say, like the apothecary, 'my poverty but not my will consents'. For a long time after this I did not have a fixed abode, and thought it not likely that I should ever have one. I regretted this profoundly.

After I had finished *Power*, I found my thoughts turning again to theoretical philosophy. During my time in prison in 1918, I had become interested in the problems connected with meaning, which in earlier days I had completely ignored. I wrote something on these problems in *The Analysis of Mind* and in various articles written at about the same time. But there was a great deal more to say. The logical positivists, with whose general outlook I had a large measure of agreement, seemed to me on some points to be falling into errors which would lead away from empiricism into a new scholasticism. They seemed inclined to treat the realm of language as if it were self-subsistent, and not in need of any relation to non-linguistic occurrences. Being invited to give a course of lectures at Oxford, I chose as my subject 'Words and Facts'. The lectures were the first draft of the book published in 1940 under the title *An Inquiry into Meaning and Truth*.

We bought a house at Kidlington, near Oxford, and lived there for about a year, but only one Oxford lady called. We were not respectable. We had later a similar experience in Cambridge. In this respect I have found these ancient seats of learning unique.

LETTERS

To Maurice Amos

16th June 1930

Dear Maurice

You wrote me a very nice letter last October and I have not answered it yet. When you wrote it I was touring America, which leaves one no leisure for anything beyond the day's work. I meant to answer your letter, but as the right moment went by, the impulse died.

I like Jeans's book. It is amusing how the physicists have come round to poor old Bishop Berkeley. You remember how when we were young we were taught that although idealism was, of course, quite the thing, Bishop Berkeley's form of it was rather silly; now it is the only form that survives. I do not see how to refute it, though temperamentally I find it repulsive. It ought, of course, in any case to be solipsism. I lectured on this subject at Harvard, with Whitehead in the Chair, and I said it seemed to me improbable that I had composed the parts of his books which I could not understand, as I should be compelled to believe if I were a solipsist. Nevertheless I have never succeeded in finding any real evidence that I did not do so.

I am very much interested in what you say about your book on the British Constitution, and especially amused that you had written 46,000 out of the 50,000 requisite words before you reached Parliament. Parliament has become a somewhat unimportant body. In the 19th century the Prime Ministers resigned when defeated in Parliament until Gladstone altered the practice; now by the threat of dissolution they terrorise Parliament. The Constitution would not be appreciably changed if the Prime Minister were directly elected, selected the Government, and had to seek re-election either after five years or when a leader appeared against him in his own Party Press.

I think you are entirely right in what you say about the Labour Party. I do not like them, but an Englishman has to have a Party just as he has to have trousers, and of the three Parties I find them the least painful. My objection to the Tories is temperamental, and my objection to the Liberals is Lloyd George. I do not think that in joining a Party one necessarily abrogates the use of one's reason. I know that my trousers might be better than they are; nevertheless they seem to me better than none.

It is true that I had never heard of Holdsworth's *History of English Law*, but in fact I have never read any books at all about law except one or two of Maitland's.

Since I returned from America I have been very much tied here, but I expect to be in London occasionally during the autumn and I should very much like to see you then.

Sanger's death was a great grief to me.

> *Ever yours affectionately*
> *Bertrand Russell*

From and to Bronislaw Malinowski, the anthropologist

The London School of Economics
13th November 1930

Dear Russell

On the occasion of my visit to your School I left my only presentable brown hat in your anteroom. I wonder whether since then it has had the privilege of enclosing the only brains in England which I ungrudgingly regard as better than mine; or whether it has been utilised in some of the juvenile experimentations in physics, technology, dramatic art, or prehistoric symbolism; or whether it naturally lapsed out of the anteroom.

If none of these events, or shall we rather call them hypotheses, holds good or took place, could you be so good as to bring it in a brown paper parcel or by some other concealed mode of transport to London and advise me on a post card where I could reclaim it? I am very sorry that my absentmindedness, which is a characteristic of high intelligence, has exposed you to all the inconvenience incidental to the event.

I do hope to see you some time soon.

Yours sincerely
B. Malinowski

15th Nov. 1930

Dear Malinowski

My secretary has found a presentable brown hat in my lobby which I presume is yours, indeed the mere sight of it reminds me of you.

I am going to the School of Economics to give a lecture to the Students' Union on Monday (17th), and unless my memory is as bad and my intelligence as good as yours, I will leave your hat with the porter at the School of Economics, telling him to give it to you on demand.

I too hope that we may meet some time soon. I made the acquaintance of Briffault[1] the other day, and was amazed by his pugnacity.

Yours sincerely
Bertrand Russell

From and to G. E. Moore

86, Chesterton Road
Cambridge
Mar. 9/30

Dear Russell

The Council of Trinity made a grant to Wittgenstein last June to enable him to carry on his researches on the foundations of Mathematics. There is now a question of making him a further grant; & they wish, before they decide, to have expert reports on the work he has done since the last grant was made. They have authorised me to ask you to make such a report for them. I'm afraid it will involve a good deal of trouble. Wittgenstein has written a great deal; but he says it would be absolutely necessary for him to explain it to you in conversation, if you are to understand it. I think he would be very glad to have an opportunity of doing this, but it would no doubt take up a good deal of your time. I hope very much that you will nevertheless be willing to do it; for there seems to be no other way of ensuring him a

[1] Briffault was a general practitioner from New Zealand who ventured into sociology, and for whose book *Sin and Sex* I did an introduction in 1931.

sufficient income to continue his work, unless the Council do make him a grant; and I am afraid there is very little chance that they will do so, unless they can get favourable reports from experts in the subject; and you are, of course, by far the most competent person to make one. They would, of course, pay a fee for the report.

There would be no need for you to come here to see Wittgenstein. He would arrange to go to see you, when & where it suited you best.

Yours fraternally
G. E. Moore

Beacon Hill School
Harting, Petersfield
11th March 1930

Dear Moore

I do not see how I can refuse to read Wittgenstein's work and make a report on it. At the same time, since it involves arguing with him, you are right that it will require a great deal of work. I do not know anything more fatiguing than disagreeing with him in an argument.

Obviously the best plan for me would be to read the manuscript carefully first, and see him afterwards. How soon could you let me have his stuff? I should like if possible to see him here before the 5th of April: on that date I shall be going to Cornwall for Easter, and I do not want to have any work to do while there, as I have been continuously very busy since the end of last summer. I do not know how long it will be necessary to argue with him. I could spare three days, say the Friday, Saturday and Sunday preceding April 5th, but it would be difficult for me to spare more. Do you think this would be enough?

Yours fraternally
Bertrand Russell

86, Chesterton Road
Cambridge
March 13/30

Dear Russell

Wittgenstein says that he has nothing written which it would be worth while to let you see: all that he has written is at present in too confused a state. I am sorry that I had not clearly understood this when I wrote to you before. What he wants is merely to have a chance of explaining to you some of the results which he has arrived at, so that you might be able to report to the Council whether, even if you thought them mistaken, you thought them important & such that he ought to be given a chance of going on working on the same lines; and I hope that a report of this kind would be sufficient for the Council. And I should think 3 days would be ample for this, & that it wouldn't be necessary for you to argue with him much. He is wiring to you now to ask if he could see you on Saturday either at Harting or in London (if you should be there), so as to try to make some arrangement with you. I think he will be in Austria on April 5th.

> *Yours fraternally*
> G. E. Moore

17th March 1930

Dear Moore

Wittgenstein has been here for the weekend, and we have talked as much as there was time for.

I should be glad to know what is the latest date for reporting to the Council, since my impressions at the moment are rather vague, and he intends while in Austria to make a synopsis of his work which would make it much easier for me to report adequately. If it is impossible to wait another month or so, I will do my best to draw up a report on the basis of our conversations, but I hope this is not necessary. He intends to visit me again in Cornwall just before the beginning of the May term, with his synopsis.

> *Yours fraternally*
> Bertrand Russell

5th May 1930

Dear Moore

I had a second visit from Wittgenstein, but it only lasted thirty-six hours, and it did not by any means suffice for him to give me a synopsis of all that he has done. He left me a large quantity of typescript, which I am to forward to Littlewood as soon as I have read it. Unfortunately I have been ill and have therefore been unable to get on with it as fast as I hoped. I think, however, that in the course of conversation with him I got a fairly good idea of what he is at. He uses the words 'space' and 'grammar' in peculiar senses, which are more or less connected with each other. He holds that if it is significant to say 'This is red', it cannot be significant to say 'This is loud'. There is one 'space' of colours and another 'space' of sounds. These 'spaces' are apparently given *a priori* in the Kantian sense, or at least not perhaps exactly that, but something not so very different. Mistakes of grammar result from confusing 'spaces'. Then he has a lot of stuff about infinity, which is always in danger of becoming what Brouwer has said, and has to be pulled up short whenever this danger becomes apparent. His theories are certainly important and certainly very original. Whether they are true, I do not know; I devoutly hope they are not, as they make mathematics and logic almost incredibly difficult. One might define a 'space', as he uses the word, as a complete set of possibilities of a given kind. If you can say 'This is blue', there are a number of other things you can say significantly, namely, all the other colours.

I am quite sure that Wittgenstein ought to be given an opportunity to pursue his work. Would you mind telling me whether this letter could possibly suffice for the Council? The reason I ask is that I have at the moment so much to do that the effort involved in reading Wittgenstein's stuff thoroughly is almost more than I can face. I will, however, push on with it if you think it is really necessary.

> *Yours fraternally*
> *Bertrand Russell*

> 86, Chesterton Road
> Cambridge
> May 7/30

Dear Russell

I don't think your letter to me, as it stands, will quite do as a report to the Council; but I don't think it is necessary that you should spend any more time in reading Wittgenstein's synopsis. What I think is important is that you should write a formal report (which they might, perhaps, want to keep in their Report-Book), not necessarily any longer than your letter, but stating quite clearly & expressly some things which are only implicit in your letter. I think the report should state quite clearly just how much you have been able to do by way of discovering what work W. has been doing since last June, i.e. partly reading of the Synopsis & partly W.'s verbal explanations; and should emphasise that your opinion of its importance, & that W. ought certainly to be given an opportunity of continuing it, is based upon what you have been able to learn of the nature of this new work itself, & not merely on your previous knowledge of W. You see the Council already know that you have a very high opinion of W.'s work in general, and what they want is your opinion as to the importance of this particular new work, not merely based on a presumption that anything W. does is likely to be important. I think you should try to state, very briefly, what its nature is & what its originality & importance consists in.

I'm afraid that to write such a report will be troublesome; but I hope it wouldn't take you very long; and I do think it's important that it should be done.

> *Yours fraternally*
> *G. E. Moore*

> Beacon Hill School
> Harting, Petersfield
> 8th May 1930

Dear Moore

I have just sent Wittgenstein's typescript to Littlewood with a formal report which he can pass on to the Council. It says just the same things as my letter to you, but it says them in grander language, which the Council will be able to understand. I enclose a copy.

I find I can only understand Wittgenstein when I am in good health, which I am not at the present moment.

Yours fraternally
Bertrand Russell

My report to the Council of Trinity on Wittgenstein's work:
Beacon Hill School
Harting, Petersfield
8th May 1930

Owing to illness I have been prevented from studying Wittgenstein's recent work as thoroughly as I had intended to do. I spent five days in discussion with him, while he explained his ideas, and he left with me a bulky typescript, *Philosophische Bemerkungen*, of which I have read about a third. The typescript, which consists merely of rough notes, would have been very difficult to understand without the help of the conversations. As it is, however, I believe that the following represents at least a part of the ideas which are new since the time of his *Tractatus*:

According to Wittgenstein, when anything is the case there are certain other things that might have been the case in regard, so to speak, to that particular region of fact. Suppose, for example, a certain patch of wall is blue; it might have been red, or green, or &c. To say that it is any of these colours is false, but not meaningless. On the other hand, to say that it is loud, or shrill, or to apply to it any other adjective appropriate to a sound, would be to talk nonsense. There is thus a collection of possibilities of a certain kind which is concerned in any fact. Such a collection of possibilities Wittgenstein calls a 'space'. Thus there is a 'space' of colours, and a 'space' of sounds. There are various relations among colours which constitute the geometry of that 'space'. All this is, in one sense, independent of experience: that is to say, we need the kind of experience through which we know what 'green' is, but not the kind through which we know that a certain patch of wall is green. Wittgenstein uses the word 'grammar' to cover what corresponds in language to the existence of these various 'spaces'. Wherever a word denoting a region in a certain 'space' occurs, the word denoting another region in that 'space' can be substituted without producing nonsense, but a word denoting any region belonging to any other 'space' cannot be substituted without bad grammar, i.e. nonsense.

A considerable part of Wittgenstein's work is concerned with the interpretation of mathematics. He considers it false to say that mathematics is logic or consists of tautologies. He discusses 'infinity' at considerable length and links it with the conception of possibility that he has developed in connection with his various 'spaces'. He believes in 'infinite possibility', as he calls it, but not in actual 'infinite classes' or 'infinite series'. What he says about infinity tends, obviously against his will, to have a certain resemblance to what has been said by Brouwer. I think perhaps the resemblance is not so close as it appears at first sight. There is much discussion of mathematical induction.

The theories contained in this new work of Wittgenstein's are novel, very original, and indubitably important. Whether they are true, I do not know. As a logician who likes simplicity, I should wish to think that they are not, but from what I have read of them I am quite sure that he ought to have an opportunity to work them out, since when completed they may easily prove to constitute a whole new philosophy.

Bertrand Russell

To W. W. Norton, publisher

27th Jan. 1931

Dear Norton

Thank you for your letter of January 14th . . .

With regard to *The Meaning of Science*, I have an abstract of it and have done some 10,000 words. I am afraid I could not do the sort of conclusion that you suggest. I do not believe that science *per se* is an adequate source of happiness, nor do I think that my own scientific outlook has contributed very greatly to my own happiness, which I attribute to defecating twice a day with unfailing regularity. Science in itself appears to me neutral, that is to say, it increases men's power whether for good or for evil. An appreciation of the ends of life is something that must be superadded to science if it is to bring happiness. I do not wish, in any case, to discuss individual happiness, but only the kind of society to which science is apt to give rise. I am afraid you may be disappointed that I am not more of an apostle of science, but as I grow older, and no doubt as a result of the decay of my tissues, I begin to see the good life more and more as a matter of balance and to dread all over-emphasis upon any one ingredient. This has always been the view of elderly men and must therefore have a physiological source, but one cannot escape from one's physiology by being aware of it.

I am not surprised at what people thought of *The Conquest of Happiness* on your side of the Atlantic. What surprised me much more was that English highbrows thought well of it. I think people who are unhappy are always proud of being so, and therefore do not like to be told that there is nothing grand about their unhappiness. A man who is melancholy because lack of exercise has upset his liver always believes that it is the loss of God, or the menace of Bolshevism, or some such dignified cause that makes him sad. When you tell people that happiness is a simple matter, they get annoyed with you.

All best wishes,

> *Yours sincerely*
> *Bertrand Russell*

17th Feb. 1931

Dear Norton

Thank you for your letter of February 9th. My method of achieving happiness was discovered by one of the despised race of philosophers, namely, John Locke. You will find it set forth in great detail in his book on education. This is his most important contribution to human happiness; other minor contributions were the English, American, and French revolutions.

The abstract [of *The Scientific Outlook*] that I sent you is not to be taken as covering all the ground that I shall, in fact, cover. Certainly education must be included in technique in society, though I had regarded it as a branch of advertising. As for behaviourism, I have included it under Pavlov. Pavlov did the work which Watson has advertised.

I have now done 36,000 words of the book, but after I have finished it, I shall keep it by me until the end of May for purposes of revision, and of adding malicious foot-notes.

I have already done a chapter on 'Science and Religion', which is explicitly atheistical. Do you object to this? It would, of course, be possible to give the whole thing an ironical twist, and possibly this might make it better literature. One could go through the arguments of the scientists, Eddington, Jeans, and their accomplices, pointing out how bad they are, and concluding that fortunately our faith need not depend upon them, since it is based upon the impregnable rock of Holy Scripture. If you prefer this as a literary form, I am prepared to re-cast the chapter in that sense. At present it is straightforward, sincere, and full of moral earnestness.

Unless I hear from you to suggest an earlier date, I propose to mail the manuscript, or to hand it to Aannestad if he is still in England, during the second week in June. It is perfectly feasible to send it sooner, but I can always improve it so long as I keep it.

I much enjoyed seeing Aannestad.

> *Yours sincerely*
> *Bertrand Russell*

11th March 1931

Dear Norton

You will have seen that my brother died suddenly in Marseilles.

I inherit from him a title, but not a penny of money, as he was bankrupt. A title is a great nuisance to me, and I am at a loss what to do, but at any rate I do not wish it employed in connection with any of my literary work. There is, so far as I know, only one method of getting rid of it, which is to be attainted of high treason, and this would involve my head being cut off on Tower Hill. This method seems to me perhaps somewhat extreme, but I am sure I can rely upon you not to make use of my title in the way of publicity.

> *Yours sincerely*
> *Bertrand Russell*

To Mr Runham Brown

21st March 1931

Dear Mr Runham Brown

Einstein's pronouncement on the duty of Pacifists to refuse every kind of military service has my most hearty agreement, and I am very glad that the leading intellect of our age should have pronounced himself so clearly and so uncompromisingly on this issue.

For my part I do not expect, much as I desire it, that any very large number of men will be found to take up the position of refusing to bear arms in wartime, nor do I think that a refusal on the part of two per cent would be sufficient to prevent war. The next war will, I think, be more fierce than the war which as yet is still called 'Great', and I think Governments would have no hesitation in shooting the pacifist two per cent. A more effective form of war resistance would be strikes among munition workers. But on the whole I expect more from international agreements than from the actions of individual pacifists. While, therefore, I agree with Einstein as to the duty of pacifists, I put a somewhat different emphasis upon the political and individual factors respectively.

There is one point upon which perhaps I disagree, on principle, with him and with many other Pacifists. If an international authority existed and possessed the sole legal armed forces, I should be prepared to support it even by force of arms.

> *Yours sincerely*
> *Bertrand Russell*

To Dr Steinbach

19th May 1931

Dear Dr Steinbach

I am afraid I have nothing very helpful to say about the English language. I notice that literary persons in America tend to study it as one studies a dead language, that is to say, it does not occur to them that the written word can be merely the spoken word transcribed.

For my part, while I am willing to read good authors for the sake of their rhythms, and also to enrich my vocabulary, it would not occur to me to read them with any grammatical purpose.

I should define correct English in the year nineteen hundred and thirty-one as the habits of speech of educated people in that year, and I see no point in making a distinction between speech and writing. When once a distinction of this sort is allowed to creep in, one soon arrives at the condition of the literary Chinese. I knew a learned Chinese who was very keen on substituting the vernacular (as it is called) for the classical language. I asked him whether this movement made much progress; he replied that there are times when it does and times when it does not. 'For example,' he said, 'it made great progress during the thirteenth century.' I do not know Chinese, but I inferred that classical Chinese corresponded to Latin, and that the vernacular corresponded to Chaucer. I do not wish this sort of thing to happen to those who speak English.

> *Yours very truly*
> *Bertrand Russell*

This and the following letter are the long and the short of it.

From and to Will Durant

> 44, North Drive
> Great Neck, N.Y.
> June 8th, 1931

Earl Bertrand Russell
Carn Voel, Porthcurno
Cornwall, England

Dear Earl Russell

Will you interrupt your busy life for a moment, and play the game of philosophy with me?

I am attempting to face, in my next book, a question that our generation, perhaps more than most, seems always ready to ask, and never able to answer – What is the meaning or worth of human life? Heretofore this question has been dealt with chiefly by theorists, from Ikhnaton and Lao-tse to Bergson and Spengler. The result has been a species of intellectual suicide: thought, by its very development, seems to have destroyed the value and significance of life. The growth and spread of knowledge, for which so many reformers and idealists prayed, appears to bring to its devotees – and, by contagion, to many others – a disillusionment which has almost broken the spirit of our race.

Astronomers have told us that human affairs constitute but a moment in the trajectory of a star; geologists have told us that civilisation is a precarious interlude between ice ages; biologists have told us that all life is war, a struggle for existence among individuals, groups, nations, alliances, and species; historians have told us that 'progress' is a delusion, whose glory ends in inevitable decay; psychologists have told us that the will and the self are the helpless instruments of heredity and environment, and that the once incorruptible soul is only a transient incandescence of the brain. The Industrial Revolution has destroyed the home, and the discovery of contraceptives is destroying the family, the old morality, and perhaps (through the sterility of the intelligent) the race. Love is analysed into a physical congestion, and marriage becomes a temporary physiological convenience slightly superior to promiscuity. Democracy has degenerated into such corruption as only Milo's Rome knew; and our youthful dreams of a socialist utopia disappear as we see, day after day, the inexhaustible acquisitiveness of men. Every invention strengthens the strong and weakens the weak; every new mechanism displaces men, and multiplies the horrors of war. God, who was once the consolation of our brief life, and our refuge in bereavement and suffering, has apparently vanished from the scene; no telescope, no microscope discovers him. Life has become, in that total perspective which is philosophy, a fitful pullulation of human insects on the earth, a planetary eczema that may soon be cured; nothing is certain in it except defeat and death – a sleep from which, it seems, there is no awakening.

We are driven to conclude that the greatest mistake in human history was the discovery of truth. It has not made us free, except from delusions that comforted us, and restraints that preserved us; it has not made us happy, for truth is not beautiful, and did not deserve to be so passionately chased. As we look upon it now we wonder why we hurried so to find it. For it appears to have taken from us every reason for existing, except for the moment's pleasure and tomorrow's trivial hope.

This is the pass to which science and philosophy have brought us. I, who have loved philosophy for many years, turn from it now back to life itself, and ask you, as one who has lived as well as thought, to help me understand. Perhaps the verdict of those who have lived is different from that of those who have merely thought. Spare me a moment to tell me what meaning life has for you, what help – if any – religion gives you, what keeps you going, what are the sources of your inspiration and your energy, what is the goal or motive-force of your toil; where you find your consolations and your happiness, where in the last resort your treasure lies. Write briefly if you must; write at

leisure and at length if you possibly can; for every word from you
will be precious to me.

Sincerely
Will Durant

Author of *The Story of Philosophy, Transition, The Mansions of Phil-*
osophy, Philosophy and the Social Problem, etc.
Formerly of the Dept. of Philosophy, Columbia University; Ph.D.
(Columbia); L.H.D. (Syracuse).

P.S. A copy of this letter is being sent to Presidents Hoover and
Masaryk; the Rt. Hons. Ramsay MacDonald, Lloyd George, Winston
Churchill, and Philip Snowden; M. Aristide Briand; Signors Benito
Mussolini, G. Marconi and G. d'Annunzio; Mme. Curie, Miss Mary
Garden and Miss Jane Addams; Dean Inge; and Messrs. Josef Stalin,
Igor Stravinsky, Leon Trotzky, M. K. Gandhi, Rabindranath Tagore,
Ignace Paderewski, Richard Strauss, Albert Einstein, Gerhardt
Hauptmann, Thomas Mann, Sigmund Freud, G. B. Shaw, H. G.
Wells, John Galsworthy, Thomas Edison, Henry Ford and Eugene
O'Neill.

The purpose in view is purely philosophical. I trust, however, that
there will be no objection to my quoting from the replies in my
forthcoming book *On the Meaning of Life*, one chapter of which will
attempt to give some account of the attitude towards life of the most
eminent of living men and women.

20th June 1931

Dear Mr Durant

I am sorry to say that at the moment I am so busy as to be convinced
that life has no meaning whatever, and that being so, I do not see how
I can answer your questions intelligently.

I do not see that we can judge what would be the result of the
discovery of truth, since none has hitherto been discovered.

Yours sincerely
Bertrand Russell

From and to Albert Einstein

Caputh bei Potsdam
Waldstr. 7/8
den 14. Oktober 1931

Lieber Bertrand Russell!
Ich habe schon lange den Wunsch, Ihnen zu schreiben. Nichts anderes

wollte ich dabei, als Ihnen meine hohe Bewunderung ausdrücken. Die Klarheit, Sicherheit, and Unparteilichkeit, mit der Sie die logischen, philosophischen und menschlichen Dinge in Ihren Büchern behandelt haben, steht nicht nur in unserer Generation unerreicht da.

Dies zu sagen hätte ich mich immer gescheut, weil Sie die objektiven Dinge so auch dies selber schon am besten wissen und keine Bestätigung nötig haben. Aber da löst mir ein kleiner Journalist, der mich heute aufsuchte, die Zunge. Es handelt sich da um ein internationales journalistisches Unternehmen (Cooperation) dem die besten Leute als Mitarbeiter angehören, und das sich die Aufgabe gestellt hat, das Publikum in allen Ländern in internationalem Sinne zu erziehen. Mittel: Artikel von Staatsmännern und Journalisten, welche einschlägige Fragen behandeln, werden systematisch in Zeitungen aller Länder veröffentlicht.

Herr Dr J. Révész geht in kurzem nach England, um für diese Sache zu wirken. Es würde nach meiner Ueberzeugung wichtig sein, wenn Sie ihm eine kurze Unterredung gewährten, damit er Sie in dieser Angelegenheit informieren kann. Ich richte eine solche Bitte nicht leichthin, an Sie, sondern in der Ueberzeugung, dass die Angelegenheit Ihrer Beachtung wirklich wert sei.

In freudiger Verehrung
Ihr
A. Einstein

P.S. Einer Beantwortung dieses Briefes bedarf es nicht.

(Translation by Otto Nathan):

October 14, 1931

Dear Bertrand Russell

For a long time I have had the wish to write you. All I wanted to do, was to express my feeling of high admiration of you. The clarity, sureness, and impartiality which you have brought to bear to the logical, philosophical and human problems dealt with in your books are unrivalled not only in our generation.

I have always been reluctant to say this to you because you know about this yourself as well as you know about objective facts and do not need to receive any confirmation from outside. However, a little-known journalist who came to see me today has now given me an opportunity to open my heart to you. I am referring to an international journalistic enterprise (Cooperation) to which the best people belong as contributors and which has the purpose of educating the public in all countries in international understanding. The method to be used is to publish systematically articles by statesmen and journalists on pertinent problems in newspapers of all countries.

The gentleman in question, Dr J. Révész, will visit England in the near future to promote the project. I believe it would be important if you could grant him a short interview so he could inform you about the matter. I have hesitated to ask of you this favour, but I am convinced that the project really deserves your attention.

With warm admiration,

Yours
A. Einstein

P.S. There is no need to reply to this letter.

Telegraph House
Harting, Petersfield
7.1.35

Dear Einstein

I have long wished to be able to invite you for a visit, but had until recently no house to which to ask you. Now this obstacle is removed, & I very much hope you will come for a week-end. Either next Saturday (12th) or the 19th would suit me; after that I shall be for 6 weeks in Scandinavia & Austria, so if the 12th & 19th are both impossible, it will be necessary to wait till the second half of March. I can scarcely imagine a greater pleasure than a visit from you would give me, & there are many matters both in the world of physics & in that of human affairs on which I should like to know your opinion more definitely than I do.

Yours very sincerely
Bertrand Russell

From and to Henri Barbusse

Vigilia
Miramar par Théoule
(Alpes-Maritimes)
10 *février* 1927

Cher et éminent confrère

Permettez-mois de joindre un appel personnel à celui que vous trouverez ci-inclus et auquel je vous demande de bien vouloir adhérer. Votre nom est un de ceux qui s'imposent dans une ligue de grands honnêtes gens qui se lèveraient pour enrayer et combattre l'envahissante barbarie du fascisme.

J'ai rédigé cet appel spontanément, sans obéir à aucune suggestion d'ordre politique ou autre. Je n'ai écouté que le sentiment de la solidarité et la voix du bon sens: le mal n'est pas sans remède; il y a 'quelque chose à faire'; et ce qu'on peut faire surtout et avant tout devant les proportions effrayantes qu'a prises le fascisme, c'est de dresser une force morale, de mobiliser la vraie conscience publique, et de donner une voix explicite à une réprobation qui est répandue partout.

Je dois ajouter que, sur la teneur de cet appel, j'ai échangé des vues avec Romain Rolland, qui est de tout coeur avec moi, et qui estime comme moi qu'une levée des esprits libres, qu'une protestation des personnes éclairées et respectées, est seule susceptible, si elle organisée et continue, de mettre un frein à un état de choses épouvantable.

Je tiens enfin à vous dire que j'ai l'intention de créer très prochainement une revue internationale: Monde, *qui aura pour but de diffuser de grands principes humains dans le chaos international actuel, de lutter contre l'esprit et la propagande réactionnaires. Cette publication peut devenir, sur le plan intellectuel, artistique, moral et social, une importante tribune, si des personnalités comme vous le veulent bien. Elle servira de véhicule à la voix du Comité, et donnera corps à sa haute protestation.*

Je vous serais reconnaissant si vous me disiez que vous acceptez d'être considéré comme un collaborateur éventuel de Monde.

Je vous serais également obligé de me répondre au sujet de l'appel par une lettre dont je pourrais faire état le cas échéant, en la publiant en son entier ou en extraits.

Croyez à mes sentiments de haute considération dévouée.

Henri Barbusse

> Sylvie
> Aumont par Senlis
> (Oise)
> 12 décembre 1932

Mon cher Russell

Le Comité Tom Mooney voulant profiter du changement de gouvernement aux Etats-Unis pour arriver à la solution de l'affaire Tom Mooney, au sujet de laquelle de nouvelles révélations viennent encore de se produire, a décidé l'envoi au Président Roosevelt de la lettre ci-jointe qui bien que conçue en termes officiels et très déférents, quoique fermes, nous paraît susceptible d'apporter réellement un terme au scandaleux martyre de Tom Mooney et de Billings.

Je vous demandé de bien vouloir y apposer votre signature et de me la renvoyer d'urgence.

Croyez à mes sentiments amicaux.

Henri Barbusse

Je vous envoie d'autre part une brochure éditée par le Comité Tom Mooney.

> 47 Emperor's Gate
> S.W.7
> 16th December 1932

Dear Barbusse

I am at all times willing to do anything that seems to me likely to help Mooney, but I have a certain hesitation about the draft letter that you have sent me.

You will, of course, remember that in the time of Kerensky the Russian Government made an appeal to President Wilson on the subject, and that he, in consequence, had the Mooney case investigated by a number of eminent legal authorities who reported favourably to Mooney. The State of California, however, pointed out that the President had no right to interfere with State administration of justice.

I do not think there is very much point in appealing to the President Elect, as he will merely take shelter behind his lack of legal power. In any case it would be no use presenting the letter until after he becomes President, which will, I think, be on March 4th. There is no doubt also that at this moment American public opinion is not feeling particularly friendly to either your country or mine, and I doubt whether we can usefully intervene until passions have cooled.

> *Yours sincerely*
> *Bertrand Russell*

This letter shows that I was not always impetuous.

From Count Michael Károlyi

The White Hall Hotel
70 Guildford St, W.C.1
5th Feb. 1935

My dear Russell

I want to thank you for the brilliant letter you wrote for the defence of Rákosi.[1] The trial is still on, and the final sentence may come any day now. If he does not get a death sentence it will be due in very great part to your intervention. I fear in this case, however, that he will be imprisoned for life. Of course, we will try to save him even so – perhaps we can succeed in getting him exchanged for something or other from the Soviet government.

The last time I saw you, you invited me to spend a week-end with you. If I am not inconveniencing you I should like to come and see you, not this Sunday, but any other time which would suit you.

There are so many things to talk over with you – please let me know.

My new address is as above, and my telephone number is Terminus 5512.

> *Yours very sincerely*
> *M. Károlyi*

---

[1] Mátyás Rákosi, a Hungarian communist, re-arrested upon his release from a long prison sentence. His life was saved but he was again imprisoned. In 1940 Russia obtained him in exchange for Hungarian flags captured in 1849. Later Rákosi became Deputy Prime Minister of Hungary.

From Gerald Brenan, author of   June 1st 1935
The Spanish Labyrinth and other   Churriana
books   [Malaga]

Dear Bertie

I see that I have to say something really very stupid indeed to draw a letter from you. My letter was written late at night, when ones thoughts and fears tend to carry one away, and I regretted it afterwards. I spent the next day in penance reading an account of de Montford's campaign.

It is easy enough to *sympathise* with the destructive desires of revolutionaries; the difficulty in most cases is to agree that they are likely to do any good. What I really dislike about them are their doctrinaire ideas and their spirit of intolerance. The religious idea in Communism, which is the reason for its success, (the assurance it gives of Time that is God, being on ones side) will lead in the end perhaps to a sort of Mohammedan creed of brotherhood & stagnation. The energy and combativeness of Christian nations comes, I suspect, from the doctrine of sin, particularly Original Sin and the kind of struggle that must go on for redemption (or for money). But for Augustine's Manichaeanism we should have been a more docile but less interesting lot. I am opposed to this Communist religion, because I think that Socialism shd be a matter of administration only. Any religious ideas that get attached to it will be impoverishing, unless of course they are treated lightly, as the Romans treated the worship of Augustus or the Chinese treated Confucianism. But that of course may [not] be the case. – Anyhow since one has in the end to accept or reject these things en bloc, I shall support Communism when I see it is winning – and I shall *always* support it against Fascism.

Out here every day brings news of the disintegration of the Popular Front. Moderate Socialists, Revolutionary Socialists and Syndicalists are all at loggerheads. Disorders go on increasing and I think that the most likely end is dictatorship. I incline to think that the best thing for the country would be a Dictatorship of the moderate left (present government with Socialists) for, say, ten years. I understand that the agricultural unemployment cannot be solved until large areas at present unirrigated have been made irrigateable. Dams have been begun, but many more are wanted and fifteen years must elapse till they are ready. The plan is for the Govt to control investments & direct them upon these dams, repaying the lenders by a mortgage on the new irrigated land.

The weather is delicious now and every moment of life is a pleasure. Besides health and weather – which is Nature's health – very little matters. It would be nice if you rented a house out here & brought out some of your books. If everything in Spain is uncertain – what about the rest of Europe?

With love from us both to you & Peter

ever yrs
Gerald Brenan

Public opinion in England seems alarmingly warlike. I favour the dropping of sanctions and conclusion of a Mediterranean pact, which would be a check to Mussolini. But then we must be ready to go to war if he takes a Greek island.

In England the importance of Austria's not going Nazi is always underestimated. *The Times* refused to look at Central Europe at all. The English are priggish about everything beyond Berlin – Vienna – Venice. I suspect that you think as I do.

From Mrs Gerald Brenan

Bell Court
Aldbourne, Marlborough
[Nov. 1938]

My dear Bertie

I thought of you very much in those really horrible days – which must have been dreadful to you going further & further away from your children and leaving them behind in such a world. It is the kind of thing you might dream of in an evil nightmare – but it was one of those modern nightmares in which you are still awake.

I share your difficulties. I am and always shall be a pacifist. But sometimes they seem to 'cry Peace Peace when there is no peace'. What a world we live in.

Power is having wonderful reviews, I see, and is a best seller. I am so glad. I hope to read it soon.

We have had an Anarchist from Holland staying with us, the Secretary of the AIT. He was a charming & very intelligent man, & had been a good deal in Spain with the CNT.

He was a great admirer of yours. He said that he had recently written an article on Anarchism for an Encyclopedia. In the Bibliography at the end he included 'All the works of Bertrand Russell' because, he explains, though they are not actually Anarchist they have 'the tendency' as old Anarchists say.

I was pleased – for whatever Anarchist parties are in practice 'the tendency' I'm sure is right. We went to Savernake Forest one day. The autumn leaves were beginning to fall but the day was warm & bright. I wished for you & Peter & John & Kate. Perhaps we will walk there again another day.

I hope you & Peter are as happy as it is possible to be so far from home & in such days.

With love to you both

> *Yours ever*
> *Gamel*

> Bell Court
> Aldbourne, Marlborough
> [Winter 1938–9]

My dear Bertie

I was so glad to get your letter and to think that you will be coming home now before so very long and we shall see you again.

Yes, we must somehow meet more often. We must have picnics in Savernake Forest – and find some charming place to come together half way between Kidlington and Aldbourne. Gerald and I are going to take to bicycles this summer, so we can meet anywhere.

I am sure America is very difficult to be in now. I was afraid you and Peter would find it trying in many ways – the tremendous lionising must be very exhausting and very tiresome in the end however well they mean.

Longmans Green are going to bring out my book some time in the late spring I think. I am glad, for I think in a small way it is a useful book. It is such a painful picture of the war state of mind. It is to be called *Death's Other Kingdom*, from T. S. Eliot's line 'Is it like this in Death's other kingdom?'

Gerald and I have both read *Power* with great interest and great admiration. It has made a great impression, I gather, not only from the reviews, but from the fact that almost every intelligent person I meet happens somehow in some connection to mention it.

I can understand how you long to be in England. And I am so glad that you will soon be coming home.

With much love to you all,

> *Yours*
> *Gamel*

I am delighted to learn the real provenance of my name – but I am not sure how I feel about its nearness to Camel.

From Mrs Bernard Berenson

> The Mud House
> Friday's Hill, Haslemere
> July 28, 1936

My dear Bertie

Might I motor over & call upon you and your wife on Thursday or Friday of this week, or sometime next week?

I've been very ill, and one of the results of illness is to make me understand what things have been precious in my life, and you were one of the most precious. I do not want to die without seeing you again & thanking you for so many things.

Yours affectionately
Mary Berenson

To and from Lion Fitzpatrick

Telegraph House
Harting, Petersfield
21.12.36

Dear Lion

It was very disappointing that I was ill just when we were coming to you – it was gastric flu, brief but incapacitating. We look forward to seeing you towards the end of January.

As Alys is going to stay with you, I wonder whether you could say some little word of a friendly sort from me. I am the more anxious for this because Mrs Berenson said a number of very critical things about Alys, to which I listened in stony silence; & I dare say she went away saying I had said them. I don't want to make mischief, so that there would be no point in mentioning Mrs Berenson to Alys; but I should be sorry if Alys thought that I said or felt unfriendly things about her.

Yours
B R

The Warden's Lodgings
All Souls College, Oxford
Dec. 28. 36

Dear Bertie

All right. I'll try to do that. But it isn't easy to inform Alys about you. She likes to think she knows everything about you. At bottom she is intensely interested in you but she still seems raw even after all these years. I expect she cares quite a lot about you still. People *are* queer. If they are without humour they either dry up or get rather rancid. I feel that to be able to regard yourself as somewhat of a joke is the highest virtue.

I'll ask (?) [illegible word] over when Alys & Grace Worthington and after them the Wells go – It will be in Feb. I am afraid unless I could come in between visits. But I generally have to go to bed then – oh Lord how unadaptable the English are and how unimpressionable the u.s. (?) [illegible word]. These people here are Scottish & Ulster. Much more flexible breed.

I have a rather miserable spot in my sub-conscious about your book on philosophy. I do wish you could get it out of you before you die – I think it would be important! – after all that is what you ought to be doing – not pot boilers. Bill Adams (the son of the Warden here) has been listening to you somewhere on physics and says your brain is the clearest in England – (Is this great praise in a country where brains are nearly all muddled and proud of it sir ?)

My regards to Lady Russell – I hope she is well – I write to her later –

Lion

Lion Fitzpatrick, the writer of the preceding letter, was a close friend of Alys's and later also of mine. 'Lion' was a nickname given to her on account of her mane of black hair. Her father had been a Belfast business man, who, owing to drink, had first gone bankrupt and then died. She came to England penniless, and was employed by Lady Henry Somerset on philanthropic work in Somerstown (St Pancras). I met her first on June 10, 1894, at a Temperance Procession which I attended because of Alys. We quarrelled about the Mission to Deep Sea Fishermen, concerning which I made some disparaging remark. Shortly afterwards she followed the example of Bernard Shaw by standing for the St Pancras Vestry (which corresponded to what is now the Borough Council). She lived up a back staircase in a slum, and as I had my Cambridge furniture to dispose of, I gave some of it to her.

Meanwhile, through Alys, she came to know a young man named Bobby Phillimore, who had proposed to Alys but been refused. He was at Christchurch, and was the son of Lord Phillimore, a very rich Liberal Law Lord and a close friend of Mr Gladstone. Bobby, I think under Logan's influence, became Socialist and a poet. He was the original of the poet in Shaw's *Candida*. He decided that he wanted to marry Lion, but he was not going to repeat the mistake of precipitancy which he had committed with Alys. So he got himself elected to the St Pancras Vestry and carefully prepared his approaches. Shortly after Alys and I were married, when we were living in Berlin, I got a letter from Lion asking my advice as to whether she should accept him. I wrote back at once giving twelve reasons against. By return of post I got a letter from her saying that she had accepted him.

In the following spring, when Alys and I were staying with her sister at Fiesole, Lion and Bobby came to see us on their return from their honeymoon in North Africa. I then for the first time learned why she had accepted him. After she had resolutely refused him for some time, he developed heart trouble, and eminent medical men gave it as their opinion that if she persisted he would die. His father pleaded with her, but in vain. Finally, in response to impassioned requests from Lord Phillimore, Mr Gladstone, though eighty and nearly blind, climbed her slummy staircase in person to urge her to abandon the role of Barbara Allen. This was too much for her, and she accepted her love-sick swain.

So far, so good – a pleasant King Cophetua story. But in Fiesole, after her honeymoon, she told a surprising sequel. Alys and I noticed at once that she had become profoundly cynical, and amazingly obscene in her conversation, so we naturally pressed her as to what produced such a change. She told us that, as soon as she and Bobby were married, he told her he had deceived the doctors, and had nothing the matter with his heart;[1] further that, though he had been determined to marry her, he did not love her and never had loved her. I believe the marriage was never consummated.

Bobby's father owned Radlett, at that time a picturesque country village; he owned also a rather beautiful country house between Radlett and Elstree. He gave Bobby the house and a free hand in managing the estate. The poet and the Socialist receded into the background, and were replaced by a very hard-headed business man, who proceeded to develop Radlett by putting up vast numbers of cheap, ugly, sordid suburban villas, which brought in an enormous profit. Years later he really did become ill. His wife nursed him devotedly for about three years, at the end of which he died. After his death she told me she would marry any man who would promise to be always ill, because she had grown so used to nursing that she did not know how to fill her days without it.

She did not, however, marry again. She published anonymously a book which had a considerable success, called *By an unknown disciple*. She had an abortive affair with Massingham. She took a great interest in psychical research. Being left a rich widow, she devoted a large part of her income to support of the Labour Party. I saw little of her in her last years, because she demanded that one should treat seriously things that I regard as nonsense – sentimental religiosity, second sight, the superior intuitions of the Irish, and so on. But I regretted these obstacles, and tried to see her without either quarrels or insincerity.

To W. V. Quine, the Harvard logician

Telegraph House
Harting, Petersfield
6-6-35

Dear Dr Quine

Your book [*System of Logistic*] arrived at a moment when I was over-worked and obliged to take a long holiday. The result is that I have only just finished reading it.

[1] However, he died of heart disease some years later.

I think you have done a beautiful piece of work; it is a long time since I have had as much intellectual pleasure as in reading you.

Two questions occurred to me, as to which I should be glad to have answers when you have time. I have put them on a separate sheet.

In reading you I was struck by the fact that, in my work, I was always being influenced by extraneous philosophical considerations. Take e.g. descriptions. I was interested in 'Scott is the author of Waverley', and not only in the descriptive functions of PM.[1] If you look up Meinong's work, you will see the sort of fallacies I wanted to avoid; the same applies to the ontological argument.

Take again notation (mainly Whitehead's): we had to provide for the correlators in Parts III and IV. Your α_β for our R|S would not do for three or more relations, or for various forms (such as R‖S) we needed.

I am worried – though as yet I cannot put my worry into words – as to whether you really have avoided the troubles for which the axiom of reducibility was introduced as completely as you think. I should like to see Induction and Dedekindian continuity explicitly treated by your methods.

I am a little puzzled as to the status of classes in your system. They appear as a primitive idea, but the connection of α with $\hat{x}(\phi x)$ seems somewhat vague. Do you maintain that, if $\alpha = \hat{x}(\phi x)$, the prop. xα, is identical with ϕx? You must, if you are to say that all props are sequences. Yet it seems obvious that 'I gave sixpence to my son' is not the *same* as 'my son is one of the people to whom I gave sixpence'.

And do you maintain that an infinite class can be defined otherwise than by a defining function? The need of including infinite classes was one of my reasons for emphasising functions as opposed to classes in PM.

I expect you have good answers to these questions.

In any case, I have the highest admiration for what you have done, which has reformed many matters as to which I had always been uncomfortable.

Yours very truly
Bertrand Russell

To G. E. Moore

Telegraph House
Harting, Petersfield
Feb. 8, 1937

Dear Moore

I have become very desirous of returning to purely philosophic work; in particular, I want to develop the ideas in my paper on 'The

[1] *Principia Mathematica.*

Limits of Empiricism', & to investigate the relation of language to fact, as to which Carnap's ideas seem to me very inadequate. But I am in the unfortunate position of being legally bound to pay between £800 & £900 a year to other people, & having only £300 a year of unearned income. I cannot therefore work at philosophy unless I can get some academic job. I suppose there is no possibility at Cambridge? I should be very glad if there were, as my desire to get back to philosophy is very strong.

> *Yours*
> *Bertrand Russell*

> Telegraph House
> Harting, Petersfield
> Feb. 18, 1937

Dear Moore

Thank you for your letter, which shows the position to be much as I supposed. I think perhaps, at the moment, it is hardly worth proceeding in the matter, as the chance of success seems small, & there are other possibilities elsewhere. I am very grateful to you for being willing to recommend me, & if other things fail I will write to you again. In the meantime, I think it will be best to do nothing.

The Leverhulme Fellowships are settled in June; till then, I shall not know. In any case they only last two years.

> *Yours*
> *Bertrand Russell*

From Desmond MacCarthy

> 25 Wellington Square
> S.W.3
> March 16. 37

Dear Bertie

I am relieved that you thought my review likely to wet the public appetite: that is what I tried to do. I did not write it well: I wrote it too quickly and only had time to make perfunctory corrections, but I think it will persuade people that *The Amberley Papers* are very interesting. I went to Trinity Commem: and dined in Hall on Sunday night. I found the review was working there.

What I am pleased about is that I got G. M. Young to write about it in the *Observer*. He wanted to write about it in the S. T. & I got him, by grabbing the book from him, to offer his comments to Garvin.

I don't expect that you hope for a large sale, but I think it may have a very respectable one & go on selling.

I am interested to hear that you have sold Telegraph House, & long to hear particulars. I am afraid the price was not not [*sic*] good or you would have written with more elation. It does not mean – does it that your worst money worries are at an end? Do you remember what a fuss Schopenhauer made about having to pension the woman he pushed down stairs for the term of her natural life? And he had only a brown poodle dependent on him, (Its name was Butz) and you have never pushed a woman down stairs. Do you remember his triumphant entry in his diary after many years, *Obit anus, abit onus?* I look forward to getting *two* postcards from you, soon, with these words on them.

It is of the utmost importance that you should have leisure to write your book clearing up the relation of grammar and philosophy and many things beside. Is it true that you could manage on £500 a year till you can write those post-cards? Your admirers ought to be able to raise that. Would you object to being pensioned? I shouldn't if my prospects were as good as yours of writing something valuable.

Time is getting short now. I don't mean that death is necessarily near either of us, but the slow death is near; the softening and relaxing of the faculty of attention which in its approach feels so like wisdom to the victim.

I met Shaw not long ago & he talked about his latest works, which exhibit all his astonishing aptitudes – except grip. I had an impulse to say (but I thought it too unkind) 'Aren't you afraid though of letting out the deadly secret – that you can no longer *care*?' I guessed the nature of that secret from having observed what was threatening me. But with you & me it is still only a threat – You, especially, can still care, for your power of feeling has always been stronger than mine. Still, time is short. We are all (and I mean also people neither of us know) [anxious] that you should philosophise, and write your book before the power to write it begins to be insensibly sucked away in the fat folds of that hydra, old age.

I stayed with Moore and we were happy – grey-beards at play, most of the time. He made me read a paper by Wisdom on Definition but I didn't get the hang of it. It was Wittgensteinian. I wanted to talk about myself and make Moore talk about himself, but we didn't care enough to get over the discomfort of leaving the pleasant shore of memories. But damn it I'll do it next time (This isn't the first time though, I've said that). Do please send me word when you are *next* in London & come to lunch or in the morning or in the afternoon, or to dinner – any time. We cd put you up. Dermod is a ships doctor, his room is empty. And I will come to you for a visit in May after my Leslie Stephen lecture. Give my affectionate & best wishes to 'Peter' for a happy delivery –

> Yours always,
> Desmond

Chapter 13

America. 1938–1944

In August 1938, we sold our house at Kidlington. The purchasers would only buy it if we evacuated it at once, which left us a fortnight in August to fill in somehow. We hired a caravan, and spent the time on the coast of Pembrokeshire. There were Peter and me, John and Kate and Conrad, and our big dog Sherry. It poured with rain practically the whole time and we were all squashed up together. It was about as uncomfortable a time as I can remember. Peter had to prepare the meals, which she hated doing. Finally, John and Kate went back to Dartington, and Peter and Conrad and I sailed for America.

In Chicago I had a large Seminar, where I continued to lecture on the same subject as at Oxford, namely, 'Words and Facts'. But I was told that Americans would not respect my lectures if I used monosyllables, so I altered the title to something like 'The Correlation between Oral and Somatic Motor Habits'. Under this title, or something of the sort, the Seminar was approved. It was an extraordinarily delightful Seminar. Carnap and Charles Morris used to come to it, and I had three pupils of quite outstanding ability – Dalkey, Kaplan, and Copilowish. We used to have close arguments back and forth, and succeeded in genuinely clarifying points to our mutual satisfaction, which is rare in philosophical argument. Apart from this Seminar, the time in Chicago was disagreeable. The town is beastly and the weather was vile. President Hutchins, who was occupied with the Hundred Best Books, and with the attempt to force neo-Thomism on the philosophical faculty, naturally did not much like me, and when the year for which I had been engaged came to an end was, I think, glad to see me go.

I became a professor at the University of California at Los Angeles. After the bleak hideousness of Chicago, which was still in the grip of winter, it was delightful to arrive in the Californian spring. We arrived in California at the end of March, and my duties did not begin until September. The first part of the intervening time I spent in a lecture tour, of which I remember only two things with any vividness. One is that the professors at the Louisiana State University, where I lectured, all thought well of Huey Long, on the ground that he had raised their salaries. The other recollection is more pleasant: in a purely rural region, I was taken to the top of the dykes that enclose the Mississippi. I was very tired with lecturing, long journeys, and heat, I lay in the grass, and watched the majestic river, and gazed, half hypnotised, at water and sky. For some ten minutes I experienced peace, a thing which very rarely happened to me, and I think only in the presence of moving water.

In the summer of 1939, John and Kate came to visit us for the period of the school holidays. A few days after they arrived the War broke out, and it became impossible to send them back to England. I had to provide for their further education at a moment's notice. John was seventeen, and I entered him at the University of California, but Kate was only fifteen, and this seemed young for the University. I made enquiries among friends as to which school in Los Angeles had the highest academic standard, and there was one that they all concurred in recommending, so I sent her there. But I found that there was only one subject taught that she did not already know, and that was the virtues of the capitalist system. I was therefore compelled, in spite of her youth, to send her to the University. Throughout the year 1939–40 John and Kate lived with us.

In the summer months of 1939 we rented a house at Santa Barbara, which is an altogether delightful place. Unfortunately, I injured my back, and had to lie flat on my back for a month, tortured by almost unendurable sciatica. The result of this was that I got behind hand with the preparations for my lectures, and that throughout the coming academic year I was always overworked and always conscious that my lectures were inadequate.

The academic atmosphere was much less agreeable than in Chicago; the people were not so able, and the President was a man for whom I conceived, I think justly, a profound aversion. If a lecturer said anything that was too liberal, it was discovered that the lecturer in question did his work badly, and he was dismissed. When there were meetings of the Faculty, the President of the University used to march in as if he were wearing jack-boots, and rule any motion out of order if he did not happen to like it. Everybody trembled at his frown, and I was reminded of a meeting of the Reichstag under Hitler.

Towards the end of the academic year 1939–40, I was invited to become a professor at the College of the City of New York. The matter appeared to be settled, and I wrote to the President of the University of California to resign my post there. Half an hour after he received my letter, I learned that the appointment in New York was not definitive and I called upon the President to withdraw my resignation, but he told me it was too late. Earnest Christian taxpayers had been protesting against having to contribute to the salary of an infidel, and the President was glad to be quit of me.

The College of the City of New York was an institution run by the City Government. Those who attended it were practially all Catholics or Jews; but to the indignation of the former, practically all the scholarships went to the latter. The Government of New York City was virtually a satellite of the Vatican, but the professors at the City College strove ardently to keep up some semblance of academic freedom. It was no doubt in pursuit of this aim that they had recommended me. An Anglican bishop was incited to protest against me, and priests lectured the police, who were practically all Irish Catholics, on my responsibility for the local criminals. A lady, whose daughter attended some section of the City College with which I should never be brought in contact, was induced to bring a suit, saying that my presence in that institution would be dangerous to her daughter's virtue. This was not a suit against me, but against the Municipality of New York.[1] I endeavoured to be made a party to the suit, but was told that I was not concerned. Although the Municipality was nominally the defendant, it was as anxious to lose the suit as the good lady was to win it. The lawyer for the prosecution pronounced my works 'lecherous, libidinous, lustful, venerous, erotomaniac, aphrodisiac, irreverent, narrow-minded, untruthful, and bereft of moral fiber'. The suit came before an Irishman who decided against me at length and with vituperation. I wished for an appeal, but the Municipality of New York refused to appeal. Some of the things said against me were quite fantastic. For example, I was thought wicked for saying that very young infants should not be punished for masturbation.

A typical American witch-hunt was instituted against me,[2] and I became taboo throughout the whole of the United States. I was to have been engaged in a lecture tour, but I had only one engagement, made before the witch-hunt had developed. The Rabbi who had made this engagement broke his contract, but I cannot blame him. Owners of halls refused to let them if I was to lecture, and if I had appeared anywhere in public, I should probably have been lynched by a Catholic mob, with the full approval of the police. No newspaper or magazine would publish anything that I wrote, and I was suddenly deprived of all means of earning a living. As it was legally impossible to get money out of England, this produced a very difficult situation, especially as I had my three children dependent upon me. Many liberal-minded

[1] Information about this suit will be found in *The Bertrand Russell Case*, ed. by John Dewey and Horace M. Kallen, Viking Press, 1941; and also in the Appendix to *Why I am not a Christian*, ed. by Paul Edwards, George Allen & Unwin, 1957.

[2] The Registrar of New York County said publicly that I should be 'tarred and feathered and driven out of the country'. Her remarks were typical of the general public condemnation.

professors protested, but they all supposed that as I was an earl I must have ancestral estates and be very well off. Only one man did anything practical, and that was Dr Barnes, the inventor of Argyrol, and the creator of the Barnes Foundation near Philadelphia. He gave me a five-year appointment to lecture on philosophy at his Foundation. This relieved me of a very great anxiety. Until he gave me this appointment, I had seen no way out of my troubles. I could not get money out of England; it was impossible to return to England; I certainly did not wish my three children to go back into the blitz, even if I could have got a passage for them which would certainly have been impossible for a long time to come. It seemed as if it would be necessary to take John and Kate away from the University, and to live as cheaply as possible on the charity of kind friends. From this bleak prospect I was saved by Dr Barnes.

The summer of 1940 offered for me an extraordinary contrast between public horror and private delight. We spent the summer in the Sierras, at Fallen Leaf Lake near Lake Tahoe, one of the loveliest places that it has ever been my good fortune to know. The lake is more than 6000 feet above sea-level, and during the greater part of the year deep snow makes the whole region uninhabitable. But there is a three-months' season in the summer during which the sun shines continually, the weather is warm, but as a rule not unbearably hot, the mountain meadows are filled with the most exquisite wild flowers, and the smell of the pine trees fills the air. We had a log cabin in the middle of pine trees, close to the lake. Conrad and his nursery governess slept indoors, but there was no room for the rest of us in the house, and we all slept on various porches. There were endless walks through deserted country to waterfalls, lakes and mountain tops, and one could dive off snow into deep water that was not unduly cold. I had a tiny study which was hardly more than a shed, and there I finished my *Inquiry into Meaning and Truth*. Often it was so hot that I did my writing stark naked. But heat suits me, and I never found it too hot for work.

Amid all these delights we waited day by day to know whether England had been invaded, and whether London still existed. The postman, a jocular fellow with a somewhat sadistic sense of humour, arrived one morning saying in a loud voice, 'Heard the news? All London destroyed, not a house left standing!' And we could not know whether to believe him. Long walks and frequent bathes in many lakes helped to make the time endurable, and, by September, it had begun to seem that England would not be invaded.

I found in the Sierras the only classless society that I have ever known. Practically all the houses were inhabited by university professors, and the necessary work was done by university students. The young man, for instance, who brought our groceries was a young man to whom I had been lecturing throughout the winter. There were also many students who had come merely for a holiday, which could be enjoyed very cheaply as everything was primitive and simple. Americans understand the management of tourists much better than Europeans do. Although there were many houses close to the lake, hardly one could be seen from a boat, since all were carefully concealed in pine trees; and the houses themselves were built of pine logs, and were quite inoffensive. One angle of the house in which we lived was made of a live and growing tree; I cannot imagine what will happen to the house when the tree grows too big.

In the autumn of 1940 I gave the William James lectures at Harvard. This engagement had been made before the trouble in New York. Perhaps Harvard regretted having made it, but, if so, the regret was politely concealed from me.

My duties with Dr Barnes began at the New Year of 1941. We rented a farmhouse about thirty miles from Philadelphia, a very charming house, about two hundred years old, in rolling country, not unlike inland Dorsetshire. There was an orchard, a fine old barn, and three peach trees, which bore enormous quantities of the most delicious peaches I have ever tasted. There were fields sloping down to a river, and pleasant woodlands. We were ten miles from Paoli (called after the Corsican patriot), which was the limit of the Philadelphia suburban trains. From there I used to go by train to the Barnes Foundation, where I lectured in a gallery of modern French paintings, mostly of nudes, which seemed somewhat incongruous for academic philosophy.

Dr Barnes was a strange character. He had a dog to whom he was passionately devoted and a wife who was passionately devoted to him. He liked to patronise coloured people and treated them as equals, because he was quite sure that they were not. He had made an enormous fortune by inventing Argyrol; when it was at its height, he sold out, and invested all his money in Government securities. He then became an art connoisseur. He had a very fine gallery of modern French paintings and in connection with the gallery he taught the principles of aesthetics. He demanded constant flattery and had a passion for quarrelling. I was warned before accepting his offer that he always tired of people before long, so I exacted a five-year contract from him. On December 28th, 1942, I got a letter from him informing me that my appointment was terminated as from January 1st. I was thus reduced once again from affluence to destitution. True, I had my contract, and the lawyer whom I consulted assured me that there was no doubt whatever of my getting full redress from the courts. But obtaining legal redress takes time, especially in America, and I had to live through the intervening period somehow. Corbusier, in a book on America, tells a typical story about Barnes's behaviour. Corbusier was on a lecture tour, and wished to see Dr Barnes's gallery. He wrote for permission, which Dr Barnes always accorded very grudgingly. Dr Barnes replied that he could see it at nine o'clock on a certain Saturday morning, but at no other time. Corbusier wrote again saying that his lecture engagements made that time impossible and would not some other time be suitable. Dr Barnes wrote an exceedingly rude letter, saying it was then or never. To this Corbusier sent a long answer, which is printed in his book saying that he was not averse from quarrels, but he preferred to quarrel with people who were on the other side in matters of art, whereas he and Dr Barnes were both in favour of what is modern, and it seemed a pity that they should not agree. Dr Barnes never opened this letter, but returned it, with the word '*merde*' written large on the envelope.

When my case came into court, Dr Barnes complained that I had done insufficient work for my lectures, and that they were superficial and perfunctory. So far as they had gone, they consisted of the first two-thirds of my *History of Western Philosophy*, of which I submitted the manuscript to the judge, though I scarcely suppose he read it. Dr Barnes complained of my treatment of the men whom he called Pithergawras and Empi-Dokkles. I observed the judge taking notice, and I won my case. Dr Barnes, of course, appealed as often as he could, and it was not until I was back in England that I actually got the money. Meanwhile he had sent a printed document concerning my sins to the Master and each of the Fellows of Trinity College, to warn them of their folly in inviting me back. I never read this document, but I have no doubt it was good reading.

In the early months of 1943 I suffered some financial stringency, but not so much as I had feared. We sublet our nice farmhouse, and went to live in a cottage intended for a coloured couple whom it was expected that the inhabitants of the farmhouse would employ. This consisted of three rooms and three stoves, each of which had to be stoked every hour or so. One was to warm the place, one was for cooking, and one was for hot water. When they went out it was several hours' work to get them lighted again. Conrad could hear every word that Peter and I said to each other, and we had many worrying things to discuss which it was not good for him to be troubled with. But by this time the trouble about City College had begun to blow over, and I was able to get occasional lecture engagements in New York and other places. The embargo was first broken by an invitation from Professor Weiss of Bryn Mawr to give a course of lectures there. This required no small degree of courage. On one occasion I was so poor that I had to take a single ticket to New York and pay the return fare out of my lecture fee. My *History of Western Philosophy* was nearly complete, and I wrote to

W. W. Norton, who had been my American publisher, to ask if, in view of my difficult financial position, he would make an advance on it. He replied that because of his affection for John and Kate, and as a kindness to an old friend, he would advance five hundred dollars. I thought I could get more elsewhere, so I approached Simon and Schuster, who were unknown to me personally. They at once agreed to pay me two thousand dollars on the spot, and another thousand six months later. At this time John was at Harvard and Kate was at Radcliffe. I had been afraid that lack of funds might compel me to take them away, but thanks to Simon and Schuster, this proved unnecessary. I was also helped at this time by loans from private friends which, fortunately, I was able to repay before long.

The *History of Western Philosophy* began by accident and proved the main source of my income for many years. I had no idea, when I embarked upon this project, that it would have a success which none of my other books have had, even, for a time, shining high upon the American list of Best Sellers. While I was still concerned with ancient times, Barnes had told me that he had no further need of me, and my lectures stopped. I found the work exceedingly interesting, especially the parts that I knew least about beforehand, the early Medieval part and the Jewish part just before the birth of Christ, so I continued the work till I had completed the survey. I was grateful to Bryn Mawr College for allowing me the use of its library which I found excellent, especially as it provided me with the invaluable work of the Rev. Charles who published translations of Jewish works written shortly before the time of Christ and in a great degree anticipating His teaching.

I was pleased to be writing this history because I had always believed that history should be written in the large. I had always held, for example, that the subject matter of which Gibbon treats could not be adequately treated in a shorter book or several books. I regarded the early part of my *History of Western Philosophy* as a history of culture, but in the later parts, where science becomes important, it is more difficult to fit into this framework. I did my best, but I am not at all sure that I succeeded. I was sometimes accused by reviewers of writing not a true history but a biased account of the events that I arbitrarily chose to write of. But to my mind, a man without a bias cannot write interesting history – if, indeed, such a man exists. I regard it as mere humbug to pretend to lack of bias. Moreover, a book, like any other work, should be held together by its point of view. This is why a book made up of essays by various authors is apt to be less interesting as an entity than a book by one man. Since I do not admit that a person without bias exists, I think the best that can be done with a large-scale history is to admit one's bias and for dissatisfied readers to look for other writers to express an opposite bias. Which bias is nearer to the truth must be left to posterity. This point of view on the writing of history makes me prefer my *History of Western Philosophy* to the *Wisdom of the West* which was taken from the former, but ironed out and tamed – although I like the illustrations of *Wisdom of the West*.

The last part of our time in America was spent at Princeton, where we had a little house on the shores of the lake. While in Princeton, I came to know Einstein fairly well. I used to go to his house once a week to discuss with him and Gödel and Pauli. These discussions were in some ways disappointing, for, although all three of them were Jews and exiles and, in intention, cosmopolitans, I found that they all had a German bias towards metaphysics, and in spite of our utmost endeavours we never arrived at common premises from which to argue. Gödel turned out to be an unadulterated Platonist, and apparently believed that an eternal 'not' was laid up in heaven, where virtuous logicians might hope to meet it hereafter.

The society of Princeton was extremely pleasant, pleasanter, on the whole, than any other social group I had come across in America. By this time John was back in England, having gone into the British Navy and been set to learn Japanese. Kate was self-sufficient at Radcliffe, having done extremely well in her work and acquired a small teaching job. There was therefore nothing to keep us in America except the difficulty of obtaining a passage to England. This difficulty, however, seemed for a long time insuperable. I went to Washington to argue that I must be allowed to perform my duties in the House of Lords, and tried to persuade the authorities that my desire to do so was very ardent. At last I discovered an argument which convinced the British Embassy. I said to them: 'You will admit this is a war against Fascism.' 'Yes', they said; 'And', I continued, 'you will admit that the essence of Fascism consists in the subordination of the legislature to the executive'. 'Yes,' they said, though with slightly more hesitation. 'Now,' I continued, 'you are the executive and I am the legislature and if you keep me away from my legislative functions one day longer than is necessary, you are Fascists.' Amid general laughter, my sailing permit was granted then and there. A curious difficulty, however, still remained. My wife and I got A priority, but our son Conrad only got a B, as he had as yet no legislative function. Naturally enough we wished Conrad, who was seven years old, and his mother to travel together, but this required that she should consent to be classified as a B. No case had so far occurred of a person accepting a lower classification than that to which they were entitled, and all the officials were so puzzled that it took them some months to understand. At last, however, dates were fixed, for Peter and Conrad first, and for me about a fortnight later. We sailed in May 1944.

LETTERS

To Charles Sanger's wife   'The Plaisance'
                                       On the Midway at Jackson
                                       Park – Chicago
                                       Nov. 5, 1938

My dear Dora

Thank you for your letter, which, after some wanderings, reached me here.

I quite agree with you about the new war-cry. I was immensely glad when the crisis passed, but I don't know how soon it may come up again. Here in America, nine people out of ten think that we ought to have fought but America ought to have remained neutral – an opinion which annoys me. It is odd, in England, that the very people who, in 1919, protested against the unjust frontiers of Czechoslovakia were the most anxious, in 1938, to defend them. And they always forget that the first result of an attempt at an armed defence would have been to expose the Czechs to German invasion, which would have been much worse for them than even what they are enduring now.

I had forgotten about Eddie Marsh at the Ship in 1914, but your letter reminded me of it. Everybody at that time reacted so characteristically.

Ottoline's death was a very great loss to me. Charlie and Crompton and Ottoline were my only really close friends among contemporaries, and now all three are dead. And day by day we move into an increasingly horrible world.

Privately, nevertheless, my circumstances are happy. John and Kate are everything that I would wish, and Conrad Crow (now 19 months old) is most satisfactory. America is interesting, and solid, whereas England, one fears, is crumbling. Daphne[1] must have had an interesting time in Belgrade.

I shall be home early in May, and I hope I shall see you soon there. All good wishes,

                             Yours ever
                             Bertrand Russell

To W. V. Quine   212 Loring Avenue
                                       Los Angeles, Cal.
                                       16 Oct., 1939

Dear Dr Quine

I quite agree with your estimate of Tarski; no other logician of his generation (unless it were yourself) seems to me his equal.

                 [1] The Sangers' daughter.

I should, consequently, be very glad indeed if I could induce the authorities here to find him a post. I should be glad for logic, for the university, for him, and for myself. But inquiries have shown me that there is no possibility whatever; they feel that they are saturated both with foreigners and with logicians. I went so far as to hint that if I could, by retiring, make room for him, I might consider doing so; but it seemed that even so the result could not be achieved.

I presume you have tried the East: Harvard, Princeton, Columbia, etc. Princeton *should* be the obvious place. You may quote me anywhere as concurring in your view of Tarski's abilities.

> *Yours sincerely*
> *Bertrand Russell*

From an anonymous correspondent   Newark, N.J.
                                   March 4, 1940

Bertrand Russell

Just whom did you think you were fooling when you had those hypocritically posed 'family man' pictures taken for the newspapers? Can your diseased brain have reached such an advanced stage of senility as to imagine for a moment that you would impress anyone? You poor old fool!

Even your publicly proved degeneracy cannot overshadow your vileness in posing for these pictures and trying to hide behind the innocence of your unfortunate children. Shame on you! Every decent man and woman in the country loathes you for this vile action of yours more than your other failings, which, after all, you inherited honestly enough from your decadent family tree. As for your questions and concern regarding Church and State connections in this country – just what concern has anything in this country got to do with you? Any time you don't like American doings go back to your native England (if you can!) and your stuttering King, who is an excellent example of British degenerate royalty – with its ancestry of barmaids, and pantry-men!

Or did I hear some one say you were thrown out of that country of liberal degeneracy, because you out-did the royal family. HAW!

> *Yours*
> *Pimp-Hater*

P.S. – I notice you refer to some American Judge as an 'ignorant fellow'. If you are such a shining light, just why are you looking for a new appointment at this late date in your life? Have you been smelling up the California countryside too strongly?

From Aldous Huxley   Metro-Goldwyn-Mayer
                                             Pictures
                                        Culver-City, California
                                        19.III.40

Dear Bertie

Sympathy, I'm afraid, can't do much good; but I feel I must tell you how much I feel for you and Peter in the midst of the obscene outcry that has broken out around your name in New York.

                                        Ever yours
                                        Aldous H.

Press statement by the Student Council, College of the City of New York

                                        March 9, 1940

To the Editor

The appointment of Bertrand Russell to the staff of the City College has brought forth much discussion in the press and has evoked statements from various organisations and individuals. We do not wish to enter any controversy on Prof. Russell's views on morals and religion; we feel that he is entitled to his own personal views.

Prof. Russell has been appointed to the staff of the City College to teach mathematics and logic. With an international reputation, he is eminently qualified to teach these subjects. He has been lecturing at the University of California and has been appointed visiting professor at Harvard University before he comes to the City College in February 1941. The student body, as well as the faculty, are of the opinion that the addition of Prof. Russell to the faculty cannot but help to raise the academic prestige and national standing of our college.

Nobody questioned public school teachers or City College instructors about their belief on the nature of the cosmos – whether they were Catholics, Protestants, Jews, atheists or worshippers of the ancient Greek Pantheon – when they were appointed. The American public education system is founded on the principle that religion has nothing to do with secular education and theoretically the religious beliefs of teachers have nothing to do with their jobs. Religious groups are free to expound their views. Why not educators ?

By refusing to yield to the pressure being brought to bear and by standing firm on the appointment of Prof. Russell, the Board of Higher Education will be saving City College an academic black eye and doing its duty to the community in the highest sense.

We wish to stress again in the words of President Mead that Prof. Russell has been appointed to the City College to teach mathematics and logic and not his views on morals and religion.

City College has long been subject to attack from various sources seeking to modify or destroy our free higher education; the attack on Bertrand Russell is but another manifestation of this tendency.

Executive Committee
Student Council
The City College

To Bernard Goltz,
Secretary, the Student
Council, C.C.N.Y.   March 22, 1940

Dear Mr Goltz

I am very happy to have the support of the student council in the fight. Old York was the first place where Christianity was the state religion, and it was there that Constantine assumed the purple. Perhaps New York will be the last place to have this honour.

Yours sincerely
Bertrand Russell

To William Swirsky,   212 Loring Avenue
a student at C.C.N.Y.   West Lost Angeles, California
                                       March 22, 1940

Dear Mr Swirsky

Thank you very much for your letter, and for the enclosures from *The Campus.* I am very glad indeed that the students do not share Bishop Manning's views about me; if they did it would be necessary to despair of the young. It is comforting that the Board of Higher Education decided in my favor, but I doubt whether the fight is at an end. I am afraid that if and when I take up my duties at the City College you will all be disappointed to find me a very mild and inoffensive person, totally destitute of horns and hoofs.

Yours gratefully
Bertrand Russell

From M. F. Ashley-Montagu   The Hahnemann Medical
                                       College and
                                       Hospital of Philadelphia
                                     31 March 1940

Dear Professor Russell

I owe you so much that I feel I could never adequately repay you for the part which your writings have played in my own intellectual development. Having acquired my share of inhibitions under the English 'system' of miseducation, I have since 1930 gradually relieved myself of what used to be termed 'a natural reluctance' to address people to whom I had not been formally introduced. At this rather trying period in your life I want to reassure you. It was really Mrs

Russell's remark (as reported in *The New York Times*) which is responsible for precipitating this letter. This *is* a strange land, but you are not strangers here. Your friends here number millions, and as you have obviously known for a long time, this is really the most humane, and fundamentally the most decent land in the world. That is why there is every hope, every reason to believe, that the decision of a single jurist will ultimately be faithfully evaluated for what it is worth, and your appointment to the faculty of City College maintained. When situations such as yours are given a thorough airing I have noted that justice is practically always done. It is only under the cloaca of local departmental privacy that injustice succeeds and may prosper, I have on more than one occasion suffered the consequences of such private tyranny, but you are in far different case. There are many of us who, both as individuals and as members of societies for the preservation of academic and intellectual freedom, will fight your case, if necessary, to the last ditch. I can predict, with a degree of probability which amounts to certainty that despite the barking of the dogs of St Ernulphus, common decency will prevail.

I can well realise how full your mailbag must be, so please don't attempt to acknowledge this letter. Your sense of humour will look after you, and you can leave the rest to us.

With all good wishes,　　　　　*Ever yours sincerely*
　　　　　　　　　　　　　　　M. F. Ashley-Montagu
　　　　　　　　　　　　　　　Associate Professor of Anatomy

To Mr Harry W. Laidler,
of the League for Industrial Democracy

April 11, 1940

Dear Mr Laidler

The undersigned members of the Department of Philosophy at U.C.L.A. are taking the liberty to answer your letter of inquiry addressed to Miss Creed. We have all attended lectures or seminars conducted by Mr Russell on this campus, and have therefore first hand knowledge of the character and the content of his teaching here. We find him to be the most stimulating teacher we have known, and his intellectual influence upon the student is remarkable. The general effect of his teaching is to sharpen the student's sense of truth, both by developing his desire for truth and by leading him to a more rigorous application of the tests of truth. Also unusual is the influence of Mr Russell's moral character upon the student. It is impossible to know Mr Russell without coming to admire his complete fairness, his unfailing and genuine courtesy and his sincere love of people and of humanity.

We may add that there has not been any criticism of Mr Russell's teachings on this campus. This Department, in recommending Mr Russell's appointment, was aware that there would be some criticism on the part of outsiders of such action by the University. But in no case has there been any objection based upon Mr Russell's work here. In inviting Mr Russell to join us we did so in the faith that the individual instructor is entitled to his individual opinion on political, moral and other social issues, and that unorthodox opinions in such matters are no ground for banning an individual from public life.

You may use this letter in any way you think fit.

> *Yours sincerely*
> *Hans Reichenbach*
> *Isabel P. Creed*
> *J. W. Robson*
> *Hugh Miller, Acting Chairman*

From and to William Ernest Hocking, 16 Quincy Street
Professor of Philosophy Cambridge, Massachusetts
Harvard University April 30, 1940

Dear Russell

I answered part of your letter of April 14 by telegram: 'No possible objection to engagement at Newark.'

For the other part, which called equally for an answer – the part in which you expressed the 'hope that Harvard doesn't mind too much' – I thought it best to wait until I could send you something tangible.

The enclosed clipping from Sunday's *Boston Herald* gives a statement issued Saturday evening by our governing body ('The President and Fellows', commonly dubbed 'The Corporation'), standing by the appointment. It will also give you a hint of the kind of attack which instigated the statement. The page from Monday's *Crimson* shows more of the inside.

Please consider what I say in comment as purely personal. Individual members of the department have taken action, as you have noticed; but the department has formulated no attitude, and I am speaking for myself alone.

It would be foolish for me to pretend that the university is not disturbed by the situation. Harvard is not a 'state university' in the sense that it draws its major support from legislative grants (as in Indiana, Michigan, etc.). But it is a state institution, with certain unique provisions for its government set into the constitution, so that political interference with our working is legally possible. The suit promised by Thomas Dorgan, legislative agent for the City of Boston, has some footing in the law of the Commonwealth, though the University is prepared to meet it. But beyond that, there are possibilities of further legislation which might be serious for an institution already an object of dislike on the part of certain elements of the public.

As to the suit itself, the university is not proposing to contest it on the ground of 'freedom of speech' or 'freedom of teaching' (for this would make the university appear as protagonist of a claim of right on your part to teach your views on sex-morals at Harvard, a claim certainly uncontemplated in our arrangements and probably untenable at law). The university is simply holding the ground of the independence of our appointing bodies from outside interference. This is a defensible position, if we can show that we have exercised and are exercising that independence with a due sense of responsibility to our statutory obligations. This line will explain the emphasis in the university's statement on the scope of your lectures, and on the restriction of your teaching to advanced students; under the circumstances we shall have to abide by this limitation.

(The number of lectures mentioned in the university's statement was taken from the words of the founding bequest, which reads 'not less than six': in practice the lectures have run to ten or twelve, partly, I suppose, because of the shift to a biennial plan.)

We are all terribly sorry that this hue and cry has arisen, both because of the distress to you, and because it gives capital prominence to what (I presume) we were both considering background stuff, in which we are definitely not interested. For myself, I am equally sorry that you are making the issue one of freedom of speech in the New York situation. For if you lose, you lose; and if you win, you lose also. And the colleges will lose, too: for the impression already in the public mind will be deepened, that the colleges insist on regarding all hypotheses as on the same level, – none are foolish and none are immoral: they are all playthings of debate for a lot of detached intellects who have nothing in common with the intuitions of average mankind. Personally I am with the average man in doubting whether all hypotheses are on the same level, or can escape the invidious adjectives.

Largely because of this, I have had, so far, nothing to say in public on this question. I have been cultivating the great and forgotten right of the freedom of silence, which it is hard to maintain in this country. If I were talking, I should agree in the main with the first paragraph of the editorial in the *New York Times* of April 20, which you have doubtless seen, and whose refrain is that 'mistakes of judgment have been made by all the principals involved'.

Your scheme of lecture titles has come, and it looks splendid to me, – many thanks. I shall write again when the department has had a chance to look it over.

Sincerely yours
Ernest Hocking

212 Loring Avenue
Los Angeles, Cal.
May 6 1940

Dear Hocking

Thank you for your letter. It makes me wish that I could honourably resign the appointment to the William James lectures, but I do not see how I can do so without laying myself open to the charge of cowardice and of letting down the interests of the whole body of teachers.

I almost wish, also, that the President and Fellows had not re-affirmed the appointment, since as you say, and as appears in the newspaper quotation you sent me, the opposition has considerable basis in law. From my point of view it would be better to be dismissed now, with financial compensation, than to be robbed both of the appointment and of compensation after long anxiety and distress.

I did not seek the appointment, and I am not so fond of the role of martyr as to wish continuously and without respite to suffer for a cause which concerns others so much more than me. The independence of American universities is their affair, not mine.

Some one seems to have misled you as to the line that I and the Board of Higher Education in New York have taken about my appointment there. I have never dreamed of claiming a right to talk about sexual ethics when I am hired to talk about logic or semantics; equally, a man hired to teach ethics would have no right to talk about logic. I claim two things: 1. that appointments to academic posts should be made by people with some competence to judge a man's technical qualifications; 2. that in extra-professional hours a teacher should be free to express his opinions, whatever they may be. City College and the Board of Higher Education based their defense solely on the first of these contentions. Their defense was therefore identical with that which you say is contemplated by Harvard.

The principle of free speech was raised by other people, in my opinion rightly. I am afraid that Harvard, like the New York Board, cannot prevent popular agitation based on this principle; though it is of course obvious that in both cases the official defense of the appointment is rightly based on the independence of duly constituted academic bodies and their right to make their own appointments.

I ask now, in advance, that I may be officially notified of any legal proceedings taken against the University on account of my appointment, and allowed to become a party. This was not done in the New York case, because of the hostility of the Corporation Counsel, who handled their defence. I cannot endure a second time being slandered and condemned in a court of law without any opportunity of rebutting false accusations against which no one else can adequately defend me, for lack of knowledge.

I hope that Harvard will have the courtesy to keep me informed officially of all developments, instead of leaving me to learn of matters that vitally concern me only from inaccurate accounts in newspapers.

I should be glad if you would show this letter to the President and Fellows.

> *Yours sincerely*
> *Bertrand Russell*

To the Editor of the *Harvard Crimson* 212 Loring Avenue
Los Angeles, Cal.
May 6 1940

Dear Sir

I hope you will allow me to comment on your references in the *Harvard Crimson* of April 29 to the recent proceedings concerning my appointment to the City College of New York.

You say 'Freedom of speech will not be the point under argument, as was the case in the proceedings against City College of New York, when the latter based an unsuccessful defense of its Russell appointment on the assertion that Russell should be permitted to expound his moral views from a lecture platform'.

In fact freedom of speech was not the defense of City College and the New York Board of Higher Education. The Board and College based their defense on the principle of academic freedom, which means simply the independence of duly constituted academic bodies, and their right to make their own appointments. *This, according to your headline, is exactly the defense contemplated by the Corporation of Harvard.* Neither the Board of Higher Education nor the faculty of City College at any time made the claim that I 'should be permitted to expound my moral views from a lecture platform'. On the contrary, they stated repeatedly and with emphasis that my moral views had no possible relevance to the subjects I had been engaged to teach.

Even if I were permitted to expound my moral views in the classroom, my own conscience would not allow me to do so, since they have no connection with the subjects which it is my profession to teach, and I think that the classroom should not be used as an opportunity for propaganda on any subject.

The principle of freedom of speech has been invoked, not by the New York Board of Higher Education as their legal defense, but by many thousands of people throughout the United States who have perceived its obvious relation to the Controversy, which is this: the American constitution guarantees to everyone the right to express his opinions whatever these may be. This right is naturally limited by

any contract into which the individual may enter which requires him
to spend part of his time in occupations other than expressing his
opinions. Thus, if a salesman, a postman, a tailor and a teacher of
mathematics all happen to hold a certain opinion on a subject unrelated
to their work, whatever it may be, none of them should devote to
oratory on this subject time which they have been paid to spend in
selling, delivering letters, making suits, or teaching mathematics. But
they should all equally be allowed to express their opinion freely and
without fear of penalties in their spare time, and to think, speak and
behave as they wish, within the law, when they are not engaged in their
professional duties.

This is the principle of free speech. It appears to be little known.
If therefore anyone should require any further information about it
I refer him to the United States Constitution and to the works of the
founders thereof.

> *Yours faithfully*
> *Bertrand Russell*

To Kingsley Martin
editor of the *New Statesman*

212 Loring Avenue
Los Angeles, Cal.
May 13 1940

Dear Kingsley Martin

Thanks for your kind paragraph about my New York appointment.
We still hope to appeal, but the Mayor and corporation counsel, from
respect for the Catholic vote, are doing their best to prevent it. A similar fuss is promised over my appointment to give the William James
lectures at Harvard in the autumn.

Actually I am being overwhelmed with friendship and support, but
in this country the decent people are terrifyingly powerless and often
very naive. This fuss is serving a useful purpose in calling attention to
the sort of thing that happens constantly to people less well known.

The news from Europe is unbearably painful. We all wish that we
were not so far away, although we could serve no useful purpose if
we were at home.

Ever since the war began I have felt that I could not go on being a
pacifist; but I have hesitated to say so, because of the responsibility
involved. If I were young enough to fight myself I should do so, but
it is more difficult to urge others. Now, however, I feel that I ought
to announce that I have changed my mind, and I would be glad if you
could find an opportunity to mention in the *New Statesman* that you
have heard from me to this effect.

> *Yours sincerely*
> *Bertrand Russell*

To Professor Hocking from John   1 West 89th St NY City
  Dewey   May 16th, 40

Dear Hocking

I have seen a copy of your letter to Russell and I cannot refrain from saying that I am disturbed by one portion of it – especially as coming from you.

Of course I do not feel qualified to speak from the Harvard point of view or to give advice on the matter as far as it is Harvard's administrative concern. But I am sure of one thing: Any weakening on the part of Harvard University would strengthen the forces of reaction – ecclesiastical and other – which are already growing too rapidly, presumably on account of the state of fear and insecurity now so general. I don't think it is irrelevant to point out that the NY City Council followed up its interference in the City College matter with a resolution in which they asked for the dismissal of the present Board of Higher Education and the appointment of a new one – the present Board being mainly La Guardia's appointments and sticking by the liberal attitudes on acct of which they were originally appointed – in spite of the Mayor's recent shocking cowardice. Tammany and the Church aren't now getting the educational plums they want and used to get. In my opinion (without means of proof) the original attack on Russell's appointment, and even more so the terms of McGeehan's decision were *not isolated* events. The reactionary catholic paper in Brooklyn, *The Tablet*, openly expressed the hope that the move might be the beginning of a movement to abolish all municipal colleges in Greater New York – now four in number. A policy of 'appeasement' will not work any better, in my judgment, with this old totalitarian institution than it has with the newer ones. Every weakening will be the signal for new attacks. So much, possibly irrelevant from your point of view, regarding the Harvard end of the situation.

The point that disturbed me in your letter was not the one contained in the foregoing gratuitous paragraph. That point is your statement of regret that Russell raised the issue of freedom of speech. In the first place, he didn't raise it; it was raised *first* by McGeehan's decision (I can't but wonder if you have ever seen that monstrous document), and then by other persons, originally in New York institutions but rapidly joined by others throughout the country, who saw the serious implications of passively sitting by and letting it go by default. As far as the legal side is concerned the issue has been and will be fought on a ground substantially identical with that you mention in the case of the Harvard suit. But the educational issue is wider, much wider. It was stated in the courageous letter of Chancellor Chase of NY University in a letter to the *Times* – a letter which finally evoked from them their first editorial comment – which though grudging and ungracious did agree the case should be appealed. If men are going to be kept out of American colleges because they express unconventional, unorthodox or even unwise views (but who is to be the judge of widsom or lack of wisdom?) on political, economic, social or moral matters, expressing those views in publications addressed to the general public, I am heartily glad my own teaching days have come to an end. There will always be some kept prostitutes in any institution; there are always [the] more timid by temperament who take to teaching as a kind of protected calling. If the courts, under outside group pressures, are going to be allowed, without protest from college teachers, to confine college faculties to teachers of these two types, the outlook is dark indeed. If I express myself strongly it is because I feel strongly on this issue. While I am extremely sorry for the thoroughly disagreeable position in which the Russells have been personally plunged, I can't but be grateful in view of the number of men of lesser stature who have been made to suffer, that his case is of such importance as to attract wide attention and protest. If you have read McGeehan's decision, I suppose you would feel with some of the rest of us that no self-respecting person would do anything – such as the *Times* editorial suggested he do – that would even remotely admit the truth of the outrageous statements made – statements that would certainly be criminally libellous if not protected by the position of the man making them. But over and above that I am grateful for the service Russell renders the teaching body and educational interests in general by taking up the challenge – accordingly I am going to take the liberty of sending a copy of this letter to Russell.

> *Very sincerely yours*
> *John Dewey*

Dear Mr Russell
   The above is self-explanatory – I know how occupied you are and it needs no reply.

> *Sincerely, & gratefully yours*
> *John Dewey*

From Alfred North Whitehead   1737 Cambridge St
                                       Cambridge, Mass.
                                       April 26, 1940

Dear Bertie
   Evelyn and I cannot let this occasion pass without telling you how greatly we sympathise with you in the matter of the New York appointment. You know, of course, that our opinions are directly opposed in

many ways. This note is just to give you our love and deep sympathy
in the personal troubles which have been aroused –

With all good wishes from us both.

> *Yours ever*
> *Alfred Whitehead*

Controversy over my appointment to C.C.N.Y. did not end in 1940.

From *The Times*, November 23rd and 26th, 1957, on the publication
of *Why I am not a Christian:*

To the Editor of *The Times*   10, Darlington Street, Bath
Sir

In a letter to *The Times* which you published on October 15, Lord
Russell complains that in 1940 Protestant Episcopalians and Roman
Catholics in New York City prevented him from denying in court
what he terms their 'libels'.

The official record of the decision declaring him ineligible for
the professorship in question makes it clear that his counsel submitted a brief on his behalf which was accepted by the court. His
subsequent application to re-open the case was denied by the court
on the grounds, among others, that he gave no indication of being able
to present new evidence which could change the decision, which was
unanimously upheld by two Courts of Appeal.

He could also have brought an action for libel against anyone for
statements made out of court, but he failed to do this.

In these circumstances is it fair to state, as Lord Russell does, that
Protestant Episcopalians and Roman Catholics prevented him from
denying in court the charges which were largely based on his own
writings ?

> *Yours truly*
> *Schuyler N. Warren*

To the Editor of *The Times*   Plas Penrhyn
                                      Penrhyndeudraeth
                                      Merioneth

Sir

In your issue of Novebemer 23 you publish a letter from Mr
Schuyler N. Warren which shows complete ignorance of the facts.
I shall answer his points one by one.

First as to 'libels'. I wrote publicly at the time: 'When grossly
untrue statements as to my actions are made in court, I feel that I
must give them the lie. I never conducted a nudist colony in England.
Neither my wife nor I ever paraded nude in public. I never went in

for salacious poetry. Such assertions are deliberate falsehoods which must be known to those who make them to have no foundation in fact. I shall be glad of an opportunity to deny them on oath.' This opportunity was denied me on the ground that I was not a party to the suit. The charges that I did these things (which had been made by the prosecuting counsel in court) were not based on my own writings, as Mr Warren affirms, but on the morbid imaginings of bigots.

I cannot understand Mr Warren's statement that *my* counsel submitted a brief on my behalf. No counsel representing me was heard. Nor can I understand his statement that two Courts of Appeal upheld the decision, as New York City refused to appeal when urged to do so. The suggestion that I could have brought an action for libel could only be made honestly by a person ignorant of the atmosphere of hysteria which surrounded the case at that time. The atmosphere is illustrated by the general acceptance of the prosecuting counsel's description in court of me as: 'lecherous, libidinous, lustful, venerous, erotomaniac, aphrodisiac, irreverent, narrow-minded, untruthful, and bereft of moral fiber.'

> *Yours truly*
> *Russell*

From and to Schuyler N. Warren

10, Darlington Street
Bath
10th January, 1958

Dear Lord Russell

I am writing with regard to your letter which appeared in the *Times* on November 26th. In this letter dealing with the controversy and subsequent litigation over your appointment as a Professor of Philosophy in the college in the City of New York you contradicted statements made by me in a letter that was published in the *Times* on November 23rd.

I enclose photostats of both decisions of the Supreme Court for your information, one revoking your appointment and the second denying your application to reopen the case. I also enclose copy of the letter from Mr Charles H. Tuttle, then as now, a member of the Board of Higher Education.

In view of your denials that no counsel representing you was heard, and that no appeal was made on your behalf, the enclosed decisions confirm the correctness of my statements. In the appendix of the volume *Why I am Not a Christian*, Professor Edwards mentions Mr Osmund K. Fraenkel as having been your Attorney and of his unsuccessful appeals to the Appellate Division and to the Court of Appeals.

> *Very truly yours*
> *Schuyler N. Warren*

Plas Penrhyn
13 January, 1958

Dear Mr Warren

Your letter of January 10 with the enclosed photostats does not bear out your stated view as to what occurred in my New York case in 1940. The appeal which you mentioned was not an appeal to the substance of the case, but on whether I should be allowed to become a party. You have not quite grasped the peculiarity of the whole affair. The defendants wished to lose the case – as at the time was generally known – and therefore had no wish to see McGeehan's verdict reversed on appeal. The statement that I was kept informed of the proceedings is perhaps in some narrow legal sense defensible, but I was held in Los Angeles by my duties there, the information as to what was happening in New York was sent by surface mail, and the proceedings were so hurried-up that everything was over before I knew properly what was happening. It remains the fact that I was not allowed to become a party to the case, that I was unable to appeal, and that I had no opportunity of giving evidence in court after I knew what they were saying about me. Mr Fraenkel, whom you mentioned, was appointed by the Civil Liberties Union, not by me, and took his instructions from them.

Yours truly
Russell

From Prof. Philip P. Wiener

The City College
New York 31, N.Y.
Department of Philosophy
Oct. 4, 1961

To the Editor of the New York Times

For myself and many of my colleagues I wish to express our distress at the unfairness and the poor taste shown by your Topics' editor's attempted comical rehashing of the Bertrand Russell case. It is well known that the educated world on moral grounds condemned Judge McGeehan's character assassination of one of the world's greatest philosophers, and that the courts did not allow Russell to enter the case. Now that this great man is almost ninety years old and fighting for the preservation of humanity (though some of us do not agree with his unilateral disarmament policy[1]), we believe your columnist owes him and the civilised world an apology.

Philip P. Wiener
Professor and Chairman

[1] I advocated unilateral disarmament at this time only for Britain.

289 Convent Avenue
New York City
Dec. 8, 1940

Dear Professor Russell

After having enjoyed your timely lecture before the P.E.A.[1] and friendly chat at the Penn. R.R. terminal, I reported to my colleagues that we had indeed been filched of a great teacher who would have brought so much of light and humanity to our students that the harpies of darkness and corruption might well have cringed with fear of a personality so dangerous to their interests. John Dewey is working on an analysis of the McGeehan decision in so far as it discusses your books on education. That will be Dewey's contribution to the book to be published by Barnes. Our department has offered to co-operate with the editors, but we have not yet heard from Horace Kallen, who appears to be directing the book.

The Hearst papers link your appointment to City College with that of the communists named by the State Legislative Committee investigating subversive political activities of city college teachers, in order to condemn the Board of Higher Education and recommends its reorganisation under more reactionary control. You may have noticed in yesterday's *N.Y. Times* that President Gannon of Fordham University recommended that 'subversive *philosophical* activities' in the city colleges be investigated!

I noted with interest your plan to devote the next four years to the history of philosophy. I always regarded your work on Leibniz next in importance only to your *Principles of Mathematics* and *Principia Mathematica*. If you made similar analytical and critical studies from primary sources of the most influential philosophers – even if only a few – e.g. Plato, Aristotle, Aquinas, Hobbes, Hume, Kant and Hegel, you would have contributed to the *critical* history of philosophy what only a philosopher equipped with modern instruments of analysis and a direct knowledge of the texts could do. This would be philosophically significant as a union of analytical and historical methods of investigating pervasive ideas like that of freedom (which exists mainly as an idea).

I should like to have a chance to discuss this matter with you, since the whole subject lies close to my chief interest and activity connected with the *Journal of the History of Ideas*. I may be in Philadelphia for the Amer. Philosophical Assoc. Symposium, Dec. 28, 1940, and should like to phone you if you are free that evening or the next day (Sunday, Dec. 29).

Yours sincerely
Philip P. Wiener

[1] Progressive Education Association.

P.S. – Professor Lovejoy might be free to come along to see you if I knew when you were free to talk history of philosophy.

To and from Robert Trevelyan   212 Loring Avenue
                                            Los Angeles, Cal., U.S.A.
                                            22.12.39

Dear Bob

Ever since I got your letter a year ago I have meant to write to you, but I felt like God when he was thinking of creating the world: there was no more reason for choosing one moment than for choosing another. I have not waited as long as he did.

I am established here as Professor of Philosophy in the University of California. John and Kate came out for the summer holidays, and stayed when the war came, so they are having to go to the university here. John has a passion for Latin, especially Lucretius; unfortunately your Lucretius is stored in Oxford with the rest of my books. (I had expected to come back to England last spring.)

Thank you very much for the list of misprints.

I wonder what you are feeling about the war. I try hard to remain a pacifist, but the thought of Hitler and Stalin triumphant is hard to bear.

C.A. [Clifford Allen]'s death must have been a great sorrow to you. I do not know what his views were at the end.

Americans all say 'you must be glad to be here at this time', but except for the children's sake that is not how we feel.

Much love to both you and Bessie from us both. Write when you can – it is a comfort to hear from old friends.

                                    Yours ever affectionately
                                    Bertrand Russell

                                    The Shiffolds
                                    Holmbury St Mary, Dorking
                                    11 Febr. 1940

Dear Bertie

It was very nice hearing from you the other day, and to know that all is well with Peter and you and the children (I suppose they are hardly children any longer now). We are fairly all right here – at present at any rate. Bessie keeps quite cheerful, though her eye is no better. I read to her in the evening now, instead of her reading to me.

We are very glad the children are staying in America, I hope it won't be for ever, though. At present things look pretty hopeless. I have sent you a copy of my Lucretius for John, as it might be a help to him. I have also sent my Poems and Plays, as a Christmas present. Of course, I don't expect you to read them from the beginning to the end: in fact, my advice, is, if you feel you must read in them at all, that you should begin at the end, and read backwards (not line by line backwards, but poem by poem), until you get exhausted.

I don't think I shall write much more poetry. If I do, it will perhaps be Whitmaniac, in form, I mean, or rather in formlessness; though no one had a finer sense of form than W. W., when he was inspired, which he was as much as or more than most poets. I have quite come back to my old Cambridge love of him, of his prose as well as his poetry. His *Specimen Days* seems to me (especially the part about the Civil War) one of the most moving books I know. I've been reading, another American book, which will hardly be popular in California, I mean *Grapes of Wrath*. It may be unfair and exaggerated about the treatment of the emigrants, I can't tell about that; but it seems to me a rather great book, in an epic sort of way. We are now reading aloud Winifred Holtby's *South Riding*, which also seems to me very nearly a great book, though perhaps not quite.

I am bringing out a book of translations of Horace's *Epistles* and two Montaigne essays, which I will send you some time this year, unless the Cambridge Press is bombed, which hardly seems likely. I have a book of prose too getting ready; but that will hardly be this year. I cannot think of a title – it is a 'Miscellany', but all the synonyms (Hotch potch, Olla Podrida etc.) sound undignified, and some of the material is highly serious. Bessie won't let me call it 'A Faggot of sticks', as she says that suggests it only deserves to be burnt.

Bessie is, I believe, intending to write to you soon, and after that I hope another year won't pass before we hear from you again. We have had the Sturge Moores here since the war began. He is rather an invalid now. We had a pleasant visit from G. E. M. in August. He is lecturing at Oxford to large audiences. Francis Lloyd says a lot of Dons go, and are amused or shocked. She seems to get a lot out of his lectures. We have also an Italian boy, a Vivante, a nephew of L. de Bosis, to whom I teach Latin and Greek. He's just got a scholarship at Pembroke Oxford. It is clear to me now I ought to have been a school-master.

Much love to you both from B. and me.

Yours ever affectionately
Bob

212 Loring Avenue
Los Angeles, Cal., U.S.A.
19 May 1940

Dear Bob

Thank you very much for the fine volumes of your works, which arrived safely, and which I am delighted to have.

At this moment it is difficult to think of anything but the war. By the time you get this, presumably the outcome of the present battle will have been decided. I keep on remembering how I stayed at Shiffolds during the crisis of the battle of the Marne, and made you walk two miles to get a Sunday paper. Perhaps it would have been better if the Kaiser had won, seeing Hitler is so much worse. I find that this time I am not a pacifist, and consider the future of civilisation bound up with our victory. I don't think anything so important has happened since the fifth century, the previous occasion on which the Germans reduced the world to barbarism.

You may have seen that I am to be hounded out of teaching in America because the Catholics don't like my views. I was quite interested in this (which involves a grave danger of destitution) until the present battle began – now I find difficulty in remembering it.

Yes, I have read *Grapes of Wrath*, and I think it a very good book. The issue of the migrant workers is a burning one here, on which there is much bitter feeling.

John and Kate are settling in to the university here, and Conrad (just 3) is flourishing and intelligent. We are all desperately homesick, and hope to return as soon as it is financially feasible.

Give my love to Bessie and tell her it will be very nice to hear from her. John was *most* grateful for Lucretius.

> *Yours affectionately*
> *Bertrand Russell*

> The Shiffolds
> 3 May 1941

My dear Bertie

We were so glad to hear from you about you and yours. I put in this line just before the post goes. Yes Plato was a comic poet. He did also apparently write some none too serious pseudo-philosophical dialogues, which got taken too seriously. Some scholars say there were two Platos; but scholars will say anything.

I am sending you a small book of Leopardi translations. I should never have started them but for you asking me to do that passage from the Ginestra, so you may look upon yourself as their 'onlie begetter'.

Bessie keeps fairly well, though she is getting rather blinder. I go on trying to work, and have lately been translating more Montaigne, not being able to write poetry. Much love to you and all yours.

> *Yours ever*
> *Bob*

Little Datchet Farm
Malvern R.D.1.
Pennsylvania
20 August 1941

My dear Bob

I was delighted to have your Leopardi translations, which I thought *very* good. I am glad to think I had a share in bringing them about.

A very short time after writing to you, I came across an allusion to Plato the comic poet. He had been till then completely unknown to me.

How does George enjoy his new dignity?[1] I have only seen him once since August 4, 1914. In old Butler's days I once stayed at the Lodge and slept in Queen Anne's bed. Is it still there?

What led you to Montaigne? Do you disapprove of Florio? I was pleased to find that 'Lead Kindly Light', vulgarly attributed to Newman, was really written by Cleanthes in the 3rd century BC. There are whole chunks of the New Testament in the Stoics.

I enclose a letter to Bessie. I hope her eyesight won't go on getting worse.

Yours ever
Bertrand Russell

The Shiffolds
Holmbury St Mary, Dorking
2 October 1941

My dear Bertie

It was a great pleasure to hear from you again. Bessie no doubt will be writing or has written. She is very well, except for her eyes. I am now reading to her Nevinson's memoirs in the evening, which are not at all bad. We read a Willa Cather novel, which we both liked. I have not written much poetry lately, but what I have written I shall soon be sending you in a volume with some old ones, as all my collected poems were burnt in Longman's fire. There are two or three quasi-philosophical poems among them, perhaps rather too Santayanaish to meet with your approval. I have lately been reading his book on the *Realm of Spirit*, which, though sometimes a bit wordy, pleases me more than most philosophy – but then I'm not a philosopher. I wish I could understand your last book, but it is rather too difficult for me. I liked, though, your little book of essays (most of which I knew before), and felt in agreement with most of what you say.

As to Montaigne, I wonder whether you have ever compared Florio with the French; if so I think you would see why I think it worthwhile

[1] He had become Master of Trinity.

translating him again – though I am only doing the Essays, or parts of Essays, I like best. I am also writing some prose myself, short essays and reminiscences; also I want to write about a few of my friends, who are dead such as Tovey, C. A., Goldie and Roger.[1] So you see I can't do you yet; but I may come to living friends if they don't disappear soon enough. George[2] did not want to be Master, but his *nolo episcopari* was brushed aside by Churchill, and now he enjoys being Master a lot. The Lodge has been done up, as it was in fearful disrepair, and now is quite pleasant and well-furnished. I slept in the Junior Judge's room. Queen Anne's bed is still there, though I think the bed-tester is gone. We enjoyed our three days visit there. George is cheerful when in company, but often sinks into gloom when alone. He feels the world he cared for is at an end. I don't quite feel like that myself, at least not often. He has written a book on Social England, leaving out wars and politics etc. What I saw was quite good. It will be out soon I suppose. His son Humphrey has written a book on Goethe, which will be very good when it comes out (by which I don't mean that 'coming out' will make it good, though perhaps that's true too). Flora Russell and her sister called last week, and they talked affectionately of you, and Flora said you had written to her, which had evidently pleased her a lot. She is getting older and is rather crippled. I haven't seen Desmond[3] since July, but hope he will come to see us soon. He is getting older, and had a bad illness this spring, but he is as charming as ever. We liked Virginia Woolf's Life of Roger very much.

Well, you must write to us again before long, and then we will write to you. I do hope you are both well, and that you both like America fairly well. G. E. Moore, it seems, likes America and Americans very much. I am very glad he is staying there this winter. I hope the children are both* well. I suppose they are hardly children now. Much love to you both from

Yours affectionately
R. C. Trevelyan

* Conrad is an infant, not a child; but I hope he is well too.

Little Datchet Farm
Malvern, R.D.1
Pennsylvania
9 July 1942

My dear Bob
For the last 6 months I have been meaning to write to you and Bessie,

[1] Donald Tovey, Clifford Allen, Goldie Dickinson, Roger Fry.
[2] His brother.
[3] Desmond MacCarthy.

but have kept on putting it off for a moment of leisure. How very sad that your Collected Poems were burnt in Longman's fire. I am all the more glad that my copy is intact. I love getting your poems – if you don't get thanks, please attribute it to enemy action.

I haven't read Santayana on the *Realm of Spirit*, as I had just finished writing on him when it appeared. I was glad to find he liked what I wrote on him. Philosophers in this country lack something I like, and I have come to the conclusion that what they lack is Plato. (Not your friend the comic poet.) I can't free myself of the love of contemplation *versus* action.

Did you realise that at a certain time Thales and Jeremiah were both in Egypt, probably in the same town? I suggest your composing a dialogue between them.

I wrote to George about the possibility of my son John going to Trinity after the war, and what would be his standing if he did; he wrote a very kind answer, showing he had taken a good deal of trouble. John is at Harvard, and he is to be allowed to complete his course there (which ends in February) before returning to England to join the British forces. For a long time this was in doubt; we were very glad when it was settled. He will presumably be in England in March. He knows a great deal of history, and reads both Latin and Greek for pleasure. I am ploughing through my history of philosophy from Thales to the present day. When Scotus Erigena dined *tête-à-tête* with the King of France, the King asked 'what separates a Scot from a sot?' 'Only the dinner-table' said the philosopher. I have dined with 8 Prime Ministers, but never got such a chance. Goodbye, with all good wishes.

> *Yours affectionately*
> *Bertrand Russell*

The Shiffolds
Holmbury St Mary, Dorking
3 January 1942 [1943]

My dear Bertie

I have long owed you a letter. Your last letters to us were written to us in July. For nearly two months I have been in hospital, as a consequence of my bravery in crossing Hyde Park Corner diagonally during the blackout and so getting knocked over. It might have been much worse; for now, after a month at home, I can walk about much as usual, though I easily get tired. You were only knocked over by a bicycle; I by an army-taxi. An army-lorry would have been more honourable, though perhaps less pleasant.

Ted Lloyd was to have come to tea today, but has influenza, so only Margaret and John came.[1] I expect you know Ted is going East. It seems he is sorry not to come back to America. We hope to see him next Sunday and then we shall hear from him about you both. I am very glad you are writing some sort of history of philosophy and philosophers. No one could do it better than you. You will no doubt trace the influence of Jeremiah upon the cosmology of Thales. Yes, a dialogue between them might be well worth doing; but at present I know almost nothing of Jeremiah and his little book. By the way, if you want a really first-rate book on the Greek Atomists, you should have a look at Cyril Bailey's *Greek Atomists* (Clarendon Press) 1928. But I dare say you know it. It seems to me he really does understand Epicurus, which our friend Benn never[2] did. Bailey is, I think very good too about Leucippus, Democritus etc.

I have not written any poetry for nearly two years; and not much prose; though I am bringing out a book of Essays and Dialogues some time this year, which I will send you, if I can manage to get it to you. All the mental effort I have been able to make lately is a little easy 'mountaineering', by which I mean translating Montaigne – not all of him, but the less dull parts. Sometimes he can be really good. For instance, I have just translated a famous sentence of his: 'When all is said, it is putting an excessively high value on one's conjectures, to cause a man to be roasted alive on account of them.'

If you can get hold of a copy, you should read Waley's translation of *Monkey* a 15th century Chinese fairy story about Buddhism, Taoism, and human nature generally, a superbly Rabelaisian, Aristophanic, Biblical Voltairian book. It came out last summer (Allen & Unwin).

When John comes over here, I hope we may have some opportunity of seeing him. We still take in the *Manch. Guardian*, so have seen your and P's letters, with which we are quite in agreement.

We wish you could have spent Christmas here with us. Perhaps next Christmas ? – but hardly so soon I fear.

There's an amusing Life of B. Shaw by Hesketh Pearson, but mostly written by G.B.S. himself. Yet I got a little tired of Shaw before I came to the end. Raymond Mortimer's Essays are not at all bad (*Channel Packet*). There's a good review of the *Amberley Papers*; but I expect you have seen that. It's just on dinner-time, so I must stop. Much love to you both from Bessie and me,

Yours affectly
Bob

Desmond was quite ill this autumn; but he seems fairly well again now.

---

[1] His wife, my cousin Margaret Lloyd, my Uncle Rollo's daughter, and her eldest son John.
[2] A. W. Benn, the classical scholar.

To and from Gilbert Murray

The West Lodge
Downing College, Cambridge
3.3.37

Dear Gilbert

Thank you for your letter. C.A. lies in his throat. The speech was against armaments, & it is nonsense to suggest that Tory Peers are against armaments.

Spain has turned many away from pacifism. I myself have found it very difficult, the more so as I know Spain, most of the places where the fighting has been, & the Spanish people, & I have the strongest possible feelings on the Spanish issue. I should certainly not find Czecho-Slovakia more difficult. And having remained a pacifist while the Germans were invading France & Belgium in 1914, I do not see why I should cease to be one if they do it again. The result of our having adopted the policy of war at that time is not so delectable as to make me wish to see it adopted again.

You feel 'They ought to be stopped'. I feel that, if we set to work to stop them, we shall, in the process, become exactly like them & the world will have gained nothing. Also, if we beat them, we shall produce in time some one as much worse than Hitler as he is worse than the Kaiser. In all this I see no hope for mankind.

Yours ever
B.R.

Yatscombe
Boar's Hill, Oxford
Jan. 5th. 1939

My dear Bertie

A man has written to the Home University Library to say that there ought to be a book on the Art of Clear Thinking. There is plenty written about theoretic logic, but nothing except perhaps Graham Wallas's book about the actual practice of clear thought. It seems to me that the value of such a book would depend entirely on the writer; I found Wallas's book, for instance, extremely suggestive and helpful, and I think that if you felt inclined to write something, it might make a great hit and would in any case be of real value. It might be a little like Aristotle's *Sophistici Elenchi*, with a discussion of the ways in which human thought goes wrong, but I think it might be something more constructive. I wonder if the idea appeals at all to you.

I read *Power* the other day with great enjoyment, and a wish to argue with you about several points.

Give my respects to your University. Once when I was in New York, there was a fancy dress dinner, to which people went as celebrated criminals. One man was dressed as a trapper, but could not be identified till at the end of the evening he confessed he was the man who discovered Chicago.

Yours ever
G.M.

University of Chicago
January 15th 1939

My dear Gilbert
Thank you for your letter of January 5th. I think a book about how to think clearly might be very useful, but I do not think I could write it. First, for external reasons, that I have several books contracted for, which I am anxious to write and which will take me some years. Secondly – and this is more important – because I haven't the vaguest idea either how I think or how one ought to think. The process, so far as I know it, is as instinctive and unconscious as digestion. I fill my mind with whatever relevant knowledge I can find, and just wait. With luck, there comes a moment when the work is done, but in the meantime my conscious mind has been occupied with other things. This sort of thing won't do for a book.

I wonder what were the points in *Power* that you wanted to argue about. I hope the allusions to the Greeks were not wholly wrong.

This University, so far as philosophy is concerned, is about the best I have ever come across. There are two sharply opposed schools in the Faculty, one Aristotelian, historical, and traditional, the other ultra-modern. The effect on the students seems to me just right. The historical professors are incredibly learned, especially as regards medieval philosophy.

I am only here till the end of March, but intellectually I enjoy the place very much.

Yours ever
B.R.

212, Loring Avenue
Los Angeles
21.4.40

My dear Gilbert
It is difficult to do much at this date in America for German academic refugees.[1] American universities have been very generous, but are by now pretty well saturated. I spoke about the matter of Jacobsthal to Reichenbach, a German refugee who is a professor here, and whom I admire both morally and intellectually. He knew all

---

[1] Murray had appealed to me on behalf of a German anti-Nazi Professor named Jacobsthal.

about Jacobsthal's work, which I didn't. The enclosed is the official reply of the authorities of this university. I must leave further steps to others, as I am at the moment unable to save my own skin. In view of the German invasion of Norway, I suppose it is only too likely that Jacobsthal is by now in a concentration camp.

Yes, I wish we could meet and have the sort of talk we used to have. I find that I cannot maintain the pacifist position in this way. I do not feel sufficiently sure of the opposite to say anything publicly by way of recantation, though it may come to that. In any case, here in America an Englishman can only hold his tongue, as anything he may say is labelled propaganda. However, what I wanted to convey is that you would not find me disagreeing with you as much as in 1914, though I still think I was right then, in that this war is an outcome of Versailles, which was an outcome of moral indignation.

It is painful to be at such a distance in war-time, and only the most imperative financial necessity keeps me here. It is a comfort that my three children are here, but the oldest is 18, and I do not know how soon he may be needed for military service. We all suffer from almost unbearable home-sickness, and I find myself longing for old friends. I am glad that you are still one of them.

Please give my love to Mary even if she doesn't want it. And do write again, telling me something of what you feel about the whole ghastly business.

> *Yours ever*
> *Bertrand Russell*

July 29th, 1940

My dear Bertie

I was very glad to get your letter, though I feel greatly distressed by it. I should have thought that the obviously unjust attack on you as a teacher would have produced a strong and helpful reaction in your favour; there was quite a good article about it in the *Nation* (American). I still hope that it may have the result of making your friends more active.

I do not suppose you are thinking of coming back here. It would be easy enough if you were alone, but children make all the difference. I suppose this country is really a dangerous place, though it is hard for the average civilian to realise the fact; life goes on so much as usual, with no particular war hardship except taxes, only news every day about battles in the air and a general impression that we are all playing at soldiers. I am inclined to think that one of the solid advantages of the English temperament is that we do not get frightened or excited beforehand as Latins and Semites do, we wait till the danger comes before getting upset by it. I suppose this is what people call lack of imagination.

One development that interests me is this: assuming that the war is in a sense a civil war throughout the world, or a war of religions or what they now call ideologies, for a long time it was not quite clear what the two sides were: e.g. some people said it was Communism or Socialism against Fascism, others that it was Christianity against ungodliness. But now, as far as ideas are concerned, it is clearly Britain and America with some few supporters against the various autocracies, which means Liberalism v Tyranny. I found Benes saying much the same the other day; he had been afraid that the war would come on what he called a false issue, of Communism v Fascism. Now he thinks it is on the right one.

If ever I can be of any use to you, please let me know.

Yours ever
Gilbert Murray

(As from) Harvard University
Cambridge, Mass. U.S.A.
September 6th 1940

Dear Gilbert

Thank you very much for your letter of July 29. My personal problems have been solved by a rich patron (in the eighteenth-century style) who has given me a teaching post with little work and sufficient salary. I cannot return to England, not only on account of my children, but also because I could not earn a living there. Exile at such a time, however, is infinitely painful. Meanwhile, we have spent the summer in a place of exquisite beauty, like the best of the Tyrol, and I have finished a big book, *An Inquiry into Meaning and Truth* – Hume plus modern logic. Sometimes I think the best thing one can do is to salvage as much as possible of civilisation before the onset of the dark ages. I feel as if we were living in the fifth century.

I quite agree with what you say about the war of ideologies. The issue became clear when Russia turned against us. Last time the alliance with the Czar confused the issue.

Sympathy in this country is growing more and more emphatic on our side. My belief, is that if we pull through this month, we shall win. But I am not optimistic as to the sort of world that the war will leave.

Yours ever
Bertrand Russell

(Permanent address)
Little Datchet Farm
Malvern, R.D.1. Pa; U.S.A.
January 18th 1941

My dear Gilbert

I was very glad to get your good letter of October 23. I am now established in a small country house 200 years old – very ancient for this part of the world – in lovely country, with pleasant work. If the world were at peace I could be very happy.

As to the future: It seems to me that if we win, we shall win completely: I cannot think the Nazis will survive. America will dominate, and will probably not withdraw as in 1919; America will not be war-weary, and will believe resolutely in the degree of democracy that exists here. I am accordingly fairly optimistic. There is good hope that the militaristic régime in Japan will collapse, and I do not believe China will ever be really militaristic. Russia, I think, will be the greatest difficulty, especially if finally on our side. I have no doubt that the Soviet Government is even worse than Hitler's, and it will be a misfortune if it survives. There can be no permanent peace unless there is only one Air Force in the world, with the degree of international government that that implies. Disarmament alone, though good, will not make peace secure.

Opinion here varies with the longitude. In the East, people are passionately pro-English; we are treated with extra kindness in shops as soon as people notice our accent. In California they are anti-Japanese but not pro-English; in the Middle West they were rather anti-English. But everywhere opinion is very rapidly coming over to the conviction that we must not be defeated.

It is rather dreadful to be out of it all. I envy Rosalind [his daughter] as much as I admire her.

I am giving a 4-year course of lectures on history of philosophy in relation to culture and social circumstances, from Thales to Dewey. As I can't read Greek, this is rather cheek; but anyway I enjoy it. I divide it into 3 cycles, Greek, Catholic, Protestant. In each case the gradual decay of an irrational dogma leads to anarchy, and thence to dictatorship. I like the growth of Catholicism out of Greek decadence, and of Luther out of Machiavelli's outlook.

I remember your description of Sophocles (which you afterwards denied) as 'a combination of matricide and high spirits'. I remember, also, when I besought you to admit merit in 'hark, hark the lark' you said it ought to go on 'begins to bark'. I disagree with you about Shakespeare; I don't know enough about Sophocles to have an opinion. At the moment, I am full of admiration for Anaximander, and amazement at Pythagoras, who combined Einstein and Mrs

Eddy. I disapprove of Plato because he wanted to prohibit all music except Rule Britannia and The British Grenadiers. Moreover, he invented the Pecksniffian style of the *Times* leading articles.

Do write again. Goodbye.

Yours ever
Bertrand Russell

Little Datchet Farm
Malvern, R.D. 1
Pennsylvania
June 18th 1941

Dear Gilbert

Thank you very much for your letter of 23 April, which reached me safely. I humbly acknowledge my error about quadruplicity! I agree with everything you say in your letter, and particularly with what you say about the 'Christian tradition'; I have been feeling the attraction of conservatism myself. There are, however, some things of importance to note. First: the tradition in question is chiefly represented in this country by the Catholic Church, which, here, has none of the culture one associates with that body historically. (On this, Santayana writes convincingly.) The Church lost much at the Reformation, more when intellectual France turned free-thinking; it has not now the merits it had. Generally, a conservative institution ceases to be good as soon as it is attacked.

I should regard Socialism in its milder forms as a natural development of the Christian tradition. But Marx belongs with Nietzsche as an apostle of disruption, and unfortunately Marxism won among socialists.

The Romantic Movement is one of the sources of evil; further back, Luther and Henry VIII.

I don't see much hope in the near future. There must first be a World-State, then an Augustan age, then slow undramatic decay. For a while, the yellow races may put vigour into the Hellenic–Roman tradition; ultimately, something new may come from the negroes. (I should like to think St Augustine was a negro.)

It seems to me that everything good in Christianity comes from either Plato or the Stoics. The Jews contributed bad history; the Romans, Church Government and Canon Law. I like the Church of England because it is the most purely Platonic form of Christianity. Catholicism is too Roman, Puritanism too Judaic.

Life here, with the job I have, would be very pleasant if there were no war. The country is like inland Dorsetshire; our house is 200 years old, built by a Welshman. My work is interesting, and moderate in amount. But it all seems unreal. Fierceness surges round, and everybody seems doomed to grow fierce sooner or later. It is hard to feel that anything is worth while, except actual resistance to Hitler, in which I have no chance to take a part. We have English friends who are going back to England, and we envy them, because they are going to something that feels important. I try to think it is worth while to remain civilised, but it seems rather thin. I admire English resistance with all my soul, but hate not to be part of it. Goodbye. Do write again.

> *Yours ever*
> *Bertrand Russell*

Little Datchet Farm
Malvern, R.D. 1
Pennsylvania
March 23rd 1942

My dear Gilbert

I have had a letter of yours on my desk for a shamefully long time, but I have been appallingly busy. You wrote about physics and philosophy. *I* think the effect of physics is to bolster up Berkeley; but every philosopher has his own view on the subject. You wrote also about post-war reconstruction. I think the irruption of Japan has changed things. Anglo–American benevolent imperialism won't work: 'Asia for the Asiatics' must be conceded. The only question is whether India and China shall be free or under Japan. If free, they will gravitate to Russia, which is Asiatic. There will be no cultural unity, and I doubt whether Russia and USA can agree about any form of international government, or whether, if they nominally do, it will have any reality. I am much less hopeful of the post-war world than before Japan's successes.

In my survey of the history of culture – alternatively, 'Sin, from Adam to Hitler' – I have reached Charlemagne. I find the period 400–800 AD very important and too little known. People's conscious thoughts were silly, but their blind actions founded the institutions under which England still lives – e.g. Oxford, and the Archbishops. There were many lonely men in those days – Archbishop of Canterbury Theodore, educated at Athens, trying to teach Greek to Anglo-Saxons; English St Boniface and Irish St Virgil disputing, in the wilds of the German forests, as to whether there are other worlds than ours; John the Scot, physically in the 9th century, mentally in the 5th or even 4th. The loss of Roman centralisation was ultimately good. Perhaps we need 400 years of anarchy to recover. In a centralised world, too few people feel important.

Very interesting struggles are going on in this country. The Government is compelled to control the capitalists, and they, in turn, are trying to get the trade unions controlled. There is much more fear here than in England of 'planned economy', which is thought socialistic and said to lead to Fascism; and yet the necessities of the war compel it. Everybody in Washington realises that a great deal of planning will be necessary after the war, but the capitalists hope then to get back to laissez-faire. There may be a good deal of difficulty then. There is a great deal of rather fundamental change going on here, which is worth studying. But I wish I could be at home.

All good wishes,

> *Yours ever*
> *Bertrand Russell*

> Little Datchet Farm
> Malvern, R.D. 1
> Pennsylvania
> 9 April 1943

My dear Gilbert

Thank you for your letter of March 13, which arrived this morning; also for your earlier letter about Barnes. He is a man who likes quarrels; for no reason that I can fathom, he suddenly broke his contract with me. In the end, probably, I shall get damages out of him; but the law's delays are as great as in Shakespeare's time. Various things I have undertaken to do will keep me here till the end of October; then (D.V.) I shall return to England – Peter & Conrad too, if the danger from submarines is not too great. We can't bear being away from home any longer. In England I shall have to find some means of earning a livelihood. I should be quite willing to do Government propaganda, as my views on this war are quite orthodox. I wish I could find a way of making my knowledge of America useful; I find that English people, when they try to please American opinion, are very apt to make mistakes. But I would accept any honest work that would bring in a bare subsistence for 3 people.

It is not growing fanaticism, but growing democracy, that causes my troubles. Did you ever read the life of Averroes? He was protected by kings, but hated by the mob, which was fanatical. In the end, the mob won. Free thought has always been a perquisite of aristocracy. So is the intellectual development of women. I am sorry to hear Mary has to do the housework. My Peter's whole time is absorbed in housework, cooking, & looking after Conrad; she hardly ever has time to read. The eighteenth & nineteenth centuries were a brief interlude in the normal savagery of man; now the world has reverted to its usual condition. For us, who imagined ourselves democrats, but were in fact the pampered products of aristocracy, it is unpleasant.

I am very sorry to hear about Lucy Silcox[1]; if you see her, please give her my love & sympathy.

[1] A well-known liberal schoolmistress.

Our reason for coming home is that we don't want to send Conrad to an American school. Not only is the teaching bad, but the intense nationalism is likely to cause in his mind a harmful conflict between home & school. We think submarines, bombs, & poor diet a smaller danger. But all this is still somewhat undecided.

I shall finish my big History of Philosophy during the summer – you won't like it, because I don't admire Aristotle.

My John is in England, training for the navy. Kate is still at College, at Radcliffe. She wants, after the war, to get into something like Quaker Relief work – She specialises in German, & is unable to feel prescribed hatreds.

Give my love to Mary – It would be a real happiness to see you again – old friends grow fewer.

> *Yours ever*
> *Bertrand Russell*

From Sir Ralph Wedgwood, the brother of Col. Josiah [Jos] Wedgwood who was later Lord Wedgwood of Barlaston.

> Aston House
> Stone, Staffordshire
> 29.7.41

Dear Russell

Jos has now returned safely to this country, and the first thing he did was to tell me that he had seen you, and send me your letter to him as corroborative evidence. It set me thinking of Cambridge days of long ago, – a thing that I find myself rather apt to do now that I have passed the limit of 65 which I had always hoped would be the term of my active life. This was to be the really good time of life, when one's conscience being satisfied, and work done, one could pick up old tastes, and perhaps find old friends. Besides, I have been reading your last book of essays, and that alone made me want to write to you to tell you what a delight they are. Many of them are new to me, and I cannot decide whether I like the new or the old best – only I am sure they are most enjoyable of all when read together.

I *should* like to meet you again, and to make the acquaintance of your wife. Are you ever likely to be in England again! Not until after the war I suppose in any event. Nor shall I be in America before that (speaking wishfully) happy event. So many of our friends have gone – and some have become altogether too reactionary! George Moore is the only one who goes on unchanged, and I expect you have seen him in America. He too seems likely to stay there for the duration, but he is a great loss to Cambridge. I stayed a night last month with the new Master of Trinity at the Lodge – not so formidable as it sounds. He is a dear, but one has to avoid so many subjects like the

plague. However we discussed old days, and listened to the nightin-
gales, – and so escaped shipwreck. Desmond McCarthy I used to see
from time to time, but war-time puts an end to all such social meetings – everybody is left to work or chafe in his own compartment. If you
can find time, do write and tell me about yourself. I shall ask Jos all
about his visit to you when I see him: he was rather ominously silent
in his letter about his visit to USA as a whole. I am afraid the Wheeler
episode has rather embittered it all for him. Goodbye, and best wishes.

> *Yours fraternally*
> *Ralph Wedgwood*

To Ely Culbertson, the Bridge expert

January 12 1942

Dear Culbertson

After a great deal of thought, I have come to more or less definite
opinions about international government and about your scheme.

As regards international government, I think it far and away the
most important question at present before the world. I am prepared to
support any scheme which seems to me likely to put a large pre-
ponderance of armed force on the side of international law; some would
please me more than others, but I should support whichever had a good
chance of being adopted. The matter will ultimately be decided by
Roosevelt, Stalin, and Churchill (or his successor); or perhaps without
Stalin. Roosevelt and Churchill will be much influenced by public
opinion in their own countries, but also by their officials. They are
almost certain to modify any scheme they adopt.

I feel, in these circumstances, that my job is to advocate the *principle*
of international government, not this or that special scheme. Special
schemes are very useful, in order that the thing can be done, but I
should not wish to get into controversy as between one scheme and
another.

You are, as you must know, extraordinarily persuasive, and I
thought I could throw in my lot publicly with you, but reflection has
led me, very regretfully, to the conclusion that my points of disagreement are too important for this. The most important are the following.

(1) Your plan of regional federations with leader States has difficulties. You yourself make France and Italy equal in the Latin
Federation; South Americans would resent acknowledged inferiority
of status to that of the US; Germany ought not to be put above the
smaller Teutonic countries, which are much more civilised, and much
more favourable to a World Federation.

(2) I cannot agree to your suggestion as regards India. I have been
for many years an advocate of Indian freedom, and cannot abandon
this just when it has a good chance of realisation.

(3) I don't like your fixing the quotas of military power 'for ever', or even for 50 years; 25 years is the utmost that would seem to me wise. This is part of a wider objection, that you have not, to my mind, a sufficient mechanism for *legal* change, yet this is essential if violence is to be made inattractive.

You may say that the points I do not like in your scheme make it more likely to be adopted. I do not think so. It seem to me that that nucleus of any practicable plan will be Anglo-American cooperation, and that a number of small countries will quickly join themselves on as satellites. One might hope the same of China and of a resurrected France. I expect therefore, at first, a Federation from which ex-enemy countries will be excluded, and from which Russia will probably hold aloof. As for the ex-enemy countries, there should be no difficulty about Italy, which is not deeply Fascist. Japan, I think, will disintegrate, and need armies of occupation to keep order; behind these armies, a new civilisation could be introduced. Germany, no doubt, will take a considerable time, but could, I think, be brought in within 20 years. As for Russia, one must wait and see.

The upshot is that I don't think we can get *everything* in the Peace Treaty. Better a nucleus of Powers in genuine agreement, and then a gradual growth, always assuming that the nucleus, at the time of the peace, has overwhelming military superiority, and the means of keeping it for some time.

As I said before, I favour *any* plan of international government that is not too like Hitler's, and I should be very glad if yours were adopted, though I still prefer the one I outlined in the *American Mercury*. I should still be very glad, if you desire it, to go over any work of yours, with a view to criticisms *from your point of view*. There might be details that could advantageously be modified. I should also, as soon as your scheme is public, speak of it as having very great merits, whenever I had occasion to talk or write on international government. But I cannot be paid by you for any public appearance, as I find this would involve too much sacrifice of intellectual independence.

I am very sorry about this, both because I found the prospect of working with you very attractive, and because it will diminish my opportunities for advocating international government. For both these reasons I was anxious to throw in my lot with you, and thought I could; but I am not good at sub-ordinating my judgment to anybody else, and if I tried to do so I feel that it wouldn't answer.

The above applies in particular to a possible lecture at Columbia Teachers' Training College about which I wrote.

I should be very sorry indeed if anything I have said in this letter impaired our personal relations. Our talks have been a great intellectual stimulus to me, and I should like to hope that, by bringing up objections, I might be of some reciprocal use to you. Apart from all that, I should like to feel that there is a real friendship between us.

Yours sincerely
Bertrand Russell

My wife asks me to send her regards.

From Pearl Buck, author of *The*   R.D. 3
Good Earth and other books   Perkasie,
           Pennsylvania
           October 23, 1942

My dear Mr Russell

I was so impressed with your attitude the other Sunday that I have been thinking of whether I might not write you.

Then Wednesday Lin Yutang spoke of your letter in PM, which he thought very fine indeed. I have not yet seen it myself – I shall try to get a copy – but he told me enough about it to make me feel that indeed I must write you.

I have for a long time – for many months, in fact – been deeply perturbed because of the feeling toward England in the minds of many Americans. I knew it was certain to rise over the India situation. I think I knew that years ago when I was in India, and saw for myself what would be inevitable if war came, and even then war seemed pretty clearly ahead.

You may ask why I have taken my share in discussions about India, if I deplored any lack of warmth between our two countries. I have done so in spite of my devotion to England, because as an American it has seemed to me my duty to do all I could, first, to see if something could not be devised to bring India wholeheartedly into the war effort, and second, because I knew there must be some sort of strong reassurance to China that we were not all thinking along the same old lines. For the latter reason I have welcomed the excellent stand that the English have taken in regard to American color segregation in our armed forces in England.

Now I feel that what has been done in India is done and the question ahead is no longer to discuss who was right and who was wrong there but to plan together, all of us, how to cope with the disaster ahead. I hope that you will read, if you have not already done so, Edgar Snow's article in the current *Saturday Evening Post*, entitled 'Must We Beat Japan First?' It is so grave that all of us must take thought together.

This alienation between Americans and English, it seems to me, must not be allowed to continue. I don't think we will get over India, especially as our losses of men in the Far East grow more severe, as they must, since India will not be mobilised to help us. I fear both the professional anti-English persons and those who have been alienated by the failure to bring India wholeheartedly into the war. I fear even more those who will grow angry when they see what the loss of India will cost us.

I don't think that Americans are particularly pro-Indian – if at all – I know I am not. But there is just something in the average American that heartily dislikes the sort of thing that has been going on in India, and this in spite of our equally wrong behaviour to our own colored folk. We are, of course, full of contradictions, but there it is. What can be done to mend the situation between our two countries?

I think of one thing which ought not to be too difficult. Granting that Churchill cannot and will not change, it would help a great deal if we could see another kind of Englishman and see him in some numbers and hear him speak. As you know, the liberal English opinion has been fairly rigidly censored. Here in America we have not been allowed to hear dissenting voices in England and the sort of official Englishman we have here, and all his propaganda, does little or nothing to mend the rift in the common man.

What can we do, English and Americans together, who know the necessity of human equality, to make known our unity of thought and purpose?

The time has come for us to find each other and to stand together for the same sort of world. We cannot yield to each other's faults and prides, but we can speak together against them, and together determine a better way and so reaffirm before our enemies and before our doubting allies everywhere the essential unity of our two peoples.

Very sincerely yours
Pearl S. Buck

My views at that time on India were that it would be necessary to persuade the British Government to renew negotiations with India. It was difficult, however, to see how this could be done while Churchill remained in power. Also, Indian leaders should be persuaded to end the civil disobedience movement and cooperate in negotiations. Possibly the latter could be done through Nehru. I took for granted that India should be free of all foreign domination, whether British or other.

From and to Mrs Sidney Webb   Passfield Corner
                                      Liphook, Hants.
                                      December 17th 1942

My dear Bertrand

I was so glad to see in that remarkable book – *I meet America* – by W. J. Brown MP that you were not only intent on winning the war but wished to reconstruct the world after the war. We were also very much interested that you had decided to remain in the USA and to encourage your son to make his career there rather than in Great Britain. If you were not a peer of the realm and your son a possible great statesman like his great grandfather I should think it was a wise decision but we want you both back in Great Britain since you are part and parcel of the parliamentary government of our democracy. Also I should think teachers who were also British Peers were at some slight disadvantage in the USA so far as a public career is concerned as they would attract snobs and offend the labour movement? But of course I may be wrong.

Sidney, I am glad to say, is very well and happy though of course owing to his stroke in 1938 he is no longer able to take part in public affairs. I go on writing, writing, writing for publication. But I am old and tired and suffer from all sorts of ailments from swollen feet to sleepless nights.

I send you our last booklet which has had a great sale in Great Britain and is being published by the New York Longman firm. Probably you will not agree with it but I think you will be interested and Bernard Shaw's Preface is amusing. Like ourselves the Bernard Shaws are very old and though Shaw goes on writing Charlotte is a hopeless invalid and rather an unhappy one. Shaw is writing a book – *What's What to the Politicians.* He has been writing it for many months and would have gone on writing a longer and longer book if he had not been pulled up by the shortness of paper.

Whether you stay in the USA or not I do hope you and your two clever young people will pay a visit to Great Britain and that we shall have the pleasure of seeing you and your wife. Pray give her my greetings; I wonder how she likes America.

> *Your affectionate friend*
> *Beatrice Webb*
> *(Mrs Sidney Webb)*

P.S. I don't think you know our nephew Sir Stafford Cripps – but he represents a new movement growing up in Gt Britain, which combines the Christian faith ... [words missing] – which might interest you. He left the Cabinet over India!

> Little Datchet Farm
> 31 Jan 1943

My dear Beatrice

Thank you very much for your letter of Dec. 17. I was delighted to have news of you and Sidney, and to know that he is well. I am sorry you suffer from 'ailments'. I suppose it is inevitable after a certain age – to which I shall soon attain.

I don't know what gave W. J. Brown the idea that I meant to settle in America. I have never at any time thought of doing such a thing. At first I came for 8 months, then jobs came in my way. Then, with the war, I thought it better for Conrad (now aged 5) to be here. But all these reasons are nearing their end.

John (Amberley) is finished with Harvard, and returning to England in a few days, to go into the Navy if he can, and, if not, the Army. My daughter Kate is at Radcliffe; she always does as well as possible in everything she studies. Her hope, after the war, is to get into some kind of relief work on the Continent. I myself am kept here for the moment by various engagements, but I may come home fairly soon, leaving Peter and Conrad here till the end of the war.

I was much disappointed that India rejected Cripps' offer. People here are ignorant about India, but have strong opinions. I have been speaking and writing to try to overcome anti-English feeling as regards India, which in some quarters is very strong.

Thank you very much for your most interesting booklet on Russia. Whether one likes the régime or not, one can't help immensely admiring the Russian achievement in the war.

I do hope to see you again when I get back to England. Peter sends greetings and thanks for your message.

> *Yours affectionately*
> *Bertrand Russell*

From Dr & Mrs A. N. Whitehead
1737 Cambridge St.
Cambridge, Mass.
Jan. 3. 1944

Dear Bertie

We have just read – in the minutes of the Trinity Council – that you have been re-elected to a Fellowship and Lectureship. The minutes also emphasised that the election was unanimous. Our warmest congratulations. It is exactly what ought to have happened.

> *Yours ever*
> *Alfred and Evelyn Whitehead*

1944–1967

Preface

This book is to be published while the great issues that now divide the world remain undecided. As yet, and for some time to come, the world must be one of doubt. It must as yet be suspended equally between hope and fear.

It is likely that I shall die before the issue is decided – I do not know whether my last words should be:

> The bright day is done
> And we are for the dark,

or, as I sometimes allow myself to hope,

> The world's great age begins anew,
> The golden years return. . . .
> Heaven smiles, and faiths and empires gleam,
> Like wrecks of a dissolving dream.

I have done what I could to add my small weight in an attempt to tip the balance on the side of hope, but it has been a puny effort against vast forces.

May others succeed where my generation failed.

During the year 1944, it became gradually clear that the war was ending, and was ending in German defeat. This made it possible for us to return to England and to bring our children with us without serious risk except for John, who was liable for conscription whether he went home or stayed in America. Fortunately, the end of the war came soon enough to spare him the awkward choice which this would have entailed.

My life in England, as before, was a mixture of public and private events, but the private part became increasingly important. I have found that it is not possible to relate in the same manner private and public events or happenings long since finished and those that are still continuing and in the midst of which I live. Some readers may be surprised by the changes of manner which this entails. I can only hope that the reader will realise the inevitability of diversification and appreciate the unavoidable reticences necessitated by the law of libel.

Chapter 14

Return to England

Crossing the Atlantic in the first half of 1944 was a complicated business. Peter and Conrad travelled on the *Queen Mary* at great speed but with extreme discomfort, in a ship completely crowded with young children and their mothers, all the mothers complaining of all the other children, and all the children causing the maximum trouble by conduct exposing them to the danger of falling into the sea. But of all this I knew nothing until I myself arrived in England. As for me, I was sent in a huge convoy which proceeded majestically at the speed of a bicycle, escorted by corvettes and aeroplanes. I was taking with me the manuscript of my *History of Western Philosophy*, and the unfortunate censors had to read every word of it lest it should contain information useful to the enemy. They were, however, at last satisfied that a knowledge of philosophy could be of no use to the Germans, and very politely assured me that they had enjoyed reading my book, which I confess I found hard to believe. Everything was surrounded with secrecy. I was not allowed to tell my friends when I was sailing or from what port. I found myself at last on a Liberty ship, making its maiden voyage. The Captain, who was a jolly fellow, used to cheer me up by saying that not more than one in four of the Liberty ships broke in two on its maiden voyage. Needless to say, the ship was American and the Captain, British. There was one officer who whole-heartedly approved of me. He was the Chief Engineer, and he had read *The ABC of Relativity* without knowing anything about its author. One day, as I was walking the deck with him, he began on the merits of this little book and, when I said that I was the author, his joy knew no limits. There was one other passenger, a business man, whom the ship's officers did not altogether like because they felt that he was young enough to fight. However, I found him pleasant and I quite enjoyed the three weeks of inactivity. There was considered to be no risk of submarines until we were approaching the coast of Ireland, but after that we were ordered to sleep in trousers. However, there was no incident of any kind. We were a few days from the end of our journey on D-day, which we learned about from the wireless. Almost the whole ship's crew was allowed to come and listen. I learned from the wireless the English for 'Allons, enfants de la patrie, le jour de gloire est arrivé.' The English for it is: 'Well, friends, this is it.'

They decanted us at a small port on the northern shore of the Firth of Forth on a Sunday. We made our way with some difficulty to the nearest town, where I had my first glimpse of Britain in that war-time. It consisted, so far as I could see at that moment, entirely of Polish soldiers and Scotch girls, the Polish soldiers very gallant, and the Scotch girls very fascinated. I got a night train to London, arrived very early in the morning, and for some time could not discover what had become of Peter and Conrad. At last, after much frantic telephoning and telegraphing, I discovered that they were staying with her mother at Sidmouth, and that Conrad had pneumonia. I went there at once, and found to my relief, that he was rapidly recovering. We sat on the beach, listening to the sound of naval guns off Cherbourg.

Trinity College had invited me to a five-year lectureship and I had accepted the invitation. It carried with it a fellowship and a right to rooms in College. I went to Cambridge and found that the rooms were altogether delightful; they looked out on the bowling green, which was a mass of flowers. It was a relief to find that the beauty of Cambridge was undimmed, and I found the peacefulness of the Great Court almost unbelievably soothing. But the problem of housing Peter and Conrad remained. Cambridge was incredibly full, and at first the best that I could achieve was squalid rooms in a lodging house. There they were underfed and miserable, while I was living luxuriously in College. As soon as it became clear that I was going to get money out of my law-suit against Barnes,[1] I bought a house at Cambridge, where we lived for some time.

VJ-day and the General Election which immediately followed it occurred while we were living in this house. It was also there that I wrote most of my book on *Human Knowledge, its Scope and Limits*. I could have been happy in Cambridge, but the Cambridge ladies did not consider us respectable. I bought a small house at Ffestiniog in North Wales with a most lovely view. Then we took a flat in London. Though I spent much time in visits to the Continent for purposes of lecturing, I did no work of importance during these years. When, in 1949, my wife decided that she wanted no more of me, our marriage came to an end.

Throughout the forties and the early fifties, my mind was in a state of confused agitation on the nuclear question. It was obvious to me that a nuclear war would put an end to civilisation. It was also obvious that unless there were a change of policies in both East and West a nuclear war was sure to occur sooner or later. The dangers were in the back of my mind from the early 'twenties. But in those days, although a few learned physicists were appreciative of the coming danger, the majority, not only of men in the streets, but even of

[1] Cf. page 464.

scientists, turned aside from the prospect of atomic war with a kind of easy remark that 'Oh, men will never be so foolish as that'. The bombing of Hiroshima and Nagasaki in 1945 first brought the possibility of nuclear war to the attention of men of science and even of some few politicians. A few months after the bombing of the two Japanese cities, I made a speech in the House of Lords pointing out the likelihood of a general nuclear war and the certainty of its causing universal disaster if it occurred. I forecast and explained the making of nuclear bombs of far greater power than those used upon Hiroshima and Nagasaki, fusion as against the old fission bombs, the present hydrogen bombs in fact. It was possible at that time to enforce some form of control of these monsters to provide for their use for peaceful, not warlike, ends, since the arms race which I dreaded had not yet begun. If no controls were thought out, the situation would be almost out of hand. It took no great imagination to foresee this. Everybody applauded my speech; not a single Peer suggested that my fears were excessive. But all my hearers agreed that this was a question for their grandchildren. In spite of hundreds of thousands of Japanese deaths, nobody grasped that Britain had escaped only by luck and that in the next war she might be less fortunate. Nobody viewed it as an international danger which could only be warded off by agreement among the Great Powers. There was a certain amount of talk, but no action was taken. This easy-going attitude survives among the laity even down to the present day. Those who try to make you uneasy by talk about atom bombs are regarded as trouble-makers, as people to be avoided, as people who spoil the pleasure of a fine day by foolish prospects of improbable rain.

Against this careless attitude I, like a few others, used every opportunity that presented itself to point out the dangers. It seemed to me then, as it still seems to me, that the time to plan and to act in order to stave off approaching dangers is when they are first seen to be approaching. Once their progress is established, it is very much more difficult to halt it. I felt hopeful, therefore, when the Baruch Proposal was made by the United States to Russia. I thought better of it then, and of the American motives in making it, than I have since learned to think, but I still wish that the Russians had accepted it. However, the Russians did not. They exploded their first bomb in August, 1949, and it was evident that they would do all in their power to make themselves the equals of the United States in destructive – or, politely, defensive – power. The arms race became inevitable unless drastic measures were taken to avoid it. That is why, in late 1948, I suggested that the remedy might be the threat of immediate war by the United States on Russia for the purpose of forcing nuclear disarmament upon her. I have given my reasons for doing this in an Appendix to my *Common Sense and*

Nuclear Warfare. My chief defence of the view I held in 1948 was that I thought Russia very likely to yield to the demands of the West. This ceased to be probable after Russia had a considerable fleet of nuclear planes.

This advice of mine is still brought up against me. It is easy to understand why Communists might object to it. But the usual criticism is that I, a pacifist, once advocated the threat of war. It seems to cut no ice that I have reiterated *ad nauseum* that I am not a pacifist, that I believe that some wars, a very few, are justified, even necessary. They are usually necessary because matters have been permitted to drag on their obviously evil way till no peaceful means can stop them. Nor do my critics appear to consider the evils that have developed as a result of the continued Cold War and that might have been avoided, along with the Cold War itself, had my advice to threaten war been taken in 1948. Had it been taken, the results remain hypothetical, but so far as I can see it is no disgrace, and shows no 'inconsistency' in my thought, to have given it.

None the less, at the time I gave this advice, I gave it so casually without any real hope that it would be followed, that I soon forgot I had given it. I had mentioned it in a private letter and again in a speech that I did not know was to be the subject of dissection by the press. When, later, the recipient of the letter asked me for permission to publish it, I said, as I usually do, without consideration of the contents, that if he wished he might publish it. He did so. And to my surprise I learned of my earlier suggestion. I had, also, entirely forgotten that it occurred in the above-mentioned speech. Unfortunately, in the meantime, before this incontrovertible evidence was set before me, I had hotly denied that I had ever made such a suggestion. It was a pity. It is shameful to deny one's own words. One can only defend or retract them. In this case I could, and did, defend them, and should have done so earlier but from a fault of my memory upon which from many years' experience I had come to rely too unquestioningly.

My private thoughts meanwhile were more and more disturbed. I became increasingly pessimistic and ready to try any suggested escape from the danger. My state of mind was like a very much exaggerated nervous fear such as people are apt to feel while a thunder-storm gathers on the horizon and has not yet blotted out the sun. I found it very difficult to remain sane or to reject any suggested measures. I do not think I could have succeeded in this except for the happiness of my private life.

For a few years I was asked yearly to give a lecture at the Imperial Defence College in Belgrave Square. But the invitations stopped coming after the lecture in which I remarked that, knowing that they believed you could not be victorious in war without the help of religion,

I had read the Sermon on the Mount, but, to my surprise, could find no mention of H-bombs in it. My audience appeared to be embarrassed, as they were good Christians as well as, of course, warriors. But, for myself, I find the combination of Christianity with war and weapons of mass extinction hard to justify.

In 1948, the Western Powers endeavoured to create a union which should be the germ of a World Government. The Conservative Party approved and wished Britain to become a member. The Labour Party, after some hesitation, opposed the scheme, but left individual members free to support it or not, as they thought fit. I joined and made a possibly somewhat excessive attack upon one of the few Communists present at the international Congress assembled at The Hague to consider the scheme. In his speech he had maintained that Communists have a higher ethic than other men. This was just after the fall of the Democratic Government of Czechoslovakia and my remarks had the complete agreement of the bulk of the people present. The younger Masaryk's suicide as a result of his rough handling by the Communists had shocked us all, and almost all of us had the conviction that co-operation with the East was for the present impossible. I said: 'If you can persuade me that hounding your most eminent citizen to his death shows a higher ethical outlook than that of the West, I shall be prepared to support you, but, till that time comes, I shall do no such thing.'

Towards the end of the war, after my return to England, and for some time thereafter, the Government used me to lecture to the Forces. The Forces had become more pacific than I expected as the war neared its end, and I remember that Laski and I were sent together on one occasion to speak to some of the air men. Laski was more radical than I was, and they all agreed with him. In the middle of my lecture I suddenly realised that half of my audience was creeping out of the hall and I wondered if I had offended them in some way more drastic than merely failing to be sufficiently radical. Afterwards, I was told that the men had been called away to combat the last of the German air raids against England.

At the time of the Berlin air lift, I was sent by the Government to Berlin to help to persuade the people of Berlin that it was worth while to resist Russian attempts to get the Allies out of Berlin. It was the first and only time that I have been able to parade as a military man. I was made a member of the armed forces for the occasion and given a military passport, which amused me considerably.

I had known Berlin well in the old days, and the hideous destruction that I saw at this time shocked me. From my window I could barely see one house standing. I could not discover where the Germans were living. This complete destruction was due partly to the English and partly to the Russians, and it seemed to me monstrous. Contemplation of the less accountable razing of Dresden by my own countrymen sickened me. I felt that when the Germans were obviously about to surrender that was enough, and that to destroy not only 135,000 Germans but also all their houses and countless treasures was barbarous.

I felt the treatment of Germany by the Allies to be almost incredibly foolish. By giving part of Germany to Russia and part to the West, the victorious Governments ensured the continuation of strife between East and West, particularly as Berlin was partitioned and there was no guarantee of access by the West to its part of Berlin except by air. They had imagined a peaceful co-operation between Russia and her Western allies, but they ought to have foreseen that this was not a likely outcome. As far as sentiment was concerned, what happened was a continuation of the war with Russia as the common enemy of the West. The stage was set for the Third World War, and this was done deliberately by the utter folly of Governments.

I thought the Russian blockade was foolish and was glad that it was unsuccessful owing to the skill of the British. At this time I was *persona grata* with the British Government because, though I was against nuclear war, I was also anti-Communist. Later I was brought around to being more favourable to Communism by the death of Stalin in 1953 and by the Bikini test in 1954; and I came gradually to attribute, more and more, the danger of nuclear war to the West, to the United States of America, and less to Russia. This change was supported by developments inside the United States, such as McCarthyism and the restriction of civil liberties.

I was doing a great deal of broadcasting for the various services of the BBC and they asked me to do one at the time of Stalin's death. As I rejoiced mightily in that event, since I felt Stalin to be as wicked as one man could be and to be the root evil of most of the misery and terror in, and threatened by, Russia, I condemned him in my broadcast and rejoiced for the world in his departure from the scene. I forgot the BBC susceptibilities and respectabilities. My broadcast never went on the air.

In the same year that I went to Germany, the Government sent me to Norway in the hope of inducing Norwegians to join an alliance against Russia. The place they sent me to was Trondheim. The weather was stormy and cold. We had to go by sea-plane from Oslo to Trondheim. When our plane touched down on the water it became obvious that something was amiss, but none of us in the plane knew what it was. We sat in the plane while it slowly sank. Small boats assembled round it and presently we were told to jump into the sea and swim to a boat – which all the people in my part of the plane did. We later learned that all the nineteen passengers in the non-smoking compartment had been killed. When the plane had hit the water a hole had been made in the plane and the water had rushed in. I had told a friend at Oslo who was finding me a place that he must find me a place where I could smoke, remarking jocularly, 'If I cannot smoke, I shall die'. Unexpectedly, this turned out to be true. All those in the smoking compartment got out by the emergency exit window beside which I was sitting. We all swam to the boats which dared not approach too near for fear of being sucked under as the plane sank. We were rowed to shore to a place some miles from Trondheim and thence I was taken in a car to my hotel.

Everybody showed me the utmost kindness and put me to bed while my clothes dried. A group of students even dried my matches one by one. They asked if I wanted anything and I replied, 'Yes, a strong dose of brandy and a large cup of coffee'. The doctor, who arrived soon after, said that this was quite the right reply. The day was Sunday, on which day hotels in Norway were not allowed to supply liquor – a fact of which I was at the time unaware – but, as the need was medical, no objection was raised. Some amusement was caused when a clergyman supplied me with clerical clothing to wear till my clothes had dried. Everybody plied me with questions. A question even came by telephone from Copenhagen: a voice said, 'When you were in the water, did you not think of mysticism and logic ?' 'No', I said. 'What did you think of ?' the voice persisted. 'I thought the water was cold', I said and put down the receiver.

My lecture was cancelled as the man who had been intended to be the Chairman had been drowned. Students took me to a place in the nearby mountains where they had an establishment. In going and coming, they walked me about in the rain and I remarked that Trondheim was as wet out of the water as in it, a remark which seemed to please them. Apart from the rain, which turned to snow in the region of the mountains, I found Trondheim a pleasant place, but I was a little puzzled when I learnt that the Bishop pronounced the place one way and the Mayor another. I adopted the Bishop's pronunciation.

I was astonished by the commotion caused by my part in this adventure. Every phase of it was exaggerated. I had swum about one hundred yards, but I could not persuade people that I had not swum miles. True, I had swum in my great-coat and lost my hat and thrown my attaché case into the sea. The latter was restored to me in the course of the afternoon – and is still in use – and the contents were dried out. When I returned to London the officials all smiled when they saw the marks of sea water on my passport. It had been in my attaché case, and I was glad to recover it.

When I had returned to England in 1944, I found that in certain ways my outlook had changed. I enjoyed once more the freedom of discussion that prevailed in England, but not in America. In America, if a policeman addressed us, my young son burst into tears; and the same was true (*mutatis mutandis*) of university professors accused of speeding. The less fanatical attitude of English people diminished my own fanaticism, and I rejoiced in the feeling of home. This feeling was enhanced at the end of the forties when I was invited by the BBC to give the first course of Reith lectures, instead of being treated as a malefactor and allowed only limited access to the young. I admired more than ever the atmosphere of free discussion, and this influenced my choice of subject for the lectures, which was 'Authority and the Individual'. They were published in 1949 under that title and were concerned very largely with the lessening of individual freedom which tends to accompany increase of industrialism. But, although this danger was acknowledged, very little was done either then or since to diminish the evils that it was bringing.

I proposed in these lectures to consider how we could combine that degree of individual initiative which is necessary for progress with the degree of social cohesion that is necessary for survival. This is a large subject, and the remarks that I shall make upon it here are no more than annotations on the lectures and sometimes expansions of subjects that have interested me since writing the book.

The problem comes down, in my view, to the fact that society should strive to obtain security and justice for human beings and, also, progress. To obtain these it is necessary to have an established framework, the State, but, also, individual freedom. And in order to obtain the latter, it is necessary to separate cultural matters from the Establishment. The chief matter in which security is desirable now is security of nations against hostile enemies, and to achieve this a world government must be established that is strong enough to hold sway over national governments in international matters.

Since no defence is possible for a single nation against a more powerful nation or a group of such nations, a nation's safety in international matters must depend upon outside protection. Aggression against a single nation by another nation or group of nations must be opposed by international law and not left to the wilful initiative of some warlike State. If this is not done, any State may at any moment be totally destroyed. Changes in weapons may frequently alter the balance of power. It happened, for example, between France and England in the fifteenth century when the Powers ceased to defend castles and came to depend upon moving armies with artillery. This put an end to the feudal anarchy which had until then been common. In like manner, nuclear weapons must, if peace is to exist, put an end to war between nations and introduce the practical certainty of victory for an international force in any possible contest. The introduction of such a reform is difficult since it requires that the international Power should be so armed as to be fairly certain of victory in warfare with any single State.

Apart from this connection with the dangers of war now that weapons of mass destruction were being developed, these lectures were important in my own life because they give the background of a subject which has absorbed me in one way and another, especially since 1914: the relation of an individual to the State, conscientious objection, civil disobedience.

The prevention of war is essential to individual liberty. When war is imminent or actually in progress various important liberties are curtailed and it is only in a peaceful atmosphere that they can be expected to revive. As a rule, the interference with liberty goes much further than is necessary, but this is an inevitable result of panic fear. When Louis XVI's head was cut off other monarchs felt their heads insecure. They rushed to war and punished all sympathy with the French Revolution. The same sort of thing, sometimes in a less violent form, happened when Governments were terrified by the Russian Revolution. If the individual is to have all the liberty that is his due, he must be free to advocate whatever form of government he considers best, and this may require the protection of an international authority, especially since nuclear weapons have increased the power of nations to interfere with each other's internal affairs. Individual liberty in war-time should extend to personal participation in war.

In the course of these lectures, I gave a brief résumé of the growth and decay of governmental power. In the great days of Greece there was not too much of it: great men were free to develop their capacities while they lived, but wars and assassinations often cut short their labours. Rome brought order, but at the same time brought a considerable degree of eclipse to the achievement of individuals. Under the Empire, individual initiative was so curtailed as to be incapable of resisting new attacks from without. For a thousand years after the fall of Rome, there was too little authority and also too little individual initiative. Gradually, new weapons, especially gunpowder, gave strength to governments and developed the modern State. But with this came excessive authority. The problem of preserving liberty in a world of nuclear weapons is a new one and one for which men's minds are not prepared. Unless we can adapt ourselves to a greater search for liberty than has been necessary during the last few centuries, we shall sink into private lethargy and fall a prey to public energy.

It is especially as regards science that difficult problems arise. The modern civilised State depends upon science in a multitude of ways. Generally, there is old science, which is official, and new science, which elderly men look upon with horror. This results in a continual battle between old men, who admire the science of their fathers, and the young men who realise the value of their contemporaries' work. Up to a point this struggle is useful, but beyond that point it is disastrous.

In the present day, the most important example of it is the population explosion, which can only be combated by methods which to the old seem impious.

Some ideals are subversive and cannot well be realised except by war or revolution. The most important of these is at present economic justice. Political justice had its day in industrialised parts of the world and is still to be sought in the unindustrialised parts, but economic justice is still a painfully sought goal. It requires a world-wide economic revolution if it is to be brought about. I do not see how it is to be achieved without bloodshed or how the world can continue patiently without it. It is true that steps are being taken in some countries, particularly by limiting the power of inheritance, but these are as yet very partial and very limited. Consider the vast areas of the world where the young have little or no education and where adults have not the capacity to realise elementary conditions of comfort. These inequalities rouse envy and are potential causes of great disorder. Whether the world will be able by peaceful means to raise the conditions of the poorer nations is, to my mind, very doubtful, and is likely to prove the most difficult governmental problem of coming centuries.

Very difficult problems are concerned with the inroads of war against liberty. The most obvious of these is conscription. Military men, when there is war, argue that it cannot be won unless all men on our side are compelled to fight. Some men will object, perhaps on religious grounds or, possibly, on the ground that the work they are doing is more useful than fighting. On such a matter there is liable to be, or at any rate there ought to be, a division between the old and the young. The old will say they are too aged to fight, and many of the young ought to say that their work is more useful towards victory than fighting.

The religious objection to taking part in warfare is more widespread. Civilised people are brought up to think it is wicked to kill other people, and some do not admit that a state of war puts an end to this ethical command. The number who hold this view is not very large, and I doubt whether any war has ever been determined by their action. It is good for a community to contain some people who feel the dictates of humanity so strongly that even in war-time they still obey them. And, apart from this argument, it is barbarous to compel a man to do acts which he considers wicked. We should all admit this if a law were proposed to punish a man for being a vegetarian, but when it is a human being whose life is at stake, we begin to wonder whether he is a friend or an enemy and, if the latter, we think we are justified in compelling the law to punish him.

In addition to those who consider all war wrong, there are those who object to the particular war that they are asked to fight. This happened with many people at the time of the Korean War and later in regard to the Vietnam War. Such people are punished if they refuse to fight. The law not only punishes those who condemn all war, but also those who condemn any particular war although it must be obvious that in any war one side, at least, is encouraging evil. Those who take this position of objecting to a certain war or a certain law or to certain actions of governments may be held justified because it is so doubtful that they are not justified. Such considerations, it will be said, since they condemn the punishment of supposed malefactors, throw doubt upon the whole criminal law. I believe this is true and I hold that every condemned criminal incurs a certain measure of doubt, sometimes great and sometimes small. This is admitted when it is an enemy who is tried, as in the Nuremberg Trials. It was widely admitted that the Nuremberg prisoners would not have been condemned if they had been tried by Germans. The enemies of the German Government would have punished with death any soldier among themselves who had practised the sort of civil disobedience the lack of which among Germans they pleaded as an excuse for condemning Germans. They refused to accept the plea made by many of those whom they condemned that they had committed criminal acts only under command of those in superior authority. The judges of Nuremberg believed that the Germans should have committed civil disobedience in the name of decency and humanity. This is little likely to have been their view if they had been judging their own countrymen and not their enemies. But I believe it is true of friend as well as foe. The line between proper acceptable civil disobedience and inacceptable civil disobedience comes, I believe, with the reason for it being committed – the seriousness of the object for which it is committed and the profundity of the belief in its necessity.

Some years before I gave the Reith Lectures, my old professor and friend and collaborator in *Principia Mathematica*, A. N. Whitehead, had been given the OM. Now, by the early part of 1949, I had become so respectable in the eyes of the Establishment that it was felt that I, too, should be given the OM. This made me very happy for, though I dare say it would surprise many Englishmen and most of the English Establishment to hear it, I am passionately English, and I treasure an honour bestowed on me by the Head of my country. I had to go to Buckingham Palace for the official bestowal of it. The King was affable, but somewhat embarrassed at having to behave graciously to so queer a fellow, a convict to boot. He remarked, 'You have sometimes behaved in a way which would not do if generally adopted'. I have been glad ever since that I did not make the reply that sprang to my mind: 'Like your brother.' But he was thinking of things like my having been a conscientious objector, and I did not feel that I could let this remark pass in silence, so I said: 'How a man should behave depends upon his profession. A postman, for instance, should knock at all the doors in a street at which he has letters to deliver, but if anybody else knocked on all the doors, he would be considered a public nuisance.' The King, to avoid answering, abruptly changed the subject by asking me whether I knew who was the only man who had both the KG and the OM. I did not know, and he graciously informed me that it was Lord Portal. I did not mention that he was my cousin.

In the February of that year I had been asked to give an address, which I called 'L'Individu et l'Etat Moderne', at the Sorbonne. In the course of it I spoke warmly and in most laudatory terms of Jean Nicod, the brilliant and delightful young mathematician who died in 1924.[1] I was very glad after the lecture that I had done so, for I learnt that, unknown to me, his widow had been in the audience.

At the end of June, 1950, I went to Australia in response to an invitation by the Australian Institute of International Affairs to give lectures at various universities on subjects connected with the Cold War. I interpreted this subject liberally and my lectures dealt with speculation about the future of industrialism. There was a Labour Government there and, in spite of the fact that the hatred and fear of China and, especially, Japan, was understandably fierce, things seemed better and more hopeful than they appeared to become in the following sixteen years. I liked the people and I was greatly impressed by the size of the country and the fact that ordinary private conversations, gossips, were conducted by radio. Because of the size, too, and people's relative isolation, the libraries and bookshops were impressively numerous and good, and people read more than elsewhere. I was taken to the capitals, and to Alice Springs which I wanted to see because it was so isolated. It was a centre for agriculture and inhabited chiefly by sheep owners. I was shown a fine gaol where I was assured that the cells were comfortable. In reply to my query as to why, I was told: 'Oh, because all the leading citizens at one time or another are in gaol.' I was told that, expectedly and regularly, whenever possible, they stole each other's sheep.

I visited all parts of Australia except Tasmania. The Korean War was in full swing, and I learnt to my surprise that the northern parts of Queensland had, when war broke out, been evacuated, but were again inhabited when I was there.

The Government, I found, treated the Aborigines fairly well, but the police and the public treated them abominably. I was taken by a public official whose duty it was to look after Aborigines to see a village in which all the inhabitants were native Australians. One complained to us that he had had a bicycle which had been stolen, and he displayed marked unwillingness to complain to the police about it. I asked my conductor why, and he explained that any native who

[1] Cf. page 327.

appealed to the police would be grossly ill-treated by them. I observed, myself, that white men generally spoke abusively to the Aborigines.

My other contact with the Government concerned irrigation. There is a chain of hills called 'Snowy Mountains' and there was a Federal scheme to utilise these mountains for purposes of irrigation. When I was there the scheme was bogged down by the operation of States which would not benefit by it. A scheme was being pushed to advocate the proposed irrigation on the grounds of defence rather than of irrigation, thus avoiding conflicts of States which are a standard problem in Australian politics. I spoke in favour of this scheme.

I was kept very busy making speeches and being interviewed by journalists and, at the end of my stay, I was presented with a beautifully bound book of press cuttings which I cherish, though I do not like much of what the journalists report me as saying of myself. I had advocated birth control on some occasion and naturally the Roman Catholics did not approve of me, and the Archbishop of Melbourne said publicly that I had been at one time excluded from the United States by the United States Government. This was not true; and I spoke of suing him, but a group of journalists questioned him on the point and he admitted his error publicly, which was a disappointment, since it meant that I had to relinquish the hope of receiving damages from an Archbishop.

On my way home to England my plane stopped at Singapore and Karachi and Bombay and other places. Though I was not permitted to visit any of these places, beyond their airports, as the plane did not stop long enough, I was called upon to make radio speeches. Later, I saw from a cutting from *The Sydney Morning Herald* for August 26th, an account of my speech at Singapore. It reported my saying: 'I think that Britain should withdraw gracefully from Asia, as she did in India, and not wait to be driven out in the event of a war . . . In this way goodwill will be won and a neutral Asian bloc could be formed under the leadership of Pandit Nehru. This is the best thing that can happen now, and the strongest argument in its favour is that it would be a strategic move.' This, though unheeded, seems to me to have been good advice.

Soon after my return from Australia. I went again to the United States. I had been asked to 'give a short course' in philosophy for a month at Mt Holyoak College, a well-known college for women in New England. From there I went to Princeton where I, as usual, delivered a lecture and again met various old friends, among them Einstein. There I received the news that I was to be given a Nobel Prize. But the chief memory of this visit to America is of the series of three lectures that I gave on the Matchette Foundation at Columbia University. I was put up in luxury at the Plaza Hotel and shepherded about by Miss Julie Medlock, who had been appointed by Columbia to bear-lead me.

Her views on international affairs were liberal and sympathetic and we have continued to discuss them, both by letter and when she visits us as she sometimes does.

My lectures, a few months later, appeared with other lectures that I had given originally at Ruskin College, Oxford, and the Lloyd Roberts Lecture that I had given in 1949 at the Royal Society of Medicine, London, as the basis of my book called *The Impact of Science on Society*. The title is the same as that of the three lectures that Columbia University published separately, which is unfortunate as it causes bewilderment for bibliographers and is sometimes a disappointment to those who come upon only the Columbia publication.

I was astonished that, in New York, where I had been, so short a time before, spoken of with vicious obloquy, my lectures seemed to be popular and to draw crowds. This was not surprising, perhaps, at the first lecture, where the audience might have gathered to have a glimpse of so horrid a character, hoping for shocks and scandal and general rebelliousness. But what amazed me was that the hall should have been packed with enthusiastic students in increasing numbers as the lectures proceeded. There were so many that crowds of those who came had to be turned away for lack of even standing room. I think it also surprised my hosts.

The chief matter with which I was concerned was the increase of human power owing to scientific knowledge. The gist of my first lecture was contained in the following sentence: 'It is not by prayer and humility that you cause things to go as you wish, but by acquiring a knowledge of natural laws.' I pointed out that the power to be acquired in this way is very much greater than the power that men formerly sought to achieve by theological means. The second lecture was concerned with the increase of power men achieve by the application of scientific technique. It begins with gunpowder and the mariners' compass. Gunpowder destroyed the power of castles and the mariners' compass created the power of Europe over other parts of the world. These increases of governmental power were important, but the new power brought by the Industrial Revolution was more so. I was largely concerned in this lecture with the bad effect of early industrial power and with the dangers that will result if any powerful State adopts scientific breeding. From this I went on to the increase of the harmfulness of war when scientific methods are employed. This is, at present, the most important form of the application of science in our day. It threatens the destruction of the human race and, indeed, of all living beings of larger than microscopic size. If mankind is to survive, the power of making scientific war will have to be concentrated in a supreme State. But this is so contrary to men's mental habits that, as yet, the great majority would prefer to run the risk of extermination. This is the supreme danger of our age. Whether a World Government will be established in time or not is the supreme question. In my third lecture I am concerned chiefly with certain views as to good and evil from which I dissent although many men consider that they alone are scientific. The views in question are that the good is identical with the useful. I ended these lectures with an investigation of the kind of temperament which must be dominant if a happy world is to be possible. The first requisite, I should say, is absence of dogmatism, since dogmatism almost inevitably leads to war. I will quote the paragraph summing up what I thought necessary if the world is to be saved: 'There are certain things that our age needs, and certain things that it should avoid. It needs compassion and a wish that mankind should be happy; it needs the desire for knowledge and the determination to eschew pleasant myths; it needs, above all, courageous hope and the impulse to creativeness. The things that it must avoid and that have brought it to the brink of catastrophe are cruelty, envy, greed, competitiveness, search for irrational subjective certainty, and what Freudians call the death wish.'

I think I was mistaken in being surprised that my lectures were liked by the audience. Almost any young academic audience is liberal and likes to hear liberal and even quasi-revolutionary opinions expressed by someone in authority. They like, also any jibe at any received opinion, whether orthodox or not: for instance, I spent some time making fun of Aristotle for saying that the bite of the shrewmouse is dangerous to a horse, especially if the shrewmouse is pregnant. My audience was irreverent and so was I. I think this was the main basis of their liking of my lectures. My unorthodoxy was not confined to politics. My trouble in New York in 1940 on sexual morals had blown over but had left in any audience of mine an expectation that they would hear something that the old and orthodox would consider shocking. There were plenty of such items in my discussion of scientific breeding. Generally, I had the pleasant experience of being applauded on the very same remarks which had caused me to be ostracized on the earlier occasion.

I got into trouble with a passage at the tail end of my last Columbia lecture. In this passage, I said that what the world needs is 'love, Christian love, or compassion'. The result of my use of the word 'Christian' was a deluge of letters from Free-thinkers deploring my adoption of orthodoxy, and from Christians welcoming me to the fold. When, ten years later, I was welcomed by the Chaplain to Brixton Prison with the words, 'I am glad that you have seen the light', I had to explain to him that this was an entire misconception, that my views were completely unchanged and that what he called seeing the light I should call groping in darkness. I had thought it obvious that, when I spoke of *Christian* love, I put in the adjective 'Christian' to distinguish it from sexual love, and I should certainly have supposed that the context made this completely clear. I go on to say that, 'If you feel this you have a motive for existence, a guide in action, a reason for courage, and an imperative necessity for intellectual honesty. If you feel this, you have all that anybody should need in the way of religion.' It seems to me totally inexplicable that anybody should think the above words a description of Christianity, especially in view, as some Christians will remember, of how very rarely Christians have shown Christian love. I have done my best to console those who are not Christians for the pain that I unwittingly caused them by a lax use of the suspect adjective. My essays and lectures on the subject have been edited and published in 1957 by Professor Paul Edwards along with an essay by him on my New York difficulties of 1940, under the title *Why I am not a Christian*.

When I was called to Stockholm, at the end of 1950, to receive the Nobel Prize – somewhat to my surprise, for literature, for my book *Marriage and Morals* – I was apprehensive, since I remembered that, exactly three hundred years earlier, Descartes had been called to Scandinavia by Queen Christina in the winter time and had died of the cold. However, we were kept warm and comfortable, and instead of snow, we had rain, which was a slight disappointment. The occasion, though very grand, was pleasant and I enjoyed it. I was sorry for another prize winner who looked utterly miserable and was so shy that he refused to speak to anyone and could not make himself heard when he had to make his formal speech as we all had to do. My dinner companion was Madame Joliot-Curie and I found her talk interesting. At the evening party given by the King, an Aide-de-Camp came to say that the King wished to talk with me. He wanted Sweden to join with Norway and Denmark against the Russians. I said that it was obvious, if there were a war between the West and the Russians, the Russians could only get to Norwegian ports through and over Swedish territory. The King approved of this observation. I was rather pleased, too, by my speech, especially by the mechanical sharks, concerning whom I said: 'I think every big town should contain artificial waterfalls that people could descend in very fragile canoes, and they should contain bathing pools full of mechanical sharks. Any person found advocating a preventive war should be condemned to two hours a day with these ingenious monsters.' I found that two or three fellow Nobel prize-winners listened to what I had to say and considered it not without importance. Since then I have published it in Part II of my book *Human Society in Ethics and Politics* and a gramophone record has been made of it in America. I have heard that it has affected many people more than I had thought which is gratifying.

1950, beginning with the OM and ending with the Nobel Prize, seems to have marked the apogee of my respectability. It is true that I began to feel slightly uneasy, fearing that this might mean the onset of blind orthodoxy. I have always held that no one can be respectable without being wicked, but so blunted was my moral sense that I could not see in what way I had sinned. Honours and increased income which began with the sales of my *History of Western Philosophy* gave me a feeling of freedom and assurance that let me expend all my energies upon what I wanted to do. I got through an immense amount of work and felt, in consequence, optimistic and full of zest. I suspected that I had too much emphasised, hitherto, the darker possibilities threatening mankind and that it was time to write a book in which the happier issues of current disputes were brought into relief. I called this book *New Hopes for a Changing World* and deliberately, wherever there were two possibilities, I emphasised that it *might* be the happier one which would be realised. I did not suggest that either the cheerful or the painful alternative was the more probable, but merely that it is impossible to know which would be victorious. The book ends with a picture of what the world may become if we so choose. I say: 'Man, in the long ages since he descended from the trees, has passed arduously and perilously through a vast dusty desert, surrounded by the whitening bones of those who have perished by the way, maddened by hunger and thirst, by fear of wild beasts, by dread of enemies, not only living enemies, but spectres of dead rivals projected on to the dangerous world by the intensity of his own fears. At last he has emerged from the desert into a smiling land, but in the long night he has forgotten how to smile. We cannot believe in the brightness of the morning. We think it trivial and deceptive; we cling to old myths that allow us to go on living with fear and hate – above all, hate of ourselves, miserable sinners. This is folly. Man now needs for his salvation only one thing: to open his heart to joy, and leave fear to gibber through the glimmering darkness of a forgotten past. He must lift up his eyes and say: "No, I am not a miserable sinner; I am a being who, by a long and arduous road, have discovered how to make intelligence master natural obstacles, how to live in freedom and joy, at peace with myself and therefore with all mankind." This will happen if men choose joy rather than sorrow. If not, eternal death will bury man in deserved oblivion.'

But my disquietude grew. My inability to make my fellow men see the dangers ahead for them and all mankind weighed upon me. Perhaps it heightened my pleasures as pain sometimes does, but pain was there and increased with my increasing awareness of failure to make others share a recognition of its cause. I began to feel that *New Hopes for a Changing World* needed fresh and deeper examination and I attempted to make this in my book *Human Society in Ethics and Politics*, the end of which, for a time, satisfied my craving to express my fears in an effective form.

What led me to write about ethics was the accusation frequently brought against me that, while I had made a more or less sceptical inquiry into other branches of knowledge, I had avoided the subject of ethics except in an early essay expounding Moore's *Principia Ethica*. My reply is that ethics is not a branch of knowledge. I now, therefore, set about the task in a different way. In the first half of the book, I dealt with the fundamental concepts of ethics; in the second part, I dealt with the application of these concepts in practical politics. The first part analyses such concepts as moral codes; good and bad, sin, superstitious ethics, and ethical sanctions. In all these I seek for an ethical element in subjects which are traditionally labelled ethical. The conclusion that I reach is that ethics is never an independent constituent, but is reducible to politics in the last analysis. What are we to say, for example, about a war in which the parties are evenly matched? In such a context each side may claim that it is obviously in the right and that its defeat would be a disaster to mankind. There would be no way of proving this assertion except by appealing to other ethical concepts such as hatred of cruelty or love of knowledge or art. You may admire the Renaissance because they built St Peter's, but somebody may perplex you by saying that he prefers St Paul's. Or, again, the war may have sprung from lies told by one party which may seem an admirable foundation to the contest until it appears that there was equal mendacity on the other side. To arguments of this sort there is no purely rational conclusion. If one man believes that the earth is round and another believes that it is flat, they can set off on a joint voyage and decide the matter reasonably. But if one believes in Protestantism and the other in Catholicism, there is no known method of reaching a rational conclusion. For such reasons, I had come to agree with Santayana that there is no such thing as ethical *knowledge*. Nevertheless, ethical concepts have been of enormous importance in history, and I could not but feel that a survey of human affairs which omits ethics is inadequate and partial.

I adopted as my guiding thought the principle that ethics is derived from passions and that there is no valid method of travelling from passion to what ought to be done. I adopted David Hume's maxim that 'Reason is, and ought only to be, the slave of the passions'. I am not satisfied with this, but it is the best that I can do. Critics are fond of charging me with being wholly rational and this, at least, proves that I am not entirely so. The practical distinction among passions comes as regards their success: some passions lead to success in what is desired; others, to failure. If you pursue the former, you will be happy; if the latter, unhappy. Such, at least, will be the broad general rule. This may seem a poor and tawdry result of researches into such sublime concepts as 'duty', 'self-denial', 'ought', and so forth, but I am persuaded that it is the total of the valid outcome, except in one particular: we feel that the man who brings widespread happiness at the expense of misery to himself is a better man than the man who brings unhappiness to others and happiness to himself. I do not know any rational ground for this view, or perhaps, for the somewhat more rational view that whatever the majority desires is preferable to what the minority desires. These are truly ethical problems, but I do not know of any way in which they can be solved except by politics or war. All that I can find to say on this subject is that an ethical opinion can only be defended by an ethical axiom, but, if the axiom is not accepted, there is no way of reaching a rational conclusion.

There is one approximately rational approach to ethical conclusions which has a certain validity. It may be called the doctrine of compossibility. This doctrine is as follows: among the desires that a man finds himself to possess, there are various groups, each consisting of desires which may be gratified together and others which conflict. You may, for example, be a passionate adherent of the Democratic Party, but it may happen that you hate the presidential candidate. In that case, your love of the Party and your dislike of the individual are not compossible. Or you may hate a man and love his son. In that case, if they always travel about together, you will find them, as a pair, not compossible. The art of politics consists very largely in finding as numerous a group of compossible people as you can. The man who wishes to be happy will endeavour to make as large groups as he can of compossible desires the rulers of his life. Viewed theoretically, such a doctrine affords no ultimate solution. It assumes that happiness is better than unhappiness. This is an ethical principle incapable of proof. For that reason, I did not consider compossibility a basis for ethics.

I do not wish to be thought coldly indifferent to ethical considerations. Man, like the lower animals, is supplied by nature with passions and has a difficulty in fitting these passions together, especially if he lives in a close-knit community. The art required for this is the art of politics. A man totally destitute of this art would be a savage and incapable of living in civilised society. That is why I have called my book *Human Society in Ethics and Politics*.

Though the reviews of the book were all that could be hoped, nobody paid much attention to what I considered most important about it, the impossibility of reconciling ethical feelings with ethical doctrines. In the depths of my mind this dark frustration brooded constantly. I tried to intersperse lighter matters into my thoughts, especially by writing stories which contained an element of fantasy. Many people found these stories amusing, though some found them too stylised for their taste. Hardly anyone seems to have found them prophetic.

Long before this, in the beginning of the century, I had composed various stories and, later, I made up stories for my children to while away the tedious climb from the beach to our house in Cornwall. Some of the latter have since been written down, though never published. In about 1912, I had written a novel, in the manner of Mallock's *New Republic*, called *The Perplexities of John Forstice*. Though the first half of it I still think is not bad, the latter half seems very dull to me, and I have never made any attempt to publish it. I also invented a story that I never published.

From the time when Rutherford first discovered the structure of the atom, it had been obvious that sooner or later atomic force would become available in war. This had caused me to foresee the possibility of the complete destruction of man through his own folly. In my story a pure scientist makes up a little machine which can destroy matter throughout the universe. He has known hitherto only his own laboratory and so he decides that, before using his machine, he must find out whether the world deserves to be destroyed. He keeps his little machine in his waistcoat pocket and if he presses the knob the world will cease to exist. He goes round the world examining whatever seems to him evil, but everything leaves him in doubt until he finds himself at a Lord Mayor's Banquet and finds the nonsense talked by politicians unbearable. He leaps up and announces that he is about to destroy the world. The other diners rush at him to stop him. He puts his thumb in his waistcoat pocket – and finds that in changing for dinner he forgot to move the little machine.

I did not publish this story at the time as it seemed too remote from reality. But, with the coming of the atom bomb, its remoteness from reality vanished, so I wrote other stories with a similar moral, some of which ended in atomic destruction, while others, which I called 'nightmares', exemplified the hidden fears of eminent men.

The writing of these stories was a great release of my hitherto unexpressed feelings and of thoughts which could not be stated without mention of fears that had no rational basis. Gradually their scope widened. I found it possible to express in this fictional form dangers that would have been deemed silly while only a few men recognised them. I could state in fiction ideas which I half believed in but had no good solid grounds for believing. In this way it was possible to warn of dangers which might or might not occur in the near future.

My first book of stories was *Satan in the Suburbs*. The title story was in part suggested to me by a stranger whom I met in Mortlake and who, when he saw me, crossed the road and made the sign of the Cross as he went. It was partly, also, suggested by a poor mad lady who I used to meet on my walks. In this story there was a wicked scientist who by subtle means caused people, after one lapse from virtue, to plunge into irretrievable ruin. One of these people was a photographer who made photography an opportunity for blackmail. I modelled him upon a fashionable photographer who had come to make a picture of me. He died shortly afterwards, and I then learnt that he practised all the sins of which I had accused him in the story. In one of the other stories, the hero proclaims a curse in which he mentions Zoroaster and the Beard of The Prophet. I got an indignant letter from a Zoroastrian saying how dare I make fun of Zoroaster. This story I had written, as a warning of what might befall her, for my secretary (a completely innocent young woman) who was about to go to Corsica on a holiday. It was published anonymously in a magazine with a prize offered for guessing the authorship. Nobody guessed right. One of the characters in the story is General Prz to whose name there is a footnote saying, 'pronounced Pish', and the prize was given to a man who wrote to the magazine: 'This is Trz (pronounced Tosh).' Another story portrayed a fight to the death between human beings and Martians. In this there is an eloquent appeal in the style of Churchill, calling upon all human beings to forget their differences and rise in defence of MAN. I had great fun proclaiming this speech, as nearly as possible in Churchill's manner, for a gramophone record.

A year later, I wrote another series of stories which I called *Nightmares of Eminent Persons*. These were intended to illustrate the secret fears that beset the Great while they sleep. A long short story that I published with *Nightmares* is called 'Zahatopolk' and concerns the hardening of what begins as a career of freedom of thought in to a hard persecuting orthodoxy. This has hitherto been the fate of all the great religions; and how it is to be avoided in the future I do not know. When my secretary was typing the story she reached the point where the semi-divine king makes a sacrificial breakfast of a lovely lady. I went in to see how she was getting on and found her gibbering in terror. Various people have dramatised this story both for film and theatre production, as they have others that occur in my writings, but, when it has come to the point, no one has been willing to produce them or I have been unwilling to have them produced because of the particular dramatisation, sometimes offensively frivolous. I regret this and regret especially that none of the *Nightmares* have been made into ballets. Various of the stories pose, and occasionally answer, various questions that I should like to call to people's attention.

I had an amusing experience with one of the *Nightmares* while I was composing it. The hero was a Frenchman who lamented his sad fate in French verse. One evening at dinner in the Ecu de France I started to declaim his last words in what I hoped was the best French classical style. The restaurant, being French, had a clientele mainly composed of Frenchmen. Most of them turned round and gazed at me in astonishment, then whispered together, wondering whether I was an unknown

French poet whom they had hit upon by accident. I do not know how long they went on wondering.

Another *Nightmare* was inspired by a psycho-analytic doctor in America who was somewhat dissatisfied by the use commonly made of psycho-analysis. He felt that everyone might be brought to humdrum normality, so I tried portraying Shakespeare's more interesting heroes after they had undergone a course of psycho-analysis. In the dream, a head of Shakespeare speaks, ending with the words, 'Lord, what fools these mortals be.' I had an approving letter from the American doctor.

I found a reluctance on the part of both editors and readers to accept me in the role of a writer of fiction. They seemed, just on the face of it, to resent the fact that I was trying my hand at something they had not grown used to my doing. Everybody wanted me to continue as a writer of doom, prophesying dreadful things. I was reminded of what the learned men of China said when I asked what I should lecture on and they replied: 'Oh, just what you say in your last book.' Authors are not allowed by their public to change their style or to part widely from their previous subjects.

My defence for writing stories, if defence were needed, is that I have often found fables the best way of making a point. When I returned from America in 1944, I found British philosophy in a very odd state, and, it seemed to me, occupied solely with trivialities. Everybody in the philosophical world was babbling about 'common usage'. I did not like this philosophy. Every section of learning has its own vocabulary and I did not see why philosophy should be deprived of this pleasure. I therefore wrote a short piece containing various fables making fun of this cult of 'common usage', remarking that what the philosophers really meant by the term was 'common-room usage'. I received a letter when this was published from the arch offender saying that he approved, but that he could not think against whom it was directed as he knew of no such cult. However, I noticed that from that time on very little was said about 'common usage'.

Most of my books, I find on looking back over them, have myths to enforce the points. For instance, I turned up the following paragraph recently in *The Impact of Science on Society*: 'What I do want to stress is that the kind of lethargic despair which is now not uncommon is irrational. Mankind is in the position of a man climbing a difficult and dangerous precipice, at the summit of which there is a plateau of delicious mountain meadows. With every step that he climbs, his fall, if he does fall, becomes more terrible; with every step his weariness increases and the ascent grows more difficult. At last, there is only one more step to be taken, but the climber does not know this, because he cannot see beyond the jutting rocks at his head. His exhaustion is so complete that he wants nothing but rest. If he lets go, he will find rest in death. Hope calls: "one more effort – perhaps it will be the last effort needed." Irony retorts: "Silly fellow! Haven't you been listening to hope all this time, and see where it has landed you." Optimism says: "While there is life, there is hope." Pessimism growls: "While there is life, there is pain." Does the exhausted climber make one more effort, or does he let himself sink into the abyss? In a few years, those of us who are still alive will know the answer.'

Others of my stories, nightmares and dreams and so forth, later formed the fiction part of my book *Fact and Fiction*. I had expected reviewers to make witticisms at my expense in regard to the title and contents of this book, but this did not occur. My 'Maxims of La Rochefoucauld' contained in it afforded me considerable amusement and I have added to them periodically. The making of my *Good Citizens' Alphabet* entertained me greatly. It was published at their Gabberbochus (which, I am told, is Polish for Jabberwocky) Press by my friends the Themersons with exceedingly clever and beautifully executed illustrations by Franciszka Themerson which heighten all the points that I most wanted made. They also published my *jeu d'esprit* on the end of the world, a short *History of the World*, for my ninetieth birthday in a little gold volume. My only venture into verse was published by the Humanists of America and is called – with apologies to Lewis Carroll – 'The Prelate and The Commissar'.

LETTERS

To and from Lucy Donnelly

> 212 Loring Avenue
> Los Angeles, Cal.
> Dec. 22, 1939

My dear Lucy

Ever since I got your nice letter I have been meaning to write to you, but have been terribly busy. It is the custom of this country to keep all intelligent people so harassed & hustled that they cease to be intelligent, and I have been suffering from this custom. The summer at Santa Barbara, it is true, was peaceful, but unluckily I injured my back & was laid up for a long time, which caused me to get behind hand with my lectures. – John & Kate, who came for the summer holidays, stayed when war broke out; it is a comfort to have them here, but John does not find the university of California a satisfactory substitute for Cambridge. I think of sending them both East to some less recent university, but last September there was no time for that. Apart from home sickness & war misery, we all flourish.

I am, when I can find time, writing a book on 'Words & Facts', or 'semantics' as it is vulgarly called. The only thing to be done in these times, it seems to me, is to salvage what one can of civilisation, personally as well as politically. But I feel rather like a strayed ghost from a dead world.

The visit to you was delightful. As time goes on, one values old friends more & more.

Remember me to Miss Finch. With love to yourself,

> *yours aff*
> *Bertrand Russell*

> New Place
> Bryn Mawr
> Pennsylvania
> 29 April 1940

My dear Bertie

Week by week I have sympathised with you & regretted bitterly that you have not been allowed to live and work in peace in America. Then, after all the muddlement & disgusting publicity, came your admirable letter in the *New York Times* – so wise, so right in feeling & so to the point at the close. Something was needed from you personally in reply to the Editorial distributing blame judiciously all round & very suspiciously avoiding the issue. Too bad of the *Times*: Your article in the *American Mercury* I also rejoiced in as just right & very useful. But this cause célèbre which scores for academic freedom for our country, I fear will have cost you yourself dear in many ways & have seriously upset your plans for the next year. I am very sorry.

I think of you always & hope to see you when you come to the East again – and perhaps your family with you. They look one & all of them delightful in their pictures. In these bad times your children must be a joy & hope. Your letter at Christmas was a happiness to me, when I remember all the people in the world to whom you have given happiness & enlightenment I marvel the more over this last confusion.

> *Ever yours with love*
> *Lucy Donnelly*

P.S. The cutting I enclose from the *College News*, our student paper, is Bryn Mawr's modest testimony to the cause in your name.

> Fallen Leaf Lodge
> Lake Tahoe, Cal.
> August 25, 1940

My dear Lucy

Peter is terribly busy, & I have finished my book, so I am answering your very nice letter to her.

We are leaving here in about a fortnight, & expect to get to Philadelphia about the 12th of September, except John & Kate, who go back to Los Angeles. I expect to be in Philadelphia only a few days, & then to go to Harvard, but Peter, with Conrad & the governess (Miss Campbell), means to stay somewhere near Philadelphia & hunt for a house. I have accepted the Barnes Institute; there was no other prospect of any post, however humble. No university dare contemplate employing me.

You once offered to put us up if we were in Philadelphia, & it would be very pleasant for us if you could have us for a few days from about the 12th, but I don't know if you have two spare rooms, one for Peter & me & one for Conrad and Miss Campbell. Still less do I know whether you would want a boy of three, whose behaviour might not always be impeccable. Please be *quite* frank about this.

Yes, I know Newman of John's. I have found him, on occasion, a very valuable critic.

I am sorry you will have to put up with us as a feeble substitute for the Renoirs. Perhaps in time I shall be able to soften Barnes's heart.

With Peter's thanks & my love,

> *Yours affectionately*
> *Bertrand Russell*

April 15, 1941

My dear Lucy

I blush with shame in the middle of the night every time I think of my outrageous behaviour at your dinner, when I deafened you by shouting at your ear. Please forgive me. Since the New York row I have been prickly, especially when I encounter the facile optimism which won't realise that, but for Barnes, it would have meant literal starvation for us all – But that is no excuse for abominable behaviour. I used, when excited, to calm myself by reciting the three factors of $a^3 + b^3 + c^3 - 3abc$; I must revert to this practice. I find it more effective than thoughts of the Ice Age or the goodness of God.

> *Yours affectionately*
> *Bertrand Russell*

Peacock Inn
Twenty Bayard Lane
Princeton, N.J.
May 14, 1944

My dear Lucy

This is a goodbye letter, with great regret that I can't bid you goodbye in person. After months of waiting, we are being suddenly shipped off at a moment's notice – Peter and Conrad are already gone & I go in

2 or 3 days. It was nice being your neighbours, & your house seemed almost a bit of England. Please tell Helen[1] I am very sorry not to write to her too – & give my love (or whatever she would like better) to Edith.

> *Ever yours aff*
> *B.R.*

> Trinity College
> Cambridge
> Oct. 7, 1944

My dear Lucy

It was nice to get your letter written in August. Coming to your house always seemed almost like coming home; it & its contents, animate & inanimate, were so much more English than one could find elsewhere in USA.

D. S. Robertson is a man I know only slightly, but he has a considerable reputation. How Keynes has expanded since he used to come & stay at Tilford! Last time I saw him he had an enormous paunch – but this was not the sort of expansion I had in mind!

John is still in London, learning Japanese forms of politeness. One would have thought forms of rudeness more useful. He will go to the East before the end of this year, & probably be there a long time. Kate has been home about a month. She ended in a blaze of glory, with a $250 prize, an offer from Radcliffe to go on their staff, & from a Southern University to become a Professor, though not yet of age. Now the British Government pays her to read Goebbels.

The Robot bombs have been trying, & have not quite ceased, but they are no longer very serious. We all flourish. Love to Edith. Much love and friendship to yourself.

> *Ever yours*
> *Bertrand Russell*

> New Place
> Bryn Mawr, Penna.
> February 20th 45

My dear Bertie

Edith's great pleasure in your two letters I have shared. I am especially glad that you thought well of her book – whatever of M.C.T. [M. Carey Thomas] herself. After living under the two presidents who have succeeded at the College, I confess that my opinion of her has risen a good deal. The new ways on the Campus make it strange and *unheimlich* to me. O, for 'the Culture' of the '90's! . . .

---

[1] Helen Thomas Flexner.

The world all round now is a very grim one, as you say, and bitter to those of us who once lived in a happier time. Here in America of course we are among the fortunate ones, well fed, well housed & all the rest, but we do not grow wiser, more gruesome minded I fear. Everywhere it seems we can depend only on old affections and tried loyalties.

I turn to you, who have for so long added to my life so much interest and pleasure, & to my happiness in hearing that you are planning to write your autobiography. You will make a great and important book. I hope from my very heart that I may live to read it. Your letters of course I will look up and send along for any help they can give you. Notes & reminders are useful ...

I have long wanted to write and to hear from you again but seem away here to have nothing worth saying. Edith and I and other friends of course often talk of you and wish you back. Our neighborhood fell into dullness when you left. We drove out, Edith & I, one day in the autumn in a *pietas* to Little Datchett, now alas painted up in all colours and newly named 'Stone Walls' on a sign at the gate. But the wide Jeffersonian view was the same and very delightful. Are either of your elder children still in America? Conrad of course will have grown beyond my recognition. Will you not send me some word of them and of Peter. I hope that she is better in health and able to get proper food.

Even the London where you are living is almost unknown to me, though I remember once walking up and down Gloucester Place, looking out the house where Lady Louisa Stuart lived in old age: and you must be near Portman Square and Mrs Montagu's grand mansion there. The late eighteenth Century in England is a safe retreat in these days for one lost in the America of Bob Taft and Henry Wallace and the rest of all you know from the papers.

Alas, that Edith and I are too poor to go to England this summer to breathe its air again and to see our friends. How I wish it were not so.

> *Affectionately yours*
> *Lucy Donnelly*

P.S. Barnes has been as quiet as a mouse these last years.

> Hotel Bellerive au Lac
> Zurich
> June 23, 1946

My dear Lucy

Thank you for your letter. I had not heard of Simon Flexner's death, which is sad. I don't know Helen's address; if I did, I would write to her. Will you please give her my very sincere sympathy, & tell her how greatly I admired & respected Simon.

What you say about my History of Philosophy is very pleasant reading. I am glad you like my Chap. on Plotinus, as I rather fancied it myself!

I am at the moment doing a short lecture tour in Switzerland; I return to Peter & Conrad in N. Wales in a week for the long vacation, after which I shall be back in Trinity, where I have been inhabiting Newton's rooms. I go about with the feeling that within 20 years England will have ceased to exist. It makes everything hectic, like the approach of closing time at a party in a hotel – 'We are for the night.' A few bombs will destroy all our cities, & the rest will slowly die of hunger.

In America, large sections of the rural middle west & the desert south-west will probably survive. But not much of your America. Three cheers for Patagonia, the future centre of world culture.

Meanwhile Rabbis & Muftis, Jinnah & Nehru, Tito & the Italians, etc., play their silly games. I am ashamed of belonging to the species Homo Sapiens.

The Swiss are passionately Anglophile, & very glad to be liberated from Nazi encirclement. I try not to depress them.

You & I may be thankful to have lived in happier times – you more than I, because you have no children.

> *Ever yours affectionately*
> *Bertrand Russell*

> Penralltgoch
> Llan Ffestiniog
> Merioneth
> March 17, 1948

My dear Lucy

Thank you for your good letter. It was a great pleasure to get it.

I enclose a letter to Helen, as I am not sure whether I have deciphered correctly the address you gave me. If not, will you please alter it as may be necessary. I have started on my autobiography, & find it an immense task. I shall be infinitely grateful for your batch of letters. It doesn't matter whether you send them to above address or to London.

My daughter Kate has just married an American named Charles Tait. She still lives in Cambridge Mass. I don't know him, but all I hear of him sounds nice.

I am terribly busy with international affairs, & have not time to write proper letters. Give nice messages to Edith. With love,

> *Yours aff*
> *B.R.*

> New Place
> Bryn Mawr College
> Bryn Mawr
> Pennsylvania
> May 8, 1948

My dear Bertie

I am sorry to have been so long in complying with any request of yours. This has been a bad and busy year here in Bryn Mawr and though I keep very well for my age, I am so easily tired and do everything so slowly, I accomplish little in a day.

In a word, I have only been able in the last fortnight to go through the papers & letters stored in the attic. The task was formidable and painful as well as happy. Many letters from you I found, dating from 1902 on, and have put aside to send you if you still want them. From your letter some time ago, I was uncertain whether you ask for all letters, or particularly for the one written to Helen on the last day of the Nineteenth Century.

All that you wrote to me I seem to have treasured down to the merest notes. They are wonderfully friendly, wise, kind letters, sympathetic almost beyond belief with my personal concerns and small Bryn Mawr affairs, while bringing in an invigorating breath from a larger freer world. I well remember the vivid pleasure of their coming, one after another, and the strength & interest they were to me. – A lifetime of gratitude I send back to you for them. – Whether they would be useful to you I cannot tell, possibly for dates, plans places & whatnot, and as a record of your own friendliness. Your memory is extraordinarily good & you have written so much that is wise & witty & important. Will you say whether you want the packet, & they really shall go off to you at once. In that case I should like to have them back when you are done with the letters. They are a precious record of a long friendship to me, though as I understand, your property . . .

All is well I hope with you, as well as may be with the world in desperate confusion. Here we are in the midst of strikes, Presidential primaries, indecisions about Palestine, [indecipherable] bills & all that you can guess.

Edith asks me to give you her love with mine. & all good wishes for the Summer. We plan to go to Canada,[1] the nearest we are able to get to the British flag.

> *Affectionately yours*
> *Lucy*

[1] Where she died in the Summer of 1948.

From the 12th Duke of Bedford

> Froxfield House
> Woburn
> Bletchley
> April 16th. 1945

Dear Lord Russell

Many thanks for your kind letter. I should have been very pleased for you to see Woburn but unluckily the abbey is infested by a government War Department of a very 'hush-hush' description and I am not allowed to enter the sacred precincts myself without a permit & suitable escort! Most of the pictures etc. are stored away, so I am afraid you will have to postpone your visit until the brief interlude between this war & world-war no. 3. – if there *is* an interlude!! I am so sorry.

> *Yours sincerely*
> *Bedford*

From H. G. Wells

> 13, Hanover Terrace
> Regent's Park, N.W.1
> May. 20th '45

My dear Russell

I was delighted to get your friendly letter. In these days of revolutionary crisis it is incumbent upon all of us who are in any measure influential in left thought to dispel the tendency to waste energy in minor dissentions & particularly to counter the *systematic & ingenious* work that is being done to sabotage left thought under the cloak of critical reasonableness. I get a vast amount of that sort of propaganda in my letter box. I get more & more anarchistic & ultra left as I grow older. I enclose a little article 'Orders is Orders' that the *New Leader* has had the guts, rather squeamish guts, to print at last. What do you think of it?

We must certainly get together to talk (& perhaps conspire) & that soon. What are your times & seasons? My daughter in law Marjorie fixes most of my engagements and you & Madame must come to tea one day & see what we can do.

I have been ill & I keep ill. I am President of the Diabetic Soc'y & diabetes keeps one in & out, in & out of bed every two hours or so. This exhausts, and this vast return to chaos which is called the peace, the infinite meanness of great masses of my fellow creatures, the wickedness of organised religion give me a longing for a sleep that will have no awakening. There is a long history of heart failure on my paternal side but modern palliatives are very effective holding back that moment of release. Sodium bicarbonate keeps me in a grunting state of protesting endurance. But while I live I *have* to live and I owe a lot to a decaying civilisation which has anyhow kept alive enough of the spirit of scientific devotion to stimulate my curiosity [and] make me its debtor.

Forgive this desolation. I hope to see you both before very long & am yours most gratefully.

H. G. Wells

From Clement Attlee

10, Downing Street
Whitehall
11 October, 1945

My dear Russell

Many thanks for your letter of October 9 and for sending me your article – 'What America could do with the Atomic Bomb'. I have read this with interest and I am grateful to you for bringing it to my notice. I need hardly tell you that this is one of the most difficult and perplexing problems with which statesmen have ever been faced and I can assure you that all the points you have made are present in my mind.

Yours sincerely
C. R. Attlee

The following is the account that I wrote to my wife Peter immediately after the plane accident in which I was involved. It is dated October 1948.

You will no doubt have learnt that I was in an accident to-day – luckily one in which I suffered no damage beyond loss of suit-case etc. I was sure the newspapers would exaggerate so I telegraphed to you at once. I came from Oslo in a sea-plane, and just as it touched the water on arrival here a sudden wind blew it onto its side and let the water in. Boats were sent out instantly, and we had to jump from a window and swim till they reached us, which was only about a minute. I did not know till later that some who could not swim were drowned. It did me no harm whatever. My writing is queer because my pen is lost. I went to bed because I had no dry clothes. The Consul has now brought me some and the Vice-Consul has lent me a suit till mine is dry. Everybody has made far more fuss of me than the occasion warranted. I was struck by the good behaviour of the passengers – all did exactly as they were told without any fuss.

I will try to relate everything.

The weather was stormy, heavy rain and a gale of wind. The seaplane had just touched the water of the fjord when there was a violent jerk and I found myself on the floor with some inches of water in which hats, coats, etc. were floating. I exclaimed 'well, well!' and started looking for my hat, which I failed to find. At first I thought a wave had broken in at a window; it didn't occur to me it was serious.

I was in the very back of the plane, the only part where one could smoke; this turned out to be the best place to be. After a few minutes the crew opened a door and got the passengers from the back through to an open window, and shoved us one by one into the sea. By this time their haste had made me realise that things were serious. I jumped, clutching my attache case, but had to let go of it to swim. When I got into the water I saw there was a boat close by. We swam to it and were pulled on board. When I looked round, nothing was visible of the plane except the tip of a wing. The swim was about 20 yards. I saw nothing of what happened at the other end of the plane; I imagine they jumped through another window. I gather the people killed were stunned when the accident happened. One of them was a Professor concerned in arrangements about my lecture. I pointed out my floating attache case to the people on the boat, and last night a policeman brought it. The things in it were all right, except that the silly books were somewhat damaged. No other piece of luggage was rescued.

The people who had come to the airport to meet me were very solicitous, and drove me at breakneck speed to the hotel, where I got my wet clothes off, went to bed, and consumed large quantities of brandy and coffee, after which I went to sleep. The Consul brought me socks, shirt, etc., and the Vice-Consul lent me a suit. My own will be wearable to-morrow. Then came an avalanche of journalists. One from Copenhagen asked what I thought while in the water. I said I thought the water was cold. 'You didn't think about mysticism and logic?' 'No' I said, and rang off.

I was not brave, only stupid. I had always thought a sea-plane would float. I did not realise there was danger, and was mainly concerned to save my attache case. My watch goes as well as ever, and even my matches strike. But the suitcase, with a suit, shirts, etc. is gone for ever. I am writing with a beastly pen, because mine is lost.

To Willard V. Quine

18 Dorset House
Gloucester Place, N.W.1
Feb. 4, 1949

Dear Dr Quine

Thank you for your kind letter, and for your paper on 'What There is' – a somewhat important subject. When I first sent my theory of description to *Mind* in 1905, Stout thought it such rubbish that he almost refused to print it.

I am glad you noticed the allusion to yourself on p. 140.

I was lucky in the aeroplane accident, as nearly half those on the plane ceased to be among 'what there is'.

Yours sincerely
Bertrand Russell

After my return to England I paid several visits to my first wife at her invitation, and received the following letters from her. The friendly correspondence lasted till her death very early in 1951.

25 Wellington Square
Chelsea, S.W.3
June 9. 1949

Dearest Bertie

I feel I must break the silence of all these years by sending thee a line of congratulation on thy OM. No one can rejoice in it more heartily than I do, just as no one was more sorry for the prison sentence and thy difficulties in America. Now I hope thee will have a peaceful old age, just as I am doing at 81, after a stormy time with Logan. I miss dear Lucy Donnelly's letters very much, but am glad they have raised over $50,000.00 to endow a Scholarship in English in her memory.

As ever, affectionately thine
Alys

25 Wellington Square
Chelsea, S.W.3
Sept. 30 1949

Dearest Bertie

I found these letters and this article of thine among my papers, and think thee may like to have them. I think I must have destroyed all thy other letters. Our scrapbook about the Sozial-Demokrats in Berlin in 1895 I presented to the London School of Economics, but have borrowed it back now as the BBC may want a Talk on it. I have told them thee could give it much better than I.

I have been told thee is writing thy Autobiography, which ought to be deeply interesting. (I don't care for B. B. [Bernard Berenson]'s but like George Trevelyan's.) I am also writing some Memoirs, and enclose a copy of what I think of saying about our marriage. But if thee thinks it incorrect, or wounding to thee, I could make it much shorter.

Thine ever
Alys

I hope thee will be interested in these recently published Letters of Mother's.

What Alys wrote of our marriage:

Bertie was an ideal companion, & he taught me more than I can ever repay. But I was never clever enough for him, & perhaps he was too sophisticated for me. I was ideally happy for several years, almost deliriously happy, until a change of feeling made our mutual life very difficult. A final separation led to a divorce, when he married again. But that was accomplished without bitterness, or quarrels, or recriminations, & later with great rejoicing on my part when he was awarded the OM. But my life was completely changed, & I was never able to meet him again for fear of the renewal of my awful misery, & heartsick longing for the past. I only caught glimpses of him at lectures or concerts occasionally, & thro' the uncurtained windows of his Chelsea house, where I used to watch him sometimes reading to his children. Unfortunately, I was neither wise enough nor courageous enough to prevent this one disaster from shattering my capacity for happiness & my zest for life.

> 25 Wellington Square
> Chelsea, S.W.3
> Jan. 13. 1950

Dearest Bertie

In September I sent thee a book of Mother's Letters, *A Religious Rebel*, with a 1909 packet of thy own letters to me, and a note from myself. I could not understand why I had no reply, but now the packet has been returned to me – my name was on the outside and it was addressed to the Hon. Bertrand Russell, OM, Penralltgoch, Llan Ffestiniog, Merioneth but marked 'not known'. I should like it to reach thee if I knew thy address.

> *Thine ever*
> *Alys*

> 25 Wellington Square
> Chelsea, S.W.3
> Feb. 14. '50

Dearest Bertie

I enjoyed thy visit immensely, & hope we can be friends & see each other soon again. I wrote to B. B. about thy coming here, & he sends thee a warm invitation to go & stay with him at any time. He says there is no man alive whom he would rather be seeing and talking with than thee, & that he practically always agrees with everything thee writes. He has asked me to lend thee his book on Aesthetics, which I will do, tho' I do not think thee will care for it. The Autobiography is better, tho' not well written.

I should like to know thy opinion of Bob Gathorne-Hardy's *Recollections of Logan*, & will send thee my extra copy, if thee has not already seen it. It has been very well reviewed, & B. B. calls it 'a masterpiece'.

> *Ever thine*
> *Alys*

> 25 Wellington Square
> Chelsea, S.W.3
> Mar. 9. 1950

Dearest Bertie

Thanks for thy letter. I was not surprised at thy not answering mine of Sept. 30th. as I thought thee probably preferred not to have any intimate talk of the past, but I am thankful that thee did not feel unduly censured, nor that my radiant memories of our life together should be marred. Please do come & have lunch with me again as soon as thee can possibly spare time. I shall count the days till then, as I have so many questions I want to discuss with thee, & I hope it will be soon. Ring up before 9.30 or after 12.

I don't think I want thy letters from Paris, nor the German volumes, as the BBC decline a talk on Germany in 1895.

> *Thine ever*
> *Alys*

> 25 Wellington Square
> Chelsea, S.W.3
> April 14. 1950

Dearest Bertie

I have so enjoyed our two meetings & thee has been so friendly, that I feel I must be honest & just say once (but once only) that I am utterly devoted to thee, & have been for over 50 years. My friends have always known that I loved thee more than anyone else in the world, & they now rejoice with me that I am now able to see thee again.

But my devotion makes no claim, and involves no burden on thy part, nor any obligation, not even to answer this letter.

But I shall still hope thee can spare time to come to lunch or dinner before very long, & that thee will not forget May 18th.

> *Thine ever*
> *Alys*

> 25 Wellington Square
> Chelsea, S.W.3
> June 8. 1950

Dearest Bertie

Thanks for my book returned, with the address I wanted on a very small slip of paper, & now for thy two volumes. I am immensely pleased to have them from thee (tho' I hope thee doesn't think I was hinting!) & shall enjoy them very much, & send my warmest thanks. Florence Halévy is delighted thee should have my copy of Elie's posthumous book, & sends thee her kindest remembrances & regards.

If thee can spare a minute before the 18th., do telephone about breakfast time any day to give me thy address in Australia. I should like to write to thee on my b. day in July.

> *Ever thine*
> *Alys*

> 25 Wellington Square
> Chelsea, S.W.3
> July 21. 1950

Dearest Bertie

I have had a nice 83rd birthday with many callers with flowers & books & fruits & telegrams, & it would have been perfect if there had been a letter from thee. But I know thee must be desperately busy, & worse still desperately worried over Korea & this awful drift to War. We can hardly think or talk of anything else, but I try to keep serene & to distract my visitors from too much worry, when there seems nothing we can any of us do, & I think I have been successful today. This little poem was a help, by Helen Arbuthnot & the friend she lives with: 'Alys Russell, hail to thee! Angel of the Square, where would Wellontonia be If thou were not there.' (The rest too fulsome to quote. I tried to write a poem to thee on May 18th. but got no further than 'Bertrand Russell, hail to thee! Darling of the BBC'. – but cld. get no further.) I have only just read thy *Conquest of Happiness* & some of the chapters would have helped me very much in my talk on 'Being over 80'. But nothing thee says cld. equal my concluding paragraph, wh. I think thee missed, literally taken from *The Times*, my wished-for epitaph 'In loving memory of John & Mary Williams who lived such beautiful lives on Bromley Common'.

This letter will be full of happy events, as my last was full of woes, & I hope it will distract thee for a few minutes.

1. My kind Irish housekeeper, of 30 years service, is better from a bad heart attack, & will be back soon.
2. My Tennyson Talk was a great success, with much approval from the 3rd Prog. Producers, & Bob G. H. [Gathorne-Hardy] wrote to me: 'Your Broadcast was absolutely delicious, like an enchanting, exquisite, complete little short story, with a perfect twist at the end "How we must have bored him!".'
3. Karin seems quite well again, & is writing a book on 'Despair'.

Desmond is speaking, I hear, on the despair of old age, which is a pity and not good news, & Hugh Trevor-Roper writes that the Berlin Congress (on Cultural Freedom ?) would not have been sponsored by thee if thee had known how it would turn out, being a political demonstration, which the Eng. representatives (following the now classical tradition of Oxford Dons) did their best to disrupt. I am surprised at his criticism, as he is himself a narrow Oxford Don.

I could write on forever, but must walk up to the King's Rd. & post this letter. I have said nothing about thy cruel private grief in not seeing Conrad, & perhaps thy fear that John may have to go back to the Navy. I do feel for thee, but hope thee is somehow managing to conquer happiness.

> Thine ever
> Alys

> 25 Wellington Square
> Chelsea, S.W.3
> July 24. 1950

Dearest Bertie

Thy letter of the 16th arrived too late for my b. day, but is most welcome. I am glad the Australians are friendly & appreciative, but wish I cld. hear the details of the Cath. B. Control invigorating fight. I remember Cath. trouble at the Wimbledon Election, but think it was over Education. Thee may not remember my little Cardiff friend, Maud Rees Jones, who helped us at Wimbledon. She only remembers wanting to pick up the windblown stamps in thy room, & thy begging her not to, saying 'If you scrounge for them I shall have to scrounge too, but if we leave them, Alys will pick them up', wh. I did presently, – I can't find Chas. Wood's name in Edith Finch's book, only on p. 35 'He (Blunt) saw much of the 2 younger Stanley sisters, Kate & Rosalind. Beautiful & vivid they whirled him away in an orgy of lively talk with all the piquancy of enthusiastic prejudice. Nothing in heaven & earth passed unquestioned or undiscussed. They stimulated in him an intellectual activity that had much to do with the later individuality of his views, & that, more immediately proved disconcerting during his life in Germany', where in 1861 he became very intimate with Lady Malet who troubled him by her constant speculation on religious troubles.

Here is an amusing extract from one of my honeymoon letters from The Hague: 'I have sewed 2 buttons on Bertie's shirts & he doesn't mind my sewing as much as he thought he would.'

I envy thee seeing a Coral Island. Did we read together Curzon's

Monasteries of the East? Robt. Byron, that clever yng. writer killed in the War, has had republished his excellent book on Mt Athos, beautifully written & deeply interesting. – Another b. day poem ends with:

> 'So here's a toast & drink it up
> In lemonade or cyder cup
> (For Auntie's Temperance)
> That decades on we still shall be
> Blessed by her merry company
> Her lovely countenance.'

But not 'merry' now with the attack on Formosa, & defeats in Korea, alas!

Thine ever
Alys

25 Wellington Square
Chelsea, S.W.3
Nov. 19. 1950

Dearest Nobel Lord

I am enchanted with thy new Honour, & am only sorry I was not sure enough of thy address to cable my congratulations. I knew of it on the 7th., when a Swedish journalist friend came here for information about thee. (I lent him Leggatt's book, tho' it has been trans^d into Swedish I believe.) He told me incidentally that Churchill & Croce were thy runners-up, but thee won. The papers here have been very enthusiastic, including a BBC Talk to children, calling thee 'an apostle of humanity & of free speech'. The American papers must have gone wild over thee. I hope thee will not share the Prize with the Amer. dentist's wife, tho' she must be feeling rather flat.

Thanks for thy letter from Swarthmore. I am shocked at thy account of poor Evelyn [Whitehead]! & feel most sorry for her without her angelic Alfred to care for her. I hope her children are some comfort. I look forward to seeing thee before or after Stockholm, but agree that Scandinavia is unhealthy for philosophers. But anyhow the present King will not get thee up at 5 a.m., nor force thee to sit on or in a stove for warmth. (He is a '*connustur*' friend of B.B.'s bye the way, & has paid a fairly recent visit to I Tatti. B. B. telegraphed his congratulations to thee thro' me, & I hope thee remembered to send him thy Essays.) I send on some cuttings thee may have missed, & also a letter from Florence Halévy. Also Desmond on Shaw. Has thy article on Shaw appeared yet?

I am glad thee doesn't mean to travel again, as I feel thee shd. not have the strain of it, & that thee can better serve the cause of

Internationalism, for which I have worked passionately for 30 years, by broadcasting at home, & writing.

Also it will save me from buying thee a new sponge bag for Xmas, which I felt sure thee must need!

> *Thine devotedly*
> *Alys*

From and to T. S. Eliot

> 24 Russell Square, W.C.1
> 10 June 1949

Dear Bertie

Permit me to add my sincere felicitations to your others; on the occasion of your joining this small and odd miscellaneous order. It is a fitting though belated tribute to the author of *The Philosophy of Leibnitz*, the *Principia* and the other works on which I fed thirty-five years ago. And also to the author of the Reith Lectures – who is one of the few living authors who can write English prose.

> *Yours ever*
> *T. S. Eliot*

The Master of Trinity recommends safety pins in the ribbon; but a neat tuck on each side is much better.

> Ffestiniog, N. Wales
> 13.6.49

Dear Tom

Thank you very much for your nice letter. In old days when we were huddled together in Russell Chambers, we could hardly have expected that lapse of time would make us so respectable.

I will test your opinion against George Trevy's as soon as I get the chance.

> *Yours ever*
> *B.R.*

> Faber and Faber Ltd.
> 24 Russell Square
> London W.C.1
> 20th May, 1964

The Rt. Hon. The Earl Russell, OM
Plas Penrhyn
Penrhyndeudraeth
Merionethshire

Dear Bertie

My wife and I listened the other night to your broadcast interview and thought it went over extremely well.

As you may know, I disagree with your views on most subjects, but I thought that you put your beliefs over in a most dignified and even persuasive way. I wanted you to know this as you are getting on so far, and as I myself am, I hope, somewhat mellowed by age.

With grateful and affectionate memories,

> *Yours ever*
> *Tom*

> Plas Penrhyn
> 23 May, 1964

Dear Tom

Many thanks for your letter of May 20. I am glad that you found my broadcast remarks 'dignified and even persuasive'. It was nice to hear from you again.

> *Yours ever*
> *Bertie*

From N. B. Foot
General Secretary of the New Commonwealth Society

> (President British Section:
> The Rt. Hon. Winston S.
> Churchill, OM, CH, MP)
> 25 Victoria Street
> London S.W.1
> September 25th, 1947

Dear Lord Russell

I am sending you this letter on the eve of your departure for the Continent in the hope that it may provide you with a little information about the New Commonwealth which you may find useful. In the first place, however, I should like to reiterate our thanks to you for having taken on this journey. We are deeply appreciative of the honour you are doing us in acting as our representative, and we feel confident that your visit will be quite invaluable in arousing interest in the Society's proposals. I hope the arrangements which Miss Sibthorp has made for you will prove satisfactory in every way.

It was very kind of you to provide us with a precis of your address. I have read it with the greatest admiration and, if I may venture to say so without presumption, it seems to me to provide a masterly analysis of the problems that confront us and of the solution which it is our purpose to offer. As you know, we have always laid stress on the urgent need for the internationalisation of the major weapons of war and the creation of machinery for the peaceful settlement of all disputes, political as well as judicial. We believe, as you do, that the establishment of a full-fledged World Parliament is likely to prove a distant goal, and probably the most distinctive feature of our programme is the proposal that until such a development becomes feasible, the legislative function to which you refer in your address should be entrusted to a completely impartial Tribunal. We fully admit that this Tribunal would not be a perfect instrument, but we are convinced that it would be infinitely more suitable for the just settlement of non-judicial issues than either the Security Council or the Permanent Court, bearing in mind that the former is made up of politicians whose first job is to further the interests of their own countries and the latter of lawyers who have little knowledge or experience outside the purely legal field.

With regard to the Society itself, we differ from UNA and other such organisations in that we have always endeavoured to function as an international Movement in the sense that our activities have never been confined to Great Britain. Before the war we had managed to build up embryonic national sections of the Movement in most of the European countries, and these were linked together in what we called our International Section. We are now faced with the task of rebuilding this machinery, and there can be no doubt that your visit to the Low Countries will be of the greatest value in helping us to carry that task a stage further.

In Holland the foundations of a New Commonwealth Committee have already been laid with Dr van de Coppello as its President and Dr Fortuin as its Honorary Secretary. You will, of course, be meeting these gentlemen during your visit, and it occurred to me that you might wish to be informed of their special connection with the Movement. I should also like to mention the names of Dr Peter de Kanter and his wife Mrs de Kanter van Hettinga Tromp who are members of our Committee and who have always played a leading part in New Commonwealth activity.

In Belgium we have not as yet been able to establish any sort of organism though we hope to be able to do so in the near future.

In apologising for bothering you with this letter, may I say again how deeply grateful we are to you for having consented to undertake this journey on our behalf.

> *Yours sincerely*
> *N. B. Foot*

From the Netherlands Section of the New Commonwealth Society

> Amsterdam, October 7th 1947
> Beursgebouw, Damrak 62A

Dear Lord Russell

Now that your tour through the continent of Western Europe has come to an end and you are back again in England, we want to express you once more our great thankfulness for the lectures you delivered to the Netherlands Section of The New Commonwealth in Amsterdam and The Hague. It was an unforgettable event to hear you – whom many of us already knew by your numerous important writings – speak about the question which occupies and oppresses our mind: the centuries-old problem of war or peace. We cannot say that your words have removed all our concern; on the contrary, to whatever we may have got used since the thirties, your supreme analysis of the present situation has considerably increased our anxiety. But we know now that you also joined those who are anxious to construct a state of international justice which will aim at the establishment of rules of law and in which the transgressor will be called to order by force, if necessary.

You will have learnt from the number of your auditors and the many conversations you had that your visit to our country has been a great success. There is no Dutch newspaper nor weekly that failed to mention your visit and your lectures.

Thank you for coming, Lord Russell; we shall not forget your words!

> *Yours very truly*
> *Dr van de Coppello*
> *President*
> *Dr Fortuin*
> *Secretary*

From Gilbert Murray

> Yatscombe
> Boar's Hill Oxford
> Sep. 12 1951

Dear Bertie

I was greatly touched by that letter you wrote to the Philosophic Society Dinner about our fifty years of close friendship. It is, I think, quite true about the fundamental agreement; I always feel it – and am proud of it.

I had explained that I preferred you to other philosophers because, while they mostly tried to prove some horrible conclusion – like Hobbes, Hegel, Marx etc, you were, I believe, content if you could really prove that $2+2 = 4$, and that conclusion, though sad, was at least bearable ('To think that two and two are four, and never five or three The heart of man has long been sore And long is like to be.')

Have you read the life of Jos Wedgwood (*The Last of the Radicals*) by his niece? He sent a questionnaire to a great list of people in which one question was: 'To what cause do you attribute your failure?' The only one who said he had not failed was Ld Beaverbrook! Interesting and quite natural.

Providence has thought fit to make me lame by giving me blisters on my feet so that I can not wear shoes; a great nuisance.

Yours ever, and with real thanks for your letter, which made me for a moment feel that I was not completely a failure.

G.M.

From General Sir Frank E. W. Simpson, KCB, KBE, DSO

> Imperial Defence College
> Seaford House
> 37, Belgrave Square
> S.W.1
> 16th July, 1952

Dear Lord Russell

May I introduce myself to you as the present Commandant of this College, having taken over from Admiral Sir Charles Daniel at the beginning of this year.

I am writing to ask whether you could possibly spare the time to visit us again this year in December and give your excellent talk on 'The Future of Mankind'. Admiral Daniel has told me how valuable and stimulating your talks to this College have been in recent years.

The date I have in mind is Thursday, 4th December next, and the time 10.15 a.m. You know our usual procedure.

I much hope that you will agree to come and that the above date will be convenient for you.

> *Yours sincerely*
> *F. E. W. Simpson*

From the *Manchester Guardian*, 22nd April 1954

ATOMIC WEAPONS

Sir

In a leading article of your issue of April 20 you say: 'The United States is not so foolish or wicked as to fire the first shot in a war with atomic weapons.' This statement as it stands is ambiguous. If you mean that the United States would not fire the first shot, the statement may be correct. But if you mean that the United States would not be the first to use atomic weapons, you are almost certainly mistaken. The United States authorities have declared that any aggression anywhere by Russia or China will be met by all-out retaliation, which certainly means the bomb. It is apparently the opinion of experts that in a world war the Western Powers will be defeated if they do not use the bomb, but victorious if they use it. If this is the view of the Russian authorities, they will abstain at the beginning of a war from using the bomb and leave to our side the odium of its first employment. Can anybody seriously suggest that the Western Powers will prefer defeat ? There is only one way to prevent the necessity for this choice, and that is to prevent a world war.

Yours &c.
Bertrand Russell

[Our point was simply that China, knowing the scruples which limit American action, could disregard an American threat to retaliate with atomic weapons if China did not desist from intervening in Indo-China. With Lord Russell's general point we are in agreement. – Ed. *Guard.*]

From my cousin, Sir Claud Russell

Trematon Castle
Saltash, Cornwall
12 July '52

Dear Bertie

I was given to read (in *Vogue*) by Flora your childhood's Memories, which I did with interest, and the more so, no doubt, as they evoked memories of my own. There must be few survivors of the Pembroke Lodge days. I think my parents went there fairly frequently on a Sunday, driving from London in a hired one-horse brougham (they never owned a carriage in London) and took one or two children with 'em. But I remember better an occasional weekend there, and no doubt your grandmother and my parents thought, with reason, that our association would be pleasant, and beneficial, to both. Your grandfather was dead before those days. I never saw him, but I remember my father telling my mother at breakfast in Audley Square 'Uncle John is dead'; and also that it fell to my father to return his KG to the Queen, and that some important part of the insignia – the Star or the Garter – could not be found, which my. father had to tell the Queen, who said: 'that doesn't matter.' I would like to see Pembroke Lodge again, and walk about the grounds. I believe it is in a dilapidated state, and no longer the home of a deserving servant of the State. I remember Windsor Castle, and that Henry VIII saw from Richmond Hill the gun fired that told him Anne Boleyn was executed. I recall the family prayers, and my embarrassment at having to sing the hymn audibly. I wonder in how many houses are family prayers now the rule ? The last I recall were at Sir Ernest Satow's. He was my Chief in Peking, and I went to see him in his retirement. He was a bachelor, an intellectual, who had read all there is, and a man of encyclopaedic knowledge. Yet, I believe an undoubting Christian. I formed this impression of him from his demeanour in the Legation Chapel at Peking, and the family prayers confirmed it. His Japanese butler, cook and housemaid, appeared after dinner, and he led the prayers. My only unpleasant memory of Pembroke Lodge arises from two boy friends of yours of the name of Logan. They conceived, I suppose, a measure of contempt for me, and made no secret of it. Perhaps they thought me a 'milk-sop', or 'softy'. However, I didn't see them often. *Per contra*, like you, I have a happy memory of Annabel (Clara we called her)[1] and I was often at York House. When her parents were in India, she came to us for her holidays (she was at school) and I was much in love with her – I being then about 15–16 years old. I wonder what became of the furniture and pictures etc. at Pembroke Lodge. I suppose Agatha had them at Haslemere. I remember particularly a statue, a life-size marble of a female nude, in the hall.[2] I think a gift from the Italian people to your grandfather, in gratitude for his contribution to the liberation and union of Italy. Like you, I owe to the Russells shyness, and sensitiveness – great handicaps in life, but no metaphysics, tho' I have tried to feebly – my father and elder brother had the latter, but not professionally, like you. What I owe to my French progenitors I leave others to judge. I noted lately in a volume of Lord Beaconsfield's letters one written from Woburn in 1865, to Queen Victoria, in which he says: 'The predominant feature and organic deficiency of the Russell family is shyness. Even Hastings is not free from it, though he tries to cover it with an air of uneasy gaiety.' *I* am much too shy for that.

I am happy to know of my family link with the heroic defender of Gibraltar – my great aunt's great uncle. Athenais and I have taken to spending the winter at Gib. If ever, with advancing years, you want to escape the English winter, I recommend it. A better climate than the Riviera, and in a sterling area.

Excuse this long letter. One thing led to another.

Yours ever
Claud

Trematon Castle
Saltash, Cornwall
9 Aug. '52

Dear Bertie

Thank you for your letter, and I fully share your indignation at the fate of Pembroke Lodge. Can it be that what you call 'Bumbledom' is now the Crown? All the same, I hope when I'm in London to go and see the old place again, and may:

[1] A daughter of Sir Mounstuart Grant Duff.
[2] This statue had an inscription on the pedestal:
   A Ld John Russell
   Italia riconoscente.

'Fond memory bring the light'
'Of other days around me',

or will I (more probably):

'Feel like one'
'Who treads alone'
'Some banquet hall deserted'
'Whose lights are fled' etc.

But did not Agatha wisely leave the Italia that I remember, to Newnham, where such a work of art could excite admiration, but never, I trust, an unruly thought.

I hope we may see you at Gib. next winter, if you want to escape the English one. The climate is more equable and healthy than that of the Riviera, and being British soil, if you have a bank balance at home, you can draw on it – or overdraw, for that matter. The Gibraltarians, tho' not typical Englishmen, are amiable and loyal. They know which side their bread is buttered, and there is no irredentism among them. O si sic omnes!

The Rock Hotel is the place to stay – well run, but not exactly cheap.

Yours ever
Claud

To and from Albert Einstein

41 Queen's Road
Richmond
Surrey
20 June, 1953

Dear Einstein

I am in whole-hearted agreement with your contention that teachers called before McCarthy's inquisitors should refuse to testify. When *The New York Times* had a leading article disagreeing with you about this, I wrote a letter to it supporting you. But I am afraid they are not going to print it. I enclose a copy, of which, if you feel so disposed, you may make use in any way you like.

Yours very sincerely
Bertrand Russell

Translation

Princeton
28.vi.53

Dear Bertrand Russell

Your fine letter to *The New York Times* is a great contribution to a good cause. All the intellectuals in this country, down to the youngest student, have become completely intimidated. Virtually no one of 'prominence' besides yourself has actually challenged these absurdities in which the politicians have become engaged. Because they have succeeded in convincing the masses that the Russians and the American Communists endanger the safety of the country, these politicians consider themselves so powerful. The cruder the tales they spread, the more assured they feel of their reelection by the misguided population. This also explains why Eisenhower did not dare to commute the death sentence of the two Rosenbergs, although he well knew how much their execution would injure the name of the United States abroad.

I have read your latest publications, 'Impact' and 'Satan . . .', with great care and real enjoyment. You should be given much credit for having used your unique literary talent in the service of public enlightenment and education. I am convinced that your literary work will exercise a great and lasting influence particularly since you have resisted the temptation to gain some short lived effects through paradoxes and exaggerations.

With cordial greetings and wishes,

> *Yours*
> *A. Einstein*

> 41 Queen's Road
> Richmond
> Surrey
> 5 July, 1953

Dear Einstein

Thank you very much for your letter, which I found most encouraging. Rather to my surprise *The New York Times* did at last print my letter about you. I hope you will be able to have an influence upon liberal-minded academic people in America. With warmest good wishes,

> *Yours very sincerely*
> *Bertrand Russell*

Albert Einstein on Russell – 1940 (time of College of the City of New York row)

> *Es wiederholt sich immer wieder*
> *In dieser Welt so fein und bieder*
> *Der Pfaff den Poebel alarmiert*
> *Der Genius wird executiert.*

Translation

> It keeps repeating itself
> In this world, so fine and honest:
> The Parson alarms the populace,
> The genius is executed.

Albert Einstein on Russell's *History of Western Philosophy*, 1946

Bertrand Russell's 'Geschichte der Philosophie' ist eine koestliche Lektuere. Ich weiss nicht, ob man die koestlische Frische und Originalitaet oder die Sensitivitaet der Einfuehlung in ferne Zeiten und fremde Mentalitaet bei diesem grossen Denker mehr bewundern soll. Ich betrachte es als ein Glueck, dass unsere so trockene und zugleich brutale Generation einen so weisen, ehrlichen, tapferen und dabei humorvollen Mann aufzuweisen hat. Es ist ein in hoechstem Sinne paedagogisches Werk, das ueber dem Streite der Parteien und Meinungen steht.

Translation

Bertrand Russell's 'History of Philosophy' is a precious book. I don't know whether one should more admire the delightful freshness and originality or the sensitivity of the sympathy with distant times and remote mentalities on the part of this great thinker. I regard it as fortunate that our so dry and also brutal generation can point to such a wise, honourable, bold and at the same time humorous man. It is a work that is in the highest degree pedagogical which stands above the conflicts of parties and opinions.

'A LIBERAL DECALOGUE'[1]
by
Bertrand Russell

Perhaps the essence of the Liberal outlook could be summed up in a new decalogue, not intended to replace the old one but only to supplement it. The Ten Commandments that, as a teacher, I should wish to promulgate, might be set forth as follows:

1. Do not feel absolutely certain of anything.

2. Do not think it worth while to proceed by concealing evidence, for the evidence is sure to come to light.

3. Never try to discourage thinking for you are sure to succeed.

4. When you meet with opposition, even if it should be from your husband or your children, endeavour to overcome it by argument and not by authority, for a victory dependent upon authority is unreal and illusory.

5. Have no respect for the authority of others, for there are always contrary authorities to be found.

6. Do not use power to suppress opinions you think pernicious, for if you do the opinions will suppress you.

[1] This first appeared at the end of my article 'The Best Answer to Fanaticism – Liberalism', in *The New York Times Magazine*, December 16, 1951.

7. Do not fear to be eccentric in opinion, for every opinion now accepted was once eccentric.

8. Find more pleasure in intelligent dissent than in passive agreement, for, if you value intelligence as you should, the former implies a deeper agreement than the latter.

9. Be scrupulously truthful, even if the truth is inconvenient, for it is more inconvenient when you try to conceal it.

10. Do not feel envious of the happiness of those who live in a fool's paradise, for only a fool will think that it is happiness.

From the *News Chronicle*, 1st April, 1954

HE FORETOLD IT

In November, 1945, in a speech in the House of Lords on the atomic bomb, Bertrand Russell said:

It is possible that some mechanism, analogous to the present atomic bomb, could be used to set off a much more violent explosion which would be obtained if one could synthesise heavier elements out of hydrogen. All that must take place if our scientific civilisation goes on, if it does not bring itself to destruction: all that is bound to happen.

From the *News Chronicle*, 1st April 1954

THE BOMB:
WHERE DO WE GO FROM HERE?

Bertrand Russell, mathematician, philosopher, answers the questions that everyone is asking (in an interview with Robert Waithman).

Bertrand Russell sat very upright in his armchair, smoking a curved pipe and talking gently about the hydrogen bomb. But there was nothing gentle about his conclusions.

Britain's greatest living philosopher, whose mind and intellectual courage have moved the twentieth century since its beginning, is now 81. His hair is white and his voice is soft; and his opinions, as always, are expressed with a memorable clarity. I put a succession of questions to him and he answered them thus:

Is there any justification for alarm at the thought that some disastrous miscalculation may occur in the H-bomb tests?

Though, obviously, there will come a time when these experiments are too dangerous, I don't think we have reached that point yet.

If there were a hydrogen-bomb war it is quite clear that practically everybody in London would perish. A shower of hydrogen bombs would almost certainly sterilise large agricultural areas, and the resulting famine would be fearful.

But we are talking of the current tests, in peace-time. I do not expect disaster from them. I think those who may have been showered with radio-active ash, whose fishing catches have been damaged or destroyed, undoubtedly have every right to complain.

But I do not foresee a rain of radio-active ash comparable with the phenomena we saw after the explosion of the Krakatoa Volcano in 1883 (which I remember well), I do not think that, so long as the explosions are few, marine life will be grievously affected.

It is affected now by oil pollution, isn't it – though that is much less dramatic a story ?

Do you think that a feeling of dread and uncertainty at the back of people's minds might have an evil social effect ?

Well, you know, it isn't an effect that lasts long. As with the atom bomb at first, people get into a state; but after a little while they forget it.

If you have perpetually mounting crises, of course, it will be different. The truth is, though, that the thought of an old peril, however great, will not distract people from their daily jobs.

You will have observed that since the first atom bombs were exploded the birth rate has continued to go up. That is a reliable test.

I should say that the fear of unemployment, which is something everyone understands, has a much greater social effect than the fear of atom bombs.

And the international effects ? Do we seem to you to have reached a strategic stalemate ? Is there now a new basis for discussion between Russia and the West ?

I think the existence of the hydrogen bomb presents a perfectly clear alternative to all the Governments of the world. Will they submit to an international authority, or shall the human race die out ?

I am afraid that most Governments and most individuals will refuse to face that alternative. They so dislike the idea of international government that they dodge the issue whenever they can.

Ask the man in the street if he is prepared to have the British Navy partly under the orders of Russians. His hair will stand on end.

Yet that is what we must think about.

You see no virtue in any proposal that the experiments should be stopped ?

None whatever, unless we have found a way of causing the Russian experiments to be stopped, too.

In my opinion, there is only one way. It is to convince the Russians beyond doubt that they can win no victory: that they cannot ever Communise the world with the hydrogen bomb.

Perhaps they are beginning to feel that. It seems to me to be significant that the Russian leaders are now allowing the Russian people to know of the devastation to be expected from an atomic war.

But I would hasten the process. I would invite all the Governments of the world, and particularly the Russians, to send observers to see the results of the American tests. It ought to be made as plain as it can be made.

There is one more thing we should do. We should diminish the anti-Communist tirades that are now so freely indulged in. We should try hard to bring about a return to international good manners. That would be a great help.

And if – or when – the Russians are convinced?

I think it ought to be possible to lessen the tension and to satisfy the Russians that there is no promise for them in atomic war. Then the first, vital step will have to be taken.

We shall have to set up an arrangement under which all fissionable raw material is owned by an international authority, and is only mined and processed by that authority. No nation or individual must have access to fissionable raw material.

And there would have to be an international inspectorate to ensure that this law is maintained.

The Russians have a morbid fear of being inspected. We shall have to help them to overcome it. For until they are agreeable to it nothing can be effectively done.

The H-bomb tests must be helping to persuade them. Hence to put off the tests would simply be to put off the day of agreement. It goes without saying that we, too, must always be ready to negotiate and to agree.

Once this first, vital agreement has been reached it should be possible, gradually, to extend international control.

That is the only answer I can see.

Chapter *15*

At Home and Abroad

More important than anything in pulling me through the dark apprehensions and premonitions of these last two decades is the fact that I had fallen in love with Edith Finch and she with me. She had been a close friend of Lucy Donnelly whom I had known well at the turn of the century and had seen something of during my various American visits as I had of Edith during my years in the United States in the thirties and forties. Lucy was a Professor at Bryn Mawr, where Edith also taught. I had had friendly relations with Bryn Mawr ever since I married a cousin of the President of that College. It was the first institution to break the boycott imposed on me in America after my dismissal from the City College of New York. Paul Weiss of its Department of Philosophy wrote asking me to give a series of lectures there, an invitation which I gladly accepted. And when I was writing my *History of Western Philosophy*, the Bryn Mawr authorities very kindly allowed me to make use of their excellent library. Lucy had died and Edith had moved to New York where I met her again during my Columbia lectures there in 1950.

Our friendship ripened quickly, and soon we could no longer bear to be parted by the Atlantic. She settled in London, and, as I lived at Richmond, we met frequently. The resulting time was infinitely delightful. Richmond Park was full of reminiscences, many going back to early childhood. Relating them revived their freshness, and it seemed to me that I was living the past all over again with a fresh and happier alleviation from it. I almost forgot the nuclear peril in the joys of recollection. As we walked about the grounds of Pembroke Lodge and through Richmond Park and Kew Gardens, I recalled all sorts of things that had happened to me there. There is a fountain outside Pembroke Lodge at which the footman, employed to make me not afraid of water, held me by the heels with my head under water. Contrary to all modern views, this method was entirely successful: after the first application, I never feared water again.

Edith and I each had family myths to relate. Mine began with Henry VIII, of whom the founder of my family had been a protégé, watching on his Mount for the signal of Anne Boleyn's death at the Tower. It continued to my grandfather's speech in 1815, urging (before Waterloo) that Napoleon should not be opposed. Next came his visit to Elba, in which Napoleon was affable and tweaked his ear. After this, there was a considerable gap in the saga, until the occasion when the Shah, on a State visit, was caught in the rain in Richmond Park and was compelled to take refuge in Pembroke Lodge. My grandfather (so I was told) apologised for its being such a small house, to which the Shah replied: 'Yes, but it contains a great man.' There was a very wide view of the Thames valley from Pembroke Lodge marred, in my grandmother's opinion, by a prominent factory chimney. When she was asked about this chimney, she used to reply, smiling: 'Oh, that's not a factory chimney, that's the monument to the Middlesex Martyr.'

Edith's family myths, as I came to know them, seemed to me far more romantic; an ancestor who in 1640 or thereabouts was either hanged or carried off by the Red Indians; the adventures of her father among the Indians when he was a little boy and his family for a short time lived a pioneering life in Colorado; attics full of pillions and saddles on which members of her family had ridden from New England to the Congress at Philadelphia; tales of canoeing and of swimming in rocky streams near where Eunice Williams, stolen away by the Indians in the great massacre at Deerfield, Massachusetts, was killed. It might have been a chapter from Fennimore Cooper. In the Civil War, Edith's people were divided between North and South. Among them were two brothers, one of them (a Southern General) at the end had to surrender his sword to his brother, who was a Northern General. She herself had been born and brought up in New York City, which, as she remembered it, seemed very like the New York of my youth of cobbled streets and hansom cabs and no motor cars.

All these reminiscences, however entertaining, were only some of the arabesques upon the cake's icing. Very soon we had our own myths to add to the collection. As we were strolling in Kew Gardens one morning, we saw two people sitting on a bench, so far away that they seemed tiny figures. Suddenly, one of them jumped up and ran fast towards us and, when he reached us, fell to his knees and kissed my hand. I was horrified, and so abashed that I could think of nothing whatsoever to say or do; but I was touched, too, by his emotion, as was Edith, who pulled herself together enough to learn that he was a German, living in England, and was grateful to me for something; we never knew for what.

We not only took long walks in the neighbourhood of Richmond and in London, along the River and in the Parks and in the City of a Sunday, but we sometimes drove farther afield for a walk. Once on the Portsmouth Road we met with an accident. Through no fault of ours we were run into by a farm lorry and our car was smashed to bits. Luckily, at the time there were plenty of observers of our guiltlessness. Though shaken up, we accepted a lift from some kind passers-by into

Guildford where we took a taxi to Blackdown to have our intended walk. There I recalled my infant exploits. My people had taken Tennyson's house during a summer's holiday when I was two years old, and I was made by my elders to stand on the moor and recite in a heart-rending pipe,

> O my cousin, shallow-hearted! O my Amy, mine no more!
> O the dreary, dreary moorland! O the barren, barren shore!

We went to plays, new and old. I remember particularly *Cymbeline*, acted in Regent's Park, Ustinov's *Five Colonels*, and *The Little Hut*. My cousin Maud Russell invited us to a party celebrating the achievement of the mosaic floor designed by Boris Anrep in the National Gallery. My portrait summoning Truth from a well occurs there with portraits of some of my contemporaries. I enjoyed sittings to Jacob Epstein for a bust that he asked to make of me which I now have.

These small adventures sound trivial in retrospect, but everything at that time was bathed in the radiant light of mutual discovery and of joy in each other. Happiness caused us for the moment to forget the dreadful outer world, and to think only about ourselves and each other. We found that we not only loved each other entirely, but, equally important, we learned gradually that our tastes and feelings were deeply sympathetic and our interests for the most part marched together. Edith had no knowledge of philosophy or mathematics; there were things that she knew of which I was ignorant. But our attitude towards people and the world is similar. The satisfaction that we felt then in our companionship has grown, and grows seemingly without limit, into an abiding and secure happiness and is the basis of our lives. Most that I have to relate henceforth may be taken, therefore, to include her participation.

Our first long expedition was to Fontainebleau when the only reminder of public squabbles was owing to Mussadeq's attempt to secure a monopoly of Persian oil. Apart from this, our happiness was almost as serene as it could have been in a quiet world. The weather was sunny and warm. We consumed enormous quantities of *fraises du bois* and *crème fraîche*. We made an expedition into Paris where, for past services, the French radio poured unexpected cash upon me that financed an epic luncheon in the Bois, as well as solemner things, and where we walked in the Tuileries Gardens and visited Notre Dame. We never visited the Château at Fontainebleau. And we laughed consumedly – sometimes about nothing at all.

We have had other holidays in Paris since then, notably one in 1954 which we determined should be devoted to sight-seeing. We had each lived in Paris for fairly long periods, but I had never visited any of the things that one should see. It was pleasant to travel up and down the river in the *bateaux mouches*, and to visit various churches and galleries and the flower and bird markets. But we had set-backs: we went to the Ste Chapelle one day and found it full of Icelanders being lectured to on its beauties. Upon seeing me, they abandoned the lecture and crowded about me as the 'sight' of most importance. My remembrance of the Ste Chapelle is somewhat garbled. We retreated to the terrace of our favourite restaurant opposite the Palais de Justice. The next day we went to Chartres which we both love. But, alas, we found it turned – so far as it could be – into a tourists' Mecca full of post-cards and souvenirs.

In the spring of fifty-two we visited Greece where we spent some time in Athens and then ten days or so driving through the Peloponesus. As everyone does, we at once set off for the Acropolis. By mistake and thinking to take a short cut, we approached it from the back. We had to scramble up a cliff by goat paths and through barbed wire to get there. We arrived scratched and breathless, but triumphant. We returned again often by more orthodox routes. It was very beautiful by moonlight. And very quiet; till suddenly, at my elbow, I heard a voice say: 'Mis-ter Russ-ell, is it not?', with the accent portentous upon each syllable. It was a fellow tourist from America.

The mountains were still snow-capped, but the valleys were full of blossoming fruit trees. Kids gambolled in the fields, and the people seemed happy. Even the donkeys looked contented. The only dark spot was Sparta which was sullen and brooding beneath Taygetus from which emanated a spirit of frightening evil. I was thankful to reach Arcadia. It was as Arcadian and lovely as if born of Sidney's imagination. At Tiryns, the guardian of the ancient citadel bemoaned the fact that it had been very badly restored. Upon being asked when this distressing renovation had taken place, he replied, 'During the Mycenaean times'. Delphi left me quite unmoved, but Epidaurus was gentle and lovely. Oddly enough its peace was not broken by a bus-load of Germans who arrived there shortly after us. Suddenly, as we were sitting up in the theatre dreaming, a beautiful clear voice soared up and over us. One of the Germans was an operatic Diva and, as we were, was enchanted by the magic of the place. On the whole, our fellow tourists did not trouble us. But the United States army did. Their lorries were everywhere, especially in Athens, and the towns were noisy with the boisterous, cock-sure, shoutings and demands of their men. On the other hand, the Greeks whom we met or observed in passing, seemed gentle and gay and intelligent. We were impressed by the happy way in which they played with their children in the Gardens at Athens.

I had never before been in Greece and I found what I saw exceedingly interesting. In one respect, however, I was surprised. After being impressed by the great solid achievements which everybody admires, I found myself in a little church belonging to the days when Greece was part of the Byzantine Empire. To my astonishment, I felt more at home in this little church than I did in the Parthenon or in any of the other Greek buildings of Pagan times. I realised then that the Christian outlook had a firmer hold upon me than I had imagined. The hold was not upon my beliefs, but upon my feelings. It seemed to me that where the Greeks differed from the modern world it was chiefly through the absence of a sense of sin, and I realised with some astonishment that I, myself, am powerfully affected by this sense in my feelings though not in my beliefs. Some ancient Greek things, however, did touch me deeply. Among these, I was most impressed by the beautiful and compassionate Hermes at Olympia.

In 1953, Edith and I spent three weeks in Scotland. On the way we visited the house where I was born on the hills above the Wye valley. It had been called Ravenscroft, but is now called Cleddon Hall. The house itself was kept up, but during the war the grounds had got into a sorry condition. My parents had, at their own instructions, been buried in the adjoining wood, but were later at the family's wish, transported to the family vault at Chenies. On the way, too, we visited Seatoller in Borrowdale, where I had spent five weeks as a member of a reading party in 1893. The party was still remembered, and the visitor's book contained proof of a story that I had told Edith without obtaining belief, namely that Miss Pepper, who had waited on us, subsequently married a Mr Honey. On arriving at St Fillans (our destination) I told the receptionist that I had not been there since 1878. She stared, and then said: 'But you must have been quite a little boy.' I had remembered from this previous visit various landmarks at St Fillans such as the wooden bridge across the river, the house next to the hotel which was called 'Neish', and a stony bay which I had imagined to be one of the 'sun-dry places' mentioned in the Prayer Book. As I had not been there since 1878, the accuracy of my memories was considered established. We had many drives, sometimes along no more than cart tracks, and walks over the moors that remain memorable to us. One afternoon, as we climbed to the crest of a hill, a doe and her fawn appeared over the top trotting towards us and, on our way down, on the shore of a wild little tarn, a proud and very tame hoopoe alighted and looked us over. We drove home to St Fillans through the gloomy valley of Glencoe, as dark and dreadful as if the massacre had just taken place.

Two years later we went again to St Fillans. This time, however, we had a far less carefree time. We had to stop on the way in Glasgow for me to make a speech in favour of the Labour candidate for Rotherglen, a tireless worker for World Government. Our spirits were somewhat damped by the fact that I had gradually developed trouble with my throat which prevented me, from swallowing properly, a trouble which I take pleasure in saying, resulted from my efforts to swallow the pronouncements of politicians. But much more distressing than any of this was the fact that my elder son had fallen seriously ill. We were beset by worry about him during the whole of this so-called 'holiday'. We were worried, too, about his three young children who were at that time more or less, and later almost wholly, in our care.

When Peter left me I had continued to live at Ffestiniog, happily working there in a house on the brow of the hill with a celestial view down the valley, like an old apocalyptic engraving of Paradise. I went up to London only occasionally, and when I did, I sometimes visited my son and his family at Richmond. They were living near the Park in a tiny house, much too small for their family of three little children. My son told me that he wanted to give up his job and devote himself to writing. Though I regretted this, I had some sympathy with him. I did not know how to help them as I had not enough money to stake them to an establishment of their own in London while I lived in North Wales. Finally I hit upon the scheme of moving from Ffestiniog and taking a house to share with my son and his family in Richmond.

Returning to Richmond, where I spent my childhood, produced a slightly ghostly feeling, and I sometimes found if difficult to believe that I still existed in the flesh. Pembroke Lodge, which used to be a nice house, was being ruined by order of the Civil Service. When they discovered, what they did not know until they were told, that it had been the home of famous people, they decided that everything possible must be done to destroy its historic interest. Half of it was turned into flats for park-keepers, and the other half into a tea shop. The garden was cut up by a complicated system of barbed wire, with a view, so I thought at the time, to minimising the pleasure to be derived from it.[1]

I had hoped vaguely that I might somehow rent Pembroke Lodge and install myself and my family there. As this proved impossible, I took a largish house near Richmond Park, turning over the two lower floors to my son's family and keeping the top two for myself. This had worked more or less well for a time in spite of the difficulties that almost always occur when two families live at close quarters. We had a pleasant life there, living separately, each having our own guests, and coming together when we wished. But it made a very full life, with the family coming and going, my work, and the constant stream of visitors.

Among the visitors were Alan and Mary Wood who came to see me about a book that he wished to write on my philosophical work. He soon decided to do a life of me first. In the course of its preparation

---

[1] Later, I changed my opinion of their proceedings and thought that they had done the adaptation very well if it had to be done.

we saw much of both him and his wife and came to be very fond of them and to rely upon them. Some of the encounters with visitors, however, were odd. One gentleman from America who had suggested coming to tea, turned up accompanied by a mistress of the American McCarthy whose virtues she extolled. I was angry. Another was an Indian who came with his daughter. He insisted that she must dance for me while he played her accompaniment. I had only a short time before returned from hospital and did not welcome having all the furniture of our sitting-room pushed back and the whole house shake as she cavorted in what, under other circumstances, I might have thought lovely gyrations.

That visit to the hospital became one of the myths to which I have already referred. My wife and I had gone on a long walk in Richmond Park one morning and, after lunch, she had gone up to her sitting-room which was above mine. Suddenly I appeared, announcing that I felt ill. Not unnaturally, she was frightened. It was the fine sunny Sunday before the Queen's coronation. Though my wife tried to get hold of a neighbour and of our own doctors in Richmond and London, she could get hold of no one. Finally, she rang 999 and the Richmond police, with great kindness and much effort, came to the rescue. They sent a doctor who was unknown to me, the only one whom they could find. By the time the police had managed to get hold of our own doctors, I had turned blue. My wife was told by a well-known specialist, one of the five doctors who had by then congregated, that I might live for two hours. I was packed into an ambulance and whisked to hospital where they dosed me with oxygen and I survived.

The pleasant life at Richmond had other dark moments. At Christmas, 1953, I was waiting to go into hospital again for a serious operation and my wife and household were all down with flu. My son and his wife decided that, as she said, they were 'tired of children'. After Christmas dinner with the children and me, they left, taking the remainder of the food, but leaving the children, and did not return. We were fond of the children, but were appalled by this fresh responsibility which posed so many harassing questions in the midst of our happy and already very full life. For some time we hoped that their parents would return to take up their rôle, but when my son became ill we had to abandon that hope and make long-term arrangements for the children's education and holidays. Moreover, the financial burden was heavy and rather disturbing: I had given £10,000 of my Nobel Prize cheque for a little more than £11,000 to my third wife, and I was now paying alimony to her and to my second wife as well as paying for the education and holidays of my younger son. Added to this, there were heavy expenses in connection with my elder son's illness; and the income taxes which for many years he had neglected to pay now fell to me to pay. The prospect of supporting and educating his three children, however pleasant it might be, presented problems.

For a time when I came out of the hospital I was not up to much, but by May I felt that I had recovered. I gave the Herman Ould Memorial Lecture to the PEN Club called 'History as an Art'. We were asked to supper afterwards by the Secretary of the Club and I enjoyed indulging my literary hates and loves. In particular, my great hate is Wordsworth. I have to admit the excellence of some of his work – to admire and love it, in fact – but much of it is too dull, too pompous and silly to be borne. Unfortunately, I have a knack of remembering bad verse with ease, so I can puzzle almost anyone who upholds Wordsworth.

A short time later, on our way home to Richmond from Scotland, we stopped in North Wales where our friends Rupert and Elizabeth Crawshay-Williams had found a house, Plas Penrhyn, that they thought would make a pleasant holiday house for us and the children. It was small and unprententious, but had a delightful garden and little orchard and a number of fine beech trees. Above all, it had a most lovely view, south to the sea, west to Portmadoc and the Caernarvon hills, and north up the valley of the Glaslyn to Snowdon. I was captivated by it, and particularly pleased that across the valley could be seen the house where Shelley had lived. The owner of Plas Penrhyn agreed to let it to us largely, I think, because he, too, is a lover of Shelley and was much taken by my desire to write an essay on 'Shelley the Tough' (as opposed to the 'ineffectual angel'). Later, I met a man at Tan-y-Ralt, Shelley's house, who said he had been a cannibal – the first and only cannibal I have met. It seemed appropriate to meet him at the house of Shelley the Tough. Plas Penrhyn seemed to us as if it would be an ideal place for the children's holidays, especially as there were friends of their parents living nearby whom they already knew and who had children of their own ages. It would be a happy alternative, we thought, to cinemas in Richmond and 'camps'. We rented it as soon as possible.

But all this was the daily background and the relief from the dark world of international affairs in which my chief interest lay. Though the reception accorded *Human Society in Ethics and Politics* was so amiable, its publication had failed to quiet my uneasiness. I felt I *must* find some way of making the world understand the dangers into which it was running blindly, head-on. I thought that perhaps if I repeated parts of *Human Society* on the BBC it would make more impression than it had hitherto made. In this, however, I was thwarted by the refusal of the BBC to repeat anything that had already been published. I therefore set to work to compose a new dirge for the human race.

Even then, in the relatively early days of the struggle against nuclear destruction, it seemed to me almost impossible to find a fresh way of putting what I had already, I felt, said in so many different ways. My first draft of the broadcast was an anaemic product, pulling all the punches. I threw it away at once, girded myself up and determined to say exactly how dreadful the prospect was unless measures were taken. The result was a distilled version of all that I had said theretofore. It was so tight packed that anything that I have since said on the subject can be found in it at least in essence. But the BBC still made difficulties, fearing that I should bore and frighten many listeners. They asked me to hold a debate, instead, with a young and cheerful footballer who could offset my grim forebodings. This seemed to me utterly frivolous and showed so clearly that the BBC Authorities understood nothing of what it was all about that I felt desperate. I refused to accede to their pleadings. At last, it was agreed that I should do a broadcast in December by myself. In it, as I have said, I stated all my fears and the reasons for them. The broadcast, now called 'Man's Peril', ended with the following words: 'There lies before us, if we choose, continual progress in happiness, knowledge, and wisdom. Shall we, instead, choose death, because we cannot forget our quarrels? I appeal, as a human being to human beings: remember your humanity, and forget the rest. If you can do so, the way lies open to a new Paradise; if you cannot, nothing lies before you but universal death.'

The broadcast had both a private and a public effect. The private effect was to allay my personal anxiety for a time, and to give me a feeling that I had found words adequate to the subject. The public effect was more important. I received innumerable letters and requests for speeches and articles, far more than I could well deal with. And I learned a great many facts that I had not known before, some of them rather desolating: a Battersea County Councillor came to see me and told me of the provisions that the Battersea Council had promulgated that were to be followed by all the inhabitants of that district in case of nuclear attack. Upon hearing the warning siren, they were to rush to Battersea Park and pile into buses. These, it was hoped, would whisk them to safety in the country.

Almost all the response to the broadcast of which I was aware was serious and encouraging. But some of my speeches had farcical interludes. One of them I remember with some smug pleasure: a man rose in fury, remarking that I looked like a monkey; to which I replied, 'Then you will have the pleasure of hearing the voice of your ancestors'.

I received the prize given by Pears' Cyclopaedia for some outstanding work done during the past year. The year before, the prize had been given to a young man who ran a mile in under four minutes. The prize cup which I now have says 'Bertrand Russell illuminating a path to Peace 1955'.

One of the most impressive meetings at which I spoke was held in April, 1955, in memory of the Jews who died at Warsaw in February, 1943. The music was tragic and beautiful, and the emotion of the assembled company so deep and sincere as to make the meeting very moving. There were records made of my speech and of the music.

Among the first organisations to show a pronounced interest in my views were the World Parliamentarians and, more seriously perhaps, the Parliamentary World Government Association with whom I had many meetings. They were to hold joint meetings in Rome in April, 1955, at which they invited me to speak. We were put up, oddly enough, in the hotel in which I had stayed with my Aunt Maude on my first trip to Rome over a half century before. It was a cold barracks that had ceased to provide meals for its guests, but was in a pleasant part of the old city. It was Spring and warm. It was a great pleasure to wander about the city and along the Tiber and up the Pincio for the otherwise unprovided meals. I found the Roman meetings very moving and interesting. I was happy that my speeches seemed to affect people, both at the meeting in the Chamber of Deputies and elsewhere. At all of them there were very mixed audiences. After one, I was held up by a man almost in tears because he had not been able to understand what had been said because he spoke no English. He besought me to translate what I had said into Esperanto. Alas, I could not. I enjoyed, too, meeting a number of friendly and notable literary and political figures in whose work I had been interested but with whom I had never before had a chance to discuss matters.

I had hoped, on the way north from Rome, to pay a visit to Bernard Berenson at Settignano. In this I was prevented by the pressure of work. Later, I learned that he took my defection very ill, especially as he had felt me, he said, to be arrogant and unfriendly at our last meeting. I was extremely sorry for this since my feelings towards him were, as they had always been, most friendly and I felt anything but arrogant towards him. But the last meeting to which he alluded had been a somewhat trying occasion to me. His wife Mary had asked me to lunch with them and I had gone. At the time of my separation from her sister Alys, she had written me a cutting letter saying that they did not wish to have anything further to do with me. Her invitation to lunch came many years later. I was glad to accept as I had never wished any break in our friendship, but I felt a little awkward and shy as I could not forget entirely her previous letter. Bernard Berenson had evidently never known of the letter or had forgotten it. I myself had felt that the luncheon had healed the breach and had been glad when he begged me to come to I Tatti again as I should have liked to do.

Meantime, as I assessed the response that my broadcast had achieved and considered what should be done next, I had realised that the point that I must concentrate upon was the need of co-operation among nations. It had occurred to me that it might be possible to formulate a statement that a number of very well-known and respected scientists of both capitalist and communist ideologies would be willing to sign calling for further joint action. Before taking any measures, however, I had written to Einstein to learn what he thought of such a plan. He had replied with enthusiasm, but had said that, because he was not well and could hardly keep up with present commitments, he himself could do nothing to help beyond sending me the names of various scientists who, he thought, would be sympathetic. He had begged me, nevertheless, to carry out my idea and to formulate the statement myself. This I had done, basing the statement upon my Christmas broadcast, 'Man's Peril'. I had drawn up a list of scientists of both East and West and had written to them, enclosing the statement, shortly before I went to Rome with the Parliamentarians. I had, of course, sent the statement to Einstein for his approval, but had not yet heard what he thought of it and whether he would be willing to sign it. As we flew from Rome to Paris, where the World Government Association were to hold further meetings, the pilot announced the news of Einstein's death. I felt shattered, not only for the obvious reasons, but because I saw my plan falling through without his support. But, on my arrival at my Paris hotel, I found a letter from him agreeing to sign. This was one of the last acts of his public life.

While I was in Paris I had a long discussion about my plan with Frédéric Joliot-Curie. He warmly welcomed the plan and approved of the statement except for one phrase: I had written, 'It is feared that if many bombs are used there will be universal death – sudden only for a fortunate minority, but for the majority a slow torture of disease and disintegration'. He did not like my calling the minority 'fortunate'. 'To die is *not* fortunate', he said. Perhaps he was right. Irony, taken internationally, is tricky. In any case, I agreed to delete it. For some time after I returned to England, I heard nothing from him. He was ill, I learned later. Nor could I induce an answer from various other important scientists. I never did hear from the Chinese scientist to whom I had written. I think the letter to him was probably misaddressed. Einstein had advised me to enlist the help of Niels Bohr who, he thought, would certainly be in favour of my plan and my statement. But I could achieve no reply from him for many weeks in spite of repeated letters and telegrams. Then came a short letter saying that he wished to have nothing to do with either plan or statement. The Russian Academicians, still suspicious of the West, also refused to sign, although they wrote commending the plan with some warmth. After some correspondence, Professor Otto Hahn refused to sign, because, I understood, he was working for the forthcoming 'Mainau Declaration' of scientists. This declaration was already in preparation, but seemed to me to be somewhat emasculated by the fact that it was intended to include among its signatories only scientists of the West. Fortunately, others who signed the Mainau Declaration agreed with me and signed both. My most personal disappointment was that I could not obtain the signature of Lord Adrian, the President of the Royal Society and Master of my College, Trinity. I knew that he agreed with the principles in my broadcast, which were those of the manifesto that I hoped he would sign. He had himself spoken publicly in similar vein. And I had been pleased when I learned that Trinity wished to have in its Library a manuscript of 'Man's Peril'. But when I discussed my statement or manifesto with him I thought I understood why he was reluctant to sign. 'It is because it is too eloquent, isn't it ?' I asked. 'Yes', he said. Many of the scientists to whom I wrote, however, at once warmly agreed to sign, and one, Linus Pauling, who had heard of the plan only at second hand, offered his signature. I was glad to accept the offer.

When I look back upon this time I do not see how the days and nights provided time to get through all that I did. Journeys to Rome and Paris and again to Scotland, family troubles, arrangements to settle in North Wales for the holidays, letters, discussions, visitors, and speeches. I wrote innumerable articles. I had frequent interviews and much correspondence with an American, R. C. Marsh, who was collecting and editing various early essays of mine which appeared the following year under the title *Logic and Knowledge*. And I was also preparing my book *Portraits from Memory* for publication in 1956. In January, 1955, I gave a lecture at the British Academy on J. S. Mill, which I had considerable difficulty in composing. I had already spoken so often about Mill. But the speech had one phrase that I cherish: in speaking about the fact that propositions have a subject and a predicate, I said it had led to 'three thousand years of important error'. And the speech was acclaimed in a most gratifying manner. The audience rose, thumped and clapped.

June came and still all the replies to my letters to the scientists had not been received. I felt that in any case some concrete plan must be made as to how the manifesto should be publicised. It seemed to me that it should be given a dramatic launching in order to call attention to it, to what it said and to the eminence of those who upheld it. After discarding many plans, I decided to get expert advice. I knew the editor of the *Observer* slightly and believed him to be liberal and sympathetic. He proved at that time to be both. He called in colleagues to discuss the matter. They agreed that something more was needed than merely publishing the fact that the manifesto had been written and signed by a number of eminent scientists of varying ideologies. They suggested that a press conference should be held at which I should read the document and answer questions about it. They did far more than this. They offered to arrange and finance the conference with the proviso that it not become, until later, public knowledge that they had done so. It was decided finally that the conference should take place on July 9th (1955). A room was engaged in Caxton Hall a week before. Invitations were sent to the editors of all the journals and to the representatives of foreign journals as well as to the BBC and representatives of foreign radio and TV in London. This invitation was merely to a conference at which something important of world-wide interest was to be published. The response was heartening and the room had to be changed to the largest in the Hall.

It was a dreadful week. All day long the telephone rang and the doorbell pealed. Journalists and wireless directors wanted to be told what this important piece of news was to be. Each hoped, apparently, for a scoop. Three times daily someone from the *Daily Worker* rang to say that their paper had not been sent an invitation. Daily, three times, they were told that they had been invited. But they seemed to be so used to being cold-shouldered that they could not believe it. After all, though they could not be told this, one purpose of the manifesto was to encourage co-operation between the communist and the non-communist world. The burden of all this flurry fell upon my wife and my housekeeper. I was not permitted to appear or to speak on the telephone except to members of the family. None of us could leave the house. I spent the week sitting in a chair in my study trying to read. At intervals, I was told later, I muttered dismally, 'This is going to be a damp squib'. My memory is that it rained during the entire week and was very cold.

The worst aspect of the affair was that not long before this I had received a letter from Joliot-Curie saying that he feared that, after all, he could not sign the manifesto. I could not make out why he had changed. I begged him to come to London to discuss the matter, but he was too ill. I had been in constant touch with Dr E. H. S. Burhop in order that the manifesto should not in any way offend those of communist ideology. It was largely due to his efforts that the night before the conference was scheduled to take place Monsieur Biquard came from Paris to discuss with Burhop and myself Joliot-Curie's objections. Monsieur Biquard has since taken Joliot-Curie's place in the World Federation of Scientific Workers. They arrived at 11.30 p.m. Sometime after midnight we came to an agreement. The manifesto could not be changed from the form it had had when Einstein had signed it and, in any case, it was too late to obtain the agreement of the other signatories to a change. I suggested, therefore, that Joliot-Curie's objections be added in footnotes where necessary and be included in my reading of the text the following morning. I had hit upon this scheme in dealing with an objection of one of the Americans. Joliot-Curie's emissary at last agreed to this and signed the manifesto for him, as he had been empowered to do if an agreement could be reached.

Another difficulty that had beset me was the finding of a chairman for the meeting who would not only add lustre to the occasion but would be equipped to help me in the technical questions that would surely be asked. For one reason or another everyone whom I approached refused the job. I confess that I suspected their refusal to have been the result of pusillanimity. Whoever took part in this manifesto or its launching ran the risk of disapproval that might, for a time at any rate, injure them or expose them to ridicule, which they would probably mind even more. Or perhaps their refusal was the result of their dislike of the intentional dramatic quality of the occasion. Finally, I learned that Professor Josef Rotblat was sympathetic. He was, and still is, an eminent physicist at the Medical College of St Bartholomew's Hospital and Executive vice-President of the Atomic Scientists' Association. He bravely and without hesitation agreed to act as Chairman and did so when the time came with much skill. From the time of that fortunate meeting I have often worked closely with Professor Rotblat and I have come to admire him greatly. He can have few rivals in the courage and integrity and complete self-abnegation with which he has given up his own career (in which, however, he still remains eminent) to devote himself to combating the nuclear peril as well as other, allied evils. If ever these evils are eradicated and international affairs are straightened out, his name should stand very high indeed among the heroes.

Amongst others who encouraged me at this meeting were Alan Wood and Mary Wood who, with Kenneth Harris of the *Observer*, executed a variety of burdensome and vexatious drudgeries to make the occasion go off well. And in the event it did go well. The hall was packed, not only with men, but with recording and television machines. I read the manifesto and the list of signatories and explained how and why it had come into being. I then, with Rotblat's help, replied to questions from the floor. The journalistic mind, naturally, was impressed by the dramatic way in which Einstein's signature had arrived. Henceforth, the manifesto was called the Einstein-Russell (or *vice versa*) manifesto. At the beginning of the meeting a good deal of scepticism and indifference and some out and out hostility was shown by the press. As the meeting continued, the journalists appeared to become sympathetic and even approving, with the exception of one American journalist who felt affronted for his country by something I said in reply to a question. The meeting ended after two and a half hours with enthusiasm and high hope of the outcome of the call to scientists to hold a conference.

When it was all over, however, and we had returned to our flat at Millbank where we were spending the weekend, reaction set in. I recalled the horrid fact that in making various remarks about the signatories I had said that Professor Rotblat came from Liverpool. Although he himself had not seemed to notice the slip, I felt ashamed. The incident swelled to immense proportions in my mind. The disgrace of it prevented me from even speaking of it. When we walked to the news hoardings outside of Parliament to see if the evening papers had noted the meeting and found it heralded in banner headlines, I still could not feel happy. But worse was to come. I learned that I had omitted Professor Max Born's name from the list of signatories, had, even, said that he had refused to sign. The exact opposite was the truth. He had not only signed but had been most warm and helpful. This was a serious blunder on my part, and one that I have never stopped regretting. By the time that I had learned of my mistake it was too late to rectify the error, though I at once took, and have since taken, every means that I could think of to set the matter straight. Professor Born himself was magnanimous and has continued his friendly correspondence with me. As in the case of most of the other signatories the attempt and achievement of the manifesto took precedence over personal feelings.

Word continued to pour in of the wide news coverage all over the world of the proclamation of the manifesto. Most of it was favourable. My spirits rose. But for the moment I could do nothing more to forward the next step in opposition to nuclear armament. I had to devote the next few weeks to family matters. During the dreadful week before the proclamation when the telephone was not ringing about that subject it was ringing to give me most distressing news about my elder son's illness. I now had to devote all my mind to that and to moving my family for the summer to our new house in North Wales. The latter had been painted and refurbished during our absence under the kind auspices of Rupert and Elizabeth Crawshay-Williams. The necessary new furnishing to augment what we had bought from the estate of the former tenant had been bought in London during five afternoons at the end of June. So all was more or less ready for us. We went there to prepare for the coming of the three grandchildren as soon as possible. I was glad to escape from London. Most people seem to think of me as an urban individual, but I have, in fact, spent most of my life in the country and am far happier there than in any city known to me. But, having settled the children with the nurse who had for some years taken care of them at Richmond, I had to journey to Paris again for another World Government Conference. It was held in the Cité Universitaire and the meetings proved interesting. There were various parties in connection with it, some official and some less so. One was at the Quai d'Orsay. At one, a cocktail party held in the house of the great couturière Schiaparelli, I went out into the garden where I was quickly surrounded by a group of women who thought that women should do something special to combat nuclear warfare. They wished me to support their plans. I am entirely in favour of anyone doing what they can to combat nuclear warfare, but I have never been able to understand why the sexes should not combat it together. In my experience, fathers, quite as much as mothers, are concerned for the welfare of their young. My wife was standing on a balcony above the garden. Suddenly she heard my voice rise in anguished tones: 'But, you see, I am not a mother!' Someone was dispatched at once to rescue me.

After this Paris conference at the end of July, we returned to Richmond for another congress. The Association of Parliamentarians for World Government had planned in June to hold a congress for both Eastern and Western scientists and others if they could manage it during the first days of August. They, as I did, believed that the time had come for communists and non-communists to work together. I had taken part in their deliberations and was to speak at the first meeting. Three Russians came from the Moscow Academy as well as other people, particularly scientists, from many parts of the world. The Russians were led by Academician Topchiev of whom I was later to see much and whom I grew to respect and greatly like. This was the first time since the war that any Russian Communists had attended a conference in the West and we were all exceedingly anxious to have the meetings go well. In the main they did so. But there was a short time when, at a committee meeting towards the end of the second day, the Russians could not come to agreement with their Western colleagues. The organisers telephoned me and asked if I could do anything to soothe matters. Fortunately agreement was managed. And at the final meeting I was able to read the resolutions of the conference as having been reached unanimously. Altogether, the conference augured well for co-operation. I could return to Wales for a few weeks of real holiday with the happy feeling that things were at last moving as one would wish.

Naturally, all work did not stop even during the holiday. I had already been considering with Professors Rotblat and Powell how we could implement the scientists' manifesto which had called for a conference of scientists to consider all the matters concerning and allied to the nuclear dangers. Professor Joliot-Curie, who was himself too ill to take active part in our plans, encouraged us at long distance. We were fairly sure by this time of being able to get together a good group of scientists of both East and West.

In the early days of preparing the manifesto, I had hoped that I might be supported in it by the Indian scientists and Government. At the beginning of Nehru's visit to London in February, 1955, my hope of it soared. Nehru himself had seemed most sympathetic. I lunched with him and talked with him at various meetings and receptions. He had been exceedingly friendly. But when I met Dr Bhabha, India's leading official scientist, towards the end of Nehru's visit, I received a cold douche. He had profound doubts about any such manifesto, let alone any such conference as I had in mind for the future. It became evident that I should receive no encouragement from Indian official scientific quarters. After the successful promulgation of the manifesto, however, Nehru's more friendly attitude prevailed. With the approval and help of the Indian Government, it was proposed that the first conference between Western and Eastern scientists be held in New Delhi in January, 1957.

Throughout the early part of 1956, we perfected, so far as we could, our plans for the conference. By the middle of the year we had sent off invitations over my name to about sixty scientists. But 1956 was a year of bits and pieces for me, taken up chiefly by broadcasts and articles. An endless and pleasant stream of old friends and new acquaintances came and went. We decided to sell our Richmond house and move permanently to North Wales. We kept, however, as a *pied à terre* in London, our flat in Millbank, with its wonderful view of the river in which I delighted. Later, we were turned out of this flat for the modernisation of Millbank. Politically, I took part in numberless meetings concerned with a variety of affairs, some to do with the troubles in Cyprus, some to do with World Government. (The World Government Association gave a dinner in my honour in February at the House of Commons. I have never felt sure how many of the people at the dinner knew that it had been announced as a dinner in my honour. At any rate, some of the speeches might have turned my head happily if only I could have believed them.) I was especially concerned with a campaign about the imprisonment of Morton Sobell in the United States.

At the time of the Rosenbergs' trial and death (one is tempted to say assassination) in 1951, I had paid, I am ashamed to say, only cursory attention to what was going on. Now, in 1956, in March, my cousin Margaret Lloyd brought Mrs Sobell, Morton Sobell's mother, to see me. Sobell had been kidnapped by the United States Government from Mexico to be brought to trial in connection with the Rosenberg case. He had been condemned, on the evidence of a known perjurer, to thirty years' imprisonment, of which he had already served five. His family was trying to obtain support for him, and his mother had come to England for help. Several eminent people in America had already taken up cudgels on his behalf, but to no avail. People both here and in the United States appeared to be ignorant of his plight and what had led up to it. I remember talking of the case with a well-known and much admired Federal Court Judge. He professed complete ignorance of the case of Morton Sobell and was profoundly shocked by what I told him of it. But I noted that he afterwards made no effort to get at the facts, much less to do anything to remedy them. The case seemed to me a monstrous one and I agreed to do all I could to call people's attention to it. A small society had already been formed in London to do this, and they agreed to help me. I wrote letters to the papers and articles on the matter. One of my letters contained the phrase 'a posse of terrified perjurers', which pleased me and annoyed those who did not agree with me. I was inundated by angry letters from Americans and others denying my charges and asking irately how I could be so bold as to call American justice into question. A few letters came from people, including members of the above-mentioned London group, who agreed with me, though no one in England, so far as I know, upheld my point of view publicly. I was generally and often venomously charged with being anti-American, as I often have been when I have criticised adversely any Americans or anything American. I do not know why, since I have spent long periods in that country and have many friends there and have often expressed my admiration of various Americans and American doings. Moreover, I have married two Americans. However – ten years later it had come to be generally agreed that the case against Morton Sobell did not hold water. The Court of Appeals pronounced publicly on the case in 1962–63. On reading the judges' verdict, I understood them to say that it was not worth granting Sobell a new trial. On appealing for advice from Sobell's defence lawyers on my interpretation of the verdict, I was informed: 'It was terrible, though not quite as crude as you'd imagined.' The defence lawyers had argued that 'Ethel Rosenberg's constitutional Fifth-Amendment rights had been violated during the trial, and that this had been fully established in a subsequent Supreme Court decision, known as the "Grunewald" decision. This decision indicated that Ethel Rosenberg had been entitled to a new trial; and since her innocence would have established her husband's and Sobell's, they too were entitled to new trials ... The Rosenbergs, alas, were no longer around, but Sobell should have his day in court.' Although his family continue their long, brave fight to obtain freedom for him, Morton Sobell remains in prison.

Early in 1947 I had said in the House of Lords that in America 'any person who favours the United Nations is labelled as a dangerous "Red" '. I was alarmed by such uncritical anti-communism, especially as it was adopted increasingly by organisations purporting to be liberal. For this reason I felt obliged, early in 1953, to resign from the American Committee for Cultural Freedom. I remained Honorary President of the International Congress for Cultural Freedom. Three years later I was sent the proof of a book called *Was Justice Done ? The Rosenberg–Sobell Case* by Malcolm Sharp, Professor of Law at the University of Chicago. It made it quite clear to me, and I should have thought to anyone, that there had been a miscarriage of justice. I denounced in the press the hysteria and police-state techniques which had been used against the Rosenbergs and Sobell. The response of the American Committee for Cultural Freedom seems even more absurd in the light of the evidence which has mounted during the intervening years than it seemed at the time. 'There is no evidence whatsoever', the American Committee pronounced, 'that the Federal Bureau of Investigation committed atrocities or employed thugs in the Rosenberg case. There is no support whatever for your charge that Sobell, an innocent man, was the victim of political hysteria. There is no ground whatever for your contention that either Sobell or the Rosenbergs were condemned on the word of perjurers, terrified or unterrified . . . Your remarks on American judicial procedure, the analogy you draw between the technique of the Federal Bureau of Investigation and the policy [*sic*] methods of Nazi Germany or Stalin's Russia, constitute a major disservice to the cause of freedom and democracy.' Having learned that the American branch approved of cultural freedom in Communist countries but not elsewhere, I resigned from the Congress for Cultural Freedom.

But in the summer of 1956 things seemed to be moving in our direction so far as the proposed conference of scientists was concerned. Then, in October, two misfortunes overtook the world: the first was the Hungarian Revolt and its suppression;[1] the second was the Suez affair. In relation to the latter I felt shocked, as I said publicly, and sickened by our Government's machinations, military and other. I welcomed Gaitskell's speech, dry and late in coming though it was, because it said more or less officially a number of things that should have been said. But the loss of influence in international affairs which Great Britain must suffer in consequence of this ill-advised Suez exploit seemed to me well-nigh irreparable. In any case, it was obviously impossible to take the Western participants in the conference by the round-about route then necessary to arrive in India in January 1957. So we had to re-plan our next move.

The problem was how the work was to be carried out and where such a conference should be held and, above all, how it could be financed. I felt very sure that the conference should not be bound by

[1] I am sometimes asked why I did not at the time fulminate against the Russian suppression of the Hungarian Revolt. I did not because there was no need. Most of the so-called Western World was fulminating. Some people spoke out strongly against the Suez exploit, but most people were acquiescent.

the tenets of any established body and that it should be entirely neutral and independent; and the other planners thought likewise. But we could find no individual or organisation in England willing, if able, to finance it and certainly none willing to do so with no strings attached. Some time before, I had received a warm letter of approbation for what I was doing from Cyrus Eaton in America. He had offered to help with money. Aristotle Onassis, the Greek shipping magnate, had also offered to help if the conference were to take place at Monte Carlo. Cyrus Eaton now confirmed his offer if the conference were to be held at his birthplace, Pugwash in Nova Scotia. He had held other sorts of conferences there of a not wholly dissimilar character. We agreed to the condition. Plans went ahead fast under the guidance of Professors Rotblat and Powell. They were greatly helped by Dr Burhop and, then and later, by Dr Patricia Lindop, a physicist of St Bartholomew's Medical College. Her informed and dedicated devotion to the causes of peace and co-operation among scientists was, I found, comparable even to Professor Rotblat's. She managed her work, her children and household and the scientists with apparently carefree grace and tact. And the first conference took place in early July, 1957, at Pugwash.

I was unable to go to this first conference because of my age and ill health. A large part of my time in 1957 was devoted to various medical tests to determine what was the trouble with my throat. In February, I had to go into hospital for a short time to find out whether or not I had cancer of the throat. The evening that I went in I had a debate over the BBC with Abbot Butler of Downside which I much enjoyed, and I think he did also. The incident went off as pleasantly as such a trying performance could do and it was discovered conclusively that I did not have cancer. But what did I have? And so the tests continued and I continued to have to live on baby's food and other such pabulum.

Since that time I have made several journeys abroad, though none so long as that to Pugwash. I fight shy of longer journeys partly because I fear if I go to one country people in other countries who have pressed me to go there will be affronted. The only way around this, for one who is not an official personage, is to renounce distant travels. In 1958, however, I journeyed to a Pugwash conference in Austria. I stayed on after the meetings and, with my wife, made a journey by motor car. We drove along the Danube to Durnstein which I had wished to see ever since my boyhood delight in Richard Coeur de Lion. I was greatly impressed by the magnificent bleak grandeur of Melk on its bluff about the river and by the beauty of its library. Then we drove in a large circle through the mountains back to Vienna. The air was delicious and spicy. It seemed like a journey into the story books of my youth, both in the countryside, which is that of fairy books, and in the kindness and simplicity and gaiety of the people. Above one little village there was a great lime tree where the villagers gathered to gossip of an evening and on Sunday. It was a magical tree in a magical meadow, calm and sweet and full of peace. Once, as we drove along a narrow lane beside a dashing stream at the foot of a mountain, we were held up by a landslide. Great trunks of fir trees were piled up across the road. We stopped, wondering how to turn or to pass it. Suddenly, men and women appeared, as if sprung from the ground, from the nearby farms and set to work, laughing and joking, to move the obstruction. In a trice, it seemed to me, the road was free and we were being waved on by smiling people.

But to return to Pugwash – I was kept in close touch by letter and telephone with the proceedings of the first conference and was pleased with what I heard. We had decided that not only physicists but biological and social scientists should be invited to attend. There were twenty-two participants in all – from the United States, the Soviet Union, China, Poland, Australia, Austria, Canada, France, Great Britain, and Japan. The meetings were carried on in both English and Russian. It pleased me especially that it showed that real co-operation such as we had hoped, could be achieved among scientists of extremely divergent 'ideologies' and apparently opposing scientific as well as other views.

The conference was called the Pugwash Conference of Scientists and for the sake of continuity the movement has continued to be identified by the name Pugwash. It established among other things a 'Continuing Committee' of five members of which I was the Chairman to organise further conferences. More important, it established a form that future conferences followed. A number of plenary meetings were held at which important papers were read. There were a greater number of meetings of the small committees set up at the start, at which particular aspects of the general subjects were discussed and decided. Most important of all, it was held in an atmosphere of friendliness. Perhaps the unique characteristic of this and subsequent Pugwash Conferences was the fact that the members consorted with each other in their spare time as well as during the scheduled meetings and grew to know each other as human beings rather than merely as scientists of this or that potentially inimical belief or nation. This most important characteristic was in large part made possible by the astute understanding by Cyrus Eaton of the situation and what we wished to accomplish and by his tactful hospitality.

As I was not present, I shall not attempt to describe in detail the action or findings of this or any of the other conferences. Professor Rotblat compiled an excellent and comprehensive history of this and the following seven conferences that were held up to the time of its publication in 1962. Suffice it to say here, that there were three committees at the first conference: (1) on the hazards arising from the use of atomic energy; (2) on the control of nuclear weapons, which outlined the general objectives of disarmament which subsequent conferences discussed in detail; and (3) on the social responsibilities of scientists. The findings of the first, as Professor Rotblat points out, probably comprise the first agreement reached between scientists of East and West on the effects of nuclear tests. The third committee summarised its findings in eleven items of common belief which became, little more than a year later, the basis of what is known as the 'Vienna Declaration'. This first Pugwash conference published a statement that was formally endorsed by the Soviet Academy of Sciences and warmly welcomed in China, but less publicised and more slowly in the West.

The Continuing Committee first met in London in December, 1957, and a further and similar conference, again made possible by Cyrus Eaton, was held at Lac Beauport in Canada in the spring of 1958. Then came a more ambitious endeavour: a large conference in September, 1958, at Kitzbühel in Austria. It was made possible through the good offices of Professor Hans Thirring, under the auspices of the Theodor-Koerner Foundation. It was followed by meetings held in Vienna. At the former conferences no press or observers had been permitted to attend. At this third conference not only were observers present but they included members of the families of the participants. At the great meetings at Vienna the press was in evidence. At the meeting in the Austrian Academy of Sciences on the morning of September 20th the Vienna Declaration was promulgated. It was a statement that had been accepted with only one abstention by all the members of the conference at Kitzbühel and it forms, as Professor Rotblat has said, the *credo* of the Pugwash movement. It is too long to be included here, but may be found in his history. The meeting was opened by the President of Austria, Dr Adolf Schaef, for the conference had been given a very generous welcome by the Austrian State. Amongst others of both East and West I spoke in my capacity of president of the movement and chairman of the Continuing Committee. It seemed to me an impressive and unforgettable formal occasion. In my speech I recalled my grandfather's speech at a Congress (also in Vienna) during the Crimean War in which he spoke in favour of peace, but was overruled. Following the great meeting, we attended the President's lunch in the Alter Hof. Then came an important meeting when ten of the participants in the conference addressed ten thousand people at the Wiener Stadthalle – but this I could not attend.

The most obvious achievement of the Pugwash movement has been the conclusion, for which it was largely responsible, of the partial Testban Treaty which forbade nuclear tests above ground in peace time. I, personally, was not and am not happy about this partial ban. It seems to me to be, as I should expect it to be, a soother of consciences and fears that should not be soothed. At the same time, it is only a slight mitigation of the dangers to which we are all exposed. It seemed to me more likely to be a hindrance than a help towards obtaining the desired total ban. Nevertheless, it showed that East and West could work together to obtain what they wished to obtain and that the Pugwash movement could be effective when and where it desired to be. It was rather a give-away of the *bona fides* of the various 'Disarmament Conferences' whose doings we have watched with some scepticism for a good many years.

The Pugwash movement now seems to be firmly established and part of the respectable progress of scientific relations with international affairs. I myself have had little to do directly with its progress in the last years. My interest turned to new plans towards persuading peoples and Governments to banish war and in particular weapons of mass extermination, first of all nuclear weapons. In the course of these fresh endeavours, I felt that I had become rather disreputable in the eyes of the more conservative scientists. The Pugwash movement held a great meeting of scientists from all over the world in London in September, 1962. I was to speak about the founding of the movement and I warned my friends that I might be hissed – as I was fully convinced that I should be. I was deeply touched by being given a standing ovation when I rose to speak which included, I was told, all the participants, all, that is, save Lord Hailsham. He was present in his capacity as the Queen's Minister of Science. He was personally, I think, friendly enough to me, but, weighed down by office, he sat tight. That was the last occasion on which I have taken public part in a Pugwash conference.

LETTERS

From Bernard Berenson

> I Tatti
> Settignano
> Florence
> March 29, 1945

Dear Bertie

Mary died the 23d, & as I know that she remained very fond of you to the end, I wish you to hear of her end. It was a liberation, for she suffered distressingly, & increasingly in recent years.

Not many months ago, I read out to her yr. article in *Horizon* about America. It delighted her & me as well.

Of other publications of yours we have seen nothing in years. We have been cut off from the Western World for a good five years. I learned with pleasure that you had returned to your Cambridge & to Trinity. It makes me believe that we may meet again some day. It will have to be here, as I doubt whether I shall get to England soon.

You must have a grown up son by now. What of him ?

With affectionate remembrance.

> *Sincerely yours*
> *B.B.*

> Hotel Europa e Britannia
> Venezia
> June 1, 54 till July

Dear Bertie

I hear from Mrs Sprigge that you would like to revisit I Tatti. It would give me real pleasure to see you again, and your wife whom I remember. I propose your coming for ten days or a fortnight at any time between Dec. 1 and April 1. The other months we are either away or too crowded & I want you to myself. For many years I have been reading what you published about things human, feeling as if nobody else spoke for me as you do.

Do not delay, for in these weeks I shall be reaching my 90th year & *le Grand Peut-être* may want me any day.

With affectionate remembrance.

> *Ever yrs*
> *B.B.*

> I Tatti
> Settignano
> Florence
> July 12 '54

Dear Bertie

Thank you for *Nightmares*. I have enjoyed yr. wit, your evocation, your *Galgenhumors*. *Continuez !*

Yes, any time between Jan. 10 & March 1 would suit me best. I should by happy if you could stay a fortnight.

> *Sincerely yours*
> *B.B.*

P.S. Later, you will give me precise dates. B.B.

> I Tatti
> Settignano
> Florence
> Nov. 16, '54

Dear Bertie

Your note of the 12th grieves me. I looked forward to seeing you, the last of my near-contemporaries, & one with whom I have so much in common.

Unless work chains you to London you could carry it on at least as well here as at home. I never see guests except at meals, or if they want to join me in my now so short walks.

If Jan. 15–March 15 are impossible is there another time that would suit you better.

Could you come in the summer? We three are at Vallombrosa in a paradise but rustic, & far less roomy & comfy.

Incline yr. heart toward my proposal.

> Sincerely
> B.B.

P.S. I never shall cross the Alps again. London, Paris, New York etc. are far, far too tiring for me now.

> Saniet Volpi-Tripoli
> May 8, 55

Dear Bertie

Of course I knew you were in Rome, & I had a faint hope that you might find time to spend a day or two with me in Florence. I was disappointed that you could not make it.

Let me urge you again to come for a fortnight or so any time between Nov. 15 & March 15, preferably Jan. 15 to March 15. You could work as well as at home for I never see guests except at meals & evenings – if they care to keep me company after dinner.

It would be a joy to live over the remembered days of so long ago. Of your wife too I retain pleasant remembrance & should be happy to renew our acquaintance.

Do you really hope that disaster can be averted? I fear experiments can not be avoided, & damn the consequences.

> Sincerely yrs.
> B.B.

I wrote the following soon after going to live in Richmond in the house which I shared with my son and his family.

> May 12th, 1950

I have been walking alone in the garden of Pembroke Lodge, and it has produced a mood of almost unbearable melancholy. The Government is doing great works, all bad. Half the garden is incredibly lovely: a mass of azaleas and bluebells and narcissus and blossoming may trees. This half they have carefully fenced in with barbed wire (I crawled through it), for fear the public should enjoy it. It was incredibly like

Blake's Garden of Love, except that the 'priests' were bureaucrats.
 I suffer also from entering into the lives of John and Susan. They
were born after 1914, and are therefore incapable of happiness. Their
three children are lovely: I love them and they like me. But the parents
live their separate lives, in separate prisons of nightmare and despair.
Not on the surface; on the surface they are happy. But beneath the
surface John lives in suspicious solitude, unable to believe that anyone
can be trusted, and Susan is driven beyond endurance by sharp stabs
of sudden agony from contemplation of this dreadful world. She finds
relief in writing poetry, but he has no relief. I see that their marriage will
break up, and that neither will ever find happiness or peace. At moments I can shut out this terrifying intuitive knowledge, but I love them
both too much to keep on thinking about them on a level of mundane
common sense. If I had not the horrible Cassandra gift of foreseeing
tragedy, I could be happy here, on a surface level. But as it is, I suffer.
And what is wrong with them is wrong with all the young throughout
the world. My heart aches with compassion for the lost generation –
lost by the folly and greed of the generation to which I belong. It is a
heavy burden, but one must rise above it. Perhaps, by suffering to the
limit, some word of comfort may be revealed.

To Charles W. Stewart, the illustrator of my Nightmares of Eminent
Persons. *I longed to find a Daumier or, better still, a Goya to point up the
savage irony of this book as well as the warning contained in my* Human
Society in Ethics and Politics.

20 Nov. 1953

Dear Mr Stewart
 Thank you for the roughs. I like them very much and shall be glad
to have you do the pictures. I note what you say about Stalin and am
assuming that the picture will be somewhat different from the rough. I
particularly like the existentialist's nightmare and the one in Zahatopolk
where the lady is being burnt. In the other Zahatopolk picture I like it
all except that I think the valley ought to be more smiling and full of
flowers, but perhaps it will be so when you have finished the picture.
In the picture of Dr Southport Vulpes I suppose the things in the sky
are aeroplanes, and I think it might be a good thing if they were somewhat larger and more emphatic. I quite agree to your suggestion of a
single heading for every other nightmare, and I have no objection to
having Vulpes put between Eisenhower and Acheson as you suggest. I
am looking forward with pleasure to a picture of the quarrel between
the two ladies in Faith and Mountains. As this story is at the printers, I
am sending you a spare typescript which, however, I should like to have
back when you have finished with it.

I am engaged on another book, not of stories, but on ethics and politics, to be called *Human Society: Diagnosis & Prognosis*. I want in this book to have three pictures, or one picture in three parts, like a triptych, illustrating the uses of intelligence in the past, present and future. If you feel inclined to undertake this and if Stanley Unwin is agreeable, I shall be very glad. Any time within the next four months would do. I should like all three as savage and bitter as possible.

I return the roughs herewith.

> *Yours sincerely*
> *Bertrand Russell*

From Ion Braby about *The Good Citizen's Alphabet*

> Queensland
> St Nicholas-at-Wade
> near Birchington, Kent
> March 31 1953

Dear Lord Russell

Thank you so much for the book. It is delightful. I am not sure whether the drawings are worthy of the text or the text worthy of the drawings. In either event they could hardly be better. I think FOOLISH, GREEDY and JOLLY are my favourites, but I am very fond of UNFAIR, ERRONEOUS and DIABOLIC and many more. And, also, of the opening address (I feel that is the word) and its illustrations. I am sure you and the artist will be due for a triple dose of hemlock, for you will be accused of corrupting not only the young but the middle-aged and elderly too – and corrupting the latter two is very wrong, as they have less time to recover. Anyway, I am very glad to be subverted by it; thank you again.

I sent my book off to The Bodley Head at the end of the week before last, and hope to get an answer soon. I need hardly say once more how much I appreciate your interest and help.

> *With best wishes*
> *Yours sincerely*
> *Ion*

From Rupert Crawshay-Williams

> Castle Yard
> Portmeirion
> Penrhyndeudraeth
> Merioneth
> August 1, 1953

Dear Bertie

I was so delighted by your story – and especially as I read most of it in a remarkably dingy cubicle in a Divinity students' hostel in Dublin – that I determined to write you a letter long enough for comment on the particular bits I liked; and I've been putting this off – largely because my holiday in Ireland did not do as a holiday is supposed to, but somehow put me into a state of mind in which all my work was worse – and much slower – than it had been before. (But this may have been a bit because revising, and particularly cutting down, is so much more boring than the actual working out of ideas.)

Anyway *Faith and Mountains* is certainly my favourite of all your stories so far. I suppose this is partly because its theme is a cup of tea just up my street. But I think you have worked it out beautifully, with just the right amount – not too much – of pastiche and exaggeration. The pseudo-scientific plausibility of the two opposing doctrines is delightful, especially in the light of Mr Wagthorne's later point about man's ability to believe what afterwards appears to have been nonsense. Incidentally, that whole paragraph on p. 43 builds up with beautifully timed comic effect to all the names beginning with M. The timing of your effects in general – for instance, the moments you choose for understatement or for sharp statement – is now technically most efficient. (The Professor's opening speech at the grand meeting; the conciseness of the paragraph at the beginning of Chapter VII in which his future is outlined – nice bit about Tensing!; 'And with that they fell into each other's arms'.)

Also there are a nice lot of sly digs put over with a straight face (which is one of your finger-prints, of course): The Magnets' dismissal of *mere* brawn; the believers finally remaining in out of the way suburbs. And I liked the conceits about the very narrow valley and about Mr Thorney's use of a sextant. And the TLS pastiche, with its 'shallow certainty' and 'deeper sources of wisdom' and 'the coldly critical intellect'.

Your 'message' of course is highly commendable; and as a matter of fact Zachary's answer to his father at the end is most concise and decisive. But, for me, even more decisive – because it made me laugh out loud (and also Elizabeth, who sends her love and entire agreement) – is the last paragraph. You have caught so neatly and ludicrously the dingy commonplaceness of so many hymns. (Now I come to think of it, part of the effect comes from the slight confusion of thought between third and fourth lines: diseases of *the* chest and Makes *our* muscles grow.) And then comes – perfectly correctly – the word 'Sublimities' in the last line.

I was glad to see, by the way, your emphasis, in a review in the *Sunday Times* some weeks ago, upon the role of power politics rather than ideologies – and also your re-emphasis upon the way in which science and scientific method have conditioned (all that is 'best' in) Western Values. It is maddening the way in which the opposite 'soupy' belief is accepted even by most unsoupy people.

My word 'soupy' was used the other day – in exactly my sense – by a novelist called Angus Wilson when reviewing a book on Georges Sand in the *Observer*. I very much hope this is a sign that it is spreading; Angus Wilson is I believe a friend of Cyril Connolly's to whom I did once introduce the word.

The names Tomkins and Merrow (together) ring a faint bell in my mind. Should it be a loud bell, and should I recognise it ?

> *Yours ever*
> Rupert

It's now Sunday, and I've just remembered that the local post office box won't take large envelopes. So I'll send the MS back to-morrow.

From J. B. S. Haldane

> University College London
> Department of Biometry
> 5th November, 1953

Dear Russell

Thank you very much for your information. I have, of course, altered the passage to bring it into line with the facts. In my old age I am getting rather interested in animal behaviour, and have even done something to 'decode' the bees' language (of which a fair account is to be found in Ribband's *The Behaviour and Social Life of Honeybees*). As you know, bees returning from a rich source of food dance. The class of all dances is a propositional function with four variables, which may be rendered

'There is a source of food smelling of A, requiring B workers, at a distance C in direction D.'

A is indicated by demonstration, B, C, and D symbolically. I have brought a little precision into the translation of the symbols for C. The paper will be sent you in due course. If, however, bees are given honey vertically above them they cannot communicate this fact, though they dance in an irregular manner. There are undanceable truths, like the ineffable name of God.

The political system of bees, discovered by Lindauer, is even more surprising. He has records of a debate as to a nest site which lasted for five days.

You will perhaps correct me if I am incorrect in describing a propositional function as a class of propositions. If one comes to them 'from outside' as in the observation of bees, this seems a natural way of looking at the matter.

Meanwhile various Germans (not v. Frisch and Lindauer) are plugging the fixity of animal behaviour in a rather Nazi manner (v.

reprint by my wife). The word 'imprinting', due to Thorpe, is used for long-lasting changes in conduct due to a juvenile experience (e.g. the following of Spalding by chickens).

Yours sincerely
J. B. S. Haldane

From H. McHaigh Esq.

87 Orewa Rd.
Auckland, N.Z.
17/viii/'51

Dear Sir

I had the pleasure of lecturing you last year: while you were in Sydney. But, one evening this week you were closer: here, in Auckland, I heard your voice – reproduced from 1.Y.A. Auck. Radio broadcast.

Now I understand how, or why, the 'Bulletin' artist was able to depict so terribly the vile personality shewn in that weekly's columns – labelled with your name: as well as seeing you in the flesh, he must have heard you speak.

Frequently, while the radio is turned on, I have wondered whether members of Broadcasting Boards have ears; or, whether, having ears, they have a grain of good taste amongst them. But, as soon as the announcer named you as the person emitting those dreadfully disgusting sounds, I knew that, ears or no ears, those men are utterly careless about inflicting pain – and about disclosing the shocking ruin that (as in your case) a human being can make of himself. For unless thoroughly bestialised, no man could possibly give out such sounds from his mouth.

When, or if, you ever entertain shame and self-disgust (and I pray it may be soon), I suggest that you gather and destroy every sound-record of your voice: you owe that reparation at least.

God help you.

Yours truly
H. McHaigh

From and to H. N. Brailsford

37 Belsize Park Gardens
London
N.W.3
19 May 1952

My Dear Russell

You have been overwhelmed, I'm sure, with congratulations, and yet I would like to add mine, for few can have come from friends who knew you in the last century. I recall vividly our first meeting at the Court-neys during the Boer War. I welcome this birthday because it gives me a happy occasion to thank you for all I have gained from your writings. Best of all in these days were the courage and optimism of your recent broadcasts.

Evamaria joins me in sending you, with our gratitude, our warmest greetings.

> Yours ever
> Noel Brailsford

[undated] May 1952

My dear Brailsford

Thank you for your letter of May 19. I owe much to you. Your review of my *Social Reconstruction* encouraged me more than any other at a time when I very much needed encouragement. I caused fury in Cambridge by quoting from your *War of Steel and Gold* a passage showing how much parsons and such were making out of armaments. The fury was of a sort of which I was glad to cause. I am very glad you have liked my recent broadcasts. Please convey my thanks to Mrs Brailsford as well as to yourself.

> Yours ever
> Bertrand Russell

From Ernest Jones, the psycho-analyst

> The Plat
> Elsted, Nr. Midhurst, Sx.
> February 20, 1955

Dear Bertrand Russell

What pleasure you have given to a host of people by your characteristically courageous, forthright and penetrating observations in today's *Observer*. You and W. K. Clifford greatly resemble each other in these attributes. I wonder how much the study of mathematics conduced to them in both of you. Your concluding paragraph might be a paraphrase of the concluding one in his *Lectures and Essays*, a copy of which I enclose in case you have mislaid his book. Many of his Essays could very well be reprinted to-day. It is sad to think that the eighty years since he wrote them have shown such little progress in the apprehension of the clear principles he enunciated.

By the way, he quotes elsewhere Coleridge's pungent aphorism: 'He who begins by loving Christianity better than Truth, will proceed by loving his own sect or Church better than Christiantiy, and end in loving himself better than all.'

> Yours very sincerely
> Ernest Jones

The Plat
Elsted, Nr. Midhurst. Sx.
April 25, 1955

Dear Bertrand Russell

In your luminous essay on Einstein in the *Observer* there is one sentence which I am a little inclined to question: it is about his being surprisingly indifferent to empirical confirmations. The following is a quotation from a letter he wrote to Freud in April 1936:

'*Bis vor Kurzem war mir nur die spekulative Kraft Ihrer Gedankengänge sowie der gewaltige Einfluss auf die Weltanschauung der Gegenwart klar geworden, ohne mir über den Wahrheitswert Ihrer Theorien klar werden zu können. In letzter Zeit aber hatte ich Gelegenheit von einigen an sich geringfügigen Fällen zu hören, die jegliche abweichende Auslegung (von der Verdrängungslehre abweichend) ausschliessen. Dies empfand ich als beglückend; denn es ist stets beglückend, wenn eine grosse und schöne Idee sich als in der Wirklichkeit zutreffend erweist.*'[1]

I had taken the concluding sentence to be based on his own experience, such as the 1919 bending of light, etc.

If a subscription or the use of my name could make any contribution to the magnificent campaign you inaugurated in Rome pray command me.

Yours sincerely
Ernest Jones

Miss Graves was a deeply religious lady who surprised me by her tolerance. I first came in contact with her over Chinese affairs. Afterwards she was chiefly concerned with Latin America.

From Anna Melissa Graves

921 Jahncke Ave.
Covington, Louisiana
USA
February 24, 1957

Dear Lord Russell

I have not heard from Victor Haya de la Torre, that is I have not had

---

[1] 'Until recently I could only apprehend the speculative power of your train of thought, together with its enormous influence on the *Weltanschauung* of the present era, without being in a position to form a definite opinion about the amount of truth it contains. Not long ago, however, I had the opportunity of hearing about a few instances, not very important in themselves, which in my judgment exclude any other interpretation than that provided by the theory of repression. I was delighted to come across them; since it is always delightful when a great and beautiful conception proves to be consonant with reality.'

a letter, but he sent me an account of himself which appeared in *The Observer*, and from that account or 'interview' he had evidently made the pilgrimage to see you. I am glad for I am sure that seeing you and meeting you was – or should have been – of real benefit to him. I hope you did not think the time you gave him wasted.

In this 'interview' he said you were so 'true' and 'hopeful'. He does not need the example of optimism, having always been a believer in a better time coming; but most Latin Americans – perhaps all politicians of every land need the example of anyone to whom Truth means as much as it does to you. I am very glad he recognised *that* first of all in you.

I wonder if you remember I asked you if you could to return his letter to me, asking me to ask you to receive him. It was enclosed in my second note to you and you answered the first note. It would be very natural if you thought the second note did not need an answer; but if you have not destroyed or mislaid Victor's letter I should be grateful if you could return it; but if it is lost that would not be at all a serious matter.

I should also be grateful if you told me your impression of him. I think I am going to Los Angeles, California, to live with Anna Louise Strong. I think I can do more for the Negroes here after having lived here than I could if I stayed. If one does what one longs to do, one often gets them into trouble. I think the condition here is worse than it is (or rather worse than it was when Reginald Reynolds wrote his book) worse here than in South Africa, of course not worse than in Kenya, but in South Africa the non-Africans (British and Boers) who wish to treat the Africans justly seem freer to – seemed freer to – work for justice than one is here. Eastland is very determined to call all who are working for justice to the Negroes – 'Communists', 'Agents of Moscow'. But it is not the Eastlands who are so dangerous, it is the cultured charming 'White-Southerners'. They could end all the injustice, but then they would not be themselves if they did. They can't open their eyes, because they don't dare.

Very sincerely yours, and gratefully for giving time to Victor
Anna Melissa Graves

From Clement Davies

31 Evelyn Mansions
Carlisle Place
London S.W.1
[Dec. 24, 54]

My dear Bertrand Russell
May I be allowed to say 'thank you' for your splendid Broadcast speech last night. I say my 'thank you' most sincerely. What memories

you stirred!! and how my thoughts went speeding along with yours at a super-sonic rate. Yes, we have accomplished much that I longed to see done 50 and more years ago – and how one battled in those days against great odds, while, today, those very opponents not only are on our side but actually are so enthusiastic about the reforms that they claim they originated them.

The remembrance of those days and the changes that have been brought about and secured, hearten me with regard to the International Situation. The odds against your and my ideals and against adopting Reason instead of Force as the arbiter in human differences are so apparently strong that our struggles might seem hopeless. But here again, we shall see and see soon a great change and if our experience in home affairs is repeated in International affairs, then those who today oppose us and reject our remedies, will not only accept the remedies but claim that they and they alone were responsible for them and that they brought to suffering humanity the Peace which all men & women desire.

Well; I hope I am right, and I shall cheer them loud and long, just as I today cheer my opponents who long ago said they would not lick stamps.

Again my most grateful thanks. With our united warmest regards & wishes to you both

Very sincerely yours
Clement Davies

31 Evelyn Mansions
Carlisle Place
London, S.W.1
Sept. 19, 55

My dear Bertrand Russell

You have tempted me into reminiscence by recalling your excursion into the political arena against the redoubtable Joe Chamberlain and his raging tearing propaganda in favour of tariffs and ultra nationalism.

My first effort was also against the formidable Joe. It was in November 1899 and I was of the very ripe experienced age of 15. I went on the platform at a Tory meeting to denounce the South African War – my oratory was not allowed to last long in spite of a strenuous effort, and I returned home with black eyes (two) and a bloody nose. It was not so much an anti-war effort as a Defence of the Boers. Little did I dream that they would misuse the Freedom which we wanted them to have and which we restored to them in 1906 – to the disadvantage of the Black and Coloured Africans.

With warmest regards & best wishes from us to you both

Ever yours sincerely
Clement Davies

PRESS CONFERENCE

by

THE EARL RUSSELL

at

Caxton Hall, Westminster

on

Saturday, 9th July, 1955

Professor J. ROTBLAT: Ladies and gentlemen, this conference was called by Lord Bertrand Russell in order to make public a statement signed by a number of scientists on the significance of nuclear warfare. I hope that each of you received a copy of the statement. I am going to call on Lord Russell to give you a short summary of this statement and afterwards it will be open to you to ask questions relating to this topic. Lord Russell.

Earl RUSSELL: Ladies and gentlemen, the purpose of this conference is to bring to your notice, and through you to the notice of the world, a statement signed by eight of the most eminent scientists in the field cognate to nuclear warfare, about the perils that are involved in nuclear warfare and the absolute necessity therefore of avoiding war.

I will just read you a brief abstract here which I think you already have:

'The accompanying statement, which has been signed by some of the most eminent scientific authorities in different parts of the world, deals with the perils of a nuclear war. It makes it clear that neither side can hope for victory in such a war, and that there is a very real danger of the extermination of the human race by dust and rain from radio-active clouds. It suggests that neither the public nor the governments of the world are adequately aware of the danger. It points out that an agreed prohibition of nuclear weapons, while it might be useful in lessening tension, would not afford a solution, since such weapons would certainly be manufactured and used in a great war in spite of previous agreements to the contrary. The only hope for mankind is the avoidance of war. To call for a way of thinking which shall make such avoidance possible is the purpose of this statement.

The first move came as a collaboration between Einstein and myself. Einstein's signature was given in the last week of his life. Since his death I have approached men of scientific competence both in the East and in the West, for political disagreements should not influence men of science in estimating what is probable, but some of those approached have not yet replied. I am bringing the warning pronounced by the signatories to the notice of all the powerful Governments of the world in the earnest hope that they may agree to allow their citizens to survive.'

Now I should like to say just a little about the genesis of this statement. I think it was an outcome of a broadcast which I gave on the 23rd December last year on the BBC on the perils of nuclear war. I had appreciative letters from various people, among others from Professor Joliot-Curie, the eminent French man of science, and I was particularly pleased at getting an appreciative letter from him because of his being a noted Communist.

I thought that one of the purposes that I had in view was to build a bridge between people of opposing political opinions. That is to say, to unite men of science on a statement of facts which would leave out all talk of what people thought in the matter of politics. I wrote to Einstein suggesting that eminent men of science should do something dramatic about nuclear war, and I got a reply from him saying that he agreed with every word. I therefore drew up a draft, after consultation with a certain number of people, which I sent to Einstein and he – being already not in very good health – suggested, I quote his own phrase, that I 'should regard myself as dictator of the enterprise' because I think chiefly his health was not equal to doing it. When I sent him the draft he replied, 'I am gladly willing to sign your excellent statement'. I received this letter on the very day of his death and after I had received news of his death, so that this was I suppose about the very last public act of his life.

The aims of drawing up the statement were to keep to what men of science as such can pronounce upon, to avoid politics and thus to get signatures both from the Right and from the Left. Science ought to be impartial, and I thought that one could get a body of agreement among men of differing politics on the importance of avoiding nuclear war, and I think that in that respect this document is fairly successful.

There are, apart from myself, eight signatories[1] of the document. All eight are exceedingly eminent in the scientific world. Most of them are nuclear physicists, some in a field which is very important in this connection, geneticists, and men who know about mutations caused by radiation, a very important subject which arises when you are considering nuclear warfare. But they were chosen solely and only for their scientific eminence and with no other view.

I applied to eighteen, I think, altogether and of these, half, or nearly half, eight[2] in fact, agreed. Some I have not yet heard from for various reasons. In particular, I applied to the most eminent of Chinese physicists, Dr Le Szi Kuang, and I have not yet had his answer. None of the

[1] Ten – Prof. Max Born and Prof. Linus Pauling to be added.
[2] Ten.

answers I have received were unsympathetic. Those who did not sign had various good reasons, for instance, that they had official positions or were engaged in some official work which made it difficult, but nobody either of Right or of the Left replied in a manner that was unsympathetic.

I had one signature from Professor Infeld of the University of Warsaw, who was joint author with Einstein of two books. I had not a signature, but a very sympathetic letter, from Skobeltsyn of Moscow. Professor Joliot-Curie was, in the first-place, son-in-law of the discoverer of radium, but he does not depend on that for his fame, he is a Nobel prizewinner. He is the sixth of the eight who has got the Nobel Prize for work of scientific character; and the other two I think probably will get the Nobel Prize before very long! That is the order of eminence of these men.

Mr Joliot-Curie made two reservations, one of which was of some importance, the other not so important. I spoke of the necessity for limitations of sovereignty and he wants it added that these limitations are to be agreed by all and in the interests of all, and that is a statement which I entirely agreed to. Then there is another reservation that he made. I say, 'Shall we put an end to the human race: or shall mankind renounce war ?' and he wants to say, 'Shall mankind renounce war as a means of settling differences between states ?' With these limitations he agreed to sign the document.

Professor Muller also made a very small reservation that seemed only to be explaining what I had meant.

I will say just a few words about these men, some of whom possibly are not so well known in the journalistic world as they are in the scientific world. They consist of two British scientists, two Americans – Einstein himself, whom I do not reckon among Americans, because Einstein's nationality is somewhat universal – one Pole, one Frenchman and one Japanese. Professor Rotblat I am very happy to have here. He is, as you know, Director of Research in Nuclear Physics in Liverpool.[1] He did a very interesting piece of what you might almost call detective work about the Bikini bomb. Those of you who are old enough may possibly remember that in 1945 people were quite shocked by the atom bomb. Well that seems now ancient history if you think of the atom bomb as something like bows and arrows.

We advanced from that to the H-bomb which was very much worse than the atom bomb and then it turned out, at first I think through the detective work of Professor Rotblat and afterwards by the admission of the American authorities, that the bomb exploded at Bikini was very much worse than an H-bomb. The H-bomb now is ancient history. You have a twofold trigger arrangement. You have first uranium 235 to

[1] Prof. of Physics in the University of London.

set off the hydrogen. Then you have the hydrogen to set off uranium 238, of which there are vast slag heaps discarded in producing uranium 235. Now we use uranium 238 for the purpose, it is very much cheaper to make, the bombs are very much more destructive when they are made, and so you see science advances rapidly. So far the Bikini bomb is the latest thing, but we cannot tell where we are going to come to.

I think that this statement, as I conceive it, is only a first step. It will be necessary to go on to get the men of science to make authoritative pronouncements on the facts and I think that should be followed by an International Congress of men of science from all scientific countries at which the signatories would, I hope, propose some such resolution as I have suggested at the end of this statement. I think resolutions with something of those terms could be suggested at the various national congresses that take place in due time. I think that the men of science should make the public and the governments of the world aware of the facts by means of a widespread popular campaign. You know it is a very difficult thing to get men of science to embark on popular campaigns; they are not used to that sort of thing and it does not come readily to them, but it is their duty, I think, at this time to make the public aware of things; they have to persuade the world to avoid war, at first by whatever expedients may suggest themselves, but ultimately by some international machinery that shall make the avoidance of war not a matter of day-to-day expedients but of world organisation. I think they should emphasise that science, which has come to have a rather sinister meaning in the minds of the general public, I think, if once this question of war were out of the way, would be capable of conferring the most enormous benefits upon mankind and making the world a very much happier place than it has ever been before. I think they should emphasise that as well as the dangers that arise through war.

I am here to answer questions, and I should be very happy to do my best to answer any questions that any of you may wish to ask.

Chapter 16

Trafalgar Square

During the first five months of 1957 I made a great many broadcasts for the BBC. Almost the last of these was an interview between Alan Wood and myself and a representative of the BBC in connection with Alan's publication of his biography of me. Alan was bitterly disappointed by this interview. His experience of broadcasting was less than mine and so he was considerably surprised when the lady who represented the BBC asked us questions which she had not asked at our rehearsal, indeed which concerned subjects such as my private life. We were both somewhat disconcerted by her questions. However, the book itself had a good reception in spite of being rather tepidly advertised. It seems to me to be an excellent piece of work.

I very much hope that Alan was happy in the reviews given to the book. We launched it pleasantly among some of my old friends and relations at a small party at Millbank on my birthday. This was almost the last time that I saw Alan. He fell very ill shortly after this and died in October. A little over two months later, his wife, Mary, died. It was a heart-breaking loss. They were young and happy and clever and able, and full of plans for their future and that of their two small sons. Their loss to me was incalculable. I not only was very fond of them, but had come to depend upon their knowledge of everything to do with me and their sympathetic understanding, and I greatly enjoyed their companionship.

It must be said that there were limitations to Alan's understanding of the matters discussed in my books. This showed particularly in regard to political matters. I regarded him as rather conservative, and he regarded me as more radical than I was or am. When I argued that everybody ought to have a vote, he thought that I was maintaining that all men are equal in ability. I only disabused him of this belief by pointing out that I had supported eugenics, which is concerned with differences in natural ability. Such disagreements, however, never marred our friendship, and never intruded in purely philosophical conversations.

These sad happenings and the fact that my wife fell ill of a bad heart attack in early June dislocated and slowed up our activities for some months. I got through little that could be of any conceivable public interest for some time. By November, however, my concern with international affairs had boiled up. I felt that I must again do something to urge at least a modicum of common sense to break into the policies of the two Great Powers, Russia and America. They seemed to be blindly, but with determination, careering down a not very primrose-strewn path to destruction, a destruction that might – probably would – engulf us all. I wrote an open letter, to President Eisenhower and Premier Khrushchev, addressing them as 'Most Potent Sirs'. In it I tried to make clear the fact that the things which they held in common were far more numerous and far more important than their differences, and that they had much more to gain than to lose by co-operation. I believed then, as I still believe, in the necessity of co-operation between nations as the sole method of avoiding war; and avoidance of war is the only means of avoiding disaster. This, of course, involves rather disagreeable concessions by all nations. A decade later, Russia seemed to have recognised the need of co-operation – except, possibly, in relations to her co-Marxist State, China. The United States continued to confound co-operation with domination. But, in 1958, I had hope, though slight hope, of both Great Powers coming to their senses, and in this letter I tried to lay my case before them.

Almost at once a reply came from Premier Khrushchev. No answer came from President Eisenhower. Two months later John Foster Dulles replied for him. This reply stung Premier Khrushchev into writing to me again answering various points made by Mr Dulles. All these letters appeared in the *New Statesmen*. They were soon published in book form with an introduction by that paper's editor, Kingsley Martin, and a final reply from me to Mr Dulles and Mr Khrushchev. The letters speak for themselves and my final reply gives my point of view on them. The righteously adamantine surface of Mr Dulles's mind as shown in his letter filled me with greater foreboding than did the fulminations and, sometimes, contradictions of Mr Khrushchev. The latter seemed to me to show some underlying understanding of alternatives and realities; the former, none.

During that autumn, George Kennan had been giving the Reith Lectures over the BBC and saying some excellent things drawn with acumen from his wide and first-hand knowledge of American and Russian policies. Early in December a group of us met with Kingsley Martin at his invitation to talk things over. As far as I remember it was at this meeting that the first glimmerings flickered of what was to become the Campaign for Nuclear Disarmament. A meeting of the sponsors of the National Council for the Abolition of Nuclear Weapons Tests was held at the house of Canon John Collins in Amen Court and the CND was formally started early in January, 1958. The officers were to be: Canon Collins, the Chairman; Mrs Peggy Duff, the Secretary;

and myself, the President. An Executive Committee was formed comprising some of those leaders already established in anti-nuclear movements and a certain number of other interested notables. There had been for some time various associations working to overcome the dangers with which the international scene was fraught. The CND proposed to take them all in – or at least almost all.

The CND was publicly launched at a large meeting at the Central Hall, Westminster, on February 17, 1958. So many people attended this meeting that there had to be overflow meetings. It seems now to many people as if the CND has been part of the national scene from the beginning of time, and it has lost its lustre and energy through familiarity. But in its early days its information and reasoning were not only sincere but were fresh and commanded considerable attention among a variety of individuals and circles important in the nation. And the first meeting went off with great éclat and success. Moreover, interest in the CND quickly spread. Soon there were committees formed in different parts of the country and then Regional Committees. Many meetings were held, at some of which I spoke. I remember, in particular, one at Manchester in 1959 at which Lord Simon of Wythenshawe was in the chair.

I saw much of Lord Simon in those days and until his death in October, 1960, as he was greatly concerned by the nuclear peril and worked hard to make the dangers known. He arranged a debate on the subject in the House of Lords and held a great number of meetings and press conferences at his London flat. He was a member of the executive committee of the CND and we saw eye to eye in most matters to do with it. He became, as I already was, an upholder of the activities of the Direct Action Committee. We both believed that the dangers must be called to the attention of the public in as many ways as possible and that if we stuck to merely meetings and even marches, no matter how admirable they might be, we should end by preaching only to the already converted. The chairman of the CND did not approve of civil disobedience and so, though nominally the Direct Action Committee was to be tolerated, it could not be aided openly by the CND. The latter did not, for instance, take part in the Aldermaston March, as it was staged by the Direct Action Committee in 1958. The march proved a success, and the CND took it over lock, stock and barrel the following year and made, of course, a much larger and more important thing of it. I was not able to attend the 1959 march or the subsequent meeting in Trafalgar Square, but the following year I spoke in the Square at the end of the march. I wished, in these years, that I had been young enough to take part in the marches. Later, they seemed to me to be degenerating into something of a yearly picnic. Though individual marchers were as sincere as ever in their endeavours and as admirable, the march was quite ineffective in achieving their aim, which was to call serious attention to and spread the movement. For the most part, the march became a subject of boredom or distress or hilarity, and converted very few of those hitherto unconverted. It was useful, nevertheless, as I think it still is, in continuing, if not enlarging, the movement. New and fresh forms of opposition to dangerous nuclear policies must be sought constantly in order to obtain converts and to catch and hold the interest of people of very diverse outlook.

Shortly after this 1960 Aldermaston March, the Summit Meeting between Eisenhower and Khrushchev took place – and crashed. We had all had high hopes of it and its break-up following the U2 incident was a blow to us. The more we learned of the skulduggery behind it the greater its foreboding quality became. It augured ill for progress towards co-operation, let alone towards disarmament. It seemed more than ever as if new methods must be sought to impress upon the public the increasingly precarious state of international affairs before people relapsed into frustrated apathy. But what this new means could be I did not see.

The CND had been working for unilateral disarmament, believing that if Great Britain gave up her part in the nuclear race and even demanded the departure of United States bases from her soil, other nations might follow suit. It was a slim hope, and still is, but none-the-less it was, and is, a hope. As such, it seemed worth following up. The Campaign also hoped to persuade not only the general public to this way of thinking but also the Government. As most of its upholders were drawn from the Labour Party, it went to work upon the Parliamentary Labour Party. My own view was that the matter was one that transcends Party politics and even national boundaries. As this reasonable view, as it seemed to me, failed to grip the public imagination, I was willing to uphold the Campaign in its efforts. The means towards the end that we both desired mattered less than its achievement. Perhaps, I thought, if the Labour Party *could* be persuaded to support the Campaign, we might be a short step towards the goal.

I had put my point of view clearly in the introduction to my book *Common Sense and Nuclear Warfare* which I wrote during the summer of 1958, and published early in 1959. I had been encouraged during 1958 by receiving the Kalinga Prize, at Unesco in Paris as I could not travel to India. (To be sure the French physicist who was deputed to bear-lead me on that occasion remarked comfortingly to his wife after I had been expounding my views: 'Never mind, my dear, by next year France will be able to explode her own bomb.') And the continued and growing success of the Pugwash movement, as well as the interest shown in the open correspondence with Khrushchev and Eisenhower (Dulles) were encouraging. I continued my search, as I have done since, to find fresh approaches through which to try to sway public opinion, including governmental opinion. All that I had succeeded in doing in 1958 touched only this or that relatively small circle of people. The CND at that time gave hope that a more general public could be reached. It seemed to me then as it does today that governmental policies must be regarded in the light of common sense. They must be shorn of red tape and 'tradition' and general mystique. They would be seen then to be leading, as they are, only to probable general destruction.

The policies that were needed were those dictated by common sense. If the public could be shown this clearly, I had a faint hope that they might insist upon governmental policies being brought into accord with common sense. I wrote my *Common Sense and Nuclear Warfare* in his hope. The book was fairly widely read, I believe, and commended. But it did not tackle the question as to exactly how each individual could make his opinion known and influence policy-making, a fact that left some readers dissatisfied. I had one moment of high hope when the Minister of Defence, Duncan Sandys, wrote commending the book and saying that he would like to talk with me about it. He was a Conservative, and a policy-maker in a national Government, and had collaborated in a pamphlet on the subject himself. But when I went to see him, he said, 'It is a good book, but what is needed is not only nuclear disarmament but the banning of war itself'. In vain I pointed out the passage in my book in which I had said that the only way to ensure the world against nuclear war was to end war. He continued to believe that I could not have said anything so intelligent. He cast my other arguments aside. I came away discouraged. I realised that most of the already informed people who read my book would read it with a bias so strong that they would take in only what they wished to take in. For the following months, therefore, I returned to the piecemeal business of speaking at meetings, CND and other, and broadcasting, and to the pleasures of my own life.

To celebrate my eighty-seventh birthday, we drove down through Bath and Wells and Glastonbury to Dorset. We visited the swannery and gardens at Abbotsbury where, by chance, we witnessed a peacock's nuptial dance, precisely articulated, one of the most enchanting and beautiful ballets that I have ever seen. We made a sentimental pilgrimage to the small Italianate eighteenth century Kingston Russell House which I had not seen before. I thought it most perfect and most perfectly set in its garden and valley. I wished immensely that I could myself live in it. I seldom feel this kind of envy, but Kingston Russell House touched me deeply. And I was interested in hunting out the old farm buildings and the village where my family had begun its more notable career. It was an altogether satisfactory expedition, but for some reason that I have now forgotten had to be cut short. So, to complete our allotted holiday, we went another extended drive after my birthday, this time in the Peak District. This, however, from the point of view of enjoyment was a complete failure. Places that should have been lonely and quiet were teeming with holiday-makers like ourselves; places that should have seemed full of life even though quiet, like Jane Austen's Bakewell, were tarnished by convention meetings. Perhaps it all seemed dreary because we struck the wrong note in the beginning by visiting Alderley where my Stanley grandparents had had an estate. The house had been destroyed. Only the gardens remained, in derelict state. The Government had taken it over for some unholy project. I have a small table, made for my mother and a larger one made for my father by the estate carpenter, from the Alderley Doomsday Oak when it had to be cut down. But the whole place made me melancholy. It was very desolate.

Early in 1960 we went to Copenhagen for a short time for me to receive the Sonning Prize for contribution to European Culture, bestowed by the University of Copenhagen. The speech of acceptance gave me a chance to outline my attitude towards present cultural differences, based upon the history of past changes in cultures. If this were reflected upon and adopted as being valid, as I think it is, it would change for the better present co-operation between nations and would increase the possibility of further and effective co-operation. My speech was published later under the title 'Old and New Cultures' in my book *Fact and Fiction*.

The occasion of the prize-giving was a pleasant one with a reception and a fine State dinner following it. My wife was seated between the Minister of Education, who declared himself to be unable to speak English, and Professor Niels Bohr, upon whom the burden of conversation therefore fell. He took his duties seriously and talked steadily through the banquet. He was very difficult to understand, we were told, even when speaking his native Danish to Danes; and, in English, I had always found it extremely hard to follow him as he spoke very quickly. My wife found it impossible. That was exasperating enough, since he was clearly talking of things that she would have wished to hear about. But, far worse on such an occasion, as he talked, he leaned further and further towards her, absorbed in his own words. Finally, he was eating the delicious confections from her plate and drinking her wine whilst the notable company of diners looked on, smiling and entranced. It was a tribute to his charm that she continued to like him, as I did.

I have seldom enjoyed my many speeches and articles during these years as they usually concerned nuclear matters. But now and again I have made a pleasurable excursion into other matters as I did at Copenhagen. I even ventured, a little later, into Shakespearean exigesis in a letter to *The Times*. For some weeks there had raged a discreet and venomous correspondence concerning the probable person to whom the printed sonnets were dedicated. The initials W. H. were interpreted this way and that by great stretches of imagination and with much learning. It seemed to me that, like Melchisedek, Mr W. H. was a clerical error for Mr W. S. who was, in truth, 'the onlie begetter' of the sonnets. I ventured, hesitantly and half in fun, to put this view forward. No one took it up and no further letters appeared on the subject. I fear that I spoiled the scholarly fun.

One evening I broadcast over the Asian service in company with a number of Asian students. As I walked down the corridor in the hotel where the occasion took place, a small, bird-like lady leapt from one of the huge red plush thrones placed at intervals along the wall, stood before me and declaimed, 'And I saw Shelley plain', and sat down. I tottered on, shattered, but delighted.

I did a series of TV interviews with Woodrow Wyatt as interlocutor that came out in book form as *Bertrand Russell Speaks his Mind*. It gave me a chance to say a good deal that I wanted to say about international affairs as well as much else to a wide audience in various parts of the world. In February, 1960, I had a debate with the Indian scientist Bhabha and Teller, the Father of the Bomb, at which Ed Murrow was the interlocutor on CBS. I found it a most distressing occasion. The debate was difficult, since we were each speaking from our own country and could not follow the facial expression or reaction of each other as we talked. Still more disconcerting, I was inhibited by my intense dislike of Teller and by what I felt to be disingenuous flattery. I came away from the BBC studio feeling that I had let down all those who agreed with my point of view by not putting up the better show that the facts of our case warranted. Another disappointing TV occasion was a BBC discussion of nuclear matters by Mrs Roosevelt, Lord Boothby, Mr Gaitskell, and myself. I was horrified to hear Mrs Roosevelt enunciate the belief that it would be better, and that she would prefer, to have the human race destroyed than to have it succumb to Communism. I came away thinking that I could not have heard aright. Upon reading her remarks in the next morning's papers I had to face that fact that she really had expressed this dangerous view.

I had a controversy with an American philosopher named Sidney Hook at this time that was one which both of us found difficult to conduct on logical lines. He was a Menshevic who had become apprehensive of Russia ruling the world. He thought this so dreadful that it would be better the human race should cease to exist. I combated this view on the ground that we do not know the future, which, so long as Man survives, may be immensely better than the past. I instanced the times of Genghiz Khan and Kublai Khan, separated by only a generation, but one horrible, the other admirable. But there were plenty of contrary instances that he could have adduced, in view of which a definite decision was impossible. I maintained, however, that any chance of a better world depended upon hope, and was on this account to be preferred. This was not a *logical* argument, but I thought that most people would find it convincing. Several years later, Hook again attacked me publicly, but this time in such a manner that no comment from me was necessary. It amused me, however, that for his defence of 'freedom' and his attack on my views on Vietnam, he chose as his vehicle a journal later admitted to be financed by the Central Intelligence Agency.[1]

The attitude of most of humanity towards its own destruction surprised me. In December, 1959, I had read Neville Shute's *On the Beach* and I attended a private viewing of its film. I was cast down by the deliberate turning away it displayed from the horrible, harsh facts entailed by nuclear war – the disease and suffering caused by poisoned air and water and soil, the looting and murder likely among a population in anarchy with no means of communication, and all the probable evils and pain. It was like the prettified stories that were sometimes told about trench warfare during the First World War. Yet the film was put out and praised by people who meant to make the situation clear, not to belittle the horror. I was particularly distressed by the fact that I myself had praised the film directly after seeing it in what I came to think the mistaken opinion that a little was better than nothing. All that sort of thing does, I came to think, is to make familiar and rob of its true value what should carry a shock of revulsion. Irony such as that in *Dr Strangelove* or *Oh, What a Lovely War* is a different matter. That does cause people to think, at least for a short time.

By the summer of 1960 it seemed to me as if Pugwash and CND and the other methods that we had tried of informing the public had reached the limit of their effectiveness. It might be possible to so move the general public that it would demand *en masse*, and therefore irresistibly, the remaking of present governmental policies, here in Britain first and then elsewhere in the world. For a time, however, I had to put my bothers behind me, especially as they were so shapeless

[1] The *New Leader* received 3,000 dollars from Chiang Kai-shek's treasury for publishing an article hostile to China. Later it prepared the book *The Strategy of Deception: A Study in World Wide Communist Tactics* and was secretly paid 12,000 dollars by the US Government. When the US information Agency asked a House Appropriations Sub-Committee to increase its allowance for 'book development' from 90,000 dollars to 195,000 dollars, the Agency assured the legislators that the funds would go for books 'written to our own specifications' and having 'strong anti-communist content' (*The New York Times*, May 3 1964).

and amorphous, as my daughter and her husband and their children came to visit me. I had not seen them for a long time, not since I was last in the United States. Since that time my son-in-law had become a full fledged Minister in the Episcopal Church – he had been a layman and in the State Department – and he was taking his whole family to Uganda where he had been called as a missionary. My daughter had also become very religious and was whole-heartedly in sympathy with his aspirations. I myself, naturally, had little sympathy with either of them on this score. When I had wished to send a sum of money to them shortly before they came to England, and had to go to the Bank of England to arrange the transfer, my request was greeted with smiles and sometimes laughter at so old and confirmed an atheist wishing to help someone to become a Minister of the Gospel. But about many things we agreed, especially in liberal politics, and I loved my daughter dearly and was fond of her family. They were to stay in England for two years to prepare for their mission work, and each July they came to North Wales where they were put up in one of the Portmeirion Hotel cottages and we saw them daily. This, with other smaller happenings, absorbed most of my time during these two months.

Towards the end of July, 1960, I received my first visit from a young American called Ralph Schoenman. I had heard of some of his activities in relation to CND so I was rather curious to see him. I found him bursting with energy and teeming with ideas, and intelligent, if inexperienced and a little doctrinaire, about politics. Also, I liked in him, what I found lamentably lacking in many workers in the causes which I espoused, a sense of irony and the capability of seeing the humour in what was essentially very serious business. I saw that he was quickly sympathetic, and that he was impetuous. What I came only gradually to appreciate, what could only emerge with the passage of time, was his difficulty in putting up with opposition, and his astonishingly complete, untouchable self-confidence. I believed that intelligence working on experience would enforce the needed discipline. I did not at first fully understand him but I happened to be approved of by him and, in turn, to approve of what he was then working for. And for his continued generosity towards me personally I was, and can still only be, deeply grateful. His mind moved very quickly and firmly and his energy appeared to be inexhaustible. It was a temptation to turn to him to get things done. At the particular time of our first meetings he acted as a catalyst for my gropings as to what could be done to give our work in the CND new life. He was very keen to start a movement of civil disobedience that might grow into a mass movement of general opposition to governmental nuclear policies so strong as to force its opinions upon the Government directly. It was to be a *mass* movement, no matter from how small beginnings. In this it was new, differing from the old Direct Action Committee's aspirations in that theirs were too often concerned with individual testimony by way of salving individual consciences.

The scheme seemed to me to have great possibilities and the more I talked with Schoenman the more favourable to it I became. I was aware that the chairman of the CND did not approve of civil disobedience and had little sympathy with even the Direct Action Committee. I also knew that the CND tolerated and was coming more and more to support in words if not in action its activities. I discussed the matter with the chairman. He did not dispute the possible efficiency of civil disobedience or oppose my upholding such a new movement. He only urged me not to make any announcement about this fresh effort till after the Conference of the Labour Party when he hoped that the Party might 'go unilateral' and take up at least some of our doctrines. To this I readily agreed.

Knowing that the chairman would neither oppose nor aid the new movement, it did not occur to me to consult him about our day to day preparations. I went to work with Schoenman to prepare a list of people who might be approached to uphold such a movement. Letters went out to them over my name. I was very insistent that letters should go to no one who was not known to us as being sympathetic, but, unfortunately, mistakes were made. One letter was sent to someone with a name similar to the intended recipient but with a different address and entirely, unhappily, different views. He at once sent our letter to the *Evening Standard* with a scathing letter of his own about our activities and intentions. This was published considerably before our plans were thoroughly formed or the participants gathered, and worse still, before the chairman thought the project should be revealed. There was a big meeting in Trafalgar Square on September 24th at which I spoke. Before it took place, I suggested to the chairman that I speak of the proposed new mass movement of civil disobedience within the CND. He replied that it might injure CND's chances of influencing the Labour Conference. I said that I would consult Frank Cousins, the head of the Transport Workers' Union, and if he felt it in any way dangerous to the desires of CND, I would not touch upon the subject. Frank Cousins replied to my letter briefly, saying that it did not matter one way or the other what I did or said. I informed the chairman of Cousins's letter and of my consequent intention to speak of the new movement. He accepted this, and I spoke of the new movement in Trafalgar Square.

After the announcement in the *Evening Standard* of the proposed mass movement of civil disobedience, it was necessary to hurry through our plans. But the event caused a great uproar. The chairman of CND made statements to his friends and to the Executive Committee and to the press which, in effect, charged me with starting a new movement behind his back and one not permissible within the rulings of CND. During the first week of October, I met with him daily for many hours at my house in Hasker Street to try to work out some *modus vivendi*. He brought with him to these meetings a friend who was not an upholder of methods of civil disobedience, to put it mildly, so I asked a member of the CND Executive Committee who professed then to be in sympathy with me, to come as balance. At my insistence, because there had been so many allegations as to what I had said and not said, a tape recording was taken of these meetings, a copy of which was sent to the CND offices for the chairman and the original of which I kept.

By October 7th we had come to an agreement which would permit us to continue to work together and gave a statement to that effect to the press. But within a short time it became evident to me that I could not continue in my position of president of the CND, which necessitated work with its chairman, and that, if only to preserve the harmonious working of the CND itself, I must resign. This I did in a letter to the press, following a letter to the chairman.

The result of all this was, for me, a shower – a storm – of letters and visits from upholders of the CND throughout the country, expostulating with me and, most of them, accusing me of causing a split in the CND. This surprised me, as I had no intention of doing so. Nor do I think that I did. Moreover, I observed no weakening in its work owing to my action. It seemed to me that the CND would get on better if it had officers who saw, at least broadly, eye to eye than it would do under the leadership of those who patently did not trust each other. I had no intention, as I said and continued repeatedly to say, of withdrawing my support of much CND work. I sent statements to the various branches of the CND explaining this and the reasons for my actions. So far as I know, these statements went unread. At the CND Executive Meeting on November 5th, my resignation was accepted. One member, I was told, wished me to be sued for libel because of something I had said or written. He was persuaded not to proceed – which was perhaps, for my personal reputation, a pity. I continued to speak at meetings of the CND at which I was asked to speak, and I remained at the head of the Welsh CND. I withdrew only my interest in CND policy-making and any responsibility that, as its president, I had for the actions of its officers.

Meantime, the new movement towards mass civil disobedience had come to be called the Committee of 100. I had been in frequent touch with the small company of young people who were its early upholders. Inspired largely by the enthusiasm of Ralph Schoenman, this company had grown into a fairly large and steadily expanding group. Early in September he had brought the Rev. Michael Scott to see me. Scott was an active member of the Direct Action Committee and became one of the most stalwart members of the Committee of 100. I saw him as well as Schoenman almost daily, and he and I published under our joint names a leaflet entitled 'Act or Perish' which presents the nucleus of the policy of the Committee.

The early members of the Committee of 100 were for the most part drawn from the CND and the ranks of the Direct Action Committee. There was much activity and there were daily meetings, most of which I could not, and was not expected to, attend. I spoke for the Committee, I think, only at a meeting in Friends House, Euston, in October, 1960, and, again, at a press conference held in Kingsway Hall in December. Gradually, adherents were drawn from outside the fold, a process greatly accelerated both by the opposition widely felt to the establishment of the US Polaris Base at Holy Loch, and especially, by the announcement of the first proposed demonstration of civil disobedience. This was to be a 'sit-down' – of at least two thousand people, it was hoped – outside the Ministry of Defence on February 18th, 1961. It was planned that each succeeding demonstration would demand the participation of more people, the number increasing at each fresh demonstration until a really mass movement was achieved. To ensure a good beginning it was decided to pledge as many as possible to take part in the first sit-down.

The activity of the Committee was intense during the days preceding February 18th. Posters went up (and were torn down), people were stopped in the street and approached in pubs and cafés and were argued with till they were converted to the need of the coming demonstration. But of all this I only heard. I took part only in endless discussions.

I hope that no one who reads these pages will think that I am attempting to write a history of the Committee of 100 or of the CND or, indeed, of any other movement or public event. I am trying only to recount what I remember that affected my own life.

My enthusiasm was high for the work and preparations that were being made for February 18th, and I was in complete agreement with the plans and with the aspirations of the Committee. I have already written in this volume of my views of civil disobedience, and I stated them publicly in speeches and articles at this time, notably in an article in the *New Statesman* for February 17th. My sole misgivings were connected with the hurried and piece-meal way in which our policies had been worked out owing to their premature publication and with the dread lest it might be too difficult – impossible, perhaps – to avoid violence in such a crowd, considering the opposition that might be encountered. Passive resistance, it seemed to me, might be very difficult to inculcate amid such enthusiasm. In the event, it posed no difficulty.

The morning of February 18th was dark and drizzly and cold, and our spirits plummeted. If it rained, the numbers participating in the demonstration would undoubtedly dwindle in spite of the large nucleus already pledged to take part. But when we assembled in Trafalgar Square there was a great crowd. Precisely how great it was, it is impossible to say. The median number as reckoned by the press and the police and the Committee made it about 20,000. The speeches went well and quickly. Then began the march up Whitehall preceded by a large banner and managed with great skill by the Committee's marshals. It comprised a surging but calm and serious crowd of somewhat over 5,000 of those who had been in the Square. At one point we were held up by the police who tried to stop the march on the ground that it was obstructing traffic. The objection, however, manifestly did not hold, and the march proceeded. Finally, over 5,000 people were sitting or lying on the pavements surrounding the Ministry. And there we sat for about two hours till darkness had fallen, a very solid and quiet, if not entirely mute, protest against governmental nuclear policies. A good many people joined us during this time, and more came to have a look at us, and, of course, the press and TV people flocked about asking their questions. As soon as word came that the marchers had all become seated, Michael Scott and Schoenman and I took a notice that we had prepared and stuck it on the Ministry door. We learned that the Government had asked the Fire Department to use their hoses upon us. Luckily, the Fire Department refused. When six o'clock arrived, we called an end to the sit-down. A wave of exultation swept through the crowd. As we marched back towards Whitehall in the dusk and lamplight, past the cheering supporters, I felt very happy – we had accomplished what we set out to do that afternoon, and our serious purpose had been made manifest. I was moved, too, by the cheers that greeted me and by the burst of 'for he's a jolly good fellow' as I passed.

The demonstration was much more auspicious than we had any right to expect. During the next months the fortunes of the Committee prospered. Branch Committees were established about the country and in some foreign countries; and some countries developed their own Committees. All the correspondence entailed by this activity and by the necessary printing and dissemination of 'literature' (leaflets, statements, etc.) not to speak of the need to keep some kind of office, cost a good deal. This, of course, as it always does in any organisation without fixed membership or dues, meant much time wasted in raising funds. Nevertheless, and owing to the generous and often self-sacrificing voluntary efforts of many people, the Committee grew in strength.

To show my continued support of the CND, I spoke to the Youth CND of Birmingham in mid-March and again in mid-April. One of these speeches caused turmoil because of a remark that I made about our then Prime Minister. The remark was widely quoted out of context by the press. In context, it is merely a QED to the preceding argument. Unfortunately, by the time the uproar had broken, I had fallen ill and was unable to defend myself for some weeks, too late to cut any ice. I spoke, also, at the meeting in Trafalgar Square at the end of the Aldermaston March.

Towards the end of March, I had arranged with Penguin Books, who, in turn, had arranged with my usual publisher, Sir Stanley Unwin, to write a further book for them on nuclear matters and disarmament, carrying on my *Common Sense and Nuclear Warfare* and expanding parts of it. The new book was to be called *Has Man a Future?* and I began work on it at once. But it was interrupted by a series of recordings that I made in London and by the two Birmingham meetings and then by a very bad bout of shingles which prevented my doing any work whatsoever for some time. But during my convalescence I wrote a good deal of the new book, and it was finished in time to meet its first deadline. It was published in the autumn.

On August 6th, 'Hiroshima Day', the Committee of 100 arranged to have two meetings: a ceremony in the morning of laying a wreath upon the Cenotaph in Whitehall and, in the afternoon, a meeting for speeches to be made at Marble Arch. The former was carried out with dignity. We wished to remind people of the circumstances of the nuclear bomb at Hiroshima. We also thought that, in commemorating the British dead, we might call attention to the fact that it was up to the living to prevent their deaths from going for nothing. We hoped in the afternoon's speeches to support this point of view. To many people, however, to bracket the deaths at Hiroshima and Nagasaki with the deaths of those who fought the Japanese in the Second War was blasphemous. It is doubtful if many of these same people object to the statue of General Washington or of General Smuts being given places of public honour.

The meeting in Hyde Park was a lively one. The police had forbidden us to use microphones as their use was prohibited by Park rules. This ruling had been overlooked in many previous cases, but was firmly held to in our case. We had determined to try to use microphones, partly because we knew that they would be necessary to make ourselves heard, and partly to expose the odd discrepancy in the enforcement of Park rules. We were, after all, an organisation devoted to civil disobedience. I, therefore, started to speak through a microphone. A policeman quietly remonstrated. I persisted. And the microphone was removed by the police. We then adjourned the meeting, announcing that we would march to Trafalgar Square to continue it. All this we had planned, and the plan was carried out with some success. What we had not counted on was a thunderstorm of majestic proportions which broke as the crowd moved down Oxford Street and continued throughout most of the meeting in the Square.

A month later, as we returned from an afternoon's drive in North Wales, we found a pleasant, though much embarrassed, Police Sergeant astride his motorcycle at our front door. He delivered summonses to my wife and me to be at Bow Street on September 12th to be charged with inciting the public to civil disobedience. The summons was said to be delivered to all the leaders of the Committee but, in fact, it was delivered only to some of them. Very few who were summoned refused to appear.

We went up to London to take the advice of our solicitors and, even more important, to confer with our colleagues. I had no wish to become a martyr to the cause, but I felt that I should make the most of any chance to publicise our views. We were not so innocent as to fail to see that our imprisonment would cause a certain stir. We hoped that it might create enough sympathy for some, at least, of our reasons for doing as we had done to break through to minds hitherto untouched by them. We had obtained from our doctors statements of our recent serious illnesses which they thought would make long imprisonment disastrous. These we handed over to the barrister who was to watch our cases at Bow Street. No one we met seemed to believe that we should be condemned to gaol. They thought the Government would think that it would not pay them. But we, ourselves, did not see how they could fail to sentence us to gaol. For some time it had been evident that our doings irked the Government, and the police had been raiding the Committee office and doing a clumsy bit of spying upon various members who frequented it. The barrister thought that he could prevent my wife's and my incarceration entirely. But we did not wish either extreme. We instructed him to try to prevent our being let off scot-free, but, equally, to try to have us sentenced to not longer than a fortnight in prison. In the event, we were each sentenced to two months in gaol, a sentence which, because of the doctors' statements, was commuted to a week each.

Bow Street seemed like a stage set as we walked down it with our colleagues amid a mass of onlookers towards the Court at a little before 10.30 in the morning. People were crowded into most of the windows, some of which were bright with boxes of flowers. By contrast the scene in the courtroom looked like a Daumier etching. When the sentence of two months was pronounced upon me cries of 'Shame, shame, an old man of eighty-eight!' arose from the onlookers. It angered me. I knew that it was well meant, but I had deliberately incurred the punishment and, in any case, I could not see that age had anything to do with guilt. If anything, it made me the more guilty. The magistrate seemed to me nearer the mark in observing that, from his point of view, I was old enough to know better. But on the whole both the Court and the police behaved more gently to us all than I could have hoped. A policeman, before proceedings began, searched the building for a cushion for me to sit upon to mitigate the rigours of the narrow wooden bench upon which we perched. None could be found – for which I was thankful – but I took his effort kindly. I felt some of the sentences to be quite unduly harsh, but I was outraged only by the words of the magistrate to one of us who happened to be a Jewish refugee from Germany. The police witness appeared to me to cut a poor figure in giving evidence. Our people, I thought, spoke well and with dignity and very tellingly. Neither of these observations surprised me. And I was pleased to be permitted to say most of what I had planned to say.

By the end of the morning all our cases had been heard and we were given an hour for lunch. My wife and I returned to Chelsea. We emerged from the Court into cheering crowds, and to my confusion one lady rushed up and embraced me. But from the morning's remarks of the magistrate and his general aspect, we were not hopeful of getting off lightly when we returned to receive our sentences in the afternoon. As each person in alphabetical order was sentenced, he or she was taken out to the cells where we behaved like boys on holiday, singing and telling stories, the tension of incertitude relaxed, nothing more to try to do till we were carted away in our Black Marias.

It was my first trip in a Black Maria as the last time I had been gaoled I had been taken to Brixton in a taxi, but I was too tired to enjoy the novelty. I was popped into the hospital wing of the prison and spent most of my week in bed, visited daily by the doctor who saw that I got the kind of liquid food that I could consume. No one can pretend to a liking for being imprisoned, unless, possibly, for protective custody. It is a frightening experience. The dread of particular, severe or ill treatment and of physical discomfort is perhaps the least of it. The worst is the general atmosphere, the sense of being always under observation, the dead cold and gloom and the always noted, unmistakable, prison smell – and the eyes of some of the other prisoners. We had all this for only a week. We were very conscious of the continuing fact that many of our friends were undergoing it for many weeks and that we were spared only through special circumstances, not through less 'guilt', in so far as there was any guilt.

Meantime the Committee of 100 had put out a leaflet with my message from Brixton. On the back of the leaflet was its urgent appeal to all sympathisers to congregate in Trafalgar Square at 5 o'clock on Sunday, September 17th, for a march to Parliament Square where a public assembly was to be held and a sit-down. The Home Secretary had issued a Public Order against our use of Trafalgar Square on that occasion, but the Committee had determined that this would be no deterrent. Unfortunately for us, my wife and I were still in gaol and were not released till the following day. I say unfortunately because it must have been a memorable and exhilarating occasion.

We delighted in our reunion in freedom at home very early on Monday morning. But almost at once we were besieged by the press and radio and TV people who swarmed into Hasker Street. Our continued involvement with them prevented us from learning for some time all that had been happening since the Bow Street session of the previous week. From what we had learned from the papers that we had seen in prison, we knew that all sorts of meetings and sit-downs had been held, not only in Britain, but also in many other countries, protesting against our imprisonment. Moreover, my wife had gathered from some of the prisoners at Holloway that the demonstration of the 17th was a success. They had listened to the radio and stood on the balcony above their nets in the great hall of the prison making the sign of thumbs-up to her and shouting excitedly that the sit-down was going splendidly. We learned only gradually quite how unbelievably great a success it had been.

The full story of that demonstration I must leave to some historian or participant to tell. The important part is that unprecedented numbers took part. It augured well for an approach to the mass movement that we desired. By early evening the Square and the streets leading to it were packed with people sitting down and with people coming only to observe what was going on who tried to force themselves into possible observation points. There was no question of marching to Parliament Square. No one could get through, though attempts were made. There was no violence, no hullabaloo on the part of the sitters-down. They were serious. And some of them were making what was individually an heroic gesture. For instance, Augustus John, an old man, who had been, and was, very ill (it was a short time before his death) emerged from the National Gallery, walked into the Square and sat down. No one knew of his plan to do so and few recognised him. I learned of his action only much later, but I record it with admiration. There were other cases of what amounted to heroism in testifying to a profound belief. There were also a good many ludicrous happenings, particularly, I was told, later in the evening when various notabilities arrived to see how things were going and were mistaken by the police for ardent upholders of the Committee and were piled, protesting, into Black Marias. But the police could hardly be blamed for such mistakes. In the vast crowd individual identities could not be distinguished, even in a dogcollar. The police could, however, be very much blamed for their not infrequent brutality. This could not be disputed, since there were many pictures taken which sometimes caught instances of regrettable police action.

Television and press accounts and pictures of this demonstration and of the preceding gaolings appeared in countries throughout the world. They had an excellent effect in setting people everywhere thinking about what we were doing and attempting to do and why. That was what we had hoped would happen, but we had not prepared sufficiently for the overwhelming publicity and interest that would be generated. From the beginning we had been careful to arrange that only certain of our members would expose themselves to possible imprisonment at any particular demonstration. There was always to be a corps of leaders to carry on the work. But the Government, by sentencing a large number, not for any particular misdeed at any particular time, but for the general charge of incitement, had managed to disrupt this rota. Added to this, were the arrests made during the general scrum of the September 17th sit-down when track could hardly be kept of who might be arrested and who not. The result was that there were very few experienced members of the Committee left to deal with pressing matters and future plans. I was tired and kept busy by matters that only I could deal with arising chiefly from my imprisonment. All this was a grievous pity for we had been given a great chance which we were unable to avail ourselves of fully.

At the end of the week after gaol we returned to North Wales but the barrage of press and TV interviews continued wherever we were and, of course, there were daily visitors from all over – Italians, Japanese, French, Belgian, Singalese, Dutch, South and North Americans, etc., etc. It was all wearing, and when we could we drove off into the country by ourselves. We had a number of adventures. One afternoon we walked along a sandy beach and around a rocky point to a cove. The rocks of the point were covered by dried seaweed. At first we tested the solidity of the way, but we grew careless, and unexpectedly I, who was ahead, sank to my thighs. At each move, I sank further. My wife was only at the edge of the bad patch. She managed to crawl to a rock and finally to haul me out. On other occasions, our car got stuck in the sand or in the bog and had to be pulled out – once, to our amused annoyance, by a nuclear station's van.

When we returned to London, too, we had adventures. One morning two young men and a young woman appeared upon my doorstep and demanded to see me as, they said, they wished to discuss anti-nuclear work. I discussed matters with them for some time and then intimated that it was time for them to go. They refused to go. Nothing that I or my housekeeper – we were the only people in the house – could say would budge them, and we were far from being strong enough to move them. They proceeded to stage a sit-down in my drawing-room. With some misgivings, I sent for the police. Their behaviour was impeccable. They did not even smile, much less jeer. And they evicted the sitters-down. The latter were later discovered, I was told, to be a young actress who wanted publicity and two of her admirers wishing to help her. They got the publicity and provided me with a good story and much entertainment. Some of the Committee were rather annoyed by my having called in the police.

During the next months there were a number of Committee of 100 meetings, both public and private, at which I spoke, notably in Trafalgar Square on October 29th and in Cardiff on November 1st. Demonstrations had been announced for December 9th to be held at various US air and nuclear bases in the country. But in planning this the Committee, in its inexperience of holding large demonstrations not in London but in the country, were too optimistic, especially in matters relating to transportation. For instance, they felt sure that the buses that they hired to take demonstrators from London to one of the targets, Wethersfield, would turn up since the bus drivers themselves had professed themselves sympathetic to the Committee's views. But, as some of us had feared, the bus company refused its buses to the Committee at the last minute. Some hardy and determined demonstrators made their way to Wethersfield by other means, but the loss of the buses and the lack of any alternative arrangements meant that the numbers were very much less than had been expected. The further difficulties encountered were great: The machinations of the police who had raided the Committee rooms and harried its members, and the opposition of the Government, which employed a large number of its ground and air force, its guard dogs and fire hoses to protect the Committee's targets from unarmed people pledged to non-violence. Nevertheless, the demonstration made a good showing. The Committee had made a mistake, however, in announcing beforehand that it would make a better showing than it could possibly hope to do and in not planning thoroughly for alternatives in foreseeable difficulties.

The Committee had already begun to weaken itself in other ways. Long discussions were beginning to be held amongst its members as to whether the Committee should devote itself only to nuclear and disarmament matters or should begin to oppose all domestic, social and governmental injustice. This was a waste of time and a dispersal of energies. Such widespread opposition, if to be indulged in at all, was obviously a matter for the far future when the Committee's power and capabilities were consolidated. By such projects consolidation could only be delayed. Again, this unfortunate tendency was the outcome, largely, of the practical political and administrative inexperience of the Committee added to the over-estimation of the meaning of September 17th's success. The latter should have been regarded as very great encouragement but not as, by any means, the certain promise of a *mass* civil disobedience movement. In proportion to the population of the country, the movement was still small and too unproved to stand against determined opposition. Unfortunately, the comparative failure of December 9th was considered only as a discouragement, not as a lesson towards a period of consolidation. I tried in my public statements at the time to overcome the discouragement and, privately, to inculcate the lesson. But in both attempts I failed.

The immediate aftermath of the demonstration of December 9th was the charging of five leaders of the Committee under the Official Secrets Act of 1911. It was, from a layman's point of view, a curiously conducted trial. The prosecution was allowed to present its case in full, resting on the question as to whether it was prejudicial to the safety of the nation for unauthorised people to enter the Wethersfield air field with the intention of immobilising and grounding the aircraft there. The defence's case was that such stations as Wethersfield, like all the stations engaged in nuclear 'defence' of the country, were in themsleves prejudicial to the safety of the country. Professor Linus Pauling, the physicist, and Sir Robert Watson-Watt, the inventor of radar, who had come from the United States to give evidence as to the dangers of the present nuclear policy of which Wethersfield was a part, and I were kept hanging about for many hours. Then all our testimony, like that of other defence witnesses, of whom some, I believe, were not permitted to be called at all, was declared irrelevant to the charges and ruled out. It was managed quite legally, but all loopholes were ruthlessly blocked against the defence and made feasible for the prosecution. There were a few bright moments, to be sure: when Air Commander MacGill, the prosecution's chief witness was asked how far it was from London to Wethersfield, he replied, 'in a fast plane, about fifty miles'. The jury returned the verdict guilty, though, and this is rather interesting, they were out for four and a half hours. No one had believed any other verdict possible under the circumstances. The five convicted men were given gaol sentences of eighteen months apiece; the one woman, the welfare secretary of the Committee, was given a year.

I felt keenly that I, since I had encouraged the demonstration but had not been able to take part, was as guilty as the condemned and I managed when I was finally able to speak at the trial to say so. Many others felt likewise, and, after the trial, we repaired to the Cannon Street police station to declare ourselves guilty. As was to be expected, no notice was taken of our declarations though they were received civilly by the police. The Committee held a meeting in Trafalgar Square to state the significance of the trial and its own attitude towards it. In snow and gale, Sir Robert Watson-Watt and I and a number of others spoke to a not inconsiderable audience.

For some time thereafter I had little to do in the way of public speaking for the Committee. During that last week of July the Committee as well as the CND sent participants to the 'World Disarmament Conference' held in Moscow. Just as it was about to start, I received a request from Professor Bernal pressing me to send a representative with a message to the conference. Christopher Farley, who had participated both in the planning and in the action of the Committee, went on my behalf. While he was there, he, in company with some other non-communists, held a public meeting in Red Square and handed out leaflets. This was illegal, and was vehemently opposed, by a variety of means, by the chairman of the CND who was there. It was also opposed by others, even some who at home, indulged in civil disobedience. They felt that they were guests of the Russians and should abide by the strict laws of hospitality. The meeting was dispersed, but its holders were triumphant in the belief that they had pointed out the international character of the civil disobedience movement and had been able to hold something of a debate before being dispersed. At the time, I received only hot objections, but no reasons were given for the objections. When Farley returned and I heard what he had to say, I felt that he had done the right thing in backing the meeting, and that it had helped to establish the fact that we were neutral and should invoke civil disobedience wherever we could in a cause which was international.

Towards the end of August the Committee began to put into effect its plan for a demonstration on September 9th. Taking warning from the previous December 9th, they decided to return to central London and to pledge people to take part. They announced that they would not hold the demonstration if they could not get 7,000 pledges. As September 9th drew near, it became evident that they could not procure this number of pledges in time. I felt very strongly that, in view of their public announcement, they should abandon the demonstration, especially as to hold to their promise those who had pledged would be to ask them to attend the demonstration unprotected by the promised number of co-participants. The secretary of the London Committee was very loath to give up and many members thought that it was unnecessary to do so. This flouting of a given promise disgusted me, and added itself to my growing belief that the Committee was disintegrating. In the end, the demonstration was called off.

During the time since the Secrets trial many things had been happening to me unconnected with the Committee – lunches such as the one given me by the foreign journalists in London, TV broadcasts such as the long one for United States consumption at which the interlocutor was named Susskind, visits from travelling dignitaries such as that of the five leading Russian journalists who spent an afternoon with me in Wales. We also went on a holiday drive for somewhat over a fortnight at the end of March, a holiday which was a total failure since the weather was cold, raw, and dreary and we were both ill throughout with raging colds. The most important events in relation to my own life were those centring about my ninetieth birthday on May 18th.

I looked forward to my birthday celebrations, I confess, with considerable trepidation, for I had been informed of their prospect though told nothing of the toil and anxiety that was going into their consummation. Only afterwards did I hear of the peculiar obstructions caused by impresarios and the managers of concert halls, or of the extreme kindness and generosity of conductors and orchestras and soloists. I only gradually learned of the immense amount of time and energy, thought and sheer determination to give me pleasure expended by my friends for many weeks. The most active of these was Ralph Schoenman who was chiefly responsible for all aspects of the concert, including the excellently arranged and, to me, most pleasing programme. When I did learn all this, I was deeply touched, as I was by the parties themselves. And to my surprise, I found that I enjoyed greatly being the centre of such unexpectedly friendly plaudits and encomiums.

On my birthday itself, we had a jolly family teaparty with two of my grandchildren and my London housekeeper Jean Redmond and, to celebrate, a fine cake topped appropriately by a small constable (donated by the baker) bearing one candle for good luck. In the evening, a dinner arranged by A. J. Ayer and Rupert Crawshay-Williams took place at the Café Royal. It seemed to me a happy occasion. Some of my friends made speeches: Ayer and Julian Huxley spoke most kindly of me and E. M. Forster recalled the early Cambridge days and spoke delightfully about my old friend Bob Trevelyan. And I met for the first time the Head of my family, the Duke of Bedford and his wife. I admired his determination to keep Woburn a private estate at however great cost to himself and against great odds. I also liked his unconventionality. I had been told that when asked to speak at the concert in my honour, he had accepted without hesitation. So I was prepared to like him – and I was not disappointed. The evening was not less enjoyable for me in re-establishing connection with a number of old friends such as Arthur Waley and Miles Malleson as well as in making a few new ones.

Of the celebration party at Festival Hall, under the kind aegis of its manager, T. E. Bean, that took place the next afternoon, I do not know what to say or how to say it. I had been told that there would be music and presentations to me, but I could not know beforehand how lovely the music would be, either the orchestral part under Colin Davis or the solo work by Lili Kraus. Nor could I know how touching and generous would be the presentation speeches: by Ralph Schoenman, the Master of Ceremonies; Victor Purcell; Mrs Sonning of Denmark; Ernst Willi,

the Swiss sculptor; Morley Nkosi of Africa; Vanessa Redgrave, the actress; and my cousin Ian Bedford. Some of those who could not be there had sent gifts which were presented to me – a bust of Socrates from my cousin Flora Russell and an excellent portrait of me from its painter Hans Erni. And many people had sent messages which Schoenman read out or had printed in the 'Tribute Programme'. It had a photograph of me taken by T. E. Morris of Portmadoc on its cover. I have been told that it has been sent to people all over the world. The Musicians Union refused to have the music recorded and the BBC refused to record any of the proceedings. The gifts, the programme, the record that was privately made of the proceedings, and, especially, the warm friendliness that I felt in the audience as well as in the actors, I still, and always shall, treasure. At the time I was so deeply moved that I felt I could not utter a word, much less find words that might express my feeling of gratitude and of what the occasion meant to me. But, mercifully, words came. I do not think that I can say again so freshly or with such entire, unconsidered sincerity what I felt then, so I give my speech itself, taking it from the recording:
'Friends,

'This is an occasion that I hardly know how to find words for. I am more touched than I can say, and more deeply than I can ever hope to express. I have to give my very warmest possible thanks to those who have worked to produce this occasion: to the performers, whose exquisite music, exquisitely performed, was so full of delight; to those who worked in less conspicuous ways, like my friend Mr Schoenman; and to all those who have given me gifts – gifts which are valuable in themselves, and also as expressions of an undying hope for this dangerous world.

'I have a very simple creed: that life and joy and beauty are better than dusty death, and I think when we listen to such music as we heard today we must all of us feel that the capacity to produce such music, and the capacity to hear such music, is a thing worth preserving and should not be thrown away in foolish squabbles. You may say it's a simple creed, but I think everything important is very simple indeed. I've found that creed sufficient, and I should think that a great many of you would also find it sufficient, or else you would hardly be here.

'But now I just want to say how it's difficult, when one has embarked upon a course which invites a greater or less degree of persecution and obloquy and abuse, to find instead that one is welcomed as I have been today. It makes one feel rather humble, and I feel I must try to live up to the feelings that have produced this occasion. I hope I shall; and I thank you from the bottom of my heart.'

The last formal celebration of my birthday took place the following week when Fenner Brockway most kindly invited me to a luncheon in my honour at the House of Commons. I was somewhat nervous of this as it seemed unlikely to me that any Members of either House would turn up to do me honour. My tension mounted as we waited in an ante-room to be led to the Harcourt Room where the banquet was to take place and, again, stood at the door rather wistfully watching the Members fortify themselves with preprandial drinks. But, when the party began, it was pleasant and friendly, and I thought it generous of many of those present to be there. I had not for some time been pulling my punches in regard to the activities of politicians, nor, I fear, did I on this occasion, seeing a chance and, indeed, an obligation, to speak to them direct.

When all this pleasant fuss to do with my becoming a nonagenarian had passed, we retired to Wales, returning to London only for a few days in July for the purpose of talking with U Thant about international nuclear and disarmament policies. This was the first time that I had met him and I was greatly impressed not only by his energy and clear grasp of affairs, but by his balanced objectivity and thoughtfulness and his delightful good humour. At this time, too, I paid my first visit to Woburn Abbey. I found the grandeurs of the house very pleasing and the lovely serenity of the Park, with its great trees sheltering Father David's deer and its wide quiet stretches of green turf, very calming.

The last months of that year were taken up with the Cuban crisis and then with the Sino-Indian Border dispute. Early in December, Penguin accepted my offer to write my account of these two happenings which I did in January. It was published by Penguin and Allen & Unwin in April under the title *Unarmed Victory*. I have told in it all there is to tell of any interest about my thought and action at that time, and I do not propose to repeat it all here. Perhaps I should add, however, that I regret nothing that I did at that time in relation to these two crises. My point of view upon them, in spite of further study, remains the same. I will give my critics only this olive branch: I am sorry that I did not couch my telegram of October 23rd to President Kennedy more gently. Its directness made it unlikely to cut much ice, I agree. But I had as little hope then as I should have in similar circumstances now of wise and quick withdrawal on the part of the US Government.

I had become so tried by the folly of some of the leading members of the Committee of 100 during the events of September and by the growing dissipation of the Committee's policies that, early in January, I resigned from the Main Committee in London. I did not wish, however, to go into these reasons in my public resignation. I based it upon the equally valid and conclusive reason that my increasing absences in Wales prevented me from participating usefully in the work of the Main Committee. I still have great sympathy with the early aims and actions of the Committee, and I should support any recrudescence of them if they seemed to me to stand any chance of success. Mass civil disobedience still seems to me one of the most effective ways of attacking present international policies which remain as bad as they were then, if not worse.

The British Government, meanwhile, had its own plans for what to do in the event of nuclear war. What these plans were we learned, in part, from an organisation which called itself 'Spies for Peace'. This organisation had succeeded in ascertaining the secret plans of Authority to be put into force on the outbreak of war. Britain was to be divided into a number of regions, each with its own government, each with autocratic power, each composed of a pre-arranged corps of officials who were to live in supposed safety in underground 'Regional Seats of Government' and decide (so far as the enemy allowed) what was to become of the rest of us, and, in particular, what was to be done about fall-out if and while we remained alive. It was feared that possibly the prospect of such measures might not please the populace, and must therefore be kept secret. 'Spies for Peace' had discovered some of the documents involved, and were anxious to publish them. They had no funds, and appealed to me. I gave them £50 with my blessing. As soon as possible the documents were published, and copies were distributed among the Aldermaston marchers.

Unfortunately (as I felt) the leaders of CND were shocked that secret methods should be employed by pacifists. They did what they could to impede the spread of knowledge which the 'Spies' had sought to secure. A fresh batch of documents which they had secured was taken to the editor of a leading pacifist journal under the impression that he would publicise their information. But he, horrified by the disclosures and the retribution their publication would undoubtedly call down, sent the documents to the mother of one of the 'Spies' and she, fearing a police raid, burnt them. So died our hope of learning Government plans for governmental salvation and the succour of such members of the public as might be allowed to live. This bitter blow to the clarification of our position and to a great impetus to work for peace was dealt by well-meaning and not unknowledgeable pacifists.

LETTERS

To and from Ernest Jones

> Plas Penrhyn
> 2 February, 1957

Dear Dr Jones
I enclose a copy of a letter from an eminent Anglican divine. It seems

to me a document worthy to go into your case-book. I should be very grateful if you felt inclined to send me any comments on it.

> *Yours sincerely*
> Russell

The following is the letter I sent to Dr Jones (without the Bishop's address or signature):

From the Bishop of Rochester

> Personal
> Bishopscourt
> Rochester
> Jan: 29. 1957

Dear Lord Russell

It has been laid upon my conscience to write to you, after your article in the *Sunday Times* on the 'Great Mystery' of survival after death; seeing that you at 84 stand yourself upon that threshold.

Your contemporaries, like myself, acclaim you the greatest brain of our generation. And many must believe, with me, that if only your moral stature had matched your intellectual power and other singular endowments, you could have saved us from a second World War. Instead, in your book on Companionate Marriage, *Marriage and Morals* (1929), the cloven hoof of the lecher cannot be disguised; and it is lechery that has been your Achilles heel, blinding your great mind from discerning that infinitely greater Mind behind all phenomena, such as has formed your enthralling study. Only the pure in heart can see God; and four wives, with three divorces, must be an awful and bitter humiliation, showing the man himself, entrusted with such a magnificent brain.

Moreover, I cannot but believe that you must at times be haunted by the remembrances of the murder, suicide, and untold misery, between the wars, caused by the experiments of young people with Companionate Marriage, of which you were the Apostle, with all the immense authority of your fame. I am an old man myself of 72, but with no outstanding gifts or learning; and yet I would, in humble sincerity, make my own, to you, what that Dr M. J. Routh, who died in his hundredth year as President of Magdalen, Oxford, (1854), wrote to a Quaker acquaintance in the condemned cell:

'Sir, this comes from one who, like yourself, has not long to live, being in his ninetieth year. He has had more opportunity than most for distinctly knowing that the scriptures of the New Testament were written by the Apostles of the Saviour of mankind. In these Scriptures it is expressly said that the blood of Jesus Christ cleanses from all sin, and that if we confess our sins, God, being merciful and just, will forgive us our sins on our repentance. Think, say, and do everything in your power to save your soul, before you go into another life.'

You may know that the great Bishop Joseph Butler of Durham, your peer as regards intellect, died with this verse from I John, I. 7, in his ears, and whispering: 'Oh! but this is comfortable.'

I pray God that you will recognise that, for some reason, I have been filled with a deep concern for you.

> *Yours sincerely*
> *Christopher Roffen*

> The Plat, Elsted
> Nr. Midhurst, Sx.
> Feb. 4, 1957

Dear Russell

I am a little surprised that you should find the Anglican's letter at all odd. I should have thought you received many such, and indeed I even wonder how many masses are already being said for your soul.

The interest of such letters is of course the calm identification of wickedness with sexual activity. Freud used to think that the main function of religion was to check man's innate aggressivity (the obvious source of all wickedness), but it is curious how often religious teachers bring it back again to sexuality. That makes one think there must be some deep connection between the two, and we believe nowadays that much aggressivity, possibly all, can ultimately be traced to the innumerable forms of sexual frustration. It remains noteworthy, however, that you, our leading apostle of true morality (love, charity, tolerance, etc.) should be cast into perdition for not accepting the Catholic view of marriage.

If you want a psycho-analytic comment on the letter there is a clue in the omnipotence he attributes to you (ability to stop wars, etc.). That can only point to a gigantic father figure (an earthly God), whose only sin, much resented by the son, was his sleeping with the mother. It is curious that such people are never shocked at God's adulterous behaviour with the Virgin Mary. It needs a lot of purification.

> *yours sincerely*
> *Ernest Jones*

> Plas Penrhyn
> 14 March, 1957

Dear Jones

Thank you for your very pleasant letter of February 4. Ever since I got it, I have been luxuriating in the pleasure of seeing myself as a formidable father-figure inspiring terror in the Anglican hierarchy.

What surprised me about the letter I sent you was that I had imagined eminent Anglican Divines to be usually fairly civilised people. I get hundreds of letters very similar to the one I sent you, but they are generally from people with very little education. I cannot make up my mind whether the writer of the letter is gnawed with remorse for the sins he has committed or filled with regret for those that he has not committed.

Yours sincerely
Russell

From and to Lord Russell of Liverpool

Old Warren Farm
Wimbledon Common
S.W.19
13/2[1959]

Dear Lord Russell

I am forwarding the enclosed as Monsieur Edmond Paris, and he is not alone, has got us mixed up. The first paragraph of his letter refers to you. The others are for me and I shall be replying to them. Would you please return the letter when you have read it.

Ys. truly
Russell of Liverpool

Plas Penrhyn
18 February, 1959

Dear Lord Russell

Thank you for your letter and for the enclosure which I return herewith. I have been wondering whether there is any means of preventing the confusion between you and me, and I half-thought that we might write a joint letter to *The Times* in the following terms: Sir, To prevent the continuation of confusions which frequently occur, we beg to state that neither of us is the other. Do you think this would be a good plan ?

Yours sincerely
Russell

Old Warren Farm
Wimbledon Common
S.W.19
20/2[1959]

Dear Lord Russell

Many thanks for your letter of the 18th.

I am not sure whether you are in earnest or joking about a joint letter to *The Times* but, in either event, I think it is a good idea. Even were it not effective it would provide a little light amusement, and if you would care to write such a letter I would gladly add my signature below yours.

Incidentally, *à propos* this subject, you will find pages 61/2 of a book of my reminiscences to be published on March 19 by Cassell & Co. under the title of *That Reminds Me* of some interest. They contain details of two occasions on which I was mistaken for an Earl Russell. Your elder brother in India in 1927 and yourself in 1954.

Page 60 will also interest you.

> *Yours sincerely*
> *Russell of Liverpool*

> Plas Penrhyn
> 23 February 1959

Dear Lord Russell of Liverpool

Thank you for your letter of February 20. I was both serious and joking in my suggestion of a joint letter. I enclose a draft which I have signed, but I am entirely willing to alter the wording if you think it too frivolous. I think, however, that the present wording is more likely to secure attention than a more solemn statement.

> *Yours sincerely*
> *Russell*

> Plas Penrhyn
> 23 February, 1959

To the Editor of *The Times*
Sir

In order to discourage confusions which have been constantly occurring, we beg herewith to state that neither of us is the other.

> *Yours etc.*
> *Russell of Liverpool*
> (*Lord Russell of Liverpool*)

> *Russell*
> (*Bertrand, Earl Russell*)

> Old Warren Farm
> Wimbledon Common
> S.W.19
> 25/2/59

Dear Lord Russell

I have forwarded our letter to *The Times* but I have asked them, of course, to put your name before mine.

I like the wording immensely.

> *Russell of Liverpool*

To and from A. J. Ayer

Plas Penhryn
19 January, 1957

Dear Ayer

I have just finished reading your *Problem of Knowledge*. I have read the book with a great deal of pleasure and I agree with most of it. I like your way of dissecting problems; for example, what you say on such subjects as television and precognition seems to me to combine logic and sound sense in just proportion. The only point upon which I seriously disagree with you is as to perception. My view on this subject, although to scientific people it seems a mere collection of truisms, is rejected as a wild paradox by philosophers of all schools. You need not, therefore, be in any degree disquieted by not having my support. I will, however, make one point: on page 126 you say that from the fact that the perceived qualities of physical objects are causally dependent upon the state of the percipient, it does not follow that the object does not really have them. This, of course, is true. What does follow is that there is no reason to think that it has them. From the fact that when I wear blue spectacles, things look blue, it does not follow that they are not blue, but it does follow that I have no reason to suppose they are blue.

As I find that philosophers, as opposed to men of science, unanimously misunderstand my theory of perception, I am enclosing a note on the subject with no special reference to your book.

Yours very sincerely
Russell

New College
Oxford
26 May 1961

Dear Russell

I have just heard from Routledge that you have withdrawn permission for your preface to be included in the new translation of Wittgenstein's *Tractatus*. The reason why I come in to this is that I am editor of the series in which the book is to appear.

I assume that you are taking this step because of the difficulties which are being raised by Ogden's brother. I do not know what Ogden has told you; but I do hope that I can persuade you to reconsider your decision. The most important fact, as I see it, is that this new translation will supersede the old, so that if your preface is not included in it, it will practically cease to be available. I think this would be a great pity, as quite apart from the light it throws on Wittgenstein, it is a very interesting piece of work in itself.

The authors of the new translation, Messrs Pears and McGuinness, tell me that if there [are] any conditions which you now wish to make before allowing them to use your preface, they will do their very best to meet them.

I am very sorry to hear that you have been ill and hope that you are now recovered.

> *Yours sincerely*
> *Freddie Ayer*

Pears and McGuinness say that they have made every effort to satisfy Ogden but have found him quite intractable.

> Plas Penrhyn
> 27 May, 1961

Dear Ayer

Thank you for your letter of May 26. I have never succeeded in understanding the points at issue between Ogden's brother and your party. I have no objection in principle to the reprinting of my introduction to the *Tractatus*. I was influenced by the fact that Wittgenstein and all his followers hated my introduction and that Wittgenstein only consented to its inclusion because the publishers made it a condition of their publishing the *Tractatus*. I did not know, until I received your letter this morning, that there was anyone who thought that my introduction had any value. Since you think that it has, I am quite willing again to grant permission for its republication. Would you kindly communicate the substance of this letter to Routledge.

> *Yours sincerely*
> *Russell*

> New College
> Oxford
> 31 May 1961

Dear Russell

Thank you very much for allowing us to reprint your Introduction to the *Tractatus*. Wittgenstein always complained at being misrepresented by anybody who wrote about him, and his followers simply echo what he said. But I am sure that your Introduction is an important addition to the work and the new translators entirely share my view. They were indeed very upset when they thought they were not going to be allowed to reprint it. With regard to Ogden's brother I am in the same position as yourself: I still do not understand what the substance of his grievance is.

> *Yours sincerely*
> *Freddie Ayer*

From and to Rudolf Carnap

> Department of Philosophy
> University of California
> May 12, 1962

Dear Lord Russell

Throughout my life I have followed with the greatest interest not only your philosophical work but also, especially during the last years, your political activities, and I admire your courage and your intensity of energy and devotion. Now, on the occasion of your ninetieth birthday, I wish to send you a message of best wishes and of deep gratitude for all I owe to you. Your books had indeed a stronger influence on my philosophical thinking than those of any other philosopher. I say more about this in my intellectual autobiography (in a forthcoming Schilpp-volume on my philosophy), and especially also about the inspiring effect on me of your appeal for a new method in philosophy, on the last pages of your book *Our knowledge of the external world.*

I am in complete agreement with the aims for which you are fighting at present: serious negotiations instead of the cold war, no bomb-testing, no fallout shelters. But, not having your wonderful power of words, I limit myself to participation in public appeals and petitions initiated by others and to some private letters to President Kennedy on these matters. Even such letters are difficult for me. By nature I am inclined to turn away from the insane quarrels of parties and governments, and pursue my thinking in a purely theoretical field. But at present, when the survival of civilisation is at stake, I realise that it is necessary at least to take a stand. I also admired your forceful and convincing argumentation in the debate with Edward Teller which I saw on television. I find it depressing to see a prominent scientist (in contrast to politicians from whom one has come to expect nothing better) strengthening the prejudices of the listeners.

I am going to be 71 on the same day you are having your birthday. May you have many more active years ahead, in good health, and with the satisfaction of seeing a more rational world order coming into being, to whose development you have contributed so much. I am going to retire in a few weeks from teaching and to devote myself to the further development of my theory of inductive probability, on which I have begun to publish in 1950 and which has occupied me ever since.

With deep affection and gratitude,

> *Yours*
> *Rudolf Carnap*

> Plas Penrhyn
> 21st June 1962

Dear Professor Carnap

I am immensely grateful to you for your kind letter. It pleased me greatly. I had not realised that your birthday and mine fall on the same day. I am sorry not to have sent you my own good wishes, which are sincerely felt.

I believe that your efforts to bring clarity and precision to philosophy will have an everlasting effect on the thinking of men, and I am very happy to see that you will continue your work after your retirement. Nothing would be more fitting than that you should successfully realise your theory of inductive probability. I entirely understand your diffidence with respect to letters to public officials. It is difficult to employ a language which speaks of intense and sincere fears for our world to public men who receive our words with small awareness of that which promotes them. I must confess that I am deeply troubled. I fear that human beings are intent upon acting out a vast deathwish and that it lies with us now to make every effort to promote resistance to the insanity and brutality of policies which encompass the extermination of hundreds of millions of human beings.

In this country we are having a much greater success than seems evident in the United States, although it is obvious that protest in the United States requires far greater courage and dedication than its equivalent here. Nonetheless; I am hopeful that the effect of our minority resistance may grow and find a co-ordinated international expression. We are holding a great demonstration at the Air Ministry in Whitehall involving civil disobedience this coming September 9th, and I shall be taking part in the physical demonstration itself. I believe that men are starved for an answer to the terror and that they will respond if their sense of helplessness can be overcome.

I am sincerely grateful to you for your kindness in writing and I wish you earnestly success in your great work.

With my good wishes and respect
Bertrand Russell

From *The Observer*, May 13, 1962

PROS AND CONS OF REACHING NINETY

by

Bertrand Russell

There are both advantages and disadvantages in being very old. The disadvantages are obvious and uninteresting, and I shall say little about them. The advantages seem to me more interesting. A long retrospect gives weight and substance to experience. I have been able to follow many lives, both of friends and of public characters, from an early stage to their conclusion. Some, who were promising in youth, have achieved little of value; others have continued to develop from strength to strength through long lives of important achievement. Undoubtedly, experience makes it easier to guess to which of these two kinds a young person is likely to belong. It is not only the lives of individuals, but the lives of movements that come, with time, to form part of personal experience and to facilitate estimates of probable success or failure. Communism, in spite of a very difficult beginning, has hitherto continued to increase in power and influence. Nazism, on the contrary, by snatching too early and too ruthlessly at dominion, came to grief. To have watched such diverse processes helps to give an insight into the past of history and should help in guessing at the probable future.

To come to more personal matters; it is natural for those who are energetic and adventurous to feel in youth a very passionate and restless desire for some important achievement, without any clear prevision of what, with luck, it may be. In old age, one becomes more aware of what has, and what has not, been achieved. What one can further do becomes a smaller proportion of what has already been done, and this makes personal life less feverish.

It is a curious sensation to read the journalistic clichés which come to be fastened on past periods that one remembers, such as the 'naughty nineties' and the 'riotous twenties'. Those decades did not seem, at the time, at all 'naughty' or 'riotous'. The habit of affixing easy labels is convenient to those who wish to seem clever without having to think, but it has very little relation to reality. The world is always changing, but not in the simple ways that such convenient clichés suggest. Old age, as I am experiencing it, could be a time of very complete happiness if one could forget the state of the world. Privately, I enjoy everything that could make life delightful. I used to think that when I reached old age I would retire from the world and live a life of elegant culture, reading all the great books that I ought to have read at an earlier date. Perhaps it was, in any case, an idle dream. A long habit of work with some purpose that one believes important is difficult to break, and I might have found elegant leisure boring even if the world had been in a better state. However that might have been, I find it impossible to ignore what is happening.

Ever since 1914, at almost every crucial moment, the wrong thing has been done. We are told that the West is engaged in defending the 'Free World', but freedom such as existed before 1914 is now as dim a memory as crinolines. Supposedly wise men assured us in 1914 that we were fighting a war to end war, but it turned out to be a war to end peace. We were told that Prussian militarism was all that had to be put down; and, ever since, militarism has continually increased. Murderous humbug, such as would have shocked almost everyone when I was young, is now solemnly mouthed by eminent statesmen. My own country, led by men without imagination and without capacity for adaptation to the modern world, pursues a policy which, if not changed, will lead almost inevitably to the complete extermination of all the inhabitants of Britain. Like Cassandra, I am doomed to prophesy evil and not be believed. Her prophecies came true. I desperately hope that mine will not.

Sometimes one is tempted to take refuge in cheerful fantasies and to imagine that perhaps in Mars or Venus happier and saner forms of life exist, but our frantic skill is making this a vain dream. Before long, if we do not destroy ourselves, our destructive strife will have spread to those planets. Perhaps, for their sake, one ought to hope that war on earth will put an end to our species before its folly has become cosmic. But this is not a hope in which I can find any comfort.

The way in which the world has developed during the last fifty years has brought about in me changes opposite to those which are supposed to be typical of old age. One is frequently assured by men who have no doubt of their own wisdom that old age should bring serenity and a larger vision in which seeming evils are viewed as means to ultimate good. I cannot accept any such view. Serenity, in the present world, can only be achieved through blindness or brutality. Unlike what is conventionally expected, I become gradually more and more of a rebel. I was not born rebellious. Until 1914, I fitted more or less comfortably into the world as I found it. There were evils – great evils – but there was reason to think that they would grow less. Without having the temperament of a rebel, the course of events has made me gradually less and less able to acquiesce patiently in what is happening. A minority, though a growing one, feels as I do, and, so long as I live, it is with them that I must work.

From Mrs Roosevelt

> 55 East 74th Street
> New York City
> September 22, 1960

My Lord

I am most grateful to you for taking part with me in our television program on British defence policy in London. It was a lively and exciting discussion and I feel the result was satisfying.

> *Sincerely*
> *Eleanor Roosevelt*

From and to Max Born

> Haus Filser
> Freibergstrasse
> Obersdorf (Allgäu)
> Germany
> 12.7.51

Dear Professor Russell

Your book *A History of Western Philosophy* which I never had time to read at home has accompanied me on my holiday journey and given me so much pleasure that I take the liberty to write to you a few words of thanks.

I confess that before putting the book into my suitcase I asked a few of my philosophical friends in Scotland about it, and was warned not to read it as it would give me a distorted picture of the actual men and events. When I was, a few weeks ago, in Göttingen I discussed your book with one of the local philosophers and found a still stronger negative attitude, based mainly on your treatment of Plato and of the German idealistic school. This encouraged me greatly to read your book. For I have been tortured at school with Plato, and I have always thoroughly disliked German metaphysics, in particular Hegel. Thus I decided to read your last chapter first, and as I wholeheartedly agreed to your own philosophy, I started cheerfully with page 1 and continued reading with ever increasing fascination and pleasure until I reached your moderate, though decided refutations of some of the modern schools of 'subjectivistic madness'. I was myself once a pupil of Edmund Husserl but found his 'phenomenology' unsatisfactory and its modern version by Heidegger rather disgusting. I suppose you found it not worth while to mention it.

My son and his wife who are with us on this journey share my admiration for your work and have gone so far to call their new-born boy Max Russell combining thus my name with yours.

On my way out I stayed a week with Niels Bohr at Copenhagen and had some most interesting talks with him on the philosophical foundations of quantum theory.

> *Yours sincerely*
> *Max Born*

> Marcard str. 4
> Bad Pyrmont
> 18 March, 1958

Dear Professor Russell

I have read Khrushchev's long declaration in the *New Statesman*. I find it just as depressing as the letter from Dulles published some weeks ago. The commentary by Kingsley Martin that these fellows are amazingly similar in their mental make-up is quite correct. One could just as well call them Khrushless and Dullchev, and, what they believe in, not an ideology, but an idiotology. I wonder whether you will write a summary containing your impressions of this exchange of opinions which you have originated.

Meanwhile we 'Eighteen' here are involved in the fight against rocket and nuclear armament of West-Germany. Von Weizsäecker is in Pugwash and will be back on April 17th when we meet again on the Rhine.

I have stirred up another ugly matter, concerning space travel, which is used by the military party to camouflage the expensive development of rocket missiles. All newspapers, the radio, the cinemas are full of this affair and I have a lively time. The great majority of the people are on our side but the Government (Adenauer, Strauss) are clever and use all means.

> *Yours sincerely*
> *M. Born*

> Plas Penrhyn
> 22 March, 1958

Dear Dr Born

Thank you very warmly for your letter of March 18 which expressed feelings exactly similar to mine as regards Khrushless and Dullchev and what you so aptly call their idiotology. I am sending my reflections on this matter to the *New Statesman* where they will be published shortly.

I wish you all success in your campaign about space travel.

> *Yours sincerely*
> *Bertrand Russell*

> Plas Penrhyn
> 25 November, 1961

Dear Max Born

Before it is too late for any of us to say anything, I wish to tell you that I feel for you a profound admiration, not only for your intellect which I have respected for forty years, but for your character of which my knowledge is more recent. I have found in you a kind of generosity and a kind of freedom from self-assertion which is very rare even among those whom, on the whole, I admire. You appear to me a man possessed of nobility – unfortunately a rare quality.

Forgive me for writing so openly, but what I have said is said in profound sincerity.

> *Yours very sincerely*
> *Bertrand Russell*

*The following statement launched the Committee of 100 in the autumn of
1960*

ACT OR PERISH

A call to non-violent action

by Earl Russell and Rev. Michael Scott

We are appealing for support for a movement of non-violent resistance
to nuclear war and weapons of mass extermination. Our appeal is made
from a common consciousness of the appalling peril to which Governments of East and West are exposing the human race.

DISASTER ALMOST CERTAIN

Every day, and at every moment of every day, a trivial accident, a
failure to distinguish a meteor from a bomber, a fit of temporary
insanity in one single man, may cause a nuclear world war, which, in
all likelihood, will put an end to man and to all higher forms of animal
life. The populations of the Eastern and Western blocs are, in the
great majority, unaware of the magnitude of the peril. Almost all
experts who have studied the situation without being in the employment of some Government have come to the conclusion that, if present
policies continue, disaster is almost certain within a fairly short time.

PUBLIC MISLED

It is difficult to make the facts known to ordinary men and women,
because Governments do not wish them known and powerful forces
are opposed to dissemination of knowledge which might cause dis-
satisfaction with Government policies. Although it is possible to
ascertain the probabilities by patient and careful study, statements
entirely destitute of scientific validity are put out authoritatively with
a view to misleading those who have not time for careful study. What
is officially said about civil defence, both here and in America, is
grossly misleading. The danger from fall-out is much greater than the
Authorities wish the population to believe. Above all, the imminence of
all-out nuclear war is ignorantly, or mendaciously, underestimated
both in the statements of politicians and in the vast majority of newspapers. It is difficult to resist the conclusion that most of the makers of
opinion consider it more important to secure defeat of the 'enemy' than
to safeguard the continued existence of our species. The fact that the
defeat of the 'enemy' must involve our own defeat, is carefully kept
from the consciousness of those who give only a fleeting and occasional
attention to political matters.

ACTION IMPERATIVE

Much has already been accomplished towards creating a public opinion opposed to nuclear weapons, but not enough, so far, to influence Governments. The threatening disaster is so enormous that we feel compelled to take every action that is possible with a view to awakening our compatriots, and ultimately all mankind, to the need of urgent and drastic changes of policy. We should wish every parent of young children, and every person capable of feelings of mercy, to feel it the most important part of their duty to secure for those who are still young a normal span of life, and to understand that Governments, at present, are making this very unlikely. To us, the vast scheme of mass murder which is being hatched – nominally for our protection, but in fact for universal extermination – is a horror and an abomination. What we can do to prevent this horror, we feel to be a profound and imperative duty which must remain paramount while the danger persists.

CONSTITUTIONAL ACTION NOT ENOUGH

We are told to wait for the beneficent activities of Congresses, Committees, and Summit meetings. Bitter experience has persuaded us that to follow such advice would be utterly futile while the Great Powers remain stubbornly determined to prevent agreement. Against the major forces that normally determine opinion, it is difficult to achieve more than a limited success by ordinary constitutional methods. We are told that in a democracy only lawful methods of persuasion should be used. Unfortunately, the opposition to sanity and mercy on the part of those who have power is such as to make persuasion by ordinary methods difficult and slow, with the result that, if such methods alone are employed, we shall probably all be dead before our purpose can be achieved. Respect for law is important and only a very profound conviction can justify actions which flout the law. It is generally admitted that, in the past, many such actions have been justified. Christian Martyrs broke the law, and there can be no doubt that majority opinion at the time condemned them for doing so. We, in our day, are asked to acquiesce, passively if not actively, in policies clearly leading to tyrannical brutalities compared with which all former horrors sink into insignificance. We cannot do this any more than Christian Martyrs could acquiesce in worship of the Emperor. Their steadfastness in the end achieved victory. It is for us to show equal steadfastness and willingness to suffer hardship and thereby to persuade the world that our cause is worthy of such devotion.

TOWARDS WORLD PEACE

We hope, and we believe, that those who feel as we do and those who may come to share our belief can form a body of such irresistible persuasive force that the present madness of East and West may give way to a new hope, a new realisation of the common destinies of the human family and a determination that men shall no longer seek elaborate and devilish ways of injuring each other but shall, instead, unite in permitting happiness and co-operation. Our immediate purpose, in so far as it is political, is only to persuade Britain to abandon reliance upon the illusory protection of nuclear weapons. But, if this can be achieved, a wider horizon will open before our eyes. We shall become aware of the immense possibilities of nature when harnessed by the creative intelligence of man to the purposes and arts of peace. We shall continue, while life permits, to pursue the goal of world peace and universal human fellowship. We appeal, as human beings to human beings: remember your humanity, and forget the rest. If you can do so, the way lies open to a new Paradise; if you cannot, nothing lies before you but universal death.

The following is the text of my leaflet 'On Civil Disobedience'

RUSSELL ON CIVIL DISOBEDIENCE

On April 15th, 1961, Earl Russell addressed the first Annual Conference of the Midlands Region Youth Campaign for Nuclear Disarmament, in Birmingham.

In putting the case for Civil Disobedience, Earl Russell makes a balanced appeal for nuclear disarmament in the interests of humanity, and his words will be of interest to all who support the Campaign and to those whose minds are open to rational persuasion.

Friends

My main purpose this afternoon is to set out the case for non-violent civil disobedience as one of the methods to be employed in combating the nuclear peril. Many people believe that this method is not likely to achieve its purpose, and some have moral objections to it on principle. Most of them will admit that non-violent civil disobedience is justified when the law demands the individual concerned to do something which he considers wicked. This is the case of conscientious objectors. But our case is a somewhat different one. We advocate and practise non-violent civil disobedience as a method of causing people to know the perils to which the world is exposed and in persuading them to join us in opposing the insanity which affects, at present, many of the most powerful Governments in the world. I will concede that civil disobedience as a method of propaganda is difficult to justify except in extreme cases, but I cannot imagine any issue more extreme or more overwhelmingly important than that of the prevention of nuclear war. Consider one simple fact: if the present policies of many great powers are not radically changed, it is in the highest degree improbable that any of you here present will be alive ten years hence. And that is not because your peril is exceptional. It is a universal peril.

'But', objectors will say, 'why cannot you be content with the ordinary methods of political propaganda?' The main reason why we cannot be content with these methods alone is that, so long as only constitutional methods were employed, it was very difficult – and often impossible – to cause the most important facts to be known. All the great newspapers are against us. Television and radio gave us only grudging and brief opportunities for stating our case. Politicians who opposed us were reported in full, while those who supported us were dubbed 'hysterical' or were said to be actuated by personal hostility to this or that politician. It was very largely the difficulty of making our case known that drove some of us to the adoption of illegal methods. Our illegal actions, because they had sensational news value, were reported, and here and there, a newspaper would allow us to say why we did what we did.

It was a most noteworthy fact that not only was our demonstration of February 18th very widely reported in every part of the world but, as an immediate consequence, all sorts of newspapers – both here and abroad – demanded and printed statements of our case which, until then, they would have rejected. I think also that the spectacle, even in photographs, of so very many serious people, not looking like freaks as newspapers had said we did, caused a widespread belief that our movement could not be dismissed as an outbreak of hysterical emotionalism.

Both popular and official ignorance of the main facts concerned has begun to grow less, and we hope that, in time some members of the Government, and perhaps one or two great newspapers may acquire some knowledge as to the terrible problems about which they light-heartedly dogmatise.

Some of our critics who oppose non-violent civil disobedience on principle say that we rely upon bullying and not upon persuasion. Alas, we are very far removed from being strong enough to bully anybody; and, if we ever were strong enough, present methods would have become unnecessary. I will take as typical of the arguments of our opponents a letter in *The Guardian* of March 29th from the Bishop of Willesden. You may think it rash to oppose a Bishop on a moral issue, but – greatly daring – I will attempt the task. The Bishop says that our demonstrations are intended to force our views upon the community, rather than merely to assert them. He has not, himself, experienced, as we have, the difficulty of asserting anything loud enough to

be heard when all the major organs of publicity are combined in an
attempt to prevent our case from being known. Non-violent civil
disobedience, according to the Bishop, is a use of force by a minority
to compel the majority to submit. This seems to me one of the most
far-fetched and absurd arguments that I have ever heard. How can a
minority of unarmed people, pledged to non-violence, impose their
will against all the forces of the Establishment backed by public
apathy ? The Bishop goes on to say that such methods can lead to
anarchy or dictatorship. There have, it is true, been many instances of
minorities acquiring dictatorship. The Communists in Russia and the
Nazis in Germany are outstanding examples. But their methods were
not non-violent. Our methods, which are non-violent, can only succeed by persuasion.

There are two arguments which are often employed against non-
violent civil disobedience. One is that it alienates people who might
otherwise be supporters, and the other is that it causes dissension
within the anti-nuclear movement. I will say a few words about each of
these. I have no wish whatever to see non-violent civil disobedience
adopted by *all* opponents of nuclear weapons. I think it is well that
organisations both practising and abstaining from non-violent civil
disobedience should exist to suit different temperaments. I do not
believe that the existence of an organisation practising non-violent
civil disobedience prevents anybody from joining an organisation
which does not. Some may say that they are deterred by distaste for
fanatical extremists, but I think these are all people who would in any
case find something to deter them. I think, on the contrary, that our
movement has a vigour and magnetism which attracts large numbers
who might otherwise remain indifferent.

As for dissensions, they, I agree, are regrettable, but they are totally
unnecessary. There is no reason why societies practising different
techniques should not exist side by side without finding fault with each
other. I think this has come to be recognised. I have, for my part, a very
great admiration for what the CND has done and I hope its work will
continue to prosper. But I think the work of those who believe in non-
violent civil disobedience is at least equally valuable, especially while to
the newspapers it has the attraction of novelty.

Many people say that, while civil disobedience may be justified
where there is not democracy, it cannot possibly be right where
everybody has a share of political power. This sort of argument is one
which is wilfully blind to very obvious facts. In practically every so-
called democratic country there are movements similar to ours. There
are vigorous movements in the United States. In Canada they are not
far from acquiring power. Naturally the movement in Japan is very
powerful and very convinced. Moreover, take the problem of people

under 21. If the Governments have their way, these people will all be slaughtered without having any legal means of giving weight to their wish to survive. Consider, again, the way in which opinion is manufactured in a nominally democratic country. Great newspapers belong to rich and powerful people. Television and radio have strong reasons for not offending the Government. Most experts would lose their position and their income if they spoke the truth.

For these reasons the forces that control opinion are heavily weighted upon the side of the rich and powerful. Those who are neither rich nor powerful can find no ways of counter-balancing this over-weight except such as the Establishment can decry with the support of all who profit by the *status quo*. There is in every great modern State, a vast mechanism intended to prevent the truth from being known, not only to the public, but also to the Governments. Every Government is advised by experts and inevitably prefers the experts who flatter its prejudices. The ignorance of important public men on the subject of nuclear warfare is utterly astounding to those who have made an impartial study of the subject. And from public men this ignorance trickles down to become the voice of the people. It is against this massive artificial ignorance that our protests are directed. I will give a few instances of this astonishing ignorance:

The *Daily Mail* in a report on civil defence stated that fall-out decays rapidly once it is down on the ground and that, therefore, people who had taken refuge in shelters would not have to stay there very long. As a matter of fact, to take only two of the most dangerous ingredients of fall-out – Strontium 90 has a half life of 28 years and Carbon 14 has a half life of 5,600 years. These facts make it seem as if people would have to stay in the shelters as long as from the building of the Pyramids to the present day.

To take a more important example, the Prime Minister recently stated without any qualification that 'there will be no war by accident'. I have not come across one non-Government expert who has studied this subject who does not say the opposite. C. P. Snow, who has an exceptional right to speak with authority, said in a recent article 'Within at the most ten years, some of these bombs are going off. I am saying this as responsibly as I can. *That* is a certainty.' John B. Witchell, an engineer, who resigned his position as a member of Canada's Atomic Research Board in protest against the Government's nuclear armament policies, stated in a recent speech: 'The demand for instantaneous retaliation leads to a hair-trigger situation which renders nuclear war a statistical certainty.' He went on to say that those whom he calls 'the official liars' will say that mistakes will be impossible. He replied to them: 'Let me say emphatically, positively, there can be no safeguard which can be considered adequate.'

I could give many other quotations expressing the same view, and none expressing the opposite view except from Government employees. Mr Macmillan should know these facts, but evidently does not.

I will give another example of the Prime Minister's cheerful ignorance: speaking in Ottawa quite recently he alluded to the signs of neutralism in Britain and told the Canadians not to be worried by them. He said, 'If ever the call comes to them, the young will go straight from the ranks of the neutralists into the ranks of Her Majesty's Forces, as they have so often done in the past'. They will have to be rather quick about it, as his own Government has told us that they will only have four minutes' notice. At the end of the four minutes they will be dead, whether in Her Majesty's Forces or still among the neutralists. The ancient rhetorical language associated with war is so ingrained that Mr Macmillan is quite unable to realise its complete remoteness from modern military facts.

It is not only that the organs of publicity are slow to publish facts which militate against official policy. It is also that such facts are unpleasant and, therefore, most people soon forget them. What proportion of the inhabitants of Britain know the official report by the US Defence Minister of probable casualties in a nuclear war with present armament? His official guess was 160 million in the US, 200 million in the USSR and everybody in Britain and Western Europe. He did not regard this as a reason for changing American policy. When one combines this estimate with the near certainty of a nuclear war if present policies continue, it is obviously not unjust to say that the Government of Britain is favouring a course which, if persisted in, will lead to the death of every one of us. It may seem odd that a majority of the British public supports the policy leading to this dreadful disaster. I do not think that British voters would continue to do so if the facts were brought to their notice so emphatically that they could no longer forget them. This is part of our purpose and part of what makes spectacular action necessary.

Most people in Britain are not aware of the attitude taken by armament experts in America to the British alliance and to the British desire to be a nuclear Power. The most learned and detailed account of American policy in these matters is Herman Kahn's big book *On Thermonuclear War*.

He is remarkably cold-blooded and makes careful arithmetical estimates of probable casualties. He believes that both America and Russia could more or less survive a nuclear war and achieve economic recovery in no very long time. Apparently – though on this he is vague – they are both to set to work at once on preparations for another nuclear war, and this sort of thing is to go on until not enough people are left alive for it to be possible to make a bomb. All this has shocked liberal-minded Americans who have criticised Mr Kahn with great severity, not realising, apparently, that he is only expounding official American policy.

There is, however, another aspect of his discussions which is of special interest to Britain. He holds that Britain as an ally adds nothing to the strength of America. He argues at length that, if Russia were to attack Britain without attacking the United States, the United States would not intervene in spite of obligations under NATO. He shows no objection to British neutrality, and explicitly regrets the lack of success for the suggestion that Britain should form a non-nuclear club of which it should be a member. Britons who are orthodox in armament policy do not seem to be aware of this American opinion. It hurts their national pride since it considers British military power negligible and the protection of Britain during war totally impossible. British opponents of British neutralism all argue vehemently that the West would be weakened if Britain became neutral. But, apparently, this is not the opinion of orthodox American armament experts.

It is not only unpleasant facts that the public ignores: it is also some facts which ought to be found pleasant. Khrushchev has repeatedly offered complete disarmament by agreement combined with any degree of inspection that the West may desire. The West shrugs its shoulders and says 'of course, he is not sincere'. This, however, is not the argument that really weighs with Western Governments. Khrushchev proclaims his hope that Communists will conquer the world by peaceful propaganda. Western Governments fear that they cannot produce equally effective counter-propaganda. As Dulles said, in an unguarded moment, 'We are losing this cold war, but we might win a hot one'. He did not explain what he meant by 'winning', but I suppose he meant that, at the end, there might be 6 Americans and only 4 Russians.

Doubts as to sincerity have at least as much justification if entertained by the Russians towards us as they have if entertained by us towards the Russians. The British Commonwealth has lately voted unanimously for universal and complete disarmament. Since in this matter there is complete agreement with Khrushchev, while America is adverse, it might have been thought that the vote of the British Commonwealth, including Britain, would lead to a rapprochement with the Soviet Government. Instead of this, however, Kennedy and Macmillan have recently been tightening up the alliance and proposing agreements which would make British disarmament totally impossible. We cannot therefore take the British vote in the Commonwealth as indicating the sincere wishes of the British Government.

I think that while we are engaged in campaigning for British unilateralism, it is important to bear in mind the more distant objectives which give international meaning to our efforts. Let us consider for a moment what international aims must form part of any attempt to put an end to nuclear war.

The first thing to realise is that, if there are not to be nuclear wars, there must not be wars, because any war is sure to become nuclear no matter what treaties to the contrary may have been concluded. And if there is not to be war, there must be machinery for settling disputes by negotiation. This will require an international authority which shall arbitrate disputes and be sufficiently powerful to compel obedience to its awards. None of this can possibly come about while relations between East and West are as strained as they are now, and while weapons of mass extermination keep the whole world in a state of nuclear terror. Before anything that seriously diminishes the risk of nuclear war can be achieved, there will have to be a treaty between America and Russia and China, and an agreement to ban – not only nuclear weapons – but also chemical and biological weapons. All this may seem beyond the power of Britain to help or hinder. I do not think that it is. Negotiations between East and West ever since 1945 have been abortive because only the two contesting blocs were represented in the negotiations, and each of them, from motives of prestige, felt unable to make the slightest concession to the other. If there is ever to be a détente between Russia and America, it will have to be brought about by the friendly mediation of neutrals. Britain, if neutral, could play an important part in this beneficent work, whereas Britain can do nothing in this direction while remaining a member of NATO.

These, as yet somewhat distant, vistas should, I think, be in our minds while we are engaged in what might seem an exclusively national campaign. We have to remember that weapons of mass extermination, once invented, remain a potential threat even if none are actually in being. For this reason, we have to remember, further, that, unless war is completely eliminated, the human race is doomed. To put an end to war, which has dominated human life for 6,000 years, is no easy task. It is a heroic task, a task worthy of all the energies and all the thought of every sane man throughout the world. I think this larger vista may help in difficult times to prevent discouragement and disillusion. I think that our campaign is the best thing that Britons not in Government posts can do, though it is only a small part of what the world needs.

Extempore comment added by Lord Russell to the foregoing speech

And I would like to say in conclusion that what I suppose most of us feel most strongly and what makes us willing to make sacrifices for the cause is the extraordinary wickedness of these weapons of mass destruction. We used to think that Hitler was wicked when he wanted to kill all the Jews, but Kennedy and Macmillan and others both in the East and in the West pursue policies which will probably lead to killing not only all the Jews but all the rest of us too. They are much more wicked than Hitler and this idea of weapons of mass extermination is utterly and absolutely horrible and it is a thing which no man with one spark of humanity can tolerate and I will not pretend to obey a government which is organising the massacre of the whole of mankind. I will do anything I can to oppose such Governments in any non-violent way that seems likely to be fruitful, and I should exhort all of you to feel the same way. We cannot obey these murderers. They are wicked and abominable. They are the wickedest people that ever lived in the history of man and it is our duty to do what we can.

[The last phrase of these extempore observations – 'They are the wickedest people that ever lived' – was taken up by the Press and published throughout Britain and the world, usually without the preceding extempore remarks and with no indication that they had been preceded by a carefully built up speech giving the documentation necessary to support such a conclusion.]

My Statement at Bow Street, September 12, 1961

If the Court permits, I should like to make a short statement as to the reasons for my present course. This is my personal statement, but I hope that those who are accused of the same so-called crime will be in sympathy with what I have to say.

It was only step by step and with great reluctance that we were driven to non-violent civil disobedience.

Ever since the bomb was dropped on Hiroshima on August 6th, 1945, I have been profoundly troubled by the danger of nuclear warfare. I began my attempt to warn people by entirely orthodox methods. I expressed my fears in a speech in the House of Lords three months after the bombs were dropped in Japan. I called together scientists of the highest eminence from all parts of the world and am now Chairman of their periodic meetings. They issue wise and reasoned reports concerning nuclear warfare, its probable disastrous results, and ways of preventing its occurrence. No newspaper notices these reports and they have no effect either on Governments or on public opinion. The popular Press minimises and ridicules the effort of those working against nuclear warfare, and television, with rare exceptions, is closed to us. In recent months one television company, and only one, offered me two minutes for general platitudes, but when I said I should wish to speak on Berlin the offer was withdrawn.

It has seemed to some of us that, in a country supposed to be a democracy, the public should know the probable consequences of present Great-Power policies in East and West. Patriotism and humanity alike urged us to seek some way of saving our country and the world. No one can desire the slaughter of our families, friends, our compatriots and a majority of the human race in a contest in which there will be only vanquished and no victors. We feel it a profound and inescapable duty to make the facts known and thereby save at least a thousand million human lives. We cannot escape this duty by submitting to orders which, we are convinced, would not be issued if the likelihood and the horror of nuclear war were more generally understood.

Non-violent civil disobedience was forced upon us by the fact that it was more fully reported than other methods of making the facts known, and that caused people to ask what had induced us to adopt such a course of action. We who are here accused are prepared to suffer imprisonment because we believe that this is the most effective way of working for the salvation of our country and the world. If you condemn us you will be helping our cause, and therefore humanity.

While life remains to us we will not cease to do what lies in our power to avert the greatest calamity that has ever threatened mankind.

The text of a leaflet issued while I was in Brixton Prison

A MESSAGE FROM BERTRAND RUSSELL

To all, in whatever country who are still capable of sane thinking or human feeling:

Friends

Along with valued colleagues I am to be silenced for a time – perhaps for ever, for who can tell how soon the great massacre will take place ? The populations of East and West, misled by stubborn governments in search of prestige and by corrupt official experts bent on retaining their posts, tamely acquiesce in policies which are almost certain to end in nuclear war.

There are supposed to be two sides, each professing to stand for a great cause. This is a delusion – Kennedy and Khrushchev, Adenauer and de Gaulle, Macmillan and Gaitskell, are pursuing a common aim: the ending of human life.

You, your families, your friends and your countries are to be exterminated by the common decision of a few brutal but powerful men. To please these men, all the private affections, all the public hopes, all that has been achieved in art, and knowledge and thought and all that might be achieved hereafter is to be wiped out forever.

Our ruined lifeless planet will continue for countless ages to circle aimlessly round the sun unredeemed by the joys and loves, the occa-

sional wisdom and the power to create beauty which have given value
to human life.

It is for seeking to prevent this that we are in prison.

Bertrand Russell

From Augustus John

Fryern Court,
Fordingbridge, Hants.
[postmarked 15 Feb. 1961]

Dear Lord Russell

Your message was brought to me while I was working in the studio
(not the one you knew but one further off) by the gardener. I told him
how to reply, which he said he understood but I don't know if he did so
correctly. All I wanted to say was that I believed in the object of the
demonstration and would like to go to prison if necessary. I didn't
want to parade my physical disabilities though I *still* have to follow the
instructions of my doctor, who I think saved my life when I was in
danger of coronary thrombosis. A very distinguished medical authority
who was consulted, took a *very* pessimistic view of my case, but my
local doctor, undeterred, continued his treatment and I feel sure,
saved my life.

All this I meant *privately* & am sure you understood, even if the
gardener garbled it when telephoning. I wish the greatest success for
the demonstration on the 18th although I can only be with you in
spirit.

Yours sincerely
Augustus John

P.S. This requires no answer.

My speech in Trafalgar Square, October 29, 1961

Friends

During the last decades there have been many people who have been
loud in condemnation of the Germans for having permitted the growth
of Nazi evil and atrocities in their country. 'How,' these people ask,
'could the Germans allow themselves to remain unaware of the evil?
Why did they not risk their comfort, their livelihood, even their lives to
combat it?'

Now a more all-embracing danger threatens us all – the danger of
nuclear war. I am very proud that there is in this country a rapidly
growing company of people who refuse to remain unaware of the
danger, or ignorant of the facts concerning the policies that enable, and
force, us to live in such danger. I am even prouder to be associated with
those many among them who, at whatever risk of discomfort and often

of very real hardship, are willing to take drastic action to uphold their belief. They have laid themselves open to the charges of being silly, being exhibitionist, being law-breakers, being traitors. They have suffered ostracism and imprisonment, sometimes repeatedly, in order to call attention to the facts that they have made the effort to learn. It is a great happiness to me to welcome so many of them here – I wish that I could say all of them, but some are still in prison. We none of us, however, can be entirely happy until our immediate aim has been achieved and the threat of nuclear war has become a thing of the past. Then such actions as we have taken and shall take will no longer be necessary.

We all wish that there shall be no nuclear war, but I do not think that the country realises, or even that many of us here present realise, the very considerable likelihood of a nuclear war within the next few months. We are all aware of Khrushchev's resumption of tests and of his threat to explode a 50 megaton bomb.

We all deplore these provocative acts. But I think we are less aware of the rapidly growing feeling in America in favour of a nuclear war in the very near future. In America, the actions of Congress are very largely determined by lobbies representing this or that interest. The armament lobby, which represents both the economic interests of armament firms and the warlike ardour of generals and admirals, is exceedingly powerful, and it is very doubtful whether the President will be able to stand out against the pressure which it is exerting. Its aims are set forth in a quite recent policy statement by the Air Force Association, which is the most terrifying document that I have ever read. It begins by stating that preservation of the *status quo* is not adequate as a national goal. I quote: 'Freedom must bury Communism or be buried by Communism. Complete eradication of the Soviet system must be our national goal, our obligation to all free people, our promise of hope to all who are not free.' It is a curious hope that is being promised, since it can only be realised in heaven, for the only 'promise' that the West can hope to fulfil is the promise to turn Eastern populations into corpses. The noble patriots who make this pronouncement omit to mention that Western populations also will be exterminated.

'We are determined', they say, 'to back our words with action even at the risk of war. We seek not merely to preserve our freedoms, but to extend them.' The word 'freedom', which is a favourite word of Western warmongers, has to be understood in a somewhat peculiar sense. It means freedom for warmongers and prison for those who oppose them. A freedom scarcely distinguishable from this exists in Soviet Russia. The document that I am discussing says that we should employ bombs against Soviet aggression, even if the aggression is non-nuclear and even if it consists only of infiltration. We must have, it says, 'ability to fight, win, and purposefully survive a general nuclear war'. This aim is, of course, impossible to realise, but, by using their peculiar brand of 'freedom' to cause belief in lies, they hope to persuade a deliberately uninformed public opinion to join in their race towards death. They are careful to promise us that H-bombs will not be the worst things they have to offer. 'Nuclear weapons', they say, 'are not the end of military development. There is no reason to believe that nuclear weapons, no matter how much they may increase in number and ferocity, mark the end of the line in military systems' development.' They explain their meaning by saying, 'We must utilise US space technology as a prime factor in the international power equation'. They lead up to a noble peroration: 'Soviet aims are both evil and implacable. The people (i.e. the American people) are willing to work toward, and fight for if necessary, the elimination of Communism from the world scene. Let the issue be joined.'

This ferocious document, which amounts to a sentence of death on the human race, does not consist of the idle vapourings of acknowledged cranks. On the contrary, it represents the enormous economic power of the armament industry, which is re-enforced in the public mind by the cleverly instilled fear that disarmament would bring a new depression. This fear has been instilled in spite of the fact that Americans have been assured in the *Wall Street Journal* that a new depression would not be brought about, that the conversion from armaments to manufactures for peace could be made with little dislocation. Reputable economists in other countries support this Wall Street view. But the armament firms exploit patriotism and anti-communism as means of transferring the taxpayers' money into their own pockets. Ruthlessly, and probably consciously, they are leading the world towards disaster.

Two days ago *The Times* published an article by its correspondent in Washington which began: 'The United States has decided that any attempt by East Germany to close the Friedrichstrasse crossing between West and East Berlin will be met by force.'

These facts about both America and Russia strengthen my belief that the aims that I have been advocating for some years, and upon which some of us are agreed, are right. I believe that Britain should become neutral, leaving NATO – to which, in any case, she adds only negligible strength. I believe this partly because I believe that Britain would be safer as a neutral, and without a bomb of her own or the illusory 'protection' of the American bomb, and without bases for foreign troops; and, perhaps more important, I believe it because, if Britain were neutral, she could do more to help to achieve peace in the world than she can do now. I do not believe that either America or Russia should disarm unilaterally, because whichever did not do so first would automatically become ruler of the world. I believe that they should disarm as a result of negotiations and agreement to do so. In order to achieve this agreement, I think that Britain might have a very important role to play, for I believe that it can only be brought about if the neutrals form a sort of balancing committee to put forward and argue possible compromises. Then Britain could profitably add her political experience to this committee. In the present state of affairs she can do nothing to forward governmental movement towards peace. I should like to think that the example of Britain unilaterally disarming and, untramelled, taking up the cudgels for peace would persuade some other countries to disarm unilaterally. Then we should be able to throw a heavy weight towards persuading America and Russia to disarm multilaterally.

I have heard the criticism that we uphold only negative aims. I should like to point out that the policy just outlined is quite positive. All our aims, the most immediate and the most distant, are positive – whether they happen to be stated in negative terms or not.

But to return –

The British Government is less ruthless than the American, but shrinks from open opposition to American Jingoism. It is our hope that, before it is too late, we may overcome this shrinking timidity. Our methods must be dominated by the knowledge that the time is short. We are censured as disobeying orders by the very men who, in the Nuremberg Trials, punished the Germans for *not* disobeying orders. There are Committees of 100 starting up in various parts of this country. But not only here. Since September 17th, the support given us from all parts of the world from individuals, by already established movements having similar aims, even by newly established Committees of 100 in other countries, has been astounding. All these people throughout the world must be encouraged. We must build up – and we must do it quickly – a great world-wide mass movement of people demanding the abandonment of nuclear weapons, the abandonment of war as a means of settling disputes. Although the time may be short, our movement is gaining strength day by day. I repeat, and shall go on repeating:

We *can* win, and we *must*.

Note to above speech:

[After Khrushchev's abandonment of violence in the Cuba crisis, the danger of war became less immediate, and Russian policy became somewhat milder.]

SUGGESTIONS FOR U THANT   RE: BALANCING COMMITTEE

The Assembly should empower the Secretary General to appoint a small committee consisting entirely of members of uncommitted nations which should be charged with the task of investigating matters in debate between East and West as they arise, with a view to suggesting compromise solutions which both sides could accept without loss of face. These solutions should be such as to give no net advantage to either side since if they favoured one side, the other would not accept them. They should also be such as to diminish friction at danger points such as Berlin.

This 'Balancing Committee' should publish the suggestions on whatever problems it investigated and seek to rally to the support of these suggestions first neutral opinion and then, if possible, the opinion of Eastern and Western negotiators. The members of the 'Balancing Committee' should command public respect in their several countries but should not be responsible to the national governments of the states from which they come.

The Committee should be small, since, otherwise, it will not reach decisions until they are out of date. It may be hoped that in time the suggestions of the 'Balancing Committee' would acquire moral authority and be difficult for either side to resist.

Statement re: CUBA CRISIS

YOU ARE TO DIE	Not in the course of nature, but within a few weeks, and not you alone, but your family, your friends, and all the inhabitants of Britain, together with many hundreds of millions of innocent people elsewhere.
WHY?	Because rich Americans dislike the Government that Cubans prefer, and have used part of their wealth to spread lies about it.
WHAT CAN YOU DO?	You can go out into the streets and into the market place, proclaiming: 'Do not yield to ferocious and insane murderers. Do not imagine that it is your duty to die when your Prime Minister and the President of the United States tell you to do so. Remember rather your duty to your family, your friends, your country, the world you live in, and that future world which, if you so choose, may be glorious, happy, and free.'

AND REMEMBER: CONFORMITY MEANS DEATH

                                   ONLY PROTEST

                                   GIVES A HOPE OF LIFE

                                                BERTRAND RUSSELL
                                                23rd October, 1962

The two following letters concerned with the Sino-Indian Border dispute were not published in Unarmed Victory. *I therefore publish them here.*

                                                Peking, November 24, 1962
The Earl Russell
London

My dear Lord

I have received with honour your letters dated November 16 and 19, 1962 and read with great pleasure your statement welcoming and supporting the Chinese Government's statement of November 21. I am deeply moved by your good wishes and efforts for a peaceful settlement of the Sino-Indian boundary question and your deep interest in world peace. I am sincerely grateful to you for the profound friendship for the Chinese people and the condemnation of US occupation of China's territory Taiwan, which you have expressed in your letters.

The Chinese Government issued a statement on October 24, 1962, putting forward three proposals. Unfortunately, they were repeatedly rejected by the Indian Government. In order to reverse the daily aggravating Sino-Indian border situation due to the Indian Government's refusal to enter into negotiations and its continued expansion of the armed border conflict, and in order to demonstrate its great sincerity for stopping the border conflict and settling the Sino-Indian Boundary question peacefully, the Chinese Government issued a statement on November 21, 1962, declaring three measures including the unilateral observation of cease-fire and withdrawal along the entire border by China on its own initiative. Now, I wish to tell you that as from 00:00 hours on November 22 the Chinese frontier guards have ceased fire along the entire Sino-Indian border. I believe that this accords with the desires you expressed in your messages.

You suggested in your letter of November 19: 'All troops to vacate this particular area – that which India has occupied since 1959 and until September 8, 1962, and felt by China to be her own.' I believe you have noted that the Chinese Government has declared in its statement of November 21 that, beginning from December 1, the Chinese frontier guards would withdraw to positions 20 kilometres behind the line of actual control which existed between China and India on November 7, 1959, and would then be far behind their positions prior to September 8, 1962. The Chinese Government hopes that the Indian Government will respond positively to the Chinese Government's November 21 statement and adopt corresponding measures. Once the Indian Government has done so, the Sino-Indian Border will become tranquil and a demilitarised zone 40 kilometres wide can be established between China and India. It goes without saying that administration will continue to be exercised by the administrative authorities of each side existing in the zone on their own side of the line of actual control between China and India.

The Chinese Government hopes that the Indian Government will be willing to change its past attitude and sincerely settle the Sino-Indian Boundary question through friendly negotiations. I hope that you will continue to use your distinguished influence to urge the Indian Government to respond positively to the Chinese Government's November 21 statement and adopt corresponding measures. At the same time, the Chinese Government also hopes that all friendly countries and peace-loving public figures will exert their influence to urge the Indian Government to return to the conference table. These efforts will be great contributions to peace.

Please accept my high regards.

Chou En-Lai

Prime Minister's House
New Dehli
December 4, 1962

CONFIDENTIAL
No. 2155-PMH/62
The Earl Russell
Plas Penrhyn, Penrhyndeudraeth
Merioneth, England

Dear Lord Russell
I must ask for your forgiveness for the delay in answering your letter of the 23rd November and your telegram which came subsequently. You can certainly write to me whenever you so wish, and I shall always welcome your views and advice.

I have given much thought to what you have written. I need not tell you that I am much moved by your passion for peace and it finds an echo in my own heart. Certainly we do not want this frontier war with China to continue, and even more certainly we do not want it to spread and involve the nuclear powers. Also there is the danger of the military mentality spreading in India and the power of the Army increasing.

But there are limits in a democratic society to what a Government can do. There is such strong feeling in India over the invasion by China that no Government can stand if it does not pay some heed to it. The Communist Party of India has been compelled by circumstances to issue a strong condemnation of China. Even so, the Communists here are in a bad way, and their organisation is gradually disappearing because of popular resentment.

Apart from this, there are various other important considerations which have to be borne in mind in coming to a decision. If there is a sense of national surrender and humiliation, this will have a very bad effect on the people of India and all our efforts to build up the nation will suffer a very serious setback. At present the popular upsurge all over India can be utilised for strengthening the unity and capacity for work of the nation, apart from the military aspect. There are obvious dangers about militarism and extreme forms of nationalism developing, but there are also possibilities of the people of our country thinking in a more constructive way and profiting by the dangers that threaten us.

If we go wholly against the popular sentiment, which to a large extent I share, then the result will be just what you fear. Others will take charge and drive the country towards disaster.

The Chinese proposals, as they are, mean their gaining a dominating position, specially in Ladakh, which they can utilise in future for a further attack on India. The present day China, as you know, is probably the only country which is not afraid even of a nuclear war. Mao Tse-tung has said repeatedly that he does not mind losing a few million people as still several hundred millions will survive in China. If they are to profit by this invasion, this will lead them to further attempts of the same kind. That will put an end to all talks of peace and will surely bring about a world nuclear war. I feel, therefore, that in order to avoid this catastrophe and, at the same time, strengthen our own people, quite apart from arms, etc., we must not surrender or submit to what we consider evil. That is a lesson I learned from Gandhiji.

We have, however, not rejected the Chinese proposal, but have ourselves suggested an alternative which is honourable for both parties. I still have hopes that China will agree to this. In any event we are not going to break the cease-fire and indulge in a military offensive.

If these preliminaries are satisfactorily settled, we are prepared to adopt any peaceful methods for the settlement of the frontier problem. These might even include a reference to arbitration.

So far as we are concerned, we hope to adhere to the policy of non-alignment although I confess that taking military help from other countries does somewhat affect it. But in the circumstances we have no choice.

I can assure you that the wider issues that you have mentioned are before us all the time. We do not want to do something which will endanger our planet. I do think, however, that there will be a greater danger of that kind if we surrender to the Chinese and they feel that the policy they have pursued brings them rich dividends.

Yours sincerely
Jawaharlal Nehru

Chapter 17

The Foundation

The nuclear peril represented a danger which was likely to last as long as governments possessed nuclear weapons, and perhaps even longer if such destructive objects get into private hands. At first I imagined that the task of awakening people to the dangers should not be very difficult. I shared the general belief that the motive of self-preservation is a very powerful one which, when it comes into operation, generally overrides all others. I thought that people would not like the prospect of being fried with their families and their neighbours and every living person that they had heard of. I thought it would only be necessary to make the danger known and that, when this had been done, men of all parties would unite to restore previous safety. I found that this was a mistake. There is a motive which is stronger than self-preservation: it is the desire to get the better of the other fellow. I have discovered an important political fact that is often overlooked, as it had been by me: people do not care so much for their own survival – or, indeed, that of the human race – as for the extermination of their enemies. The world in which we live is one in which there is constant risk of universal death. The methods of putting an end to this risk are obvious to all, but they involve a very tiny chance that someone may play the traitor, and this is so galling that almost everybody prefers running the risk of nuclear war to securing safety. I thought, and I still think, that, if the risk of total destruction were made sufficiently vivid, it would have the desired effect. But how was an individual, or a collection of individuals, to bring about this vividness? In company with those who thought like me, I tried various methods with varying degrees of success. I tried first the method of reason: I compared the danger of nuclear weapons with the danger of the Black Death. Everybody said, 'How true,' and did nothing. I tried alerting a particular group, but though this had a limited success, it had little effect on the general public or Governments. I next tried the popular appeal of marches of large numbers. Everybody said, 'These marchers are a nuisance'. Then I tried methods of civil disobedience, but they, too, failed to succeed. All these methods continue to be used, and I support them all when possible, but none has proved more than partially efficacious. I am now engaged in a new attempt which consists of a mixed appeal to Governments and public.

So long as I live, I shall continue the search and in all probability I shall leave the work to be continued by others. But whether mankind will think itself worth preserving remains a doubtful question.

For many years I had been interested in the persecuted minorities and those people in many countries who, I thought, had been unjustly imprisoned. I tried to help, for instance, the Naga and Sobell about whom I have already told. A little later, I became concerned with the plight of the Gypsies, being especially interested in the efforts of Grattan Puxon to give them a fit abiding place with at least the necessary amenities, such as decent sanitation and opportunity to obtain at least a minimum of proper education.

My scutcheon on the score of liberating prisoners, I confess, is not entirely unsmirched. Many years ago a young German Jewish refugee came to me asking for help. The Home Office had decreed that he was to be returned to Germany and, if he were returned, he would be executed. He seemed a silly young man but harmless enough. I went with him to the Home Office and said, 'Look, do you think that he is dangerous ?' 'Well,' they said, 'no.' They agreed not to dispatch him to his homeland but said that he must have a fresh passport. They started at once putting him through the questions to be answered for this purpose. 'Who was your father ?' 'I do not know.' 'Who was your mother ?' 'I do not know.' 'Where and when were you born ?' 'I do not know.' The Officials quailed. The only thing he was sure of was that he was a Jew. Seeing my stubborn and grim, if by this time slightly pink, visage, the officials persisted and gave him his passport. The last thing I heard of him was a message to the effect that to remain in England he knew that he had to pay his way and he had learnt that the surest means of obtaining money was to get an English girl pregnant. He could then apply for and receive a governmental hand-out. I was only slightly reassured by the comment that, up to date, he had failed in this scheme.

Many years ago, too, a young Pole appealed to me for help against imprisonment on the charge of writing obscene verse. I thought, 'A poet gaoled! Never! This cannot be!' And again I appealed to the Home Office. I then read some of his verse and found it so thoroughly disgusting that my sympathies were with the earlier verdict. But he was allowed to stay in England.

Though both these cases are somewhat embarrassing to remember, I cannot regret them. It seems to me nonsense to imprison people for silliness that is unlikely to harm the general public. If it were carried to its logical conclusion, there are few men who would be free. Moreover, to deal with obscenity by means of the law and the threat of imprisonment does more harm than good. It merely adds an aura of delightful and enticing wickedness to what may be only foolish or may be evil. It does nothing to curtail it. I feel even more strongly in the matter of political prisoners and for similar reasons. To gaol a man merely for his political views, however tempting it may be, is more likely to spread than to stop the dissemination of those views. It adds to the sum of human misery and encourages violence, and that is all. In recent years I have become, as I have said, more and more involved in work against the incarceration and the persecution of individuals and groups because of their political and religious opinions. I have received a continually increasing number of written appeals for help from individuals and organisations all over the world and almost daily visits from representatives of the latter. I have been unable to travel to distant countries myself, so, in order to have as nearly as possible first-hand objective information, I have been obliged to send representatives to the various countries.

In 1963, my interests in the resistance fighters in Greece came to a head. They had opposed the Nazis there but were still languishing in prison because most of them had been 'Communists'. A number of their representatives came to see me, among them the Greek MPs who visited England in April and May. A 'Bertrand Russell Committee of 100' had been formed in Greece and they held a march, or tried to hold one, towards the end of April to which I sent a representative. Then came the murder of the MP Lambrakis at Salonika, with, it was fairly clear, the connivance of the Authorities. This deeply shocked me, in common with other liberal-minded people. Again, at request, I sent my representative to the funeral of Lambrakis in Athens. He returned with a very moving story. By the time that the Greek Royal visit to Buckingham Palace took place in July, feeling here had mounted to boiling point. I shared it. I spoke in Trafalgar Square against the visit and took part in a demonstration. The press were shocked at such unseemly doings on the part of Her Majesty's subjects, Cabinet Ministers gobbled, and the police planted bricks in the pockets of arrested demonstrators and charged them with carrying offensive weapons. One of the most persistent and bravest of British demonstrators was Betty Ambatielos whose Greek husband had been held a prisoner for many years. Two years later, he was freed and visited us in London, but others of the prisoners remained in gaol. Later he and, for a time, his wife were re-imprisoned and many more prisoners were thrown into concentration camps by the Greek Authorities. The contemplation of what their lives must be in these camps, herded together in the blazing sunlight, without water, without sanitation, with no care of any sort, is sickening.

That same April, 1963, I sent a representative to Israel to look into the situation of the Palestine Arab refugees. We wished to form some assessment of what, if anything, might most effectively be urged to help to settle matters between Jews and Arabs concerning the question of the Palestine refugees. Since then I have, often at request, sent other representatives to both Israel and Egypt to discuss the separate and the joint problems of those countries. In turn, they have sent their emissaries to me. I was also much concerned, and still am, with the plight of the Jews in the Soviet Union, and I have carried on a considerable and continuing correspondence with the Soviet Government in regard to it. In addition, a very large number of Jewish families in Eastern Europe have been separated by the Second World War and wish to rejoin their relations abroad, usually in Israel. At first I appealed for permission for them to emigrate individually, but later, under the pressure of hundreds of requests, I began to make appeals on behalf of whole groups. As such work developed, I found myself working for the release of political prisoners in over forty countries where they are held, half forgotten, for deeds which were often praiseworthy. Many prisoners in many lands have been freed, we are told, as a result of my colleagues' and my work, but many remain in gaol and the work goes on. Sometimes I have got into difficulty about this work and had to bear considerable obloquy, as in the case of Sobell and, later, in regard to the freeing of Heintz Brandt. The abduction and imprisonment by the East Germans of Brandt, who had survived Hitler's concentration camps, seemed to me so inhuman that I was obliged to return to the East German Government the Carl von Ossietsky medal which it had awarded me. I was impressed by the speed with which Brandt was soon released. And perhaps it was my work for prisoners, in part at any rate, that won me the Tom Paine award bestowed upon me by the American Emergency Civil Liberties Committee in January, 1963.[1]

Through the last years, and especially recently, since I have been able to act in this work as part of an organisation, I have sent fact-finding representatives to many parts of the world. They have gone to most European countries, 'East' and 'West', and to many eastern countries – Cambodia, China, Ceylon, India, Indonesia, Japan, Vietnam. They have gone to Africa – Ethiopia and Egypt and the newer countries of both East and West Africa. And, of course, they have gone to countries of the Western Hemisphere, both north and south. These investigators have been generously welcomed by the Heads of the countries to which they journeyed and by many of the Government officials and heads of organisations dealing with problems in which they are interested. And, naturally, they have talked with members of the general public. I have myself carried on prolonged correspondence with the various Heads of State and officials, and have discussed in London a variety of

[1] In seeking to liberate prisoners, my colleagues and I made no distinction of party or creed, but only of the justice or injustice of the punishment inflicted and the unnecessary cruelty caused by the imprisonment.

international problems with them, particularly with those from Eastern Europe and Asia and Africa. The gatherings for the Commonwealth Conference, especially, made possible many of these meetings. Some of them were entertaining and adorned with the proper trappings – flashing eyes, robes, scimitars, jewels and tall, fierce attendants – as was my meeting with the Sheikh of Bahrein in 1965, the memory of which I rejoice in. On special subjects, of course, I am in frequent touch with the Embassies in London.

All this work steadily mounted in demand. By 1963, it was rapidly becoming more than one individual could carry on alone even with the extraordinarily able and willing help that I had. Moreover, the expenses of journeys and correspondence – written, telegraphed and telephoned – and of secretaries and co-workers was becoming more than my private funds could cover. And the weight of responsibility of being an entirely one-man show was heavy. Gradually the scheme took shape, hatched, again, I think, by the fertile mind of Ralph Schoenman, of forming some sort of organisation. This should be not just for this or that purpose. It should be for any purpose that would forward the struggle against war and the armaments race, and against the unrest and the injustices suffered by oppressed individuals and peoples that in very large part caused these. Such an organisation could grow to meet the widely differing demands. It could, also, reorientate itself as circumstances changed. A good part of my time, therefore, in 1963, was taken up with discussing plans for the formation of such an organisation. Many of my colleagues in these discussions had been working with me since the early days of the Committee of 100.

My colleagues were inexperienced in organisation and I myself am not at all good at it, but at least we brought our aims into some sort of cohesive progression, and, where we erred, it was on the side of flexibility which would permit of change and growth. We faced the fact that in the early days of the organisation our work must be carried on much as it had been, with me bearing most of the public responsibility and holding the position of final arbitrator of it. We hoped to strengthen the organisation gradually. We felt that not only the day-to-day work for it, but the responsibility and the planning should, in time, be borne by it as an entity. As I look back upon our progress, it seems to me that we achieved far more than we had dared to hope to do in its first three years.

Many people have worked to build up the Foundation, but I wish to stress not only my own but the Foundation's debt to Ralph Schoenman. He has carried on its work sometimes almost single-handed and many of its most fertile ideas are owing to him. His ingenuity, moreover, and his almost super-human energy and courageous determination have been largely responsible for carrying them out. I should like to record, also, something of both the Foundation's and my debt to another recent friend, Christopher Farley. Without his judgement and thoughtfulness we should be hard put to it to keep on as even a keel as we manage to keep. But he is reticent and unassuming and too often remains in the background. He takes a point quickly, and I thought at first that his occasional hesitation in pronouncing upon it was owing to timidity. I now know that it is owing to his extreme scrupulousness. It was some time before I realised the depth of feeling with which he pursues justice or the compassion and patience with which this pursuit is tempered. I learned only gradually that his obvious knowledge of present-day men and affairs is enriched by wide reading and a very considerable study of the past. The tendency to dogmatism and clap-trap and humbug which this combination might induce in a more superficial mind is burnt away by his intense perception of ironies and absurdity and the liveliness of his many interests. His observations are both sensitive and his own. All this makes him a helpful, interesting and delightful companion.

During the spring and early summer of 1963 we sent out letters over my name to a number of people who we thought might be willing to be sponsors of the new Foundation. By the end of the summer nine of these had agreed. With such backing, we felt ready to make our plans public, especially as there was reason to expect others to join us soon. And, in fact, soon after the establishment of the Foundation was announced, seven others did join.

We knew our aims – chief of which was to form a really inter-national organisation – and the long-term means towards them that we must strive to achieve, and the outlines of work that we must carry on, work such as we had been carrying on for some sime. We also recognised the fact that the attainment of our purposes necessitated vast sums of money. Rather against my will my colleagues urged that the Foundation should bear my name. I knew that this would prejudice against the Foundation many people who might uphold our work itself. It would certainly prejudice well-established and respectable organisations and, certainly, a great number of individuals in Britain, particularly those who were in a position to support us financially. But my colleagues contended that, as I had been carrying on the work for years, helped by them during the last few years, and my name was identified with it in many parts of the world, to omit my name would mean a set-back for the work. I was pleased by their determination, though still somewhat dubious of its wisdom. But in the end I agreed. When, however, we decided to seek charitable status for our organisa-tion, it became evident to my friends as well as to myself that it would be impossible to obtain it in Great Britain for any organisation bearing my name.

Finally, our solicitors suggested that we compromise by forming two Foundations: The Bertrand Russell Peace Foundation and the Atlantic Peace Foundation, for the second of which we obtained charitable status. These two Foundations were to work, and do work, in co-operation, but the latter's objects are purely educational. Its purpose is to establish research in the various areas concerned in the study of war and peace and the creation of opportunities for research and the publication of its results. As the Charity Commission registered this Foundation as a charity, income tax at the standard rate is recoverable on any subscription given under a seven-year covenant, which, in turn, means that such subscriptions are increased by about sixty per cent.

The Bertrand Russell Peace Foundation was to deal with the more immediately political and controversial side of the work, and contributions to it, whether large or small, are given as ordinary gifts. During its first three years of existence many thousands of pounds have been contributed to it, some from individuals, some from organisations, some from Governments. No contribution with strings tied to it is accepted. Particularly in the case of Government contributions, it is made clear to the donors that the source of the money will not in any way prejudice the methods or results of its expenditure.

Unfortunately, I fell very ill at the beginning of September when we had decided to make our plans public, but by the end of the month, on September 29, 1963, we were able to release them. After I had made a vehement statement, we gave the press men the leaflet that my colleagues had prepared about each Foundation. That concerning the Bertrand Russell Peace Foundation gave a list of the then sponsors, and a letter that U Thant had written for the purpose on the outside. I had talked with him about our plans among other things and written to him about them. He had been warmly sympathetic, but explained that he could not be a sponsor because of his position as Secretary-General of the United Nations. He offered, however, to write the carefully worded but encouraging letter which we printed.

Reading a list of our ambitious projects, the journalists asked whence we proposed to obtain the funds. It was a pertinent question and not unexpected. Since we had not wished to divulge our plans till September 29th, we had been unable to campaign for funds. Our answer could only be that we were determined to raise the necessary funds and were sure that we could, in time, do so – a reply naturally received with acid scepticism.

Looking back upon the occasion, I cannot say that I blame the assembled pressmen for their attitude, nor the press in general for the anything but encouraging start that was given us. Anyone who is willing to back his vision of the future by action should be prepared to be thought a 'crack-pot', and we were prepared. Moreover, we were elated. It was a kind of freedom to be able to work again publicly towards the ends that we had in view. And, of course, our first efforts were towards obtaining funds to carry on with.

We approached an endless number of individuals; with singularly little success among the rich: 'Oh yes', they said more often than not, 'we think that you are doing a wonderful work. We entirely believe in it and wish it success. But, of course, we already have so many commitments . . .' Though all such financial begging is always awkward and distasteful, we only occasionally met with unpleasantness and only once with virulent discourtesy. This was at a party of rich Jews given in order that I might speak of our work for the Jews in Soviet countries in whom they professed themselves mightily interested. The unpleasant occasions were unexpected since they occurred when, upon apparently knowledgeable advice, we approached people who had expressed themselves passionately interested in the special project about which we approached them and to be friendly towards us, to 'greatly admire' me and my work as it was always put. We received many surprises, both pleasant and exasperating: one morning a message came that two people were leaving in their wills their very considerable estate on the continent to the Foundation; another morning came a letter from Lord Gladwyn, a former British Ambassador in Paris, that I append to this chapter along with my reply, as it gives the tone and reasoning of part of the huge correspondence that building up the Foundation had entailed. I believe that this exchange of letters, in spite of Lord Gladwyn's suggestion, has not before been published. In his letter, it will be noted, he advocated my advancing my proposals in the House of Lords 'where they could be subjected to intelligent scrutiny'. I refrained, in my reply, from remarking that on the occasions when I had advanced proposals in the House of Lords, I had never perceived that my audience, with a few exceptions, showed any peculiar degree of intelligence – but perhaps the general level has risen since the advent of Lord Gladwyn.

However, many people in many parts of the world helped us. Artists – painters and sculptors and musicians – of different countries have been especially generous. Indeed, one of our first money-raising ventures was an art sale of their paintings and sculpture given by the artists, which took place, through the kindness of the Duke of Bedford, at Woburn Abbey. I could not attend the opening of the sale, but I went some time later, arriving, to my amusement, on the same day that the Miss World beauties were being entertained at Woburn and I was privileged to meet them. The sale was fairly successful and we have since then been given other works of art and sold them to the great profit of our work. Though musicians were generous to us, their generosity was more often than not, thwarted by their agents or impresarios and the managers of concert halls. Actors and playwrights made us many promises of benefit performances or special plays of one sort or another, but nothing came of them. We had better fortune with the Heads of Governments, perhaps because they were better able to understand what we were doing. One of the difficulties in our begging was that much of our work – that concerning special prisoners or broken families and minority groups, for instance – could not be talked of until it was accomplished, if then, or it would be automatically rendered ineffective. The same was even more true of discussions and schemes concerning international adjustments. When asked, therefore, precisely what we had to show for our work, we had to speak chiefly in vague and general terms, which carried conviction only to the astute and the already converted.

The drawback to this more or less haphazard gathering of money was that it was impossible to be sure what monies we should have when. No huge sum came in at one time which could be used as a back-log, and promises were not always kept promptly. The result was that we sometimes had enough to go ahead with fairly ambitious schemes, but sometimes we had next door to nothing. The latter periods would have been impossible to weather had it not been for the dedication to the idea and ideas of the Foundation and the dogged determination of the people working with me, especially of Ralph Schoenman and Christopher Farley and Pamela Wood. These three in their different ways held the work together and pulled it through bad as well as good times. Many others from many different countries aided our work, some as volunteers and some on the payroll, but, for one good reason or another, until the present time, they have proved to be transient workers and sometimes too dearly paid for. Now, however, a staff of colleagues has been built up that appears stable and quite capable of dealing, each with one or more of the various aspects of the work.

For the most part the British press has done very little to help us. They have treated us with silence or, if they can find something to make us look ridiculous or wicked, with covert jeers. Perhaps this is not astonishing, since we have been working, though quite legally, against our country's established policies – not those which Mr Harold Wilson's Government promised before it came to office both for the first and second time, but against the policies which it has adopted in office. For the same reason at different times the press of other countries have railed at us or refused to mention us. And, of course, journalists and commentators are apt to deal with me personally by saying that I am senile. The journalists in the United States, especially, do this since for years I have been worrying over the increase of violence in that country and most of my recent writing has been very vehemently against their Government's warlike policies. This method of diminishing my effectiveness alarms and angers my friends and affronts me, but, from the point of those who differ with me, I dare say it is about their only retort. In any case, if the charge is true, I fail to see why anyone troubles to remark on my babblings.

Those who wish to make up their own minds as to whether or not I am senile or, even, sillier than they had formerly believed me to be, have been given ample opportunity to do so as I have given countless newspaper and TV interviews and made several films. The general rule to which I adhere in determining to which requests for interviews to accede to is to refuse all those that show signs of being concerned with details of what is known as my 'private life' rather than my work and ideas. The latter, I am glad to have publicised, and I welcome honest reports and criticisms of them. The best of these TV interviews that I have seen during the last years seemed to me to be one in early October, 1963, with John Freeman; one made in early April, 1964, in which Robert Bolt was the interlocutor (there is also a later one, made in 1967, with him, but I have not seen it); and one made in September, 1965, with Ralph Milliband. But many, of course, I have never seen. The two most important public speeches that I have made have been those concerned with the perfidy of the Labour Government under the premiership of Harold Wilson, one in mid-February 1965, and one eight months later. The first deals with the general international policies of the Government, the second dwells upon its policies in regard, especially, to Vietnam and is, therefore, reprinted in my book *War Crimes in Vietnam*. At the end of the second, I announced my resignation from the Party and tore up my Labour card. To my surprise, this intensely annoyed two of the other speakers on the platform, a Member of Parliament and the Chairman of the CND. The latter remarked to the press that I had stage-managed the affair. If I had been able to do so, I do not know why I should not have done so, but, in actual fact, all the management was in the hands of the Youth CND under whose auspices the meeting was held. The MP, who had often expressed views similar to mine on Vietnam, arrived late at the meeting and stalked out because of my action. I was rather taken aback by this singular behaviour as both these people had been saying much what I said. The only difference seemed to be that they continued in membership of the Party they denounced.

There are four other charges brought against me which I might mention here since I suppose they are connected, also, with 'The folly of age'. The most serious is that I make extreme statements in my writings and speeches for which I do not give my sources. This is levelled, I believe, against my book *War Crimes in Vietnam*. If anyone cares to study this book, however, I think that they will find it well documented. If I occasionally make a statement without giving the basis of it, I usually do so because I regard it as self-evident or based upon facts noted elsewhere in the book or so well known that there is no need to name the source.

Another charge, allied to this one, is that I myself compose neither speeches nor articles nor statements put out over my name. It is a curious thing that the public utterances of almost all Government officials and important business executives are known to be composed by secretaries or colleagues, and yet this is held unobjectionable. Why should it be considered heinous in an ordinary layman ? In point of fact, what goes out over my name is usually composed by me. When it is not, it still presents my opinion and thought. I sign nothing – letters or more formal documents – that I have not discussed, read and approved.

Two other rumours which I have learned recently are being put about, I also find vexatious. They are that letters and documents sent to me are withheld by my secretaries lest they trouble me, and that my secretaries and colleagues prevent people who wish to see me from doing so. But I myself open and read all that is addressed to me at home. My mail, however, is so large that I cannot reply to everything, though I indicate to my secretary what I wish said and read the replies drafted by my secretary before they are sent. Again, it is the number of people who wish to see me about this or that which makes it impossible to see them all. During a week, for instance, that I spent in London towards the end of 1966 in order to open the preparatory meetings of the War Crimes Tribunal, I received visits each day, morning, afternoon and evening, from people wishing to talk with me. But, as well over one hundred people asked to talk with me during this week, many, over a hundred, had to be refused.

I have remarked upon these charges at such length not only because I dislike being thought to be silly, but because it exasperates me to have my arguments and statements flouted, unread or unlistened to, on such grounds. I also dislike my colleagues coming under fire for doing, most generously, what I have asked them to do.

Less than two months after the Foundation was established I, in common with the rest of the world, was shocked by the news of the murder of President Kennedy. Perhaps I was less surprised by this vicious attack than many people were because for a number of years I had been writing about the growing acceptance of unbridled violence in the world and particularly in the United States. Some of my articles on this subject were published, but some were too outspoken for the editors of the publications that had commissioned them.

As I read the press reports in regard to the President's assassination and, later, the purported evidence against Oswald and his shooting by Ruby, it seemed to me that there had been an appalling miscarriage of justice and that probably something very nasty was being covered up. When in June, 1963, I met Mark Lane, the New York lawyer who, originally, had been looking into the affair on behalf of Oswald's mother, my suspicions were confirmed by the facts which he had already gathered. Everyone connected with the Foundation agreed with my point of view, and we did everything that we could, individually and together, to help Mark Lane and to spread the knowledge of his findings. It was quite clear from the hushing-up methods employed and the facts that were denied or passed over that very important issues were at stake. I was greatly impressed, not only by the energy and astuteness with which Mark Lane pursued the relevant facts, but by the scrupulous objectivity with which he presented them, never inferring or implying meanings not inherent in the facts themselves.

We thought it better if the Foundation itself were not involved in supporting those who were ferreting out the facts of the matter and propagating knowledge of them. We therefore started an autonomous committee with the unsatisfactory name of 'The British Who Killed Kennedy ? Committee'. We got together a fair number of sponsors and even a secretary, but not without difficulty, since many people thought the affair none of our British business. A few understood what skulduggery on the part of American Authorities might portend, not only for the inhabitants of the United States, but for the rest of the world as well. Those few had a hard time. We were well and truly vilified. A threatening telephone call from the United States Embassy was received by one of our number. Committees similar to ours were set up in some other countries and some of their officers received similar warnings. Finally, the Foundation had to take our Committee under its wing, and its members toiled both night and day in consequence of this extra work. By August, when I wrote an article called '16 Questions on the Assassination', meetings were being held, and other statements and articles were being issued. Feeling ran high. Mark Lane himself travelled about this country as well as about others, including his own, recounting the facts that he was unearthing which refuted the official and generally accepted pronouncements concerning the matter. I was sent the Warren Commission's Report before it was published in September, 1965, and at once said, to the apparent annoyance of many people, what I thought of it. Word went about that I was talking through my hat and had not even read the report, and could not have done so. In point of fact, Lane had sent me an early copy which I had read and had time to consider. Now that the Warren Commission Report has been examined minutely and it is 'respectable' to criticise it, many people agree with me and have blandly forgotten both their and my earlier attitudes. At the time, they were too timid to listen to or to follow the facts as they appeared, accepting blindly the official view of them. They did all that they could to frustrate our efforts to make them known.

Since shortly before April, 1963, more and more of my time and thought has been absorbed by the war being waged in Vietnam. My other interests have had to go by the board for the most part. Some of my time, of course, is spent on family and private affairs. And once in a blue moon I have a chance to give my mind to the sort of thing I used to be interested in, philosophical or, especially, logical problems. But I am rusty in such work and rather shy of it. In 1965, a young mathematician, G. Spencer Brown, pressed me to go over his work since, he said, he could find no one else who he thought could understand it. As I thought well of what little of his work I had previously seen, and since I feel great sympathy for those who are trying to gain attention for their fresh and unknown work against the odds of established indifference, I agreed to discuss it with him. But as the time drew near for his arrival, I became convinced that I should be quite unable to cope with it and with his new system of notation. I was filled with dread. But when he came and I heard his explanations, I found that I could get into step again and follow his work. I greatly enoyed those few days, especially as his work was both original and, it seemed to me, excellent.

One of the keenest pleasures of these years has been my friendship, a friendship in which my wife shared, with Victor Purcell, and one of the losses over which I most grieve is his death in January, 1965. He was a man of humour and balanced judgement. He had both literary appreciation and attainment, and very considerable learning as well as great knowledge of the present-day scene. He had achieved much both as a Government administrator in South East Asia and as a Don at Cambridge. His talk was a delight to me. For many years I had known him through his political writings which he used to send to me from time to time and about which I would write to him. A little later I rejoiced in his witty verses written under the pseudonym of Myra Buttle (a pun for My Rebuttal). I had never met him till he spoke at the birthday party given for me at the Festival Hall in 1962. I did not even begin to know him till he was drawn into discussions with us about the Foundation's doings in relation to South East Asia. He spoke at a meeting at Manchester in April, 1964, under the auspices of the Foundation at which I spoke also, and, soon afterwards, he did an admirable pamphlet for us surveying 'The Possibility of Peace in South East Asia'. During this time we saw something of him in London, but it was not until May, 1964, that we really came to know each other when he paid us a short visit in North Wales. We talked endlessly. We capped each other's stories and quotations, and recited our favourite poems and prose to each other. We probed each other's knowledge especially of history, and discussed serious problems. Moreover, it was a comfort to find someone who understood at once what one was driving at and, even when not entirely in agreement, was willing to discuss whatever the subject might be with tolerance and sympathy. He came again to visit us in December, little more than a fortnight before his death, and suddenly we felt, as he said, that we were old friends, though we had seen each other so little. I remember, especially, about this last visit, his suddenly bursting into a recitation of *Lycidas*, most beautifully given, and again, reading his latest work by Myra Buttle, singing those lines parodied from song. He was a brave and thoughtful, a compassionate and boisterous man. It startles me sometimes when I realise how much I miss him, not only for the enjoyment but for the help that he could and, I feel sure, would have given me. It is seldom, I think that one of my age makes a new friend so satisfying and so treasured, and astonishing that all this affection and trust and understanding should have grown up in so short a time.

My book on the situation in Vietnam and its implications, called *War Crimes in Vietnam*, appeared early in January, 1967, in both cloth and paper editions. It was published in Britain by Allen & Unwin, to whose generosity and liberal attitude, in the person of Sir Stanley Unwin especially, I have owed much ever since the First World War. The book is comprised of a few of the innumerable letters, statements, speeches and articles delivered by me since 1963. To these are added an Introduction giving the general background of the situation at the beginning of 1967 and of my own attitude to it; a Postcript describing briefly the War Crimes Tribunal for which I had called; and an appendix containing some of the findings of Ralph Schoenman during one of his visits of many weeks to Vietnam. *War Crimes in Vietnam* is so thorough an account of my attitude towards the war and the facts upon which I base it, and, in any case, I have published and broadcast so much on them during the past few years, that I shall not go into them here. The book was reviewed with considerable hostility in some journals, so it was a pleasure to learn that the paperback edition was sold out within a fortnight of its publication and that the book has been published in the United States and translated and published in many languages throughout the world.

Schoenman's reports were of extreme importance since they contain not only first-hand observation but verbatim accounts given by victims of the war attested to both by the victims themselves and by the reliable witnesses present at the time the accounts were given. The reports also paved the way for the more formal investigations conducted in Indo-China by teams sent by the International War Crimes Tribunal. It was in part upon such reports as Schoenman's and of those of Christopher

Farley who, in November, 1964, was the first member of the foundation to go to Vietnam to obtain first-hand impressions, that I base my
attitude and statements in regard to the Vietnam war, as well as upon
reports of other special investigators. Chiefly, however, I base my
opinions upon the facts reported in the daily newspapers, especially
those of the United States. These reports seem to have been published
almost by chance since they appear not to have affected editorial policy.

Occasionally I have been invited by the North Vietnamese to give my
opinion about various developments in the war. They asked my advice
as to the desirability of permitting Mr Harrison Salisbury, Assistant
Managing Editor of the *New York Times*, to visit Hanoi as a journalist.
Mr Salisbury had previously attacked me in his introduction to the
Warren Commission's Report, in which he wrote of the Commission's
'exhaustive examination of every particle of evidence it could discover'.
These comments were soon seen to be ridiculous, but I suspected that
he would have great difficulty in ignoring the evidence of widespread
bombardment of civilians in North Vietnam. I recommended that his
visit was a risk worth taking, and was pleased to read, some weeks later,
his reports from Hanoi, which caused consternation in Washington
and probably lost him a Pulitzer Prize.

I have been, of course, in close touch with the two representatives of
North Vietnam who are in London and with the North Vietnamese
Chargé d'Affaires in Paris. I have corresponded with various members
of the South Vietnam National Liberation Front and with members of
the United States armed forces as well as with American civilians, both
those who support and those who oppose the war. There is no lack of
information if one wishes to have it. But there is great difficulty in
making it known to the general public and in persuading people to pay
attention to it. It is not pleasant reading or hearing.

The more I and my colleagues studied the situation, the more
persuaded we became that the United States' attitude on Vietnam was
wholly indefensible and that the war was being conducted with unprecedented cruelty by means of new methods of torture. We concluded, after careful examination of the great body of facts that we had
amassed, that the war must be ended quickly and that the only way to
end it was to support the North Vietnamese and the Liberation Front
unequivocally. Moreover, we feared that so long as the war continued
it would be used by America as an excuse for escalation which was
likely to end in a general conflagration. We set up the Vietnam Solidarity
Campaign, which brought together those groups which saw the Vietnam war as flagrant aggression by the world's mightiest nation against
a small peasant people. Supporters of the Campaign held that justice
demanded that they support the Vietnamese entirely. I delivered the
opening address to the founding of the Solidarity Campaign in June,

1966, and this was later published in my book on Vietnam. The Campaign sent speakers all over the country, together with the Foundation's photographic exhibition on the war, and formed a nucleus of support in Britain for the International War Crimes Tribunal.

The Tribunal, of which my Vietnam book told, caught the imagination of a wide public the world over. For four years I had been searching for some effective means to help make known to the world the unbelievable cruelty of the United States in its unjust attempt to subjugate South Vietnam. At the time of the Korean War I had been unable to believe in the allegations brought by Professor Joseph Needham and others charging the Americans with having used that war as a proving-ground for new biological and chemical weapons of mass destruction. I owe Professor Needham and the others my sincere apologies for thinking these charges too extreme. By 1963, I had become convinced of the justice of these allegations since it was clear that similar ones must be brought against the United States in Vietnam. Early in that year, I wrote to the *New York Times* describing American conduct in Vietnam as barbarism 'reminiscent of warfare as practised by the Germans in Eastern Europe and the Japanese in South-East Asia.' At the time this seemed too strong for the *New York Times*, which first attacked me editorially, then cut my reply and finally denied me any access to its letters columns. I tried other publications and determined to find out more about what was at that time a 'secret war'. The more I discovered, the more appalling American intentions and practice appeared. I learned not only of barbaric practices, but also of the most cynical and ruthless suppression of a small nation's desire for independence. The destruction of the Geneva Agreements, the support of a dictatorship, the establishment of a police state, and the destruction of all its opponents were intolerable crimes. The following year I started sending observers regularly to Indo-China, but their reports were continually overtaken by the enlargement of the war. The pretexts for the 'escalation', particularly the attack upon North Vietnam, reminded me of nothing less than those offered a quarter of a century earlier for Hitler's adventures in Europe. It became clear to me that the combination of aggression, experimental weapons, indiscriminate warfare and concentration camp programmes required a more thorough and formal investigation than I was able to manage.

In the summer of 1966, after extensive study and planning, I wrote to a number of people around the world, inviting them to join an International War Crimes Tribunal. The response heartened me, and soon I had received about eighteen acceptances. I was especially pleased to be joined by Jean-Paul Sartre, for despite our differences on philosophical questions I much admired his courage. Vladimir Dedijer, the Yugoslav writer, had visited me earlier in Wales, and through his wide knowledge of both the Western and Communist worlds proved a valuable ally. I also came to rely heavily on Isaac Deutscher, the essayist and political writer, whom I had not seen for ten years. Whenever there were too many requests for television and other interviews about the Tribunal, I could rely on Deutscher in London to meet the press and give an informed and convincing assessment of world affairs and of our own work. I invited all the members to London for preliminary discussions in November, 1966, and opened the proceedings with a speech to be found at the end of this chapter. It seemed to me essential that what was happening in Vietnam should be examined with scrupulous care, and I had invited only people whose integrity was beyond question. The meeting was highly successful, and we arranged to hold the public sessions of the Tribunal over many weeks in the following year, after first sending a series of international teams to Indo-China on behalf of the Tribunal itself.

When the Tribunal first proposed to send a selection of its members to investigate atrocities, the proposal was ridiculed on the ground that there were no atrocities on the American side. When this contention was shown up, it was said that American military authorities would deal with this. When this was shown up, it was said that eminent legal authorities made themselves a laughing-stock by undertaking such work. Far better, it was argued, to let the atrocities go unpunished. The Press, the military authorities, and many of the American and British legal luminaries, consider that their honour and humanity will be better served by allowing their officers to burn women and children to death than by adopting the standards applied in the Nuremberg Trials. This comes of accepting Hitler's legacy.

When our opponents saw the seriousness of what we were preparing, there was the sort of outcry to which, over the years, I have become accustomed. Three African Heads of State who had sponsored the Foundation resigned, and it was not difficult to discover the hand behind their defection. One of them even sent me a photostat of a letter which I had sent about the Tribunal to President Johnson at the White House, a piece of clumsiness which even the Central Intelligence Agency must have deplored. The next move was for various journalists to question the impartiality of our Tribunal. It amused me considerably that many of these same critics had shortly before this been among the staunchest supporters of the Warren Commission on the Assassination of President Kennedy.[1] Their new found interest in impartiality did, however, give us the opportunity to explain our own position. Clearly, we had all given considerable thought to some of the evidence we were about to assess. Our minds were not empty, but neither were they

[1] Prominent members of that Commission had been the former director of the CIA and an associate of the FBI.

closed. I believed that the integrity of the members of the Tribunal, the fact that they represented no state power and the complete openness of the hearings would ensure the objectivity of the proceedings. We also decided to accept possible evidence from any source, so I wrote to President Johnson inviting him to attend the Tribunal. Unfortunately, he was too busy planning the bombardment of the Vietnamese to reply.

All this stir concerning the Tribunal naturally caused fresh interest in the Foundation itself. The Atlantic Peace Foundation remained a registered charity; the Bertrand Russell Peace Foundation became a company limited by guarantee, and has branches in several countries: Argentina, Australia and New Zealand, France, India, Italy, Japan, the Philippines, and the United States. In London it not only retained the small central offices off the Haymarket, which it had from its inception, but it provided a larger office for the War Crimes Tribunal. It also bought a larger freehold property into which much of the work has been transferred. All this placed the work on a firmer footing and prepared the way for further developments. For perhaps the first time, I was conscious of activity, centred on the Tribunal, involving world-wide support.

In the late forties and early fifties, I had been profoundly impressed by the horror of Stalin's dictatorship, which had led me to believe that there would be no easy resolution of the cold war. I later came to see that for all his ruthlessness, Stalin had been very conservative. I had assumed, like most people in the West, that his tyranny was expansionist, but later evidence made it clear that it was the West that had given him Eastern Europe as part of the spoils of the Second World War, and that, for the most part, he had kept his agreements with the West. After his death, I earnestly hoped that the world would come to see the folly and danger of living permanently in the shadow of nuclear weapons. If the contenders for world supremacy could be kept apart, perhaps the neutral nations could introduce the voice of reason into international affairs. It was a small hope, for I overestimated the power of the neutrals. Only rarely, as with Nehru in Korea did they manage to add significant weight to pressures against the cold war.

The neutrals continued to embody my outlook, in that I consider human survival more important than ideology. But a new danger came to the fore. It became obvious that Russia no longer entertained hope of world-empire, but that this hope had now passed over to the United States. As my researches into the origins and circumstances of the war in Vietnam showed, the United States was embarking upon military adventures which increasingly replaced war with Russia as the chief threat to the world. The fanaticism of America's anti-communism, combined with its constant search for markets and raw materials, made it impossible for any serious neutral to regard America and Russia as equally dangerous to the world. The essential unity of American military, economic and cold war policies was increasingly revealed by the sordidness and cruelty of the Vietnam war. For people in the West, this was most difficult to admit, and again I experienced the silence or opposition of those who had come to accept my views of the previous decade. In the third world, however, our support was very considerable. Cruelty has not gone wholly unchallenged.

My views on the future are best expressed by Shelley in the following poem:

> O cease! must hate and death return?
>   Cease! must men kill and die?
> Cease! drain not to its dregs the urn
>   Of bitter prophecy.
> The world is weary of the past,
> O might it die or rest at last!

Final stanza of 'Hellas' (478. 1096–1107)

LETTERS

On 'The Free Man's Worship'

27 July 1962

Dear Professor Hiltz

Thank you for your letter of June 27. As regards your 3 questions: (1) I have continued to think 'The Free Man's Worship' 'florid and rhetorical' since somewhere about 1920; (2) This observation concerns only the style; (3) I do not now regard ethical values as objective, as I did when I wrote the essays. However, my outlook on the cosmos and on human life is substantially unchanged.

Yours sincerely
Bertrand Russell

Thanks to Julian Huxley for his pamphlets: 'Psychometabolism'; 'Eugenics in Evolutionary Perspective'; 'Education and the Humanist Revolution'.

Plas Penrhyn
10 March, 1963

My Dear Julian

Thank you very much for sending me your three papers which I have read with very great interest. I loved your paper about psycho-metabolism, explaining why peacocks dance and women use lipstick, both of which had hitherto been mysterious to me. I do not know enough about the matters of which this paper treats to be able to offer any criticism. You touch occasionally on the mind-body problem as to which I have very definite views which are acceptable to some physiologists but are rejected with scorn and contempt by practically all philosophers, none of whom know either physics or physiology. You might find it worth your while to read a short essay of mine called 'Mind and Matter' in *Portraits from Memory*.

What you say about eugenics has my approval up to a certain point, but no further. You seem to think that governments will be enlightened and that the kind of human being they will wish to produce will be an improvement on the haphazard work of nature. If a sperm-bank, such as you envisage, had existed during the régime of Hitler, Hitler would have been the sire of all babies born in his time in Germany. Exceptional merit is, and always has been, disliked by Authority; and obviously Authority would control the sperm-bank. Consequently, in the degree to which eugenics was efficient, exceptional merit would disappear. I am entirely with you as to what eugenics *could* achieve, but I disagree as to what it would achieve.

I have somewhat similar criticisms to make on what you say about education. For example: you dismiss silly myths which make up orthodox religion, and you do not mention that throughout the Western world nobody who openly rejects them can be a schoolmaster. To take another point: education has enormously facilitated total war. Owing to the fact that people can read, while educators have been at pains to prevent them from thinking, warlike ferocity is now much more easily spread than it was in former times.

You seem to think that governments will be composed of wise and enlightened persons who will have standards of value not unlike yours and mine. This is against all the evidence. Pythagoras was an exile because Policrates disliked him; Socrates was put to death; Aristotle had to fly from Athens as soon as Alexander died. In ancient Greece it was not hard to escape from Greece. In the modern world it is much more difficult; and that is one reason why there are fewer great men than there were in Greece.

Best wishes to both of you from both of us.

Yrs. ever
B. R.

From Sir Julian Huxley

31 Pond Street
Hampstead, N.W.3
13th March, 1963

Dear Bertie

So many thanks for your fascinating letter. I can hear you chuckling about peacocks and lipstick!

As regards the mind-body problem, I think it must be approached from the evolutionary angle. We are all of us living 'mind-body' organisations, with a long history behind us, and related to all other living organisations. To me this implies that mind and body in some way constitute a single unity.

Of course you are right as to the dangers inherent in eugenic measures or approved educational measures. On the other hand, one must do *something*! My attitude is neither purely optimistic nor purely pessimistic – it is that we and our present situation are far from perfect, but are capable of improvement, and indeed are liable to deteriorate unless something is done. This is to me the real point – that something must be done, though of course we must try to see that it is, in principle, the right thing, and also must try to safeguard it as far as possible from abuse.

Again, we must have an educational system of sorts – & I should have thought we ought to try to improve it, in spite of possible dangers –

Juliette sends her best wishes,

> *Yours ever*
> *Julian H.*

To and from Alice Mary Hilton

> Plas Penrhyn
> 9 June, 1963

Dear Miss Hilton

My warm thanks for your book on *Logic, Computing Machines and Automation*. I have, so far, only had time to read parts of it, but what I have read has interested me very much. In particular, I am grateful for the nice things you say about *Principia Mathematica* and about me. The followers of Gödel had almost persuaded me that the twenty man-years spent on the *Principia* had been wasted and that the book had better been forgotten. It is a comfort to find that you do not take this view.

> *Yours sincerely*
> *Bertrand Russell*

> 405 East 63rd Street
> New York 21, New York
> July 2, 1963

Dear Lord Russell

Thank you very much for your kind letter about my book on *Logic, Computing Machines and Automation*. It was very thoughtful of you to write to me and I can hardly express my appreciation for your interest and your kindness. Although I am aware of the fact that it doesn't matter very much what I think of *Principia Mathematica*, I am convinced that future generations of mathematicians will rate it one of the two or three major contributions to science. I have the feeling that the criticism stems from a lack of understanding rather than anything else. I cannot claim that I understand this tremendous work fully but I have been trying for several years now to learn enough so that I can at least understand basic principles. I am quite certain no great mathematician (which I am certainly not) could possibly have read the *Principia* and think that 'the twenty man-years spent on the *Principia* had been wasted and that the book had better be forgotten'. I am quite certain that it won't be forgotten as long as there is any civilisation that preserves the work of really great minds.

I mentioned to you in the past that I am planning to edit a series which is tentatively called *The Age of Cyberculture* and which is to include books by thinkers – scientists, philosophers, artists – who have a contribution to make to the understanding of this era we are entering. It seems to me that humanity has never been in so critical a period. Not only do we live in constant danger of annihilation, but even if we do survive the danger of nuclear extinction, we are standing on the threshold of an age which can become a paradise or hell for humanity. I am enclosing a very brief outline of the series. Because I believe so strongly that understanding and communication among the educated and thinking human beings of this world are so important I am presuming to ask you to write a contribution to this series. I am going further than that. I would like to ask you to serve on the editorial board. I know that you are a very busy man, and I am not asking this lightly. But I also know that you make your voice heard and I believe very strongly that this series will make a contribution and possibly have considerable impact to further the understanding among people whose work is in different disciplines and who must cooperate and learn to understand one another. It is through the contributors and the readers of this series that I hope that some impact will be made upon the political decision makers of this society and through them upon all of us who must realise our responsibility for choosing the right decision makers.

It would give me personally the greatest pleasure to be allowed to work with the greatest mind of this – and many other – century.

I would like you to know that your recording has just become available in this country ('Speaking Personally, Bertrand Russell') and that we have listened to it with great enjoyment and have spent several happy and most wonderful evenings in the company of friends listening to your words.

Thank you again for all of your kindness.

Sincerely
Alice Mary Hilton

To John Paulos

2nd August, 1966

Dear Mr Paulos

Thank you very much for your letter.

My reason for rejecting Hegel and monism in general is my belief that the dialectical argument against relations is wholly unsound. I think such a statement as 'A is west of B' can be exactly true. You will find that Bradley's arguments on this subject pre-suppose that every proposition must be of the subject-predicate form. I think this the fundamental error of monism.

With best wishes,

Yours sincerely
Bertrand Russell

To Marchesa Origo

19 January, 1966

Dear Marquesa

I have been reading your book on Leopardi with very great interest. Although I have long been an admirer of his poetry, I knew nothing of his life until I read your book. His life is appallingly tragic and most of the tragedy was due to bad institutions.

I cannot agree with Santayana's remark: 'The misfortunes of Leopardi were doubtless fortunate for his genius.' I believe that in happier circumstances he would have produced much more.

I do not know Italian at all well and have read most of his poetry in Italian; as a result I have probably missed much by doing so. I am grateful to your book for filling many gaps in my knowledge.

Yours sincerely
Bertrand Russell

To Mr Hayes

25.11.1963

Dear Mr Hayes

Thank you for your letter of November 18. The idea which has been put about to the effect that I am more anti-American than anti-Russian is one of ignorant hostile propaganda. It is true that I have criticised American behaviour in Vietnam, but I have, at the same time, been vehemently protesting against the treatment of Soviet Jews. When the Russians resumed Tests I first wrote to the Soviet Embassy to express a vehement protest & then organised hostile demonstrations against the Soviet Government. I have described the East German Government as a 'military tyranny imposed by alien armed force'. I have written articles in Soviet journals expressing complete impartiality. The only matter in which I have been more favourable to Russia than to America was the

Cuban crisis because Khrushchev yielded rather than embark upon a nuclear war. In any crisis involving the danger of nuclear war, if one side yielded & the other did not, I should think the side that yielded more deserving of praise than the other side, because I think nuclear war the greatest misfortune that could befall the human race.

In view of your letter, I am afraid I cannot write an article that would be acceptable to you as I have always expressed in print my criticisms of Russia as often & as emphatically as my criticisms of the West.

Yours sincerely
Bertrand Russell

From Arnold Toynbee

At 273 Santa Teresa
Stanford, Calif. 94305
United States
9 May, 1967

Dear Lord Russell

Your ninety-fifth birthday gives me, like countless other friends of yours who will also be writing to you at this moment, a welcome opportunity of expressing some of the feelings that I have for you all the time: first of all, my affection for you and Edith (I cannot think of either of you without thinking of you both together), and then my admiration and my gratitude.

I met you first, more than half a century ago, just after you had responded to the almost superhuman demand that Plato makes on his fellow philosophers. You had then stepped back out of the sunshine into the cave, to help your fellow human beings who were still prisoners there. You had just come out of prison in the literal sense (and this not for the last time). You had been put in prison, that first time, for having spoken in public against conscription.

It would have been possible for you to continue to devote yourself exclusively to creative intellectual work, in which you had already made your name by achievements of the highest distinction – work which, as we know, gives you intense intellectual pleasure, and which at the same time benefits the human race by increasing our knowledge and understanding of the strange universe in which we find ourselves. You could then have led a fairly quiet life, and you would have been commended unanimously by all the pundits. Of course, ever since then, you have continued to win laurels in this field. But you care too much for your fellow human beings to be content with your intellectual career alone, a splendid one though it is. You have had the greatness of spirit to be unwilling to stay 'above the battle'. Ever since, you have been battling for the survival of civilisation, and latterly, since the invention of the atomic weapon, for the survival of the human race.

I am grateful to you, most of all, for the encouragement and the hope that you have been giving for so long, and are still giving as vigorously and as fearlessly as ever, to your younger contemporaries in at least three successive generations. As long as there are people who care, as you do, for mankind, and who put their concern into action, the rest of us can find, from the example that you have set us, courage and confidence to work, in your spirit, for trying to give mankind the future that is its birthright, and for trying to help it to save itself from self-destruction.

This is why Thursday, 18 May 1967, is an historic date for the hundreds of millions of your contemporaries who are unaware of this, as well as for the hundreds of thousands who do know what you stand for and what you strive for. You have projected yourself, beyond yourself, into the history of the extraordinary species of which you are so outstanding a representative. Every living creature is self-centred by nature; yet every human living creature's mission in life is to transfer the centre of his concern from himself to the ultimate reality, whatever this may be. That is the true fulfilment of a human being's destiny. You have achieved it. This is why I feel constant gratitude to you and affection for you, and why 18 May, 1967, is a day of happiness and hope for me, among your many friends.

> *Yours ever*
> *Arnold Toynbee*

From Field Marshal Sir Claude Auchinleck, GCB

> Oswald House
> Northgate
> Beccles, Suffolk
> 1 May 64

My dear Lord Russell

I apologise for not having written earlier to thank you for your hospitality and, for me, a most interesting and inspiring visit. I have read the paper you gave me – 'A New Approach to Peace' which I found most impressive. There is nothing in it with which I could not whole-heartedly agree and support. I understand the relationship and functions of the Atlantic Peace Foundation and the Bertrand Russell Peace Foundation and I hope to be able to make a small contribution to the expenses of the former.

If I can be of help in any other way, perhaps you or your Secretary will let me know. It is an honour to have met you.

With best wishes and hopes for your success.

> *Yours sincerely*
> *C. J. Auchinleck*

From U Thant on the formation of the Bertrand Russell Peace
Foundation

Secretary General

It is good to know that it is proposed to start a Foundation in the
name of Lord Russell, to expand and continue his efforts in the cause
of peace.

Lord Russell was one of the first to perceive the folly and danger of
unlimited accumulation of nuclear armaments. In the early years he
conducted practically a one-man crusade against this tendency and he
now has a much larger following. While there may be differences of
views about the wisdom of unilateral disarmament, and other similar
ideas, I share the feeling of Lord Russell that the unrestricted manu-
facture, testing, perfecting, and stock-piling of nuclear armaments
represent one of the greatest dangers to humanity and one of the most
serious threats to the survival of the human race.

I hope, therefore, that this effort to put on an institutional basis the
crusade for peace that Lord Russell has conducted for so long and with
such dedication will be crowned with success.

U Thant

SPONSORS OF THE BERTRAND RUSSELL PEACE FOUNDATION

H.I.M. Haile Selassie
Prof. Linus Pauling, Nobel
    Prize for Chemistry and
    for Peace
Pres. Kenneth Kaunda
Pres. Kwame Nkrumah
Pres. Ayub Khan
Pres. Julius K. Nyerere
Pres. Leopold Senghor
The Duke of Bedford

Dr Max Born, Nobel Prize for Physics
Lord Boyd Orr, FRS, Nobel Peace Prize
Pablo Casals, Puerto Rico, Cellist
Danilo Dolci, Sicily
Her Majesty Queen Elizabeth of the
    Belgians
Prime Minister Jawaharlal Nehru
Vanessa Redgrave, Actress
Dr Albert Schweitzer, Lambarene,
    Nobel Peace Prize

February 1964

A NEW APPROACH TO PEACE

by

BERTRAND RUSSELL

The nuclear age in which we have the misfortune to live is one which
imposes new ways of thought and action and a new character in

international relations. Ever since the creation of the H-bomb, it has been obvious to thoughtful people that there is now a danger of the extermination of mankind if a nuclear war between two powerful nations or blocs of nations should break out. Not only would such a war be a total disaster to human hopes, but, so long as past policies persist, a nuclear war may break out at any minute. This situation imposes upon those who desire the continuation of our species a very difficult duty. We have, first, to persuade Governments and populations of the disastrousness of nuclear war, and when that has been achieved, we have to induce Governments to adopt such policies as will make the preservation of peace a possibility.

Of these two tasks, the first has been very largely accomplished. It has been accomplished by a combination of methods of agitation: peace marches, peace demonstrations, large public meetings, sit-downs, etc. These were conducted in Britain by the CND and the Committee of 100, and in other countries by more or less similar bodies. They have testified – and I am proud that I was amongst them – that nuclear war would be a calamity for the whole human race, and have pointed out its imminence and its dangers. They have succeeded in making very widely known, even to Governments, the dangers of nuclear war. But it is time for a new approach. The dangers must not be forgotten but now the next step must be taken. Ways and means of settling questions that might lead to nuclear war and other dangers to mankind must be sought and made known, and mankind must be persuaded to adopt these new and different means towards securing peace.

The culmination, so far, of the conflict between rival nuclear groups was the Cuban crisis. In this crisis, America and Russia confronted each other while the world waited for the destruction that seemed imminent. At the last moment, the contest was avoided and it appeared that neither side was willing to put an end to the human race because of disagreement as to the politics of those who would otherwise be living in Cuba. This was a moment of great importance. It showed that neither side considered it desirable to obliterate the human race.

We may, therefore, take it that the Governments of the world are prepared to avoid nuclear war. And it is not only Governments, but also vast sections, probably a majority, of the populations of most civilised countries which take this view.

The first part of the work for peace has thus been achieved. But a more difficult task remains. If there is not to be war, we have to find ways by which war will be avoided. This is no easy matter. There are many disputes which, though they may begin amicably, are likely to become more and more bitter, until at last, in a fury, they break out into open war. There is also the risk of war by accident or misinformation. Furthermore, there are difficulties caused by the one-sided character of information as it reaches one side or the other in any dispute. It is clear that peace cannot come to the world without serious concessions, sometimes by one side, sometimes by the other, but generally by both. These difficulties in the pursuit of peace require a different technique from that of marches and demonstrations. The questions concerned are complex, the only possible solutions are distasteful to one side or both, and negotiators who discuss such questions will need to keep a firm hold of their tempers if they are to succeed.

All this should be the work of Governments. But Governments will not adequately do the necessary work unless they are pushed on by a body or bodies which have an international character and are especially concerned with a search for peaceful solutions. It is work of this kind that we hope to see performed by the new Foundations, which I hereby recommend to you.

Of the two Foundations one is called The Atlantic Peace Foundation. Being a Foundation for purposes of research in matters of war and peace, it has been registered as a charity and is recognised as such by the British Inland Revenue. Income Tax at the standard rate is, therefore, recoverable on any subscription given to it under a seven-year contract, which means that such subscriptions are increased by about sixty per cent. This Foundation works in co-operation with the Bertrand Russell Peace Foundation. The latter implements the purposes of the Atlantic Peace Foundation. For this reason, I shall refer to only a single Foundation in the rest of this discussion.

It may be said: 'But such work as that is the work of the United Nations.' I agree that it should be the work of the United Nations and I hope that, in time, it will become so. But the United Nations has defects, some of them remediable, others essential in a body which represents an organisation of States. Of the former kind of defect, the most notable is the exclusion of China; of the latter kind, the equality of States in the Assembly and the veto power of certain States in the Security Council. For such reasons the United Nations, alone, is not adequate to work for peace.

It is our hope that the Foundations which we have created will, in time, prove adequate to deal with all obstacles to peace and to propose such solutions of difficult questions as may commend themselves to the common sense of mankind. Perhaps this hope is too ambitious. Perhaps it will be some other body with similar objects that will achieve the final victory. But however that may be, the work of our Foundation will have ministered to a fortunate ending.

The problems which will have to be settled are two kinds. The first kind is that which concerns mankind as a whole. Of this the most important are two: namely, disarmament and education. The second class of problems are those concerning territorial adjustments, of which Germany is likely to prove the most difficult. Both kinds must be solved if peace is to be secure.

There have been congresses concerned with the subject of disarmament ever since nuclear weapons came into existence. Immediately after the ending of the Second World War, America offered to the world the Baruch Proposal. This was intended to break the American monopoly of nuclear weapons and to place them in the hands of an international body. Its intentions were admirable, but Congress insisted upon the insertion of clauses which it was known the Russians would not accept. Everything worked out as had been expected. Stalin rejected the Baruch Proposal, and Russia proceeded to create its own A-bomb and, then, its own H-bomb. The result was the Cold War, the blockade of Berlin, and the creation by both sides of H-bombs which first suggested the danger to mankind in general. After Stalin's death, a new attempt at complete disarmament was made. Eisenhower and Khrushchev met at Camp David. But warlike elements in the Pentagon continued their work of spying, and the Russian destruction of U-2 put an end to the brief attempt at friendship. Since that time, disarmament conferences have met constantly, but always, until after the Cuban Crisis, with the determination on both sides that no agreement should be reached. Since the Cuban Crisis there has again been a more friendly atmosphere, but so far, without any tangible result except the Test-Ban Treaty. This Treaty was valuable, also, as showing that agreement is possible between East and West. The success of the negotiations involved was largely due to Pugwash, an international association of scientists concerned with problems of peace and war.

The present situation in regard to disarmament is that both America and Russia have schemes for total nuclear disarmament, but their schemes differ, and no way has, so far, been discovered of bridging the differences. It should be one of the most urgent tasks of the Foundation to devise some scheme of disarmament to which both sides could agree. It is ominous, however, that the Pentagon has again allowed one of its planes to be shot down by the Russians over Communist territory.

If peace is ever to be secure, there will have to be great changes in education. At present, children are taught to love their country to the exclusion of other countries, and among their countrymen in history those whom they are specially taught to admire are usually those who have shown most skill in killing foreigners. An English child is taught to admire Nelson and Wellington; a French child, to admire Napoleon; and a German child, Barbarossa. These are not among those of the child's countrymen who have done most for the world. They are those who have served their country in ways that must be forever closed if man is to survive. The conception of Man as one family will have to be taught as carefully as the opposite is now taught. This will not be an easy transition. It will be said that boys under such a regimen will be soft and effeminate. It will be said that they will lose the manly virtues and will be destitute of courage. All this will be said by Christians in spite of Christ's teaching. But, dreadful as it may appear, boys brought up in the old way will grow into quarrelsome men who will find a world without war unbearably tame. Only a new kind of education, inculcating a new set of moral values, will make it possible to keep a peaceful world in existence.

There will, after all, be plenty of opportunity for adventure, even dangerous adventure. Boys can go to the Antarctic for their holidays, and young men can go to the moon. There are many ways of showing courage without having to kill other people, and it is such ways that should be encouraged.

In the teaching of history, there should be no undue emphasis upon one's own country. The history of wars should be a small part of what is taught. Much the more important part should be concerned with progress in the arts of civilisation. War should be treated as murder is treated. It should be regarded with equal horror and with equal aversion. All this, I fear, may not be pleasing to most present-day educationists. But, unless education is changed in some such way, it is to be feared that men's natural ferocity will, sooner or later, break out.

But it is not only children who need education. It is needed, also by adults, both ordinary men and women and those who are important in government. Every technical advance in armaments has involved an increase in the size of States. Gunpowder made modern states possible at the time of the Renaissance by making castles obsolete. What castles were at that time, national States are now, since weapons of mass destruction have made even the greatest States liable to complete destruction. A new kind of outlook is, therefore, necessary. Communities, hitherto, have survived, when they have survived, by a combination of internal co-operation and external competition. The H-bomb has made the latter out of date. World-wide co-operation is now a condition of survivial. But world-wide co-operation, if it is to succeed, requires co-operative feelings in individuals. It is difficult to imagine a World Government succeeding if the various countries of which it is composed continue to hate and suspect each other. To bring about more friendly feelings across the boundaries of nations is, to begin with, a matter of adult education. It is necessary to teach both individuals and Governments that as one family mankind may prosper as never before, but as many competing families there is no prospect before mankind except death. To teach this lesson will be a large part of the educative work of the Foundation.

There are throughout the world a number of territorial questions, most of which divide East from West. Some of the questions are very thorny and must be settled before peace can be secure. Let us begin with Germany.

At Yalta it was decided that Germany should be divided into four parts: American, English, French and Russian. A similar division was made of Berlin within Germany. It was hoped that all would, in time, come to agree and would submit to any conditions imposed by the victorious allies. Trouble, however, soon arose. The city of Berlin was in the midst of the Russian zone and no adequate provision had been made to secure access to the Western sector of Berlin for the Western allies. Stalin took advantage of this situation in 1948 by the so-called 'Berlin Blockade' which forbade all access to West Berlin by road or rail on the part of the Western allies. The Western allies retorted by the 'Air Lift' which enabled them to supply West Berlin in spite of the Russian blockade. Throughout the period of the Berlin blockade both sides were strictly legal. Access to West Berlin by air had been guaranteed in the peace settlement, and this the Russians never challenged. The whole episode ended with a somewhat ambiguous and reluctant agreement on the part of the Russians to allow free intercourse between West Berlin and West Germany. This settlement, however, did not satisfy the West. It was obvious that the Russians could at any moment occupy West Berlin and that the only answer open to the West would be nuclear war. Somewhat similar considerations applied, rather less forcibly, to the whole of Western Germany. In this way, the problem of Germany became linked with the problem of nuclear disarmament: if nuclear disarmament was accepted by the West without adequate assurances as to disarmament in regard to conventional weapons, then Germany's defence against the East would become difficult if not impossible.

The German problem also exists in regard to Eastern Germany – and here it represents new complexities. What had been the Eastern portion of the German Reich was divided into two parts. The Eastern half was given to Russia and Poland, while the Western half was given to a Communist regime in East Germany. In the part given to Russia and Poland all Germans were evicted. Old and young, men, women and children were ruthlessly sent in over-crowded trains to Berlin, where they had to walk from the Eastern terminus to the Western terminus in queues which were apt to take as much as thirty-six hours. Many Germans died in the trains and many in the Berlin queues, but for the survivors there was no legal remedy.

And how about the part of Germany which was assigned to the

East German Government? The East German Government was a Communist Government, while the population was overwhelmingly anti-Communist. The Government was established by the Russians and sustained by their armed forces against insurrection. Eastern Germany became a prison, escape from which, after the construction of the Berlin Wall, was only possible at imminent risk of death.

It cannot be expected that Germany will tamely accept this situation. The parts of the old German Reich which were given to Russia or Poland were, for the most part, inhabited by Poles and must be regarded as justly lost to Germany whatever may be thought of the hardships suffered by excluded Germans. But the position of the Germans in what is now the Eastern portion of Germany is quite different. Eastern Germany is virtually a territory conquered by the Russians and governed by them as they see fit. This situation, combined with the natural nationalistic sympathy felt by the West Germans, is an unstable one. It depends upon military force and nothing else.

So far, we have been concerned with the German case, but the Nazis, during their period in power, inspired in all non-Germans a deep-rooted fear of German power. There is reason to dread that, if Germany were reunited, there would be a repetition of the Nazi attempt to rule the world. This apprehension is apparently not shared by the Governments of the West, who have done everything in their power to strengthen West Germany and make it again capable of another disastrous attempt at world dominion. It cannot be said that this apprehension is unreasonable.

What can be done to secure a just and peaceful solution of this problem? The West might suggest that Germany should be free and reunited and the East might, conceivably, agree, if Germany were disarmed. But the Germans would never agree to a punitive disarmament inflicted upon them alone. Only general disarmament would make German disarmament acceptable to the Germans. In this way, the question of Germany becomes entangled with the problem of disarmament. It is difficult to imagine any solution of the German problem which would be acceptable both to Germans and to the rest of the world, except reunification combined with *general* disarmament.

The next most difficult of territorial disputes is that between Israel and the Arabs. Nasser has announced that it is his purpose to exterminate Israel and that, within two years, he will be in possession of missiles for this purpose. (*Guardian*, 16.3.64.) The Western world is sure to feel that this cannot be allowed to happen, but most of Asia and, possibly, Russia would be prepared to look on passively so long as the Arabs continued to be victorious. There seems little hope of any accommodation between the two sides except as a result of outside pressure. The ideal solution in such a case is a decision by the United Nations which the countries concerned would be compelled to adopt. I am not prepared to suggest publicly the terms of such a decision, but only that it should come from the United Nations and be supported by the major powers of East and West.

In general, when there is a dispute as to whether the Government of a country should favour the East or the West, the proper course would be for the United Nations to conduct a plebiscite in the country concerned and give the Government to whichever side obtained a majority. This is a principle which, at present, is not accepted by either side. Americans do not accept it in South Vietnam, though they conceal the reason for their anti-Communist activities by pretending that they are protecting the peasantry from the inroads of the Vietcong. The attitude of the United States to Castro's Government in Cuba is very ambiguous. Large sections of American opinion hold that throughout the Western Hemisphere no Government obnoxious to the United States is to be tolerated. But whether these sections of opinion will determine American action is as yet, doubtful. Russia is, in this respect, equally to blame, having enforced Communist Governments in Hungary and Eastern Germany against the wishes of the inhabitants. In all parts of the world, self-determination by hither-to subject nations will become very much easier if there is general disarmament.

The ultimate goal will be a world in which national armed forces are limited to what is necessary for internal stability and in which the only forces capable of acting outside national limits will be those of a reformed United Nations. The approach to this ultimate solution must be piecemeal and must involve a gradual increase in the authority of the United Nations or, possibly, of some new international body which should have sole possession of the major weapons of war. It is difficult to see any other way in which mankind can survive the invention of weapons of mass extinction.

Many of the reforms suggested above depend upon the authority of the United Nations or of some new international body specially created for the purpose. To avoid circumlocution I shall speak of the United Nations to cover both those possibilities. If its powers are to be extended, this will have to be done by means of education which is both neutral and international. Such education will have to be carried out by an organisation which is, itself, international and neutral. There are, at present, in various countries, national associations working towards peace, but, so far as we are aware, the Foundation with which we are concerned is the first international association aiming at the creation of a peaceful world. The other Foundations are limited in scope – being either national or aimed towards dealing with only one or two aspects or approaches to peace. We shall support them where we can, and shall hope for their support in those areas of our work which impinge upon theirs. We shall also endeavour to diminish the acerbity of international controversy and induce Governments and important organs of public opinion to preserve at least a minimum of courtesy in their criticism of opponents.

The Government of this Foundation will be in the hands of a small body of Directors. This body is, as yet, incomplete, but should as soon as possible be representative of all the interests concerned in the prevention of war. It is supported by a body of Sponsors who approve of its general purposes, but, for one reason or another, cannot take part in the day to day work. There is to be a Board of Advisers, each having special knowledge in some one or more fields. Their specialised knowledge shall be drawn upon as it may be relevant. The Head-quarters of the Foundation will remain in London, which will also house the International Secretariat. In the near future, it is intended to establish offices in various parts of the world. Probably the first two, one in New York and one in Beirut, will be established in the immediate future. Others will follow as soon as suitable personnel can be recruited. This is, in many parts of the world, a difficult task. Many Governments, although they do not venture publicly to advocate nuclear war, are opposed to any work against it in their own territories, and many individuals, while genuinely desirous of peace, shrink from such national sacrifices as the Foundation's general policy may seem to make desirable. It is obvious that a general peace policy must demand moderation everywhere, and many friends of peace, while admitting the desirability of concessions by countries other than their own, are apt to shrink from advocating necessary concessions by their own country. Willingness for such concessions is a necessary qualification for membership of the Secretariat and for the Head of any subsidiary office. Each subsidiary office will have to collect information and first-hand knowledge on all local matters from both the ordinary population and the authorities. They will have to assess this knowledge with a view to its importance in work towards peace. And they will have to disseminate accurate knowledge and to educate both authorities and the public in attitudes and actions desirable in work towards peace. Each office will also have the task of finding suitable workers to support its own part of the general work and to collect money both for its own and the general work. It should be part of the work of the subsidiary offices to pass on information and advice so that the Central Secretariat can draw up soundly based schemes for the settlement of disputes that stand a good chance of being accepted by the disputants.

To accomplish these tasks will not be possible without a considerable expenditure in secretarial help, in offices, in means of travel, in means of publicising findings and, ultimately, when and if funds permit, in establishing a radio and newspaper of our own. Until such funds permit, the exploration of possibilities and estimates of location, plant and personnel for these needed means of publicity – in itself no mean task – must occupy the Foundation.

It will be seen that the Foundation as we hope it may become must be a gradual work. It cannot spring into being full-armoured like Athene. What exists at present is only a small seed of what we hope may come to be. We have a Head Office in London. We have a small Secretariat which is international, neutral and energetic, but too small for the work what has to be done. We have pamphlets and leaflets stating our views on various topical issues. These we supplement, when we can, by letters and articles in the Press. But what can be done in this way is, as yet, very limited since most newspapers are opposed to what must be done in this or that disturbed region if peace is to be secured there. Nevertheless, even now, we have found that there is much that we can accomplish. We can collect information, partly by means of already published facts, and partly by travels in the course of which we visit the Governments and learn their point of view. In the short five months of its existence, the Foundation has sent emissaries to various troubled spots and to the Governments concerned. We have already an enormous correspondence, partly with sympathisers in all parts of the world, and partly also, with Heads of States. From all these we derive both information and advice. Partly, too, our correspondence has been concerned with appeals for the liberation of political prisoners and the amelioration of the lot of minorities in various countries, East and West, South and North. In these last respects, our work has already met with great and unexpected success. In recounting the success of the Foundation during these first five months, however, we labour under the handicap of being unable to be specific. Negotiations such as we are conducting, as will readily be understood, cannot be talked of, since to talk of them would nullify their efficacy.

As everybody who has ever attempted to create a large organisation will understand, our chief effort during these early months has been concerned with obtaining funds, and this must continue for a considerable time since much of the work we wish to do involves very considerable expense. We are opening accounts in various countries to pay for local expenditure. We have done various things to raise money, such as a sale of paintings and sculpture generously donated to us by their creators. We are sponsoring a film. We have hope of money from various theatrical performances. But these alone will not suffice, unless supplemented by gifts from individuals and organisations. It is obvious that the more money we can collect the more nearly and adequately we can carry out our aims. We are firmly convinced that the Foundation can achieve the immense work it has undertaken provided sufficient funds become available. We are working for a great cause – the preservation of Man. In this work one might expect to have the support of every human being. This, alas, is not yet the case. It is our hope that, in time, it will become so.

From and to Erich Fromm

> Gonzalez Cosio No. 15
> Mexico 12, D.F.
> May 30th, 1962

Lord Bertrand Russell
care of Mrs Clara Urquhart
London, W.1

Dear Bertrand Russell

I know how frightfully busy you must be before the Moscow Conference, but I also believe that you will understand it if I approach you for your advice and help with regard to the fate of a man, Heinz Brandt, who was arrested last June by the East German police in East Berlin, or Potsdam, and was sentenced to thirteen years of hard labour (Zuchthaus) on the 10th of May at a secret trial for espionage against the DDR.

Brandt was a German communist before Hitler, for eleven years was in Hitler's prisons and concentration camps and severely tortured in the latter. After the War he went to East Germany and was a journalist there for the communist party. He got more and more into opposition with that party, and eventually fled to West Germany where he took a job in Frankfort as a journalist on the newspaper of the Metal Workers' Union. He was sent last year by his union to attend a union conference in West Berlin, and apparently was kidnapped or lured into East Berlin by the East German police, since nobody who knows him believes that he would have gone voluntarily to East Germany. The remarkable thing about him is that, in spite of having turned against communism he did not do what so many others have done, to become a rabid spokesman against communism in West Germany. On the contrary, he was one of the most passionate and ardent fighters against West German rearmament, for peace and for an understanding with the Soviet Union. Although his union in Frankfort is not only the biggest but also the most peace-minded union in West Germany, his courageous stand made him enemies in many places and yet he fought for his ideals without the slightest compromise.

I know that Brandt was left in a nervous condition from the tortures he underwent in the Nazi camps, he has a wife and three young children, and the sentence amounts to a life-long one or even a death sentence, considering his present age of around 55 and his condition ...

There was a great deal of protest and indignation going on since he was arrested and again now after he was sentenced. Naturally his case has been used for fanatical anti-communist propaganda by various circles. We, on the other hand, have done all we could to prevent this kind of misuse, and we have addressed ourselves in cables to Khrushchev and Ulbricht asking for Brandt's release. (These cables were signed by a number of American pacifists and leading peace workers and also by some from France (Claude Bourdet) and Germany (Professor Abendroth).) After being sentenced, it seems that the only hope for his liberation would lie in the fact that enough people, and sufficiently influential ones from the Western Hemisphere, would approach the Soviet people with the request to exert influence on the Ulbricht government to pardon Brandt and return him to his family in West Germany. I thought myself that the coming Congress in Moscow would be a good opportunity for such an attempt. I intend to go there as an observer. I cabled Professor Bernal some time ago and asked him whether, if I went, I would be free to bring up the Brandt case, and he cabled back that this was so. Naturally, the success of this action depends on one fact: How many other non-communists and Western peace people will support this step? I hope very much that you could decide to lend your support also.

I enclose the declaration of the West German Socialistischer Deutscher Studentenbund. Similar declarations have been signed by Professor W. Abendroth, Professor H. J. Heydorn, H. Brakemeier and E. Dähne. (It may be known to you that the Socialistischer Deutscher Studentenbund has been expelled from the West German Democratic Party precisely because of its stand against West German rearmament.)

I would have liked very much to talk with you before the Moscow conference, about how one could best organise a step in favour of Brandt. (I assume you will go to Moscow.) Would you be kind enough to drop me a line how long you will be in London, and when you will be in Moscow, and if you could see me for an hour to discuss this case either before you leave or in Moscow?

Yours sincerely
Erich Fromm

Encl.
cc – Mrs Clara Urquhart

1 July 1962

Dear Erich Fromm

I wish to apologise to you most sincerely for leaving your letter of May 30th unanswered until now. I shall do anything you advise with respect to Brandt. I have recently received two communications from

Khrushchev and can easily incorporate the question of Brandt in my reply.

I am not going to Moscow but I am sending a personal representative and four members of the Committee of 100 are going as delegates. I should very much wish to see you in London. I shall be in London until around July 10 when I expect to be returning to Wales. I should be delighted to see you in London at my home. Please contact me as soon as you come to London. Good wishes.

> *Yours sincerely*
> *Bertrand Russell*

To Nikita Khrushchev

4 July, 1962

Dear Mr Khrushchev

I am venturing to send to you a copy of a letter which I have written to the Moscow Conference on Disarmament, dealing with the case of Heinz Brandt. I hope you will agree with me that clemency, in this case, would further the cause of peace.

My warmest thanks for your kind letter on the occasion of my 90th birthday, which gave me great satisfaction.

> *Yours sincerely*
> *Bertrand Russell*

To the President of the Moscow Conference on Disarmament

4 July, 1962

Sir

I wish to bring to the attention of this Conference the case of Heinz Brandt who has been sentenced in East Germany to thirteen years of prison with hard labour. I do not know the exact nature of the charges against him. At first, he was to have been charged with espionage, but, when he was brought to trial, this charge was dropped. Heinz Brandt has been throughout his active life a devoted and self-sacrificing worker for peace and against West German re-armament. For eleven years during Hitler's regime, he was in prisons and concentration camps, including Auschwitz and Buchenwald. To all friends of peace and disarmament in West Germany, his arrest and condemnation by the East German Authorities were a severe blow, while to the militarists of West Germany they supplied new arguments and new reasons for bitterness. I have no doubt that, in the interests of disarmament with which this Congress is concerned, his release would be profoundly beneficial. I hope that the Congress will pass a resolution asking for his release on these grounds.

> *Bertrand Russell*

To Walter Ulbricht

12 August, 1963

Dear Herr Ulbricht

Recently I was honoured with an award for peace by your government in the name of Carl von Ossietzky. I hold Ossietzky's memory in high regard and I honour that for which he died. I am passionately opposed to the Cold War and to all those who trade in it, so I felt it important to accept the honour accorded me.

You will understand, therefore, the motives which lead me to, once more, appeal to you on behalf of Heinz Brandt. I am most deeply disturbed that I have not received so much as an acknowledgement of my previous appeals on his behalf. Heinz Brandt was a political prisoner, placed in concentration camp along with Ossietzky. He has suffered many long years of imprisonment because he has stood by his political beliefs. I do not raise the question here of the comparative merit or demerit of those beliefs. I but ask you to consider the damage that is done to the attempts to improve relations between your country and the West and to soften the Cold War by the continued imprisonment of Heinz Brandt. I appeal to you, once more, on grounds of humanity, to release this man, and I should be grateful if you would inform me of your intentions with regard to him.

Although I value the Ossietzky Medal, I am placed in an ambiguous position by the continued imprisonment of Heinz Brandt.

Yours sincerely
Bertrand Russell

On October 30, 1963, the Secretary of the East German State Council wrote to me at great length to explain that 'the spy Brandt', 'condemned for treason' had received the 'justified sentence' of thirteen years' hard labour, the sentence to expire in June, 1974. Brandt had served only two years of this sentence, and no long sentence could be conditionally suspended until at least half of it had been served. 'Reduction of the sentence by act of grace' was not justified because of the seriousness of the crimes. Herr Gotsche's letter concluded: 'I may assume that you, too, dear Mr Russell, will appreciate after insight . . . that in this case the criminal law must be fully applied . . . in the interests of humanity.'

To Walter Ulbricht

7 January 1964

Dear Mr Ulbricht

I am writing to you to tell you of my decision to return to your Government the Carl von Ossietzsky medal for peace. I do so reluctantly and after two years of private approaches on behalf of Heinz

Brandt, whose continued imprisonment is a barrier to coexistence, relaxation of tension and understanding between East and West.

My representative, Mr Kinsey, spoke recently with officials of your governing council in East Berlin and he carried a message from me.

I regret not to have heard from you on this subject. I hope that you will yet find it possible to release Brandt through an amnesty which would be a boon to the cause of peace and to your country.

> *Yours sincerely*
> *Bertrand Russell*

29 May 1964

Dear Premier Ulbricht

I am writing to convey my great pleasure at the news of the release of Heinz Brandt from prison. I realise that this was not an easy decision for your Government to make but I am absolutely convinced that it was a decision in the best interests of your country and of the cause of peace and good relations between East and West.

I wish to offer my appreciation and approval for this important act of clemency.

> *Yours sincerely*
> *Bertrand Russell*

From and to Tony and Betty Ambatielos

> Filonos 22
> Piraeus, Greece
> 7 May 1964

Dear Lord Russell

It will give my husband and I the greatest pleasure if, during a visit we hope to make to Britain soon, we are able to meet you and thank you personally for all your support over the years. Meantime, however, we send you this brief letter as a token of our deep gratitude and esteem.

We will be indebted to you always for assisting in bringing about Tony's release and we know that his colleagues who were freed at the same time would wish us to convey their feelings of gratitude towards you also. It is unfortunate that when so many hundreds were at last freed, nearly one hundred were and are still held. But we are all confident that with the continued interest and support of such an esteemed and stalwart friend as yourself, they too can be freed in the not too distant future.

With kind regards to Lady Russell and all good wishes and thanks,

> *Yours sincerely*
> *Betty Ambatielos*

692 The Autobiography of Bertrand Russell

I wish to send you these few lines to express my very deep gratitude and respect to you for the way you championed the cause of the political prisoners.

Your name is held in very high esteem among all of us.

Please accept my personal thanks for all you have done.

Yours sincerely
Tony Ambatielos

13 May, 1964

Dear Mr and Mrs Ambatielos

Thank you very much for your letter. I should be delighted to see you both in Wales or London. I have been corresponding with Papandreou, pressing him for the release of remaining prisoners and the dropping of recent charges in Salonika.

With kind regards,

Yours sincerely
Bertrand Russell

From and to Lord Gladwyn

30, Gresham Street
London, E.C.2
3rd November, 1964

Dear Lord Russell

I have read with great interest, on my return from America your letter of September 11th which was acknowledged by my secretary. It was indeed kind of you to send me the literature concerning the 'Bertrand Russell Peace Foundation' and the paper entitled 'Africa and the Movement for Peace' and to ask for my views, which are as follows:—

As a general observation, I should at once say that I question your whole major premise. I really do not think that general nuclear war is getting more and more likely: I believe, on the contrary, that it is probably getting less and less likely. I do not think that either the USA or the USSR has the slightest intention of putting the other side into a position in which it may feel it will have to use nuclear weapons on a 'first strike' for its own preservation (if that very word is not in itself paradoxical in the circumstances). Nor will the Chinese for a long time have the means of achieving a 'first strike', and when they have they likewise will not want to achieve it. We are no doubt in for a difficult, perhaps even a revolutionary decade and the West must stand together and discuss wise joint policies for facing it, otherwise we may well lapse into mediocrity, anarchy or barbarism. If we do evolve an intelligent common policy not only will there be no general nuclear war, but we shall overcome the great evils of hunger and overpopulation. Here, however, to my mind, everything depends on the possibility of organising Western unity.

Nor do I believe that 'war by accident', though just conceivable, is a tenable hypothesis. Thus the so-called 'Balance of Terror' (by which I mean the ability of each of the two giants to inflict totally unacceptable damage on the other even on a 'second strike') is likely to result in the maintenance of existing territorial boundaries (sometimes referred to as the 'Status Quo') in all countries in which the armed forces of the East and West are in physical contact, and a continuance of the so-called 'Cold War', in other words a struggle for influence between the free societies of the West and the Communist societies of the East, in the 'emergent' countries of South America, Africa and Asia. I developed this general thesis in 1958 in an essay called 'Is Tension Necessary?' and events since then have substantially confirmed it. The Balance of Terror has not turned out to be so 'delicate' as some thought; with the passage of time I should myself say that it was getting even less fragile.

In the 'Cold War' struggle the general position of the West is likely to be strengthened by the recent ideological break between the Soviet Union and China which seems likely to persist in spite of the fall of Khrushchev. Next to the 'Balance of Terror' between Russia and America I should indeed place the split as a major factor militating in favour of prolonged World Peace, in the sense of an absence of nuclear war. The chief feature of the present landscape, in fact (and it is a reassuring one), is that America and Russia are becoming less afraid of each other. The one feels that the chances of a subversion of its free economy are substantially less: the other feels that no attack can now possibly be mounted against it by the Western 'Capitalists'.

Naturally, I do not regard this general situation as ideal, or even as one which is likely to continue for a very long period. It is absurd that everybody, and more particularly the USA and the USSR, should spend such colossal sums on armaments, though it seems probable that, the nuclear balance having been achieved, less money will be devoted to reinforcing or even to maintaining it. It is wrong, in principle, that Germany should continue to be divided. Clearly general disarmament is desirable, though here it is arguable that it will not be achieved until an agreed settlement of outstanding political problems, and notably the reunification of Germany is peacefully negotiated. The truth may well be that in the absence of such settlements both sides are in practice reluctant to disarm beyond a certain point, and without almost impossible guarantees, and are apt to place the blame for lack of progress squarely on the other. What is demonstrably untrue is that the West are to blame whereas the Soviet Union is guiltless. In particular, I question your statement (in the African paper) that the Soviet Union has already agreed to disarm and to accept adequate inspection in all the proper stages, and that failure to agree on disarmament is solely the responsibility of the West. The facts are that although the Soviet Government has accepted full verification of the destruction of all armaments due for destruction in the various stages of both the Russian and the American Draft Disarmament Treaties, they have *not* agreed that there should be any verification of the balance of armaments remaining in existence. There would thus, under the Russian proposal, be no guarantee at all that retained armed forces and armaments did not exceed agreed quotas at any stage. Here the Americans have made a significant concession, namely to be content in the early stages with a system of verifying in a few sample areas only: but the Soviet Government has so far turned a deaf ear to such suggestions. Then there is the whole problem of the run-down and its relation to the Agreed Principles, as regards which the Soviet intentions have not, as yet, been fully revealed. Finally the West want to have the International Peace-Keeping Force, which would clearly be required in the event of complete disarmament, under an integrated and responsible Command, but the Soviet Government is insisting, for practical purposes, on the introduction into the Command of a power of veto.

It follows that I cannot possibly agree with your subsequent statement either that 'if we are to alter the drift to destruction it will be necessary to change *Western* policy (my italics)' – and apparently Western policy only. At the time of the Cuba crisis you circulated a leaflet entitled 'No Nuclear War over Cuba', which started off 'You are to die'. We were to die, it appeared, unless public opinion could under your leadership be mobilised so as to alter *American* policy, thus allowing the Soviet Government to establish hardened nuclear missile bases in Cuba for use against the United States. Happily, no notice was taken of your manifesto: the Russians discontinued their suicidal policy; and President Kennedy by his resolution and far-sightedness saved the world. We did not die. Some day, all of us will die, but not, I think in the great holocaust of the Western imagination. The human animal, admittedly, has many of the characteristics of a beast of prey: mercifully he does not possess the suicidal tendencies of the lemmings. What we want in the world is less fear and more love. With great respect, I do not think that your campaign is contributing to either objective.

These are matters of great moment to our people and indeed to humanity. I should hope that you would one day be prepared to advance your proposals in the House of Lords where they could be subjected to intelligent scrutiny. In the meantime I suggest that we agree to publish this letter together with your reply, if indeed you should feel that one is called for.

Yours sincerely
Gladwyn

Plas Penrhyn
14 November, 1964

Dear Lord Gladwyn

Thank you for your long, reasoned letter of November 3rd. I shall take up your points one by one.

I. You point out that the danger of a nuclear war between Russia and the West is less than it was a few years ago. As regards a direct clash between NATO and the Warsaw Powers, I agree with you that the danger is somewhat diminished. On the other hand, new dangers have arisen. All the Powers of East and West, ever since Hiroshima, have agreed that the danger of nuclear war is increased when new Powers become nuclear. But nothing has been done to prevent the spread of nuclear weapons. France and Belgium, India and China and Brazil have or are about to have nuclear weapons. West Germany is on the verge of acquiring a share in Nato weapons. As for China, you say that it will be a long time before China will be effective, but I see no reason to believe this. The West thought that it would be a long time before Russia had the A-bomb. When Russia had the A-bomb, the West thought it would be a long time before they had the H-bomb. Both these expectations turned out to be illusions.

You consider war by accident so improbable that it can be ignored. There is, however, the possibility of war by mistake. This has already almost occurred several times through mistaking the moon for Soviet planes or some such mis-reading of radar signals. It cannot be deemed unlikely that, sooner or later, such a mistake will not be discovered in time.

Moreover, it is a simple matter of mathematical statistics that the more nuclear missiles there are the greater is the danger of nuclear accident. Vast numbers of rockets and other missiles, primed for release and dependent upon mechanical systems and slight margins in time, are highly subject to accident. Any insurance company would establish this where the factors involved relate to civilian activity such as automobile transport or civilian aviation. In this sense, the danger of accidental war increases with each day that the weapons systems are permitted to remain. Nor is the danger wholly mechanical: human beings, even well 'screened' and highly trained are subject to hysteria and madness of various sorts when submitted to the extreme tensions and concentration that many men having to do with nuclear weapons now are submitted to.

Another danger is the existence of large, adventurous and very powerful groups in the United States. The US Government has run grave risks in attacks on North Vietnam forces. In the recent election some 40%, or thereabouts, of the population voted for Goldwater, who openly advocated war. Warlike groups can, at any moment, create an incident such as the U2 which put an end to the conciliatory mood of Camp David.

In estimating the wisdom of a policy, it is necessary to consider not only the possibility of a bad result, but also the degree of badness of the result. The extermination of the human race is the worst possible result, and even if the probability of its occurring is small, its disastrousness should be a deterrent to any policy which allows of it.

II. You admit that the present state of the world is not desirable and suggest that the only way of improving it is by way of Western unity. Your letter seems to imply that this unity is to be achieved by all countries of the West blindly following one policy. Such unity does not seem to me desirable. Certainly the policy to which you appear to think the West should adhere – a policy which upholds the present United States war in South Vietnam and the economic imperialism of the US in the Congo and Latin America – cannot possibly avoid a lapse into mediocrity, anarchy or barbarism, which you say you wish above all to avoid.

The United States is conducting a war in Vietnam in which it has tolerated and supervised every form of bestiality against a primitively armed peasant population. Disembowelments, mutilations, mass bombing raids with jelly-gasoline, the obliteration of over 75% of the villages of the country and the despatch of eight million people to internment camps have characterised this war. Such conduct cannot be described as an ordered bulwark against mediocrity, anarchy or barbarism. There is a large body of opinion in the United States itself that opposes this war, but the Government persists in carrying it on. The unity that you advocate would do little to encourage the US Government to alter its policy. The US policy in the Congo promises to be similar to that in Vietnam in cruelty. The Western nations show no signs of encouraging any other policy there. (I enclose two pamphlets dealing with Vietnam and the Congo in case you have not seen them.)

Universal unity, however, such as might be achieved by a World Government I am entirely persuaded is necessary to the peace of the world.

III. You find fault with me on the ground that I seem to hold the West always to blame and the Soviet Union always guiltless. This is by no means the case. While Stalin lived, I considered his policies abominable. More recently, I protested vigorously against the Russian tests that preceded the Test Ban Treaty. At present, I am engaged in pointing out the ill-treatment of Jews in the Soviet Union. It is only in certain respects, of which Cuba was the most important, that I think the greatest share of blame falls upon the United States.

IV. Your comments on the Cuban crisis are, to me, utterly amazing. You say that the way the solution was arrived at was that 'the Russians discontinued their suicidal policy; and President Kennedy by his resolution and farsightedness saved the world'. This seems to me a complete reversal of the truth. Russia and America had policies leading directly to nuclear war. Khrushchev, when he saw the danger, abandoned his policy. Kennedy did not. It was Khrushchev who allowed the human race to continue, not Kennedy.

Apart from the solution of the crisis, Russian policy towards Cuba would have been justifiable but for the danger of war, whereas American policy was purely imperialistic. Cuba established a kind of Government which the US disliked, and the US considered that its dislike justified attempts to alter the character of the Government by force. I do not attempt to justify the establishment of missiles on Cuban soil, but I do not see how the West can justify its objection to these missiles. The US has established missiles in Quemoy, in Matsu, in Taiwan, Turkey, Iran and all the countries on the periphery of China and the Soviet Union which host nuclear bases. I am interested in your statement that the Soviet Government was establishing hardened nuclear missile bases in Cuba, especially as neither Mr Macmillan nor Lord Home stated that the missiles in Cuba were nuclear, fitted with nuclear warheads or accompanied by nuclear warheads on Cuban soil.

In view of the conflict at the Bay of Pigs, it cannot be maintained that Cuba had no excuse for attempts to defend itself. In view of Kennedy's words to the returned Cuban exiles after the crisis, it cannot be said that Cuba still has no excuse.

You speak of 'the free world'. Cuba seems a case in point. The West seems little freer than the East.

You allude to my leaflet 'Act or Perish'. This was written at the height of the crisis when most informed people were expecting universal death within a few hours. After the crisis passed, I no longer considered such emphatic language appropriate, but, as an expression of the right view at the moment, I still consider it correct.

V. You say, and I emphatically agree with you, that what the world needs is less fear and more love. You think that it is to be achieved by the balance of terror. Is it not evident that, so long as the doctrine of the balance of terror prevails, there will be continually new inventions which will increase the expense of armaments until both sides are reduced to penury? The balance of terror consists of two expensively armed blocs, each saying to the other, 'I should like to destroy you, but I fear that, if I did, you would destroy me.' Do you really consider that this is a way to promote love? If you do not, I wish that you had given some indication of a way that you think feasible. All that you say about this is that you see no way except disarmament, but that disarmament is not feasible unless various political questions have first been settled.

My own view is that disarmament could now come about. Perhaps you know Philip Noel-Baker's pamphlet 'The Way to World Disarmament – Now!' In it he notes accurately and dispassionately the actual record of disarmament negotiations. I enclose it with this letter in case you do not know it. He has said, among other things that Soviet proposals entail the presence of large numbers of inspectors on Soviet territory during all stages of disarmament. In 1955 the Soviet Union accepted in full the Western disarmament proposals. The Western proposals were withdrawn at once upon their acceptance by the Soviet Union. It is far from being only the West that cries out for disarmament: China has pled for it again and again, the last time a few days ago.

As to the expense of present arms production programmes, I, naturally, agree with you. Arms production on the part of the great powers is in excess of the gross national product of three continents – Africa, Latin America and Asia.

I also agree that disarmament would be easier to achieve if various political questions were first settled. It is for this reason that the Peace Foundation of which I wrote you is engaged at present in an examination of these questions and discussions with those directly involved in them in the hope of working out with them acceptable and feasible solutions. And it is with a view to enhancing the love and mitigating the hate in the world that the Foundation is engaged in Questions relating to political prisoners and members of families separated by political ruling and red tape and to unhappy minorities. It has had surprising and considerable success in all these fields during the first year of its existence.

As to publication, I am quite willing that both your letter and mine should be published in full.

> *Yours sincerely*
> *Russell*

enc:

'Vietnam and Laos' by Bertrand Russell and William Warbey, MP
'The Way to World Disarmament – Now!' by Philip Noel-Baker
Unarmed Victory by Bertrand Russell
'The Cold War and World Poverty' by Bertrand Russell
'Freedom in Iran' by K. Zaki
'Oppression in South Arabia' by Bertrand Russell
'Congo – a Tragedy' by R. Schoenman

No reply was ever received by me to this letter to Lord Gladwyn who, so far as I know, never published either of the above letters.

16 QUESTIONS ON THE ASSASSINATION

The official version of the assassination of President Kennedy has been so riddled with contradictions that it has been abandoned and rewritten no less than three times. Blatant fabrications have received very widespread coverage by the mass media, but denials of these same lies have gone unpublished. Photographs, evidence and affidavits have been doctored out of recognition. Some of the most important aspects of the case against Lee Harvey Oswald have been completely blacked out. Meanwhile the FBI, the police and the Secret Service have tried to silence key witnesses or instruct them what evidence to give. Others involved have disappeared or died in extraordinary circumstances.

It is facts such as these that demand attention, and which the Warren Commission should have regarded as vital. Although I am writing before the publication of the Warren Commission's report, leaks to the press have made much of its contents predictable. Because of the high office of its members and the fact of its establishment by President Johnson, the Commission has been widely regarded as a body of holy men appointed to pronounce the Truth. An impartial examination of the composition and conduct of the Commission suggests quite otherwise.

The Warren Commission has been utterly unrepresentative of the American people. It consisted of two Democrats, Senator Russell of Georgia and Congressman Boggs of Louisiana, both of whose racist views have brought shame on the United States; two Republicans, Senator Cooper of Kentucky and Congressman Gerald R. Ford of Michigan, the latter of whom is leader of his local Goldwater movement, a former member of the FBI and is known in Washington as the spokesman for that institution; Allen Dulles, former director of the CIA; and Mr McCloy, who has been referred to as the spokesman for the business community. Leadership of the filibuster in the Senate against the Civil Rights Bill prevented Senator Russell attending a single hearing during this period. The Chief Justice of the United States Supreme Court, Earl Warren, who rightly commands respect, was finally persuaded, much against his will, to preside over the Commission, and it was his involvement above all else that helped lend the Commission an aura of legality and authority. Yet many of its members were also members of those very groups which have done so much to distort and suppress the facts about the assassination. Because of their connection with the Government, not one member would have been permitted under American law to serve on a jury had Oswald faced trial. It is small wonder that the Chief Justice himself remarked: 'You may never know all of the facts in your life time.' Here, then, is my first question: *Why were all the members of the Warren Commission closely connected with the* US *Government.*

If the composition of the Commission was suspect, its conduct confirmed one's worst fears. No counsel was permitted to act for Oswald, so that cross-examination was barred. Later, under pressure, the Commission appointed the President of the American Bar Association, Walter Craig, one of the leaders of the Goldwater movement in Arizona, to represent Oswald. To my knowledge he did not attend a single hearing, but satisfied himself with representation by observers. In the name of national security, the Commission's hearings were held in secret, thereby continuing the policy which has marked the entire course of the case. This prompts my second question: *If, as we are told, Oswald was the lone assassin, where is the issue of national security?* Indeed, precisely the same question must be put here as was posed in France during the Dreyfus case: *If the Government is so certain of its case, why has it conducted all its enquiries in the strictest secrecy?*

At the outset the Commission appointed six panels through which it would conduct its enquiry. They considered: (1) What did Oswald do on November 22, 1963? (2) What was Oswald's background? (3) What did Oswald do in the US Marine Corps, and in the Soviet Union? (4) How did Ruby kill Oswald? (5) What is Ruby's background? (6) What efforts were taken to protect the President on November 22? This raises my fourth question: *Why did the Warren Commission not establish a panel to deal with the question of who killed President Kennedy?*

All the evidence given to the Commission has been classified 'Top Secret', including even a request that hearings be held in public. Despite this the Commission itself leaked much of the evidence to the press, though only if the evidence tended to prove Oswald was the lone assassin. Thus Chief Justice Warren held a press conference after Oswald's wife Marina, had testified, he said, that she believed her husband was the assassin. Before Oswald's brother Robert, testified, he gained the Commission's agreement never to comment on what he said. After he had testified for two days, Allen Dulles remained in the hearing room and several members of the press entered. The next day the newspapers were full of stories that 'a member of the Commission' had told the press that Robert Oswald had just testified that he believed that his brother was an agent of the Soviet Union. Robert Oswald was outraged by this, and said that he could not remain silent while lies were told about his testimony. He had never said this and he had never believed it. All that he had told the Commission was that he believed his brother was in no way involved in the assassination.

The methods adopted by the Commission have indeed been deplorable, but it is important to challenge the entire role of the Warren Commission. It stated that it would not conduct its own investigation, but rely instead on the existing governmental agencies – the FBI, the Secret Service and the Dallas police. Confidence in the Warren Commission thus presupposes confidence in these three institutions. *Why have so many liberals abandoned their own responsibility to a Commission whose circumstances they refuse to examine?*

It is known that the strictest and most elaborate security precautions ever taken for a President of the United States were ordered for November 22 in Dallas. The city had a reputation for violence and was the home of some of the most extreme right-wing fanatics in America. Mr and Mrs Lyndon Johnson had been assailed there in 1960 when he was a candidate for the Vice-Presidency. Adlai Stevenson had been physically attacked when he spoke in the city only a month before Kennedy's visit. On the morning of November 22, the Dallas *Morning News* carried a full-page advertisement associating the President with communism. The city was covered with posters showing the President's picture and headed 'Wanted for Treason'. The Dallas list of subversives comprised 23 names, of which Oswald's was the first. All of them were followed that day, except Oswald. *Why did the authorities follow as potential assassins every single person who had ever spoken out publicly in favour of desegregation of the public school system in Dallas, and fail to observe Oswald's entry into the book depository building while allegedly carrying a rifle over four feet long?*

The President's route for his drive through Dallas was widely known and was printed in the Dallas *Morning News* on November 22. At the last minute the Secret Service changed a small part of their plans so that the President left Main Street and turned into Houston and Elm Streets. This alteration took the President past the book depository building from which it is alleged that Oswald shot him. How Oswald is supposed to have known of this change has never been explained. *Why was the President's route changed at the last minute to take him past Oswald's place of work?*

After the assassination and Oswald's arrest, judgement was pronounced swiftly: Oswald was the assassin, and he had acted alone. No attempt was made to arrest others, no road blocks were set up round the area, and every piece of evidence which tended to incriminate Oswald was announced to the press by the Dallas District Attorney, Mr Wade. In such a way millions of people were prejudiced against Oswald before there was any opportunity for him to be brought to trial. The first theory announced by the authorities was that the President's car was in Houston Street, approaching the book depository building, when Oswald opened fire. When available photographs and eye-witnesses had shown this to be quite untrue, the theory was abandoned and a new one formulated which placed the vehicle in its correct position.

Meanwhile, however, DA Wade had announced that three days after Oswald's room in Dallas had been searched, a map had been found there on which the book depository building had been circled and dotted lines drawn from the building to a vehicle on Houston Street. After the first theory was proved false, the Associated Press put out the following story on November 27: 'Dallas authorities announced today that there never was a map. Any reference to the map was a mistake.'

The second theory correctly placed the President's car on Elm Street, 50 to 75 yards past the book depository, but had to contend with the difficulty that the President was shot from the front, in the throat. How did Oswald manage to shoot the President in the front from behind? The FBI held a series of background briefing sessions for *Life* magazine, which in its issue of December 6 explained that the President had turned completely round just at the time he was shot. This, too, was soon shown to be entirely false. It was denied by several witnesses and films, and the previous issue of *Life* itself had shown the President looking forward as he was hit. Theory number two was abandoned.

In order to retain the basis of all official thinking, that Oswald was the lone assassin, it now became necessary to construct a third theory with the medical evidence altered to fit it. For the first month no Secret Service agent had ever spoken to the three doctors who had tried to save Kennedy's life in the Parkland Memorial Hospital. Now two agents spent three hours with the doctors and persuaded them that they were all misinformed: the entrance wound in the President's throat had been an exit wound, and the bullet had not ranged down towards the lungs. Asked by the press how they could have been so mistaken, Dr McClelland advanced two reasons: they had not seen the autopsy report – and they had not known that Oswald was behind the President! The autopsy report, they had been told by the Secret Service, showed that Kennedy had been shot from behind. The agents, however, had refused to show the report to the doctors, who were entirely dependent upon the word of the Secret Service for this suggestion. The doctors made it clear that they were not permitted to discuss the case. The third theory, with the medical evidence rewritten, remains the basis of the case against Oswald. *Why has the medical evidence concerning the President's death been altered out of recognition?*

Although Oswald is alleged to have shot the President from behind, there are many witnesses who are confident that the shots came from the front. Among them are two reporters from the Fort Worth *Star*

Telegram, four from the Dallas *Morning News,* and two people who were standing in front of the book depository building itself, the director of the book depository and the vice-president of the firm. It appears that only two people immediately entered the building, the director, Mr Roy S. Truly, and a Dallas police officer, Seymour Weitzman. Both thought that the shots had come from in front of the President's vehicle. On first running in that direction, Weitzman was informed by 'someone' that he thought the shots had come from the building, so he rushed back there. Truly entered with him in order to assist with his knowledge of the building. Mr Jesse Curry, however, the Chief of Police in Dallas, has stated that he was immediately convinced that the shots came from the building. If anyone else believes this, he has been reluctant to say so to date. It is also known that the first bulletin to go out on Dallas police radios stated that 'the shots came from a triple overpass in front of the presidential automobile'. In addition, there is the consideration that after the first shot the vehicle was brought almost to a halt by the trained Secret Service driver, an unlikely response if the shots had indeed come from behind. Certainly Mr Roy Kellerman, who was in charge of the Secret Service operation in Dallas that day, and travelled in the presidential car, looked to the front as the shots were fired. The Secret Service have removed all the evidence from the car, so it is no longer possible to examine the broken windscreen. *What is the evidence to substantiate the allegation that the President was shot from behind?*

Photographs taken at the scene of the crime could be most helpful. One young lady standing just to the left of the presidential car as the shots were fired took photographs of the vehicle just before and during the shooting, and was thus able to get into her picture the entire front of the book depository building. Two FBI agents immediately took the film from her and have refused to this day to permit her to see the photographs which she took. *Why has the FBI refused to publish what could be the most reliable piece of evidence in the whole case?*

In this connection it is noteworthy also that it is impossible to obtain the originals of photographs of the various alleged murder weapons. When *Time* magazine published a photograph of Oswald's arrest – the only one ever seen – the entire background was blacked out for reasons which have never been explained. It is difficult to recall an occasion for so much falsification of photographs as has happened in the Oswald case.

The affidavit by police officer Weitzman, who entered the book depository building, stated that he found the alleged murder rifle on the sixth floor. (It was at first announced that the rifle had been found on the fifth floor, but this was soon altered.) It was a German 7.65mm. Mauser. Later the following day, the FBI issued its first proclamation.

Oswald had purchased in March 1963 an Italian 6.5mm. carbine. DA Wade immediately altered the nationality and size of his weapon to conform to the FBI statement.

Several photographs have been published of the alleged murder weapon. On February 21, *Life* magazine carried on its cover a picture of 'Lee Oswald with the weapon he used to kill President Kennedy and Officer Tippett'. On page 80, *Life* explained that the photograph was taken during March or April of 1963. According to the FBI, Oswald purchased his pistol in September 1963. The *New York Times* carried a picture of the alleged murder weapon being taken by police into the Dallas police station. The rifle is quite different. Experts have stated that it would be impossible to pull the trigger on the rifle in *Life*'s picture. The *New York Times* also carried the same photograph as *Life*, but left out the telescopic sights. On March 2, *Newsweek* used the same photograph but painted in an entirely new rifle. Then on April 13, the Latin American edition of *Life* carried the same picture on its cover as the US edition had on February 21, but in the same issue on page 18 it had the same picture with the rifle altered. *How is it that millions of people have been misled by complete forgeries in the press?*

Another falsehood concerning the shooting was a story circulated by the Associated Press on November 23 from Los Angeles. This reported Oswald's former superior officer in the Marine Corps as saying that Oswald was a crack shot and a hot-head. The story was published everywhere. Three hours later AP sent out a correction deleting the entire story from Los Angeles. The officer had checked his records and it had turned out that he was talking about another man. He had never known Oswald. To my knowledge this correction has yet to be published by a single major publication.

The Dallas police took a paraffin test of Oswald's face and hands to try to establish that he had fired a weapon on November 22. The Chief of the Dallas Police, Jesse Curry, announced on November 23 that the results of the test 'proves Oswald is the assassin'. The Director of the FBI in the Dallas–Fort Worth area in charge of the investigation stated: 'I have seen the paraffin test. The paraffin test proves that Oswald had nitrates and gun-powder on his hands and face. It proves he fired a rifle on November 22.' Not only does this unreliable test not prove any such thing, it was later discovered that the test on Oswald's face was in fact negative, suggesting that it was unlikely he fired a rifle that day. *Why was the result of the paraffin test altered before being announced by the authorities?*

Oswald, it will be recalled was originally arrested and charged with the murder of Patrolman Tippett. Tippett was killed at 1.06 p.m. on November 22 by a man who first engaged him in conversation, then caused him to get out of the stationary police car in which he was sitting and shot him with a pistol. Miss Helen L. Markham, who states that she is the sole eye-witness to this crime, gave the Dallas police a description of the assailant. After signing her affidavit, she was instructed by the FBI, the Secret Service and many police officers that she was not permitted to discuss the case with anyone. The affidavit's only description of the killer was that he was a 'young white man'. Miss Markham later revealed that the killer had run right up to her and past her, brandishing the pistol, and she repeated the description of the murderer which she had given to the police. He was, she said, 'short, heavy and had bushy hair'. (The police description of Oswald was that he was of average height, or a little taller, was slim and had receding fair hair.) Miss Markham's affidavit is the entire case against Oswald for the murder of Patrolman Tippett, yet District Attorney Wade asserted: 'We have more evidence to prove Oswald killed Tippett than we have to show he killed the President.' The case against Oswald for the murder of Tippett, he continued, was an absolutely strong case. *Why was the only description of Tippett's killer deliberately omitted by the police from the affidavit of the sole eye-witness?*

Oswald's description was broadcast by the Dallas police only 12 minutes after the President was shot. This raises one of the most extraordinary questions ever posed in a murder case: *Why was Oswald's description in connection with the murder of Patrolman Tippett broadcast over Dallas police radio at 12.43 p.m. on November 22, when Tippett was not shot until 1.06 p.m.?*

According to Mr Bob Considine, writing in the New York *Journal American*, there had been another person who had heard the shots that were fired at Tippett. Warren Reynolds had heard shooting in the street from a nearby room and had rushed to the window to see the murderer run off. Reynolds himself was later shot through the head by a rifleman. A man was arrested for this crime but produced an alibi. His girl-friend, Betty Mooney McDonald, told the police she had been with him at the time Reynolds was shot. The Dallas police immediately dropped the charges against him, even before Reynolds had time to recover consciousness and attempt to identify his assailant. The man at once disappeared, and two days later the Dallas police arrested Betty Mooney McDonald on a minor charge and it was announced that she had hanged herself in the police cell. She had been a striptease artist in Jack Ruby's nightclub, according to Mr Considine.

Another witness to receive extraordinary treatment in the Oswald case was his wife, Marina. She was taken to the jail while her husband was still alive and shown a rifle by Chief of Police Jesse Curry. Asked if it was Oswald's, she replied that she believed Oswald had a rifle but that it didn't look like that. She and her mother-in-law were in great danger following the assassination because of the threat of public revenge on them. At this time they were unable to obtain a single police officer to protect them. Immediately Oswald was killed, however, the Secret Service illegally held both women against their will. After three days they were separated and Marina has never again been accessible to the public. Held in custody for nine weeks and questioned almost daily by the FBI and Secret Service, she finally testified to the Warren Commission and, according to Earl Warren, said that she believed her husband was the assassin. The Chief Justice added that the next day they intended to show Mrs Oswald the murder weapon and the Commission was fairly confident that she would identify it as her husband's. The following day Earl Warren announced that this had indeed happened. Mrs Oswald is still in the custody of the Secret Service. To isolate a witness for nine weeks and to subject her to repeated questioning by the Secret Service in this manner is reminiscent of police behaviour in other countries, where it is called brain-washing. *How was it possible for Earl Warren to forecast that Marina Oswald's evidence would be exactly the reverse of what she had previously believed?*

After Ruby had killed Oswald, DA Wade made a statement about Oswald's movements following the assassination. He explained that Oswald had taken a bus, but he described the point at which Oswald had entered the vehicle as seven blocks away from the point located by the bus driver in his affidavit. Oswald, Wade continued, then took a taxi driven by a Darryll Click, who had signed an affidavit. An enquiry at the City Transportation Company revealed that no such taxi driver had ever existed in Dallas. Presented with this evidence, Wade altered the driver's name to William Wahley. Wade has been DA in Dallas for 14 years and before that was an FBI agent. *How does a District Attorney of Wade's great experience account for all the extraordinary changes in evidence and testimony which he has announced during the Oswald case?*

These are only a few of the questions raised by the official versions of the assassination and by the way in which the entire case against Oswald has been conducted. Sixteen questions are no substitute for a full examination of all the factors in this case, but I hope that they indicate the importance of such an investigation. I am indebted to Mr Mark Lane, the New York criminal Lawyer who was appointed Counsel for Oswald by his mother, for much of the information in this article. Mr Lane's enquiries, which are continuing, deserve widespread support. A Citizens' Committee of Inquiry has been established in New York[1] for such a purpose, and comparable committees are being set up in Europe.

[1] Room 422, 156 Fifth Avenue, New York, N.Y. (telephone: YU 9–6850).

In Britain I invited people eminent in the intellectual life of the country to join a 'Who killed Kennedy Committee', which at the moment of writing consists of the following people: Mr John Arden, playwright; Mrs Carolyn Wedgwood Benn, from Cincinnati, wife of Anthony Wedgwood Benn, MP; Lord Boyd-Orr, former director-general of the UN Food and Agricultural Organisation and a Nobel Peace Prize winner; Mr John Calder, publisher; Professor William Empsom, Professor of English Literature at Sheffield University; Mr Michael Foot, Member of Parliament; Mr Kingsley Martin, former editor of the *New Statesman*; Sir Compton Mackenzie, writer; Mr J. B. Priestley, playwright and author; Sir Herbert Read, art critic; Mr Tony Richardson, film director; Dr Mervyn Stockwood, Bishop of Southwark; Professor Hugh Trevor-Roper, Regius Professor of Modern History at Oxford University; Mr Kenneth Tynan, Literary Manager of the National Theatre; and myself.

We view the problem with the utmost seriousness. US Embassies have long ago reported to Washington world-wide disbelief in the official charges against Oswald, but this has never been reflected by the American press. No US television programme or mass circulation newspaper has challenged the permanent basis of all the allegations – that Oswald was the assassin, and that he acted alone. It is a task which is left to the American people.

THE LABOUR PARTY'S FOREIGN POLICY

A speech delivered at the London School of Economics on 15th February, 1965, by Bertrand Russell

Before his speech, which begins below, Lord Russell made this emergency statement on the situation in Vietnam:

'The world is on the brink of war as it was at the time of the Cuban Crisis. American attacks on North Vietnam are desperate acts of piratical madness. The people of South Vietnam want neutrality and independence for their country. America, in the course of a war of pure domination in the South, attacked a sovereign state in the North because the US has been defeated by the resistance of the entire population in South Vietnam.

We must demand the recall of the Geneva Conference for immediate negotiations. I urge world protest at every US Embassy. And in Britain the craven and odious support for American madness by the Labour Government must be attacked by meetings, marches, demonstrations and all other forms of protest.

If this aggressive war is not ended now, the world will face total war. The issue must be resolved without a nuclear war. This is only possible by world outcry now against the United States. The American proposition that an independent Vietnam free of US control is worse than a nuclear war is madness. If America is allowed to have its cruel way, the world will be the slave of the United States.

Once more America summons mankind to the brink of world war.

Once more America is willing to run the risk of destroying the human race rather than bow to the general will.

Either America is stopped now or there will be crisis after crisis until, in utter weariness, the world decides for suicide.'

My purpose in what I am about to say is to examine the relations between the foreign policy of the Labour Party before the General Election and the policy of the Labour Government in regard to international politics. I should like to recall to you, first, the preamble to that section – almost the last – in the Labour Manifesto of last September, entitled 'New Prospects for Peace'. I take it from *The Times* of September 12th.

It begins with a very brief history of East–West relations since 1945 and says that even in 'the grimmest periods . . . Labour always regarded the Cold War strategies as second best . . . and remained faithful to its long-term belief in the establishment of East–West co-operation as the basis for a strengthened United Nations developing towards World Government.'

It castigates the Tory Government for their old-fashioned policies, especially the Tory failure to relax tensions and to halt the spread of nuclear weapons. 'The Labour Government will do all that is possible to rectify these policies.'

The Manifesto then considers the means to be taken to 'relax tensions'. 'First and foremost', it says, 'will come our initiative in the field of disarmament. We are convinced that the time is opportune for a new breakthrough in the disarmament negotiations, releasing scarce resources and manpower desperately needed to raise living standards throughout the world.'

'We shall appoint a Minister in the Foreign Office with special responsibility for disarmament to take a new initiative in the Disarmament Committee in association with our friends and allies.'

'We have', it says, 'put forward constructive proposals:
  (1) To stop the spread of nuclear weapons.
  (2) To establish nuclear-free zones in Africa, Latin America and Central Europe.
  (3) To achieve controlled reductions in manpower and arms.
  (4) To stop the private sale of arms.
  (5) To establish an International Disarmament Agency to supervise a disarmament treaty.'

The Labour Government has, to be sure, appointed a Minister in the Foreign Office with special responsibility for disarmament and even an arms control and disarmament research unit headed by a reader in international relations at the LSE. It has, indeed, appointed so many new Ministers and departments for various phases of disarmament and defence and offence that one is hard put to it to know to whom to apply for what.

As to the five proposals. Nothing, so far as the Press has told us, has been done about implementing any of them. Far from taking measures to stop the spread of nuclear weapons, the Labour Government has done quite the opposite. Nor has it taken measures to achieve controlled reductions in manpower and arms – it has turned down any suggestion of reducing the British Army in Germany. Little seems to have come out of the propositions of Mr Rapacki concerning a nuclear-free zone in Central Europe. Chinese proposals – pleas, even – for a nuclear-free zone in Asia and/or the Pacific have been passed over in apparent scorn. I know of no measures taken to stop the private sale of arms or to establish an International Disarmament Agency.

A few lines further on in the Manifesto, the following sentence occurs: 'Labour will stand by its pledge to end the supply of arms to South Africa.' 'Britain,' it says, 'of all nations, cannot stand by as an inactive observer of this tragic situation.' Admirable statements, and backed by previous admirable statements: the *Sunday Times* of January 26, 1964, reports Mrs Barbara Castle as saying, in regard to a possible order from South Africa for Bloodhound bombers, 'If an order is placed before the election we shall do all we can to stop it.' Mr Wilson has, in the past, referred to the arms traffic with South Africa as 'this bloody traffic in these weapons of oppression', and called on the people of Britain to 'Act now to stop' it ... But, on November 25, 1964, Mr Wilson announced that the Labour Government had determined to honour the contract entered into during the rule of the Tory Government for 16 Buccaneers for South Africa.

Following the five proposals that I have cited, the Manifesto says: 'In a further effort to relax tension, a Labour Government will work actively to bring Communist China into its proper place in the United Nations; as well as making an all-out effort to develop East-West trade as the soundest economic basis for peaceful co-existence.' Britain has achieved nothing since the advent of the Labour Government towards the admission of China into the UN nor has it appreciably increased East-West trade. Traders are usually ahead of politicians, Tory traders no less than Labour traders.

The Manifesto continues with an item which, in the light of the Government's actions, does not read well: it says, 'Peaceful co-existence, however, can only be achieved if a sincere readiness to negotiate is combined with a firm determination to resist both threats and pressures'. It is difficult to equate this statement with the refusal, curt and out-of-hand, given by the Labour Government to the proposals of the Chinese Government for summit discussions of disarmament and other international matters which our Press told us took place soon after the Labour Government's advent.

That the Labour Government 'will continue to insist on guarantees for the freedom of West Berlin' we do not yet know – the matter has not come to the fore during Labour's rule. Nor do we yet know how far the Labour Government will be able to implement its admirable suggestions concerning the UN nor how far it will be able to take us towards world government, which the Manifesto says is the final objective – as I believe it should be. So far, Britain under the Labour Government has done nothing to strengthen the UN, though it has been, according to *The Guardian* (27 January, 1965) 'giving close study to the question of designating specific military units for potential use in United Nations peace-keeping operations'. In the light of events during the past two or three months, I cannot, however, feel very hopeful as I read what the Manifesto has to say on these matters, much as I agree with it regarding them.

I propose to take up further on in my discussion of the Labour Government's policy the question of how far the measures which it has so far indulged in tend to relax the tensions of the Cold War, as the Manifesto says the Party wishes to do. But I will continue for a moment with the next item mentioned in the Manifesto; the Party's 'Defence Policy Outline' and its 'New Approach' to defence.

It excoriates the 'run down defences' of the Tory Government whose wastefulness and insistence upon sticking to such affairs as Blue Streak, Skybolt and Polaris, and whose inefficient policy in regard to the aircraft industry has resulted in our defences being obsolescent and meagre. It proposes to institute a revision of the Nassau agreement to buy Polaris know-how and missiles from the United States. But, in face of the storm about TSR 2 bombers and of the fact that it is continuing plans for Polaris submarines and is discussing a nuclear umbrella for South East Asia, one wonders how far the Government intends to go with such plans. It seems extraordinary that, having set itself such a programme as the Manifesto suggests, it had not examined the problems of conversion very carefully and come to some sort of plan to avoid or minimise the hardships that would be entailed in the way of unemployment and waste of machinery and money. But no evidence has been given the ordinary newspaper reader that any such basic studies were made.

It is possible that the Government will strengthen conventional regular forces in order to contribute its share to NATO and keep its peace-keeping commitments to the Commonwealth and the UN as the Manifesto says it stresses doing. This seems, however, unless it runs concurrently with cutting down in other quarters, to be contrary to the controlled reduction in arms which it also says it will strive for.

The next item is both bewildering and interesting. The Manifesto says: 'We are against the development of national nuclear deterrents and oppose the current American proposal for a new mixed-manned nuclear surface fleet (MLF). We believe in the inter-dependence of the Western alliance and will put constructive proposals for integrating all NATO's nuclear weapons under effective political control so that all the partners in the Alliance have a proper share in their deployment and control.' A little further on, when discussing the folly of the Conservatives in entering into the Nassau agreement and in talking about an 'independent British deterrent', it says: This nuclear pretence runs the risk of encouraging the 'spread of nuclear weapons to countries not possessing them, including Germany'. And yet, when the Prime Minister announced what one must suppose are the 'new constructive proposals' which the Manifesto told us to expect, they turned out to be the Atlantic Nuclear Force (ANF). The ANF is to be not merely, as was the MLF, a mixed-manned force of surface ships, but is to include other nuclear delivery systems, including aircraft and submarines. It therefore encourages the spread of nuclear weapons more enthusiastically than does the MLF – which I agree was a deplorable suggestion – and certainly encourages the spread of nuclear weapons to Germany. The remedy is, therefore, far worse than the disaster it professes to correct.

If you would like a glimpse of the chicanery indulged in, I advise you to read the reports of the Parliamentary debate on defence in the week beginning 14th December, and the report in *The Times* of 18 December entitled 'Britain to waive control of Polaris weapons', 'Our bombers over Asia' in the *Daily Worker* of the same date, and 'Britain to retain part of V-bomber force' in *The Guardian* of the previous day. Amongst other information to be gained from these various sources are the facts that Britain proposes to give a certain number of its ships and V-bombers by devious routes to NATO, but will keep others to be used by Britain outside the NATO area. The Government thereby persuades the populace that it is keeping its promise to do away with its independent deterrent and at the same time can, independently, form 'a nuclear umbrella' over South East Asia. By means of the ANF we soothe German feelings, since the Germans will participate equally with us in the control and benefits of this nuclear force and will, therefore, be distracted from pushing for an independent nuclear deterrent of their own. This scheme of the ANF has been put to the public through the Press in such a way that the layman is entirely baffled and cannot understand either what the ANF consists in or how very contrary it is to professed beliefs of the Labour Party as given in the Manifesto or as understood by the lay members of the Party. It is a bare-faced turn-about carried off, in so far as the Government has succeeded in carrying it off, by being wrapped up in a welter of words and the happy slogans that the Prime Minister did not knuckle under to the US in the matter of the MLF and Britain is once more taking the initiative in constructive pacific proposals.

The Manifesto concludes with eight paragraphs in which it first gives itself a reason for not carrying out its promises at once by saying that it does not yet know what damage inflicted upon the country by the Tories it will have to repair. It seems a little odd, perhaps, that the members of the Labour Party who aspired to office were so taken by surprise by the financial state of the country – a situation that was fairly apparent to many laymen – and had not prepared any adequate plans to cope with it. But I do not intend to go into economics and finances here. The Manifesto goes on to say that a Labour Government will first of all have to make itself more efficient than the Government which it supersedes. Presumably the rash of new offices and holders of office in the present Government is its answer to the need of efficiency. Secondly, it says that the Government will seek to establish a true partnership between the people and their Parliament; and thirdly it must foster, throughout the nation, a new and more critical spirit. 'The Government can give a lead,' it says, 'by subjecting to continuing and probing review of its own Departments of State, the administration of justice and the social services.' And here I should like to recount an experience of mine that appears to run counter to the promise contained in the statement from the Manifesto I have just cited. Three eminent Russians were appointed by the Russian Government to discuss various topics of international interest with me. In November these three Russians applied for visas to enter Britain. The Home Office at first refused visas for all three, but after protest, allowed visas for two of them. In regard to the most eminent of the three, the Chief Archivist of the Supreme Soviet, the Home Office remained adamant. I wrote to the Home Office – and I am, of course, speaking of the Labour Home Office – begging them to rescind their ban upon a visa for the Chief Archivist. After many weeks during which I was unable to learn anything of the fate of my letter, I received a reply from the Home Secretary saying that he did not feel able to grant my request. I wrote again and wrote also to the Prime Minister. After some time, I received from the Home Secretary the same reply as before, and from the Prime Minister a notification that he agreed with the Home Secretary and would not ask him to reconsider. On no occasion from beginning to end, has any reason been given me or to the Russians for the ban. If this experience is typical, it hardly bears out the claim of the Manifesto that the Government would, or does welcome criticism or open discussion with its electors and members of its Party.

The Manifesto ends with a stirring pronouncement that the Labour Government 'must put an end to the dreary commercialism and personal selfishness which have dominated the years of Conservative government' and says that 'the Labour Party is offering Britain a new way of life that will stir our hearts'.

There is a lot of ironic fun to be got out of that Manifesto now that we have seen its fruits.

So much for the Manifesto upon which the present Government was elected and for how far it has carried out its promises in certain respects. I propose now to return to one of its most important promised intentions: its determination to relax the tensions of the Cold War. And I beg of you to ask yourselves, as I recount what has been happening in certain areas of international activity, whether you consider that this activity to which the present Government has contributed and proposes to continue to contribute is calculated to relax any tensions whatever.

You doubtless know a good deal about the war in South Vietnam, but I will give a very brief outline of its progress and character. South Vietnam was part of French Cochin-China, but after a long process of civil war, the French were excluded from the whole region. A conference was summoned to meet at Geneva in 1954. The conclusions reached were sensible, and, if they had been carried out, no trouble would have arisen. Vietnam was to be independent and neutral, and was to have a parliamentary government established by a General Election. The Americans did not like this. They professed to suspect that Vietnam would become part of the Communist bloc if left to itself and that North Vietnam was already, and has continued to be, part of the Communist bloc, in spite of reiterated statements by the Government of North Vietnam that they wish to be neutral.

The Americans sent observers who decided that South Vietnam was too disturbed for a general election. There were in South Vietnam three parties; the peasants, who constituted the large majority; the Buddhists; and a tiny minority of Christians, who had been supporters of the French. The Americans decided to support this small faction. They did so at first by sending technical aid and material and 'Advisers'. It was soon seen, however, that the 'Advisers' were taking far more than a passive part in the war that ensued between the American-supported minority and the Buddhists and peasants. The war has continued now for many years and the American-supported Government – or, more outspokenly, the Americans – have steadily lost ground. It has been warfare of an incredibly brutal kind, brutal to a degree seldom equalled by any civilised Power.

Eight million people have been put in barbed wire concentration camps involving forced labour. The country – civilians, animals and crops, as well as warriors and jungle – has been sprayed with jelly gasoline and poison chemicals. Fifty thousand villages were burnt in 1962 alone. The following account was published in the Dallas *Morning News* on January 1, 1963: 'Supposedly the purpose of the fortified villages is to keep the Vietcong out. But barbed wire denies entrance and exit. Vietnamese farmers are forced at gunpoint into these virtual concentration camps. Their homes, possessions and crops are burned. In the province of Kien-Tuong, seven villagers were led into the town square. Their stomachs were slashed, their livers extracted and put on display. These victims were women and children. In another village, expectant mothers were invited to the square by Government forces to be honoured. Their stomachs were ripped open and their unborn babies removed.' And the anti-Communist Democratic Party of Vietnam told the International Control Commission that: 'Decapitation, eviscerations and the public display of murdered women and children are common.' It is, as the *Nation* of January 19, 1963, called it, 'a dirty, cruel war', and one can only agree with the leader of the Vietnamese Democratic Party when he said in an interview on CBS (reported in the Vietnamese Democratic Bulletin for September, 1963): 'It is certainly an ironic way to protect the peasant masses from Communism.'

It is generally admitted that there is no hope that the Americans can win this war. Obviously failing in South Vietnam, they are now considering extending the war to North Vietnam in spite of the fact that China has declared its support of Vietnam if that should happen, and Russia may follow suit. The Labour Party had, hitherto, been opposed to this policy which involves risk of world war. As late as June 4, 1964, the *Daily Worker* said that Mr Wilson, at the end of talks in Moscow, was opposed to carrying the war into North Vietnam as well as to North Vietnamese infiltration into the South. But, since the formation of his Government, the Labour Party has agreed with America to support that country in its war of conquest. *The Guardian* reports on December 10, 1964, that Mr Wilson told President Johnson that Britain wholly supported the legitimate role the United States is playing in South Vietnam. The Labour Government is doing this in spite of the fact that the vast majority of the inhabitants of South Vietnam are opposed to this American war and want to achieve peace and neutrality – as the North Vietnamese have repeatedly asserted that they also wish – and in spite of the extreme unparalleled brutality of the war, and in spite of the fact – and this is to be noted – that the

Americans have no shred of right in South Vietnam and are conducting a war of a type to which the Labour Party has always been passionately opposed. Moreover, if the Americans extend the war to North Vietnam, as they threaten to do, we and they will be involved in a war with China of which the consequences are bound to be horrible – possibly all-out nuclear war. For all these consequences, the Labour Government will share the responsibility.

A similar situation is developing in the Congo. Katanga is incredibly rich in valuable minerals, especially cobalt. Cobalt would be necessary for the Doomsday Bomb. When the Congo became independent, the Western Powers, especially America and Belgium, made a determined effort to preserve for the West the products of Katanga. Lumumba, who was the Congo's choice as Prime Minister, was murdered, and Tshombe, under Western pressure, was made Prime Minister of the whole country. The country rose against this decision, and the Americans and Belgians sent a military expedition to enforce their will. This expedition, the British, under the leadership of the Labour Government, supported, and they allowed it to use Ascension Island as a convenient spot from which to conduct the invasion. There is, in consequence, a war of devastation in progress throughout the Congo. The likelihood is that this will degenerate into guerilla warfare which will continue without securing victory for the West. Perhaps an excerpt from the writing of one of those who was a mercenary fighting for the West in the Congo would bring home the sort of war we are supporting there. I quote this from *News of the World* for 22 November, 1964:

'On the way to Stanleyville one of our vehicles broke down. We took our gear off it and retreated into the bush. Late in the afternoon we went back to the vehicle, but found it completely wrecked . . .

'The young English lieutenant was furious. "We will give the bastards a real lesson." He ordered us to move at once on the nearest village and take it apart.

'It was a familiar enough command. It seemed to me we had been taking villages apart, innocent villages of peaceful farming folk who did not want any part of this war, all the way along the track from far down in the south.

'We would turn up unexpectedly, open fire without warning, race through the place, burning every pathetic shanty and shack to the ground regardless of who might be inside. The idea was to spread the image of our determination and ruthlessness; to terrorise the whole area; to give the rebels an example of what they were in for . . .

'It seemed almost certain that the villagers knew nothing about the activities of the rebels. I doubted they even knew the lorry had been destroyed.

'It was just before dusk when we came. Unsuspecting women were hustling around, carrying water and going about the last of their day's chores. Children were playing in the dust, laughing and shouting to one another.

'We paused for a few minutes, and then came the order to fire. There was a great crackle of shots from machine guns and our deadly new Belgian rifles. Women screamed and fell. Little children just stood there, dazed, or cartwheeled hideously as bullets slammed into them.

'Then, as usual, we raced into the place, still firing as we went. Some of us pitched cans of petrol on to the homes before putting a match to them. Others threw phosphorus hand grenades, which turned human beings into blazing inextinguishable torches of fire.

'For a while, as we raced along, there was bedlam. Shrieks, moans, shrill cries for mercy. And, above all, the throaty, half-crazed bellowing of those commandoes among us who quite obviously utterly loved this sort of thing.

'Then, as we moved away beyond the village, the comparative silence, the distant, hardly distinguishable cries of the wounded, the acrid smell of burning flesh.'

The account continues, but I do not think that I need pursue it to illustrate my point. The cardinal point in the training of these mercenaries – and again I quote – is 'that never, in any circumstances, should prisoners be taken. "Even if men, women and children come running to you" I was told, "even if they fall on their knees before you, begging for mercy, don't hesitate. Just shoot to kill."'

I need hardly say that this young man was sickened of being a hired assassin and ceased to be one. But, in England, under the aegis of the Labour Government, we are continuing to support this slaughter. On November 20, 1964, *The Times* announced that Mr George Thomson, our Minister of State at the Foreign Office, was informed during the previous week by the Belgian Government that they were engaged in contingency planning with the US Government. Britain then gave her permission to use Ascension Island. *The Times* also announced that Belgian troops were flown to Ascension Island with British permission. The *Daily Express* of 30 November, 1964, reports: 'At one stage the Cabinet considered sending British troops. Britain was the first to suggest armed invervention to Belgium. But officials in Whitehall now say that the terrain in rebel-held areas prevents large-scale troop landings.' And on December 15, 1964, Mr George Thomson stated: 'We give outright support to Tshombe.' Yet, two days later our Minister of Defence (one of them, anyway) 'referred to "primitive barbarism" in the Congo and said that we had to see that other parts of Africa and Asia were not plunged into "a similar state of chaos."' Does this mean that we are to uphold similar bloody and unjustified slaughter otherwhere in Africa, carried on with the permission and help of the Labour Government? The record is one of which I as an Englishman cannot be proud. As a member of the Party responsible, I am sickened.

But to move on: Similar troubles are being stirred up by British initiative in the war between Malaysia and Indonesia, a war likely to be as bloody and atrocious as the two of which I have been speaking and to last as long, with no victory possible. On page 65 of the report of the 62nd Annual Conference of the Labour Party, July, 1963, you will find that Labour supported the Malaysia Bill for the relinquishment of British sovereignty over North Borneo, Sarawak and Singapore. Labour felt – and I quote – 'that the federation of Malaysia would play an important stabilising role in S.E. Asia.' On December 10 of this last year, *The Guardian* reports that Mr Wilson told President Johnson that Britain has 8,000 troops in Borneo, 20,000 in Malaysia as a whole: and the *New Statesman* of January 15, 1965, says that 'the bulk of Britain's fleet, some 700 ships including a Commando "bushfire" ship and aircraft carriers' are now in the waters near Malaysia and Indonesia. 'The Commonwealth Brigade is in Malaya facing Sumatra.'

But these are not the only places where the Labour Government is supporting Western imperialism. In both British Guiana and Aden and the South Arabian Protectorates it is following the policies of the Tory Government although it has sent its Colonial Secretary travelling to the trouble spots to study the situations once again.

All these are shameful attempts to support the tottering supremacy of Britain and America against the wishes of the populations concerned, and against the vast movement for independence which is agitating formerly subject peoples. It is a terrible fact that the Labour Government is supporting these hopeless and cruel attempts at subjugation. It is an almost worse fact that it is running the risk for us of these wars escalating to large nuclear wars. Its reception of China's overtures towards peace and disarmament is a dreary pointer to its attitude. Soon after the Labour Government took office, Premier Chou En-lai wrote to our Prime Minister proposing that the governments of the world should undertake not to use nuclear weapons, and suggesting a summit conference. Mr Wilson replied: 'I do not believe the procedure you have suggested is the best way to make progress in present circumstances.' He criticised China on two grounds: for carrying out a nuclear test in the atmosphere and for her approach being 'not realistic'. This attitude on the part of the Prime Minister hardly seems a means of relaxing tensions or of resolving differences between East and West or of halting the spread of nuclear weapons – all of which the electoral Manifesto said the Labour Government would try to do. Again it is following the dangerous policies of the past. In the past few years the West has rebuffed several overtures made by China towards nuclear disarmament and denuclearised zones. If China is not included in disarmament discussions there is little hope for peace in the world. The Labour Government might have taken – might still take – a new and more realistic attitude, taking the promises of the East, as well as the West, at face value, at least as a basis for discussion, until they have been proved to be hollow. But our new Minister for Disarmament seems to be interested chiefly in how to keep up our armed forces more cheaply than hitherto. (See his speech at Salisbury 2 February, 1965, and the extracts from it which the Labour Party appears to think important.)

In none of the actions of the Labour Government has there been evidence of the promised effort to relax the tensions of the Cold War.

What the Labour Government has accomplished in the way of carrying out the promises made in its electoral Manifesto is to appoint a Minister for Disarmament in the Foreign Office. Possibly, also, it has made the Government more efficient by the vast proliferation of new offices, ministries and committees which it has instituted.

It has done nothing apparent to implement Labour's promises in the very important fields of disarmament negotiations, the establishment of nuclear-free zones, the reduction of man-power and arms, the private sale of arms, a drastic re-examination and modification of our defence policy, a re-negotiation of the Nassau agreement, the admission of China into the UN, or the revivification of the morale and the increase of the powers of the UN. Nor does it show any signs of the self-criticism or of the welcome to criticism by their fellow Labour Party members which it advocated.

Moreover, it has directly contravened its definite statements in regard to arms for South Africa and to opposition to the spread of nuclear arms. And, perhaps worst of all, it has increased by many times and in many ways the Cold War tensions between East and West.

What are we to think of this betrayal? Is it the result of a kind of blackmail owing to the parlous state of the economy and finances of the country? But, surely, those who were about to take office must have examined the economic and financial condition of the country and the extent of its dependence upon the United States, and made plans to carry out their promises with the results of their examination in mind. Had they not the courage to attack their problems boldly – or, indeed, with the probable end-results of their actions in mind, realistically?

What hope is there for Parliamentary democracy when the leaders of a Party, upon achieving office, act in direct contradiction to their electoral promises? Those Labour Party members who do not like treachery have hitherto kept quiet in the interests of unity. But what is the use of unity in evil? The cardinal virtues in gangs of criminals are unity and loyalty. Before we are committed irrevocably – and we are rapidly being so committed – to policies leading to disaster for ourselves and for all the inhabitants of the world, we should make known in unmistakable terms our abhorrence of present policies. To wait much longer will be to wait too long. If the Labour Party is to regain any part of its former championship of vitally necessary reforms, those who voted for it on the basis of its electoral Manifesto will have to insist that the leading members of this present Government must lose hope of ever holding office again. Whatever they may have done or not done in regard to their pre-election promises, they have got us into, and propose to keep us in, at least two of the most cruel and useless wars that there have ever been – wars of extermination. Against this policy we must protest in every possible way.

SPEECH TO FIRST MEETING OF MEMBERS OF THE WAR CRIMES TRIBUNAL, NOVEMBER 13, 1966

Allow me to express my appreciation to you for your willingness to participate in this Tribunal. It has been convened so that we may investigate and assess the character of the United States' war in Vietnam.

The Tribunal has no clear historical precedent. The Nuremberg Tribunal, although concerned with designated war crimes, was possible because the victorious allied Powers compelled the vanquished to present their leaders for trial. Inevitably, the Nuremberg trials, supported as they were by State power, contained a strong element of *realpolitik*. Despite these inhibiting factors, which call in question certain of the Nuremberg procedures, the Nuremberg Tribunal expressed the sense of outrage, which was virtually universal, at the crimes committed by the Nazis in Europe. Somehow, it was widely felt, there had to be criteria against which such actions could be judged, and according to which Nazi crimes could be condemned. Many felt it was morally necessary to record the full horror. It was hoped that a legal method could be devised, capable of coming to terms with the magnitude of Nazi crimes. These ill-defined but deeply-felt, sentiments surrounded the Nuremberg Tribunal.

Our own task is more difficult, but the same responsibility obtains. We do not represent any State power, nor can we compel the policy-makers responsible for crimes against the people of Vietnam to stand accused before us. We lack *force majeure*. The procedures of a trial are impossible to implement.

I believe that these apparent limitations are, in fact, virtues. We are free to conduct a solemn and historic investigation, uncompelled by reasons of State or other such obligations. Why is this war being fought in Vietnam? In whose interest is it being waged? We have, I am certain, an obligation to study these questions and to pronounce on them, after thorough investigation, for in doing so we can assist mankind in understanding why a small agrarian people have endured for more than twelve years the assault of the largest industrial power on earth, possessing the most developed and cruel military capacity.

I have prepared a paper, which I hope you will wish to read during your deliberations. It sets out a considerable number of reports from Western newspapers and such sources, giving an indication of the record of the United States in Vietnam. These reports should make it clear that we enter our enquiry with considerable *prima facie* evidence of crimes reported not by the victims but by media favourable to the policies responsible. I believe that we are justified in concluding that it is necessary to convene a solemn Tribunal, composed of men eminent not through their power, but through their intellectual and moral contribution to what we optimistically call 'human civilisation'.

I feel certain that this Tribunal will perform an historic role if its investigation is exhaustive. We must record the truth in Vietnam. We must pass judgement on what we find to be the truth. We must warn of the consequences of this truth. We must, moreover, reject the view that only indifferent men are impartial men. We must repudiate the degenerate conception of individual intelligence, which confuses open minds with empty ones.

I hope that this Tribunal will select men who respect the truth and whose life's work bears witness to that respect. Such men will have feelings about the *prima facie* evidence of which I speak. No man unacquainted with this evidence through indifference has any claim to judge it.

I enjoin this Tribunal to select commissions for the purpose of dividing the areas of investigation and taking responsibility for their conduct, under the Tribunal's jurisdiction. I hope that teams of qualified investigators will be chosen to study in Vietnam the evidence of which we have witnessed only a small part. I should like to see the United States Government requested to present evidence in defence of its actions. The resistance of the National Liberation Front and of the Democratic Republic of Vietnam must also be assessed and placed in its true relation to the civilisation we choose to uphold. We have about five months of work before us, before the full hearings, which have been planned for Paris.

As I reflect on this work, I cannot help thinking of the events of my life, because of the crimes I have seen and the hopes I have nurtured. I have lived through the Dreyfus Case and been party to the investigation of the crimes committed by King Leopold in the Congo. I can recall many wars. Much injustice has been recorded quietly during these decades. In my own experience I cannot discover a situation quite comparable. I cannot recall a people so tormented, yet so devoid of the failings of their tormentors. I do not know any other conflict in which the disparity in physical power was so vast. I have no memory of any people so enduring, or of any nation with a spirit of resistance so unquenchable.

I will not conceal from you the profundity of my admiration and passion for the people of Vietnam. I cannot relinquish the duty to judge what has been done to them because I have such feelings. Our mandate is to uncover and tell all. My conviction is that no greater tribute can be provided than an offer of the truth, born of intense and unyielding enquiry.

May this Tribunal prevent the crime of silence.

THE AIMS AND OBJECTIVES OF THE TRIBUNAL
NOVEMBER 1966

The conscience of mankind is profoundly disturbed by the war being waged in Vietnam. It is a war in which the world's wealthiest and most powerful State is opposed to a nation of poor peasants, who have been fighting for their independence for a quarter of a century. It appears that this war is being waged in violation of international law and custom.

Every day, the world Press and, particularly, that of the United States, publishes reports which, if proved, would represent an ever growing violation of the principles established by the Nuremberg Tribunal and rules fixed by international agreements.

Moved and shocked by the suffering endured by the Vietnamese people and convinced that humanity must know the truth in order to deliver a serious and impartial judgement on the events taking place in Vietnam and where the responsibility for them lies, we have accepted the invitation of Bertrand Russell to meet, in order to examine these facts scrupulously and confront them with the rules of law which govern them.

It has been alleged that in the first nine months of 1966, the air force of the United States has dropped, in Vietnam, four million pounds of bombs daily. If it continues at this rate to the end of the year, the total will constitute a greater mass of explosives than it unloaded on the entire Pacific theatre during the whole of the Second

World War. The area bombarded in this way is no bigger than the states of New York and Pennsylvania. In the South, the US forces and their docile Saigon allies have herded eight million people, peasants and their families, into barbed wire encampments under the surveillance of the political police. Chemical poisons have been, and are being, used to defoliate and render barren tens of thousands of acres of farmland. Crops are being systematically destroyed – and this in a country where, even in normal times, the average man or woman eats less than half the food consumed by the average American (and lives to less than one third of his age).

Irrigation systems are deliberately disrupted. Napalm, phosphorus bombs and a variety of other, sadistically designed and hitherto unknown weapons are being used against the population of both North and South Vietnam. More than five hundred thousand Vietnamese men, women and children have perished under this onslaught, more than the number of soldiers the United States lost in both world wars, although the population of Vietnam had already been decimated during the Japanese and French occupations and the famine which followed the Second World War.

Even though we have not been entrusted with this task by any organised authority, we have taken the responsibility in the interest of humanity and the preservation of civilisation. We act on our own accord, in complete independence from any government and any official or semi-official organisation, in the firm belief that we express a deep anxiety and remorse felt by many of our fellow humans in many countries. We trust that our action will help to arouse the conscience of the world.

We, therefore, consider ourselves a Tribunal which, even if it has not the power to impose sanctions, will have to answer, amongst others, the following questions:

1. Has the United States Government (and the Governments of Australia, New Zealand and South Korea) committed acts of aggression according to international law?

2. Has the American Army made use of or experimented with new weapons or weapons forbidden by the laws of war (gas, special chemical products, napalm, etc.)?

3. Has there been bombardment of targets of a purely civilian character, for example hospitals, schools, sanatoria, dams, etc., and on what scale has this occurred?

4. Have Vietnamese prisoners been subjected to inhuman treatment forbidden by the laws of war and, in particular, to torture or to mutilation? Have there been unjustified reprisals against the civilian population, in particular, the execution of hostages?

5. Have forced labour camps been created, has there been deportation of the population or other acts tending to the extermination of the population and which can be characterised juridically as acts of genocide?

If the Tribunal decides that one, or all, of these crimes have been committed, it will be up to the Tribunal to decide who bears the responsibility for them.

This Tribunal will examine all the evidence that may be placed before it by any source or party. The evidence may be oral, or in the form of documents. No evidence relevant to our purposes will be refused attention. No witness competent to testify about the events with which our enquiry is concerned will be denied a hearing.

The National Liberation Front of Vietnam and the Government of the Democratic Republic of Vietnam have assured us of their willingness to co-operate, to provide the necessary information, and to help us in checking the accuracy and reliability of the information. The Cambodian Head of State, Prince Sihanouk, has similarly offered to help by the production of evidence. We trust that they will honour this pledge and we shall gratefully accept their help, without prejudice to our own views or attitude. We renew, as a Tribunal, the appeal which Bertrand Russell has addressed in his name to the Government of the United States. We invite the Government of the United States to present evidence or cause it to be presented, and to instruct their officials or representatives to appear and state their case. Our purpose is to establish, without fear or favour, the full truth about this war. We sincerely hope that our efforts will contribute to the world's justice, to the re-establishment of peace and the liberation of the oppressed peoples.

*   *   *

RESOLUTION OF THE TRIBUNAL

We are grateful to the Bertrand Russell Peace Foundation for the work which it has already done. We are sure that the preliminary steps already taken by it will help us to complete our task within a reasonable time and with considerable more efficiency than it would have been possible if its preliminary work had not helped our deliberations.

APPEAL FOR SUPPORT FOR THE INTERNATIONAL WAR CRIMES TRIBUNAL

For several years Western news media have unwittingly documented the record of crime committed by the United States in Vietnam, which comprises an overwhelming *prima facie* indictment of the American war. The terrible series of photographs, and accounts of torture, mutilation and experimental war has impelled Bertrand Russell to call us together to conduct an exhaustive inquiry into the war in all its aspects. Scientists, lawyers, doctors and world-renowned scholars will serve on commissions investigating the evidence. Witnesses will be brought from Vietnam to give their first-hand testimony. Investigating teams will travel throughout Vietnam and Indochina, gathering data on the spot. The documentation published in the West and elsewhere will be relentlessly examined. This five months' intensive work, requiring travelling scientific inquiry, and the detailed research, will cost a vast amount of money. Twelve weeks of public hearings will be even more expensive.

The International War Crimes Tribunal is determined to be financially independent. This can only be accomplished through the contributions of every individual who supports the work of the Tribunal and recognises the profound importance of the full realisation of its task.

We command no state power; we do not represent the strong; we control no armies or treasuries. We act out of the deepest moral concern and depend upon the conscience of ordinary people throughout the world for the real support – the material help, which will determine whether people of Vietnam are to be abandoned in silence or allowed the elementary right of having their plight presented to the conscience of Mankind.

POSTSCRIPT[1]

The serious part of my life ever since boyhood has been devoted to two different objects which for a long time remained separate and have only in recent years united into a single whole. I wanted, on the one hand, to find out whether anything could be known; and, on the other hand, to do whatever might be possible toward creating a happier world. Up to the age of thirty-eight I gave most of my energies to the first of these tasks. I was troubled by scepticism and unwillingly forced to the conclusion that most of what passes for knowledge is open to reasonable doubt. I wanted certainty in the kind of way in which people want religious faith. I thought that certainty is more likely to be found in mathematics than elsewhere. But I discovered that many mathematical demonstrations, which my teachers expected me to accept, were full of fallacies, and that, if certainty were indeed discoverable in mathematics, it would be in a new kind of mathematics, with more solid foundations than those that had hitherto been thought secure. But as the work proceeded, I was continually reminded of the fable about the elephant and the tortoise. Having constructed an elephant upon which the mathematical world could rest, I found the elephant tottering, and proceeded to construct a tortoise to keep the elephant from falling. But the tortoise was no more secure than the elephant, and after some twenty years of very arduous toil, I came to the conclusion that there was nothing more that *I* could do in the way of making mathematical knowledge indubitable. Then came the First World War, and my thoughts became concentrated on human misery and folly. Neither misery nor folly seems to me any part of the inevitable lot of man. And I am convinced that intelligence, patience, and eloquence can, sooner or later, lead the human race out of its self-imposed tortures provided it does not exterminate itself meanwhile.

On the basis of this belief, I have had always a certain degree of optimism, although, as I have grown older, the optimism has grown more sober and the happy issue more distant. But I remain completely incapable of agreeing with those who accept fatalistically the view that man is born to trouble. The causes of unhappiness in the past and in the present are not difficult to ascertain. There have been poverty, pestilence, and famine, which were due to man's inadequate mastery

[1] Published separately as 'Reflections on my Eightieth Birthday' in *Portraits from Memory*.

of nature. There have been wars, oppressions and tortures which have been due to men's hostility to their fellow men. And there have been morbid miseries fostered by gloomy creeds, which have led men into profound inner discords that made all outward prosperity of no avail. All these are unnecessary. In regard to all of them, means are known by which they can be overcome. In the modern world, if communities are unhappy, it is often because they have ignorances, habits, beliefs, and passions, which are dearer to them than happiness or even life. I find many men in our dangerous age who seem to be in love with misery and death, and who grow angry when hopes are suggested to them. They think hope is irrational and that, in sitting down to lazy despair, they are merely facing facts. I cannot agree with these men. To preserve hope in our world makes calls upon our intelligence and our energy. In those who despair it is frequently the energy that is lacking.

The last half of my life has been lived in one of those painful epochs of human history during which the world is getting worse, and past victories which had seemed to be definitive have turned out to be only temporary. When I was young, Victorian optimism was taken for granted. It was thought that freedom and prosperity would spread gradually throughout the world by an orderly process, and it was hoped that cruelty, tyranny, and injustice would continually diminish. Hardly anyone was haunted by the fear of great wars. Hardly anyone thought of the nineteenth century as a brief interlude between past and future barbarism. For those who grew up in that atmosphere, adjustment to the world of the present has been difficult. It has been difficult not only emotionally but intellectually. Ideas that had been thought adequate have proved inadequate. In some directions valuable freedoms have proved very hard to preserve. In other directions, especially as regards relations between nations, freedoms formerly valued have proved potent sources of disaster. New thoughts, new hopes, new freedoms, and new restrictions upon freedom are needed if the world is to emerge from its present perilous state.

I cannot pretend that what I have done in regard to social and political problems has had any great importance. It is comparatively easy to have an immense effect by means of a dogmatic and precise gospel, such as that of Communism. But for my part I cannot believe that what mankind needs is anything either precise or dogmatic. Nor can I believe with any wholeheartedness in any partial doctrine which deals only with some part or aspect of human life. There are those who hold that everything depends upon institutions, and that good institutions will inevitably bring the millennium. And, on the other hand, there are those who believe that what is needed is a change of heart, and that, in comparison, institutions are of little account. I cannot accept either view. Institutions mould character, and character transforms institutions. Reforms in both must march hand in hand. And if individuals are to retain that measure of initiative and flexibility which they ought to have, they must not be all forced into one rigid mould; or, to change the metaphor, all drilled into one army. Diversity is essential in spite of the fact that it precludes universal acceptance of a single gospel. But to preach such a doctrine is difficult especially in arduous times. And perhaps it cannot be effective until some bitter lessons have been learned by tragic experience.

My work is near its end, and the time has come when I can survey it as a whole. How far have I succeeded, and how far have I failed? From an early age I thought of myself as dedicated to great and arduous tasks. Nearly three-quarters of a century ago, walking alone in the Tiergarten through melting snow under the coldly glittering March sun, I determined to write two series of books: one abstract, growing gradually more concrete; the other concrete, growing gradually more abstract. They were to be crowned by a synthesis, combining pure theory with a practical social philosophy. Except for the final synthesis, which still eludes me, I have written these books. They have been acclaimed and praised, and the thoughts of many men and women have been affected by them. To this extent I have succeeded.

But as against this must be set two kinds of failure, one outward, one inward.

To begin with the outward failure: the Tiergarten has become a desert; the Brandenburger Tor, through which I entered it on that March morning, has become the boundary of two hostile empires, glaring at each other across a barrier, and grimly preparing the ruin of mankind. Communists, Fascists, and Nazis have successfully challenged all that I thought good, and in defeating them much of what their opponents have sought to preserve is being lost. Freedom has come to be thought weakness, and tolerance has been compelled to wear the garb of treachery. Old ideals are judged irrelevant, and no doctrine free from harshness commands respect.

The inner failure, though of little moment to the world, has made my mental life a perpetual battle. I set out with a more or less religious belief in a Platonic eternal world, in which mathematics shone with a beauty like that of the last Cantos of the *Paradiso*. I came to the conclusion that the eternal world is trivial, and that mathematics is only the art of saying the same thing in different words. I set out with a belief that love, free and courageous, could conquer the world without fighting. I came to support a bitter and terrible war. In these respects there was failure.

But beneath all this load of failure I am still conscious of something that I feel to be victory. I may have conceived theoretical truth wrongly, but I was not wrong in thinking that there is such a thing, and that it deserves our allegiance. I may have thought the road to a world of free and happy human beings shorter than it is proving to be, but I was not wrong in thinking that such a world is possible, and that it is worth while to live with a view to bringing it nearer. I have lived in the pursuit of a vision, both personal and social. Personal: to care for what is noble, for what is beautiful, for what is gentle: to allow moments of insight to give wisdom at more mundane times. Social: to see in imagination the society that is to be created, where individuals grow freely, and where hate and greed and envy die because there is nothing to nourish them. These things I believe, and the world, for all its horrors, has left me unshaken.

INDEX

A

A.B.C. of Atoms, The 387
A.B.C. of Relativity, The 387, 506
A-bomb 680, 695
Aannestad, Elling 441
Abbotsbury 599
Abel 381
Abelard, Peter 294
Aborigines 517-18
abortion 416
Abraham and Sarah 317
Abyssinia 314
academic freedom 460-3, 469-79; and H. M. Sheffer 343-6
Acheson, Dean 582
Acland, Lady Eleanor 282
Acland, Sir Francis 282
Acropolis 560
'Act or Perish' 606, 632-4, 697
Adam 496
Adams, Bill 454
Adams, Peg 393
Addams, Jane 445
Addis, Sir Charles 381
Adenauer, Konrad 642
Adrian, Lord Edgar 568
advertising 441
'Africa and the Movement for Peace' (BRPF) 692
Aiken, Clarice Lorenz, L from 415; L to 415-16
Alderley 600
Aldermaston March 597-8, 608, 619
Alexander, Samuel, L from 295
Algeria 314
Alice Springs 517
Allen, Clifford 247-8, 254, 288, 293-4, 297, 317, 327, 329, 332-5, 339-40, 347, 354, 483, 487, 490
Allen & Unwin Ltd, George 283, 377, 461, 489, 618, 665
Alps 324
Amalgamated Society of Engineers 176
Amazon River 258
Ambatielos, Betty 654; L from and to 691-2

Ambatielos, Tony, L from and to 691-2
Amberley, John, Viscount (B.R.'s father) 10-15, 21, 26, 53, 63, 79-81, 123-4, 151, 376, 408, 414, 432
Amberley, Kate, Viscountess (B.R.'s mother) 10-15, 21, 26, 74, 81, 124, 158, 232, 432, 542
Amberley Papers, The 432, 457, 489
America 11, 69, 73, 78, 94, 129, 132-5, 143-4, 146, 156, 168-9, 219-22, 242, 253-4, 274-5, 278, 282, 292-4, 296, 298, 310, 326, 337, 340, 346, 355, 358, 365, 373, 387, 389-91, 403, 408-9, 413-16, 418, 429, 433-4, 441-2, 448-9, 452-3, Ch. 13 passim, 512, 518-19, 532, 548, 596, 662, 714; anti-nuclear protests in 627; and armament lobby 644-5; and Baruch proposal 508, 680; Britain's dependence on 718; and China 361-2, 366, 376, 382-3, 394, 396-7, 648-9; and civil defence 632; and Cuban crisis 618, 647-8, 678; domination of 394, 494; fundamental change in 497; Kennedy Assassination 662-4, 699-707; McCarthyism in 511; mothers of 416; nuclear policy of 636-40, 693-5, 697, 710-11; patriotism in 276, 346, 468, 498; and Rosenberg executions 552; and Sobel case 573-5; its tolerance of opinion 345, 415, 460-2, 475-6; and Vietnam war 666-70, 696, 707-8, 713-15, 719-24; whether B.R. is anti- 674; in World War I 250-3, 256, 283-4, 309, 311, 315; see also under individual place names
American Civil Liberties

Union 481
American Civil War 484
American Committee for Cultural Freedom 574
American Emergency Civil Liberties Committee 655
American Mercury 500, 529
American Philosophical Association 482
Amos, Bonte 132, 144-5, 171
Amos, Sir Maurice Sheldon 85, 107-8, 132, 143-6, 171; L to 433-4
Amos, Mr (senior) 143-4
Amos, Mrs 101, 143-4
Analysis of Matter, The 387
Analysis of Mind, The 256, 347, 354, 378n, 387, 433
Analysis of Religious Belief, An (Amberley) 11
anarchism 323, 355, 367, 369, 389, 451
Anaximander 494
Anderson, Dame Adelaide 381
Anderson, W. C. 288
Andorra 329
Angell, Norman 268
Anglicanism 395, 461, 479, 494-5
Anglo-American cooperation 467, 493, 497, 500-4
Anglo-Boer War (see Boer War)
Anglo-Saxons 496
Ann Arbor University 221
Annalen der Naturphilosophie 353n
Annam 257
Anne, Queen 487
Annesley, Lady Clare (Colette's sister) 248
Annesley, Lady Priscilla (Colette's mother) 248
d'Annunzio, Gabriele 445
Anrep, Boris 559
Apostles, The (see Moral Science Club)
appearance and reality 313
Appolinaris Sidonius 316
Aquinas, St Thomas 459, 482
Arabs 654, 683; and Palestine refugees 654

BOOKS BY BERTRAND RUSSELL